THE ESSENE WRITINGS
FROM QUMRAN

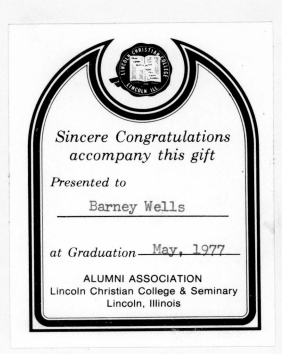

Sincere Congratulations accompany this gift

Presented to

Barney Wells

at Graduation May, 1977

ALUMNI ASSOCIATION
Lincoln Christian College & Seminary
Lincoln, Illinois

A. DUPONT-SOMMER

THE ESSENE WRITINGS FROM QUMRAN

Translated by G. Vermes

GLOUCESTER, MASS.

PETER SMITH

1973

A. DUPONT-SOMMER

André Dupont-Sommer was born in Marnes-la-Coquette, France, on December 23, 1900. One of the leading Hebrew scholars of his country, Professor Dupont-Sommer has been *directeur d'études* at the Ecole des Hautes Etudes since 1938, professor at the Sorbonne since 1945, and president of the Institut d'Etudes Sémitiques of the University of Paris since 1952. He has published many articles and a number of books, including two translated into English under the titles *The Dead Sea Scrolls: A Preliminary Survey* (1952) and *The Jewish Sect of Qumran and the Essenes* (1954).

Reprinted, 1973, by Permission of
WORLD PUBLISHING
Times Mirror

ISBN: 0-8446-2012-2

AN ORIGINAL MERIDIAN BOOK

Published by The World Publishing Company
2231 West 110 Street, Cleveland, Ohio 44102
Second Printing, December, 1967
Third Printing, August, 1969
Translated from the second revised and enlarged
edition of *Les Ecrits esseniens decouverts pres de la mer Morte*
(Les Editions Payot, Paris).
Translation copyright © 1961 by Basil Blackwell
All rights reserved
Library of Congress Catalog Card Number: 62-10171
Printed in the United States of America
3WP869

À Monsieur Charles Virolleaud
Membre de l'Institut
en homage d'admiration et de respectueuse amitié

PREFACE

The first edition of the present work appeared a year ago in French under the title, *Les Écrits esséniens découverts près de la mer Morte* (Payot, Paris, June 1959). It is essentially intended as a collection of the non-biblical Jewish sectarian documents recovered since 1947 from the caves in the region of Wadi Qumran. All the non-biblical scrolls and scroll fragments are assembled here in their entirety, in translation and with comments. The book constitutes, therefore, a corpus of the Qumran writings and, in addition, sums up all the problems raised by the new texts. The latter are provided with the introductions and explanations necessary for placing them, as far as this is possible, within their time and environment.

No corpus as complete as this, or similarly conceived, had appeared till then either in France or elsewhere, and for this reason two eminent British colleagues kindly encouraged me to translate it into English and themselves recommended the project to Mr. H. L. Schollick, a director of the publishing house of Basil Blackwell. When I was in Oxford last September, attending the Third International Congress for the Study of the Old Testament, I went to see Mr. Schollick about this and will always remember his most cordial welcome. I wish to take this opportunity to express my thanks to him, as well as to Professor G. R. Driver and Professor H. H. Rowley. In the *Book List 1960* published by the Society for Old Testament Study, the reviewer concluded his criticism of my book thus: 'No doubt an English edition of this important work will be forthcoming before long; we hope so.' This wish is now realized, thanks to Blackwell's, who have already done me the honour of publishing in 1952 the English translation of my *Aperçus préliminaires sur les manuscrits de la mer Morte* under the title, *The Dead Sea Scrolls. A Preliminary Survey*.

My thanks are also extended to Dr. G. Vermes, Lecturer in Divinity at the University of Durham, who accepted the onerous task of translating my book and has accomplished it with much devotion, intelligence and care. A translation such as this presents considerable difficulties, since for a great part it entails rendering into English a French text which is itself a translation from Hebrew or Aramaic. While keeping strictly to my interpretation, Dr. Vermes

vii

has had constant recourse to the original documents in order to determine the exact sense of my French translation and to avoid misunderstandings and blunders. The present version is not just a simple transfer of French material into English — *traduttore, traditore!* It depends also on the Hebrew and Aramaic texts, with which, as everyone is aware, Dr. Vermes is perfectly familiar. I am glad that the English translation of my book has been entrusted to such an expert. Of course it goes without saying that his competent and valuable collaboration involves him in no responsibility for the views expressed in this work, and on various points his opinions may differ from mine. His labours as a mere interpreter do him all the more credit and win the author's sincere gratitude.

Publications in the field of Qumran studies accumulate from month to month, or rather from day to day. The present English edition has been brought carefully up to date. It includes, in particular, three important supplements. The first presents a fragment of a second *Commentary on Hosea* from cave IV, published a few months after the appearance of the French edition (in the *Journal of Biblical Literature*, lxxviii, 1959, pp. 144-7); the second supplement is devoted to two fragments of a liturgical writing — equally from cave IV — the subject of a paper read in September 1959 during the Oxford Congress (see *Supplements to Vetus Testamentum*, vol. vii. Congress Volume, Oxford, 1959 [Leiden, 1960] pp. 318-45); the third supplement is a postscript to Appendix I and brings fresh information concerning the copper scrolls discovered in cave III.

Paris, June 1960

CONTENTS

LIST OF ILLUSTRATIONS

LIST OF ABBREVIATIONS

BASOR	*Bulletin of the American Schools of Oriental Research*
JBL	*Journal of Biblical Literature*
JJS	*Journal of Jewish Studies*
JNES	*Journal of Near Eastern Studies*
JQR	*Jewish Quarterly Review*
J. Sem. St.	*Journal of Semitic Studies*
JTS	*Journal of Theological Studies*
PEQ	*Palestine Exploration Quarterly*
RB	*Revue Biblique*
REJ	*Revue des Études Juives*
RHPR	*Revue d'Histoire et de Philosophie Religieuses*
RHR	*Revue de l'Histoire des Religions*
R. Paris	*Revue de Paris*
RQ	*Revue de Qumran*
TLZ	*Theologische Literaturzeitung*
TR	*Theologische Rundschau*
VT	*Vetus Testamentum*
ZAW	*Zeitschrift für die alttestamentliche Wissenschaft*
ZNW	*Zeitschrift für die neutestamentliche Wissenschaft*

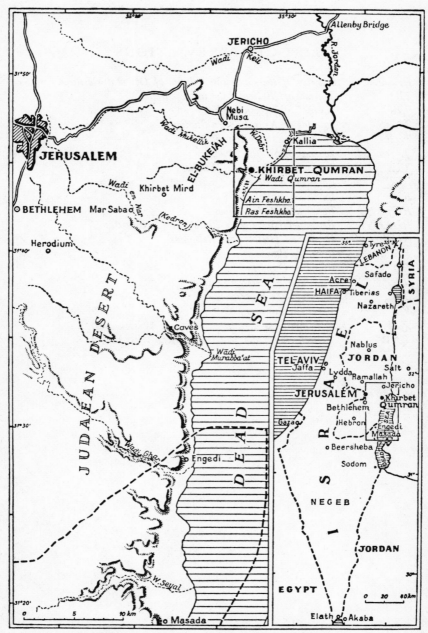

Fig. 1. Map of the Judaean Desert and Dead Sea, with inset map of Palestine.

INTRODUCTION

The discovery of the manuscripts. — General contents of the manuscripts. — Acquisition of the manuscripts and their publication. — The biblical manuscripts. Their importance to textual criticism of the Bible. — The non-biblical manuscripts. Their importance for the history of Essenism and of primitive Christianity. — Object, plan and method of the present work.

The traveller flying from Beirut to Jerusalem passes over the ravines of the plateau of Transjordan from east to west before emerging into the valley of the Jordan; and there a most lovely view meets his eyes. To his right, towards the north, the silver Jordan winds among the shrub; before him, to the west, rise the arid escarpments and the grey and tawny dunes of the desert of Judah over which he will presently cross; beneath him lies Jericho in its green oasis; and to his left, towards the south, the blue sunlit waters of the Dead Sea, bounded on either side by steep purple mountains, magnificent and wild, stretch as far as the eye can reach. The upper extremity of the lake forms a sort of semicircle, and into the middle of this the Jordan flows. But the excited traveller turns his attention to the western bank, just beyond this semicircle, to the majestic promontory of Ras Feshkha. He sees the high cliff about seven miles long, which running from north to south in its approach to the lake, ends just there. At the foot of this cliff is a patch of greenness brightening the countryside, the spring called Ain Feshkha, and quite near, to the north, on a marl terrace contiguous to the cliff and slightly dominating the coastal plain, the ruins known as Khirbet Qumran. Although from the air he rather guesses their whereabouts than sees them, this is the focus of his pilgrimage, and while waiting to set foot on this small piece of land, he eagerly feasts his eyes upon it.

Khirbet Qumran, lost in lonely spaces empty except for a few Bedouin in their tents, is mentioned and described by ancient explorers of Palestine only very summarily; yet during the last years it has become one of the most celebrated and venerable of the great memorials of the history of man.

By now, most people know the story of the Bedouin Muhammad ed Dib who, while looking for a lost sheep in the cliff near Qumran in the spring of 1947, discovered a cave containing a whole quantity of ancient Hebrew scrolls. This story, picturesque as it is true, has been told many times.[1]

The manuscripts thus found soon became known as the Dead Sea Scrolls. But this first purely accidental find was followed by many others in the same area which considerably enriched the initial lot. In February 1952, Bedouin discovered a second cave of manuscripts a few hundred yards from the first; and in the following month, archaeologists exploring the entire cliff along a distance of five miles, had the joy of locating a third cave containing curious copper scrolls engraved with a long text in square Hebrew script,[2] as well as fragments of manuscripts written on leather or papyrus.

A few months later, in September 1952, Bedouin discovered a fourth cave, this time in the side of the marl terrace on which the ruins of Qumran stand; inside, underneath a layer of earth, were thousands of manuscript fragments. One of the elders of the tribe was responsible for this find. One night he was in his tent, recalling the memories of his youth, and he told the story of how he was once tracking a wounded partridge in the neighbourhood of the ruins and had seen it disappear into a hole. Guided by the bird, he had penetrated into a cave almost inaccessible from the ground, and had picked up potsherds there, and an ancient lamp. The young men in his audience were quickly able to find this cave of the wounded partridge — a worthy rival of the cave of the lost sheep — and archaeologists arriving soon after completed the clearing of the hiding-place. In addition, they discovered near by, in the same marl terrace, a fifth cave containing the remains of manuscripts. They also succeeded in identifying, at the foot of the cliff in the Wadi Qumran, a sixth cave from which Bedouin had a little earlier taken another small quantity of manuscript fragments.

In the spring of 1955, four new caves in the flank of the marl terrace, quite near caves IV and V, yielded another small quantity of scroll fragments as well as some inscribed potsherds. And finally, at the beginning of 1956, Bedouin — fine sleuths that they are when lured by the promise of gain — found in the cliff, about half a mile north of cave I, an eleventh cave from which four new scrolls have been recovered.

Will any more caves be found? There is nothing to prevent us

---

[1] The date 1947 has, however, been challenged by a declaration signed by the same Bedouin and recently published by W. H. BROWNLEE in *JNES*, no. 4, October 1957, pp. 296 ff; according to this, the find was made in 1945.

[2] Cf. appendix 1 (pp. 379-93).

from hoping so. In any case, no one imagined ten years ago that the desert of Judah would produce the smallest manuscript or papyrus, yet from this point of view it has become another Egypt!

Besides the ten almost complete scrolls which have been found there, the eleven caves discovered so far in the Qumran region have yielded more or less important fragments of almost six hundred books. Cave I was a genuine hiding-place where a certain number of books had been concealed to keep them safe. This is proved by the fact that originally the cave had only one opening, extremely narrow and near to the roof. It was certainly not habitable.[1] The same may be said of cave IV, where entry can only be effected through a sort of chimney, and perhaps of other caves also. On the whole, however, these other caves did, it seems, serve as dwellings for pious hermits and the manuscripts found in each of them — relatively few — probably represent their personal libraries, abandoned by them when they were obliged to flee the area. Caves I and IV, on the other hand, contained far larger deposits of books which were intentionally hidden in order to preserve them from pillage and profanation. They came either from a group of hermitages (the case, perhaps, of cave I, which is situated in the cliff about three-quarters of a mile from the Qumran ruins themselves), or direct from the library of the community house (as in the case of cave IV, which is in the marl terrace and quite near to the ruins).[2]

The inventory of the manuscripts collected from the various caves is not entirely completed, but it seems clear that about a quarter of them are copies of biblical books. There are specimens of each of the books of the canonical Jewish Bible — with the exception of the Book of Esther — often in many copies. There are as many as fourteen manuscripts of Deuteronomy, fifteen of Isaiah, and seventeen of the Psalms. To these may be added the books of Tobit and Ben Sira (also called Ecclesiasticus), two works forming no part of the Jewish canon or of the Bible of the Protestant churches, but accepted into the canon of the Roman Catholic church as 'deuterocanonical' books.

All the remaining Qumran manuscripts form a vast collection of

[1] Today there is another opening in the wall, but it was cut by the searchers themselves after the discovery of the cave, in order to render access more convenient.
[2] Cf. J. T. MILIK, *Dix ans de découvertes dans le désert de Juda*, Paris, 1957, p. 23. (Eng. edn., *Ten Years of Discovery in the Wilderness of Judaea*, London, 1959, pp. 20-1.)

Jewish religious books showing such homogeneity of doctrine that they can only come from the same mystical environment, from one sect. Besides the various biblical books venerated by Jews as a whole, this sect possessed a considerable number of works of its own which it considered, though in a varying degree, to be sacred writings also. It is interesting to recall at this point a passage from IV Ezra (xiv. 37-47), which recognizes two distinct categories among the books that the legendary Ezra was supposed to have remembered and dictated to his secretaries: twenty-four books intended for 'the worthy and the unworthy', i.e. the canonical books of the Bible, and seventy intended for the 'wise' — secret books reserved to initiates. The finds at Qumran reveal almost the same proportion: one-quarter biblical manuscripts, and three-quarters non-biblical writings.

The latter are extremely varied. To begin with, they include writings known earlier called the Pseudepigrapha of the Old Testament:[1] the *Book of Jubilees*, the *Book of Enoch*, and the *Testaments of the Twelve Patriarchs*. These Jewish books were soon discarded by the Synagogue, but were held in high esteem by certain Christian communities, and different translations made by the churches have come down to us. The Qumran caves have restored fragments of these books in their original language. They were therefore part of the library of the Jewish sect of Qumran, and were, no doubt, written by some of its members.

To these known Pseudepigrapha must be added several others which had entirely disappeared. I would mention in particular the Aramaic writing called by its editors *A Genesis Apocryphon*,[2] the *Psalms of Joshua* and the *Prayer of Nabonidus*, etc.

Other works are more typically sectarian; namely, the *Rule*, the *Damascus Document*, the *War Rule of the Sons of Light*, and the *Hymns of Thanksgiving*. In addition, there are a number of writings of an apocalyptic, liturgical, sapiential, or juridical nature, about which we are as yet very inadequately informed.

Special mention must also be made of a whole series of exegetical writings of a very particular kind. These are quite unusual. The Hebrew word employed to describe them, *pesher*, means 'explanation'. They may be called 'commentaries', but these particular

[1] This is their usual title among Protestant scholars: Catholics use the expression *Apocrypha* of the Old Testament.
[2] This is the scroll from cave I which was originally and provisionally called the *Apocalypse of Lamech*.

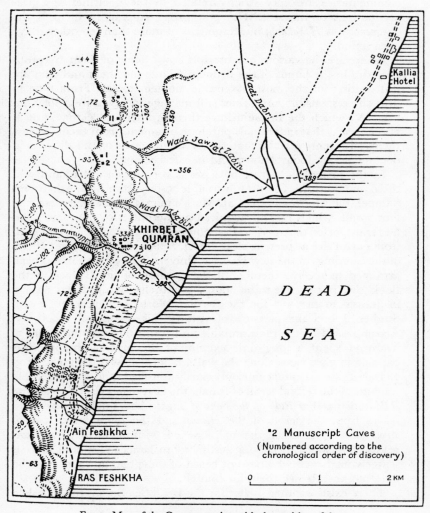

FIG. 2. Map of the Qumran region with the position of the
manuscript caves marked.

commentaries are very strictly related to the doctrines and pre-occupations of the sect. The best preserved among them is the *Commentary on Habakkuk*, but fragments of more than ten others have been found.[1]

Where are the various manuscripts now? Some of them are probably still in the hands of the Bedouin who found them and who are still waiting for the most favourable moment to sell. From time to time the responsible authorities still manage to buy a fresh lot from cave IV, which the Bedouin have therefore held since 1952, and it also happens that individuals purchase fragments from them. Nevertheless, it seems certain that the great majority of the discovered documents are today known and in safe keeping.

In the first place, Israel possesses a very important quantity of these manuscripts. The State was able to buy from Mar Athanasius Samuel, the Metropolitan of St. Mark's monastery in Jerusalem, the four scrolls which he had acquired at the outset of the affair, and had transported to America. Consequently, the seven scrolls collected from cave I are at present all in Israel. A hall in the basement of one of the buildings of the new Hebrew University in Jerusalem has been arranged to receive them until the erection of the 'Palace of the Book', where they are to be housed eventually. While I was staying in Jerusalem in 1957 for the Second World Congress for Jewish Studies, I had the pleasure of visiting this crypt and sanctuary. Accompanied by the most amiable and competent of guides, Dr. Y. Yadin, I spent a long time examining the precious manuscripts exposed in glass cases along the walls. Before me was the great scroll of Isaiah, almost intact but only partly unrolled, and the venerable remains of the second scroll of Isaiah, the *Commentary on Habakkuk*, the *Rule* and the *War Rule of the Sons of Light*. And finally, there were leaves from the scroll of the *Hymns* and the remnants of *Genesis Apocryphon*. Ever since the hall opened, visitors have passed unceasingly before this moving testimony to Israel's past, and there is scarcely an Israeli who has not heard of these manuscripts and who does not wish to see them for himself.

There exists another shelter for the Dead Sea Scrolls in Jerusalem

---

[1] A detailed inventory of the discovered manuscripts, though still incomplete and provisional, may be found in *RB*, lxiii, 1956, pp. 54-67, and in *Actes du 2e Congrès International pour l'étude de l'Ancien Testament* (Strasbourg, 1956), pp. 17-26. To be added to this list are the finds recovered from cave XI; namely, a scroll of Leviticus, a scroll of the Psalms, an ancient Targum of Job, and an apocalypse. But this information is still a little uncertain.

in the Jordan zone, on the other side of the great wall marking the armistice boundary. In the Palestine Archaeological Museum are gathered and preserved all the manuscripts and objects collected from the caves and the site of Qumran since 1948, the date of the Israeli-Arab armistice. For the Qumran region now belongs to the kingdom of Jordan, and everything found there is the legal property of the State. Some of these finds are exhibited in the Museum, but the greater part of the manuscripts are lodged in an annexe, a great austere and silent workroom where countless fragments are set out methodically under glass on long tables. All day long the members of the little team of Hebrew scholars responsible for their publication are bent over these slides. In April 1957, Father de Vaux — the leader of the team — took me into this laboratory, and under the friendly guidance of his colleagues, Father Milik and Father Starcky, I was able to spend several days looking through the various collections, still almost wholly unpublished. More than once I found myself lingering over a fragment revealing with marvellous precision some essential point of the doctrines of the Jewish sect. It is greatly to be hoped that these fragments will soon appear in print.

At present all the scrolls from cave I, as well as the manuscript fragments found there, have been scientifically published and photographed in Israel, America and Europe. As regards the finds from the other caves, the various members of the team responsible for editing them have from time to time published specimens in different scientific journals; but they are still relatively few. They constitute a mere foretaste, for it has been announced that the total publication will take years of work. Students must therefore arm themselves with patience.

In the meantime the texts already published provide matter of exceptional originality and interest for research. Articles and books devoted to the Dead Sea Scrolls have multiplied during the last ten years to an incredible degree all over the world. A German scholar, C. Burchard, has just published an entire book on the bibliography of the subject, *Bibliographie zu den Handschriften vom Toten Meer*, Berlin, 1957. His catalogue ends at the beginning of 1957, but even omitting writings of a purely popular type he already lists 1538 titles. Excluding the basic publications giving the *editio princeps* of the new documents, more than thirty books have already appeared in French, English, German, Dutch, Italian, Spanish and modern Hebrew. Philologists, historians and theologians are working intensively, and within the vast field of oriental studies a new discipline is emerging. In Germany they have even invented a name for it: Qumranology. It is clear that Qumran studies, affecting as they do all sorts of spheres — palaeographic, linguistic, literary, historical, theological — will continue to develop, and will require the co-operation of very many scholars for a long time to come, whether with regard to the biblical manuscripts or the non-biblical writings.

The biblical manuscripts are of prime importance. It should be remembered that it was not until A.D. 90, during the Rabbinic Council of Jamnia, that the text of the Hebrew Bible began to be officially established. This work of fixation and unification, entailing the addition of vowel points to the consonantal text in order to standardize the pronunciation, was completed towards the beginning of the eighth century. While establishing an official text, the Rabbinic authorities also took severe measures to ensure its faithful reproduction and to eliminate differing versions, and their method was so efficient that, in fact, the numerous biblical manuscripts still extant all reproduce, almost without variation, one and the same text, the so-called Masoretic or Traditional Text of the Bible. The oldest of these manuscripts, that of the Prophets, dates from A.D. 895 and is preserved at Cairo.

Such, at least, was the situation prior to the Dead Sea discoveries; but now, thanks to them, we have a considerable quantity of Hebrew biblical manuscripts very much more ancient. These biblical manuscripts were used by the Jewish community settled at Qumran and obviously date from before the dispersion of its members during the great Jewish War (A.D. 66-70). Most of them are copies written either during the first century B.C. or during the first two-thirds of the first century A.D., but some may go back a little further, even to the third century B.C. In any case, these biblical manuscripts, together with the biblical quotations reproduced in the various Qumran commentaries, all present a text earlier than the official one, a pre-Masoretic text. This is a fact of the greatest significance because, as has been said, until this time no Hebrew or Aramaic biblical manuscript from the pre-Masoretic period was available.

Now it is evident that however great and legitimate its authority from the point of view of the Synagogue, the Masoretic Text could never pretend to represent absolutely perfectly the original and primitive text of the various biblical books. Before they were authoritatively fixed, the Jewish writings which have become canonical were exposed, as are all writings which are copied and recopied, to multiple risks of alteration. In addition, many of them only attained their final form little by little, and sometimes but recently. Even the most sacred among them, those forming the Pentateuch (the *Torah*), were not protected from the accidental faults or intentional modifications which occur over the centuries in the transmission of texts whatever they may be.

Before the Qumran discoveries, we already possessed evidence of a certain diversity in the biblical text as it has been transmitted; namely, in the famous Samaritan Pentateuch, which, preserving the text adopted by the Samaritan sect several centuries before the establishment of the Masoretic version, presents, by comparison, numerous and important variants. Even weightier evidence, affecting all the books of the Bible, is found in the Greek version known as the Septuagint. This was composed during the last two or three centuries before the Christian era for the Jewish communities in Egypt, and it postulates the existence of a Hebrew prototype which must have been very different from the Masoretic Text. For this reason, scholars specializing in the study of the text of the Bible were led to recognize several distinct traditions during the pre-Masoretic period. Together with the tradition which served as basis for the fixing of the Masoretic Text, there must have existed, they explained, a Samaritan and a Judeo-Egyptian tradition; but this was only an hypothesis or assumption.

The essential issue resulting from the discovery of the biblical manuscripts of Qumran is that this hypothesis or assumption is now a certainty, positively demonstrated. These biblical manuscripts show that in the pre-Masoretic period, among the Jewish sect at Qumran anyway, *the three textual traditions were all represented*. Although some manuscripts show evidence in favour of the Masoretic tradition, others reveal undeniable agreement, either with the Samaritan tradition or with that of the Septuagint. It is not possible in these pages to present detailed proof, but the general fact is now quite certain. It should be added that the situation is at times very complex, for several manuscripts contain an amalgam of two, or even three, traditions; also, some variants are peculiar to Qumran.

The new documentation is still only partially known, and it is necessary to await the publication of all the biblical documents from the Qumran caves before forming a properly balanced judgment. The study it necessitates is as yet only in outline, and will call for long and detailed analysis. But it is already realized that as far as textual criticism of the Bible is concerned, although the Qumran discoveries do not, strictly speaking, predicate any essential change in the concepts and methods in practice for a long time among experienced specialists, they furnish an abundance of new material of inestimable value which will enable them to further their research in a much more solid and precise manner than hitherto.

The antiquity of the Masoretic Text so dear to the Synagogue, or rather, the antiquity of the tradition from which it derives, and its fidelity to this ancient tradition, have been proved. It has now a discernible history behind it. The recent discoveries leave it a place of honour among the various versions of the biblical text, if only for the fact that in the end it remains the only complete Hebrew text of the whole Bible which we possess.

It must, however, be recognized that the Samaritan and Greek variants have also acquired a verifiable antiquity which increases the value of their testimony and invites their consultation even more urgently than before.

Research on the Septuagint, carried out with enthusiasm for so many years, has also received crowning justification. It will spring into new and vigorous action now that we have at our disposal considerable portions of its Hebrew prototype. They have even found at Qumran some fragments several centuries older than the great codices by which it was known till now.[1] From the time of St. Jerome, the Masoretic Text has been honoured with the title 'veritas hebraica', but now that the text of the Septuagint is confirmed by the Hebrew manuscripts of Qumran, it also possesses a *veritas hebraica*. From the point of view of 'Hebrew truth', the Masoretic Text no longer enjoys an exclusive privilege.

Variants attested by the biblical manuscripts of Qumran should of course not be preferred *a priori* to the Masoretic Text. But it is more than ever important to compare all the versions of the biblical text, and to choose each reading according to its merit. This implies

---

[1] These codices date from the fourth and fifth centuries A.D. Note that various papyri have recently yielded fragments of this version which are older than the codices, in particular the Cairo papyrus Fouad 266 and the Manchester papyrus Greek 458, which appear to date from the second half, and the middle, of the second century B.C. respectively. (Cf. P. KAHLE, *The Cairo Geniza*, 2nd edn., 1959, pp. 218-22).

the inauguration of an entirely new stage in the field of that necessary introduction to the study of the Bible, textual criticism.

Nevertheless, despite the great interest of the Qumran biblical manuscripts, it is the non-biblical documents — very much more numerous, as has been pointed out — which make the Dead Sea discoveries so important. Through them we learn, directly and in detail, about the doctrines, institutions and customs of the Qumran sect, of a mystical Jewish sect that is to say, which flourished in Palestine around the beginning of the Christian era, at the very time of the appearance of Jesus and the preaching of the Christian gospel.

What was this sect? The late Professor Sukenik of the Hebrew University of Jerusalem was the first to suggest that they were Essenes. He was present in Palestine in 1947 when negotiations were begun with the Bedouin for the purchase of the scrolls found in cave I. Informed of these dealings, he was able to acquire three of the scrolls and to borrow four others, and was consequently the first scholar to examine the new documents. The idea of their Essene origin sprang to his mind immediately.

Already in 1949 a study of the first published texts, though few in number, convinced me of the Essene character of the documents as a whole.[1] When the complete Hebrew text of the *Commentary on Habakkuk* appeared in 1950 I immediately set out to place this little work, as exactly as possible, in its time and environment;[2] in my book, *Aperçus préliminaires sur les manuscrits de la mer Morte* (Eng. edn., *The Dead Sea Scrolls. A Preliminary Survey*), which appeared a few months afterwards, I devoted several pages to the demonstration of this Essene theory. The following year, as soon as the complete scroll of the *Rule* was, in its turn, published, I returned to the same argument, which the availability of this essential book in its entirety allowed me to enrich with new argument.[3]

In America, Professor W. H. Brownlee also championed the

---

[1] See my article, 'La grotte aux manuscrits du désert de Juda', in *R. de Paris*, July 1949, pp. 79-90. See also, ANDRÉ NEHER's article in *Évidences*, no. 4 (October 1949), in which the author reports the opinion then expressed by me.

[2] See my 'Observations sur le Commentaire d'Habucuc découvert près de la Mer Morte', a paper read before the Académie des Inscriptions et Belles-Lettres on May 26th, 1950 (Paris, 1950).

[3] See my 'Observations sur le Manuel de Discipline découvert près de la Mer Morte', a paper read before the Académie des Inscriptions et Belles-Lettres on June 8th, 1951 (Paris, 1951).

Essene theory from the first. But later, many other explanations were advanced. Exploring every aspect of the vast field of the ancient Jewish sects, some suggested the Hasidim of pre-Maccabean or Maccabean times, others suggested the Pharisees, others the Sadducees, others the Zealots, others the Judeo-Christian Ebionites, and others the Ḳaraites of the Middle Ages, etc. The hypotheses thus covered a period stretching from the third century B.C. to about the twelfth century A.D. In short, extreme confusion reigned and there was total disagreement!

However, as research on the Qumran texts developed and the archaeological finds from Khirbet Qumran threw fresh light on the date and character of the discoveries as a whole, the Essene theory quickly gained more and more ground. After only a few years, this view is held today by a considerable number of experts, men of a variety of schools and from every country, and although not yet accepted unanimously, and still meeting with a certain stubborn opposition, it may be said to enjoy the wide support of scholarly opinion. Having had to struggle almost alone, at the beginning of the affair, in defence of a theory which many considered almost provokingly audacious, I must confess that I am surprised by such rapid results.

As a matter of fact, before the Dead Sea discoveries the Essene question was considered one of the most obscure and even embarrassing problems of the whole of the history of religion. A vast number of books and articles have been written on the character and nature of the sect, on the role it played in the Jewish world, and on the foreign influences to which it must have been subjected. This mystic sect originated and flourished during the two centuries preceding the capture of Jerusalem by Titus and the destruction of the second Temple in A.D. 70. After this great national catastrophe, Israel reorganized itself in order to survive, and it was essentially the Rabbis — i.e. the Pharisees — who achieved this restoration and became the leaders of the new Synagogue. Deprived of its Temple, of its ancient political machinery and of its land, it had to find a principle of unity and cohesion for the communities dispersed all over the world in a fervent love of its Book, the *Torah*, and in fidelity to the traditional interpretation of Scripture. In this new Synagogue, rebuilt and controlled by the Pharisees, and obliged, in order to resist more strongly, to harden itself within a unified discipline, the Essenes — who had previously been considered by Judaism as orthodox —

found themselves cast aside, treated as undesirables, and after some time even hunted down as heretics and excommunicated. Inheriting these hostile sentiments, certain modern Jewish historians have been little inclined to show consideration for a sect which the official Synagogue formerly cursed and expelled.

Nor have Christian historians always done justice to the Essenes, though for quite different reasons. This Jewish sect seemed to present, in so far as it was known, striking analogies to the primitive Church; there were the same beliefs, the same moral and mystical ideas, and the same characteristic rites. In the eighteenth century, historical criticism bravely suggested that Christianity itself sprang from an Essene *milieu*. This point of view, which was very general at that time among philosophers, is expressed for example — a little boldly perhaps — in a letter written by Frederick II to d'Alembert on October 17th, 1770. 'Jesus', wrote the philosopher-king, 'was really an Essene: he was imbued with Essene ethics which, in their turn, owe much to Zeno.' In this form the argument certainly lacked balance. To Christian apologists it appeared a weapon, a devilish theory designed to sap the originality and transcendence of Christian revelation. It is therefore not difficult to understand the very lively opposition of a number of Christian historians, Catholic and Protestant alike, in the nineteenth century and during the first half of the twentieth. As a result, the very name Essene was suspect, and for a long time it was hardly good taste to recall the existence of the sect or to inquire into the influence which they had been able to exert. Nevertheless, some historians remained faithful to the eighteenth-century theory, or at least recognized that there was some truth in it;[1] thus, in France, Ernest Renan, though not admitting any 'direct commerce' between the Essenes and Jesus, proposed the following finely shaded definition: 'Christianity is an Essenism which has largely succeeded.' *An* Essenism, he says; but not *the* Essenism.

Such being the state of affairs, it will surprise no one to hear that in 1950 certain people welcomed rather coldly the theory of the Essene origin of the Dead Sea Scrolls; and all the more so that, in the book in which I explained this theory for the first time, I had not been able to suppress the fact that these manuscripts, while providing direct and immediate information about the history, beliefs and rites of the ancient Jewish sect, revealed numerous and extremely

[1] See the recent study by S. WAGNER, *Die Essenerforschung im 19. Jahrhundert* (Doctoral thesis, Leipzig, 1957).

significant affinities between the latter and primitive Christianity
which to a certain extent confirmed the older views of historical
criticism. In reply to my book, an influential Catholic journal
published, in February 1951, under the name of a writer known for
his work on Judaism, an article which included the following
passage: 'For years, historians inquiring into the origins of Christianity have studied every kind of document which might inform them
about the history and teaching of Jesus and his first disciples. They
have made themselves familiar with the currents of thought and
with the religious movements which, in Judaism, prepared the
coming of Christianity. . . . But, we repeat, the documents recently
discovered increase our knowledge on this point scarcely at all. . . .
The identification of the members of the New Covenant (the sect
from which the scrolls derive) with the Essenes, cannot at the
moment be stated with certainty. . . . Can we say more of the
Essenes, of their history, number, and extent, than the writers who
knew them, Pliny, Josephus, and Philo?'

Fifteen months later (in June 1952), this same journal wrote on the
subject once more, this time under the signature of a certain Jerome
(not St. Jerome, but an ingenuous pseudonym): 'It is hardly
necessary to draw attention to the immense interest of these discoveries. The Essenes emerge from the shadows which enveloped
them; we had only the testimony of Pliny the Elder, Philo and
Josephus concerning them. . . . The Qumran depository is today
connected with the Essenes; this does not establish the date of the
manuscripts, but it can throw light on their interpretation, and on
the history of the Essenes. Christians will see with joy and emotion
that the modern discoveries will bring them closer to the life of
the Jewish people living at the beginning of the Christian era. How
fortunate they will be if they can learn more about an environment
which must have been very close to that of the Baptist. Christianity
has everything to gain from a serene and objective light being thrown
on the times which saw its birth.'

This sudden change of front shows what rapid progress the Essene
theory made in circles which had proved themselves most hostile.
Owing to the Dead Sea discoveries, the name of the Essenes has
today become honourable once more, and the attention of a large
and enlightened public is turned with passionate curiosity towards
this Jewish sect, to which a few years ago only a small group of
specialists paid any attention at all.

It should be said at once that for the historian who considers the subject with the necessary broad-mindedness and serenity, this sect is undoubtedly representative of one of the most lofty and fruitful mystical movements of the ancient world, and is certainly one of the glories of ancient Judaism. On the other hand, although the Essenes, more than any other Jewish movement, were privileged to prepare the way for the institution of Christianity, the latter's originality remains impregnable despite the affinities and borrowings which the new texts reveal. But the historian concerned with Christian origins sees that the solution bristles with all sorts of problems, and that an entirely new period has opened in this field of knowledge. In future Jesus and the Christian church will be more solidly rooted in history. Such a gain is of great value, not only to the scholar, but also to those believers who are interested in the earthly and human aspects of the origins of the Christian message.

Historians studying the Jewish world in the age of Jesus, and trying to reconstruct the religious background from which Christianity sprang, may have thought until now that certain features of primitive Christianity without parallel in the Jewish world as they knew it, were entirely new and original, or else, in certain cases, were borrowed by Christianity from the various mystical teachings of the Hellenistic world. Such and such a doctrine found in the first Christian writings was not Jewish, they said, and was even incompatible with Judaism. But they were familiar mainly with Pharisaic Judaism, or Rabbinic Judaism; of Essene Judaism they had but imperfect, and more often than not, indirect knowledge. From now on, the Qumran documents take us into the heart of the Essene sect and lift the veil from its mysteries, rites and customs.

They are, of course, only a remnant of an immense corpus of literature, now largely lost. But the portion which has survived the assaults of time in the caves of Qumran and has been so happily and unexpectedly restored, the more or less mutilated scrolls and even the fragments, are all priceless to the historian of Judaism or of the beginnings of Christianity. And the golden rule for the interpretation of these Essene texts must undoubtedly be the following: read the texts exactly as they stand; feel no surprise at any of their revelations; try not to align them with doctrines current in Judaism; do not minimize *a priori* the significance of a doctrinal statement even if it is expressed very briefly and almost furtively, as, for example, in the biblical commentaries.

The main object of the present work is to introduce the reader to the non-biblical writings recovered from the various caves at Qumran of which the original text has now been published. The only omissions are the very mutilated writings and the really tiny fragments which have nothing particular to contribute to our knowledge of the sect.

The title of this book defines the documents as 'Essene writings', and in the first two chapters I will try to justify this appellation. First of all, I will set out, in a new translation, the classic accounts of the Essenes bequeathed to us by ancient literature: then I will compare, point by point, the information obtained from these accounts with that found in the new manuscripts. The following chapters, constituting the essential part of the book, will give a complete translation of these various writings, with introductions and notes designed to facilitate the reading. The last chapters will form as it were a supplement in which some fundamental historical problems, touched on in the preceding chapters, will be considered more closely and separately. They will be only brief sketches, but it seemed useful to add them to this collection of Qumran writings.

Such is the general plan. Other manuscripts found during the last few years in the same Judaean desert, though not in the Qumran region, are entirely omitted. Some were discovered in the caves of Wadi Murabba'at, a dozen miles or so south of Qumran; others in caves not yet identified with certainty but probably situated still farther to the south; and others still, from Khirbet Mird, about ten miles south-east of Jerusalem. Interesting though they are, these discoveries[1] have absolutely nothing to do with the Qumran finds, and it would be dangerous to confuse them. Some of the documents date from the time of the Second Jewish Revolt (A.D. 132-35) under the Emperor Hadrian, and others from a later period. None of them are of Essene origin or character. They therefore have no place in the present corpus of 'Essene writings'.

In 1950, in the Introduction to my book *Aperçus préliminaires ...*, I took care to emphasize that this first work on the subject had no other ambition, as its title indicated, than to present 'attempts at making use of a new documentation', 'working hypotheses and outlines of solution'. Two years later, in the Introduction to my *Nouveaux aperçus sur les manuscrits de la mer Morte* (Eng. edn., *The Jewish Sect of*

---

[1] A brief catalogue may be found in J. T. Milik's *Dix ans de découvertes ...*, pp. 16-18, 87-8, 93-5. (Eng. edn., pp. 14-16, 129-30, 135-8.)

Qumran and the Essenes), I insisted once more on the still provisory nature of the proposed explanations. 'It is clear', I wrote then, 'that we are only on the threshold of an immense research effort. The documents available to us at the present time are only a part of those found in the cave in 1947. In addition, there exist in the desert of Judah other caves containing manuscripts; some of these were explored quite recently and it seems that the material found there exceeds in importance the finds already made. The affair of the Dead Sea Scrolls, which even at the very beginning appeared of exceptional interest, assumes, therefore, greater and greater proportions. But before all this unknown material, before this mass of new texts of whose inventory, even, we are still ignorant, the scholar can only apply himself to the study of the documentation at his disposal, and formulate his opinions with reserve pending later confirmation. It is, nevertheless, his duty to try already to inject a maximum of clarity, even at the price of a certain amount of daring, into the precious texts at present before him.'

On the threshold of this new book — five years have passed since the last one was published — I feel the same need to remind the reader that on many points, in the present state of documentation, it is still not possible to give a definite verdict. Since 1952 the material has, of course, been considerably enriched: many texts have been published of which we knew nothing then. But we shall have to wait until all the Qumran texts are published, and the archaeological excavations on the site of Qumran are completed and all their results fully known, before the problems can be grappled with in their entirety, with every possible scientific guarantee. Until then, we can only mark the way; the moment has not yet come for the historian to try to write a really great and exhaustive work on the subject, making full and methodical use of all the new documents.

Until that time comes, the prudent caution which is indispensable will not prevent research from developing in every way; it is even greatly to be hoped that the most varied paths will be explored with complete freedom. But it is also to be hoped that the student engaged in these inquiries will make it a firm rule to attend to the totality of the documents and information at present at his disposal, and that writers will not simply take into account one part of the elements of a problem and then rush into fragile and evanescent hypotheses. Let them remember this basic precept from the *Discours de la Méthode* of Descartes: 'To make everywhere such complete reckonings and such

extensive surveys that I might be certain of omitting nothing.'
Applied to the field of the historical sciences, this rule means that the
greatest care must be taken not to overlook any text, any fragment.
For this reason, the present book aims above all to set before the
reader all the papers in the file, or at any rate all those known today.

Both my *Aperçus préliminaires* ... and my *Nouveaux aperçus*... resulted
from the same preoccupation, namely, to 'regroup the results of
partial inquiries into a more general picture, into an account of the
whole which will widen the perspectives and give to the various
elements of the construction their exact value'. Although I do not
repeat here what I wrote in these first essays, the work published
today is a continuation of them and a clarification. The reader who
has done me the honour of reading both books will easily realize that
this one adds something new. He will see also that the considerable
enrichment of the documentation, and the evolution of research
since 1950, have by no means obliged me to abandon my first
opinions on any essential point, or to retract any of my fundamental
views. On the contrary they have provided precious confirmation
and, to tell the truth, my research has continued and developed
along the same lines from the beginning.

Aperçus préliminaires ... acted as a pioneer; this little book had the
redoubtable honour of inaugurating what has now become a
lengthy series of books devoted to the Dead Sea Scrolls, and of
initiating discussion on this exciting subject. I take the liberty of
recalling its principal arguments: 'All the discovered manuscripts
proceed from an Essene community settled in the Qumran area,
from the Essene community mentioned by Pliny the Elder; the
story of the Teacher of Righteousness is to be placed roughly in the
first third of the first century B.C., a little before the capture of
Jerusalem by the Roman Pompey, and the community which he
founded hid its books in the neighbouring caves and left Qumran at
the time of the great Jewish War (A.D. 66-70); this Teacher, who very
probably died during the persecution directed against the sect by a
Hasmonean High Priest, was an eminent personality and the object
of his followers' fervent admiration; finally, and above all, the new
texts show that the primitive Christian church was rooted in the
Jewish Essene sect to a degree none would have suspected.'[1]

Increasing acceptance of all these theories is now evident among

---

[1] See my Preface to D. HOWLETT's book, *Les Esséniens et le Christianisme* (Paris, 1958),
p. 8.

all kinds of scholars; they have almost become traditional and, in a way, classic. Some writers even see no point nowadays in indicating their source: but no matter. Nothing reveals more clearly how much progress has been made. It is even due to this progress that I am not afraid to include the word 'Essene' in the title of the present work. Not that the Essene theory is considered as absolutely definitive, but I think it is sufficiently supported by many solid arguments to be quite clearly asserted. It can no longer be viewed as imprudent conjecture or pure possibility.

Certain people, it is true, still prefer to display a more or less total scepticism with regard to the various problems raised by the study of the Qumran texts. Others, timid by nature, are content to argue the pros and cons but do not commit themselves to taking up any particular stand. This allows them, whatever happens, to win without running any risk. Detailed and severe criticism is, of course, indispensable, but I believe it should not be confused with that negative tendency which is the worst enemy of science and its constructive effort. Scientific progress demands both daring and prudence. The illustrious scholar, Antoine Meillet, wrote: 'I have tried to formulate clear propositions; if they do not conform to the truth it will be all the easier to demonstrate their errors.' It is in this spirit that both *Aperçus*, and the present book, have been written.

Like the previous books, the present volume is meant for an enlightened public interested in the great problems of religious history, and not only for specialists. For this reason the translations given here are without the apparatus used by philologists, and I have simply referred to the special articles published by me in various scholarly journals: if the reader desires, he will be able to find there arguments which would be out of place in these pages.

It should be added that, conscientious though they are, these translations are still to a certain extent provisional; they will certainly have to be retouched here and there when the language and style proper to the documents are more completely known, as well as the environment from which they come. *Dies diem docet!* These reservations will cause no surprise to men of science. We know the remark of the physicist genius, Frédéric Joliot-Curie: the scholar, he liked to say, proceeds 'by means of successive erasures'. I am not ashamed to admit that sooner or later I shall certainly be obliged to make quite a few 'erasures' in this book; rather do I pity those who would hold this against me.

Such is the imperfect book offered to the 'benevolent reader'. May he find pleasure in following with his eyes the efforts of an historian anxious to extract from the marvellous archives of Qumran everything that may throw new light on the ancient history of Judaism and the origins of Christianity.[1]

Paris, January 1959

---

[1] The present work makes substantial use of a series of articles published in *Évidences* from 1956-58 (nos. 54-73). It is my pleasant duty to thank the editor of this journal, M. Nicolas BAUDY, for allowing them to be reproduced, as a whole or in part, in a separate publication.

CHAPTER I

THE ESSENES IN ANCIENT LITERATURE

1. PHILO OF ALEXANDRIA: *Quod omnis probus liber sit; Apologia pro Judaeis.* 2. FLAVIUS JOSEPHUS: *The Jewish War; Jewish Antiquities.* 3. PLINY THE ELDER; DIO CHRYSOSTOM.

1. PHILO OF ALEXANDRIA

The two earliest accounts of the Essenes are those written by Philo of Alexandria; one appears in his treatise *Quod omnis probus liber sit* (§§ 75-91), and the other in his *Apologia pro Judaeis.* This last book is now lost, but Eusebius of Caesarea quotes the passage on the Essenes in his *Praeparatio Evangelica,* Book VIII, Chapter 11. Although the exact date of these writings is unknown, Philo was born around 30 B.C. and pursued his literary activities until at least A.D. 40.

Quod omnis probus liber sit[1]

§ 75. Nor is Palestinian Syria, which is occupied by a considerable part of the very populous nation of the Jews, barren of virtue. Certain among them, to the number of over four thousand, are called Essaeans;[2] although this word is not, strictly speaking, Greek, I think it may be related to the word 'holiness'.[3] Indeed, they are men utterly dedicated to the service of God; they do not offer animal sacrifice, judging it more fitting to render their minds truly holy.

§ 76. First it should be explained that, fleeing the cities because of the ungodliness customary among town-dwellers, they live in villages; for they know that, as noxious air breeds epidemics there, so does the social life afflict the soul with incurable ills.

Some Essaeans work in the fields, and others practise various crafts contributing to peace; and in this way they are useful to themselves and

---

[1] The Greek text is from the L. COHN and P. WENDLAND edition of the works of Philo, vol. vi (Berlin, 1915).

[2] Instead of 'Essaeans', Josephus usually writes 'Essenes', the term at present employed in English.

[3] Philo seems here to play on the similarity between the Greek words *Essaioi,* 'Essaeans', and *osioi,* 'holy, pure'. The exact etymology of the word Essaean, or Essene, remains obscure; its root is obviously *ess-* and certainly transcribes some Semitic word. I have suggested in this connection the Hebrew word '*eẓah,* 'council, party': in the Qumran texts the Essenes are described as 'men of the Council (or Party) of God'. See below, p. 43.

to their neighbours. They do not hoard silver and gold, and do not acquire vast domains with the intention of drawing revenue from them, but they procure for themselves only what is necessary to life.

§ 77. Almost alone among all mankind, they live without goods and without property; and this by preference, and not as a result of a reverse of fortune. They think themselves thus very rich, rightly considering frugality and contentment to be real superabundance.

§ 78. In vain would one look among them for makers of arrows, or javelins, or swords, or helmets, or armour, or shields; in short, for makers of arms, or military machines, or any instrument of war, or even of peaceful objects which might be turned to evil purpose. They have not the smallest idea, not even a dream, of wholesale, retail, or marine commerce, rejecting everything that might excite them to cupidity.

§ 79. There are no slaves among them, not a single one, but being all free they help one another. And they condemn slave-owners, not only as unjust in that they offend against equality, but still more as ungodly, in that they transgress the law of nature which, having given birth to all men equally and nourished them like a mother, makes of them true brothers, not in name but in reality. But for its own greater enjoyment crafty avarice has dealt mortal blows at this human kinship, putting hostility in the place of affection, and hatred in the place of friendship.

§ 80. As regards philosophy, they first of all leave logic to word-chasers, seeing that it is useless in the acquisition of virtue; then they leave natural philosophy to street orators, seeing that it is beyond human nature, except, however, in what it teaches of the existence of God and the origin of the world. But they work at ethics with extreme care, constantly utilizing the ancestral laws, laws which no human mind could have conceived without divine inspiration.

§ 81. They continually instruct themselves in these laws but especially every seventh day; for the seventh day is thought holy. On that day they abstain from other work and proceed to the holy places called synagogues, where they sit in appointed places, according to their age, the young men below the old, attentive and well-behaved.

§ 82. One of them then takes up the books and reads, and another from among the more learned steps forward and explains whatever is not easy to understand in these books. Most of the time, and in accordance with an ancient method of inquiry, instruction is given them by means of symbols.[1]

§ 83. They learn piety, holiness, justice, the internal rule, the constitution, knowledge of what is truly good or bad or indifferent, and how to choose what must be done and how to flee from what must be avoided. In this they make use of triple definitions and rules concerning, respectively, the love of God, the love of virtue, and the love of men.

---

[1] A reference to the allegorical exegesis especially in favour in Alexandria.

§ 84. Of their love of God they give a thousand examples by constant and unceasing purity throughout the whole of life, by the rejection of oaths, the rejection of falsehood, and by the belief that the Deity is the cause of all good, but of no evil: of their love of virtue, by contempt for riches, glory and pleasure, and by their continence and endurance, and also frugality, simplicity, contentment, modesty, obedience to the rule, stability of character, and all similar virtues: of their love of men, by kindness, equality and a communal life of which, although beyond all praise, it is not out of place to speak briefly here.

§ 85. Firstly, no house belongs to any one man; indeed, there is no house which does not belong to them all, for as well as living in communities, their homes are open to members of the sect arriving from elsewhere.

§ 86. Secondly, there is but one purse for them all and a common expenditure. Their clothes and food are also held in common, for they have adopted the practice of eating together. In vain would one search elsewhere for a more effective sharing of the same roof, the same way of life and the same table. This is the reason: nothing which they receive as salary for their day's work is kept to themselves, but is deposited before them all, in their midst, to be put to the common employment of those who wish to make use of it.

§ 87. As for the sick, they are not neglected on the pretext that they can produce nothing, for, thanks to the common purse, they have whatever is needed to treat them, so there is no fear of great expense on their behalf. The aged, for their part, are surrounded with respect and care: they are like parents whose children lend them a helping hand in their old age with perfect generosity and surround them with a thousand attentions.

§ 88. Such are the athletes of virtue which this philosophy produces, a philosophy which undoubtedly lacks the refinements of Greek eloquence, but which propounds, like gymnastic exercises, the accomplishment of praiseworthy deeds as the means by which a man ensures absolute freedom for himself.

§ 89. And this is the proof. Over the course of time, many kings of diverse character and inclinations have risen against this land. Some, rivalling the most ferocious wild beasts in their cruelty, sparing no sort of atrocity, immolating their subjects in flocks, and even dismembering them alive, piece by piece, limb by limb, like butchers, never ceased until they were themselves obliged to undergo the same misfortunes beneath the blows of that Justice which watches over human destiny.

§ 90. Others, replacing frenzy and rage with another kind of wickedness, nourishing unutterable cruelty, speaking calmly yet revealing beneath their soft-worded hypocrisy a soul filled with profound hatred, caressing as dogs whose bite is poison, these authors of incurable evils left as monuments to their wickedness, from town to town, the never-to-be-forgotten calamities of those who had suffered.

§ 91. But none of them, neither the most cruel, nor the most un-principled and false, was ever able to lay a charge against the society known as Essaeans, or Saints;[1] on the contrary, they were all defeated by the virtue of these men. They could only treat them as independent individuals, free by nature, and extol their communal meals and com-munal life as beyond all praise and as the clearest demonstration of a perfect and completely happy existence.

Now follows, in an extract from his *Apologia pro Judaeis*, Philo's second account of the Essenes.[2]

§ 1. Our Law-giver[3] encouraged the multitude of his disciples to live in community: these are called Essaeans, and I think they have merited this title because of their holiness.[4] They live in a number of towns in Judaea,[5] and also in many villages and large groups.[6]

§ 2. Their enlistment is not due to race (the word race is unsuitable where volunteers are concerned), but is due to zeal for the cause of virtue and an ardent love of men.

§ 3. There are therefore no children of tender years among the Essaeans, nor even adolescents or young men, since at this age the character, be-cause of its immaturity, is inconstant and attracted to novelty; but they are men of ripe years already inclining to old age who are no longer carried away by the flux of the body nor drawn by the passions, but enjoy true and unparalleled liberty.

§ 4. Their life bears witness to this liberty. None of them can endure to possess anything of his own; neither house, slave, field, nor flocks, nor anything which feeds and procures wealth. But they set down everything in a heap in their midst, and enjoy in common the resources of them all.

§ 5. They live together in brotherhoods, having adopted the form of associations and the custom of eating in common. They employ their whole activity for the common good.

§ 6. Nevertheless, they all follow different occupations, and apply

---

[1] In Greek *osioi*; cf. above, § 75. All this oratory is perhaps partly aimed at Herod the Great, the cruel prince who nevertheless treated the Essenes with friendship and regard, and partly at the Roman authorities with their insidious and perfidious despotism. The Essenes, during the time of Philo, seem to have lived in peace with them also.

[2] Greek text from the G. DINDORFF edition of the works of Eusebius of Caesarea, vol. i (Leipzig, 1867).

[3] Moses.

[4] The same explanation of the word 'Essaean' as in the previous account (§ 75).

[5] This information contradicts the previous account in which Philo writes (§ 76): 'They flee the towns. . . .' On the other hand it agrees with JOSEPHUS, *The Jewish War*, § 124 (see below, p. 28).

[6] In Greek, *omiloi*; literally, 'societies, companies'.

themselves to them with zeal, like athletes, never offering as excuse either cold, or heat, or atmospheric changes. Performing their accustomed tasks from before sunrise, they do not leave them until the sun has almost set, devoting themselves to them with no less joy than those who train for gymnastic combat.

§ 7. Indeed, they believe their own training to be more useful to life, more agreeable to body and soul, and more lasting, than athletic games, since their exercises remain fitted to their age, even when the body no longer possesses its full strength.

§ 8. There are farmers among them expert in the art of sowing and working the land, shepherds leading every sort of flock, and bee-keepers.

§ 9. Others are craftsmen in divers trades. So they have to suffer no privation of what is indispensable to essential needs, and they never defer until the morrow whatever serves to procure for them blameless revenue.

§ 10. When each man receives his salary for these different trades, he hands it over to one person, the steward elected by them; and as soon as the steward receives this money, he immediately buys what is necessary and provides ample food, as well as whatever else is necessary to human life.

§ 11. Daily they share the same way of life, the same table, and even the same tastes, all of them loving frugality and hating luxury as a plague for body and soul.

§ 12. And not only do they have a common table, but common clothes also. In fact they have at their disposition thick coats for the winter, and inexpensive tunics for the summer; so it is simple and lawful, for whoever desires to do so, to take the garment he wishes, since it is agreed that whatever belongs to each belongs to all, and conversely, whatever belongs to all belongs to each.

§ 13. In addition, if any of them falls ill he is treated at the expense of the community, and is surrounded by the care and attention of them all. As for the aged, even if they have no children they are as fathers not only of many children but of very good ones. They usually quit life in extremely happy and splendid old age, honoured by privileges and by the regard of so many sons who care for them spontaneously rather than as a result of natural necessity.

§ 14. On the other hand, shrewdly providing against the sole or principal obstacle threatening to dissolve the bonds of communal life, they banned marriage at the same time as they ordered the practice of perfect continence. Indeed, no Essaean takes a woman because women are selfish, excessively jealous, skilful in ensnaring the morals of a spouse and in seducing him by endless charms.

§ 15. Women set out to flatter, and wear all sorts of masks, like actors on the stage; then, when they have bewitched the eye and captured the ear, when, that is to say, they have deceived the lower senses, they next lead the sovereign mind astray.

§ 16. On the other hand, if children are born, they then declare with audacious arrogance, and swollen with pride and effrontery, what they were formerly content to insinuate hypocritically by means of allusions, and shamelessly employ violence to commit actions all of which are contrary to the good of the common life.

§ 17. The husband, bound by his wife's spells, or anxious for his children from natural necessity, is no more the same towards the others, but unknown to himself he becomes a different man, a slave instead of a freeman.

§ 18. The life of the Essaeans is indeed so enviable that not only individuals but even great kings are seized with admiration before such men, and are glad to pay homage to their honourable character by heaping favours and honours upon them.

2. FLAVIUS JOSEPHUS

The Jewish historian, Flavius Josephus, makes passing mention of the Essenes in various passages of his works, but besides these brief references which may be omitted here, he has written two justly famous accounts of the Essenes, one in *The Jewish War*, and the other in *Jewish Antiquities*.

The first, from Book II, Chapter 8 of *The Jewish War* is by far the longer and more detailed of the two. It is fuller and more exact than Philo's accounts of the Essenes, concerned as they are with philosophical preoccupations and oratorical amplifications, and is very likely independent of them: the use of common sources may explain similarities between the two. In addition, the Jewish historian must have known personally, in Palestine, the Essenes whom he describes, and must have recorded personal observations in his picture of them. It should be remembered that Josephus wrote *The Jewish War*, his first work, between A.D. 70 and 75.

This important evidence is reproduced below *in extenso*. The present translation is made direct from the Greek text of Josephus.[1] There exists also an ancient Slavonic version of the Jewish historian's

---

[1] Greek text from B. NIESE's edition of the works of Josephus, vol. vi (Berlin, 1895). There is a good French translation of *The Jewish War* by RENÉ HARMAND in *Œuvres complètes de Flavius Josèphe*, vol. v (Paris, E. Leroux, 1911); but a new translation is offered here which, although inspired by Harmand's work, aims at the closest possible rendering of the Greek. (English translation by H. ST. J. THACKERAY, in the Loeb Classical Library.)

book,[1] and in this the account of the Essenes presents, by comparison with the Greek text, several curious additions to which different authors have recently drawn attention;[2] their significance remains in dispute however,[3] and I will not dwell on them here.

Another long account of the Essenes appears in the work of Hippolytus of Rome, entitled *Refutation of all heresies*,[4] and written in about A.D. 230 (IX, 18-28). This report is, on the whole, parallel to that of Josephus in *The Jewish War*; it is a sort of abridgment of the latter, and seems to have been borrowed from it. It nevertheless includes some interesting variants,[5] and I draw attention to the chief of these in the notes accompanying the translation of Josephus.

Now follows the translation: for the sake of clarity, I have myself introduced a few sub-titles into the text.

Jewish Sects

2. § 119. Indeed, there exist among the Jews three schools of philosophy: the Pharisees belong to the first, the Sadducees to the second, and to the third belong men who intend to cultivate a particularly saintly life, called Essenes.[6] They are Jews by race, but in addition they are more closely united among themselves by mutual affection than are the others.

The Essene ideal: asceticism and the common life

§ 120. The Essenes renounce pleasure as an evil, and regard continence and resistance to the passions as a virtue. They disdain marriage for themselves, but adopt the children of others at a tender age in order to instruct them;[7] they regard them as belonging to them by kinship, and condition them to conform to their own customs.

[1] The latest edition of this 'Slavonic Josephus' is the best, namely, that of A. VAILLANT and P. PASCAL, *La prise de Jérusalem de Josèphe le Juif*. Texte vieux-russe publié intégralement par V. ISTRIN, imprimé sous la direction de A. VAILLANT, traduit en français par P. PASCAL (Paris, Institut des Études slaves, 1934-38, 2 volumes).

[2] See A. RUBINSTEIN, *The Essenes according to the Slavonic Version of Josephus' Wars*, in *VT*, vi, 1956, pp. 307-8; M. PHILONENKO, *La notice du Josèphe slave sur les Esséniens*, in *Semitica*, vi, 1956, pp. 69-73.

[3] See A. VAILLANT, *Le Josèphe slave et les Esséniens*, in *Semitica*, viii, 1958, pp. 39-40.

[4] It is also currently known as *Philosophoumena*; critical edition by P. WENDLAND, *Hippolytus Werke*, Band 3 (Leipzig, 1916); collection, Die griechischen Christlichen Schriftsteller der ersten drei Jahrhunderte, vol. xxvi.

[5] See M. BLACK, 'The account of the Essenes in Hippolytus and Josephus', in *The Background of the New Testament and its Eschatology. Studies in honour of Charles Harold Dodd* (Cambridge, 1956), pp. 172-5.

[6] Josephus seems here to allude to the etymology of the word 'Essene'. Philo, as has been seen (p. 21, note 3), plays on the similarity of the Greek terms *Essaioi* and *osioi*, but Josephus quotes not the word *osioi* but another Greek word, *semnoi*, which, although meaning more or less the same, does not lend itself — directly, anyway — to the same play on words. This phrase from Josephus remains a little obscure.

[7] This contradicts Philo in *Apologia pro Judaeis*, § 3. Philo is probably less well informed on this point.

§ 121. It is not that they abolish marriage, or the propagation of the species resulting from it, but they are on their guard against the licentiousness of women and are convinced that none of them is faithful to one man.

3. § 122. They despise riches and their communal life is admirable. In vain would one search among them for one man with a greater fortune than another. Indeed, it is a law that those who enter the sect shall surrender their property to the order; so neither the humiliation of poverty nor the pride of wealth is to be seen anywhere among them. Since their possessions are mingled, there exists for them all, as for brothers, one single property.

§ 123. They regard oil as a defilement, and should any of them be involuntarily anointed, he wipes his body clean. They make a point of having their skin dry and of being always clothed in white garments.

The administrators of the common funds are elected, and each, without distinction, is appointed in the name of all to the various offices.

4. § 124. They are not in one town only, but in every town several of them form a colony. Also, everything they have is at the disposal of members of the sect arriving from elsewhere as though it were their own, and they enter into the house of people whom they have never seen before as though they were intimate friends.

§ 125. For this reason also, they carry nothing with them when they travel: they are, however, armed against brigands.[1] In every town a quaestor of the order, specially responsible for guests, is appointed steward of clothing and other necessaries.

§ 126. Their dress and outward behaviour are like those of children whose teacher rears them in fear: they do not change their garments or shoes until they are completely torn or worn out.

§ 127. They neither buy nor sell anything among themselves; each man gives what he has to whoever needs it, and receives in return whatever he himself requires. And they can even receive freely from whomsoever they like without giving anything in exchange.[2]

The daily life of an Essene

5. § 128. Their piety towards the Deity takes a particular form: before sunrise they speak no profane word but recite certain ancestral prayers to the sun as though entreating it to rise.

§ 129. After these prayers the superiors dismiss them so that each man

---

[1] This constitutes a notable diminishment of the ideal of absolute pacifism which PHILO, Q.o.p.l., § 78, attributes to the Essenes.

[2] The Essenes, therefore, could only barter without making use of money. They could also give each other gifts, pure and simple. This would seem to infer that they had some possessions at their disposal; perhaps food, or some small objects (cf. § 134). But perhaps Josephus had in mind Essenes not subject to the rule of common ownership, either because they were not yet definitely admitted into the order — postulants and novices — or because they lived, for various reasons, outside the community houses, like tertiaries.

may attend to the craft with which he is familiar. Then, after working without interruption until the fifth hour,[1] they reassemble in the same place and, girded with linen loin-cloths, bathe themselves thus in cold water. After this purification they assemble in a special building to which no one is admitted who is not of the same faith; they themselves only enter the refectory if they are pure, as though into a holy precinct.

§ 130. When they are quietly seated, the baker serves out the loaves of bread in order, and the cook serves only one bowlful of one dish to each man.

§ 131. Before the meal the priest says a prayer and no one is permitted to taste the food before the prayer; and after they have eaten the meal he recites another prayer. At the beginning and at the end they bless God as the Giver of life.

Afterwards they lay aside the garments which they have worn for the meal, since they are sacred garments, and apply themselves again to work until the evening.

§ 132. Then they return and take their dinner in the same manner, and if guests are passing through they sit at the table. No shouting or disturbance ever defiles the house; they allow each other to speak in turn.

§ 133. To those outside, this silence of the men inside seems a great mystery; but the cause of it is their invariable sobriety and the fact that their food and drink are so measured out that they are satisfied and no more.

Essene virtues

6. § 134. On the whole, therefore, they do nothing unless ordered by the superiors. Yet two things depend on themselves: aid and pity. In fact they are allowed on their own discretion to help those worthy of help[2] whenever it is asked for, and to offer food to the needy, but they have no right to subsidize members of their own family without the authority of the procurators.

§ 135. They are righteous arbiters of their anger, masters of their wrath, paragons of loyalty and peacemakers.

Every word they speak is stronger than an oath and they refrain from swearing, considering it worse than perjury; for, they say, the man who cannot be believed unless he calls on God as witness condemns himself.[3]

---

[1] About 11 a.m.

[2] This seems to infer that it was forbidden to help the unworthy, for example those who had been excommunicated (cf. § 143).

[3] Because of this prohibition, Herod dispensed the Essenes from the oath imposed by him on his subjects: cf. JOSEPHUS, *Jewish Antiquities*, XV, 10, 4, § 371. All the same, the Essenes had to take an oath on their admission into the order (see § 139), so this rule allowed for exceptions.

The Essene books

§ 136. They apply themselves with extraordinary zeal to the study of the works of the ancients[1] choosing, above all, those which tend to be useful to body and soul. In them they study the healing of diseases, the roots offering protection and the properties of stones.[2]

Admission into the sect: the preparatory stages

7. § 137. Those desiring to enter the sect do not obtain immediate admittance. The postulant waits outside for one year; the same way of life is propounded to him and he is given a hatchet,[3] the loin-cloth which I have mentioned,[4] and a white garment.[5]

§ 138. Having proved his continence during this time, he draws closer to the way of life and participates in the purificatory baths at a higher degree, but he is not yet admitted into intimacy. Indeed, after he has shown his constancy, his character is tested for another two years, and if he appears worthy he is received into the company permanently.[6]

The Essene oath

§ 139. But before touching the common food he makes solemn vows before his brethren. He first swears to practise piety towards the Deity; then to observe justice towards men and to do no wrong to any man, neither of his own accord nor at another's command; to hate the wicked always, and to fight together with the just.[7]

§ 140. He swears constant loyalty to all, but above all to those in

---

[1] There is again mention of these books in § 142; among them may be included, for example, *Enoch* and *Jubilees*.

[2] Certain plants and stones were thought to have medicinal value; various treatises of Gnostic origin on this subject have come down to us.

[3] JEROME CARCOPINO compares the Essene hatchet to the implement figuring on a number of Roman epitaphs under the name of *ascia*. He sees in it a symbol of Pythagorean origin (*Le Mystère d'un Symbole chrétien*, Paris, 1955). Note that a hatchet of the *ascia* type has been found in cave XI at Qumran. Is this 'an Essene hatchet'? See R. DE VAUX, *VT*, ix, 1959, pp. 399-407.

[4] Cf. § 129.

[5] Cf. § 123. The Pythagoreans were also dressed in white.

[6] Before being permanently received, he had therefore to spend one year as a postulant 'outside', then two years of novitiate during which he was progressively admitted to greater participation in the life of the community. At the end of each stage, he could only pass on to the next after an examination had proved his worthiness. Participation in the communal meal, the most sacred sacrament of the sect (cf. §§ 129-31), was only allowed to those who had done the two years of novitiate and sworn the solemn oath of final admission.

[7] Instead of this phrase, HIPPOLYTUS (*Refutation*, IX, § 23) reads as follows: 'To hate no man, neither the wicked nor the enemy, but to pray for them and to fight together with the good.' Is this variant in the work of the Christian author, with its elimination of the obligation 'to hate the unjust', due to some memory of the Sermon on the Mount? Or is it the more charitable version of a genuine Essene formula which had tended among the Essenes themselves to take the place of the ancient formula of a pronouncedly harsh sectarianism?

THE ESSENES IN ANCIENT LITERATURE

power; for authority never falls to a man without the will of God. He swears never to show insolence in the exercise of his duty should he ever happen to be in command himself, nor to outshine his subordinates in his dress or by increased adornment.

§ 141. He swears always to love truth and to pursue liars; to keep his hands pure from theft and his soul pure from wicked gain. Also he swears to conceal nothing from the members of the sect, and to reveal nothing to outsiders even though violence unto death be used against him.

§ 142. In addition, he swears to transmit none of the doctrines except as he himself received them, abstaining from all < alteration >,[1] and to preserve the books of their sect likewise, as also the names of the Angels.[2] Such are the oaths by which they secure the fidelity of those who enter the sect.

Exclusion from the sect

8. § 143. Those who are caught in the act of committing grave faults are expelled from the order. The individual thus excluded often perishes, the prey to a most miserable fate; for bound by his oaths and customs he cannot even share the food of others. Reduced to eating grass, he perishes, his body dried up by hunger.

§ 144. They have also out of compassion taken back many who were at their last gasp, judging this torture to death sufficient for the expiation of their faults.

Judicial power

9. § 145. In matters of judgment they are very exact and impartial. They dispense justice at assemblies of not less than a hundred, and their decisions are irrevocable.

Respect for the name of the Lawgiver

The name of the Lawgiver is, after God, a great object of veneration among them, and if any man blasphemes against the Lawgiver he is punished with death.[3]

---

[1] The Greek text has here a word signifying 'brigandage': I think it should be corrected.

[2] This shows the importance attached by the sect to the revelation of the names of the Angels, a revelation which secured for the initiates knowledge of the loftiest secrets of the divine world.

[3] It is generally explained that this Lawgiver is Moses. But I myself think rather that it refers to the Lawgiver of the sect, i.e. its Founder. His name was, 'after God, a great object of veneration': not only was it forbidden, on pain of death, to blaspheme against it, but it was also no doubt forbidden to be uttered, just as it was forbidden to pronounce the name of God (Yahweh). In the same way, the Pythagoreans were forbidden, out of respect, to pronounce the name of Pythagoras and used instead the expression, 'Master', or, quite simply, 'he' (autos epha).

Discipline

§ 146. They make it their duty to obey their elders as well as the majority; for example, when ten sit together no man speaks if the other nine oppose it.

Particular regulations

§ 147. In addition, they refrain from spitting in the middle of the company, or to the right.[1] They are also forbidden, more rigorously than any other Jew, to attend to their work on the seventh day. Not only do they prepare their food on the day before to avoid lighting a fire on that day, but they dare not even move an object, or go to stool.

§ 148. On other days, they dig a hole one foot deep with their mattocks[2] (for such is the hatchet given to the new disciples). They squat there, covered by their mantles so as not to offend the rays of God.[3]

§ 149. Then they push back the excavated soil into the hole. For this operation they choose the loneliest places. However natural the evacuation of excrement, they are accustomed to wash themselves afterwards as though defiled.[4]

The four classes of Essenes

10. § 150. They are divided into four lots according to the duration of their discipline, and the juniors are so inferior to their elders that if the latter touch them they wash themselves as though they had been in contact with a stranger.[5]

[1] The law against spitting 'in the middle of the company' may be a simple rule of cleanliness or hygiene, but the injunction against spitting 'to the right' refers to some superstitious preoccupation.

[2] Cf. § 137.

[3] This is an exact translation of the Greek text, but one would expect to read 'the rays of the sun' instead. This passage may be compared with § 128: 'Before sunrise . . . they recite certain ancestral prayers to the sun.' The Essenes considered the sun, not, of course, as a god, but as the manifestation or symbol of divine splendour. They therefore covered themselves carefully with their mantles so that the rays of the heavenly body should not reach any part of their nakedness.

[4] These various regulations are obviously inspired by Deut. xxiii. 12-14. 'You shall have a place outside the camp and you shall go out to it; and you shall have a stick with your weapons; and when you sit down outside, you shall dig a hole with it, and turn back and cover up your excrement. Because the Lord your God walks in the midst of your camp to save you and to give up your enemies before you, therefore your camp must be holy, that he may not see anything indecent among you and turn away from you.' The Essenes, in their concern for extreme purity, add to these ancient rules the double obligation of strict concealment of their nakedness when evacuating, and ablutions afterwards.

[5] It is regrettable that Josephus did not see fit to name the four 'lots', i.e. the four classes or categories to which he alludes. Perhaps, judging from §§ 137-8, they consisted of postulants, first-year novices, second-year novices, and the professed. HIPPOLYTUS, in *Refutation*, IX, § 26, gives a long variant of this passage, interpreting the division into four classes in quite a different manner. The text runs as follows: 'They are divided according to their age and do not follow the observances in the same manner, divided as they are into four classes. Indeed, some of them carry the observances to an extreme, going so far as to refuse to hold a piece of money in the hand, declaring it forbidden to carry, look at

Their longevity and their heroism in the face of death

§ 151. I think it is because of the simplicity of their way of life and their regularity that they live long, so that most of them reach the age of more than a hundred years.

Yet they despise danger: they triumph over pain by the heroism of their convictions, and consider death, if it come with glory, to be better than preservation of life.

§ 152. The war against the Romans fully revealed their souls. During it their limbs were twisted and broken, burned and shattered; they were subjected to every instrument of torture to compel them either to blaspheme against the Lawgiver[1] or to eat forbidden food.[2] But they refused to do either, or even to flatter their butchers or weep.

§ 153. Smiling amidst pain, and mocking those who tortured them, they gave up their souls cheerfully, convinced that they would recover them again.

Their beliefs concerning the soul and the hereafter

11. § 154. Indeed, it is a firm belief among them that although bodies are corruptible, and their matter unstable, souls are immortal and endure for ever; that, come from subtlest ether, they are entwined with the bodies which serve them as prisons, drawn down as they are by some physical spell;

§ 155. but that when they are freed from the bonds of the flesh, liberated, so to speak, from long slavery, then they rejoice and rise up to the heavenly world. Agreeing with the sons of the Greeks, they declare that an abode is reserved beyond the Ocean for the souls of the just; a place oppressed neither by rain nor snow nor torrid heat, but always refreshed by the

---

[1] Moses, or more likely, the Founder of the sect. Cf. the note on § 145.

[2] Forbidden either by Mosaic law or by customs proper to the Essenes (cf. § 143). What war is referred to here, and what persecution of the Essenes? The passage is generally thought to allude to the great Jewish War against the Romans in A.D. 66-70, but nothing is known of a persecution of the Essenes at that time. Some writers have suggested that the war in question may have been that of Pompey in 63 B.C., but this point remains obscure.

---

and fabricate effigies. Also, none of these dare enter a city for fear of passing through a gate surmounted by statues, esteeming it sacrilege to pass beneath an image. Certain others among them, when they hear an individual discoursing on God and His laws, make sure, if he is uncircumcised, that this individual is alone in a place, then threaten him with assassination unless he allows himself to be circumcised. If he does not wish to comply, far from sparing him, they cut his throat. It is on account of this that they have received the name of Zealots; or as some call them, Sicarii. Still others among them refuse to call any man master but God, even though they be maltreated or put to death. And those who have come later are so inferior with respect to the observances, that those who hold to the ancient customs do not even touch them. Should they do so, they wash themselves immediately, as though they have touched a stranger.' It is clear that Hippolytus connects the Essenes with the Zealots, a sect thought to have sprung later from the Essenes, and with which the latter refused to associate.

gentle breeze blowing from the Ocean.[1] But they relegate evil souls to a dark pit shaken by storms, full of unending chastisement.

§ 156. The Greeks, I think, had the same idea when they assigned their valiant ones, whom they call 'heroes' and 'demi-gods', to the Islands of the Blessed, and the souls of the bad to Hades, the place of the wicked, where according to their mythology, certain people such as Sisyphus, Tantalus, Ixion and Tityus, undergo their torment. A belief of this kind assumes in the first place that souls are eternal; next, it serves to encourage virtue and to deflect from vice.

§ 157. Indeed, the good will become better during their lives if they hope to be rewarded, even after their end; whilst the wicked will restrain their instincts out of fear if they expect to suffer eternal punishment after their dissolution even though they escape while they live.

§ 158. Such, then, are the religious teachings of the Essenes with regard to the soul: they offer them as a lure, and those who have once tasted their wisdom do not resist.[2]

Their gift of prediction

12. § 159. There are some among them who, trained as they are in the study of the holy books and the < sacred > writings,[3] and the sayings of

---

[1] This description draws its whole inspiration from HOMER (*Odyssey*, IV, 562-8).

[2] This account of Essene beliefs concerning the soul and the hereafter is, without doubt, more or less influenced by a desire to draw attention to their likeness to the doctrines of Greek spirituality, especially those of Pythagorism. Furthermore, the same passage as it appears in HIPPOLYTUS (*Refutation*, IX, § 27), expressly attributes to the Essenes belief in the resurrection of the body, final judgment and the consummation of the universe by fire at the end of time. The text is as follows: 'The doctrine of the resurrection is firmly established among them. They declare, in fact, that flesh will rise again and be immortal, just as the soul is already immortal. When the soul is separated from the body it goes to rest in a pleasantly light and airy place until the judgment. This is the place which the Greeks, who had heard tell of them, called the Isles of the Blessed. But there are still more Essene doctrines which many Greeks have appropriated to make them their own. Indeed, the Essene observances with respect to the Deity are more ancient than those of all the nations; which shows that those who have dared to speak of God, or the creation, received their doctrines from no other source than the Jewish Law. Among them, Pythagoras and the Stoics of Egypt received most in following the school of the Essenes. Furthermore, they declare that there will be a judgment and a universal conflagration, and that the wicked will be punished for ever.' The relation between Jewish Essenism and pagan Pythagorism is presented here in an ingenuously apologetical manner, and contrary to all probability: according to it, the pagan philosophers were pupils of the Jews. But JOSEPHUS had noticed a resemblance between Essenism and Pythagorism before Hippolytus. 'The Essene sect', he writes, 'practises the way of life taught by Pythagoras to the Greeks' (*Jewish Antiquities*, XV, 10, 4, § 371); he says nothing, however, of the sect's influence on Pythagoras, nor — at least not explicitly — of a Pythagorean influence on the Essenes.

[3] The Greek text reads: *kai diaphorois agneiais*, 'and by various purifications'. But what are 'purifications' doing here between 'holy books' and 'sayings of the prophets'? With Isidore Lévy, I translate *diaphorois* in the sense attested by some texts, and render it 'writings', and I correct *agneiais* to *agiais*, 'sacred'. The 'sacred books' are without doubt the canonical Bible, whilst the terms 'sacred writings' and 'sayings of the prophets' allude to religious works proper to the sect. Or else the 'sacred books' might refer here to the

the prophets, become expert in foreseeing the future: they are rarely deceived in their predictions.[1]

The order of married Essenes

13. § 160. There exists another order of Essenes who, although in agreement with the others on the way of life, usages, and customs, are separated from them on the subject of marriage. Indeed, they believe that people who do not marry cut off a very important part of life, namely, the propagation of the species; and all the more so that if everyone adopted the same opinion mankind[2] would very quickly disappear.

§ 161. Nevertheless, they observe their women for three < months >.[3] When they have purified themselves three times and thus proved themselves capable of bearing children, they then marry them. And when they are pregnant they have no intercourse with them, thereby showing that they do not marry for pleasure but because it is necessary to have children.

The women bathe wrapped in linen, whereas the men wear a loin-cloth.

Such are the customs of this order.

Besides this long account in the *Jewish War*, Josephus inserts a brief description of the Essenes into *Jewish Antiquities* (Book XVIII, Chapter 1), a book which he wrote later. This report gives certain details and features absent from the *War* but appearing in Philo. Some writers have consequently supposed that *Antiquities* borrowed directly from Philo, but it can equally well be held that both writers drew from the same sources.

---

[1] JOSEPHUS himself tells of many predictions, supposed to have been made by the Essenes in various circumstances, which came true. (*Jewish Antiquities*, XIII, 11, 2; XV, 10, 5; XVII, 13, 3.)

[2] The Greek text gives only *to genos* which may be translated (man)'kind', or 'sect' (Essene). In a parallel passage, HIPPOLYTUS (*Refutation*, IX, § 28) explicitly writes: 'the whole of mankind'. This interpretation seems the better one.

[3] The Greek text reads *trietia*, 'for three years', but the passage as a whole is only intelligible if this word is altered to *trimenoi*, 'for three months'. If the young woman menstruated for three months, she showed herself normally regular and properly nubile. Without this assurance, the husband could not have legitimate intercourse with her, since marriage has at its exclusive end the procreation of children.

---

five books of the *Torah*, and 'sacred writings' and 'sayings of the prophets' to the *Ǩetubim* (Hagiographa) and the *Nebi'im*. Although this order does not conform to that of the Hebrew Bible, it is found in the Septuagint. However this may be, the passage from Josephus informs us that the Essenes preferred to base their gift of divination and prophecy on the sacred texts themselves. They searched out by means of subtle exegesis the hidden meaning which would reveal the future to them.

Jewish Antiquities[1]

5. § 18. The Essenes like to teach that in all things one should rely on God.[2]

They also declare that souls are immortal, and consider it necessary to struggle to obtain the reward of righteousness.

§ 19. They send offerings to the Temple, but offer no[3] sacrifices since the purifications to which they are accustomed are different. For this reason, they refrain from entering into the common enclosure, but offer sacrifice among themselves.

For the rest, they are excellent men and wholly given up to agricultural labour.[4]

§ 20. Compared to all others adept in virtue, their practice of righteousness is admirable; nothing similar ever existed in any Greek or any barbarian even for a short time, yet among them it has prevailed unimpeded from a remote age.[5] They put their property into a common stock, and the rich man enjoys no more of his fortune than does the man with absolutely nothing. And there are more than 4000 men who behave in this way.[6]

§ 21. In addition, they take no wives and acquire no slaves; in fact, they consider slavery an injustice,[7] and marriage as leading to discord.[8] They therefore live among themselves and serve each other.

§ 22. They choose virtuous men to collect the revenue and gather the various products of the soil, and priests to prepare the bread and food.[9]

They live in no way different from, but as much as possible like, those < Sadducees > who are called *The Many*.[10]

---

[1] Greek text from NIESE's edition, vol. iii (Berlin, 1882).

[2] Compare this passage with another by the same writer in *Jewish Antiquities* (XIII, 5, 9, § 172): 'The Essene sect declares Destiny to be the master of all things, and that nothing happens to man except in conformity with its decision.'

[3] This negation is found only in a few manuscripts, but with many other writers I consider it probably correct. The Essenes, we read, 'sacrifice among themselves', but not in the Temple. According to PHILO (*Q.o.p.l.*, § 75), they did not sacrifice at all.

[4] Cf. PHILO, *Apologia pro Judaeis*, § 8.

[5] The Greek text for these last few words is uncertain, and the translation is conjectural.

[6] The same figure is given in PHILO, *Q.o.p.l.*, § 75.

[7] The same explanation appears in PHILO, ibid., § 79.

[8] PHILO gives the same reason in *Apologia*, § 14. JOSEPHUS, in the *War*, § 121, explains the Essene repugnance to marriage as being due to their unflattering opinion of womanly virtue.

[9] Neither the text nor the meaning of the latter part of this sentence is sure; in *War* (§ 131) the priest is to recite grace before and after the meal — which is understandable — not to prepare the bread and food — the job of the baker and the cook (§ 130).

[10] The Greek text reads, *pleistois*, meaning literally, 'very many'. I think this is a translation of the Hebrew *rabbim*, 'many' (or 'very many'), a term frequently used in the Qumran documents to describe the members of the sect or of its Council ('The Many'). Josephus no doubt means that the Essenes all lived the same kind of life in conformity to that of the *Rabbim*, the Essene group which served as a model to them all. The Greek text also gives the word *Dakōn*, 'of the Dacians', which is totally incomprehensible in this context. This is a corrupt word in which one is inclined to recognize an original *Zadok*, or rather, *Saddoukaiōn*: ' . . . those Sadducees who are called *The Many*'. In fact, the

3. PLINY THE ELDER

Pliny the Elder inserts a famous account of the Essenes into his *Natural History* (V, 17, 4). This Latin writer, it will be remembered, died in A.D. 79; he may have accompanied Titus to Palestine during the Jewish War of A.D. 70. Nevertheless his description of the Essenes probably depends on some written source rather than on direct information. In spite of its brevity, this pagan writer's evidence of the Jewish sect is of great value: accurately and colourfully he brings into relief certain of its characteristic features.

Here is the translation of this passage; it follows immediately after Pliny's description of the Dead Sea and its eastern shore.

To the west (of the Dead Sea) the Essenes have put the necessary distance between themselves and the insalubrious shore. They are a people unique of its kind and admirable beyond all others in the whole world, without women and renouncing love entirely, without money, and having for company only the palm trees. Owing to the throng of new-comers, this people is daily re-born in equal number; indeed, those whom, wearied by the fluctuations of fortune, life leads to adopt their customs, stream in in great numbers. Thus, unbelievable though this may seem, for thousands of centuries a people has existed which is eternal yet into which no one is born: so fruitful for them is the repentance which others feel for their past lives!

Pliny immediately goes on to describe two other sites on the western shore of the Dead Sea: Engedi, which is farther towards the south, and Masada, farther south still.

Below the Essenes was the town of Engada (Engedi), which yielded only to Jerusalem[1] in fertility and palm-groves but is today become another ash-heap. From there, one comes to the fortress of Masada, situated on a rock, and itself near the lake of Asphalt.

It will be seen from this text that the Essene settlement described above was situated, not only on the western shore, as Pliny explicitly mentions, but also towards the north of that shore. In fact, by

[1] This is the reading of the text, but mention of palm-groves is hardly applicable to Jerusalem. Perhaps the word should be corrected to 'Jericho'.

Essenes of Qumran gave themselves the title 'Sons of Zadok' (= Sadducees), as the discovered Hebrew documents testify, but these Essene-Sadducees were quite a different sect from the classic Sadducees. Perhaps it was this homonym which embarrassed the copyist and led him to read another word, 'Dacians', which actually means nothing here. See my article, 'On a passage of Josephus relative to the Essenes' in the *J. Sem. St.*, i, 1956, pp. 361-6.

indicating that the town of Engedi was 'below the Essenes' (*infra hos*), the author wished to say, not, as had been explained earlier, that the Essenes lived on the mountain just above Engedi, but that the town was *downstream* (to the south) of the place where the Essenes lived. It is, in fact, the same deep depression which, stretching from north to south, constitutes the valley of the Jordan and forms the bed of the Dead Sea. Pliny, by mentioning successively the Essene site on the western shore of the Dead Sea, then Engedi, and finally Masada, descends from north to south in the same direction as the flow of the Jordan itself.[1]

The existence of this Essene settlement is confirmed by Dio Chrysostom, a Greek orator and philosopher who lived a little later than Pliny the Elder. His biographer, Synesius,[2] recounts that he 'also somewhere praises the Essenes, who form an entire and prosperous city near the Dead Sea, in the centre of Palestine, not far from Sodom'.

It is generally accepted that Pliny and Dio drew from the same source. Their evidence as to the presence of a strong and prosperous Essene community near the shores of the Dead Sea is of prime importance for the identification of the Jewish sect from which the famous scrolls derive. This problem is to be examined in the next chapter.

[1] The word *infra* is often found in other passages from Pliny in the sense of 'downstream'. That it indicates the south here is because, as I have said, of the direction in which the Jordan flows. In Egypt, on the contrary, the Aramaic papyri from Elephantine use the words 'below' and 'above' to designate north and south respectively — obviously meaning downstream and upstream with respect to the Nile. I first suggested this new explanation of the words *infra hos* in Pliny's account in 1950 (see *Aperçus préliminaires* . . . , p. 106, note 3) and it is now accepted by most authors (cf. J. T. MILIK, *Dix ans de découvertes dans le désert de Juda*, 1957, p. 41; Eng. edn., pp. 44-5).

[2] Dio, 5 (ed. Petavius, p. 39 — *Dio Chrysostom* — Loeb Classical Library, vol. v, p. 378).

CHAPTER II

THE ESSENE ORIGIN OF THE QUMRAN WRITINGS

The *Damascus Document* and the Qumran Scrolls: the problem of their origin. — 1. Textual evidence. The 'Council of God'. Community life. Rites. Doctrines. Customs. — 2. Archaeological evidence. Excavations at Khirbet Qumran. Data from the Qumran writings and the ancient accounts.

When, in 1948, scholars were informed of the Hebrew scrolls found in a cave in the desert of Judah, they at first turned their attention almost exclusively to the two scrolls of Isaiah. It was a marvellous, and even a sensational find, involving as it did the recovery of copies of the biblical book about a thousand years older than the oldest manuscript of the Hebrew Bible, and pre-dating even the establishment of the Masoretic Text.

However, the same cave yielded five other scrolls, five books unknown until then which neither Synagogue nor Church had handed down to us. These five books were obviously the products of some ancient Jewish sect. There was the sect's *Rule* (its American editors have given it the title *Manual of Discipline*); a commentary on the biblical book of Habakkuk full of references to the history of the sect; a curious *War Scroll* envisaging the battle to be fought at the end of time between the 'Sons of Light', the members of the sect, and the 'Sons of Darkness', the forces of evil; a collection of *Hymns* (or Thanksgiving Psalms), i.e. a book of prayers proper to the sect; and finally, an Aramaic work at first wrongly named the 'Apocalypse of Lamech', but in fact a sort of paraphrase of the first chapters of Genesis written in the style and manner of a book known to us called the *Book of Jubilees*.

It was realized at once that this collection of books showed very great affinities of language, style and content with another Hebrew document discovered in 1896-97 among the mass of manuscripts in the *Geniza* of a synagogue in Old Cairo. This document, which was published in 1910 under the title *Fragments of a Zadokite Work*, consists of two manuscripts dating from about the tenth and twelfth centuries, and contains a long Exhortation, followed by a whole series of rules and regulations proper to the sect. Its discovery gave rise, from 1910 onwards, to a great deal of study, but because of the age of the manuscripts and their fragmentary condition, as well as the formidable obscurity of the text, widely differing hypotheses were advanced regarding the origin and nature of this sect. All that was clear was that its members called themselves 'Sons of Zadok' (whence the title *Zadokite Work*), and their association, the 'New Covenant in the Land of Damascus' (whence the title *Damascus Document*, as the writing is generally known). Since then, several fragments of this work have been found in the Qumran caves and there is no longer any doubt that the sect of the *Damascus Document* is identical with the sect of the scrolls from the desert of Judah. The 'New Covenant in the Land of Damascus' is the work of the Judaean sect itself and was written in the land of Damascus where its members had to seek refuge from persecution and where they settled for a certain time. It must be added, in its entirety, to the rest of the Dead Sea Scrolls.

It is curious to observe that, before the Qumran discoveries, among the many theories proposed by scholars regarding the origin of the *Damascus Document* not one explicitly mentioned the Essenes. The work was either related to a group of pious Jews of the pre-Maccabaean era, or to the Sadducees, or the Pharisees, or the Dositheans, or the Judeo-Christian Ebionites, or to the Karaites of the Middle Ages; to everyone, in fact, except the Essenes! They alone were overlooked, no doubt because of the sort of general academic ostracism which had been inflicted on them. Only a few critics drew attention to various affinities between the Damascus sect and the Essenes, among them the French scholars Israel Lévi and Isidore Lévy (see below, p. 145-6). But the date of the copies and the site of their discovery provided neither measuring-rod nor guide. Only the text was capable of throwing light on the problem, but unfortunately the historical allusions with which it is interspersed are fearfully sibylline, and the various implications which the rules of the sect appeared to authorize led to no certain conclusion.

Happily the discovery of the Qumran scrolls has completely altered this situation. First of all, from the very beginning the script itself suggested, and even demanded, an ancient date; even if there were some hesitation about fixing this exactly, the script obviously dated from some time in the first century B.C. — from about 150 B.C. to A.D. 50. For my part I recognized this immediately; the old theories of an Ebionite or Karaite origin were thereby excluded, though these theories were revived once more in 1950 by some scholars. But there was another essential point: since the scrolls were found in a cave near Khirbet Qumran, had they not been placed there by people living in the vicinity, or more precisely — considering the contents of the scrolls — by a sect of Jewish mystics from some desert settlement in the region of Khirbet Qumran itself? The famous text of Pliny the Elder, quoted in the preceding chapter, sprang to mind, with its exact location of the great Essene establishment near the north-western shore of the Dead Sea. Thus the Essene hypothesis was advanced, this time concretely.

The date of the scrolls as established by palaeographical criteria accorded perfectly with this hypothesis: Josephus attests the existence in about 146 B.C. of the Essene sect, together with the sects of Pharisees and Sadducees.[1] Moreover he reports the intervention, at the beginning of the reign of Aristobulus I (104 B.C.), of a famous diviner, a certain Judas, who belonged, he says, to the Essenes. This sect was, as we knew, fully active during the whole of the first century B.C. until the time of the great Jewish War (A.D. 66-70), when it was obliged to disband and began to fall into decline.

At first, certain archaeologists resisted this Essene hypothesis for some time. They asserted that the jars in which the scrolls had been found dated from the Hellenistic period and were certainly older than 100 B.C., and that the scrolls must be as old as the jars. They came, it was explained, from some small unknown group of Pharisees who had hidden their books in the Qumran caves just before disappearing at the end of the second century B.C. All possible historical contact between the sect of the scrolls and primitive Christianity was in this way eliminated. I pointed out that one of the scrolls, the *Commentary on Habakkuk*, contained definite allusions to the invasion of Palestine by the Romans, and that this scroll, anyway, could only have been written after the Roman invasion in the first century B.C.[2] But at that time this conclusion made very little impact on the dogmatism of these pottery experts. Nevertheless, and this change of front does them credit, their opposition speedily came to an end and was soon replaced by wholehearted support of the Essene hypothesis.

As a matter of fact, these same archaeologists found themselves responsible, a little while later, for the excavations on the site of Khirbet Qumran, the ruins not far from the cave where the scrolls

[1] *Antiquities*, XIII, 5, 9, § 171.   [2] See *Aperçus préliminaires . . .*, 1950, pp. 43-4.

were found. If the scrolls were of Essene origin, as I had thought myself able to establish in 1950, and probably came from the Essene settlement described by Pliny the Elder, were not the Qumran ruins the remains of this Essene establishment? I had expressly suggested this from the middle of 1951.[1] The excavation of Khirbet Qumran became imperative for the verification of the theory. The first archaeological campaign took place from November to December in 1951, and was followed by five others in the spring of 1953, 1954, 1955, 1956 and 1958. The archaeologists were quickly convinced that their first dating had been wrong: the many coins found on the site indicated an occupation of the area covering, roughly, the end of the second century B.C. to the time of the Jewish War. As for the archaeological remains uncovered by them, they accorded so well with the Essene hypothesis that these archaeologists have now become its doughtiest champions.

It must nevertheless be noted that the principal witness to their origin, the essential evidence, lies in the scrolls themselves. Despite its usefulness, and however detailed its present-day methods, archaeology as a science still remains ancillary to history: and history is essentially constructed upon texts. When archaeological exploration has no texts available to guide and enlighten it, more often than not it can only grope in the dark and arrive at indefinite and uncertain conclusions. Indeed, in research on the Dead Sea Scrolls it was primarily an examination of the texts which allowed the historian to assert the Essene character of the documents; and archaeological excavation brought subsequent confirmation. The following demonstration will therefore proceed in the same order and will deal firstly with textual, and secondly with archaeological evidence.

1. TEXTUAL EVIDENCE

The 'Council of God'

As the scrolls show, the Qumran sect was called by its members, the 'Covenant' (berīt), or 'New Covenant': these Jews were, in their own eyes, and to the exclusion of all other Jews, representatives of the only Covenant agreeable to God, the eternal and final Covenant. The old Covenant concluded under the leadership of Moses had been broken because of Israel's infidelity. The new Community was the 'little Remnant' foretold by the Prophets, i.e. the true Israel.

[1] See *R. de Paris*, August 1951, p. 98.

This 'New Covenant' is also very frequently called, in the Qumran scrolls, the 'Council of God', the 'Holy Council', the 'Council of the Community'; its followers were known as the 'Men of the Council of God'.[1] In these various expressions, the Hebrew word translated 'Council' seems to have a whole range of meanings and it is not always easy to know which one to choose. Sometimes it refers to the divine Counsel according to which the chosen are predestined; sometimes to the Council of the sect, i.e. the deliberative assembly at which all the members were entitled to assist; sometimes to a more restricted Council composed of a varying number of dignitaries; and sometimes to the Congregation or Community as a whole, as a body including all of the same opinion and the same aims; what, in fact, we should today call the Party.

The frequent occurrence of this word 'Council' in the Qumran documents is certainly remarkable. In Hebrew, the word is 'ezah. Now it is possible, as I have already noted (see above, p. 21, n. 3) that this word 'ezah, so characteristic and so frequently repeated in the scrolls, is to be seen in the word 'Essene', or 'Essaean', itself. Its root is obviously ess-, and this transcribes perfectly the Hebrew 'ezah (the -ah in 'ezah is merely a feminine ending). In order to give a Greek form to the Hebrew expression 'Men of the Council', there is little alternative but to write it as Essenoi (or Essaioi). The etymology of the word 'Essene' formerly gave rise to all sorts of hypotheses, all of them to a greater or lesser extent uncertain; for as long as there was no Hebrew document to explain the exact terminology of the sect, the hypothesis I have suggested could never have entered the mind. But if it is accepted as correct, it establishes a very precise link between the sect of the Covenant of the Qumran documents and the Essenes described by ancient writers.

Community life

But the argument to be drawn from it in favour of the Essene theory has only a problematic value. Much more important is the fact that the members of the Covenant formed, in the strictest sense of the word, a 'community'. This trait, which went as far as to entail a common ownership of property, is, as may be recalled, very strongly emphasized by Philo and Josephus, who consider it to be the distinguishing mark of the Essene sect.[2]

[1] This title appears in the *Rule Annexe* (I, 3), the *Blessings* (IV, 24) and the *Hymns* (VI, 11).
[2] See especially, PHILO, *Q.o.p.l.*, §§ 85, 91; *Apologia*, §§ 10-12. JOSEPHUS, *War*, II, § 122; *Antiquities*, XVIII, § 20.

The Qumran documents constantly return to the idea of 'community': the corresponding Hebrew word, *yaḥad*, is used in these texts with a characteristic frequency, and is the exact equivalent of the Greek *koinōnia* employed by Philo and Josephus. The sect is not only called the 'Council of the Community', but also the 'Institution of the Community', the 'Community of God', the 'Community of the Eternal Covenant', the 'Covenant of the Community', the 'Covenant of the Eternal Community'. Among the brethren, everything was held in common: in the *Rule* (VI, 2-3) we read:

> And they shall eat in common, bless in common, and deliberate in common.

The sectary belonged entirely to the Community, as regards both his soul and his possessions:

> And all the volunteers who are joined to His truth shall bring all their understanding and all their powers and all their possessions into the Community of God. . . .[1]

Common ownership of property was absolute, at any rate among the fully professed. In addition to the transfer of each man's heritage, it involved the handing over of the daily wage to the bursar of the Community.[2] It became in this way a common fund, 'the property of the Community', and any damage to Community property,[3] and above all, any deception in connection with the surrender of possessions or wages,[4] was severely punished.

It is frequently repeated that the members of the Qumran sect are 'volunteers'; this is another detail actually mentioned by Philo with regard to the Essenes. He writes:

> Their enlistment is not due to race (the word race is unsuitable in connection with volunteers), but to zeal for the cause of virtue and an ardent love of men.[5]

It was just this 'zeal for the cause of virtue' that led the faithful of Qumran to group themselves in a society apart, and to separate themselves from the rest of the Jews. The latter were the 'Congregation of perverse men'; but they themselves were a congregation of 'penitents' (this figures in Pliny the Elder's account of the Essenes), of 'saints', of 'the perfect', of 'men of perfect holiness', as appears over and over again in the Qumran writings.

[1] *Rule*, I, 11-12.   [2] *Rule*, VI, 19-20.   [3] *Rule*, VII, 6-7.
[4] *Rule*, VI, 24-5.   [5] *Apologia*, § 2.

As for the rules governing the admission of new members to Qumran, they are almost identical with those described by Josephus: one year as a postulant, followed by two years in the novitiate, and then the final admission when they were at last allowed to participate in the Community meal.[1] The *Rule* contributes various details on this subject, especially concerning the régime of common property and participation in the baths during the preparatory stages (VI, 13-23); but they in no way contradict Josephus's account. There is just one small difference between the two documents: whereas Josephus describes the postulant as having to wait for one year, the *Rule* does not fix the exact length of time. The duration of this first stage seems to have been left to the discretion of the overseer. But in mentioning one year, Josephus no doubt noted what was the usual custom in this respect; there is no contradiction. On the contrary, the general agreement between Josephus's account and the Qumran *Rule* is most striking. Josephus specifies that the new sectary,

> before touching the common food, swears solemn vows before his brethren,

and he goes on to list the essential obligations which they imposed.[2] This solemn oath, required for admission into the sect, is very clearly indicated in the Qumran texts. Thus, in the *Rule* (V, 7-11):

> When they are joined to the Community, let whosoever comes to the Council of the Community enter into the Covenant of God in the presence of all the volunteers, and let him undertake by an oath of obligation to be converted to the Law of Moses. . . . And let him undertake by the Covenant to be separated from all perverse men who walk in the way of wickedness.

There is a great deal about the 'oath of the Covenant' by which the sectary swore to 'be converted to the Law of Moses' in the *Damascus Document* also (XV, 4-XVI, 9): in no case 'even at the price of death' might he violate such an oath. Josephus speaks of 'solemn vows', but says nothing of the actual ceremony in which the catechumens bound themselves by such oaths. It is the *Rule* that describes the ritual of that solemn liturgy, with the blessings pronounced on the 'men of the lot of God', and the terrible curses, 'the curses of the Covenant', heaped on the 'men of the lot of Belial', and particularly

---

[1] *War*, II, §§ 137-9.   [2] *War*, II, §§ 139-42.

on new followers whose conversion might not be entirely sincere (I, 6-II, 18). An echo of this appears in the following menacing phrase from the *Damascus Document* (XV, 12-13):

> And when he has once undertaken to be converted to the Law of Moses with all his heart and soul, [how] terrible would [it be] for him to betray [it]![1]

One of the obligations to which the new sectary bound himself by oath was, according to Josephus,

> to conceal nothing from the members of the sect, as also to reveal nothing to any others but them, even though violence unto death be used against him.[2]

This unambiguous passage reveals the strictly esoteric character of the Essene sect. But this is also one of the most accentuated characteristics of the sect from Qumran. They had rules peculiar to themselves which it was forbidden to divulge to postulants without the permission of the overseer;[3] they possessed secret doctrines, revelations reserved to initiates, a higher Knowledge — a Gnosis of salvation — which was the privilege of the elect. From these elect, the brethren admitted to the sect, nothing was to be concealed:

> When they shall have established them (the novices) in the Institution of the Community, in perfection of the way, for two years day for day, they shall be set apart within the Council of the members of the Community (as) holy (persons), and let nothing of what was hidden from Israel, but found by the Man who sought, be hidden from them from fear of the spirit of apostasy.[4]

Initiation into this revealed Gnosis would be progressive:

> He shall guide each man in Knowledge according to his spirit (and) according to the destined moment of time; and likewise, he shall instruct them in the marvellous and true mysteries in the midst of the members of the Community. . . .[5]

---

[1] The last few words of this phrase are partially effaced and the correctness of their translation is only probable.

[2] *War*, II, § 141. [3] *Damascus Document*, XV, 10-11.

[4] *Rule*, VIII, 10-12. [5] *Rule*, IX, 18-19.

To outsiders, on the other hand, nothing was to be communicated:

But let him conceal the maxims of the Law from the midst of men of perversity.[1]

And the sectary proclaims:

With wise reflection I will conceal Knowledge. . . .[2]

The mystic community described by Josephus was governed by a principle of rigorous obedience. 'They do nothing', he writes, 'unless ordered by the superiors.'[3] And again: 'They make it their duty to obey their elders as well as the majority: for example, when ten sit together, no man speaks if the other nine oppose it.'[4] Now there is not a single characteristic mentioned in these two passages that is not confirmed by the Qumran documents. The 'superiors' appear many times in the *Rule*, and are called in Hebrew *mebaqqer*, 'overseer';[5] the *Damascus Document* describes their attributes at length (XIII, 7-16, XIV, 8-12). This religious society was subjected, like an army, to the most rigorous, systematic and strangely perfect discipline. Each man was inscribed in the register of this militia with a number corresponding to his merits and fixed each year in full assembly. Each man owed strict obedience to anyone whose number showed him to be his elder or superior;[6] whoever refused 'to obey his fellow inscribed before him' was severely punished.[7] Everything was deliberated in assembly and a majority decision ruled.[8] The 'Council' was an essential institution: the regulations for its meetings, which aimed at ensuring order and respect for the rights of precedence, are described in detail in the Qumran texts.[9] The following remark of Josephus confirms this: 'No shouting or disturbance ever defiles the house; they allow each other to speak in turn.'[10] Philo, too, writes: 'They sit in appointed places according to their age, the young men below the old, attentive and well-behaved.'[11]

[1] *Rule*, IX, 17.
[2] *Rule*, X, 24. — The text reads, 'I will conceal' ('*STR*), but also indicates as a variant, 'I will recount' ('*SPR*). The meaning of the variant is the exact contrary but it is also acceptable: *from the brethren* they were to conceal nothing of the divine revelations but were to 'recount knowledge' to them. — It should be noted, moreover, that quite a lot of fragments in *cryptic* writing have been found in the Qumran caves, which shows the sect's concern for esotericism.
[3] *War*, II, § 134.   [4] *War*, II, § 146.
[5] One would translate this into Greek as *episcopos* (bishop).
[6] *Rule*, V, 23-4.   [7] *Rule*, VI, 26.   [8] *Rule*, V, 2-3, 22.
[9] *Rule*, VI, 8-13; *Rule Annexe*, II, 11-17.   [10] *War*, II, § 132.   [11] *Q.o.p.l.*, § 81.

Even the group of ten, to which Josephus refers in the text quoted above, is mentioned in the Qumran texts. Thus we read in the *Rule* (VI, 3-4):

> And in every place where there are ten persons of the Council of the Community, let there not lack among them a man who is a priest. And let them sit before him, each according to his rank, and in the same order let them ask his advice in everything.

The same recommendation appears in the *Damascus Document* (XIII, 2-3):

> And where there are ten of them, let there not lack a man who is a priest learned in the Book of Meditation: they shall all obey his orders.

Essene society possessed its own tribunals. Josephus writes: 'In matters of judgment they are very exact and impartial. They dispense justice in assemblies of not less than a hundred and their decisions are irrevocable.'[1] Now it appears from various passages of the *Rule* that whenever there was 'trial and judgment', the same Council in which the fully initiated members participated was transformed into a court of justice: it was at 'meetings of the Many' that the guilty were tried. The *Damascus Document* describes various rules concerning judges, witnesses and the judicial oath (IX, 9-X, 10); it even contains a short fragment of the sect's penal code (XIV, 18-22). The complete penal code is preserved, except for some slight lacunae, in the *Rule* (VI, 24-VII, 25). Doubtless it differs slightly from that given in the *Damascus Document*; there are several visible corrections in the manuscript of the *Rule*, showing that the code was kept up to date and therefore fully in use. Thus, where the text originally read 'six months' punishment for something, the correction 'one year' can clearly be seen. Offences dealt with are those thought to be either most important or most common; they include loud laughter and inane conversation as well as blasphemy. The penalties were carefully regulated and were for ten days, thirty days, three months, six months, one year, or two years. The culprit had his food ration reduced and was separated from the 'Purification of the Many', which means that he was set apart, excluded from the purificatory baths of the Community.

[1] *War*, II, § 145.

The same code imposes a sentence of excommunication for the gravest faults;[1] it forbids the brethren to consort with an excommunicated person, or to assist him in any way at all on pain of his own excommunication.[2] Such severity agrees well with the famous passage from Josephus referring to excommunication among the Essenes.[3]

Rites

The Essene, as described by Josephus, was obliged to bath every day and to wash himself on various other occasions.[4] The Qumran documents also mention these rites of purification by water. The *Damascus Document* gives a whole lesson 'on purification by water' (X, 11-13), and the *Rule* refers several times to the baptismal practices of the members of the Covenant.

> Let (the wicked) not enter the water to touch the purification of the holy men: for a man is not pure unless he be converted from his malice (V, 13-14).

In another passage, it specifies that the first-year novice was not authorized to 'touch the purification of the Many' (VI, 16-17). Finally, a long and eloquent tirade warns that baptism and ablutions are insufficient; the spirit of man must show the required disposition and the Holy Spirit participate in the purification (III, 4-9). This passage does not tend to deny either the legitimacy or the necessity of purification by water, but it warns against an entirely materialist and magical interpretation of rites which only purify the flesh if the spirit is truly turned to God. Such instruction only makes sense if the Qumran sect was essentially a baptist sect.

Josephus also tells us of the importance of the common meal in the day of an Essene: it was, according to him, a sacred repast in which no one participated unless they had bathed and clothed themselves in sacred garments. The place where the brethren ate was 'as a holy place', forbidden to the profane, and an august and mysterious silence reigned there. A priest presided over the meal and prayed before and after it, and it was forbidden to eat before the initial prayer.[5] The Essene meal was, in fact, a sacrament, the holiest

---

[1] *Rule*, VII, 22-5; VIII, 20-IX, 2; cf. V, 14. There is mention of excommunication in the *Damascus Document* also, XII, 2-8.
[2] *Rule*, VII, 25.   [3] *War*, II, §§ 143-4.
[4] See especially, *War*, II, §§ 129, 138, 149, 150.   [5] *War*, II, §§ 129-33.

sacrament of the sect. Its holiness was greater even than that of baptism, since although novices were allowed to participate in the latter, the holy meal was reserved to professed brethren only.

The *Rule* from Qumran not only testifies to these communal meals of the sect, but also gives their essential liturgy.

> When they have set the table to eat, or (prepared) the wine to drink, the priest shall first stretch out his hand to pronounce a blessing on the first-fruits of bread and wine (VI, 5-6).

The initial blessing and the priest's role conform fully to Josephus's account. But the *Rule* adds one detail of an interest that will escape no one: the priest blesses the *bread and wine*. The same point appears again in the *Rule Annexe* (II, 17-22); but the interest of this second text lies in the fact that it describes the ideal Supper, the Supper over which the Priest and the Messiah of Israel will preside at the end of time — the latter being clearly subordinate to the former. Now the Priest in question here is the Priest-Messiah, the Messiah of Aaron, the Priest, that is to say, who founded the sect and was known to its members as the 'Teacher of Righteousness'. Although this Teacher suffered and was put to death, he still lived, and his followers expected him to return at the end of time with the Messiah of Israel, the King-Messiah. The supper which the members of the New Covenant celebrated each day referred essentially to the Supper which would take place later when the Kingdom of God had come. The humble daily supper was therefore a constant reminder of the revered Teacher, and the presiding priest was, so to speak, the representative of, or substitute for, the Priest *par excellence*:

> And they shall proceed according to this rite at every meal where at least ten persons are gathered together.

Another of the essential Essene rites was, according to Josephus, their morning prayer. A little before the dawn they turned towards the sun 'as though entreating it to rise'.[1] The sun was for them the manifestation or symbol of divine power and splendour. Now, in my opinion, the Qumran *Hymns* testify in detail to this practice and belief. The sectary addresses himself to God as follows:

---

[1] *War*, II, § 128.

And Thou hast appeared unto me in Thy might at daybreak
(IV, 23).

Thus as the sun rose, it was God who appeared brilliant and
mighty; it was God Himself whom the sectary encountered. The
Wisdom of Solomon (xvi. 28) alludes to this matutinal apparition,
this divine encounter which every dawn represents:

We must precede the sun to give Thee thanks, and encounter
Thee at daybreak.

Doctrines

According to Philo and Josephus, some aspects of Essene faith in
the nature or essence of God were peculiar to them. Philo reports that
for them 'the Deity is the cause of all good but nothing evil';[1] and
Josephus tells us that their favourite maxim was 'in all things rely
on God',[2] and their characteristic dogma, 'Fate is master of all,
and nothing befalls men but what is according to its decision.'[3] Not
one of these fundamental assertions is absent from the Qumran
documents; frequently and widely repeated, they typify the attitude
of the Qumran sectary with regard to God.

The prime doctrine of Qumran was, in fact, that the Spirit of
Evil, known also as the Prince or Angel of Darkness, Belial, or
Satan, is the cause of all wickedness. God is the cause of all good:
'In His hand are the laws of all (beings) and He supports them in all
their needs.'[4]

In all His works of loving-kindness God acts through the Spirit of
Good, called also the Prince of Lights, Angel of Truth; He loves this
Spirit of Good 'everlastingly, and delights in all his deeds for ever'.[5]
The two Spirits wage incessant battle, 'but the God of Israel and His
Angel of Truth succour all the sons of light'.[6]

The sectary was therefore assured of divine protection even when
plunged in anguish and distress, and the *leitmotiv* of Qumran spirituality was to do the will of God in all things and to abandon oneself
completely to Him. Only two short passages can be quoted here, the
first from the *Rule* (IX, 23-4):

He shall do the will of God in every enterprise of his hands that He
may reign over all things according to His command, and shall

---

[1] *Q.o.p.l.*, § 84.　　　[2] *Antiquities*, XVIII, § 18.　　　[3] *Antiquities*, XIII, 5, 9, § 172.
[4] *Rule*, III, 16-17.　　　[5] *Rule*, III, 26-IV, 1.　　　[6] *Rule*, III, 24-5.

gladly delight in all that He has made; and beyond the will of
God he shall desire nothing. . . .

The next quotation is from the *Hymns* (IX, 34-6) and praises
God's paternal goodness:

> . . . Until I am old Thou wilt care for me.
> For my father knew me not
> and my mother abandoned me to Thee.
> For Thou art a father to all Thy sons of truth,
> and hast put Thy joy within them
> like her that loves her babe;
> and like a foster father (holding a child) to his breast,
> so carest Thou for all Thy creatures.

This complete trust sprang from the sectary's conviction that he
belonged to the 'lot of God'. In His marvellous Counsel God had
chosen him from all eternity, just as He had at the same time
destined the wicked to damnation, to the 'lot of Belial'. The word
gōral, 'the lot', 'the fate', appears constantly in the various Qumran
texts, and the frequent use of this characteristic term reflects a truly
dominating idea, a belief in rigorous predestination. Men belong,
even before their birth, to the 'lot of light' or the 'lot of darkness':
their destiny is fixed for ever. It is even written in the stars: a very
strange fragment from cave IV gives a genuine horoscope determining, from the date of birth, the spiritual destiny of every human
being, the part to be played by the Spirits of God and Evil mingling
and struggling within him. This fatalism shows the influence of
astrological beliefs which were extraordinarily in fashion at that time
in the Hellenistic world.

For the Essenes, 'Fate is master of all things' writes Josephus; for
them, Fate was confused with divine Omnipotence. And how often,
how enthusiastically, does the Qumran sectary praise this same divine
Omnipotence in the *Hymns* and the *Rule*, and compare it to the
nothingness of man! Again and again he proclaims that justification
is entirely the work of God and the fate of man wholly in His hands.
He experiences immense joy at finding himself, because of his
adherence to the sect, in the 'lot of truth', among the elect. He is a
'Son of Light', and nothing but good can come to him because God
has chosen him. He is a 'man of the Counsel of God', marked for

salvation by a divine Plan. This is even the meaning of the word 'Essene', if the etymology I have suggested earlier is correct.

For these mystics, the purpose of earthly life was salvation and eternal life, and adherence to the sect was their gage of salvation: ' . . . the Covenant of God is for them an assurance that they will live for thousands of generations; as it is written, *He keeps unto a thousand generations the Covenant of Grace with them that love Him and keep His commandments*'.[1]

The *Rule* describes the future reward as 'eternal joy, and a crown of glory in everlasting life, and a garment of honour in eternal light' (IV, 7-8). Very different, however, is the fate of the damned; for them await 'an abundance of blows administered by all the Angels of destruction in the everlasting Pit . . . unending fear and shame without end, and the disgrace of destruction by the fire of the regions of darkness' (IV, 12-13).

These descriptions are in essential agreement with Josephus's account of Essene beliefs in the hereafter[2] — an account in which, it should be noted, a certain Greek polish must be taken into consideration. Similarly, the doctrine of the soul's opposition to the body, attributed in the same passage to the Essenes, corresponds to the distinction made between 'spirit' and 'flesh' in the Qumran texts, which frequently contrast these two component elements of man.

Neither Philo nor Josephus mentions an Essene belief in the resurrection of the body, but this omission is made good by Hippolytus, who reports their faith in resurrection, final judgment, and the destruction of the world by fire at the end of time.[3] These three themes appear quite explicitly in the Qumran writings. The idea of Judgment, or divine Visitation, crops up, so to speak, on every page, and the notion of final destruction by fire is extensively developed in the *Hymns*.[4] As for belief in the resurrection, this is openly asserted in the *War Scroll* (XII, 5).

Concerning the Essene oath, Josephus calls attention to the fact that the sectary undertook to preserve, without alteration, 'the names of the angels'.[5] This suggests that in the thought and piety of the Essenes the angelic world occupied a very important place. In fact the Qumran scrolls refer to the angels at every turn, calling them also 'holy ones', 'spirits', 'gods' (*elīm*), 'honourable ones', 'sons of

---

[1] *Damascus Document*, VII, 5-6; B I, 1-2.   [2] *War*, II, §§ 154-8.
[3] See above, p. 34, n. 2.   [4] See, for example, III, 29-36.
[5] *War*, II, § 142.

Heaven'. The member of the Covenant lived in the company of the celestial spirits all the time. The Community of the Covenant was one with the society of the angels; the Church of men was one with that of the angels. This concept is very much emphasized, especially in the *Hymns*. But in the *War Scroll* we see the whole angelic world involved in the battle (I, 10-11); the angels of holiness are present in the camp of the sons of light (VII, 6). It is the 'Great Angel' who brings them decisive support (XVII, 6), and the formations called 'towers' each bear an angelic name — Michael, Gabriel, Sariel and Raphael (IX, 15-16). The 'saints of the Covenant' are 'those that see the angels of holiness' (X, 10-11), visionaries whose eyes are accustomed to angelic apparitions. Is there anything surprising, therefore, in the fact that a description of the angelic liturgy has been found among the fragments from the Qumran caves?

Josephus also notes that the Essenes 'apply themselves with extraordinary zeal to the study of the works of the ancients'; these works were secret books which had to be guarded with scrupulous care.[1] Quite a number, though in a fragmentary state, have been recovered from the Qumran caves. Often, at the head of a scroll or at the start of an instruction, we find the words, 'For the man of understanding' (*lammaskīl*), i.e. for the initiate, for the instructor responsible for the indoctrination of new brethren: a note such as this implies that the book is secret. The Qumran library was very rich in works of this sort: in addition to the scrolls from cave I, it contained, as we have seen, the *Book of Enoch*, the *Book of Jubilees*, the *Testament of Levi* and all kinds of apocalyptic and liturgical works of which fragments of varying importance have been recovered.

Customs

The various scrolls from Qumran give an accurate picture of the sect's ethical ideal, and on every point it corresponds remarkably with the Essene ideal as described by Philo and Josephus.

To mention only a few essential points: Josephus recounts that the Essenes were 'more united by mutual affection among themselves than the others'.[2] Now the *Rule* constantly returns to the duty of 'affectionate charity'; it provides severe penalties for anyone who insults his fellow or speaks to him arrogantly — a year's punishment in the first case, and six months in the second (VII, 4-5). In the instruction on the two Spirits, it describes 'abundant affection towards all the

---

[1] *War*, II, §§ 136, 142.   [2] *War*, II, § 119.

sons of truth' as being one of the manifestations of the Spirit of Good (IV, 5).

The Essene oath, according to Josephus, prescribed that the sectaries should 'hate the wicked always and fight together with the good'.[1] The *Rule* also pronounces it a duty to 'love all the sons of light, each according to his lot in the Counsel of God', and to 'hate all the sons of darkness, each according to his fault in the Vengeance of God' (I, 9-11). This hatred, be it noted, is a holy hatred addressed to Belial and his friends, i.e. to the enemies of God and of goodness as such. It was, however, accompanied by the fundamental obligation 'to observe justice towards men, and to do no wrong to any man, neither of his own accord nor at another's command', as Josephus writes.[2] Personal retaliation was therefore prohibited. This theme is also found in the following declaration from the *Rule* (X, 17-18):

To no man will I render the reward of evil,
with goodness will I pursue each one.
For judgment of all the living is with God,
and He it is who will pay to each man his reward.

Only at the end of the world, in God's chosen time, will vengeance be exacted.

The Essenes, says Josephus again, 'renounce pleasure as an evil, and regard continence and resistance to the passions as a virtue'.[3] Compare this with the following formula from the *Rule*: 'To walk no more in the stubbornness of a guilty heart, nor with lustful eyes committing every sort of evil' (I, 6-7). And again: 'Let no man walk in the stubbornness of his heart to stray by following his heart and eyes and the thoughts of his (evil) inclination. But in the Community they shall circumcise the foreskin of the (evil) inclination. . . . (V, 4-5). This is an allusion to the propensity for evil innate in every human soul: the member of the Covenant must fight it unceasingly, avoiding everything which might pander to lust and sensual pleasure.

The Essenes, Josephus continues, 'despise riches, and their community life is admirable. . . .'[4] The initiate swears 'to keep his hands pure from theft and his soul pure from wicked gain'.[5] In the Qumran texts, contempt for riches and horror of gain are expressed

---

[1] *War*, II, § 139.   [2] *War*, II, § 139.   [3] *War*, II, § 120.
[4] *War*, II, § 122.   [5] *War*, II, 141. Cf. PHILO, *Q.o.p.l.*, § 78.

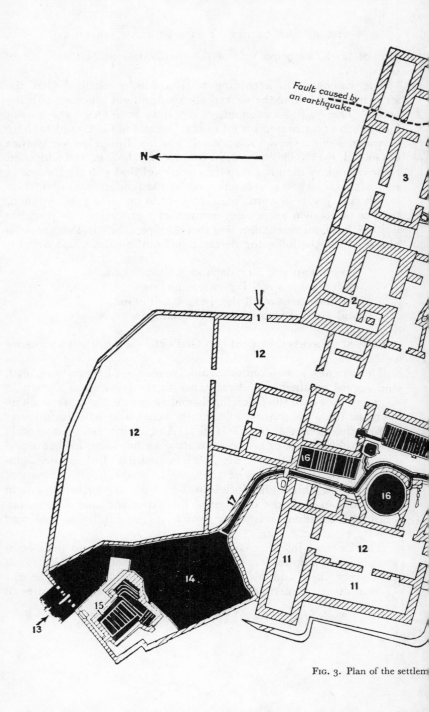

Fig. 3. Plan of the settlem

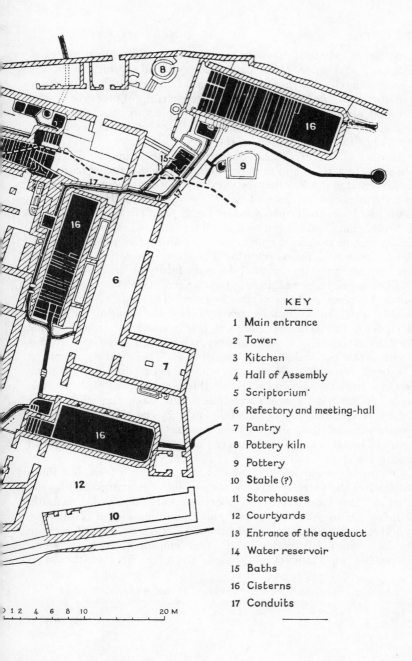

KEY

1 Main entrance
2 Tower
3 Kitchen
4 Hall of Assembly
5 Scriptorium·
6 Refectory and meeting-hall
7 Pantry
8 Pottery kiln
9 Pottery
10 Stable (?)
11 Storehouses
12 Courtyards
13 Entrance of the aqueduct
14 Water reservoir
15 Baths
16 Cisterns
17 Conduits

0 1 2   4   6   8   10   20 M

rbet Qumran (Essene period).

many times. 'My soul', says the sectary, 'will not covet the riches of violence';[1] and again, 'Everlasting hatred for all the men of the Pit (i.e. the ungodly), because of their spirit of hoarding'.[2] As has been seen above, the *Rule* imposed common ownership of property on the members of the Covenant; vowed to a simple and poor way of life, they called themselves 'the Poor', and their sect, as we read quite explicitly, 'the congregation of the Poor'.[3]

Another clause of the Essene oath was, according to Josephus, 'always to love truth and to pursue liars'.[4] Now the idea of truth is so fundamental to the *Rule* that the word 'truth' (*emet*) recurs constantly. The sectaries are 'the sons of truth', 'volunteers for His truth'; the sect is 'the House of Truth', God is 'Truth', and His Spirit the 'Spirit of Truth'. Falsehood is pursued in all its forms whether inspired by self-interest or not; in the first case the punishment is for one year, and in the second, for six months.[5] The sectary declares: 'and on my lips shall be found no criminal deceit or falsity or lies'.[6]

'They are righteous arbiters of their anger, masters of their wrath', writes Josephus apropos of the Essenes.[7] The *Rule* of Qumran is equally strict in forbidding revenge and the bearing of malice (VII, 8-9). The *Damascus Document*, laying down the procedure for the denouncement of a guilty brother, states that in no case must this denunciation be made 'in the heat of anger', before the guilty man has been reprimanded; neither was it permissible to postpone matters until the morrow because this would mean that the sun would go down on a man's wrath and thus make him guilty of sin himself (IX, 2-8). Traces of a subtle and very elaborate casuistry are apparent in all this, showing how far the Qumran sectaries took pains to be 'arbiters of their anger', in the words of Josephus, and 'masters of their wrath'.

Of course the cult of the Law was common to all Jews, but Philo emphasizes the extreme fervour with which it was practised by the Essenes. 'They work at ethics with extreme care', he says,[8] 'constantly utilizing the ancestral laws, laws which no human mind could have conceived without divine inspiration.' In these ancestral laws — in the Law, the holy *Torah* — the Essenes 'continually instruct themselves, but especially every seventh day; for the seventh day is

---

[1] *Rule*, X, 19.   [2] *Rule*, IX, 21-2.
[3] Fragment of a *Commentary on Psalm XXXVII*, col. II, line 10 (published in the *Palestin Exploration Quarterly*, vol. lxxxvi, May-September 1954, pp. 69-75). See below, p. 271.
[4] *War*, II, § 141.   [5] *Rule*, VI, 24-5, VII, 3-4.   [6] *Rule*, X, 22.
[7] *War*, II, § 135.   [8] *Q.o.p.l.*, § 80.

thought holy'.[1] He then goes on to describe the study meetings during which the Essenes, assembled about a revered teacher, listened to his instruction with passionate attention. This extreme devotion to the Law is also found in the sect at Qumran. The *Damascus Document* calls the latter 'the House of the Law', and this title was well merited in view of the oath by which new members undertook, expressly and essentially, to 'be converted to the Law of Moses with all their heart and all their soul'. Every fault against the Law, if voluntary, entailed irrevocable expulsion from the sect, and even if committed through inadvertence was heavily punished. The guilty man was separated for two years 'from Purification and from the Council', and was not readmitted until his conduct during those two years had been closely examined.[2] But in addition to all this, the study of the Law was organized at Qumran as one of its essential institutions: 'And in the place where the ten are, let there not lack a man who studies the Law day and night, constantly. . . .'[3] The group of ten, it may be recalled, was the basic unit: in each of these groups, one of the brethren was therefore discharged from every kind of material occupation, and was exclusively devoted to study and meditation on the Law. In general it was doubtless the groups' presiding priest. Furthermore, we read in the *Rule* of Qumran: 'Let the Many watch in common for a third of all the nights of the year, to read the Book and study the law and bless in common '(VI, 7-8). No doubt the brethren were divided into three lots — the night consisted of three 'watches' — and each lot watching in turn thereby ensured that a permanent vigil was maintained. During these holy watches the Law was read and interpreted and blessings recited.

As regards the observance of the Sabbath, one of the fundamental commandments of the Law, Josephus writes that the Essenes are 'forbidden more rigorously than any Jew to attend to their work on the seventh day. Not only do they prepare their food the day before to avoid lighting a fire on that day, but they dare not even move an object. . . .'[4] This rigorous observance of the Sabbath is entirely corroborated at Qumran; indeed, there is a long instruction on the Sabbath in the *Damascus Document* (X, 14-XI, 18), consisting of twenty-seven articles whose exigencies seem even more severe than the Rabbinic and Pharisaic rules.

Josephus tells of various special rules of purity observed by the

---

[1] *Q.o.p.l.*, § 81. [2] *Rule*, VIII, 20-IX, 2.
[3] *Rule*, VI, 6-7. [4] *War*, II, § 147.

Essenes. He notes, for instance, that the Essenes 'regard oil as a defilement'.[1] The *Damascus Document* also contains an allusion to 'the defilements of oil' (XII, 16). Josephus points out that the excommunicated Essene 'cannot even share the food of others' (other Jews) because of being ineradicably bound to the rules of the sect in matters of food.[2] Again, the *Damascus Document* gives a whole special instruction on clean and unclean foods (XII, 11-18). This work emphasizes, in several passages, the importance of the rules relating to purity, and this sort of insistence is quite in conformity with Josephus's account, which states that the Essenes practised purifications different from those of other Jews.[3] The Jewish historian writes that they were obliged to wash not only after contact with a stranger but even when one of the older brethren had been in contact with a younger.[4]

Finally it is as well to recall the passage in which Josephus describes the precautions against impurity taken by the Essenes when they went to stool.[5] These rules were inspired by a passage from Deuteronomy (xxiii. 12-14) which lays it down that a man must go outside the camp and dig a hole for his excrement there. It seems that the sectaries of Qumran were particularly attentive to this law of Deuteronomy. In the *War Scroll* (VII, 6-7) we read: 'And there shall be a space of about two thousand cubits between their camp and the site of the (retiring) place, and nothing shameful or ugly shall be seen in the surroundings of all their camp.' This rule makes a point, therefore, of fixing the distance exactly, whereas Josephus writes more vaguely of 'the loneliest places'. On the other hand, he specifies that the Essene had to wrap himself carefully in his mantle 'in order not to offend the rays of God', i.e. not to expose his nakedness in any way. The *Rule* appears to allude to the same preoccupation when it threatens punishment for 'the man who allows his hand[6] to protrude from beneath his garment, if this garment is in rags and exposes his nakedness'.[7]

I hope I shall be forgiven for ending this comparison of classical and Qumran texts on such an unexalted note, but for the Essenes the whole of life, even its humblest physical functions, was enveloped and penetrated by religion and concern for purity. This parallel is given merely in outline and could be developed at much greater

---

[1] *War*, II, § 123.   [2] *War*, II, § 143.   [3] *Antiquities*, XVIII, § 19.
[4] *War*, II, § 150.   [5] *War*, II, §§ 148-9.   [6] Euphemism.
[7] *Rule*, VII, 13-14.

length. But it appears to me that in all respects, whether with regard to the organization of community life, rites, doctrines, or customs, there is so much in common where essential characteristics and traits are concerned, that it is almost impossible not to identify the Qumran sect with the Essenes, or in other words, conclude that the Qumran scrolls are of Essene origin.

Moreover, in the first century B.C., when, as coins found in the ruins show, the Qumran sect was in full activity, there were, according to the testimony of Josephus, only three sects in Palestine — the Sadducees, the Pharisees and the Essenes. The sectaries of the Community of the Covenant were, however, certainly not Sadducees (in the usual meaning of the word): on the contrary, numerous Qumran texts show them to have been engaged in a violent struggle with the priests of the party of the Sadducees. Were they Pharisees? But where is there any question of common ownership, an oath of initiation, or sacred meals presided over by a priest, etc., among the Pharisees? There remain the Essenes, and here the similarities are so many, and so striking, that identification seems really inevitable.

It remains for me to show that the ruins of Qumran uncovered by the recent excavations are directly connected with the scrolls found in the neighbouring caves, and that the character and arrangement of the buildings, no less than their situation in the desert, rule out practically every other hypothesis regarding the nature of the ancient settlement except the one identifying it as the Essene establishment described by Pliny the Elder as being situated near the western shore of the Dead Sea.

2. ARCHAEOLOGICAL EVIDENCE

The Qumran ruins occupy a broad terrace dominating a ravine about three-quarters of a mile from the shore of the Dead Sea. Quite near, towards the west and parallel to the shore, is the cliff stretching from north to south in which the first cave of manuscripts was discovered. The terrace rises about 135 feet above the level of the Dead Sea and the coastal plain. The site corresponds remarkably closely to Pliny's observation: 'To the west (of the Dead Sea) the Essenes have put the necessary distance between themselves and the insalubrious shore.'

This place had been visited before by explorers; among others, the

French orientalist C. Clermont-Ganneau went there in 1873. He saw a few dilapidated walls, the ground strewn with every sort of potsherd, and a vast cemetery of about eleven hundred curious tombs which were neither Jewish, Christian, nor Muslim; but he would not risk committing himself to any theory regarding the nature or date of these strange remains. After him came the German archaeologist G. Dalman, who spoke of a Roman fort. But why such a huge and singular cemetery beside a Roman fort? The excavations begun in 1951 resulted, as I have already said, in finds of considerable importance which have at last uncovered the mystery of this enigmatic desert settlement. They were conducted by G. Lankester Harding, Director of the Jordan Department of Antiquities, and Father R. de Vaux, Director of the French School of Archaeology in Jerusalem.

From the very earliest campaign, pottery specimens were discovered similar to those found in the manuscript caves, thereby proving that there was probably some connection between the scrolls and the ancient settlement of Khirbet Qumran. This probability became a certainty as continuing excavation uncovered the entire site and revealed the various peculiarities of the buildings.

These buildings — impossible to describe in detail here — consist, among other things, of silos and storehouses, a baker's oven, a large mill, a kitchen, a laundry, workshops, kilns, as well as numerous cisterns and the water ducts supplying them: in short, they constitute all the installations necessary for the material life of a community isolated in the desert, and far from any urban centre, which has to manufacture or prepare for itself everything needed for its subsistence and support.

The terrace buildings had no dormitories or bedrooms. The members of the Community must have lodged, not in these quarters, which were reserved for the communal offices, but in tents or huts in the vicinity, and also in caves in the near-by cliff. In the neighbourhood of Khirbet Qumran, twenty-five caves have been located containing pottery remains, and the fact that these remains are of the same type as those found in the manuscript caves and in Khirbet Qumran suggests that at least some of these caves must have served as individual dwellings for members of the Qumran Community. With its tents and huts, the place must have looked like a camp, and it is precisely this word, 'camp, encampment' (in Hebrew *maḥaneh*) which the *Damascus Document* uses to describe the typical habitat of the communities of the sect of the Covenant. Philo of Alexandria reports that the Essenes lived 'in villages',[1] a description calling to mind those 'laurae' which in the Christian era, multiplied in Egypt and Palestine — in the same desert of Judah. They were, so to speak, religious hamlets inhabited by monks who assembled in the community house for offices and meals.

However, in addition to the various installations already listed, the communal buildings included other great halls; now these correspond exactly to the essential exigencies of the religious life of an Essene community. For instance, the remains of a *scriptorium* have been discovered, and of a very long narrow table (about sixteen and a half feet long), and pieces of one or two shorter tables. These were doubtless writing tables, since two inkpots were found in the same place, one of terra-cotta and the other of bronze. It therefore seems that this was the place in which the scrolls from the caves were copied. The copyists who bent over these tables and dipped their pens in these inkpots were not, as has been suggested, just ordinary secular scribes copying something for the benefit of some client or other. The Qumran caves have yielded nothing but religious writings, either biblical books proper or Jewish mystical works of a sectarian character: there is not a single secular writing among them, or even anything foreign to Essenism. And anyway, what would secular copyists be doing in a desert like this, plying their trade far from any city and clientele? No, the copying of the Essene books, which were holy and secret, required scribes recruited from among the members of the sect itself. Some inscribed potsherds have been found among the ruins, and one of these *ostraca* is most interesting. It is a little Hebrew alphabet whose letters correspond exactly to those of the scrolls found in the caves. This small document is the work of a scribe's apprentice; one or two letters have been rewritten. For it should be remembered that the Qumran scribes could not have acquired such mastery of the art of writing as seen in the discovered manuscripts without a long apprenticeship.

There is also another great hall, about 73 feet long. The ceiling was supported by pillars, and at one end, towards the west, there is a kind of stone platform which was no doubt reserved to the president of the assembly and the reader. But this hall did not only serve as a place for the Community study sessions. Another smaller annexe communicates with it on its southern side, and at the end of the annexe a whole heap of crockery was discovered, carefully piled up.

[1] *Q.o.p.l.*, § 76. Cf. *Apologia*, § 1.

There were about thirty earthenware terrines, about two hundred plates, more than seven hundred bowls, and about seventy goblets. All this tableware suggests that the adjacent great hall must have been the Community's refectory, or more exactly, given the sacred character of the Essene community meal, its 'cenacle'.

Josephus informs us[1] that the Essenes had to take a purificatory bath, a baptism, before entering the cenacle. Have such baptistries been found in the ruins of Qumran? As I have said, four large cisterns and seven small ones have been uncovered. Obviously it was necessary to have water in that desert, and even a great deal of water for the material needs of the Community, but it nevertheless seems certain — and such is the opinion of Father de Vaux — that at least two of the more carefully built pools, provided with several sets of steps, were really baths, or more exactly the Community's baptistries.

During the spring campaign of 1955 the excavators also brought to light about forty curious deposits which had been carefully buried in the earth, namely jars filled with animal bones. They were mostly the remains of sheep, goats and lambs, but there were also bones of calves and cows.[2] That they were buried in the soil of the monastery itself suggests that this must have been done in conformity with some rite, and they are doubtless the remains of a sacred meal, perhaps a sacrificial meal. But why bury them? Is it possible that they were foundation burials, like the dog and pig bones found in the soil of the Pythagorean basilica of Porto Maggiore in Rome, the remains of the foundation sacrifice offered at the consecration of the building?[3] In any case, these clearly ritual deposits are evidence of the sacred character of the Qumran establishment: it was certainly a holy place.

On the terrace itself, to the east, a large area separated from the buildings by a long wall running from north to south had been set apart for the dead. The archaeologists have opened about forty tombs. The bodies lie on their backs at the bottom of a rectangular pit with their heads pointing to the south; over each grave is an oval tumulus covered with pebbles. There is no funeral offering, no ornament, no inscription. It seems natural to think that these tombs in the middle of the desert (about eleven hundred of them) must be the cemetery of the religious community. Fragments of an entire jar identical with those found in the ruins and the caves have been

---

[1] *War*, II, § 129.   [2] See *RB*, lxiii, 1956, pp. 73-4.
[3] Cf. J. CARCOPINO, *La basilique pythagoricienne de la Porte Majeure*, pp. 91 f.

recovered from the earth in one of the graves. Their simplicity corresponds to the ideals of poverty and humility so dear to the Essenes; and at the same time the care with which the holy remains have been buried and protected manifests their faith in the resurrection of the body. The orientation of the bodies with the head to the south is particularly remarkable; the same characteristic may be seen in the Jewish Karaite sect which in many ways appears to continue ancient Essene customs.[1]

Most of the excavated tombs contain male skeletons, and only a few of them hold female remains. There is nothing surprising in the presence of a few women in this Essene cemetery. It is true that Pliny the Elder's account states that in the first century A.D., the Essenes of the Dead Sea monastery lived in strict celibacy, 'without women and renouncing love entirely'. But earlier, in the first century B.C., when the Qumran establishment was first inaugurated, the Essenes living there could very well have had their families with them. In the *Damascus Document*, and also in the *Rule Annexe* found at Qumran, there is mention of married sectaries, their wives and children. Also Josephus[2] informs us that in his time there were married Essenes: these doubtless were only continuing an ancient custom which may have been practised at Qumran in the first phase of its history. Moreover, even when the Essenes of Qumran had adopted the rule of celibacy it is not impossible to imagine that in some exceptional case a pious women may have been admitted to take her last sleep in the cemetery of the holy asceties.

Taking into account, therefore, all the archaeological indications, it not only appears that there is nothing to contradict the Essene hypothesis, but that in fact it furnishes the only satisfactory explanation of all the data confronting us. It is, in particular, the opinion of the archaeologists who, having worked on the site from 1951 to 1958, are more qualified than any others to speak with competence. So it is highly probable, to say the least, that the remains of the famous 'laura' so fortunately mentioned by Pliny the Elder have at last been discovered. The cenacle where the Essenes celebrated their

[1] According to J. T. MILIK (*RB*, lxv, 1958, p. 77, n. 1) this north-south orientation of the Qumran tombs may be explained by the fact that the Essenes located Paradise in the extreme north, as does the *Book of Enoch* which they so assiduously read: '... While they are dead, they lie with their heads to the south waiting for the day of resurrection, contemplating in the dream of passing sleep their future land. When they wake, they will arise with their faces to the north and will walk straight on to Paradise, the Holy Mountain, the Heavenly Jerusalem. ...' This explanation appears very reasonable.

[2] *War*, II, §§ 160-1.

mysterious repasts, the tables where they religiously recopied their sacred books, the baptistries where they took their purificatory baths, the oven where they baked their bread, the workshops where they laboured,[1] the caves in the side of the cliff where they lived, their burial place in the affecting necropolis whose orderly lay-out and uniform graves again reflect the discipline and fervour of their community life — today it is all there for us to see. And in the solemn quietness of the bare and torrid desert it is possible to imagine the people of penitents who led such a hard and exceedingly austere life there, the grave mature men depicted by Philo, whose strange superhuman race had, as Pliny the Elder thought, endured in these parts 'for thousands of centuries'.

It is now time to read the books which nourished their spirit, books to which they committed their mystic beliefs, apocalyptic dreams, and hopes of immortality. These books were secret, but owing to their fortuitous discovery by a Bedouin, they are now in our hands, in their authentic text, unaltered, without interpolations or later non-Essene modifications, just as they were written and copied about two thousand years ago. What wonderful luck for the historian!

It should nevertheless be noted straight away that in spite of their general striking agreement with the accounts of Philo and Josephus, the Qumran scrolls do present some rare divergences. This is not at all surprising. The accounts written by the two Jewish authors are essentially summary; they could not enter into all the complexities of situations and regulations, and necessarily tended to simplify, and also sometimes to colour, the facts according to their own taste. There may be vagueness and even some inaccuracy; are there not even a few divergences between Philo and Josephus themselves? It is quite inevitable that external evidence should fail to coincide

---

[1] In particular, a whole pottery workshop, with the kiln, the clearly recognizable site of the wheel, etc. I would also draw attention to the various installations discovered in the region of Ain Feshkhah, two miles south of Khirbet Qumran, in the 1956-58 excavations. See R. DE VAUX, *RB*, lxv, 1958, pp. 406-8: '. . . There is no doubt as regards the general interpretation of the installations brought to light. It was a dependency of Khirbet Qumran, a secondary centre, or more exactly, an agricultural centre, where those who were occupied with the community's palm-groves and flocks, and who turned the products of farming and stock-breeding to some industrial use, lived and worked. These discoveries complete our picture of the life of the community and show how they tried, within the bounds of possibility, to achieve self-sufficiency.' — Father de Vaux has recently published a fairly detailed preliminary survey of these excavations in *RB*, lxvi, 1959, pp. 225-55 and twelve plates.

absolutely rigorously with the documents themselves; the contrary would be abnormal. Every historian knows very well that wherever several witnesses of different origin and character testify to the same event, they never, so to speak, tally completely; he has therefore to interpret and explain one by the light of the other.

As far as the Qumran documents are concerned, it is necessary to add one further point. These writings are not all of the same age and can betray, from one document to the next, a certain evolution in institutions and beliefs. Traces of a similar evolution may even be seen in one and the same document, between one passage and the next, either because it may be a compilation of differently dated material, or because the primitive redaction may have been more or less modified and adapted to its present form.

Finally it should be borne in mind that the Qumran sect, i.e. the Essene sect, was both secret and esoteric. Consequently, those who spoke of it from the outside *cannot have known all.* Also they *may not have wished to say all,* for various reasons. This explains why the Qumran scrolls, although in my opinion unquestionably attesting the identity of the sect with the Essenes described by Philo and Josephus, reveal certain things unmentioned by those writers: for instance, everything relating to the religious calendar, the doctrine of the two Spirits, messianic expectations, the war-like dreams of the final battle against Belial and all his fiends, and above all, the history of the august founder and legislator of the Essenes, the mysterious Teacher of Righteousness, the priestly Messiah who suffered and was put to death about a hundred years before Jesus of Nazareth, and whose glorious return at the end of time was awaited by his disciples. All this additional information throws entirely new light on our knowledge of Essenism, as we shall see.

Chapter III

THE SCROLL OF THE *RULE*

Description of the scroll: its contents, character and date.
Translation of the *Rule*. Translation of the *Rule Annexe*. Translation of the *Book of Blessings*.

Of the various scrolls from the Qumran caves, the *Rule* is the one that should be read first: it at once admits the reader into the very heart of the sect, into the intimacy of its community life and the secret of its doctrines, ceremonies and rites.

This scroll was found in cave I in 1947. It was acquired at the end of that year by the Syriac Metropolitan of the monastery of St. Mark in Jerusalem, Mar Athanasius Samuel, and was taken to the United States. There it was studied and edited by American scholars who with laudable promptness published it in 1951 under the title, *The Dead Sea Scrolls of St. Mark's Monastery, vol. II. Fasc. 2: Plates and Transcription of the Manual of Discipline* (The American Schools of Oriental Research, New Haven). This publication is essentially a collection of photographs of the eleven columns of the scroll accompanied by a simple transcription in printed Hebrew characters; the author is Professor Millar Burrows, assisted by John C. Trever and William H. Brownlee. Towards the end of 1954, the State of Israel succeeded in buying the *Rule* from the Metropolitan, together with three other scrolls which he had acquired in 1947, and since February 1955 they have been in Jerusalem where, as I have said, they are carefully and religiously kept in one of the buildings of the Hebrew University.

The eleven columns of the *Rule* published in 1951 do not, however, constitute the whole book. In 1950, various fragments which had become detached from the scroll when it was taken from the cave, and had been sold by the Bedouin to an antique dealer in Bethlehem, were handed over by him to the Palestine Museum in Jerusalem (Jordan). These fragments have been published by Fr. D. Barthélemy and Fr. J. T. Milik in a collection of all the small finds from cave I (the first cave discovered in 1947) under the title, *Qumran Cave I* (Oxford, 1955). This is the first of seven to ten volumes in which all

the documents discovered (or still to be found) in the Judaean desert
— with the exception of the great scrolls already published in America
and Israel — are to be made available to scholars.[1] The fragments of
the *Rule* published in *Qumran Cave I* (no. 28, plates XXII-XXIX)
are, in fact, two appendices. One, consisting of two columns, is as it
were an *Annexe* to the *Rule*, and refers to particular issues; the other,
which originally consisted of at least six columns, is a collection of
Blessings. These two appendices are of the greatest importance and
their translation in these pages follows that of the *Rule* itself.

Its American editors have named this scroll *The Manual of
Discipline*. But is it really a 'manual'? We know in antiquity of the
celebrated *Manual* of Epictetus (*Encheiridion*) but in that case the
word was intended to indicate the reduced size and relatively
abridged character of the book as opposed to a lengthy treatise. This
Hebrew scroll is, however, neither abridged nor condensed; it is full
of repetition and oratorical development. Again, is it the real aim of
the work to explain the sect's 'discipline' or disciplinary rules?
Though an exposition of this kind does occupy an important place,
the scroll as a whole is of a different character. It is surely better to
call it the *Rule*, as it more and more tends to be called by analogy
with those works recording the statutes of monastic orders (*Regula* or
Regulae). In any case, the word 'rule' (*serek*) is repeated constantly in
the scroll itself, in particular at the beginning of several sections.[2]

It is nevertheless essential to bear in mind that the scroll is not
wholly a 'rule'. It opens with an introduction defining the aim and
ideals of the community (I, 1-15). Then follows a description of the
ceremony of admission into the sect (I, 16-II, 18), a rule imposing an
annual census on all the members, an exhortatory development on
the moral disposition required of them (II, 19-III, 12), and a long
instruction, catechismal in character and remarkably definite and
polished, on the theme of the two Spirits, the basis of the sect's
whole mystical doctrine and spirituality (III, 13-IV, 26). Only after
all this does the 'rule' proper begin, in the form of a statement of the
various regulations in force among the sect (V, 1-IX, 26), including
the penal code. But again this section is not entirely devoted to a
collection of statutory texts; it contains an introductory exhortation

---

[1] The general title of the collection is *Discoveries in the Judaean Desert*. From the present
state of things, the edition is expected to require from five to ten years to complete.

[2] It seems that this word even appeared in the general title at the head of the scroll, just
before the first column; what remains of it should probably read: '[. . . ru]le of the
Community and [. . .]'

to obedience, is full of doctrinal digressions, and ends with a recommendation to total submission to the will of God and the command to bless Him always. This conclusion also serves to introduce the final section of the work (X, 1-XI, 22), which is really a hymn or psalm in which the sectary, speaking in the first person, recalls poetically certain of the sect's fundamental doctrines — the celebration of feasts on the days prescribed by its own calendar, the obligation to praise God unceasingly, the conduct to be observed towards each other, the belief that justification is by God alone, the omnipotence of God compared with the nothingness of man. There is, therefore, a subtle and scholarly progression through the whole book that raises it finally to the most sublime themes of Qumran speculation. As for the appendices, the first — called the *Rule Annexe* — does in fact consist of a series of statutory texts which were apparently intended to complete those of the principal book. But the second, rightly titled the *Blessings*, is a liturgical book, a collection of benedictory formulae addressed to the members of the sect and its various dignitaries: there is nothing of a 'rule' about it.

It seems, then, that the scroll called the *Rule* is really a composite work. Although it contains a good many texts of a juridical and constitutional nature, there are others — very many more in fact — that are mystical and moral exhortations, doctrinal expositions, rituals and poetic exaltation. It should be noted at this juncture that the *Damascus Document* mentions several times a basic work of the sect, the *Book of Meditation*,[1] and orders that the judges of the Congregation and the priests presiding over each camp are to be instructed in this book and in the constitution and laws of the sect (X, 6; XIII, 2; XIV, 8). Then again, the *Rule Annexe* (I, 7) prescribes instruction in the book, as well as in the precepts of the Covenant, to children born into the sect. May not the scroll which we call the *Rule* be, purely and simply, this *Book of Meditation*? It is certainly presented as a collection of basic texts intended for constant reading and meditation. Also, the importance of the book and the favour it enjoyed in the sect is clearly demonstrated by the fact that, in addition to the scroll found in cave I, fragments of the same work corresponding to eleven different manuscripts have been found in cave IV.[2] On the other hand, unless this can be identified as the work we know as the *Rule*, nothing seems to have been found in the caves of the

---

[1] In Hebrew *SPR HHGW*.   [2] See *RB*, lxiii, 1956, pp. 60 f.

famous *Book of Meditation*. Provisionally, therefore, I will conclude that such an identification is highly probable.[1]

It is very difficult to determine when the *Rule* was written. As I have said, the work is composite; in some respects it is a compilation, a digest, and its various elements do not necessarily derive from the same author or from the same period. What part did the Teacher of Righteousness play in the formation of the collection, or in its writing? It is strange to find no mention of him, no explicit mention at least. Is this because he was himself the author, if not of the present recension, then of the basic recension from which it stems? The authority which, judging from the great number of manuscripts found in the Qumran caves, this book enjoyed, leads us to suppose that the Teacher cannot have been wholly foreign to its formation. On the other hand, passages from the *Rule* alluding to the retreat into the desert (VIII, 12-14; IX, 19-20) appear to indicate that when they were written the Community was already effectively installed at Qumran in the desert of Judah. These passages were no doubt written during the Teacher's lifetime (in my opinion, the first third of the first century B.C.) even if the Teacher himself did not write them. Besides, where there is mention in the *Rule* (IX, 9-11) of the 'first ordinances' prior to 'the coming of the Prophet and the Anointed of Aaron and Israel', one has reason to suppose that the period inaugurated by the coming of the Prophet — very likely the Teacher — had already begun, and that the 'last ordinances' had already been promulgated by him.

Then again, when describing the Supper as it is to be celebrated when the messianic age is fulfilled, the *Rule Annexe* (II, 11-12) mentions the presence at that Supper of the Priest and the Messiah of Israel: in this context, the Priest is the Messiah of Aaron — the Priest-Messiah — and in my opinion, the Teacher of Righteousness himself. As we know, he was a priest who had come already, but it was believed by his followers that he would return at the end of time together with the Messiah of Israel, the King-Messiah. Consequently, the passage in question from the *Rule Annexe* must have been written after the death of the Teacher of Righteousness, perhaps only a little while after.

In short, the *Rule* may, basically, very easily derive from the

[1] Too little remains of the general title at the head of the scroll (cf. p. 69, n. 2) for any objection to be drawn from it against the proposed identification. The words *SPR HHGW* may have disappeared either before or after the two or three words remaining.

Teacher of Righteousness himself, but may have undergone some alteration or adaptation, and also some expansion, after his death. When the fragments of the eleven manuscripts found in cave IV are published, they may show variants that will help us to solve these delicate problems.

These variants may also throw some light on certain obscurities in the Hebrew text of the scroll found in cave I. The translation suggested here cannot be final. Although improved here and there, it is the translation I prepared in 1951, as soon as the text was published, and included in *Nouveaux Aperçus sur les manuscrits de la mer Morte* (1953). But the publication of the still unedited fragments from cave IV may call for more retouching.[1] As regards the two appendices, I have taken my inspiration from the French translation attached to the *editio princeps*, but have reshaped it quite extensively, partly to bring it into line with my own style of translation, and partly to render several points more precise and exact. I have tried to see that the translation is clear and flowing, but have at the same time respected, as far as possible, its Hebraic style and colour. The sub-titles in italics are my own. The verse form is intended to emphasize, whenever it is sufficiently recognizable, the characteristics of this style with its long sententious and oratorical periods, and also the parallelism of the poetic sections. The accompanying notes do not pretend to serve as a true commentary, but are merely intended to help the reader to understand some of the sect's technical words and certain of the difficult passages.[2]

Aim and ideal of the Community

I (1) For [the man of understanding[3] that he may instruct the sai]nts to li[ve according to the ru]le of the Community;

[1] Various translations of the *Rule* have been published in French, English, German and Latin. The most useful is that of W. H. Brownlee, which appeared in 1951 in *BASOR*, Supplementary Studies, 10-12 (New Haven). P. Wernberg-Møller's, *The Manual of Discipline Translated and Annotated with an Introduction* (Leiden, 1957) reached me too late to use here.

[2] In this translation, as in those of the following chapters, words or letters enclosed in square brackets indicate a completion of accidental lacunae in the manuscript; those set between pointed brackets are corrections judged necessary to the text itself; those placed in parentheses are additions helpful to the clarity of the translation. Dots indicate a fairly extensive lacuna in the manuscript impossible to fill by conjecture. Roman numbers in bold type show the column numbers, and the bold figures in parentheses, the line numbers.

[3] I have completed the lacuna at the beginning of the scroll as *la[mmaskil]*, 'for the man of understanding', i.e. the initiate, the instructor of new brethren. This indication is frequently encountered in the Qumran documents, either at the head of the scroll or at the beginning of a section, and means that the book is a secret religious book proper to the sect as opposed to the biblical books common to all Jews.

to seek (2) God with [all their heart] and [all their soul]
[and] do what is good and right before Him,
as (3) He commanded by the hand of Moses
and all His servants the Prophets;
and to love all (4) that He has chosen
and hate all that He has despised;
and to depart from all evil
(5) and cling to all good works;
and to practise truth and righteousness and justice (6) on earth,
and to walk no more in the stubbornness of a guilty heart,
nor with lustful eyes (7) committing every kind of evil;
and to cause all the volunteers to enter[1]
who wish to practise the precepts of God (8) in the Covenant of Grace,
that they may be united in the Council of God
and behave perfectly before Him
⟨according⟩ to all (9) the revelations concerning their regular feasts;[2]
and that they may love all the sons of light,
each (10) according to his lot in the Council of God;
and that they may hate all the sons of darkness,
each according to his fault (11) in the Vengeance of God.[3]

And all the volunteers that cling to His truth
shall bring all their understanding and powers and (12) possessions
into the Community of God,
to purify their understanding in the truth of the precepts of God,
and to order their powers (13) according to the perfection of His ways,
and all their possessions according to His righteous Counsel.[4]

[1] The sectaries were 'volunteers' who enlisted freely and spontaneously; cf. PHILO on the Essenes (*Praep. evang.*, VIII, 11, § 2): 'Their enlistment is not due to race — the word race is unsuitable where volunteers are concerned.'

[2] The Essenes attached the greatest importance to their special calendar, which was to be followed when fixing the dates of the religious feasts. This calendar was regarded as having been revealed by God and as genuinely conforming to the divine Law of the World. Because the other Jews followed another calendar, they were considered as having fallen into gravest error; unaware of the real dates, they celebrated all the Sabbaths and feasts at the wrong times, and thereby continually violated God's true time. The *Rule* returns over and over again to this basic question of the religious calendar. The *Book of Jubilees* and the *Book of Enoch* tell us most about the Essene calendar, which was based entirely on a division of the year into four seasons of 3 months; each season consisted of exactly 13 weeks (91 days), and consequently the whole year contained 52 weeks (364 days). For further discussion on the Essene calendar, see *Nouveaux aperçus sur les manuscrits de la mer Morte* (Paris, 1953), pp. 141-56. (Eng. edn., pp 104-17.)

[3] Cf. JOSEPHUS, *War*, II, § 139: 'He (the Essene) swears . . . to hate the wicked always and to fight together with the good.' The 'sons of light' are the just, i.e. the sectaries, and the 'sons of darkness' the unjust, the ungodly, all who do not belong to the sect. The 'lot', i.e. the destiny, of both is fixed from all eternity; the sons of light are predestined to be men of the 'Counsel of God', and the others to be sons of the 'Vengeance of God'.

[4] The Essene belonged entirely, body and soul, to the Community. He had even to surrender his possessions to it (cf. VI, 19, 22; IX, 8-9, 22). This obligation is clearly and strongly emphasized by Philo and Josephus.

And they shall make no single step
(**14**) from all the words of God concerning their times,
they shall not anticipate their times,
nor delay them (**15**) for any of their feasts.[1]
And they shall not depart from His precepts of truth
to walk either to right or to left.

The ceremony of entry into the Covenant

(**16**) And all who decide to enter into the rule of the Community shall pass into the Covenant[2] in the presence of God, (undertaking) to act (**17**) according to all His commands and not to turn back from Him on account of fear, or fright, or any affliction whatever, (**18**) if tempted by the dominion of Belial.[3]

And when they pass into the Covenant, the priests (**19**) and Levites shall bless the God of deliverances and all His works of truth. And all (**20**) who pass into the Covenant shall say after them, Amen, Amen!

(**21**) And the priests shall recount the deeds of God in His mighty works (**22**) and proclaim all the favours of (divine) mercy towards Israel. And the Levites shall recount (**23**) the iniquities of the sons of Israel and all their guilty rebellions and the sins (which they have committed) under the dominion (**24**) of Belial.

And all who pass into the Covenant shall make their confession after them, saying:
We have been sinful, (**25**) we have rebelled,
we have sinned, we have been wicked,
we and our fathers before us,
by going (**26**) against the precepts of truth.
And just is God who has fulfilled His judgment
against us and against our fathers.
II (**1**) But He extends His gracious mercy towards us for ever and ever.

And the priests shall bless all (**2**) the men of the lot of
God who walk perfectly in all His ways, and shall say:
May He bless thee with all (**3**) goodness,
and keep thee from all evil!
May He enlighten thy heart with understanding of life,
and favour thee with everlasting Knowledge!
(**4**) May He lift His gracious face towards thee
to grant thee eternal bliss!

---

[1] Feasts had to be celebrated on the exact date fixed by the sect's calendar. No attempt had to be made to make these dates conform to the common calendar of official Judaism.

[2] The New Covenant as constituted by the Essene Community.

[3] Belial, or Satan, is the Evil Spirit, the Angel of Darkness, the Commander of the Army of Evil. See below, the instruction on the two Spirits (III, 13-IV, 26).

And the Levites shall curse the men (5) of the lot of Belial, and shall speak and say:

Be thou cursed in all the works of thy guilty ungodliness!
(6) May God make of thee an object of dread
  by the hand of all the Avengers of vengeance!
May He hurl extermination after thee
  by the hand of all the Executioners (7) of punishment!
Cursed be thou, without mercy,
  according to the darkness of thy deeds!
Be thou damned
  (8) in the night of eternal fire!
May God not favour thee when thou callest upon Him,
  and may He be without forgiveness to expiate thy sins!
(9) May He lift His angry face to revenge Himself upon thee,
  and may there be for thee no (word) of peace
  on the lips of all who cling (to the Covenant) of the Fathers!
  (10) And all who pass into the Covenant shall say after those that bless and those that curse, Amen, Amen!

(11) And the priests and Levites shall say again:

Cursed be he when he passes, together with the idols of his heart, (12) who enters into this Covenant leaving before him whatever causes him to fall into iniquity and to turn away (from God)! Behold, (13) as he listens to the words of this Covenant, he blesses himself in his heart, saying: May peace be with me (14) when I walk in the stubbornness of my heart! But his spirit shall be torn out, the dry with the humid, without (15) forgiveness.
May the Wrath of God and the Zeal of His judgment
  burn him in eternal destruction!
May there cling to him
  all (16) the curses of this Covenant!
May God set him apart for evil,
  and may he be cut off from the midst of the sons of light,
because he has turned away (17) from God
  on account of his idols and of that which causes him to stumble into sin!
May He place his lot
  among the eternally damned!
  (18) And all who enter into the Covenant shall speak after them and say, Amen, Amen![1]

---

[1] All this ritual obviously takes its inspiration from Deut. xxvii-xxx (blessings and curses accompanying the making of the Mosaic Covenant).

The annual census

(**19**) This is what they shall do, year by year, during all the time of the dominion of Belial. The priests shall pass (**20**) first, in order, according to (the degree of the excellence of) their spirits, one after another, and the Levites shall pass after them; (**21**) and thirdly, all the people shall pass, in order, one after another, by Thousands and Hundreds (**22**) and Fifties and Tens,[1] that every man of Israel may know the place he must occupy in the Community of God, (**23**) that of the eternal Counsel. And no man shall go down from the place he must occupy, nor raise himself above the place to which his lot assigns him.[2]

(**24**) For they shall all be in the Community of truth and virtuous humility and loving charity and scrupulous justice (**25**) one towards another, in the Council of holiness as sons of the everlasting Company.

But whoever scorns to enter (**26**) the ways of God in order to walk in the stubbornness of his heart, he shall not pass into His Community of truth.[3]

For **III** (**1**) his soul has loathed the teachings of Knowledge,
he has not established (within him) the ordinances of righteousness by
[conversion of his life.
Therefore he shall not be counted among upright men,
(**2**) and his understanding and powers and possessions
shall not be brought into the Council of the Community.[4]
For his silence (is invaded) by confusion of wickedness
and defilements (**3**) (are hidden) within his calm.
When he dissembles the stubbornness of his heart he shall not be justified,
nor when he beholds the ways of light (being himself) darkness;
and ⟨among⟩ the perfect[5] (**4**) he shall not be counted.
He shall not be absolved by atonement,
nor purified by lustral waters,
nor sanctified by seas (**5**) and rivers,

---

[1] The Essene Community, like the official Synagogue, was divided into three categories: priests, Levites and laity. The laity were divided again into Thousands, Hundreds, Fifties and Tens, as in the time of Moses according to Exod. xviii. 21, 25, and Deut. i. 15.

[2] The place or rank of every member of the Community was believed to have been fixed by God, by Destiny, and he had to adhere to it scrupulously. On the classification of the sectaries of Qumran, see also V, 20-4. This classification was examined and altered every year.

[3] The member of the Covenant had to surrender himself entirely to the Community, to be perfectly obedient and disciplined, and to renounce his own will, otherwise he did not truly belong to it. Despite his external adherence, if the required interior disposition was wanting, the purificatory rites of the sect would have no effect on him. This is the meaning of the section that follows (III, 1-12).

[4] Such a man was unfit to figure on the Community register and had to be excluded, excommunicated. See below, V, 13-20.

[5] The text reads: 'in the fount (B'TN) of the perfect'. This seems a curious expression and instead of B'TN I propose W'M, 'and among the perfect . . .'.

nor cleansed by all the waters of washing.
Unclean, unclean shall he be
for as long as he scorns the ordinances (6) of God
and allows not himself to be taught by the Community of His Council.
For by the Spirit of true counsel concerning the ways of man
shall all (7) his sins be atoned
when he beholds the light of life.
By the Holy Spirit of the Community, in His truth,
shall he be cleansed of all (8) his sins;
and by the Spirit of uprightness and humility
shall his iniquity be atoned.
By his soul's humility towards all the precepts of God
shall (9) his flesh be cleansed
when sprinkled with lustral water
and sanctified in flowing water.[1]
And he shall establish his steps to walk perfectly
(10) in all the ways of God,
according to His command concerning His regular feasts;[2]
and he shall step aside neither to right nor to left,
and (11) shall make no single step from all His words.
Then will he please God with agreeable expiation,
and it will obtain for him the Covenant (12) of the eternal Community.

The instruction on the two Spirits[3]

(13) For the man of understanding, that he may instruct and teach all
the sons of light concerning the nature of all the sons of men:[4] (14) all the
spirits which they possess, with their distinctive characters;[5] their works,

[1] An evident allusion to the baptismal practices of the sect.

[2] Another allusion to the sect's religious calendar.

[3] This instruction is of prime importance. It is, so to speak, introduced by the preceding
declamation underlining the essential role played by the 'Spirit of true counsel', the 'holy
Spirit', the 'Spirit of uprightness and humility' in the purification and sanctification of
man. The doctrine set out in the present section is very strongly influenced by Zoroastrian
speculation: on the subject of this Persian influence, see my *Nouveaux Aperçus* . . . , pp.
157-72. (Eng. edn., pp. 118-30.)

[4] This lesson on the two Spirits — Good and Evil — had to be learnt and continually
meditated on by 'all the sons of light', i.e. by all the members of the sect. It deals with the
primordial and fundamental problem of the nature of man and the human condition and
explains it by the presence and action of the two Spirits. It is because of these two Spirits
that man's life is a struggle and a fight, a profound drama.

[5] Every man has his spirit which partakes at the same time, though in unequal proportions, of both the Spirits (cf. IV, 16, 23-6); consequently all the variety of the human
spirit derives fundamentally from the two Spirits. The quality of each man's spirit,
whether good or bad, is to be recognized by signs and distinctive characteristics. The art of
'discernment of spirits' was of considerable importance in the sect; before admitting a new
member, 'they shall examine his spirit in common (distinguishing) between one and the
other according to his understanding and his works . . . ' (V, 20-1). Then after admission
'they shall examine their spirit and works year by year . . . ' (V, 23-4). Broadly speaking,

with their classes;[1] and the Visitation in which they are smitten, together
with (**15**) the times when they are blessed.[2]

Prologue: God and Creation

From the God of Knowledge comes all that is and shall be,
and before (beings) were, He established all their design.
(**16**) And when they are, they fulfil their task according to their statutes,
in accordance with His glorious design, changing nothing within it.[3]
In His hand (**17**) are the laws of all (beings)
and He upholds them in all their needs.[4]
It is He who made man
that he might rule (**18**) over the earth.[5]

The two Spirits and man

And He allotted unto man two Spirits
that he should walk in them until the time of His Visitation;[6]
they are the Spirits (**19**) of truth and perversity.
The origin of Truth is in a fountain of light,
and the origin of Perversity is from a fountain of darkness.[7]
(**20**) Dominion over all the sons of righteousness
is in the hand of the Prince of light;
they walk in the ways of light.
All dominion over the sons of perversity
is in the hand of the Angel of (**21**) darkness;
they walk in the ways of darkness.[8]

[1] A reference to the double catalogue — of virtues (IV, 2-6) and vices (IV, 9-11) —
contained in this instruction, i.e. the 'ways' of both Spirits.

[2] A reference to the two kinds of retribution appearing in the instruction — reward for
the good (IV, 6-8) and chastisement for the wicked (IV, 11-14). The word 'Visitation' in
the Bible, as well as in the Qumran documents, generally signifies divine retribution.

[3] This idea of the order of the universe and of its laws is especially developed in Ecclus.
(xvi. 24-8), *Enoch* (II), *Testament of Naphtali* (III), and *Psalms of Solomon* (XVIII, 11-14).

[4] An affirmation of divine Providence.

[5] The idea that man has received authority from God to rule over creation is biblical.
See Gen. i. 26-8, Ps. viii. 7-9. For the Hellenistic period, see Ecclus. xvii. 2-4, Wisd. of Sol.
ix. 1-2.

[6] Until the Last Judgment when the Evil Spirit will be destroyed for ever.

[7] As in Zoroastrian teaching, light is the symbol of truth and justice and darkness the
symbol of lies and perversity.

[8] Each of the two Spirits rules over part of humanity — the Good Spirit over the sons of
righteousness (or light), and the Evil Spirit over the sons of perversity (or darkness). This
division of humanity into two lots, or parties — into two camps — is one of the governing
concepts of the *Gatha*. These constitute the oldest part of the *Avesta*, and are generally
attributed to Zoroaster himself or to his immediate disciples.

the instructor had to 'separate and weigh the sons of righteousness according to their
spirits' (IX, 14).

And because of the Angel of darkness
(22) all the sons of righteousness go astray;
and all their sin and iniquities and faults,
and all the rebellion of their deeds,
are because of his dominion,
(23) according to the Mysteries of God until the end appointed by Him.
And all the blows that smite them,
(and) all the times of their distress,
are because of the dominion of his malevolence.[1]
(24) And all the spirits of his lot
cause the sons of light to stumble;
but the God of Israel and His Angel of truth
succour all (25) the sons of light.[2]

Truly, the Spirits of light and darkness were made by Him;
upon these (Spirits) He has founded every work,
(26) upon their [counsels] every service,
and upon their ways [every Visit]ation.
The one, God loves **IV** (1) everlastingly,
and delights in all his deeds for ever,
but the counsel of the other He loathes,
and He hates all his ways for ever.

The Good Spirit: its ways and reward

(2) And these are the ways of these (Spirits) in the world.
It is ⟨of the Spirit of truth⟩ to enlighten the heart of man,
and to level before him the ways of true righteousness,
and to set fear in his heart of the judgment (3) of God.
And (to it belong) the spirit of humility and forbearance,
of abundant mercy and eternal goodness,
of understanding and intelligence,
and almighty wisdom with faith in all (4) the works of God
and trust in His abundant grace,
and the spirit of knowledge in every design
and zeal for just ordinances,
and holy resolution (5) with firm inclination

---

[1] Thus no one, even among the just, escapes sin or the blows of the Angel of Darkness. The two Spirits live together within every man and are engaged in constant struggle (IV, 24). This mixture of Good and Evil that characterizes the present human condition will not cease until the Day of Judgment appointed by God when Evil will be destroyed.

[2] The 'sons of light' are assailed by all the evil spirits, but their allies in this superhuman struggle are 'the God of Israel' (who, in this Jewish instruction, takes the place of Ahura Mazda) and 'His Angel of Truth' (an amalgam of the Spirit of Good with the ancient biblical representation of the 'Angel of Yahweh').

and abundant affection towards all the sons of truth,
and glorious purification from hatred of all the idols of defilement,
and modesty (6) with universal prudence,
and discretion concerning the truth of the Mysteries of Knowledge.
Such are the counsels of the Spirit to the sons of truth in the world.

And as for the Visitation of all who walk in this (Spirit),
it consists of healing (7) and abundance of bliss,
with length of days and fruitfulness,
and all blessings without end,
and eternal joy in perpetual life,
and the glorious crown (8) and garment of honour in everlasting light.[1]

The Evil Spirit: its ways and reward

(9) But to the Spirit of perversity belong cupidity,
and slackness in the service of righteousness,
impiety and falsehood,
pride and haughtiness,
falsity and deceit,
cruelty (10) and abundant wickedness,
impatience and much folly,
and burning insolence,
(and) abominable deeds committed in the spirit of lust,
and the ways of defilement in the service of impurity,
(11) and a blaspheming tongue,
blindness of eye and hardness of ear,
stiffness of neck and heaviness of heart
causing a man to walk in all the ways of darkness,
and malignant cunning.

And as for the Visitation (12) of all who walk in this (Spirit),
it consists of an abundance of blows administered by all the Angels of
[destruction
in the everlasting Pit[2] by the furious wrath of the God of vengeance,
of unending dread and shame (13) without end,

---

[1] The instruction first mentions earthly rewards, and then eternal ones. This is also the teaching of 1 Tim. (iv. 8): 'Piety is profitable to all things: it possesses the promises of present life and those of the life that is to come.' The final 'in everlasting light' is an excellent conclusion to the list of rewards promised to the just; on this everlasting light, cf. *Enoch*, LVIII, 6: 'And there will be light immeasurable, and (the elect) will not enter into a limited number of days, for darkness will first have been dissipated and the light of truth established for ever before the Lord of Spirits.'

[2] The Pit of Hell where the wicked suffer unending punishment. Cf. Josephus on the Essenes (*War*, II, § 155): '. . . they relegate evil souls to a dark pit. . . .' The wicked are referred to as the 'sons of the Pit' (IX, 16, 22; X, 19).

and of the disgrace of destruction by the fire of the regions of darkness.[1]
And all their times from age to age
are in most sorrowful chagrin and bitterest misfortune,
in calamities of darkness till (14) they are destroyed
with none of them surviving or escaping.

The struggle between the two Spirits

(15) In these (two Spirits) walk the generations of all the sons of men,
and into their (two) divisions all their hosts are divided from age to age.
They walk in their (two) ways;
and all the reward (16) of their works is by their (two) classes,
according to the share of each,
according to whether he has much or little,
throughout all ages.
For God has allotted these (two Spirits) in equal parts until the
and has set between their divisions eternal hatred.   [(17) final end,
An abomination to Truth are the deeds of Perversity,
and an abomination to Perversity are all the ways of Truth.
And a fighting (18) ardour (sets one against the other) on the subject of
for they walk not together.   [all their ordinances,

But in His Mysteries of understanding and in His glorious Wisdom
God has set an end for the existence of Perversity;
and at the time (19) of the Visitation He will destroy it for ever.[2]
Then Truth shall arise in the world for ever;
for (the world) has defiled itself in the ways of wickedness under the
until (20) the time of final Judgment.   [dominion of Perversity
Then God will cleanse by His Truth all the works of every man,
and will purify for Himself the (bodily) fabric of every man,
to banish all Spirit of perversity from his (21) members,
and purify him of all wicked deeds by the Spirit of holiness;
and He will cause the Spirit of Truth to gush forth upon him like lustral
All lying abominations shall come to an end,   [water.[3]

[1] The fire of Hell; cf. II, 7-8: 'Be damned in the night of everlasting fire!' Fire is here an evil element that burns without dissipating the darkness. Cf. *Book of Enoch*, CIII, 8: 'And your soul shall enter into darkness and into bonds and burning flame where there shall be great chastisement; and the great chastisement shall endure for all the generations of the world. . . .'
[2] The doctrine developed here (IV, 18-23) of the final destruction of the Evil Spirit and the eternal triumph of the Spirit of Good at the Last Judgment is typically Zoroastrian. PLUTARCH (*De Iside et Osiride*, § 47) describes it as follows: 'There will come a fatal moment when Arimanios (Ahriman, the Spirit of Evil), bringing pest and famine, must be completely destroyed by them and disappear.'
[3] The body of the elect will be purified, cleansed of all spirit of perversity and filled with the Spirit of holiness and truth. It will be a 'spiritual body' and no longer a 'body of flesh'.

(and) defilement (**22**) by the Spirit of defilement.
The just will comprehend the Knowledge of the Most High,
and the perfect of way[1] will have understanding
of the wisdom of the Sons of Heaven.[2]
For God has chosen them for an everlasting Covenant
(**23**) and all the glory of the Man is theirs.[3]
Perversity will exist no more:
shame upon all the works of deceit!

Till now the Spirits of truth and perversity battle in the hearts of every
(**24**) (they) walk in Wisdom and Folly.   [man;
And according to each man's share of Truth and Righteousness,
so does he hate Perversity.
And according to his portion in the lot of Perversity,
and (according to) the wickedness (which is) in him,
so does (**25**) he abominate Truth.
For God has allotted these (Spirits) in equal parts
until the final end, the time of Renewal.
He knows the reward of their works throughout all (**26**) ages,
and He has divided these (Spirits) among the sons of men
that they may know Good [and Evil]
[and that] the destiny of every creature [may be] decreed in accordance
on [the day of Judgment and] Visitation.   [with his spirit

The rule of the Community: obedience

V (**1**) And this is the rule for the members of the Community,
for those who volunteer to be converted from all evil
and to cling to all His commands according to His will;
to separate themselves from the congregation (**2**) of perverse men,
to become a Community in the Law and with regard to property and
                                                                    [⟨laws⟩
under the authority of the sons of Zadok the priests who keep the Covenant,
and under the authority of the majority of the members (**3**) of the Com-
they who cling to the Covenant.   [munity,
Under their authority shall destiny be decreed in all things,
whether it concern the Law, or property, or justice.
They shall practise truth in common, and humility,
(**4**) and righteousness and justice and loving charity,
and modesty in all their ways.

        [1] The elect endowed with a spiritual body will possess perfect Gnosis like the angels
themselves.
        [2] The angels.
        [3] 'The Man' is here the biblical Adam, the lord of creation; but also, no doubt, mythical
Man, the Anthropos of Gnostic speculation.

Let no man walk in the stubbornness of his heart
to stray by following his heart (5) and eyes and the thoughts of his (evil)
[inclination.
But in the Community they shall circumcise the foreskin of the (evil)
[inclination and disobedience
in order to lay a foundation of truth for Israel,
for the Community of the (6) everlasting Covenant;
that they may atone for all who are volunteers
for the holiness of Aaron and for the House of truth in Israel,
and for those who join them to live in community
and to participate in trials and judgments
(7) destined to condemn all those who transgress a precept.

The oath of admission into the Covenant

And this is the norm of their conduct concerning all these precepts.
When they join the Community, let whoever comes to the Council of
the Community (8) enter into the Covenant of God in the presence of all
the volunteers, and let him undertake by oath of obligation to be converted
to the Law of Moses according to all His commands, with all (9) his heart
and all his soul, following all that is revealed of it to the sons of Zadok the
priests who keep the Covenant and seek His will, and to the majority of
the members of their Covenant, (10) they who volunteer together for His
truth and to walk in His will. And let him undertake by the Covenant to
be separated from all perverse men who walk (11) in the way of wickedness.

For they are not counted in His Covenant:
for they have not inquired nor sought Him concerning His precepts
in order to know the hidden matters in which they have (12) guiltily
and they have treated with insolence matters revealed   [strayed;
that Wrath might rise unto Judgment
and Vengeance be exercised by the curses of the Covenant,
and (13) solemn judgment be fulfilled against them unto eternal destruc-
leaving no remnant.   [tion,
Let not (the wicked) enter the water
to touch the Purification of the holy,[1]
for a man is not pure (14) unless he be converted from his malice.
For he is defiled for as long as he transgresses His word.
Let no man join him in work or possessions
lest he cause him to bear (15) the iniquity of a fault,
but in all things let him keep far from him.
For thus it is written: *Keep far from every false thing.*[2]

[1] i.e. the purificatory baths which the Essenes had to take daily.
[2] Exod. xxiii. 7.

And let no member (16) of the Community answer their questions
concerning any law or ordinance;
and let him neither eat nor drink anything of theirs.
And let him receive nothing at all from their hand (17) unless he pay its
[price,
according to that which is written: *Turn away from the man in whose nostrils
for of what account is he?*[1]   [*is nothing but breath,*
For (18) all who are not counted in His Covenant
shall be set apart, together with all that is theirs;
and the holy shall not rely on any work (19) of vanity.
For they are all vanity who know not His Covenant,
and He will destroy from the world all them that despise His word;
all their deeds are defilement (20) before Him,
and their possessions wholly unclean.[2]

Classification of the members of the Community

And if any man enters the Covenant to act according to these precepts
by joining the holy Congregation, they shall examine (21) his spirit in
common, (distinguishing) between one and the other according to his
understanding and his works with regard to the Law. The decision shall
lie with the sons of Aaron who volunteer in common to establish (22) His
Covenant and to attend to all the commandments which He has commanded, together with the majority of Israel who volunteer to be converted in common to His Covenant. (23) And they shall inscribe them in
order, one before the other, according to their intelligence and their works,
that they may all obey each other, the lower (obeying) the higher.

And they (24) shall examine their spirit and works year by year, in
order to promote each man according to his understanding and the
perfection of his conduct, or to demote him according to the faults which
he has committed.

Concerning reproof

They shall (25) reprove each other in truth and humility and loving
charity one towards the other.

Let no man speak to his ⟨brother⟩ with anger, or ill-temper, (26) or
disrespect, or impatience, or a spirit of wickedness. And let no man hate
him [in the perver]si[ty] of his heart; he shall be reproved on the very same
day. And thus a man **VI** (1) shall not bear a fault because of him. Also,

---

[1] Isa. ii. 22.
[2] The member of the Covenant must live absolutely separate from non-members who
are, in consequence, ungodly, wicked. Every contact and every relation with them constitutes a defilement; even their possessions are impure. The sectarian spirit could hardly
go further.

let no cause be brought before the Many,[1] by one man against another, unless reproof has been made before witnesses.

The common life

In these (precepts) (2) shall walk those that are together in all their dwelling-places. And in whatever concerns work or property, the lower shall obey the higher. And they shall eat in common, (3) bless in common, and deliberate in common.

And in every place where there are ten persons of the Council of the Community,[2] let there not lack among them a man (4) who is a priest. And let them sit before him, each according to his rank, and in the same order let them ask their advice in everything.

And then when they set the table to eat, or (prepare) the wine (5) to drink, the priest shall first stretch out his hand to pronounce a blessing on the first-fruits of bread and wine ⟨   ⟩.[3]

(6) And in the place where the ten are, let there not lack a man who studies the Law night and day, (7) continually, concerning the duties of each towards the other.[4]

And let the Many watch in common for a third of all the nights of the year, to read the Book and study the law (8) and bless in common.[5]

The assemblies

This is the rule for an assembly of the Many.

Let each man sit according to his rank! Let the priests sit in the first (place), and the elders in the second, and then the rest (9) of all the people; let them sit according to their ranks![6] And let them likewise inquire

---

[1] The Hebrew word thus translated is *rabbīm*. This expression, which appears several times in the *Rule*, is a technical term used to designate the members of the sect. It appears to allude to the large number of brethren who enjoyed equal-rights and formed, *en masse*, the Council of the Community. *Rabbīm* may also be translated 'the Great Ones'; this interpretation would make it a title of respect accorded to members of the holy Council, but I think this sense is less suitable.

[2] The group of ten constituted the basic unit. Cf. JOSEPHUS, *War*, II, § 146.

[3] The text of the manuscript adds: 'to drink, the priest shall first stretch out his hand to pronounce a blessing on the first-fruits of bread and wine'. This is obviously an accidental repetition of part of the previous sentence. On the Essene community meal, see *Rule Annexe* (II, 17-22). Cf. JOSEPHUS, *War*, II, §§ 129-31.

[4] The translation 'concerning the duties . . . ' is a little uncertain. The order formulated here refers to that given by God to Joshua: 'This book of the Law shall not depart out of your mouth, but you shall meditate on it day and night' (i. 8): also, in the Ps. (i. 2), the man is blessed who ' . . . meditates on his Law day and night'.

[5] The brethren were no doubt divided into three groups which watched in relays all during the night, thereby ensuring a permanent vigil. An institution of this kind reveals the extreme fervour of the Essene Community and shows how careful they were not to interrupt for an instant, even during the night, the reading and study of the Law and the recital of the blessings.

[6] Cf. PHILO on the Essenes, *Q.o.p.l.*, § 81: 'They sit in appointed places according to their age, the young men below the old. . . .'

concerning the law and concerning every kind of counsel and matter to do with the Many, each man bringing his knowledge (**10**) to the Council of the Community. Let no man interrupt the words of another before he has finished speaking. Also, let no man speak out of turn. Let whoever is inscribed (**11**) before one, the man who is questioned, speak in his turn. And let no man speak a word in the assembly of the Many without the consent of the Many unless he is (**12**) the overseer of the Many. And unless he is in office, whoever has something to say to the Many, whoever desires to put a question to the Council (**13**) of the Community, shall rise to his feet and say: I have something to say to the Many. If they order him to speak, he shall speak.[1]

Admission into the Community: preparatory stages[2]

And whoever, born of Israel, volunteers (**14**) to join the Council of the Community, he shall be examined on his intelligence and deeds by the man who is the overseer at the head of the Many; and if he is suited to the discipline, he will bring him (**15**) into the Covenant that he may be converted to the truth and turn away from all perversity: he shall instruct him in all the ordinances of the Community. And when he later comes to present himself to the Many, they shall (**16**) all consider his case, and according to whatever fate decrees, following the decision of the Many he shall either approach or depart.

And when he approaches the Council of the Community, he shall not touch the Purification (**17**) of the Many until he has been examined concerning his spirit and deeds, and until he has completed one full year. Also, let him not mingle his property with that of the Many.[3] (**18**) Then when he has completed one year within the Community, the Many shall consider his case concerning his intelligence and deeds with regard to the Law, and if fate decrees (**19**) that he approach the Company of the Community, following the decision of the priests and the majority of the members of their Covenant, his property and also his wages shall be handed over to the (**20**) overseer of the revenues of the Many;[4] but it shall be inscribed to his credit, and shall not be spent to the profit of the Many.[5]

---

[1] Cf. JOSEPHUS on the Essenes, *War*, II, § 132: 'They allow each other to speak in turn.'

[2] Compare JOSEPHUS, *War*, II, §§ 137-8.

[3] The 'mingling of property' did not begin until the end of the first year of novitiate (see lines 19-20). It only came into force completely at the end of the second year of the novitiate, from the time when the novice was finally admitted (see line 22). The expression 'mingling of property' is a technical term meaning common ownership; it appears in JOSEPHUS, *War*, II, § 122: 'Since their possessions are mingled, there exists for them all, as for brothers, one single property.'

[4] The treasurer or bursar of the Community. Cf. JOSEPHUS, *War*, II, §§ 123, 125; *Antiquities*, § 22.

[5] The novice's possessions were not irrevocably handed over to the Community until final admission; if he quitted the sect they were all returned to him.

He shall not touch the Banquet of the Many until (21) he has completed a second year in the midst of the members of the Community.

When he has completed the second year, they shall examine him. According to the decision of the Many, and if fate decrees (22) that he approach the Community, he shall be regularly inscribed in his rank among his brethren in whatever concerns the Law and justice and Purification and the mingling of his property; and he may give his opinion (23) to the Community together with his judgment.

The penal code

(24) And these are the ordinances by which they shall judge in an inquiry of the Community, according to the decision of the texts.

If there is a man among them who lies (25) in matters of property,[1] and does this knowingly, he shall be separated from the midst of the Purification of the Many for one year, and shall be punished with regard to one quarter of his food.

And whoever answers (26) his fellow disrespectfully, or speaks (to him) impatiently, going so far as to [vio]late his brother's formal order by refusing to obey his fellow inscribed before him, (27) [or (whoever) metes] out justice with his own hand, shall be punished for one year [and separated].

[And] whoever makes any mention whatever of the name of the Being venerated above all other venerated beings, [shall be put to death].[2] **VII** (1) But if he has blasphemed from fright, or under the blow of distress, or for any other reason whatever while reading the Book or

---

[1] Particularly in declaring his property or his income, which had to be handed over to the Community. Cf. Acts v. 1-11 (the story of Ananias and Sapphira).

[2] In the Synagogue it was forbidden to pronounce the name of God, Yahweh; perhaps this is also the name alluded to in the sect's ban on any mention of the name 'of the Being venerated above all other venerated beings'. The terms of punishment have disappeared in the lacuna at the end of the line, but they were certainly very heavy considering that the penalty in the following case, where there is a question of attenuating circumstances, is final excommunication. The only punishment exceeding this is death, expressly prescribed by Lev. xxiv. 6 for whoever 'blasphemes against the name of Yahweh'. It should be remembered, however, that according to JOSEPHUS (*War*, II, § 145), for the Essenes 'the name of the Lawgiver is, after God, a great object of veneration (*sebas mega*) and if any man blasphemes against the Lawgiver, he is punished with death'. Thus any blasphemy with regard to the name of the Lawgiver was punished among the Essenes by death, just as blasphemy against the name of Yahweh was punished in the Law. Now the Lawgiver in the text from Josephus is probably, as has been explained earlier (p. 31, n. 3), not Moses but the Lawgiver of the sect: it was as forbidden to speak his name as it was forbidden to utter the name of Yahweh. In fact, although the name of Moses is mentioned quite clearly in the Qumran documents without any sort of interdiction, the name of the sect's lawgiver is never given. He is generally spoken of as the 'Teacher of Righteousness', and is sometimes given other titles, but his proper name is never divulged and remains unknown to us. Consequently, I think it very likely that the ban on any mention 'of the name of the Being venerated above all other venerated beings' in the Qumran penal code, really refers to the name of the Teacher of Righteousness rather than to that of God.

pronouncing the Blessings, he shall be separated (2) and shall return no more to the Council of the Community.[1]

And if he speaks irritably against one of the priests inscribed in the book,[2] he shall be punished for one year (3) and set apart by himself from the Purification of the Many. But if he has spoken inadvertently, he shall be punished for six months.

And whoever lies knowingly (4) shall be punished for six months.

And the man who insults his fellow unjustly (and) knowingly shall be punished for one year (5) and separated.

And whoever speaks to his fellow arrogantly, or knowingly deceives, shall be punished for six months.

And if (6) he shows himself negligent to the detriment of his fellow, he shall be punished for three months. And if he shows himself negligent to the detriment of the property of the Community to the point of causing its loss, he shall reimburse them (7) entirely. (8) And if his hand is unable to reimburse them, he shall be punished for sixty days.[3]

And whoever bears malice towards his fellow unjustly shall be punished for six months:[4] (9) and likewise for whoever takes revenge for any reason whatever.

---

[1] The beginning of this phrase, from which two or three words have been intentionally deleted in the manuscript, is not very clear. The text does not define the person or name against whom the guilty man has blasphemed. Is it against the name of Yahweh, or that of the Teacher of Righteousness? It may perhaps refer to both here. JOSEPHUS speaks of torture inflicted on the Essenes during a persecution 'to compel them to blaspheme against the Lawgiver' (War, II, § 152). The words of the penal code of Qumran correspond closely to this passage: '. . . if he has blasphemed from fright or under the blow of distress. . . .' On the other hand, when the same code continues, 'or for any other reason whatever while reading the Book (the Bible, obviously) or pronouncing the Blessings', it seems rather to allude to the name of Yahweh, which it is natural to encounter frequently in the Bible and in the blessings, and which one consequently runs the risk of uttering by mistake instead of replacing it, as must be done, by another name (God, Adonai, Heaven, the Name, etc.). However this may be, fright and inadvertence are considered as attenuating circumstances and final excommunication is substituted for the death penalty.

[2] Doubtless the register in which the priestly members of the sect were inscribed. It should be noted that cave VI has, in fact, yielded a genealogical list of priests — very likely of priests inscribed in the sect (see RB, lxiii, 1956, p. 55). Of course, the respect due to priests did not protect those who did not belong to the sect from every kind of censure and attack; they were wicked priests. The Commentary on Habakkuk, in particular, does not hesitate to castigate in the most pointed way 'the Wicked Priest', i.e. the High Priest, the leader of the Jewish nation and persecutor of the sect of the Covenant.

[3] The words 'sixty days' are an addition. On the other hand, after 'he shall reimburse them', two or three words have been intentionally deleted and replaced by 'entirely'; this word seems to have been written by another hand. It is curious to find the guilty man required to reimburse the Community for loss, since, according to the Rule itself, the members possessed nothing of their own. It must, however, be noted that the rule concerning the 'mingling of property' was imposed neither on postulants nor on novices (even the second-year novice retained his possessions), but only on the fully professed. Therefore the obligation to reimburse the Community was applicable to some of the members anyway. Perhaps those who had surrendered their belongings were put to additional work in order to make good the loss; or else they were simply punished without making restitution.

[4] The text shows the addition 'one year' written in another hand.

And whoever utters a foolish word from out of his mouth: three months.

And for whoever interrupts the words of another: (10) ten days.

And whoever stretches out and sleeps during the assembly of the Many: thirty days. And likewise for whoever leaves the assembly of the Many (11) without permission and without reason: for up to three times during the assembly, he shall be punished for ten days, but if he is called to order (?) (12) and leaves, he shall be punished for thirty days.

And whoever goes naked before his fellow without being gravely ill[1] shall be punished for six months.

(13) And the man who spits in the midst of the assembly of the Many shall be punished for thirty days.[2]

And whoever allows his hand to protrude from beneath his garment, if this garment (14) is in rags and reveals his nakedness he shall be punished for thirty days.[3]

And whoever laughs stupidly (and) loudly shall be punished for thirty (15) days.

And whoever brings out his left hand to describe his thoughts with it shall be punished for ten days.[4]

And the man who goes about calumniating his fellow (16) shall be separated from the Purification of the Many for one year. And whoever goes about calumniating the Many shall be sent away from them (17) and shall not return.

And the man who murmurs against the Institution of the Community shall be sent away and shall not return. But if it is against his fellow that he murmurs (18) unjustly, he shall be punished for six months.

And the man whose spirit fears the Institution of the Community to the point of betraying the Truth (19) and of walking in the stubbornness of his heart, if he returns he shall be punished for two years: during the first

---

[1] The translation 'gravely ill' is a little uncertain. It is nevertheless plausible; in cases of grave illness care of the invalid might require him to be undressed. JOSEPHUS emphasizes that the Essenes were obliged to wear a loin-cloth during their ritual baths and that the women had to wrap themselves in cloths (*War*, II, § 161).

[2] Cf. JOSEPHUS, *War*, II, § 147.

[3] The word 'hand' is a euphemism for penis. When the Essene relieved himself, he was obliged to squat down and wrap himself in his mantle 'in order not to offend the rays of God', i.e. not to expose his nakedness (JOSEPHUS, II, § 148). If this garment were in rags and revealed 'his nakedness', the fault, due to carelessness of dress, was punished by a sentence of thirty days. The comparative lightness of this sentence rules out any question of grave or intentional indecency.

[4] The inference seems to be that the sectaries should use their *right* hand, and not the left, to gesticulate and express their opinion. PHILO of Alexandria (*De Vita Contemplativa*) reports that the Theraputae — a sect more or less related to the Essenes — showed their disagreement with an orator 'by lifting the tip of the little finger of the *right* hand'. The ban on the use of the left hand, which is of superstitious origin, is interesting to note. The right side is the noble side; according to JOSEPHUS (*War*, II, § 147) the Essenes were forbidden to spit to the right.

year he shall not touch the Purification of the Many, (20) and during the second year he shall not touch the Banquet of the Many and shall be seated after all the members of the Community. Then when the two years are accomplished (21) for him, day for day, the Many shall consider his case, and if he is directed to approach, he shall be inscribed in his rank, and afterwards he may question concerning the law.[1]

(22) And no man who is in the Council of the Community for more than ten whole years (23) and whose spirit turns back to the point of betraying the Community, and who goes out from before the (24) Many to walk in the stubbornness of his heart, shall return again to the Council of the Community.[2] And whoever among the members of the Commun[ity] mingles (25) with him in his purification and possessions with[out the permission?] of the Many, his case shall be the same as his: he shall be s[ent away and shall not return].[3]

The Twelve and the Three

VIII (1) In the Council of the Community (there shall be) twelve men and three priests,[4] perfect in all that is revealed of all (2) the Law, to practise truth, righteousness, justice, loving charity, and modesty one towards the other, (3) to guard the faith upon earth with a firm inclination and a contrite spirit, and to expiate iniquity among those that practise justice (4) and undergo distress of affliction, and to behave towards all men according to the measure of truth and the norm of the time.

---

[1] Anyone who left the sect might, at his own request, be readmitted if the reason for his departure had been discouragement because of the severity of the community life; this discouragement, or 'fear', might excuse his fault. But he then had to go through the whole of the two years' novitiate again (VI, 15-21). The procedure was the same as for the sectary who sinned inadvertently against the Law (see VIII, 24-IX, 2).

[2] This case differs from the previous one in that it concerns a person who has been among the brethren 'for more than ten whole years'. It was considered that such a veteran must be broken in to the discipline and to the ascetic life, and that there could therefore be no excuse for his departure. His excommunication was consequently irrevocable.

[3] By consorting with an *excommunicatus vitandus*, a member became liable to excommunication himself. There is further mention of penalties and excommunication in VIII, 16-IX, 2.

[4] The text is ambiguous. Does it mean that there was a college of twelve members, three of whom had to be priests? Or else a college of fifteen members, twelve of them laymen and three priests? The second interpretation is undoubtedly the one most likely to be right, since the figure fifteen is distinctly given on a fragment from cave IV, still unpublished, in an apparently parallel passage (see MILIK, *Dix ans de découvertes . . .*, p. 111; Eng. edn., p. 96): the twelve laymen would represent the twelve tribes, and the three priests the three Levitical clans — Gershon, Kohath and Merari. The functions of the supreme Essene College, which consisted of twelve or fifteen members, are not clearly defined in this passage; its members were required to have perfect knowledge of all the revelations possessed by the sect, to observe the Essene virtues perfectly, and to behave judiciously and with sound judgment towards all the other sectaries.

Holiness of the Community

When these things come to pass in Israel,[1]
(5) the Council of the Community shall be established in truth
It is the House of holiness for Israel   [as an everlasting planting.[2]
and the Company of infinite (6) holiness for Aaron;
they are the witnesses of truth unto Judgment
and the chosen of Loving-kindness
appointed to offer expiation for the earth
and to bring down (7) punishment upon the wicked.[3]
It is the tried wall, the precious corner-stone;[4]
(8) its foundations shall not tremble
nor flee from their place.
It is the Dwelling of infinite holiness (9) for Aaron
in ⟨eternal⟩ Knowledge unto the Covenant of justice
and to make offerings of sweet savour;
(it is) the House of perfection and truth in Israel
(10) to establish the Covenant according to the everlasting precepts.
And they shall be accepted as expiation for the earth
and to decree the judgment of wickedness
with no perversity remaining.

Communication of secret doctrine during the novitiate

When they have established them in the Institution of the Community, in perfection of way, for two years day for day,[5] (11) they shall be set apart (as) holy (persons) within the Council of the members of the Community; and let nothing of that which was hidden from Israel, but found by the Man (12) who sought,[6] be hidden from them out of fear of the spirit of apostasy.

[1] This expression, unfortunately very vague, recurs at the beginning of two other passages (VIII, 12, IX, 3; cf. IX, 5). It seems to allude to circumstances of some gravity — no doubt those which obliged the sect to settle in Qumran in the desert, far from a Jerusalem given over to wickedness, and to organize itself apart from the official Synagogue in order to establish and perpetuate there the true Israel until the Day of Judgment. This move to Qumran seems to have taken place during the reign of Alexander Jannaeus (103-76 B.C.) who, as Josephus informs us, persecuted the Pharisees. Very likely this repression constituted a serious threat to the Essenes themselves, for they can scarcely have been less hostile towards him than the Pharisees.
[2] An expression used by the sect to describe the Community (cf. XI, 8; *Damascus Document*, I, 7; *Jubilees*, I, 16, VII, 34, XXI, 24; *Enoch*, X, 16, LXXXIV, 6, XCIII, 2; *Psalms of Solomon*, XIV, 3). It is inspired by Isa. lx. 21.
[3] These are the elect, the members of the sect who are to condemn the wicked at the Last Judgment. This concept, which recurs in line 10, is expressed many times in the various writings of the sect.
[4] Inspired by Isa. xxviii. 16.
[5] A reference to the two years' novitiate; cf. VI, 16-21. The novices had to be instructed in all the sect's secret doctrine, even before the final admission.
[6] This may refer to the Teacher of Righteousness, the Seeker of the Law and Prophet

Retreat into the desert

And when these things come to pass for the Community in Israel (13) at these appointed times, they shall be separated from the midst of the habitation of perverse men to go into the desert to prepare the way of 'Him':[1] (14) as it is written,

In the wilderness prepare the way of . . . . Make straight in the desert a highway for our God.

(15) This (way) is the study of the Law which He has promulgated by the hand of Moses, that they may act according to all that is revealed, season by season, and (16) according to that which the Prophets have revealed by His Holy Spirit.[2]

Temporary exclusion and reintegration into the Community[3]

And no man among the members ⟨   ⟩ of the Covenant (17) of the Community who has turned aside from all that is laid down, in any way whatever, shall touch the Purification of the men of holiness (18) or know anything of all their Council until his deeds are purified of all perversity and he walks in perfection of way. Then he shall be made to approach (19) the Council, following the decision of the Many, and afterwards inscribed in his rank. And it shall be according to this ordinance for all those who join the Community.

Faults against the Law: expulsion, or in the case of inadvertence, exclusion for two years

(20) And these are the ordinances in which the men of perfect holiness shall walk, one beside the other.[4]

[1] The name Yahweh, forbidden to be uttered, is replaced by the pronoun 'Him' (*hūhā*).
In the subsequent quotation from Isa. xl. 3, four dots are substituted for the four letters of this name, as in two passages of the scroll of Isaiah A discovered in cave I.
[2] The retreat into the desert is no doubt meant to be taken here in its literal sense; it is the retreat of the Essenes to Qumran. As for the way that must be prepared in the desert, this is, figuratively, the search or study (*midrash*) of the Law from which proceed the revelations granted by God to His elect 'season by season', the same revelations as those made known by the Prophets throughout the ages.
[3] This short section is a sort of supplement to the penal code (VI, 24-VII, 25); it does not allude to faults committed against the Law (these are dealt with in the following section), but to infringements of the sect's rules, those that were punished, according to the penal code, by the temporary 'separation' of the guilty man. The present passage defines this 'separation' as consisting of exclusion from Purification (purificatory baptism), and from the Council. It states also that having paid the penalty, the guilty man was not to be taken back into the Community except on the decision of the Many — a decision which presupposes an inquiry into the sinner's improvement.
[4] This section concerns sectaries guilty of violating the Mosaic Law itself. Punishment

par excellence, the possessor of all revealed Knowledge. It can also be translated 'but which the seeker finds' — a general aphorism which would not specially allude to the Teacher.

(21) Among all those who have entered the Council of holiness to walk in perfection of way according to His command, any man (22) who deliberately, or through slackness, sins against the Law of Moses, shall be expelled from the Council of the Community (23) and shall not return. And no man among the men of holiness shall mingle with his possessions or counsel in any (24) matter.

But if he has acted through inadvertence, he shall be separated from Purification and from the Council. Then the case shall be examined. (25) Let him judge no man, nor question any decision for two years day for day. If his conduct is perfect, (26) (it shall be considered) in assembly, at an inquiry and in the Council, whether, according to the decision of the Many, he has committed any inadvertence before the two years were accomplished for him (27) day for day. IX (1) For one inadvertence alone, he shall be punished for two years; but any man who has acted deliberately shall not return. Only the man who has committed an inadvertence (2) shall be tried for two years day for day concerning the perfection of his conduct and counsel, according to the decision of the Many. And afterwards, he shall be inscribed in his rank in the holy Community.

Spiritual cult

(3) When these things come to pass in Israel according to all the appointed times for the Institution of the Spirit of holiness (founded) in accordance with (4) eternal Truth, they shall expiate guilty rebellion and sinful infidelity and (procure) Loving-kindness upon earth without the flesh of burnt offering and the fat of sacrifice, but the offering (5) of the lips in accordance with the law shall be as an agreeable odour of righteousness, and perfection of way shall be as the voluntary gift of a delectable oblation.[1]

---

[1] By retiring to Qumran, far from the Temple which they considered profaned by the wickedness of the official priesthood, the members of the sect had to renounce offering the usual sacrifices there. JOSEPHUS writes that the Essenes 'fulfil their sacrifices among themselves' (Antiquities, XVIII, 1, 5, § 19), whereas according to PHILO (Q.o.p.l., § 75), they offered no sacrifice at all. It appears from various Qumran writings that the sect did not in principle condemn sacrifices absolutely; they accorded them a place in religion. But the present section of the Rule shows that, for the Essenes, 'the offering of the lips', i.e. divine praise, and perfect conduct, were sufficient to secure God's loving-kindness and to take the place of expiatory sacrifice. This doctrine can cite the authority of Amos, Hosea and Isaiah; but it accorded also with the spiritual leanings of the religious élite of the ancient world. Thus Zoroaster abolished blood-sacrifice, and among the Pythagoreans some forbade it rigorously, alleging that the veto stemmed from Pythagoras himself (cf. J. CARCOPINO, La basilique pythagoricienne de la Porte Majeure, p. 234). The neo-Pythagorean Apollonius of Tyana forbade the offering of any sacrifice whatever to the 'great god who

---

for this was final excommunication, the guilty man becoming even excommunicatus vitandus· But if the fault was committed inadvertently, punishment was reduced to temporary expulsion for two years.

Separation of priests and laity: authority of the priests

In those days, they shall separate the members (6) of the Community (into) the House of holiness for Aaron that infinite holiness may be assembled together, and (into) the House of community for Israel for those that walk in perfection.

(7) The sons of Aaron alone shall command in matters of justice and property, and it is under their authority that fate shall be decreed in every decision concerning the members of the Community.[1]

Separation of the property of the perfect

(8) Concerning the property of the men of holiness who walk in perfection, let their possessions not be mingled with those of the men of deceit who (9) have not purified their way to be separated from perversity and walk in perfection of way.[2]

Respect for the Law and for the first ordinances

And they shall not depart from any maxim of the Law to walk (10) in all the stubbornness of their heart.

And they shall be governed by the first ordinances in which the members of the Community began their instruction, (11) until the coming of the Prophet and the Anointed of Aaron and Israel.[3]

---

[1] This paragraph plainly marks the predominance of priest over layman in Essene society. It was for the priests alone to fix the laws, i.e. the jurisprudence of the sect, and to administer the Community's revenues; also, it was a priest who presided over, and commanded, each group of ten (cf. VI, 3-4).

[2] Separation from the wicked was incomplete unless it extended to their property and fortune. For this reason, the sectaries of the Covenant were forbidden to possess anything in common with the wicked, or to depend on them materially or economically (cf. V, 16-20).

[3] This passage appears to refer to two essential stages in the history of the sect — the beginning, when only the 'first ordinances' were in force, and then the period inaugurated by 'the coming of the Prophet'. The expression 'first ordinances' only makes sense if there were also 'last ordinances'; there is, in fact, mention of the 'first and last ordinances' in the *Testament of Judah*, XXIV, 3, and also in the *Damascus Document* B, II, 8-9. The 'last ordinances' were doubtless those promulgated by the Prophet himself, but their effect was not to abolish the earlier ones, which the present passage of the *Rule* emphasizes as being still in force. Who was this Prophet whose coming inaugurated a new phase? No doubt he was 'the Prophet like Moses' promised to Israel in Deut. xviii. 15-18; 1 Macc. iv. 45-6, xiv. 41 (cf. also ix. 27) alludes to this expectation of the Prophet's coming. The expression in the *Rule*, 'until the coming of the Prophet and the Anointed of Aaron and Israel', suggests that the Prophet's appearance, and the consequent inauguration of the eschato-

---

is above all things. That man honours him worthily who, without immolating victims and without lighting fire, offers him only the wordless *logos*, the mightiest of all, and solicits the most noble Being with what is most noble in us, the mind'. The idea of spiritual sacrifice is general in Hermetic Gnosticism, e.g. *Poimandres*, § 31: 'Receive pure sacrifices in the words which a pure soul offers unto Thee, a heart held out towards Thee, O Unutterable One, O Unspeakable One. . . .' Cf. *Testament of Levi*, III, 6: 'the sacrifice of words, and unbloody'.

Duties of the instructor: seasons and spirits

(**12**) These are the precepts for the man of understanding, that he may walk in them in the company of all the living in accordance with the rule proper to every season and the weight of every man.[1]

(**13**) He shall do the will of God according to all that has been revealed, season by season, and he shall teach all understanding discovered throughout time, together with (**14**) the Decree of Time.[2]

He shall separate and weigh the sons of righteousness[3] according to their spirits, and he shall cling to the elect of the time in accordance with the decision (**15**) of His will, according to His command.

He shall judge each man according to his spirit, and shall cause each man to approach according to the purity of his hands; and according to (their) understanding (**16**) shall he cause them to go forward.

And as his love is, so shall his hatred be.[4]

The doctrine to be concealed from the wicked but taught to the just

And let him not rebuke the men of the Pit nor dispute with them; (**17**) let him conceal the maxims of the Law from the midst of the men of perversity.

And let him keep true Knowledge and right Justice for them that have chosen (**18**) the Way.[5] He shall guide each man in Knowledge according

---

[1] Here the 'man of understanding', *maskil*, is the instructor, the guide, the catechist. He must estimate each man's worth according to his 'weight', i.e. according to his exact value from the spiritual and moral viewpoint. Cf. Dan. v. 27: 'You have been weighed in the balance and have been found too light.' *Book of Enoch*, XLI, 1: '. . . and how the deeds of men will be weighed in the balance'.

[2] The 'Decree of Time' is the divine Law governing the regular succession of periods, seasons and hours. The sect's doctrine involves a mystical representation of Time. Every action must be made at the right moment, the moment foreseen and determined by God, the Sovereign Lord of time. God Himself distributes His revelations throughout the course of time. Cf. *Commentary on Habakkuk*, VII, 13-14: 'All the seasons of God come to pass at their appointed time, according to His decree concerning them in the Mysteries of His Prudence.

[3] Obviously the members of the sect. The Hebrew text presents an anomaly here, and some correct it to, 'sons of Zadok'.

[4] Love for members of the sect, hatred for the others.

[5] The members of the sect were not only 'chosen' (i.e. the 'elect'), but also 'choosers': they chose the Way of God and Goodness. This theme of the two ways of virtue and vice is absolutely fundamental to the sect: see above, the instruction on the two Spirits (III, 13-IV, 16). It was particularly current in Pythagorism; there the sacred letter *Υ*, with its two diverging branches, symbolized the opposition of the two ways.

---

logical era, would be followed after a fairly brief delay by the coming of the two Anointed of Aaron and Israel (the Priest-Messiah and the King-Messiah). This passage from the *Rule* seems to infer that the eschatological age had begun and that the Prophet had already appeared. For the sectaries of the Covenant, however, this Prophet could scarcely be anyone but the Teacher of Righteousness himself. It nevertheless seems that *in this passage* the Teacher is identified as the Prophet, but not yet as the Priest-Messiah, as he will be later (see *Rule Annexe*, II, 11-21).

to his spirit (and) according to the appointed moment of time; and likewise, he shall instruct them in the marvellous and true Mysteries in the midst (19) of the members of the Community, that they may walk with one another in perfection in all that has been revealed to them.

This is the time to *prepare the way*[1] (20) to go into the desert. And he shall instruct them in all that has been found that they may do it at this time, and that they may be separated from all who have not departed (21) from all perversity.

Contempt for riches

And these are the norms of conduct for the man of understanding in these times, concerning what he must love and how he must hate.

Everlasting hatred (22) for all the men of the Pit because of their spirit of hoarding![2] He shall surrender his property to them and the wages of the work of his hands, as a slave to his master and as a poor man in the presence (23) of his overlord.[3] But he shall be a man full of zeal for the Precept, whose time is for the Day of Vengeance.[4]

Submission to the will of God[5]

He shall do the will of God in every enterprise of his hands,
(24) that He may reign over all things according to His command;
and he shall gladly delight in all that He has made,
and beyond the will of God he shall desire nothing.
(25) [And] he shall delight [in all] the words of His mouth,
and shall covet nothing of that which He has not command[ed].
And he shall constantly watch for the Judgment of God.
(26) [And in all that be]falls, he shall bless Him who did it,
and in all that befalls, he shall tell [of His deeds]
and shall bless Him [with the offering] of the lips.

[1] Cf. Isa. xl. 3. On the retreat into the desert, see above, VIII, 12-16.

[2] The translation is uncertain. Others translate: 'in the spirit of secrecy'. The Hebrew word *seter*, 'hiding-place', appears here to signify, not concealment of doctrine but of treasure. The context suggests this meaning because in the next sentence abandonment of wealth is recommended. The piling-up of riches characterizes 'the men of the Pit' just as disdain for wealth is an cssential virtue of a member of the Covenant.

[3] On the sectary's humility and submissiveness towards masters and rich men, see below, XI, 1-2. He must show total detachment from material possessions, and if the wicked claim anything belonging to him, or argue about it, then he must be ready to hand it over — in so far, obviously, as he still possesses anything (cf. above p. 88, n. 3).

[4] Entirely detached from concern for material things, the sectary is zealous only for the fulfilment of the Law and defers all his hope and all his need of justice to the Day of Vengeance. He lives in constant expectation of this Day when he will be rewarded and the wicked punished (cf. below, X, 17-21).

[5] Total submission to the will of God was a fundamental virtue among the Essenes, as PHILO and JOSEPHUS point out (*Q.o.p.l.*, § 84, *Antiquities*, XIII, § 172, XVIII, § 18).

Celebration of the holy times

X (1) I will sing the Decree[1] with the seasons:
at the beginning of the dominion of light, during its circling,
and when it vanishes towards its appointed dwelling-place;
at the beginning (2) of the watches of darkness
when He opens their reservoir and sets them up on high,
and in their circling when they vanish before the light;
when (3) the (heavenly) lights appear from out of the realm of holiness,
(and) when they vanish towards the dwelling-place of glory;
at the seasons' entry, on the days of the new moon,
the circling of the seasons being in harmony with (4) the bonds binding
          [one new moon to another,
for the moons are renewed and grow according to the infinite holiness of
according to the key of His everlasting favour,   [the sign N,[2]
according to the beginning (5) of the seasons for all time to come;
at the beginning of the months according to the seasons on which they
and (on the) days of holiness,[3] on their appointed date   [depend;
with reference to the seasons on which they depend.

(6) With the offering of the lips will I bless Him
according to the Decree that is graven for ever:
at the beginnings of the years[4] and in the circling of the yearly seasons,
while the Decree is fulfilled (7) assigning to them an appointed date,

---

[1] The 'Decree' — or as it appears below, 'the Decree that is graven for ever' (line 6), 'the graven Decree (line 8) — is here 'the Decree of Time' (cf. IX, 14), the divine Law regulating the order of the world and the harmonious succession of the seasons. The 'Decree' is 'graven' — an allusion to the divine tables on which all destiny and all the appointed times are inscribed: they are frequently mentioned in *Jubilees* and *Enoch*. This conception of cosmic Law is in the same category as that of Inevitability, Destiny and Order general among Gnostics of the Hellenistic era. The development which follows, lyrical in tone, describes with emphasis the various sacred seasons as they were celebrated within the sect in conformity with its own calendar (see above, p. 73, n. 2). This passage, which is not without obscurity, consists, as it were, of two verses. The first (lines 1-5) is concerned with the two holy periods of the day, dawn and dusk, and then with the sacred times of the year: the start of the seasons, the beginning of the months, and the Sabbaths. The second verse (lines 6-8), is concerned with the sacred seasons marking the succession of the years: the beginning of the years, sabbatical years, years of jubilee. On the whole of this passage, see my *Nouveaux Aperçus* . . . (Paris, 1953), pp. 141-56 (Eng. edn., pp. 104-17).

[2] The Hebrew letter *nun*, whose numerical value is 50. The number 50, as PHILO of Alexandria says, was considered by the Pythagoreans as 'the holiest and most substantial of numbers, since it formed the power (the square) of the right-angled triangle, the principle of the generation of the universe'. The Essene calendar, which was basically founded on the principle of the division of the year into four seasons of three months, seems to have been connected, by means of subtle reasoning, with this sacrosanct number.

[3] This expression may refer to all the feasts of the liturgical year, but I think it alludes particularly to the Sabbaths. The text emphasizes that these Sabbaths were fixed 'with reference to the seasons'; each season had, in fact, thirteen Sabbaths (91 days).

[4] i.e. New Year's Day.

on the regular day of each of them[1] one with respect to the other;
the season of harvest with respect to summer,
and the season of sowing with respect to the season of germination;
(on the) feasts of years according to the weeks of years;[2]
(8) and at the beginning of the weeks of weeks of years, at the time of
[Release.[3]
For the whole of my life the graven Decree shall be upon my tongue
as a fruit of praise and the offering of my lips.

God to be praised at all times and in all circumstances

(9) I will sing in Knowledge,[4]
and my whole lyre shall throb to the Glory of God,
and my lute and harp to the holy Order which He has made.
I will raise the flute of my lips because of His righteous measuring-cord.

(10) When day comes and the night, I will enter the Covenant of God;[5]
when night and morning depart, I will recite His precepts,
and for as long as they are, I will establish in them (11) my realm of no
I will pronounce my judgment according to my iniquities,   [return.[6]
my rebellions shall be before my eyes like the graven Decree.[7]
But to God I will say, My righteousness!
(12) (and) to the Most High, Support of my goodness!

[1] This refers to 'the days of the seasons' (*Jubilees*, VI, 23), the four days in the year marking the start of each new season; these were the Ember Days of the Essene liturgy. The seasons enumerated here correspond to the four seasons popularized in the world from the Hellenistic period onwards: harvest (spring), summer, seed-time (autumn), and germination (winter). The Hebrew names are connected with the agricultural cycle in Palestine. The ancient Jewish world distinguished only two annual seasons — summer (the hot dry season) and winter (the cold and rainy season); the introduction of the four seasons into the Essene calendar seems to have been due to the influence of Hellenism.

[2] This refers to sabbatical years, i.e. those celebrated every seven years (Lev. xxv. 1-7).

[3] A reference to the years of jubilee when slaves were to be liberated (Lev. xxv. 8-55). The jubilee cycle lasted 49 years: every fiftieth year was a year of jubilee. The fiftieth year was at the same time the first year of the new jubilee cycle. Weeks of years and jubilees are the basis of the chronological system of the book called *Jubilees*.

[4] Or 'with understanding'. Cf. 1 Cor. xiv. 15: 'I will sing with the spirit and I will sing with the understanding also.' There is nothing more lyrical than this song of the soul, this spiritual symphony: the poet names the lyre, the lute, the harp and the flute.

[5] The sectary had to pray at dawn and at dusk (cf. X, 1-3). Contemplating the rising and setting sun, he raised himself in spirit towards the invisible light and renewed the pledge binding him as a 'son of light' to the Covenant of God.

[6] In the presence of the immutable laws governing the course of the stars, the sectary's whole soul is in communion with the eternal and marvellous incorruptibility of the heavenly world. This astral mysticism, born of new advances in the knowledge of astronomy, was very widespread in Hellenistic times.

[7] The sectary acknowledges his guilt and his unceasing inclination towards rebellion, and contrasts this primordial tendency to disorder and evil with the unchanging Order of the world obedient to the 'graven Decree'. Given man's evil inclination, it is only God who can justify him. This is what the psalmist proclaims in the following verse; he develops this basic theme a little further on (XI, 12-15).

Source of Knowledge! Fountain of Holiness!
Infinite Glory and Might of Eternal Majesty!
I will choose whatever (**13**) He teaches me
and will delight in His judgment of me.

At the beginning of every enterprise of my hands or feet
I will bless His Name;
at the beginning of every activity, when I go out and return,
(**14**) when I sit and rise up
and when I retire to bed
I will utter cries of joy unto Him.
And I will bless Him with the offering of that which issues from out of
because of the table laid for men,   [my lips
(**15**) and before I lift my hands to nourish me
with the delicious fruits of the earth.[1]

(When) a prey to fear and dread,
in the depth of distress, in full desolation,
(**16**) I will bless Him.
I will confess Him because He is marvellous
and will meditate on His Might;
and I will lean on His favours every day.
I know that in His hand is judgment (**17**) of all the living
and that all His works are truth;
when distress is unfurled I will praise Him,
and when He saves me I will likewise shout with joy.

The perfect sectary

To no man will I render the reward (**18**) of evil,
with goodness will I pursue each one;
for judgment of all the living is with God,
and He it is who will pay to each man his reward.[2]

---

[1] An allusion to the blessing preceding the sacred meal (VI, 4-5; *Rule Annexe*, II, 17-22).

[2] The sectary must never take his own revenge but must leave it to God. He must 'pursue each one' with goodness, i.e. render good for evil. This is also the teaching of the *Testaments of the Twelve Patriarchs*, a work connected with the Qumran sect. Thus in the *Testament of Joseph*, XVIII, 2 we read: 'And if a man wishes to harm you, do good to him and pray for him, and you will be delivered from all evil by the Lord.' In the *Testament of Benjamin*, IV, 2-4 is another saying to the same effect: 'For the good man has no eye of darkness, but he has pity on all, even if they are sinners. Even if they have no loving-kindness towards him, he can conquer evil by doing good, and he is protected by God. He loves the unjust as himself.' It may be recalled that according to HIPPOLYTUS (*Elenchos*, IX, § 23), the Essenes were required 'to hate no man, neither the unjust nor the enemy, but to pray for them'.

I will not envy from a spirit (**19**) of wickedness
and my soul shall not covet the riches of violence.[1]

As for the multitude of the men of the Pit,
I will not lay hands on them till the Day of Vengeance;
but I will not withdraw my anger (**20**) far from perverse men,
I will not be content till He begins the Judgment.[2]
I will be without malice and wrath towards those that are converted from
[rebellion,
but merciless (**21**) to those that have turned aside from the way;
I will not comfort them that are smitten until their way is perfect.[3]
And I will not keep Belial in my heart;
no folly shall be heard within my mouth,
(**22**) and on my lips shall be found
no criminal deceit or falsity or lies.[4]
But on my tongue shall be fruit of holiness
and (**23**) no abominations shall be found on it.
I will open my mouth in thanksgiving,
and my tongue shall ever recount the deeds of God,
together with the unfaithfulness of men until the destruction (**24**) of their
I will cause vain words to cease from my lips,   [rebellion.
and defilement and perfidy from the understanding of my heart.
With wise reflection I will conceal Knowledge;[5]
(**25**) with understanding prudence I will guard [it] within firm bounds,
to keep the faith and the law strictly according to the righteousness of God.

I will apportion (**26**) the Precept with the measuring-cord of the times[6]
and [. . .] righteousness

[1] Cf. *Testament of Benjamin*, IV, 3: 'If any man becomes proud, let him not envy him;
if any man is rich, let him not be jealous of him.'

[2] The sectary must do no violence to the 'men of the Pit', i.e. the wicked, the enemies of
the sect. He must await Judgment Day: this will be the time for the reward and punishment demanded by divine justice. The sectary must therefore hate the wicked, preserve
in his heart a holy wrath against them, and pray for the 'Day of Vengeance'. But this
sectarian sentiment, which is very marked in the Qumran documents, is explicitly toned
down by an effective tolerance which, pending the Judgment, not only forbids the sectaries
to do any wrong to the wicked, but commands them to do good.

[3] The duty of charity towards the unjust has its inevitable limits. For example, the
sectary is required to show no exaggerated pity, but just severity towards the excommunicated, towards the man who has been justly chastised; punishment must be allowed
to run its course. Cf. Matt. xviii. 17: 'And if he refuses to listen even to the church, let him
be to you as a Gentile and a tax collector.'

[4] The love of truth, loyalty and integrity were for the Essenes essential virtues. Cf.
JOSEPHUS, *War*, II, § 135: 'Every word they speak is stronger than an oath.' And § 141:
'He swears always to love truth and to pursue liars.'

[5] On the reading 'I will conceal' see above, p. 47, n. 2.

[6] This phrase seems to mean that it is necessary to know how to measure out the obligations to be imposed on the brethren for the perfect practice of the Law by taking into
account the aptitude of each one at any given moment.

full of loving charity towards the disheartened
and strengthening the hands of those whose [heart] is troub[led];
[teaching] **XI** (1) understanding to those whose spirit has gone astray,
instructing in the doctrine those that murmur,[1]
answering with humility the proud of spirit,
and with a contrite spirit, those that brandish (2) a stick,
that point the finger and utter wounding words[2]
and have possessions.

Justification the work of God, not of man

For to God belongs my justification,[3]
and the perfection of my way,
and the uprightness of my heart
are in His hand:
(3) by His righteousness are my rebellions blotted out.

For He has poured forth from the fount of His Knowledge
the light that enlightens me,
and my eye has beheld His marvels
and the light of my heart pierces the Mystery (4) to come.

The everlasting Being is the stay of my right hand;
the way of my steps is on a stout rock,
nothing shall be fearsome before me.
For God's truth is (5) the rock of my steps
and His power, the stay of my right hand,
and from the fount of His Righteousness comes my justification.

From His wondrous Mysteries is the light in my heart,
in the everlasting Being (6) has my eye beheld Wisdom:
because Knowledge is hidden from men
and the counsel of Prudence from the sons of men.
The fountain of righteousness, the reservoir (7) of power, and the dwelling-
are denied to the assembly of flesh;[4]   [place of glory
but God has given them as an everlasting possession

---

[1] Inspired by Isa. xxix. 24. The sectary must meekly and patiently lead back into the right path those who have temporarily gone astray.

[2] Inspired by Isa. lviii. 9. The sectary of the Covenant is a 'poverello'; in the presence of the great and powerful he must be all humility.

[3] The Hebrew word *mishpaṭ* is translated 'justification' throughout this passage. This definite meaning seems more suitable here than the general sense of 'justice'.

[4] This expression describes the multitude of the damned living in sin and according to the flesh, as opposed to the assembly of the Elect, the sect of the Covenant; cf. line 9, 'the assembly of perverse flesh'. According to this teaching, there are two assemblies just as there are two armies, two parties.

to those whom He has chosen.
He has granted them a share in the lot (8) of the Saints,[1]
and has united their assembly, the Council of the Community,
with the Sons of Heaven.
And the assembly of the holy Fabric shall belong to an eternal planting
for all (9) time to come.[2]

As for me, I belong to wicked humanity,
to the assembly of perverse flesh;
my iniquities and rebellion and sin
together with the iniquity of my heart
(10) (belong to) the assembly doomed to worms,
(the assembly) of men who walk in darkness.[3]

For is man master of his way?[4]
No, men cannot establish their steps,
for their justification belongs to God,
and from His hand comes (11) perfection of way.
By His understanding all things are brought into being,
by His thought every being established,
and without Him nothing is made.

And I, if (12) I stagger,
God's mercies are my salvation for ever;
and if I stumble because of the sin of the flesh,
my justification is in the righteousness of God
which exists for ever.
(13) If He unfurl distress upon me,
He will draw back my soul from the Pit
and establish my steps in the way.

He has caused me to approach by His Mercy
and by His favours He will bring (14) my justification.

[1] The Saints and the Sons of Heaven are the Angels, the blessed spirits whose lot is
heavenly life.
[2] The earthly Community is in communion with the whole angelic and celestial world.
This is what is obviously meant by 'an eternal planting' (cf. VIII, 5); 'the assembly of the
holy Fabric' seems to allude to heaven, i.e. the whole body of angelic beings.
[3] The sectary of the Covenant is essentially a 'penitent'; he is always aware of the
depths of sin within him. His tendency to evil, in some way ineradicable, joins him to
wicked humanity, to the camp of the 'sons of darkness', even though divine election has
made of him a 'son of light'. Justification and salvation can only come from God. This
rending of the soul in two, and this anguish and expectation of divine salvation, are
fundamental to the various forms of ancient Gnosticism.
[4] Compare Jer. x. 23: 'For the way of man is not in himself.' The negative may have
disappeared accidentally from this passage of the *Rule*. But the phrase can also be read
interrogatively, as I have done: the sense is then the same.

He has justified me by His true justice
and by His immense goodness He will pardon all my iniquities.
And by His justice He will cleanse me of the defilement (15) of man
and of the sin of the sons of men,
that I may acknowledge His righteousness unto God
and His majesty unto the Most High.

The omnipotence of God and the nothingness of man

Blessed be Thou, O my God,
who hast opened unto Knowledge (16) the heart of Thy servant!
Establish all his works in righteousness,
and according to Thy loving-kindness to the elect among men
grant to the son of thy handmaid
that he may (17) watch before Thee for ever.

For without Thee no way is perfect,
and without Thy will nothing is done.
It is Thou who hast taught (18) all Knowledge,
and all that is brought into being exists by Thy will.
And there is none other beside Thee
to dispute Thy decision
and to comprehend (19) all Thy holy Thought
and to contemplate the depth of Thy Mysteries
and to understand all Thy Marvels and the power (20) of Thy Might.

Who then shall contain Thy Glory?
And what is the son of man himself
amidst all Thy marvellous works?
(21) And he that is born of woman,
what is his worth before Thee?
Truly, this man was shaped from dust
and his end is to become the prey of worms.
Truly, this man is a mere frail image (22) in potter's clay
and inclines to the dust.
What shall clay reply, the thing which the hand fashions?
What thought can it comprehend?

THE *RULE ANNEXE*

Title

I (1) And this is the rule for all the Congregation of Israel[1] at the end of days, when they shall join [the Community to wa]lk (2) in obedience to the law of the sons of Zadok the priests and of the members of their Covenant who have refus[ed to walk in] the way (3) of the people: they are the men of His Counsel[2] who keep His Covenant in the midst of wickedness in order to aton[e for the ear]th.

Instruction of new arrivals

(4) On their arrival, they shall gather them all together, including the children and the women, and shall read into [their] ea[rs] (5) all the precepts of the Covenant and shall instruct them in all their ordinances lest they stray in [their] st[ray]ing.[3]

---

[1] The editors of the *Rule Annexe* (in *Qumran Cave I*, no. 28ᵃ), give it the title 'The Rule of the Congregation', following the heading of the text itself. They hold that 'the Congregation of Israel', to which the two columns of the present *Annexe* refer, is not, strictly speaking, the Community to which the *Rule* proper is addressed, the eleven columns of which are translated above. To distinguish between them, they prefer to call the latter 'The Rule of the Community'. The 'Congregation', in their opinion, is the congregation of the Hasidaeans of the time of Judas Maccabee, whereas the 'Community' describes the Essene sect, itself probably sprung from the Hasidaean movement. So the 'Rule of the Congregation' is *older* than the 'Rule of the Community'. This opinion seems to me to rely on very insubstantial argument. Although the *Rule* employs the word 'Community' more frequently, it also describes this 'Community' as a 'Congregation' (V, 20, 'the holy Congregation'); and on the other hand, although the *Rule Annexe* uses the word 'Congregation' constantly, it also employs the word 'Community' several times (I, 26, 27, II, 2, 11, 17, 18, 21). It is my belief that in reality 'Congregation' and 'Community' are identical. The relative preference given to one or the other may simply be due to the respective redactors, or to a certain terminological evolution, there being no specific intention to differentiate between the two: does not the redundancy of the expression 'the Congregation of the Community', which appears in the *Annexe* (II, 21), show that the terms are practically synonymous? Contrary to the editors, I think that in its present form the *Rule Annexe* is not earlier, but *later* (perhaps only a little later) than the *Rule* proper — later than its primitive version anyway. Perhaps this *Annexe* was originally a more extensive document than the one preserved in the two columns; it may be that only those passages were retained which appeared usefully to complete the *Rule*.

[2] On this expression, see above p. 43. We are reminded of Isa. xlvi. 11, where Yahweh calls Cyrus 'the man of His Counsel', i.e. the man whom He has chosen and called to carry out His designs.

[3] This passage alludes to a mass arrival of new members complete with their families. It will be remembered that JOSEPHUS clearly mentions the existence of an order of married Essenes (*War*, II, §§ 160-1); the *Damascus Document* also refers in various passages to members of the sect who were married and had children. This was probably the situation among a great number of Essenes during the first phase of the sect's existence; the people

Education of children and promotion to various offices

(**6**) And this is the rule for all the hosts of the Congregation, concerning every native in Israel.[1]

From [his] you[th] (**7**) [he shall be in]structed in the Book of Meditation[2] and shall be taught the precepts of the Covenant in accordance with his age, and [shall receive] (**8**) his [edu]cation in their ordinances for ten years [from] the time of entry into the children's [class].[3]

Then at the age of twenty [he shall be subject] (**9**) [to] the census: he shall enter into the lot in the midst of his clan (to live) in community in the holy Congregation.[4] And he shall not [approach] (**10**) a woman to know her sexually unless he is twenty years old when [she] knows [good] (**11**) and evil;[5] and this being so, she shall be admitted to invoke the ordinances of the Law against him, and to take her place at the hearing of the ordinances (**12**) and among the crowd which is there.[6]

Then at the age of twenty-five years he may take his place among the foundations of the (**13**) holy Congregation to ensure the service of the Congregation.[7]

---

[1] An expression taken from Lev. xxiii. 42; it describes the Israelite as opposed to a foreigner. The sect drew its recruits from among the Jews: 'They are Jews by race', states JOSEPHUS (*War*, II, § 119). Nevertheless, the *Damascus Document* finds place for proselytes (XIV, 4).

[2] On this 'Book of Meditation', see above, p. 70.

[3] JOSEPHUS (but not Philo) draws attention to the presence among the celibate Essenes of children whom they adopted in order to raise them in the rule of the sect (*War*, II, § 120). In the present text where there is question of married Essenes, the children spoken of are probably nearly all the offspring of Essene parents. Their education lasted for ten years: since it normally ended at the age of twenty, as the following sentence seems to indicate, they no doubt entered the 'children's class' at the age of ten. Before that age there could scarcely have been any question of an Essene education proper.

[4] Cf. *Damascus Document*, XV, 5-6: 'let his sons who have reached the age to pass before the census pledge themselves by the oath of the Covenant'.

[5] According to my interpretation, two conditions were necessary for the consummation of marriage: the bridegroom had to be twenty years old and the bride had to 'know good and evil'. In the Bible, this expression means to possess discernment, to have reached the age of reason (cf. Isa. vii. 15-16). In the present context it must have another meaning. It may be a euphemism for puberty; JOSEPHUS (*War*, II, § 161) writes that the Essenes made sure that their brides could bear children before 'marrying' them.

[6] This phrase is also difficult to interpret. I take it to mean that once the girl was recognized as nubile, fit to bear children, and the marriage was consummated, she possessed the right to invoke the Law against her husband (e.g. if he should wish to take another wife, which was forbidden by the laws of the sect, cf. *Damascus Document*, IV, 21), and also to assist as a listener at the Community assemblies for the study of the ordinances.

[7] It was not until he was twenty-five years old that the Essene was able to exercise any office involving special responsibility; but the superior offices, the chief posts in the various scales of the hierarchy, could only be entrusted to men who were thirty and over as the following sentence indicates. Note that in the *Damascus Document* the judges must be between twenty-five and sixty years old (X, 6-7), the overseer between thirty and sixty

who joined it at the beginning could hardly have been expected to abandon their wives and children. The practice of celibacy at Qumran itself must have been established and have spread later. A little below, in lines 9-12, there is question of the marriage of young people who have lived among the Congregation since their infancy.

Then at the age of thirty years he may be promoted to arbitrate at law-suits (**14**) and trials, and to take his place among the chiefs of the Thou-sands of Israel, and the chiefs of the Hundreds, the chiefs of the Fi[ft]ies, (**15**) [the chiefs] of the Tens, the judges, and the officers, according to their tribes, in all their clans, [according to the de]cision of the sons (**16**) [of Aar]on the priests and of all the heads of family of the Congregation.

Whoever is destined to take his place in the offices (**17**) shall go out and enter before the Congregation. And according to his understanding and the perfection of his conduct, he shall strengthen his loins in the pos[ition (which he occupies) in order to ful]fil (**18**) the office confided to his care in the midst of his brethren. They shall all be honoured, one more than another, [according to whether they] have much or little.[1]

The aged

(**19**) And when a person is old, duty in the [servi]ce of the Congregation shall be entrusted to him in proportion to his strength.

The simple

And let no person that is simple (minded) (**20**) enter into the lot to have access to a higher post in the Congregation of Israel in matters of law[suit and tr]ial, nor to assume any duty in the Congregation, (**21**) nor to fill any place in the war that is destined to crush the nations.[2] His clan shall merely inscribe him in the register of the army (**22**) and he shall fulfil his service in fatigue-duty in proportion to his capacity.

Role of the Levites

And each of the sons of Levi shall remain at his post (**23**) under the orders of the sons of Aaron to cause all the Congregation to come in and go out, each in his rank, under the leadership of the heads (**24**) of family of the Congregation, the chiefs, the judges, and the officers, according to

---

[1] On this strict hierarchy within the sect, see *Rule*, II, 19-23, V, 21-4. It was based on each man's merit and excellence, 'according to whether they have much or little'. We find an analogous expression in *Rule*, IV, 16: 'according to the share of each (of Truth and Righteousness, cf. IV, 24), according to whether he has much or little'.

[2] A reference to the final eschatological war; it was with this in mind that the *War Scroll* was written.

---

years (XIV, 6-7), and the 'overseer in charge of all the camps' between thirty and fifty years old (XIV, 8-9). See other indications of the age necessary for various military functions or posts in *War Scroll*, VI, 14-VII, 3.

the number of all their hosts, under the orders of the sons of Zadok the priests (25) [and of all the h]eads of family of the Congregation.[1]

Sanctification before the Assembly

And when the order is given to (gather) the whole Assembly (together) to dispense justice, or (26) for the Council of the Community, or for military mobilization,[2] they shall sanctify them for three days so that every member may be (27) rea[dy].

Composition of the Council of the Community

[The]se are the persons convoked to the Council of the Community ... [3] all (28) the [wise] men of the Congregation, and the understanding, and the learned, perfect of conduct and able-bodied men, together with (29) [the chiefs of the tri]bes and all their judges and officers, and the chiefs of the Thousands, the chiefs [of the Hundreds,] II (1) and of the Fifties, and of the Tens, and the Levites, (each) in the mid[st of] his [divi]sion of service. Such are (2) the men of renown called to the Assembly gathered for the Council of the Community in Israel (3) in the presence of the sons of Zadok the priests.[4]

Persons excluded from the Assembly

And let no person smitten with any (4) human impurity whatever enter the Assembly of God.[5] And every person smitten with these impurities, unfit (5) to occupy a place in the midst of the Congregation, and every (person) smitten in his flesh, paralysed in his feet or (6) hands, lame or

---

[1] This passage describes the Levites as being strictly subordinate to the priests, and as acting as a sort of police force within the Congregation which was placed under the direct supervision of lay leaders. Basically, therefore, they were in charge of the administration and enforcement of the rule; authority proper was invested solely in the priests and in the 'heads of family of the Congregation'.

[2] For the final battle against the nations, or in preparation for that war.

[3] In the Hebrew scroll the word *MBN* appears here, followed by the two letters *'ain* and *shin* and a blank about half an inch wide. *'ain* and *shin* may represent the word *'ash*, which in Job ix. 9 means a constellation — Orion perhaps, or the Great Bear. The translation would then read 'by the Son of Orion' (?), an expression which would apply to the Messiah, like the expression 'Son of the Star'. But this interpretation is most uncertain. The editors suppose that the end of the word, and of the phrase 'from the age of tw[enty years'], have been omitted — an hypothesis no less uncertain than the other one.

[4] According to this passage, the Council of the Community composed of 'men of renown' included the 'wise men', the lay leaders, the Levites, and obviously the priests, since the others were gathered together in their presence: these seem to be listed so that the highest dignitaries are mentioned last. A little further on, however, in II, 11-17, the members of the Council are listed in the opposite way — priests, lay leaders, 'wise men' (the Levites are omitted).

[5] The word 'Assembly' (*qahal*) is here practically synonymous with the terms Congregation, Council of holiness, Council of the Community, Congregation of the Community, which appear here and there in the *Rule Annexe*.

blind or deaf, or dumb or smitten in his flesh with a blemish (7) visible to the eye, or any aged person that totters and is unable to stand firm in the midst of the Congregation: (8) let these persons not en[ter] to take their place in the midst of the Congregation of men of renown, for the Angels (9) of holiness are [in] their [Congrega]tion. And if [one of] them should have somethi[ng] to say to the Council of holiness, (10) [then] he shall be questioned privately; but that person shall not enter into the midst [of the Congregation], for he is smitten.

Precedence in the Council of the Community

(11) [Concerning the mee]ting of the men of renown [called] to assembly for the Council of the Community when [Adonai] will have begotten (12) the Messiah among them.[1]

[The Priest][2] shall enter [at] the head of all the Congregation of Israel, then all (13) [the chiefs of the sons] of Aaron the priests called to the assembly, men of renown; and they shall sit (14) [before him], each according to his rank.

And afterwards, [the Mess]iah of Israel [shall enter]; and the chiefs (15) of [the tribes of Israel] shall sit before him, each according to his rank, according to their [position] in their camps and during their marches; then all [16] the heads of fa[mily of the Congre]gation, together with the wise me[n of the holy Congregation], shall sit before them, each according to (17) his rank.

The Community meal

And [when] they gather for the Community tab[le], [or to drink w]ine, and arrange the (18) Community table [and mix] the wine to drink, let no man [stretch out] his hand over the first-fruits (19) of bread and [wine] before the Priest; for [it is he who] shall bless the first-fruits of bread (20) and w[ine, and shall] first [stretch out] his hand over the bread. And after[wards], the Messiah of Israel shall [str]etch out his hands (21) over

---

[1] 'The Messiah' is doubtless the 'Messiah of Israel' mentioned in lines 14 and 20, i.e. the King-Messiah or lay Messiah. He has not yet come, but is expected in the near future. The expression 'when Adonai will have begotten the Messiah', refers to Ps. ii. 7: 'Yahweh said to me: Thou art my son, I myself have begotten thee today.' According to the terminology of the Psalm, therefore, this Messiah will be the 'son of God'.
[2] This word has disappeared in a lacuna; it is reinserted here following line 19, where 'the Priest' is the first to bless the first-fruits of bread and wine. This Priest has manifest precedence over the Messiah of Israel and must be the Messiah of Aaron, i.e. the Priest-Messiah. He is the Priest *par excellence*, and probably the Teacher of Righteousness himself, who, as we know, was a priest: he has come already, but has been taken away and will return at the end of time together with the Messiah of Israel. It was above all on the coming of this Messiah of Israel that the messianic expectation of the sect was focused, for a time at least, and this is why he is also called, quite briefly, 'the Messiah'.

the bread. [And afterwards,] all the Congregation of the Community shall [bl]ess, ea[ch according to] his rank.

And they shall proceed according to this rite (22) at every mea[l where] at least ten persons [are as]sembled.[1]

---

[1] This passage on the Community meal is to be compared with the briefer description in the *Rule*, VI, 4-5. The present text refers to the ideal Supper as it is to be celebrated at the end of time when the two Messiahs are present. But, meanwhile, the daily supper in every community of at least ten members (cf. *Rule*, VI, 3-4), with a priest presiding, draws its inspiration from this ideal liturgy of the messianic meal, of which it is, as it were, both a reflection and an anticipation.

THE *BOOK OF BLESSINGS*

Blessing of the faithful[1]

I (1) Words of blessi[ng] for the man of understanding
to bless those who fear [God and do] His will,
who observe His commandments (2) and cling firmly to His holy
and walk perfectly [in all] His [ways of tru]th;   [Covenant
whom He has chosen for the (3) everlasting Covenant
wh[ich shall re]main for ever.

May A[donai] bless thee [from His holy dwelling-place!]
May He open for thee from the heights of heaven
the everlasting spring (4) which shall n[ever run d]ry! . . .
(5) And may He favour thee with all the [heavenly] bless[ings]
[and instru]ct [thee] in the Knowledge of the Saints! . . .

. . . .

Blessing of the High Priest[2]

II . . . .
(24) may He favour thee with the Spirit of holiness . . .
(25) and may He favour thee with the everlasting Covenant . . .
(26) and may He favour thee with righteous judgment . . .
(27) and may He favour thee in all thy works . . .
(28) [in] everlasting truth . . .
III (1) May Adonai raise His face towards thee,
and may the sweet o[dour of thy sacrifices . . .]
[and that in al]l those who dwell . . . (2) He may delight
and that He may give heed to thy holy offerings . . .
. . . . all thy seed;

---

[1] The *Book of Blessings* annexed to the *Rule* is preserved in a very incomplete state: only a few fragments of five columns remain. Furthermore, there was originally at least a sixth column, since the last sentence of the last line of column V is clearly unfinished. To their credit, the editors have succeeded in putting a little order and clarity into what remains of the collection. First comes the Blessing of the members of the sect, then that of the High Priest, then that of the priests, and finally there is the Blessing of the 'Prince of the Congregation'. In the present translation I have omitted certain words and scraps of phrases which, because of the lacunae, are of practically no interest.

[2] The title of this Blessing has disappeared in the lacunae. From the few phrases remaining, the editors — rightly I think — believe that this blessing was intended for the High Priest, and probably for the 'Messiah of Aaron' himself; i.e. the Priest-Messiah, the supreme spiritual leader of the Congregation.

[and may He raise] (3) His face towards all thy Congregation!
May He set upon thy head [the diadem . . .]
(4) [and may He sanc]tify thy seed unto eternal glory . . .
(5) May he grant thee eternal [bl]iss . . .
and may the sovereignty . . .
(6) and that in the company of the Angels of hol[iness . . .]
(7) may He fight [before] thy Thousands . . .

. . . .

(18) [to ensl]ave many people unto thee . . .
(19) . . . all the riches of the world . . .
(20) For God has laid soundly all the foundations of . . .
(21) He has established thy bliss unto eternal ages.

Blessing of the priests

(22) Words of blessing for the man [of understanding]
[to bless] the sons of Zadok the priests
whom (23) God has chosen to establish His Covenant for [ever]
[and to t]est all His ordinances in the midst of His people
and to instruct them (24) according to His command;
who have founded [His Covenant] in truth
and heeded in righteousness all His precepts
and walked according to (25) His will.

May Adonai bless thee from His [ho]ly [dwelling-place]
and make of thee a splendid ornament in the midst (26) of the Saints!
[May He re]new for thee the Covenant of the [everlasting] priesthood
and grant thee a place [in the abode] (27) of holiness!
May He j[udge all] the nobles by thy works,
and by that which comes from thy lips, all [the leaders] (28) of the
[peoples!
May He grant thee a share in the first-fruits of [all deli]cious [food]
and bless the counsel of all flesh by thy hand!
IV . . . .
(23) to raise up (the voice) at the head of the Saints
and to bl[ess] thy people . . .
. . . by thy hand (24) the men of the Council of God . . . [1]
And thou, (25) thou shalt be as an Angel of the Face in the dwelling-place
for the glory of Elohim of hos[ts . . .]   [of holiness
[and thou shalt] be in the company of God, ministering in the (26) royal
[palace,

---

[1] i.e. the members of the sect. The same expression is used in the *Rule Annexe*, I, 3.

and decreeing fate in the company of the Angels of the Face;[1]
and the Council of the Community . . .
for everlasting time and for all ages for ever;
for (27) [all] His judgments [are truth].
And may He make of thee an object of holin[ess] in the midst of His
and a torch [. . . to shine] upon the world in Knowledge   [people,
and to enlighten the face of many (28) [. . .]
[And may He make of thee] an object vowed to infinite holiness;
for thou, [thou] art [con]secrated to Him
and wilt glorify His Name and Holiness . . .
V   .   .   .   .

Blessing of the Prince of the Congregation[2]

(20) For the man of understanding
to bless the Prince of the Congregation who . . .
(21) and for whom He will renew the Covenant of the Community,
that he may restore the kingdom of His people for ev[er]
[and judge the poor with justice,]
(22) [and] that he may rule with e[quity the hum]ble of the land
and walk before Him perfectly in all the ways [of truth . . .]
(23) and that he may restore [His holy] Coven[ant at the time] of the
                                    [distress of those who seek [Him].

May Adonai [rai]se [thee] to everlasting heights,
and as a forti[fied] tower upon a (24) steep wall!

[1] The Angels of the Face (or of the Presence) mentioned several times in the books of
Jubilees and *Enoch* and in the *Testaments of the Twelve Patriarchs*, are celestial beings continually occupied in the service of God. The priests are compared to them in *Jubilees*,
XXXI, 14: 'May the Lord cause thee to approach Him, thou (Levi) and thy seed, to
serve in His sanctuary like the Angels of the Face. . . .' The 'royal palace', and also the
'dwelling-place of holiness', are Heaven, where God dwells and reigns: it can also be
translated 'Temple of the kingdom (of Heaven)'. Together with the Angels of the Face,
we read, the priest will decree 'destiny'. I think this expression should be compared to the
following passage from the *Rule*, IV, 26: '. . . and that the destiny of every creature may
be decreed in accordance with his spirit, on the day of Judgment and Visitation'. It
would then allude to the justiciary role, the role *par excellence* of the priests at the Last
Judgment.
[2] The 'Prince of the Congregation' is the supreme temporal leader, the lay leader.
This title appears also in the *Damascus Document* (VII, 20) and in the *War Scroll* (V, 1).
The present passage gives valuable help in recognizing the role and attributes of this
person: it is he who will restore the Kingdom of God (line 21), it is he who will restore the
holy Covenant (line 23). This passage paraphrases and applies to him the celebrated
oracle from Isa. (xi. 1-5) concerning the Messiah sprung from the stem of Jesse, i.e. the
son of David. It is therefore clear that this 'Prince of the Congregation' is the 'Messiah of
Israel', the lay Messiah mentioned in the *Rule Annexe* (II, 11-22), as we have seen above.
This Davidic Messiah, King-Messiah, has not yet come; his coming is ardently expected,
for it is this King-Messiah who will finally crush the nations and the wicked and will
inaugurate the fullness of the messianic age. This expectation of the coming of the Davidic
Messiah is expressed perfectly clearly in the *Psalms of Solomon* (XVII, 23-51; XVIII, 6-14),
where he is described very much as in this Blessing.

And [thou shalt strike the peoples] by the might of thy [mouth];
thou shalt devastate the earth by thy sceptre,
and by the breath of thy lips (25) shalt thou slay the ungodly.
[The Spirit of couns]el and eternal might [shall be upon thee],
the Spirit of Knowledge and of the fear of God.
And righteousness shall be (26) the girdle [of thy loins],
[and faith] the girdle of thy haunches.
May He make thy horns of iron
and thy shoes of bronze!
(27) May thou toss like a [young] bull [. . .]
[and trample the peopl]es like the mud of the streets!
For God has established thee as a sceptre[1] (28) over the rulers . . .
[and all the peo]ples shall serve thee,
and He shall exalt thee by His holy Name.
(29) And thou shalt be as a l[ion . . .]

· ·

(Here ends the surviving portion of the scroll of the *Rule*.)

[1] An allusion to the oracle of Balaam in Num. xxiv. 17-19: '. . . a sceptre has risen out of Israel. . . .' This oracle is recalled in the *Damascus Document*, VII, 19-21, where the sceptre is identified with the 'Prince of all the Congregation'; it is cited also in the *War Scroll* (XI, 6-7). It is the 'Prince of the Congregation', i.e. the lay Messiah, the King-Messiah, who is to conquer the nations and enslave them to Israel. The expectation and exaltation of the second Messiah as conqueror of the nations and founder of the Kingdom of God is all the better understood among the sectaries in that the first Messiah, the priestly Messiah, i.e. the Teacher of Righteousness, had been put to death and, on the temporal level, his work had ended in failure.

CHAPTER IV

THE DAMASCUS DOCUMENT

Description of the two manuscripts from the Cairo Geniza; analysis of the book. — 1. *The Exhortation*. General contents and date. Translation of Manuscript A. Translation of Manuscript B. — 2. *The Ordinances*. Their composite character, date, Essene origin. Translation.

From the *Rule* it is no doubt advisable to turn to the reading and study of the *Damascus Document*. It should be remembered that this is a conventional abridgement of the full title which, complete, should read, 'The Document of the New Covenant in the Land of Damascus'— the 'New Covenant in the Land of Damascus' being the name given to the sect in the work itself. As has already been explained,[1] this sect was the Jewish sect of the Covenant which, driven out of Judaea by persecution, sought refuge in the region of Damascus and remained there for a certain time before returning to its own country. Convinced that the Teacher of Righteousness, whom the High Priest had put to death, would return at the end of time, his disciples regrouped and reorganized themselves, and settled in their land of exile to await the great Day of God's supreme Visitation. The *Damascus Document* is witness to this phase of the history of the Essene church.[2]

To tell the truth, we do not know the original title of this work; the fragments discovered in 1896-97 by Solomon Schechter in the Geniza of a synagogue in Old Cairo, and published by him in 1910, are of no help to us in this respect. Their editor named them 'Fragments of a Zadokite Work'[3] because the sect claimed to be in some way the 'sons of Zadok'. Following Schechter's example, many writers, especially in England and America, still speak of the

---

[1] See above, p. 40.
[2] See my *Aperçus préliminaires* . . . (Paris, 1950), p. 68. (Eng. edn., p. 54).
[3] These fragments are preserved in the Cambridge University Library. The complete title of SCHECHTER's publication is, *Documents of Jewish Sectaries, vol. I. Fragments of a Zadokite Work, edited from Hebrew Manuscripts in the Cairo Genizah Collection now in possession of the University Library, Cambridge, and provided with an English translation, introduction, and notes* (Cambridge, 1910).

'Zadokite fragments', or — which comes to the same thing — 'Sadducean fragments'. But the words 'Zadokite' and 'Sadducean' are dangerously equivocal because both the Sadducees proper (mentioned by Josephus and the New Testament), and the sectaries of Qumran and Damascus, were known by that name: yet although the latter arrogated to themselves the glorious title of 'sons of Zadok', they were in reality the sworn enemies of the Sadducees. It is wiser, therefore, to drop 'Zadokite' and 'Sadducean' from the title of the work found in the Cairo Geniza, and to call it instead the 'Document of the New Covenant in the Land of Damascus' — or more briefly, and as German writers mostly do, the *Damascus Document (Damaskusschrift, Damaskusdokument)*.

The fragments from the Cairo Geniza consist, on the one hand, of eight leaves of parchment written upon both sides (these sixteen pages of script all appear to have been written by the same scribe) and on the other, of one leaf of larger format. This is also written upon both sides but by another less skilful hand. These fragments derive, therefore, from two distinct manuscripts: the first (A) dates from approximately the tenth century A.D. and the second (B) from one or two centuries later. Of the eight leaves of Manuscript A, the first four (pages i to viii) contain an important part of a long Exhortation; the text runs on without interruption from one leaf to the next, but one or more leaves may be missing from the beginning, and those giving the end of the Exhortation have certainly disappeared. The four remaining leaves of Manuscript A (pages ix to xvi) present a series of ordinances, but although the text of the first three leaves of this group (pages ix to xiv) is unbroken, one or more leaves are probably missing between the third and the fourth (between pages xiv and xv). Moreover, it is possible that we are without the beginning and the end of this collection of ordinances. As regards the fragment from Manuscript B, this gives only a part of the Exhortation, and in a different recension from that of Manuscript A; furthermore, commencing *ex abrupto* in the middle of a phrase, this fragment first of all presents a text parallel to that of leaf IV of Manuscript A (pages vii and viii), but afterwards continues alone, giving, it seems, the end of the Exhortation.

Besides the fragments from Cairo, the *Damascus Document* is attested today by several other Hebrew fragments from the Qumran caves: caves IV and VI, which were discovered in 1952, almost sixty years after the Cairo find, have yielded a considerable number of remains of at least eight manuscripts of the same Essene book.[1] Fragments of seven manuscripts have been found in cave IV: their text conforms to that of Manuscript A, but they contain sections which have not been preserved in the Cairo manuscripts. As a matter of fact, we are assured that two fragments from two different manuscripts contain 'a text which certainly preceded the present beginning of the *Damascus Document*' (i.e. the Exhortation). Furthermore, two other manuscripts restore the missing end of the work (i.e. of the collection of ordinances) with a section beginning: 'And this is the exact tenor of the ordinances which they shall follow during all the time of ungodliness.' The section ends with the words: '. . . the last interpretation of the Law'. Finally we are told: 'Almost all the manuscripts contain, in the body of the text, rules which do not appear in the Cairo manuscripts.' None of these fragments from cave IV have been published yet. As regards cave VI, five small fragments found there were published recently: four of them contain scraps of text corresponding to various passages from the Cairo Manuscript A, but the other one, in which appear a few words of a phrase forbidding sodomy, has no parallel among the Cairo manuscripts.[2]

Clearly all these ancient fragments of the *Damascus Document* are of the utmost importance. Deriving from manuscripts which date, at the latest, from the first century A.D., they will allow us to assess the fidelity of the copies found in Cairo, which are only medieval. Then again, their supplements to both the Exhortation and the collection of ordinances may be extremely valuable. It is to be hoped that the text of all these ancient fragments will be communicated to scholars as soon as possible. Until then any study of the *Damascus Document*, a basic work of the Essene sect, can — in part — lead only to provisional conclusions, and the efforts of students will continue to be considerably impeded.

There are a certain number of obvious mistakes in the text of the Cairo fragments, but in the following translation I have felt it my duty to make as few corrections as possible. Conjecture, which may be recommended elsewhere, must here be reduced to the minimum; the philologist has still only a part of the existing evidence at his

---

[1] Cf. *RB*, 1956, pp. 55, 61.
[2] See M. BAILLET, *RB*, 1956, pp. 513-23. The first four fragments correspond to the following passages from the Cairo Manuscript A: IV, 19-21; V, 13-14; V, 18; VI, 2; VI, 20; VII, 1.

disposal and, with the exception of the fragments from cave VI, even that is of later date and consequently the least reliable.[1]

As I have shown in my analysis of the Cairo Manuscript A, the *Damascus Document* is essentially in two parts: an Exhortation and a collection of ordinances. These two parts are closely linked together, or rather, the first part acts as a sort of introduction to the second. I think it is a mistake to speak, as Rabin does,[2] of 'two entirely different writings which the scribe of Manuscript A happened to copy out in the same book'. In reality, the whole purpose of the Exhortation is to advise the members of the sect to obey its ordinances. These ordinances are an interpretation of the Mosaic Law, an authentic and revealed commentary; they constitute the Essene *halakhah*. Every Essene had to submit and rigorously conform to them. In the *Rule Annexe* (I, 5) it is explicitly stated that they are to be carefully taught to new members; and the *Damascus Document* itself (XIV, 7-8) orders that every priest acting as an overseer must know them thoroughly as well as the 'Book of Meditation' — the latter being, in my opinion, the scroll of the *Rule*.[3]

In this chapter on the *Damascus Document* we will first examine the Exhortation, and then the Ordinances.

1. The Exhortation

As far as can be judged from the two Cairo manuscripts, the Exhortation follows no rigid design. It is dominated by a few central ideas, namely, absolute obedience to the sect's ordinances, the eminent authority and holiness of both the sect and its founder, the criminal wickedness of those who have not joined the sect or who have left it, the imminence of final Judgment when the faithless and

---

[1] After SCHECHTER, the text of the Cairo fragments was established with the aid of photography by L. ROST, *Die Damaskusschrift* (Berlin, 1933); the photographic facsimiles of these fragments were not published until the appearance of S. ZEITLIN's booklet, *The Zadokite Fragments. Facsimile of the manuscripts in the Cairo Genizah Collection in the possession of the University Library, Cambridge, England; with an Introduction* (Philadelphia, 1952). Since then, C. RABIN, in his recent work *The Zadokite Fragments* (Oxford, 1954), has presented a new edition of the text based on a direct study of the originals and also on an examination of a new set of photographs; it is accompanied by an English translation and copious philological notes. I have made a great deal of use of this important study, as well as of various earlier translations, in particular those of ISRAEL LÉVI (*REJ*, 1911, pp. 161-205), J. M. LAGRANGE (*RB*, 1912, pp. 203-40), and R. H. CHARLES (*The Apocrypha and Pseudepigrapha of the Old Testament*, 1913, II, pp. 799-834). I have also been helped by the frequently pertinent remarks of P. WERNBERG-MØLLER published in the *J. Sem. St.*, April 1956, pp. 110-28.

[2] op. cit., p. x.

[3] See above, p. 70.

the apostates will be chastised. These themes return time and again: there is no attempt to avoid repetition. The tone and manner are those of a preacher who addresses the faithful, not to teach them *ex professo* the doctrines of the sect, but to stimulate their fervour and to put them on their guard against discouragement and betrayal. He reminds them ceaselessly of the known truths; ceaselessly, too, he alludes to recent events, to happenings of their own time. His style is rich in biblical reminiscence, but the frequent quotations, explicit and implicit, are entirely at the service of a mind vigorously directed towards a specific, concrete end, which is to hold the members of the sect to their faith and their obedience.

These he calls his 'sons' (II, 14); without any doubt, this preacher was one of the sect's principal personalities, and even perhaps its supreme chief, the 'overseer of all the camps', whose role and function are described in the ordinances (XIV, 8-11). Is not the overseer like a 'father' to the sectaries (cf. XIII, 9)? The supreme chief of the sect seems to be the person most qualified to assemble the authentic ordinances by which its members were governed, and to place at the head of this collection a solemn introduction. It is no doubt due to this high authority that the book ranked among the essential works of the sect, as is proved by the large number of copies identified among the fragments from the Qumran caves.

This person's name is unknown to us. When did he write his book? As I have said, the Exhortation is full of allusions to recent and contemporary history, but in harmony with the usual style of this sect of apocalypticists, they are, alas, deliberately sibylline; it is very difficult for us to decipher all these enigmas today. Nevertheless it is obvious that they were at one time understood easily enough and if we set ourselves to reconstruct the sect's historical *milieu* we may hope to rediscover the key. Actually the style is no more enigmatic than that of the vision of Daniel and other Jewish apocalyptic writings: if modern criticism has succeeded in revealing precisely which people, and which historical facts, are alluded to in chapter xi of Daniel, why should we be unable to unravel the mystery of the historical allusions with which the *Damascus Document* teems?

Many attempts of this kind were made before the discoveries at Qumran, but the opinions advanced were of such diversity as to arouse some scepticism concerning their chance of success. The position today is different: the *Commentary on Habakkuk*, in particular, provides us, I believe, with a few quite reliable pointers. The *Damascus Document*, for instance, mentions several times two outstanding characters, the 'Teacher of Righteousness' and the 'Man of Lies'; the former was the founder of the sect, and the latter its enemy, the Teacher's persecutor. Now these two people figure again in the *Commentary on Habakkuk*; in that work, the 'Man of Lies' is also called the 'Wicked Priest'. Various indications have led me to identify this 'Wicked Priest' as Hyrcanus II, who succeeded his father Alexander Jannaeus as High Priest in 76 B.C., and ascended the throne on the death of his mother Alexandra in 67 B.C. He was supplanted for a time by his brother Aristobulus II. Then after the capture of Jerusalem in 63 B.C., Pompey nominated him High Priest once more, and he filled this office until 40 B.C., when he was dispossessed by Antigonus and taken prisoner by the Parthians. As for the Teacher of Righteousness, it is my belief that he probably began his ministry towards the end of the second century B.C., and continued it during the whole of the reign of Alexander Jannaeus (103-76 B.C.), not without suffering a certain amount of persecution at the hands of this High Priest. But the main persecution was conducted by Hyrcanus II, who put the Teacher to death some time between 65 and 63 B.C. It was then that the sect that he had founded was obliged to seek refuge in the land of Damascus, out of reach of the Jewish High Priest. The sectaries no doubt remained there at least until the end of the pontificate of Hyrcanus II in 40 B.C. A little later they returned to Judaea, and to Qumran in the desert of Judah in particular, the site of their original settlement. There they stayed until the time of the great Jewish Revolt, or more precisely, until A.D. 68.

This chronological outline seems to provide the key to various allusions and historical presuppositions in the *Damascus Document*. I think the enemy against whom the author of the Exhortation constantly directs his violent and bitterly hostile attacks is this Hyrcanus II, who, after killing the Teacher of Righteousness and plundering the various communities, forbade the faithful ever to enter the country again or to reinstall themselves in the houses of their order. The Congregation of the Man of Lies, whose impiety and crimes the Exhortation denounces, is the official Synagogue, the Jewish nation governed by Hyrcanus II. Thanks to the skilful diplomacy of the High Priest, it recovered little by little. How could the sectaries of the Covenant in their distant exile have avoided the temptation to desert and return 'with the Man of Lies'? Their leader insists that they must persevere; the hour of great Judgment is near, when the wicked and the traitors will be destroyed and only those who have held out until the end will be saved. And to fill them with salutary fear, he reminds them several times of a great event still fresh in their memories, an unforgettable catastrophe that had recently struck the wicked congregation. The instrument of this Vengeance was a person whom the author describes as 'Chief of the Kings of Yāwān', i.e. Greece, the Hellenized Orient (A, VIII, 1-13; B, I, 15-26). I think this person must have been Pompey, and the catastrophe alluded to, the capture of Jerusalem in 63 B.C. which resulted in horrible massacre and marked the onset of the Roman domination of Palestine and the loss of Jewish independence.[1] I feel that such an allusion provides a sound pointer for the dating of the Exhortation; it must have been written after the capture of Jerusalem by Pompey. Furthermore, it is stated that during this 'first Visitation', the impious Jews were delivered to the sword whereas the pious were saved (A, VII, 21-VIII, 1; B, I, 10-13). This indication is best explained if the Damascus exile began, as I think it did, a little before the siege of Jerusalem by Pompey; by leaving Judaea, the sectaries of the Covenant escaped death.

The same view is expressed in the *Psalms of Solomon*, a pseudepigraphic collection also emanating from the sect of the Covenant. 'The arm of the Lord', we read (XIII, 2-4), 'has saved us from the raised sword and from famine and from the death of sinners. Wild beasts hurled themselves upon them (the wicked); they tore their flesh with their teeth and with their molar teeth they ground their bones. But from all this the Lord has preserved us.' Nobody doubts today that the *Psalms of Solomon* contain many references to the great catastrophe of 63 B.C. and to Pompey the Great; the siege of Jerusalem and the pride of the Roman general are described in several passages. Some famous verses even celebrate the miserable death, in 48 B.C., of this 'Wicked Man' justly smitten by God. The *Damascus Document*, which still gives Pompey the splendid title of 'Chief of the Kings of Yāwān', was no doubt written a little before 48 B.C. So unless I am wrong it originated between 63 and 48 B.C., whereas the *Rule*, the work of the Teacher of Righteousness himself (basically at any rate), must have been composed before 63 B.C.

---

[1] See my article, 'Le chef des rois de Yâwân dans l'*Écrit de Damas*', in *Semitica*, vol. v, pp. 41-57.

Now follows the translation of the first part of the *Damascus Document*. I give first of all the complete translation of Manuscript A, followed by the complete translation of Manuscript B.

TRANSLATION OF MANUSCRIPT A

A reminder of divine Judgment

I (1) Therefore hear now, all you who know justice,
and comprehend the words (2) of God!
For He tries all flesh
and will judge all those who scorn Him.

The origin of the Community and the Teacher of Righteousness

(3) For because of the unfaithfulness of those who abandoned Him
He hid His face from Israel and its Sanctuary
(4) and delivered them up to the sword.[1]
But remembering the Covenant of the Patriarchs,
He left a remnant (5) to Israel
and did not deliver them to destruction.
And in the time of wrath,
three hundred and (6) ninety years after He had delivered them
into the hand of Nebuchadnezzar king of Babylon,
(7) He visited them,
and caused a root of planting to spring from Israel and Aaron
to possess (8) His land
and to grow fat on the good things of His earth.[2]

---

[1] An allusion to the capture of Jerusalem by Nebuchadnezzar (586 B.C.), as is explicitly stated below (lines 5-6).

[2] The 'root of planting' which God caused 'to spring from Israel and Aaron' is the sect of the Covenant founded '390 years' after the capture of Jerusalem by Nebuchadnezzar. This figure appears to have been borrowed from Ezek. iv. 5, where the number of days during which the prophet must bear the sin of the house of Israel is given as 390; it is a symbolical figure, and it is useless to try to attach any value to it in determining the real date of the sect's origin. It should be noted, moreover, that the *Damascus Document* explicitly provides two other indications of the same kind: 'twenty years' between the foundation of the sect and the appearance of the Teacher of Righteousness (A, I, 10), and 'forty years' between his disappearance and the final Visitation (B, II, 14-15). Forty years is taken here, as customary in the Bible, to describe the span of one generation, and refers to the writer's own generation, the 'last generation'. But before this last generation, between the appearance and disappearance of the Teacher of Righteousness — during, that is to say, the lifetime of the Teacher — there is another period of forty years, the life-span of another generation. So the total number of years from the capture of Jerusalem to the final Visitation works out as follows: 390+20+40+40 = 490. This figure corresponds exactly to the seventy weeks of years in the prophecy of Dan. ix. 2, 24, a sacred number which appears again in the *Testament of Levi* (XIV, 1). If my interpretation is acceptable, the purpose of this reckoning was to show the sectaries to whom the *Damascus Document* was addressed that they truly belonged to the last generation and that final Judgment

And they understood their iniquity,
and recognized that (9) they were guilty men.
But they were like blind men,
and like men who groping seek their way
(10) for twenty years.[1]
And God considered their works,
for they had sought Him with a perfect heart;
(11) and He raised up for them a Teacher of Righteousness
to lead them in the way of His heart
and to make known (12) to the last generations
what He ⟨would do⟩ to the last generation,
the congregation of traitors.[2]

The 'congregation of traitors' and the 'Man of Mockery'; their punishment

(13) They are those that have departed from the way;
it is the time of which it is written,
Like a stubborn heifer Israel was stubborn,[3]
(14) when the Man of Mockery[4] arose who by his preaching
let flow over Israel (15) the waters of falsehood
and led them astray in the roadless desert,
bringing low the everlasting heights
and departing (16) from the paths of righteousness
and removing the bound which their forefathers
had established in their inheritance,
that (17) the curses of His Covenant might cling to them,
delivering them up to the avenging sword,
the avenger (18) of the Covenant.[5]

Because they sought pleasant things
and chose illusion,

[1] 'Twenty years' describes the period covering the beginning of the sect's existence before the coming of the Teacher of Righteousness. I would repeat that this is essentially an artificial figure.

[2] A reference to the official Synagogue, the Jewish nation governed by the High Priest. In the eyes of the sectaries of the Covenant, those Jews were traitors and 'ungodly' who did not follow them into schism but remained faithful to the High Priest.

[3] Hos. iv. 16.

[4] The High Priest in office in Jerusalem, the persecutor of the sect and consequently wicked — in my opinion, Hyrcanus II. He is also called the 'Man of Lies', the 'Prophet of Lies', and (in the *Commentary on Habakkuk*) the 'Wicked Priest'. The author of the *Damascus Document* heaps obloquy and every kind of reproach on this detested person.

[5] An allusion to the divine chastisement — in my opinion, the capture of Jerusalem by Pompey — of the Jewish nation which had connived at the crimes committed by the High Priest.

was close. Once again, it is of no help in establishing any exact dates but, like all analogous apocalyptic calculations, is essentially artificial.

and because they spied out (**19**) breaches
and chose the beauty of the neck,
and because they declared the wicked righteous
and the righteous wicked,
(**20**) and because they transgressed the Covenant
and violated the Precept,
and because they threatened the life of the just,
and because their soul loathed all them that walk in perfection,
(**21**) and because they persecuted them by the sword,
and because they stirred up civil strife:[1]
II (**1**) then the Anger of God was kindled against their congregation,
ravaging all their multitude,[2]
and their works were as a defilement before Him.

God's treatment of the elect and the wicked; predestination

(**2**) Therefore hear now, all you who have entered the Covenant,
and I will uncover your ear concerning the ways (**3**) of the wicked.
God loves Knowledge.
He has established Wisdom and Counsel before Him;
(**4**) Prudence and Knowledge are His ministers.
Longanimity is with Him
together with fullness of pardon
(**5**) to forgive them that are converted from sin.
But (He wields) Might and Power and towering Fury
in the midst of flames of fire
(**6**) by ⟨the hand of⟩ all the Angels of destruction
against them that have departed from the way
and loathed the Precept,
with no remnant remaining of them (**7**) nor survivor.
For God has not chosen them from former times, from days of old,
(**8**) and before they were made He knew their works.
And He loathed the generations born of blood
and hid His face from the land,
(**9**) from (days of old) until they ended.
And He knows the years of life and the number,
together with the exact date of the times of all (**10**) the events of the ages,
and the things to come, all that comes to pass
in the seasons of all the everlasting years.

---

[1] The gravest crime of the High Priest and his party was their violent persecution of the Teacher of Righteousness and his sect. Note that this was a bloody persecution 'by the sword' which doubtless led to martyrdom and, in particular, to the death of the Teacher of Righteousness himself.

[2] JOSEPHUS writes that twelve thousand Jews perished during the siege of Jerusalem by Pompey, and that an even greater number were led into captivity.

(11) And in all these (times) He raised up for Himself
men named with a name,
in order to leave survivors upon the earth
and to fill (12) the face of the world with their posterity.
And He made known to them His Holy Spirit
by the hand of His Anointed[1]
and He showed (13) the truth;
and ⟨He established⟩ their names with exactness.
But as for those whom He hated, He led them astray.

Exhortation to the perfect life

(14) Therefore hear me now, O sons,
and I will uncover your eyes that you may see
and that you may understand the works (15) of God;
and that you may choose that which He desires
and reject that which He hates;
that you may walk in perfection (16) in all His ways,
and that you may not be drawn by the thoughts of the guilty inclination
and by lustful eyes.

The lessons of history[2]

For many (17) went astray because of this,
and valiant heroes stumbled because of this
from former times until now
because they walked in the stubbornness (18) of their heart.
The ⟨Watchers⟩ of Heaven fell because of this;
they were taken because they had not kept the commandments of God.[3]
(19) And their sons as tall as cedar trees
whose bodies were like mountains

---

[1] The 'Anointed' are here the Prophets who, throughout the ages, had transmitted divine revelations to the elect. Further on (VI, 1), they are called 'the Anointed of holiness'. The present passage may also be translated: 'And He instructed them by the hand of the Anointed of His Holy Spirit.'

[2] In the whole of this section, the words 'because of this' mean 'because of the stubbornness of heart', i.e. because of obstinacy and disobedience towards God's commandments. The author gives historical proof that this kind of attitude has always drawn down heavy punishment from heaven, and his argument is perfectly appropriate in an Exhortation introducing a list of the sect's rules — an Exhortation whose sole aim is to preach a strict and steadfast observance of these same divinely revealed rules, outside which there is no salvation. The only exceptions in this sombre picture of past history recalling the countless acts of disobedience committed by men, and even angels, throughout the course of time, are the three great Patriarchs, Abraham, Isaac and Jacob (III, 2-4).

[3] The 'Watchers' are the angels; they are given this name in Daniel, *Jubilees*, *Enoch* and the *Testaments of the Twelve Patriarchs*. The story of the fall of the angels guilty of marrying the daughters of men (cf. Gen. vi. 1-4) occupies an important place in the Pseudepigrapha, especially in *Enoch*.

fell ⟨because of this⟩.[1]
(20) All flesh on dry land died ⟨because of this⟩;[2]
they were as though they had not been
because they did (21) their own will
and did not keep the commandments of their Maker,
so that His Anger was kindled against them.
III (1) The sons of Noah and their families went astray because of this,
they were cut off because of this.[3]

(2) Abraham did not walk in this
and was rai[sed to be a Fr]iend of God[4]
because he kept the commandments of God
and did not choose (3) the will of his own spirit.
And he handed them down to Isaac and Jacob who kept them
and were inscribed as Friends (4) of God
and party to the Covenant for ever.

The sons of Jacob strayed because of this
and were punished ⟨according to⟩ (5) their straying.[5]
And their sons walked in Egypt in the stubbornness of their heart,
plotting against (6) the commandments of God,
each doing what was good in his own eyes;
and they ate blood.
Then were (7) their males cut off in the desert.
⟨And⟩ at Kadesh ⟨when He said⟩ to them, *Go up and possess* ⟨*the land*⟩,[6]
⟨they chose the will⟩ of their own spirit
and did not heed (8) the voice of their Maker.
They did not keep the commandments of their Teacher[7]
and murmured in their tents.
Then the Anger of God was kindled (9) against their congregation.
And because of this their sons perished,
and because of this their kings were cut off,
and because of this their heroes (10) perished,
and because of this their land was ravaged.[8]

[1] From the marriage of the angels with the daughters of men were born the Giants, as appears in Gen. vi. 4 and the Pseudepigrapha. The story is told in the *Book of Enoch* (XIV, 6) of how these Giants were struck down by the sword before the eyes of their parents.
[2] An allusion to the universal Flood, a punishment for man's wickedness.
[3] Cf. *Jubilees*, X-XI.
[4] Abraham is called 'Friend of God' in Isa. xli. 8; this title is given to him in *Jubilees*, XIX, 9, and also in the Koran.
[5] Cf. *Testaments of the Twelve Patriarchs: Reuben* (I, 7), *Simeon* (II, 12), *Judah* (XIII, 8).
[6] Cf. Deut. ix. 23. Several words have been omitted by the copyist in this passage: I have restored them by conjecture.
[7] God Himself, or Moses.
[8] A summary of the history of Israel during the time of the Judges and the Kings.

And because of this the first to enter the Covenant ⟨were rendered guilty⟩[1]
and were delivered up (11) to the sword;
because they had abandoned the Covenant of God,
and because they had chosen their own will,
and because they had let themselves be drawn
by the stubbornness (12) of their heart,
each one doing his own will.

Institution of the New Covenant

But because of those who clung to the commandments of God
(13) (and) survived them as a remnant,
God established His Covenant with Israel for ever,
revealing to them (14) the hidden things
in which all Israel had strayed:
His holy Sabbaths and His (15) glorious feasts,
His testimony of righteousness, and His ways of truth,
and the desires of His will
which man must fulfil (16) that he may live because of them.
He opened (this) before them,
and they dug a well of abundant waters,[2]
(17) and whoever despises these waters shall not live.
But they, they defiled themselves by the sin of man
and by the ways of defilement,
(18) and they said, This is ours![3]
And God in His marvellous mysteries
forgave their iniquity
and blotted out their sin;
(19) and He built for them a sure House in Israel[4]
such as did not exist from former times till (20) now.

They who cling to it are (destined) for everlasting life
and theirs shall be all the glory of the Man,
as (21) God has assured them by the hand of the prophet Ezekiel:

---

[1] The members, perhaps, of the Ancient Covenant who were 'delivered up to the sword' in the time of Nebuchadnezzar; this catastrophe is recalled at the beginning of the Exhortation (I, 4). 'The first' could also be taken to refer to the first disciples of the Teacher (as in IV, 6, 8, 9; VIII, 17); those among them who deserted 'were delivered up to the sword' when Pompey took Jerusalem.

[2] This well is the Law, as is expressly stated in VI, 4.

[3] 'This' seems to mean 'our Way', 'our conduct'. But in the eyes of the sectary, man is not master of his way (*Rule*, XI, 2). Compare this with the *War Scroll* (XI, 5): 'Thine is the combat. . . . No, (the combat) is not ours.'

[4] The Community of the Covenant is 'the House of the Law' (B, II, 10, 13), 'the House of truth in Israel' (*Rule*, V, 6), 'the House of holiness for Israel' (*Rule*, VIII, 5), 'the House of holiness for Aaron . . . and the House of Community for Israel' (*Rule*, IX, 6).

The priests and the Levites and the sons **IV** (1) *of Zadok*
who kept the charge of my sanctuary
while the children of Israel went (2) *astray from me*
shall come near ⟨*to me to serve me*
and shall stand before me to offer⟩ *me fat and blood.*[1]
The priests are the converts of Israel
(3) who went out from the land of Judah;
and ⟨the Levites are⟩ those who joined them.[2]
And the sons of Zadok are the chosen (4) of Israel,
the (men) named with a name who shall stand at the end of days.
This is the accurate list (5) of their names
according to their lineage
and the time of their existence
and the number ⟨of the days⟩ of their afflictions
and of the years (6) of their exile,
and the accurate account of their works.[3]

. . . .

⟨Such are the fir⟩st ⟨men⟩ of holiness
whom God pardoned,
(7) who declared the just man just
and the wicked, wicked;
then all those who entered (the Covenant) after them
(8) to act according to the exact tenor of the Law
in which the first had been instructed[4]
until the consummation (9) of time
⟨according to the number⟩ of those years.[5]

[1] Ezek. xliv. 15; the copyist has accidentally omitted several words from this quotation. The Hebrew Masoretic Text reads at the beginning, *The levitical priests, the sons of Zadok,* and not, *The priests and the Levites and the sons of Zadok.* But the conjunction 'and' allows the author, by interpreting the biblical text subtly and artificially, to distinguish, so to speak, three groups among the sect's members: those who left the land of Judah to form the first nucleus of the new Covenant in the land of Damascus ('the priests'); those who joined the Community after this first lot ('the Levites'); and finally, all those who are to belong to it at the end of time, at the consummation of the world ('the sons of Zadok').

[2] In Hebrew, NLWYM, a pun on the word 'Levites', LWYM, inspired by Num. xviii. 2, 4 (cf. *Jubilees*, XXXI, 16).

[3] There seems to be a lacuna here. Originally the text must have continued with a list of the sect's members (or of the chief men among them), with their genealogy, dates and titles. This list, borrowed no doubt from the sect's register in which the names of all its members were inscribed, began with the names of 'the first' (contemporaries of the Teacher of Righteousness himself), and then continued with the names of those who joined later. The medieval copyist must have thought it useless to reproduce this ancient list; from our point of view this is very regrettable.

[4] Cf. *Rule*, IX, 10-11: 'And they shall be governed by the first ordinances in which the members of the Community began their instruction.'

[5] The same formula appears in lines 10-11. It may be recalled that in B, II, 13-15, the time given between the disappearance of the Teacher of Righteousness and the end of the world is about 'forty years'; it was for this intermediate period, 'the time of wickedness', and in view of the final ordeal, that the Community of the New Covenant was founded.

According to the Covenant which God established with the first,
(**10**) pardoning their sins,
thus shall God pardon them.[1]
And at the consummation of time,
according to the number of (**11**) those years,
there shall be no more consort with the House of Judah,[2]
but each man shall stand on (**12**) his ⟨fortification⟩:[3]
the wall is built, the boundary carried far.[4]

The present time: the three nets of Belial

And in all those years[5] (**13**) Belial shall be unleashed against Israel;
as God said by the hand of the prophet Isaiah son of (**14**) Amoz,
Terror and pit and snare are upon thee, O inhabitant of the land.[6]
The explanation of this (is that) (**15**) these are Belial's three nets,
of which Levi son of Jacob spoke,[7]
(**16**) by which he (Belial) ensnared Israel,
(**17**) and which he set [be]fore them as three sorts of righteousness:
the first is lust,
the second is riches,
(and) the third (**18**) is defilement of the Sanctuary.
Whoever escapes this is caught by that,
and whoever escapes that one is caught (**19**) by this.[8]

The builders of the wall,[9] they who walked after '*zaw*' — [10]
'*zaw*' is a preacher (**20**) of whom He said, *They only preach* — [11]
have been caught by lust in two things:

[1] This evidently refers to those members of the sect who entered after 'the first'; they will enjoy divine pardon like 'the first'.
[2] It has fallen and been replaced by the Community of the Covenant, henceforth the only 'sure House in Israel'.
[3] Cf. Hab. ii. 1. The 'fortification' upon which each man must stand is the Community of the Covenant itself; only there will he be safe at the time of Judgment.
[4] Inspired by Mic. vii. 11.
[5] During the time preceding the consummation of the world — for the author, the present time.
[6] Isa. xxiv. 17.
[7] This seems to be an allusion to the *Testament of Levi*, but the passage referred to does not appear in its present text. However, the basic ideas are to be found in various passages of the *Testaments of the Twelve Patriarchs*.
[8] Inspired by Isa. xxiv. 18.
[9] This expression, borrowed from Ezek. xiii. 10, describes the followers of the High Priest, the enemies of the sect; cf. VIII, 12 ('Those who build the wall and cover it with whitewash'), 18. It stigmatizes the fragility of their construction — their work — whose cracks they mask with the help of a deceptive veneer.
[10] Cf. Hos. v. 11; the significance of the Hebrew word *zaw* in this passage from Hosea is uncertain. But in Isa. xxviii. 10, 13, it is a sort of onomatopoeia to describe ironically a prophet's prating. Here our author applies this title, 'the Preacher of Lies', to the persecuting High Priest; cf. above, I, 14.
[11] Mic. ii. 6.

by marrying (21) two women during their lifetime,[1]
whereas nature's principle is
Male and female created He them.[2]
V (1) And those who entered the ark (of Noah),
Two and two they went into the ark.[3]
And concerning the prince it is written,
(2) *He shall not multiply wives for himself.*[4]

As for David, he did not read the sealed book of the Law which was
(3) in the ark (of the Covenant). For it was not opened in Israel from the
day that Eleazar (4) and Joshua ⟨   ⟩ and the Elders died,[5] when
(the children of Israel) began to serve Ashtoreth; and it remained hidden
(5) ⟨and⟩ was ⟨not⟩ revealed until the coming of Zadok. And the deeds
of David rose up (to God), with the exception of the murder of Uriah;
(6) and God left them to him.[6]

Moreover, they defile the Sanctuary[7]
inasmuch as they (7) do not distinguish in accordance with the Law,
and lie with her who sees the blood of her flux.[8]

And they marry (8) every one the daughter of his brother or the daughter
of his sister. Now Moses said, *Thou shalt not approach* (9) *the sister of thy*

---

[1] Doubtless to be understood as 'in the lifetime of both women'. The sect condemns all polygamy and even seems to forbid divorce followed by a second marriage if the first wife is still alive. This rule was completely new to Judaism; it is revived in the New Testament (Matt. xix. 3-9; Mark x. 2-12).

[2] Gen. i. 27; the same biblical text is cited in Matt. xix. 4 and Mark x. 6.

[3] Cf. Gen. vii. 9.

[4] Deut. xvii. 17.

[5] After the death of Joshua and Eleazar and the elders of their generation, the children of Israel abandoned Yahweh to serve Baal and Astarte (Ashtoreth); cf. Joshua xxiv. 29-31, 33; Judges ii. 7-10, 13. During the time of apostasy, 'the sealed book of the Law' remained hidden 'until the coming of Zadok'. This Zadok seems to be the priest Zadok who lived in the time of David; it was he who, supplanting the priest Abiathar, anointed Solomon just before David's death. According to the present passage, this Zadok made known again the authentic text of the Law: this praise of his rule is an interesting feature.

[6] The purpose of the whole of this passage is to explain why David had many wives in spite of polygamy being unlawful. The reason given is that it was because he did not, and could not, know 'the sealed book of the Law' hidden 'until the coming of Zadok', i.e. until towards the end of his life. Because of his involuntary ignorance, God counted his good deeds in his favour and allowed their merit to remain. Nevertheless, in spite of the author's excuses and justifications, he concedes that the murder of Uriah remains a blot on the saint's memory.

[7] Before this passage on 'the defilement of the Sanctuary' one would have expected to find, following IV, 17-18, a dissertation on 'riches'; this has probably disappeared accidentally. Also, in connection with 'lust', after having dealt with the first point (polygamy) one would have expected the author to go straight on to develop the second point announced in IV, 20. This second point may have concerned the marriage of an uncle with his niece, which is, in fact, discussed in V, 7-11.

[8] Cf. Lev. xv. 19.

mother; it is the flesh of thy mother.[1] The law of incest (**10**) is written for men but also for women, and if a brother's daughter uncovers the nakedness of the brother (**11**) of her father, whereas it is the flesh ⟨. . .⟩.[2]

Moreover, they have defiled their Holy Spirit,
and with a (**12**) blaspheming tongue have opened their mouth
against the precepts of the Covenant of God,
saying, They are not true!
But it is an abominable thing (**13**) they utter concerning them.
They are all kindlers of fire and lighters of brands;[3]
their webs are (**14**) spider webs
and their eggs are adder eggs.[4]
Whoever approaches them (**15**) shall not go unpunished . . .[5]

Israel's past and present infidelity

For formerly ⟨also⟩ God visited (**16**) their works,
and His anger was kindled against their forfeits.
For this is a people without understanding;[6]
(**17**) they are a nation void of counsel
for there is no understanding among them.[7]
For formerly (**18**) Moses and Aaron arose
by the hand of the Prince of Lights;
but Belial raised up Jannes and (**19**) his brother, in his cunning,
when Israel was saved for the first time.[8]

(**20**) And in the time of the desolation of the land,
the removers of bounds rose up
and led Israel astray.
(**21**) And the land was ravaged,

---

[1] Lev. xviii. 13. This Mosaic law explicitly forbids the marriage of a nephew to his aunt; but the sect forbids also the marriage of a niece to her uncle. It justifies itself in this by arguing that although the law may seem to involve men only because it is addressed to men, in reality it concerns women (nieces) as well.

[2] The phrase is incomplete.

[3] Isa. l. 11.

[4] Isa. lix. 5.

[5] A short phrase follows here, but its text has been altered and is unintelligible.

[6] Isa. xxvii. 11.

[7] Cf. Deut. xxxii. 28.

[8] At the time of the Exodus. Moses was then confronted by two sorcerers, Jannes and Jambres (cf. 2 Tim. iii. 8), who performed the same miracles as he did before Pharaoh (Exod. vii). It was the Prince of Lights (the Good Spirit) who raised up Moses, and Belial (the Evil Spirit) who raised the two brothers against him. In the following phrase, 'the time of the desolation of the land' refers to the present time: the 'removers of bounds' who have 'led Israel astray' and 'prophesied falsely' are the national leaders hostile to the sect (cf. I, 13-16). It seems that they are being implicitly compared here to Jannes and his brother. Is the author alluding to Hyrcanus II and his brother Aristobulus II?

for they preached rebellion against the commandments of God
(revealed) by the hand of Moses and also **VI** (1) by ⟨the hands of the⟩
Anointed of holiness;[1]
and they prophesied falsely
to turn Israel away from following (2) God.

The new Covenant and the new Lawgiver

And God remembered the Covenant of the Patriarchs
and raised out of Aaron men of understanding
and out of Israel (3) sages,
and He caused them to hear (His voice) and they dug the well:
The well which the princes dug,
which (4) *the nobles of the people delved with a rod.*[2]
The well is the Law,
and those who dug it (5) are the converts of Israel
who went out from the land of Judah
and were exiled in the land of Damascus;
(6) all of whom God called princes,
for they sought Him
and their ⟨glory⟩ is denied (7) by the mouth of no man.
And the rod (the Lawgiver) is the Seeker of the Law;[3]
as (8) Isaiah said, *He has made a tool for His work.*[4]
And the nobles of the people are they (9) that come to dig the well
with the help of the Lawgiver's precepts,[5]
(10) that they may walk in them during all the time of wickedness,
and without which they shall not succeed
until the coming (11) of the Teacher of Righteousness at the end of days.[6]

The essential obligations of the members of the Covenant; their reward

And none of those who have entered the Covenant
(12) shall enter the Sanctuary to kindle His altar in vain,

---

[1] The prophets; cf. II, 12.

[2] Num. xxi. 18.

[3] 'Rod', *meḥōqeq*, means both 'leader' and 'lawgiver'; the author is here making a pun on the word. The 'Seeker of the Law' is the Teacher of Righteousness; he is given this title also in VII, 18. He is the student of the Law *par excellence*.

[4] Isa. liv. 16. The 'tool' is the rod, i.e. the Teacher of Righteousness, the new Lawgiver.

[5] The rules of the sect promulgated by the Teacher of Righteousness. The author distinguishes between 'the princes' who dug the well (the first disciples of the Teacher) and 'the nobles of the people' who continue to delve (those who have continued to rally to the sect since the Teacher's death and the Damascus exile).

[6] The Teacher of Righteousness is dead but will reappear 'at the end of days', i.e. at the end of the world, when 'all the time of wickedness' will have ended. This expectation of the Teacher's return, formulated so clearly here, was one of the fundamental articles of belief in the credo of the New Covenant.

but they shall close (**13**) the door; as God said,
Who among you will close his door?
And you shall not kindle my altar (**14**) *in vain.*[1]
Truly, they shall be careful to act
according to the exact tenor of the Law in the time of wickedness,
to separate themselves (**15**) from the sons of the Pit,
and to keep themselves from the unclean riches of iniquity
(got) with a vow or anathema,[2]
(**16**) or by robbing the goods of the Sanctuary,
or by stealing from the poor of His people
to make of widows their prey
(**17**) and to murder the fatherless;[3]
and to distinguish between the unclean and the clean,
and to make known (the distinction) between (**18**) sacred and profane,
and to observe the Sabbath day according to its exact tenor,
and the feasts, (**19**) and the Day of Fasting[4]
according to the ⟨commands⟩ of those who have entered the New
[Covenant in the land of Damascus;
(**20**) to set holy things apart according to their exact tenor;
to love each man his brother (**21**) as himself,
and to support the hand of the needy, the poor, and the stranger,
and to seek each man the well-being **VII** (**1**) of his brother,
and not to betray, each man him who is flesh of his flesh;
to keep from lust (**2**) according to the ordinance;
to reprove each man his brother according to the commandment,
and to bear no malice (**3**) from one day to the next;
and to be separated from all uncleanness according to their ordinance,
and not to defile (**4**) each man his Holy Spirit
according to the distinctions which God has made for them.
For all who walk (**5**) in these (precepts) in holy perfection,
obeying all His instructions,
the Covenant of God is assurance
(**6**) that they will live for a thousand generations.[5]

[1] Mal. i. 10. The sectaries of the New Covenant exiled in Damascus were obliged to dissociate themselves from the Temple worship. But this rupture was only provisional; at the end of time, during the messianic age proper, Jerusalem — a new and purified Jerusalem — would become once more the centre of worship (cf. the fragments of a description of the new Jerusalem mentioned below, chapter XI, pp. 328-9). Meanwhile, the sectaries of the Covenant must live apart, and perfectly, during 'the time of wickedness' and the long phrase which follows (VI, 14-VII, 4) lists, point by point, the principal obligations of Essene life representing 'the exact tenor of the Law'.

[2] Cf. XVI, 13-16.

[3] Cf. Isa. x. 2.

[4] i.e. the Day of Atonement, which the sect appears to have celebrated with particular fervour.

[5] The expression is borrowed from Deut. vii. 9; in the present context it refers to the eternal life promised to the sectaries of the Covenant.

Married members

And if they live in camps according to the rule of the land[1]
and take (**7**) a wife and beget children,
they shall walk in obedience to the Law,
and according to the ordinance (**8**) concerning ⟨pledges⟩,
according to the rule of the Law;
according to that which He said, *Between a man and his wife,
and between a father* (**9**) *and his child.*[2]

Punishment of unfaithful members; the first Visitation

But when God visits the earth,
all those who despise (the commandments)
shall draw down on themselves the reward of the wicked;
(**10**) when the word shall come that is written in the words of the prophet
[Isaiah son of Amoz,
(**11**) who said, *There shall come upon thee and thy people,
and upon thy father's house,
days such as* (**12**) *have* ⟨*not*⟩ *come
since the day when Ephraim departed from Judah.*[3]
When the two houses of Israel were separated,
(**13**) Ephraim ruled over Judah,
and all those who fell back were delivered up to the sword,
whereas those who held firm (**14**) escaped to the land of the north;
as He said, *I will exile the 'Sikkuth' of your king*

---

[1] Doubtless the land of Judah. The parallel passage from Manuscript B (I, 3) reads:
'According to the rule of the land which existed formerly.' The allusion to this 'former'
rule seems to indicate that the members of the sect already lived in 'camps' in Judah,
before their Damascus exile. The *Rule*, as we have seen, makes several allusions to the
retreat into the desert, and probably to the Qumran establishment itself: contrary to the
opinion of some, it therefore seems that the *Damascus Document* as a whole is later than
the *Rule*. The Essenes exiled in the region of Damascus—a certain number of them anyway
—lived there in the same manner, and following the same basic rules, as in the desert
of Judah.

[2] These words appear in Num. xxx. 17 (though the Masoretic Text reads, 'between a
father and his daughter'). This chapter from Numbers deals with the vows and pledges of
women; there is a short passage on this subject in the Ordinances (XVI, 10-12).

[3] Isa. vii. 17, also quoted in XIV, 1. This passage is applied to the contemporary situation. 'The day when Ephraim departed from Judah' is the day on which the members of
the sect ('Ephraim') separated themselves from the mass of the Jews ('Judah'), and left
the land of Judah for the north, for the land of Damascus. Punning on the double significance of the Hebrew word *sar*, 'departed' and 'ruled', the author explains that in these
circumstances Ephraim ruled over Judah, meaning by this that the fate of the sectaries
was a far happier one than that of the other Jews. This explains the rest of the phrase:
whereas the Jews who remained in Jerusalem — including the sectaries who refused to
leave and fell into apostasy — were delivered to the sword (during the capture of the city
by Pompey), the sect's followers escaped punishment and were saved. Thus will it be
again, the author concludes (VIII, 1-2), at the time of the final Visitation; those who have
not persevered to the end will be wiped out.

(**15**) *and the 'Kiyyun' of your images*
⟨*and the Star of your God*⟩
from my tent in Damascus.[1]

The books of the Law are the hut (*sukkath*) (**16**) of the king; as He said, *I will raise up the hut of David which is fallen.*[2]

The king (**17**) is the Assembly;
⟨   ⟩ and the faithfulness (*kēwān*) of the images is the books of the (**18**) whose words Israel has despised.[3]   [prophets

And the Star is the Seeker of the Law[4]
(**19**) who came to Damascus; as it is written,
A star has journeyed out of Jacob
and a sceptre is risen (**20**) *out of Israel.*[5]

---

[1] Amos v. 26-7. The text of this quotation, on which the author bases his clever explanation, does not conform exactly to the Masoretic Text.

[2] Amos ix. 11. The author makes a pun on the similarity of the words *Sikkuth* and *sukkath*, 'hut': he explains that 'the *Sikkuth* of your king', which God transports from Jerusalem to Damascus, is 'the hut of the King', i.e. the Law. God promised to 'raise up the hut of David which is fallen', and at Damascus, thanks to the Congregation of the Covenant, the 'House of the Law', the Law is restored and re-established in all its purity. In this exegesis, therefore, the expression 'hut of David' in the Amos ix quotation means the Law: the word 'David' is taken as a simple synonym of 'King', and the word 'King', as the author expressly claims, really signifies 'the Assembly', i.e. the Congregation of the Covenant in so far as it possesses a royal prerogative and authority.

[3] Again the author makes a pun on the Hebrew words *Kiyyun* and *kēwān*, 'truth, fidelity'. He explains that the books of the prophets are 'the faithfulness of the images', i.e. faithful images — images, of course, of the Mosaic Law or divine Truth. The sectaries venerate both the Law and the Prophets, whereas the great mass of the Jews betray the Law and despise the words of the Prophets.

[4] i.e. the Teacher of Righteousness: cf. VI, 7. He is called here 'the Star', doubtless a messianic title in the sect; the biblical quotation which follows was, in effect, interpreted by them messianically (see *Qumran Cave I*, p. 121). The words 'who came to Damascus' may also be translated 'who will come to Damascus'. Did the Teacher of Righteousness himself lead his people into exile there? Or is this a reference to his mystic presence among the Damascus exiles? Or does it mean that when he returns at the end of time he will go to Damascus to find his disciples and lead them to Jerusalem?

[5] Num. xxiv. 17, as also the quotation that follows, 'he will break down all the sons of Seth'. The 'sceptre' signifies here 'the Prince of all the Congregation': this is the title given to the lay Messiah, the 'Messiah of Israel' in the *Book of Blessings* (V, 20; see above, chapter III, p. 112). The blessing addressed to this personage reads as follows: 'Thou shalt devastate the earth by thy sceptre' (V, 24). It is the Prince of all the Congregation who must fight and conquer the nations and the wicked in the great war at the end of time. We are unable to say whether this 'Prince of all the Congregation', this Messiah of Israel, is confused and identified in this text with 'the Star', the Teacher of Righteousness, or whether he is someone else. Whereas the *Rule* (IX, 11) speaks of the coming of two 'Anointed of Aaron and Israel', i.e. the two Messiahs, the *Damascus Document* mentions only one 'Anointed of Aaron and Israel', both in Manuscript A (XII, 23; XIV, 19) and in Manuscript B (I, 10-11; II, 1). In the present state of documentation, it is, I think, unwise to correct this singular form to the plural, as some critics do. It may very well be that the sect's doctrine on the question of messianism was not rigorously uniform, and that two tendencies showed themselves — one attributing the sacerdotal (or spiritual) and kingly (or temporal) functions to two different Messiahs, and the other transferring both these roles to one and the same Messiah. We should remember that the *Testaments of the Twelve Patriarchs* speak sometimes of two distinct Anointed (the Messiah son of Levi and the Messiah son of Judah), and sometimes of a single Anointed who will be at the same time both Priest and King. See my *Nouveaux aperçus* ... pp. 78-80. (Eng. edn., pp. 51-4.)

The sceptre is the Prince of all the Congregation,
and at his coming *he will break down* (21) *all the sons of Seth.*
They were saved at the time of the first Visitation,[1]
VIII (1) but those who fell back were delivered up to the sword.
And such shall be the lot of all who enter His Covenant
but do (2) not hold firm to these (precepts)
when He visits them for destruction by the hand of Belial.

More about the punishment of unfaithful sectaries: the Chief of the kings of Yāwān

That will be the day (3) when God will visit; ⟨as He said⟩,
The princes of Judah were ⟨*like those who remove the bound*⟩,
upon whom Anger shall pour.[2]
(4) For they shall be sick ⟨without⟩ any healing
and all the ⟨chastisings shall crush⟩ them
because they did not depart from the way (5) of traitors,
and because they defiled themselves in the ways of lust
and in the riches of iniquity,
and because they took revenge and bore malice
(6) each towards his brother,
and because each man hated his fellow,
and because they refused their help,
each man to him who is flesh of his flesh,
(7) and because they had shameful commerce,
and because they made themselves strong for the sake of riches and gain,
and because each man did what was good in his eyes,
(8) and because each man chose the stubbornness of his heart,
and because they kept not themselves from the people
but lived in licence deliberately,
(9) walking in the way of the wicked, of whom God said,
Their wine is the poison of serpents
(10) *and the head of asps is cruel.*[3]

[1] The punishment that struck the unfaithful Jews in 63 B.C. — a prelude, as it were, to the second Visitation at the end of time.

[2] Hos. v. 10. The tirade which follows is directed at apostate sectaries, as the parallel passage in Manuscript B (I, 16-17) clearly shows. The description of the conduct of the wicked in the present passage is a sort of counterpart of the description given a little earlier of the conduct of the perfect sectary (VI, 14-VII, 4).

[3] Deut. xxxii. 33. The second half of the phrase should really read 'and the cruel poison (*rōsh*) of asps', but the author, punning on the double meaning of the Hebrew word *rōsh*, 'poison' and 'head', interprets it quite differently — 'and the head of asps is cruel'. From there, he can go on to explain that 'the head of asps' is the Chief of the kings of Yāwān, since the word 'head' signifies in Hebrew, as in many other languages, the man in command, 'the chief'. I would repeat that, in my opinion, this leader is the Roman Pompey, the Chief of the kings of Yāwān (Greece, the Hellenized Orient)—that same Pompey who invaded Palestine and took Jerusalem in 63 B.C. For an interpretation of the whole of this passage, see my article in *Semitica*, v, 1955, pp. 41-57.

The serpents are the kings of the peoples
and their wine is (11) their ways;
and the head of asps is the Chief of the kings of Yāwān
who came to wreak (12) vengeance upon them.
But those who build the wall and cover it with whitewash
did not understand all this.
For (13) a man who raises the wind and preaches lies,[1]
against the whole of whose congregation the Anger of God was kindled,
had preached for them.

God's love for the sectaries of the Covenant and His hatred for the 'builders of the wall'

(14) But that which Moses said,
Not because of thy righteousness or the uprightness of thy heart
art thou going in to inherit (15) *those nations,*
but because He loved thy Fathers
and because he kept the oath,[2]
(16) so is it with the converts of Israel
(who) have departed from the way of the people;
because of God's love for (17) the first
who ⟨testified⟩ in His favour
He loves those who have followed after,[3]
for theirs is the (18) Covenant of the Fathers.
But because of His hatred for the builders of the wall
His Anger is kindled.

Excommunication of unfaithful sectaries

(19) And it is likewise for whoever despises the commandments of God
and abandons them and turns away in the stubbornness of his heart;
(20) this is the word which Jeremiah spoke to Baruch son of Neriah,
and (which) Elisha (spoke) (21) to his servant Gehazi.[4]
All the men who entered the New Covenant in the land of Damascus[5]
. . . .

[1] Cf. Mic. ii. 11. This 'Preacher of Lies' is the persecuting High Priest (cf. I, 14; IV, 19).

[2] Deut. ix. 5 and vii. 8.

[3] 'The first' are the first disciples of the Teacher of Righteousness; 'those who followed after' describes the following generation of sectaries, i.e. the present generation. Cf. IV, 6-10.

[4] An allusion to unknown pseudepigraphical works.

[5] Here ends, on an unfinished sentence, the preserved portion of the Exhortation in Manuscript A. The rest of the phrase, as well as the end of the Exhortation, appears in Manuscript B (from I, 34, onwards).

TRANSLATION OF MANUSCRIPT B[1]

. . . .

(the Covenant of God) **I** (**1**) is for them assurance
that they will live for thousands of generations;
as it is written, *He keeps the Covenant and Grace* (**2**) *for a thousand generations*
with those who love ⟨him⟩ and keep his commandments.[2]

Married members

And if they live in camps according to the rule (**3**) of the land which
[existed formerly,
and take a wife according to the direction of the Law and beget children,
(**4**) they shall walk in obedience to the Law
and according to the ordinance concerning ⟨pledges⟩,
according to the rule of the Law; (**5**) as He said,
Between a husband and his wife and between a father and his child.

Punishment of unfaithful sectaries: the first Visitation

But all who despise the commandments (**6**) and precepts
shall draw down upon themselves the reward of the wicked
when God visits the earth,
(**7**) when the word shall come that is written . . .[3]
. . . ⟨as He said⟩ by the hand of the prophet Zechariah,
Awake O sword against (**8**) *my shepherd,*
and against the man who is my companion, oracle of God!
Strike the shepherd and the sheep will be scattered,
(**9**) *but I will turn my hand to the little ones.*[4]

---

[1] I would remind the reader that only one leaf remains of this Manuscript B, written
upon on both sides: two pages of script, therefore. I have marked these B I and B II. Schechter,
however, numbers them XIX and XX (the sixteen pages of Manuscript A being numbered
I-XVI). Nothing seems to justify this method which leaves pages XVII and XVIII
entirely unaccounted for. Rost and Rabin, in their editions of the *Damascus Document*, and
even the various translators of this work, have followed Schechter's numbering for
Manuscript B (XIX and XX); as for Zeitlin, he has rather oddly numbered the first page
XVII-XVIII, and the second, XIX-XX. Is it not clearer and more logical to number
them B I and B II?

[2] Deut. vii. 9. The parallel passage in Manuscript A (VII, 6) gives no explicit quotation
and retains only the words 'a thousand generations' of the biblical text.

[3] In the parallel section in Manuscript A there is a long passage at this point (VII,
10-VIII, 1) beginning with a quotation from Isa. vii. 17. It has probably disappeared
from Manuscript B by accident.

[4] Zech. xiii. 7. This text is quoted in the Gospels, where 'shepherd' is applied to Jesus
(Matt. xxvi. 31; Mark xiv. 27). Is the author thinking of the Teacher of Righteousness,
struck down and slain by his enemies? The whole of the passage is missing from Manuscript
A, and the long lacuna in Manuscript B, just before the Zechariah quotation, prevents us
from answering this question with any certainty.

Now those who heed Him are the poor of the flock;[1]
(10) they will be saved at the time of Visitation.
But the others will be delivered up to the sword
when the Anointed (11) of Aaron and Israel comes,
as came to pass at the time of the first Visitation;
as He said (12) by the hand of Ezekiel,
A mark shall be put on the forehead of those who sigh and groan;[2]
(13) but the others were delivered up to the avenging sword, the avenger
[of the Covenant.
And such will be the lot of all who enter (14) His Covenant
but hold not firm to these precepts,
when He visits them for destruction by the hand of Belial.

More punishment of unfaithful sectaries: the Chief of the kings of Yāwān

(15) That will be the day when God will visit; as He said,
The princes of Judah were like those who remove (16) the bound,
I shall pour out Anger upon them like water.[3]
For they entered the Covenant of conversion
(17) but did not depart from the way of traitors;
and they defiled themselves in the ways of lust
and in the riches of iniquity;
(18) and they took revenge and bore malice, each towards his brother,
and each man hated his fellow,
and they refused their help (19) each man to him who is flesh of his flesh,
and they had shameful commerce
and made themselves strong for the sake of riches and gain,
and (20) each man did what was good in his eyes,
and each one chose the stubbornness of his heart,
and they kept not themselves from the people (21) and its sin
but lived in licence deliberately,
walking in the ways of the wicked; of whom (22) God said,
Their wine is the poison of serpents
and the head of asps is cruel.
The serpents are (23) the kings of the peoples
and their wine is their ways:
and the head of asps is the Chief (24) of the kings of Yāwān
who came among them to wreak vengeance.
But all this they did not understand
who build (25) the wall and cover it with whitewash;

---

[1] Cf. Zech. xi. 11. 'The poor of the flock' are the sectaries; God will save them 'at the time of (the final) Visitation', as is declared in the following phrase.

[2] Ezek. ix. 4.

[3] Hos. v. 10; the biblical text is quoted more exactly than in the parallel passage (A, VIII, 3).

for he walks after the wind and raises whirlwinds
and preaches (26) lies to men,[1]
against all of whose congregation the Anger of God was kindled.

God's love for the sectaries of the Covenant and His hatred for the 'builders of the wall'

But as Moses said (27) to Israel,
*Not because of thy righteousness or the uprightness of thy heart
art thou going in to inherit those (28) nations,
but because he loved thy Fathers
and because he has kept the oath,*
so it is (29) with the converts of Israel
(who) have departed from the way of the people.
Because of God's love for the first
(30) who testified against the people in favour of God,
He loves those who have followed after;
for theirs is (31) the Covenant of the Fathers.
But He hates and loathes the builders of the wall,
and His Anger is kindled against them
and against all (32) who follow after them.

Excommunication of unfaithful sectaries

And it is likewise for whoever despises the commandments of God
(33) and abandons them, and turns away in the stubbornness of his heart.
Similarly, none of all those men who have entered the New Covenant
but have turned back and betrayed (it)   [(34) in the land of Damascus[2]
and departed from the Well of living waters,
(35) shall be counted in the Assembly of the people
or inscribed in their register
from the day when **II** (1) the Unique Teacher was taken,
till the coming of the Anointed sprung from Aaron and Israel.[3]

It is likewise also for whoever has entered (2) the Congregation of men of
[perfect holiness
and has become discouraged from practising the precepts of the just;
(3) he is a man who has melted in the midst of the furnace.

[1] Compare this with the parallel passage, A, VIII, 13.
[2] From now on, we are indebted to Manuscript B alone for the text of the Exhortation.
[3] 'The Unique Teacher' is the Teacher of Righteousness, the sect's founder and law-giver. He is dead but will return at the end of time, as A, VI, 10-11, declares. Here there is the question of the coming of the 'Messiah sprung from Aaron and Israel': in my view, there is nothing to contradict the identification of this Messiah with the Teacher of Righteousness himself, reappearing at the end of time. Note that according to Acts ii. 36, it was only after his death that Jesus became 'Lord and Messiah'.

When his works appear, he shall be expelled from the Congregation
(4) as one whose lot has not fallen among the Disciples of God.
According to his unfaithfulness shall the men (5) of Knowledge rebuke
[him
until the day when he returns to take his place among the men of perfect
(6) And when his works appear,   [holiness.
in accordance with the interpretation of the Law in which (7) the men of
[perfect holiness walk,
let no man consort with him in whatever concerns property and labour,
(8) for all the saints of the Most High have cursed him.

And it is likewise for all who despise (the ordinances),
the first (9) or the last,
who have set idols upon their heart
and have gone in the stubbornness (10) of their heart;
(there is) for them no share in the House of the Law.
Like their companions who turned back (11) with the men of mockery,
they will be judged for uttering words of straying against the precepts of
[righteousness,
and for having despised (12) the Covenant and the Pact which they made
in the land of Damascus,
which is the New Covenant;
(13) and there shall be for them and their families
no share in the House of the Law.

The final Visitation

Now from the day when (14) the Unique Teacher was taken,
until the overthrow of all the fighting men
who turned back (15) with the Man of Lies,[1]
(there shall pass) about forty years.
And at that time (16) God's Anger will be kindled against Israel;
as He said,[2] *No king and no prince*,
no judge, nor (17) anyone to rebuke with justice.
But those who are converted from the sin of J[a]c[ob],
who have kept the Covenant of God,
they will then speak one (18) with another
to justify each man his brother

---

[1] Cf. Deut. ii. 14. A reference to the sectaries who deserted and joined the party of the
persecuting High Priest; they will all be destroyed on Judgment Day. One generation will
elapse between the death of the Teacher and the Last Judgment, i.e. in round figures,
forty years. This same time-limit of forty years until the final destruction of the wicked is
indicated in a fragment of the *Commentary on Psalm XXXVII*, published in the *PEQ*,
lxxxvi, 1954, pp. 69-74; see below, pp. 270-1.
[2] Hos. iii. 4.

by supporting their steps in the way of God.
And God will heed (19) their words and will hear,
and a reminder will be written [before Him] of them that fear God
and of them that revere (20) His Name,[1]
until Salvation and Justice are revealed to them that fear [God].
[And] you will distinguish anew between the just (21) and the wicked,
between him that has served God and him that has served Him not.[2]
And He will be merciful to [thousands],
to them that love Him (22) and to them that heed Him,
for a thousand generations.[3]
The House of Peleg (?)[4] are those that went out of the Holy City
(23) and leaned upon God
at the time when Israel was unfaithful
and defiled the Sanctuary,
and were converted to (24) God.
B[ut] in the holy Council the people will be judged with few words,
each one of them according to his spirit.
(25) And all among those who have entered the Covenant
who have breached the bound of the Law,
when the Glory of God appears (26) to Israel
they will be cut off from the midst of the camp,
and with them all those of Judah who have done wickedly
(27) in the days of ⟨their⟩ trials.
But all who have clung to those ordinances,
going (28) and coming in accordance with the Law,
and have heeded the voice of the Teacher,[5]
and have confessed themselves before God (saying),
Truly, (29) we have been wicked, we and our fathers,
by walking against the commands of the Covenant;
justice (30) and truth are Thy judgments towards us;[6]
and who have not raised their hand against His precepts of holiness
and His ordinances (31) of righteousness
and His testimonies of truth,
and who have let themselves be instructed in the first ordinances
by which (32) the men of the Unique (one) were judged,[7]
and who have lent their ear to the voice of the Teacher of Righteousness,

---

[1] The whole passage from 'They will speak then' is inspired by Mal. iii. 16.
[2] Mal. iii. 18.
[3] Exod. xx. 6 and Deut. vii. 9.
[4] The meaning of this expression is uncertain; even the text is unsure.
[5] The Teacher of Righteousness; cf. below, line 32.
[6] Form of confession analogous to that appearing in the *Rule* (I, 24-6).
[7] i.e. the followers of the 'Unique Teacher' (cf. B, I, 1). Some correct this to 'the men (the members) of the Community'. Cf. *Rule*, IX, 10: 'And they shall be governed by the first ordinances in which the members of the Community began their instruction.'

and have not disputed (33) the precepts of righteousness when hearing
they will rejoice and be glad   [them,
and their heart will be strong
and they will bear it away (34) over all the sons of the world.
And God will forgive them,
and they will see His salvation
because they sought refuge in His holy Name.

2. The Ordinances

As I have said, the leaves of Manuscript A found in the Cairo
Geniza contain only a part of the collection of ordinances; the end,
in particular, is missing. Various fragments from cave IV fill some
of the lacunae, but as yet they are still unpublished. Nevertheless,
what we have learned of the Essene code from the Cairo manuscript is extensive enough to provide a firm basis for a few preliminary observations.

It should be noted first of all that this Code is essentially composite: it is a compilation, a digest, a collection of decisions which
may date from different epochs. The case is exactly analogous to
that of the ancient codes of Israel preserved in the Bible — the Code
of the Covenant, the Deuteronomic Code, the Priestly Code. In
each of them modern criticism distinguishes different redactional
layers, additions and corrections. It is the same with the Talmudic
Code, which is an extraordinary conglomeration of decisions and
juridical opinions contributed by various authors at different times.
This collection of Essene ordinances, also, is a veritable and very
complex corpus; I think it would be a grave mistake to overlook this
fundamental fact, and to try to interpret the ordinances as though
they must all reflect exactly the same period and the same situation.

The *Damascus Document* itself draws attention in the Exhortation
(B, II, 31) to 'the first ordinances by which the men of the Unique
(one) were judged'; these seem to be the same ordinances as those
mentioned in the *Rule* (IX, 10) — 'the first ordinances in which the
members of the Community began their instruction'. The mention
of 'first ordinances' presupposes, I think, that the sect must have
possessed 'last ordinances' also. In point of fact, the *Damascus
Document* actually refers in the Exhortation (B, II, 8-9) to the 'first
and last ordinances', an expression found once more in another of
the sect's writings, the *Testament of Judah* (XXIV, 3). Moreover,
fragments of the *Damascus Document* found in cave IV at Qumran

contain, as I have explained, the final section of the Code, which ends with these words: 'the last interpretation of the Law'.[1] A 'last interpretation' postulates a 'first interpretation', older ordinances. The present Code juxtaposes, and in some cases amalgamates, these 'first' and 'last' ordinances, usually without indicating their date or origin. There are successive layers among them; some of the 'first' ordinances may have preserved their primitive redaction, and others have undergone some subsequent modification with a view to adapting them to altered circumstances.

When was the present Code of the *Damascus Document* formed? What connection is there between this Code and the *Rule*? No one will deny the affinities and striking resemblances between the two works; very many expressions, and even entire sentences, are identical. But which of them was written first? Since the *Rule* and the Code are both — though to a varying degree — composite, the answer is not easy, but it seems to me that the *Rule* as a whole is the older of the two. It dates (basically at any rate) from the lifetime of the Teacher of Righteousness himself,[2] whereas in its present form, the Code must have been written at the same time as the Exhortation that precedes it; therefore after the disappearance of the Teacher.[3] From this it follows that the Code must date approximately from the time when the two columns of the *Rule Annexe* were written, the two columns, that is, constituting the first Appendix to the *Rule*.[4]

But I would emphasize that the Code contains a number of 'first ordinances', i.e. archaic rules dating from before the Damascus exile, and even before the redaction of the *Rule* and the ministry of the Teacher. That these ancient ordinances were preserved must have been out of respect for their very antiquity. Some of them may have become practically inapplicable because they no longer corresponded to later circumstances or the later situation; they may also have been thought necessary for enforcement in the future when circumstances would have altered. But the presence of these archaic ordinances in no way authorizes us, I think, to conclude — as some writers have done — that the *Damascus Document* as a whole is older than the *Rule*, or that the Damascus exile preceded that of the settlement at Qumran.[5] Conclusions like these collapse the

---

[1] See above, p. 116.   [2] See above, p. 71.   [3] See above, p. 120.
[4] For the date of this *Rule Annexe*, see p. 71.
[5] G. VERMÈS, *Les manuscrits du désert de Juda*, pp. 53, 66.

moment one recognizes that the Code is a corpus of rules ancient and new.

Some critics have even gone so far as to refuse, despite the close affinities existing between the two works, to attribute the Code of the *Damascus Document* to the same community as that responsible for the *Rule*. Rabin, for example, emphasizes that whereas the *Rule* is addressed to cenobites subject to a strict régime of common owner-ship of property, certain of the Code's ordinances in the *Damascus Document* are aimed at people who are farmers (XII, 10), wage-earners (XIV, 13), owners of property and even of slaves (XI, 12). He concludes from this that the two communities cannot have been exactly the same. The same writer even believes that the two parts of the *Damascus Document* must be considered as 'two entirely different writings'; most of the Code's ordinances show special affinities with Rabbinic laws, and various traits rule out any identification with the Essene world proper.[1]

This, in my view, is to draw from a few correct observations conclusions which are exaggerated. The Code of the *Damascus Document* is, as I have shown,[2] closely bound to the Exhortation: the two parts form one and the same work. Then again, those ordinances which appear to postulate individual ownership of property may belong to an archaic layer dating from before the institution of common ownership. Besides, even where the régime of common property was in force there was still some reason for such ordinances. A régime such as this was only fully obligatory for the fully initiated; neither postulants nor novices were subject to it (second-year novices were partially affected by it) and they may have been relatively numerous. Thus the *Rule* orders the total reimbursement of all damage caused to the 'property of the Community' by a member of the sect (VIII, 6-8): if reimbursement was provided for, it was because the delinquents, some of them anyway, were judged to have the means to perform it. It may also be thought, as Isidore Lévy judiciously observes,[3] that in addition to its cenobites living in monasteries and subject to a strict communism of production and consumption, the Essene sect also included members who were in a way seculars, living 'in the world' and holding merely to the practice of solidarity. We know that an analogous situation existed among the

---

[1] *The Zadokite Documents*, pp. x-xi, *et passim*.
[2] See above, p. 117.
[3] *La légende de Pythagore de Grèce en Palestine*, p. 274.

followers of Pythagoras who were divided into cenobites and simple hearers, into 'Pythagoreans' who practised common ownership of property and lived in perpetual community, and 'Pythagorists' who followed a régime of private ownership. Therefore, although some of the *Damascus Document* ordinances postulate private ownership of property, this in no way excludes Essene responsibility for the collection as a whole, if this Essene origin is otherwise solidly established.

Against this, as I have said, Rabin raises the objection that the ordinances resemble Rabbinic laws. But, in fact, the differences are more apparent than the similarities. The Code is generally more severe, and a number of its rules are concerned with a particular way of life and with sectarian preoccupations without equivalent in Pharisaic jurisprudence. If similarities do exist, they can be explained quite easily without it being necessary to renounce the Essene hypothesis: the Essene sect and the sect of the Pharisees may share some distant common origin, or one of them may quite simply — either generally, or on some particular point — have influenced the other to a greater or lesser extent. The Essene character of the ordinances is in my opinion unquestionable; the links between the Code of the *Damascus Document* and the Qumran document as a whole are too close to allow for any other source of origin.

It is true that before the Qumran discoveries very few critics thought that the *Damascus Document* could be an Essene work; instead, some excellent specialists worked hard to connect these ordinances with either Rabbinic or Karaite legislation. Such research was not without interest or purpose, but it by-passed the essential fact that the Code is actually Essene, and neither Pharisaic nor Karaite. This curious aberration may be explained, partially at least, by a sort of 'Essenophobia' with which most historians of Judaism and primitive Christianity were for a long time affected. However, as early as 1912, an author as erudite and discerning as Israel Lévi did not fail explicitly to connect the sect of the *Damascus Document* with the Essenes, particularly with regard to the functions of the 'overseer'. He even wrote the following, at that time singularly prophetic, words: 'The whole question of the origins of Essenism must be revived and reconsidered in the light of the document studied by us here (the *Damascus Document*). Another reconsideration is equally necessary, that of the origin of the first Christian communities. . . . '[1] To this, Fr. Lagrange immediately replied, with evident ill-humour: 'We were not to be spared from meeting the inevitable Essenes in this affair.'[2] And in a few sentences he dispatched the Essene hypothesis which Israel Lévi had with such remarkable perspicacity just suggested. Now that the various Qumran scrolls bring us greater understanding of the *Damascus Document*, once so enigmatic, nothing of this condemnation remains, but it is only right to pay homage to the scholar who guessed the truth from the beginning.[3]

In fact the existence of a code of Essene ordinances is quite normal and exactly what might have been expected. Philo had already informed us that the Essenes 'work at ethics with extreme care, constantly utilizing the ancestral laws, laws which no human mind could have conceived without divine inspiration'.[4] Fundamentally, these divinely revealed 'ancestral laws' are the Law, the Mosaic Law, but they are also ordinances which the Essenes derived from the Law, and which constituted their own legal code. Their exegesis of the Law in the Code of the *Damascus Document* appears to us excessively subtle, distorted and twisted, but in their eyes it was inspired and prophetic. Their code was guaranteed by divine revelation and represented 'the exact tenor of the Law',[5] 'all that is revealed of it';[6] even their religious calendar was thought to have been revealed by God.[7]

To obtain these divine revelations it was necessary to 'seek'

---

[1] *REJ*, lxiii, 1912, p. 10. I would recall the following lines written by the eminent historian (art. cit., p. 9): 'Another comparison appears to be even more indispensable, chiefly in connection with the functions of Mebaker, between our sect and the Essenes. Among these, executive power was also vested in a principal to whom Josephus gives the name of *epimeletes*, a term which adapts itself perfectly to that of Mebaker. . . . But resemblances do not end here: there is the same abundance of precautions for the admission of proselytes, the same oath imposed on neophytes to honour and serve God with all their heart and to reveal nothing of the affairs of the sect, the same punishment of the guilty — expulsion from the community. Their common horror of sensual pleasure should also be noted, and their equal contempt of riches. But what is even more striking is the same rigorousness in the observance of the Sabbath. What Josephus explicitly says of the Essenes, namely, that in this respect they are more severe than the other Israelites, and that they do not even dare to move an object from its place on the Sabbath day, is equally true of the Damascus sect. Finally, to cap everything, the priest plays a religious role among the Essenes also.'

[2] *RB*, 1912, p. 344.

[3] Isidore Lévy must share in this homage. In 1927, in his *Légende de Pythagore* . . . (pp. 290-1) he showed that on a number of points the sectaries of Damascus 'recall the Essenes'. I would add that Isidore Lévy — I have it from his own mouth — had, from 1912, helped and advised his teacher and friend Israel Lévi (cf. *REJ*, lxiii, p. 7, n. 1, p. 9, n. 2) and had come to the same conclusion regarding the Essenes.

[4] *Q.o.p.l.*, § 80.   [5] *Damascus Document*, IV, 8; XIII, 6.

[6] *Rule*, V, 9; VIII, 1; *Damascus Document*, XV, 13.   [7] *Rule*, I, 9.

(*darash*), that is to say, to study — this word being understood in a highly religious and mystical sense. The way of God which the Essenes were to 'prepare in the desert' was, as they explain, 'the study (*midrash*) of the Law which He promulgated by the hand of Moses, that they may act according to all that is revealed, season by season, and according to that which the prophets have revealed by His Holy Spirit'.[1] The fruit of this study were the ordinances themselves, which they call 'the *midrash* of the Law'[2] and which, concretely, is an interpretation or commentary on the Law.

But although by studying the Law every Essene enjoyed divine revelations, the 'Seeker of the Law' *par excellence* was the Teacher of Righteousness; in the *Damascus Document* (VI, 7; VII, 18), it will be remembered, this title is given to him twice. The Teacher sought better than any other, and also found better than any other. The sect observed with extreme care the ordinances derived from the Law which the Teacher promulgated. In the eyes of his followers, he was the Lawgiver,[3] the new Moses; outside his precepts there was no salvation. While waiting for his glorious return, they must unceasingly listen to his voice and walk in his commandments.[4] The corpus of Essene ordinances certainly includes rules for which he was not directly responsible; there are some, in particular, which doubtless antedate him, those referred to in the texts as 'the first ordinances'. But the Teacher extends his supreme authority over them all; they are, as appears in many passages, 'precepts of holiness', 'ordinances of righteousness', 'testimonies of truth'. The collection of the sect's ordinances was thus endowed with an extraordinary prestige, like the Mosaic Law itself. Whoever wished to do the will of God had to submit strictly not only to the Law, but also to the revealed code which was, as it were, the development and fulfilment of the Law in which all God's wishes were infallibly recorded.

Now follows the translation of the Essene code as transmitted to us in Manuscript A from Cairo (pages IX-XVI). The reader may be surprised and even discouraged by its meticulous aridity; but the style of canon law cannot be the same as that of the Sermon on the Mount or of the Gospel parables. Such as it is, this collection gives precious information concerning many details of Essene life, and

---

[1] *Rule*, VIII, 15-16.
[2] *Damascus Document*, B, II, 6; inedited fragments of the *Damascus Document* also speak, as I have said, of 'the last interpretation (*midrash*) of the Law'.
[3] *Damascus Document*, VI, 7-9.
[4] *Damascus Document*, B, II, 28, 32; A, VI, 10-11.

shows above all the extreme fervour of a sect wholly dedicated to the cult of the divine Law. The Teacher of Righteousness could have said, like Jesus the Nazarene: 'Think not that I am come to abolish the Law and the prophets; I am not come to abolish but to fulfil. Truly, I say to you: until heaven and earth pass away, not one iota, not one dot, will pass from the Law until all is accomplished. Whoever violates one of these commandments shall be called small in the kingdom of Heaven; but whoever does them and teaches them shall be called great in the kingdom of Heaven' (Matt. v. 17-19).

TRANSLATION

Concerning capital punishment

IX (1) In all cases when anathema is pronounced against a man, it is by the orders of the Gentiles that this man shall be put to death.[1]

Concerning vengeance and reproof

(2) And concerning that which He said, *Thou shalt take no revenge and shalt bear no malice against the sons of thy people*,[2] any man from among the members (3) of the Covenant who brings an action against his fellow without having reproved him before witnesses, (4) or brings this action in the heat of anger, or tells (the matter) to his elders to dishonour him, is a man who takes revenge and bears malice; (5) whereas it is written (that) only *he (God) takes vengeance on his adversaries and bears malice against his enemies*.[3]

---

[1] This ordinance was no doubt preceded by a certain number of others; it would be surprising if the collection started like this, *ex abrupto*, with no title. In the present Manuscript A, the beginning of the Code may have figured on one or several vanished leaves. However this may be, the first phrase is difficult to interpret, and the explanation I suggest is inspired by that of C. RABIN (*The Zadokite Documents*, p. 44). The text should be compared with the law of Lev. xxvii. 29: 'No man vowed by anathema shall be redeemed; he shall be put to death.' The present ordinance specifies that when the Jewish tribunal has pronounced sentence of death, it is not for Jews to execute it, but Gentiles. This only makes sense if Palestine was at that time under foreign domination (under Roman rule, in fact). We may recall in this context the words spoken by the Jews to Pilate at the trial of Jesus: 'It is not lawful for us to put any man to death' (John xviii. 31).

[2] Lev. xix. 18. The present ordinance concerns the application of this Mosaic law in legal matters. Anyone who brings an action against his fellow without having reproved him before witnesses, or without having overcome his anger, or who slanders him before 'his elders', revenges himself and bears malice and consequently sins against the Law. The Penal Code of the *Rule* (VII, 8) imposes a penalty of six months' punishment for the bearing of malice and the taking of revenge.

[3] Nahum i. 2. The word 'He' at the beginning of the quotation replaces 'Yahweh' in the Masoretic Text; the same substitution appears in *Rule*, VIII, 13. The Nahum text is

(6) If he has kept silence towards his fellow from one day to another (without reproving him), or has spoken against him in the heat of his anger, it is in an action liable to (punishment by) death (7) that he will have witnessed against himself, since he has not fulfilled the commandment of God which has said to him, *Thou shalt* (8) *rebuke thy neighbour and thou shalt not bear a sin because of him.*[1]

Concerning the judicial oath

Concerning the oath.

As for that which (9) He said, *Thou shalt not mete out justice with thine own hand,*[2] the man who causes another to swear in the country, (10) and not in the presence of the judges or on their order, will have meted out justice by his own hand.

And any object that is lost (11) without it being known who stole it from among the ⟨people⟩ of the camp from which it was stolen, its owner

---

[1] Lev. xix. 17. The biblical text is interpreted to mean that a man, on pain of sin, must reprove his fellow on the day itself, and not denounce him under the stress of anger; to behave otherwise is to violate a commandment of God and to render himself liable to the death penalty. Cf. *Rule*, V, 26-VI, 1: 'He shall be reproved on the very same day. And thus a man shall not bear a fault because of him'; *Damascus Document*, VII, 2-3: 'to reprove each man his brother according to the commandment, and to bear no malice from one day to another'. Compare this with St. Paul's precept (Eph. iv. 26): 'Let not the sun go down upon your wrath!' The gravity of speaking in anger recalls Matt. v. 32: 'Whoever is angry with his brother will be liable to condemnation. Whoever says to his brother 'Raka' will be subject to the jurisdiction of the Sanhedrin. Whoever says to him 'Fool' will be liable to the Gehenna of fire'.

[2] Cf. 1 Sam. xxv. 26; the *Rule* (VI, 27) also alludes to this same biblical verse. It is applied here to the judicial oath which must only be sworn 'in the presence of the judges or on their order'. Only judges could demand such an oath, and for a man himself to require one from an adversary was tantamount to dispensing justice himself and he would thereby incur guilt. The present passage, as we see, is concerned to limit swearing of oaths; another passage further on carefully fixes the form (XV, 1-5). According to JOSEPHUS, the Essenes had to abstain from swearing (*War*, II, § 135), but this rule allowed for some exceptions; the historian himself describes the oath of entry into the sect (ibid. §§ 139-42). The *Damascus Document* deals specially with this oath later (XV, 5-XVI, 12), as well as with the oath by which a man swore to observe the Law. As for the judicial oath, it would have been very difficult even for an Essene tribunal to do without it. But the casuistry of the oath in the Essene sect may have evolved more and more towards a total interdiction; compare this with Matt. v. 33-7 and Jas. vi. 12.

---

interpreted to mean that the sectaries must leave vengeance to God alone; they must not take revenge themselves. Cf. *Rule*, X, 17-18: 'To no man will I render the reward of evil, with goodness will I pursue each one. For judgment of all the living is with God and He will pay to each man his reward.' The obligation to reprove a brother before denouncing him to the tribunal appears already in the *Rule* (VI, 1). It may also be read in Matt. xviii. 15-17: 'If your brother has sinned against you, go and find him and reprove him between you and him alone; if he listen, you will have gained your brother; if he does not listen to you, take with you one or two others that the whole affair may be ordered according to the opinion of two or three witnesses. If he does not listen to them, tell it to the Church. And if he refuses to listen to the Church, let him be for you like a heathen and a publican.'

shall be made to swear (**12**) by the oath of malediction, and whoever hears shall be guilty if he knows the thief and does not denounce him.[1]

(**13**) If there is no owner of any object obtained unlawfully which a man wishes to return, whoever returns it shall ⟨confess⟩ to the priest, (**14**) and all of it shall belong to him independently of the ram of sacrifice offered for the offence.[2]

And likewise, any lost object that is found again and has no (**15**) owner shall belong to the priests when the man who has found the object does not know to whom it lawfully belongs; (**16**) if its owner has not (yet) been found, the priests shall be its keepers.[3]

Concerning witnesses[4]

For every infringement which a man commits (**17**) against the Law, and which his fellow has seen, being alone, if it is a matter liable to the death (penalty), reproving him, the witness shall denounce the culprit (**18**) to the overseer in his presence; and the overseer shall inscribe him with his own hand, waiting until he commits (**19**) another (infringement) before one person alone, and he again denounces him to the overseer. If he relapses and is caught in the act (a third time) before (**20**) one person alone, his case is juridically complete.

And if the witnesses are two, but (each) testifies to (**21**) a different deed, the culprit shall be separated from Purification only on condition that they are trustworthy (**22**) and that they denounce the thing to the overseer the very day on which they see the culprit.

---

[1] An application of Lev. v. 1 to the case of an object stolen in the camp. The 'camp' in the Code and in the Exhortation (cf. VII, 6; B, I, 2) was the sort of *laura* where the Essenes lived in community in the desert. For the 'oath of malediction' see Num. v. 21.

[2] An ordinance derived from Num. v. 8: the Mosaic law provides for an offended owner who has died without leaving an heir, but here this law is extended to cover every occasion where the owner is unknown.

[3] This ordinance extends the preceding one concerning stolen objects to cover anything found whose owner is unknown; the priests are to take it for themselves. However, as long as the owner is being sought, they are only to look after it, and must return it as soon as he is discovered.

[4] The following ordinances concerning the number of witnesses necessary for judgment are based on these two passages from Deuteronomy: 'A man shall be put to death only on the evidence of two or three witnesses; he shall not be put to death on the evidence of one witness alone' (xvii. 6). 'The evidence of a single witness shall not be held against an accused, for no matter what crime or misdemeanour; a fact can only be established on the evidence of two or three witnesses' (xix. 15). On the basis of these biblical texts, the Essene code appears to lay down that if in the case of some capital charge the offence has been seen by only one witness, two more witnesses are needed, each of them denouncing the culprit for a new offence: three witnesses in all, therefore. If there are altogether only two witnesses, each denouncing him for a different action, the death penalty cannot be pronounced, but only the punishment of 'separation', i.e. exclusion (compare the expression 'separated from Purification' in *Rule* VI, 25; VII, 3). In matters of property, i.e. civil suits, it is specified that two witnesses are also required for the pronouncement of punishment by 'separation'. The interpretation of the whole of passage IX, 16-23, remains a little uncertain.

And if it concerns property, let two (**23**) trustworthy witnesses be accepted and ⟨not⟩ one alone, to separate ⟨from⟩ Purification.

And let no witness be accepted **X** (**1**) by the judges for condemnation to death on his evidence unless he has reached the age required to pass before (**2**) the census as Godfearing.[1]

Let no man be judged trustworthy (**3**) as a witness against his fellow if he has transgressed any commandment deliberately, unless he has been purified by repentance.

Concerning judges

(**4**) And this is the rule concerning the judges of the Congregation.[2]

(Let them be) to the number of ten men, periodically chosen (**5**) by the Congregation: four for the tribe of Levi and Aaron, and for Israel (**6**) six. They must be learned in the Book of Meditation and in the constitutions of the Covenant, and aged from twenty-five (**7**) to sixty years old.[3]

And let no man be in office from (**8**) sixty years and over as judge of the Congregation; for because of the unfaithfulness of men (**9**) their days are diminished, and in the heat of His anger against the inhabitants of the earth God has ordained that (**10**) their understanding should decline before their days are fulfilled.

Concerning purification by water

Let no man (**11**) bathe in dirty water or in a quantity too little to cover a man completely.[4]

(**12**) Let no man purify a vessel with this water.

And any pool in a rock in which there is not enough water (**13**) to cover ⟨a man⟩ completely, if an unclean person has touched it he defiles the water of the pool ⟨as⟩ he would defile the water in a vessel.

---

[1] i.e. twenty years old; cf. *Rule Annexe*, I, 8-9.

[2] The function of these 'judges' is not entirely clear. Besides the dispensation of justice, they were no doubt invested with other important offices in the Congregation; according to XIV, 13, it was they who, with the 'overseer', held and administered the funds destined for charity. Is this college of 'judges' the same institution as the College of Fifteen mentioned in *Rule*, VIII, 1-4? If so, the institution must have developed, for in the *Rule* it consists, I think, of fifteen members, three priests and twelve laymen, and in the *Damascus Document*, of ten members — four priests (or Levites) and six laymen. But it is more likely that two different institutions are involved.

[3] According to the *Rule Annexe* (I, 12-16), although the Essene could take his place 'among the foundations of the Congregation', he could not accede to the rank of leader, judge, or administrator until he was thirty. It is not indicated in this document when these offices had to be relinquished; it is only said (I, 19) that 'when a person is old' he must be given a job commensurate with his strength. In the present passage retirement age is given as sixty; note that in Lev. xxvii. 7, this is the age at which a man's value diminishes. The considerations which follow, justifying the retirement of judges (lines 7-10), recall very closely *Jubilees*, XXIII, 1.

[4] A reference to the ritual baths or baptisms in favour among the Essenes.

Concerning the Sabbath[1]

(**14**) Concerning the Sabbath, that it may be observed according to the ordinance regarding it.

Let no work be done (**15**) on the sixth day from the moment the sun's disc (**16**) is removed in its fullness from the gate where it goes down; for He has said, *Observe* (**17**) *the Sabbath day to sanctify it.*[2]

And on the Sabbath day let no (**18**) foolish or vain word be spoken.

Let a man lend nothing to his fellow.

Let there be no discussion on matters of riches or gain.

(**19**) Let there be no talk of work or of labour to be done on the morrow.

(**20**) Let no man walk in the country to carry out his task on (**21**) the Sabbath ⟨day⟩.[3]

Let no man walk further than a thousand cubits outside his town.[4]

(**22**) Let only that be eaten on the Sabbath day which has been prepared (on the previous day).[5]

And whatever is lost (**23**) in the fields, ⟨   ⟩ let it not be eaten.

And let no man drink if he is not in the camp. XI (**1**) ⟨But if a man is⟩ travelling and goes down to bathe, he may drink there where he is; but let no (water) be drawn up (to be poured) into (**2**) any vessel.[6]

Let no man require a stranger to do his task on the Sabbath day.

(**3**) Let no man put on himself soiled garments (that have been) sent back to the store unless (**4**) they have been washed in water or rubbed with incense.

Let no man ⟨fast⟩ voluntarily on (**5**) the Sabbath.[7]

[1] This long series of ordinances relative to the Sabbath is on the whole distinguished by a severity greater than the Rabbinic laws on the same subject. This agrees with JOSEPHUS's observation (*War*, II, § 147): 'They (the Essenes) are also forbidden, more rigorously than any Jew, to attend to their work on the seventh day. . . .'

[2] Deut. v. 12. The word 'observe' is taken in the sense of 'to watch' for the exact moment when the Sabbath rest begins; that is to say, when the sun touches the horizon at the end of the sixth day.

[3] The meaning of this is not quite clear; although walking was permitted (within the limits of the following ordinance), it must have nothing to do with one's work.

[4] The law against travelling on the Sabbath derives from Exod. xvi. 29 ('Let each man remain where he is, let no man go out of his place on the seventh day'); the distance of one thousand cubits comes from Num. xxxv. 4. Rabbinic law authorizes a walk of two thousand instead of one thousand cubits, in accordance with Num. xxxv. 5. This is the figure given in XI, 5-6 in this collection, for the distance over which it was permitted to graze the flocks. For the walk, therefore, the Essene code is more severe than Rabbinic law.

[5] This Essene rule is formally attested by JOSEPHUS (*War*, II § 147): 'They prepare their food the day before to avoid lighting a fire on that day (the Sabbath).' The same law is found in *Jubilees* (II, 29; L, 9).

[6] Compare *Jubilees*, L, 8: 'And whoever draws water on that day without having prepared it for himself on the sixth day . . . shall die.' This Essene ordinance also forbids the drawing of water on the Sabbath; the sectaries could therefore drink only in the camp, where the water had been prepared the day before. But they could drink outside the camp if they were bathing in a cistern or a stream and were not obliged to draw up water.

[7] The same rule against fasting on the Sabbath appears in *Jubilees*, L, 12; cf. also L, 10: '. . . they must eat and drink and enjoy themselves on this feast day. . . .'

Let him not go after the herd to pasture it outside the town (6) except to two thousand cubits.[1]

Let no man raise his hand to strike it with his fist; if it (7) is stubborn, let it not be made to go out of its house.

Let nothing be carried from the house (8) to the outside, or from outside to the house. Even if a man is in a hut, let nothing be taken out of it (9) and nothing be taken in.[2]

Let no sealed vessel be opened on the Sabbath.

Let no man wear (10) perfumes upon himself when going and coming on the Sabbath.

Let there be lifted in the dwelling-place no (11) stone nor dust.

Let no foster-father carry his foster-child when going and coming on the Sabbath.

(12) Let no man irritate his slave or maidservant or employee on the Sabbath.

(13) Let no beast be helped to give birth on the Sabbath day; and if it fall into a cistern (14) or into a pit, let it not be lifted out on the Sabbath.[3]

Let not the Sabbath be celebrated in the vicinity (15) of Gentiles on the Sabbath (day).[4]

Let not the Sabbath be profaned for matters of riches and gain on the Sabbath (day). (16) But every human being who falls into a place full of water, or into a place (17) ⟨from which he cannot climb out⟩, let ⟨him be made to climb out⟩ with the help of a ladder or a rope or some other object.[5]

Let nothing be offered on the altar on the Sabbath (18) except the Sabbath burnt offering; for it is written, *Besides your Sabbaths*.[6]

Various regulations

Let there be sent (19) to the altar of holocaust neither offering nor incense nor wood by the hand of a man defiled by any (20) defilement whatsoever, permitting him thus to render the altar unclean; for it is

---

[1] Cf. above, p. 152, n. 4.

[2] Compare *Jubilees*, L, 8: 'And whoever lifts a burden to carry it out of his tent or out of his house . . . shall die.'

[3] In Matt. xii. 11, Jesus appears more liberal: 'If one of you has a sheep and it falls on the Sabbath day into a pit, will he not seize it to take it out?'

[4] All contact with heathens must be avoided on that day.

[5] The text is partly corrupt. As it stands, it should be translated: 'But every human being who falls into a place full of water, or into a place [*sic*], let him not be made to climb out. . . .' I have adopted the correction proposed by GINZBERG and RABIN. It obviously mitigates the inhumanity of the ordinance and renders it more probable, but it is only a conjecture.

[6] Lev. xxiii. 38; but the biblical text is given an entirely forced meaning. This ordinance no doubt refers to the time when the sect had not yet cut itself off from Temple service.

written, *The sacrifice* (**21**) *of the wicked is an abomination, but the prayer of the just is like a delectable offering.*[1]

And whoever enters (**22**) the House of Prostration,[2] let him not enter in a state of uncleanness; let him wash himself.

And when the trumpets of Assembly sound, (**23**) whether it is early or late all work shall not cease; it [is not a] **XII** (**1**) holy time.[3]

Let no man lie with a woman in the city of the Sanctuary for fear of defiling (**2**) the city of the Sanctuary with their defilement.[4]

Every man who is governed by the spirits of Belial (**3**) and utters words of rebellion shall be judged according to the ordinance concerning the spirits of the dead and spectres.[5]

And whoever strays (**4**) by profaning the Sabbath or the feasts, he shall not be put to death but it shall be incumbent on men (**5**) to watch him; and if he is cured of this sin, he shall be watched for a period of seven years, and afterwards he (**6**) shall enter the Assembly (once more).[6]

Let no man stretch out his hand to shed the blood of any Gentile (**7**) for

---

[1] Prov. xv. 8. This biblical quotation seems here to mean that rather than send defiled offerings to the Temple — which would happen if they were brought by any unclean person — it is better merely to pray to God. This prayer would take the place of sacrifice, as is stated in the *Rule* (IX, 4-5). Note that only a member of the sect could be pure, and consequently serve as an emissary. JOSEPHUS specifies (in *Antiquities*, XVIII, § 19) that although the Essenes do not offer sacrifice in the Temple 'they send offerings there'; the present ordinance alludes to just this sending of offerings to the Temple.

[2] Probably the Temple.

[3] For the 'trumpets of Assembly', i.e. trumpets serving to convoke the Assembly, see Num. x. 2-7. The meaning of this ordinance is unclear because of the lacuna from the end of line 23, but if my conjecture is right it refers to the announcement of feasts and Sabbaths by the Temple trumpets. If this announcement does not conform to the authentic calendar, the sect's calendar — this is what is meant, I think, by 'whether it is early or late' (compare *Rule*, I, 14) — there is no reason to stop all work, i.e. to observe the ritual rest, because it is not a genuine feast day. The Essenes were not to regulate their liturgical life by the calendar of the official Synagogue but by their own.

[4] The city of the Sanctuary is Jerusalem. According to Lev. xv. 18, a man and a woman who have had intercourse must wash themselves, and are in a state of impurity until the evening. The present ordinance forbids all sexual relations in Jerusalem in order not to defile the Holy City. Observe that according to *Jubilees* (L, 8) it is similarly forbidden to have intercourse on the Sabbath in order not to defile the holy day.

[5] This refers, after Deut. xiii. 6, to the man who preaches rebellion against God and the Law; he is considered as being possessed by the spirits of Belial, i.e. by evil spirits, and is to be treated as one possessed by the spirit of a dead man or a ghost, and stoned to death in conformity with the law of Lev. xx. 27.

[6] The fault envisaged here cannot, in my view, be the violation pure and simple of the Sabbath or the feasts; the penalty for such a sin could only be death. It refers rather to the celebration of Sabbaths and feasts *on dates not conforming to the sect's calendar*. Cf. *Jubilees*, VI, 37: 'They will make of the day of testimony an abominable day, and of a feast day an ungodly day, and they will confuse all the days, the holy with the impure and the impure with the holy; for they will err in what concerns the months and the Sabbaths and the feasts and the jubilees.' This kind of offence, involving dates, is obviously less grave than pure and simple violation. But so anxious was the sect to ensure respect for its religious calendar that it was punished very severely all the same, with at least seven years' exclusion before readmittance into the Community. I would emphasize that there is no question here of a sin committed against the Law 'through inadvertence'; this is provided for in the *Rule* (VIII, 24-IX, 2), and is punished with two years' exclusion.

the sake of riches and gain. And let him also take none of their possessions, that they may (8) not blaspheme, unless it is the order of the Council of the Association of Israel.

Let no man sell clean beasts (9) or birds to the Gentiles, that they may not sacrifice them.

And the contents of his granary (10) or his vat; let a man refuse with all his strength to sell them anything from them.

And concerning his slave and his maidservant; let no man sell them to them (11) because they have entered with him into the Covenant of Abraham.[1]

Let no man defile himself (12) with any animal or creeping creature by eating them, from the larvae of bees to all (13) living creatures which creep in water.[2]

And as for fish, let them not be eaten unless they have been split (14) alive and their blood spilt.

And as for all the locusts in their various species, let them be put into fire or water (15) alive; for such is the ordinance according to their nature.[3]

And as for all wood, stones, and (16) dust defiled by man's uncleanness from defilement by oil,[4] like them, according (17) to their uncleanness, shall every man be who touches them.

And every object, nail, or peg (fixed) in the wall, (18) which are with a dead man in a house, shall be defiled with the defilement of any other working tool.[5]

(19) Rule concerning the constitution of the towns of Israel.[6]

It is according to these ordinances that they shall distinguish between

---

[1] Slaves of foreign origin were obliged by the Law to be circumcised; from then on, like Jewish slaves, they could not be sold to Gentiles.

[2] Honey and liquids had to be filtered.

[3] It was forbidden to eat locusts found dead; they must be cooked alive or drowned.

[4] With ROST, I read the Hebrew word ŠMN, and not ŠMW. According to this interpretation, allusion is made here to uncleanness caused by defilement by oil; a man thus defiled communicates his uncleanness to objects which, in their turn, communicate it again to whoever touches them. This curious oil taboo is observed among the Essenes by JOSEPHUS (*War*, II, § 123): 'They regard oil as a defilement, and should any of them be involuntarily anointed, he wipes his body clean.'

[5] On uncleanness caused by contact with the dead, or by the presence of a dead man in a house, see Num. xix. 11-12. The jurists considerably extend the contamination resulting from this; according to this ordinance it even affects the nails and pegs fixed into the house walls as well as the utensils found there, especially working tools (cf. Lev. xi. 32).

[6] This is the title of a section, and is parallel to the title appearing a little further on (lines 22-3): 'And this is the rule relating to the constitution of the camps.' Why is there mention in one place of the 'towns of Israel' and, in another, of the 'camps'? The reason for this is that there are probably two sets of rules, one for the 'towns' and the other for the 'camps'; cf. PHILO, *Apologia pro Judaeis*, § 1: 'They (the Essenes) live in a number of towns in Judaea, and also in many villages and large groups.' But although the title announcing rules for the constitution of the camps is in fact followed by such ordinances (XII, 23-XIII, 19), the present title is followed by none at all. The copyist seems to have eliminated a whole passage, as happened also in the Exhortation (IV, 6).

(**20**) the clean and the unclean, and shall make known (the distinction) between the sacred and the profane.[1]

And these are the precepts (**21**) for the man of understanding, that he may walk in them in the company of all the living according to the law proper to each time; and it is according to this law that (**22**) the race of Israel shall walk that it may not be cursed.[2]

Concerning the organization of the camps

And this is the rule concerning the constitution (**23**) of the camps.

(Let) those who walk in these (ordinances) during the time of ungodliness until the coming of the Anointed of Aaron **XIII** (**1**) and Israel,[3] (be) in groups of at least ten men, by Thousands and Hundreds and Fifties (**2**) and Tens.[4]

And where there are ten of them, let there not lack a man who is a priest learned in the Book of Meditation; (**3**) they shall all obey his orders.[5]

And if he is not expert in all these matters, but a man from among the Levites is expert (**4**) in them, fate will have wished that all the members of the camp go and come under the orders of this Levite.[6]

But if (**5**) there appear in anyone a case which comes under the law of leprosy, the priest shall come and stay in the camp, and the overseer shall instruct the priest (**6**) in the exact tenor of the Law. Even if the priest be simple, it is he who shall cause the sick man to be enclosed, for to them belongs (**7**) the judgment.[7]

---

[1] This phrase seems to be either the beginning or the end of a section, which has also disappeared, relating to a series of rules concerning purity and impurity.

[2] Another title announcing a series of ordinances which appear to have been omitted by the copyist. The first sentence reproduces, almost word for word, *Rule*, IX, 12, but there the title is followed by a series of maxims.

[3] Compare VI, 10: 'until the coming of the Teacher of Righteousness at the end of days'.

[4] The same divisions as in the *Rule* (II, 21-2), the *Rule Annexe* (I, 14-15), and the *War Scroll* (IV, 1-4).

[5] The same basic group of ten persons in charge of a priest as in the *Rule* (VI, 3-5); cf. *Rule Annexe*, II, 22.

[6] This eventual replacement of a priest by a Levite as leader of the group of ten is not mentioned in the *Rule*; perhaps this arrangement only became necessary after the composition of the latter work, when it had become difficult to find among the priests leaders suitable for all the groups of ten because their number had diminished during the exile in Damascus.

[7] Cf. Hos. v. 1: 'for the judgment pertains to you' (the priests); also, according to Deut. xxi. 5, it is for the 'priests the sons of Levi' to decide 'in every dispute and every scourge'. The present ordinance seems to rely on these two passages to establish that even when the group is commanded by a Levite it is still the priest who must apply the law relating to leprosy, and in particular to pronounce the order confining the sick man (Lev. xiii.) The Hebrew text reads literally 'the law of the scourge' — the Hebrew word 'scourge' serving usually to designate leprosy. In such an event, a priest ill-instructed in the Law and even unintelligent (since it is for these reasons that he has not been able to take over the leader-

And this is the law concerning the overseer of the camp.[1]

He shall instruct the Many in the works (8) of God
and shall teach them His marvellous deeds
and shall recount before them the happenings of former times. . . .[2]
(9) And he shall have pity on them as a father of his children
and shall carry them in all their despondency as a shepherd his flock.[3]
(10) He shall unloose all the bonds which bind them[4]
that there may no more be any oppressed or broken among his congrega-
[tion.

(11) And whoever joins his congregation, he shall examine him on his
deeds and strength and power and possessions, (12) and he shall be
inscribed in his place according to whatever he is in the lot of Tr[uth].[5]
Let no (13) member of the camp arrogate to himself the right to introduce
any man into the Congregation [agai]nst the decision of the overseer of
the camp.

---

[1] There is also the question of the 'overseer' — the title given to the leaders of the
Congregation — in the *Rule* (VI, 12, 14, 20). Judging from their prerogatives, they seem
to have been priests (or at least Levites, when there were no suitable priests available);
cf. *Rule*, IX, 7: 'The sons of Aaron alone shall command in matters of justice and property,
and under their authority fate shall be decreed in every decision concerning the members
of the Community.' The present passage from the *Damascus Document* first defines the
functions of the overseer as those of a teacher and shepherd, and then as the person concerned with the admission of new members and as being responsible for the various
commercial transactions.

[2] The Hebrew text adds the word BPRTYH. This word is considered corrupt by all the
critics, who suggest various alternatives. It has, however, one meaning, namely 'in
Parthia' (i.e. in the land of the Parthians), and if this is preserved, the phrase reads: 'and
he shall recount before them the events that came to pass in Parthia'. Bearing in mind the
role played by the Parthians in the first century B.C. (the same century as that in which
the *Damascus Document* was written), in general political and religious history as well as in
Jewish history, the reading of the manuscript should not, I think, be rejected so easily. It
may in fact refer to some event or deed in the history of the Parthians which occurred in
some region of the Parthian empire and was of special interest to the sect; (remember, for
example, the story of Tobit). In any case, the generally obvious influence of the Persian
world on the doctrines of the sect, and no doubt also on its rites, invites us, I think, to pay
at least some attention to this mention of 'Parthia' attested by Manuscript A of the
Damascus Document.

[3] Cf. Isa. xl. 11 and Ezek. xxxiv. 12. As RABIN points out, in this passage the verb BQR
(from which the word *mebaqqer*, 'overseer', derives) is repeated several times.

[4] Cf. Isa. lviii. 6. This seems to be a reference to spiritual bonds, the bonds of sin; the
overseer has the power to 'unloose' these chains in order that all the members of his
congregation, oppressed by Belial and weighed down by the consciousness of their sin, may
know liberty and spiritual joy. Cf. Matt. xvi. 19; xviii. 18.

[5] On this examination of the postulant by the overseer, see also the *Rule* (VI, 13-15).

---

ship of a group) must receive from the 'overseer', i.e. probably from the Levite replacing
him as leader, the necessary teaching so as to carry out correctly all the rather complex
legal procedure. The reader will notice in this passage a concern both to safeguard the
privileges of the priesthood and to further the strict application of the Law.

(**14**) And let no member of the Covenant of God have any dealings with the sons of the Pit except (**15**) (by paying) from hand to hand.[1]

And let no association be formed for buying or selling without making it known (**16**) to the overseer who is in the camp, and without acting loyally.[2]

And [. . .] (**17**) [. . .]

And let it be likewise for whoever is expelled; and let him [. . .] (**18**) [. . .] let them answer him, that with loving charity he may bear them no malice [. . .] (**19**) [. . .] and whoever is not bound by [. . .][3]

(**20**) And this is ⟨the rule⟩ concerning the constitution of the camps for all [the time of ungodliness; and those who] (**21**) [do not persevere in the]se (ordinances) shall not be fit to dwell in the land [when the Messiah of Aaron and Israel comes] (**22**) [at the end of days.][4]

[And these] are the [ordinance]s for the man of understanding, [that he may walk in them in the company of all the living until] (**23**) [God visits the earth; as He has said, *Days will come upon thee and upon thy people and upon the house of thy father*] **XIV** (**1**) *such as have not come since Ephraim was separated from Judah.* And concerning all those who walk in these (ordinances, (**2**) the Covenant of God is assurance for them that He will save them from all the snares of the Pit; but ⟨the foolish⟩ will be punished.[5]

Concerning the organization of all the camps

(**3**) And (the) rule concerning the constitution of all the camps.[6]

Let them all be counted by name: the priests first, (**4**) and the Levites

---

[1] The 'sons of the Pit' are those destined to the Pit of Hell, strangers to the sect; commerce with them was forbidden except on 'cash' terms; there was to be no association, no contract at all.

[2] The reference here is to commercial contracts and associations between the members of the sect themselves — between those of them, obviously, who were not bound by a strict community of property but only by certain rules of solidarity (see below, XIV, 12-16). Even over these the overseer exercised control as far as their commercial activities were concerned.

[3] In this paragraph there are so many lacunae that it is impossible to reconstruct the meaning exactly. It seems to allude again to the relationship between the overseer and his subordinates: he must show 'loving charity' to 'whoever is expelled' (from the Congregation? or his country?), as well as to 'whoever is not bound' (by sin?).

[4] The lacunae are completed by conjecture with the help of parallel passages. This is probably a title heading a new series of ordinances, omitted by the scribe as above, in XII, 19-22.

[5] A new heading recalling XII, 20-1. I have followed RABIN in filling the lacunae in lines 22-3; cf. VII, 9-12. For the expression, 'the Covenant of God is assurance for them', cf. VII, 5 (B, I, 1). Here again only the title seems to have been preserved.

[6] The whole of this section (lines 3-12) concerns the organization of all the camps, as the title indicates, i.e. the organization of the whole of the Essene Church: a general classification of the members, the qualities required in the overseers, the qualities required in the 'overseer in charge of all the camps'.

second, and the sons of Israel third, and the proselytes fourth. And let them be inscribed by name (5) one after the other: the priests first, the Levites second, and the sons of Israel (6) third, and the proselytes fourth. And let them be seated in this order, and in this order let them question on all matters.[1]

And the priest who is overseer of (7) the Many shall be aged between thirty and sixty years, learned in the Book (8) [of Meditation] and in all the ordinances of the Law, to lead them according to the law that is theirs.[2]

And the overseer in charge (9) of all the camps shall be aged between thirty and fifty years, having mastered all (10) the secrets of men and all the tongues which their various clans speak.[3] The members of the Congregation shall enter at his command, (11) each in his turn. And for everything which a man has to say, let him say it to the overseer (12) concerning every dispute and judgment.

Concerning funds allotted to charity

And [this is] the rule concerning the Many to provide for all their needs. The wage (13) of at least two days a month, this is what they shall pay into the hands of the overseer and the judges.[4] (14) They shall set apart a portion of this sum for [orph]ans, and with the other they shall support the hand of the poor and the needy and the old man (15) [dy]ing, and the man that is a fugitive and him that is taken captive into a foreign nation,

[1] A reference to the annual census of the sect as mentioned in *Rule*, II, 19-23. It is worth noting that in this passage from the *Rule* only the priests, Levites, and the people are mentioned. That the *Damascus Document* finds place for proselytes, too, means that during the Damascus exile, i.e. when it was in a pagan land, the sect had no doubt attracted a certain number of proselytes, whereas this kind of recruitment was necessarily more restricted in Judaea. For the inscription of members, see *Rule*, V, 23. For good order at meetings, see *Rule*, VI, 8-13.

[2] I.e. the priest placed at the head of each camp as overseer. Cf. XIII, 2-3. He must be between thirty and sixty years old; the 'judge', on the other hand, must be between twenty-five and sixty (X, 4-7).

[3] This is the general overseer whose jurisdiction extended to all the camps and also, it seems, to each member of the order individually. That he was not allowed to be older than fifty (instead of sixty for an ordinary overseer) was no doubt due to the weight of his task which required among other things a great deal of moving about. He must be master 'of all the secrets of men and of all their tongues'; these words probably mean that rather than the gifts, even exceptional ones, of the psychologist and the polyglot, he must possess the supernatural talents of insight into the minds of men and of 'speaking with tongues'. This was the way that Peter, for example, was able miraculously to read the hearts of Ananias and Sapphira, and to convict them of untruth (Acts v. 1-11), and that the Twelve, filled with the Holy Spirit on the day of Pentecost, 'began to speak in other tongues as the Spirit gave them utterance' (ibid., ii, 1-15).

[4] This ordinance can of course only concern those Essenes who were not subject to common ownership of property, since the others had to hand over all their goods and wages to the bursar of the Community (cf. *Rule*, VI, 19-20). The contribution demanded from the brethren (the wages of at least two days in the month, i.e. approximately 8 per cent of their income) went to swell the funds of solidarity and charity. There follows, in an almost lyrical vein, the list of the principal works of charity.

and the virgin (16) [with no] near kin and the you[ng woman wh]om no man seeks (in marriage). All the service of the Association they (17) [. . .]

And this is the exact tenor ⟨of the rule⟩ concerning the constitution of the [camps . . .] (18) [. . .]¹

The penal code²

And this is the exact tenor of the ordinances [by] which [they shall judge during the time] (19) [of ungodliness until the Anoint]ed of Aaron and Israel [arises] and expiates their iniquity [. . .]

(20) [If there is among them a man] who [li]es in matters of property, and does so knowingly, and [. . .] (21) [. . . he shall] be punished for six days.

And whoever sa[ys . . .]

(22) [And whoever bears malice towards his fellow u]njustly, [shall be punished for one] year [. . .] (23) [. . .]

. . . .

Concerning the oath by the curses of the Covenant³

[. . . that by . . . does not] **XV** (1) [sw]ear, neither by *Aleph* and *Lamed*, nor by *Aleph* and *Daleth*, but the oath of [. . .] (2) by the curses of the Covenant. And let there be no mention of the Law of Moses, for [. . .] (3) and if a man swears and breaks (his oath), he will profane the Name. But if [he sw]ears by the curses of the Covenant [before] (4) the judges, and if he breaks (his oath), he will be guilty of an offence and shall confess

¹ Once again, this is probably the title of a section which has disappeared.

² This penal code should be compared to the one in the *Rule* (VI, 24-VII, 25). Unfortunately, we have only the beginning of the code, for it very probably lacks one or several leaves between pages XIV and XV; and even so, this beginning is mutilated. It seems, however, that the first offence (lying in matters of property) is the same in both codes; but the penalty indicated in the *Damascus Document*, namely 'six days', is surprising since the *Rule* punishes the same fault with 'one year', and besides, its minimum penalty is ten days. This may be a copyist's error. At the end of line 22, the penalty of one year may obviously correspond to various misdemeanours; I have followed RABIN's conjecture and completed the lacuna by following the *Rule* (VII, 8): 'And whoever shall bear malice against his fellow. . . .' RABIN observes that although the *Rule* indicates a sentence of 'six months' for this offence, another hand has superimposed the words 'one year'. Is this an amendment of the primitive text of the *Rule* based on the (later) *Damascus Document*?

³ The beginning of this section has disappeared together with the preceding leaf of the manuscript, so the general sense is not easy to determine. It no doubt alludes to the judicial oath, the 'oath of malediction' which has already been mentioned in IX, 9-12. The present passage fixes the formula for this oath; it is forbidden to swear by the name of God (this must have been stated at the end of the vanished leaf), or even by the initials of the word Elohim (*Aleph* and *Lamed*), or of the name Adonai (*Aleph* and *Daleth*), or by the Law of Moses, but 'by the curses of the Covenant'. Compare this casuistry with Matt. v. 34-6: 'But I say to you, do not swear at all, either by heaven, for it is the throne of God; or by the earth, for it is His footstool; or by Jerusalem, for it is the city of the Great King. And do not swear by your head, for you cannot make one hair white or black.'

and make restitution; but he shall take no [sin] upon himself [and shall (5) not] di[e].[1]

Concerning the oath of entry into the Covenant[2]

And whoever has entered the Covenant appointed for all Israel for ever, let his sons who have reached the age (6) to pass before the census pledge themselves by the oath of the Covenant.[3]

And likewise is (7) the case during all the time of ungodliness for whoever is converted from his corrupted way. On the day on which he speaks (8) with the overseer of the Many, he shall be counted by (swearing) the oath of the Covenant which Moses concluded (9) with Israel,[4] the Covenant which consists of [his conversion] to the Law of Moses with all his heart [and all] (10) his soul to whatever of it is to be done during al[l the ti]me [of ungodliness.]

And let (11) not the ordinances be made known to him until he has presented himself before the overseer, in case he should be judged simple by the overseer when he examines him.

(12) And when once he has undertaken to be converted to the Law of Moses with all his heart and soul, (13) [how] terrible would it be for him to be[t]ray [it]![5]

And all that is revealed of the Law for Knowledge (14) [. . .] if he is worthy of it, let the overseer [teach] him, and let him give orders concerning him, and let him [. . .] (15) for a whole year on the decision of [. . .] (16-23) [. . .][6]

[. . .] **XVI** (1) *with you a Covenant and also with all Israel.*[7] For this reason

---

[1] All this phrase is obscure. It seems that the violation of an oath sworn 'by the curses of the Covenant' was not to be considered true perjury, liable to the death penalty; the fault could be expiated by confession to the priest, and by the restitution of whatever had been evilly acquired, as in Lev. v. 1-7.

[2] There is also mention of this oath in the *Rule* (V, 7-11).

[3] When a boy was twenty he had to be counted in the census. Compare this ordinance obliging the children of Essene parents to make their personal pledge by the oath of the Covenant, with *Rule Annexe*, I, 8-9.

[4] The procedure for admission as described here seems to include none of the preparatory stages (postulant, novice) described in the *Rule* (VI, 13-23) and by JOSEPHUS (*War*, II, §§ 137-8). Perhaps this is a reference to some archaic procedure in force before these preparatory stages were organized.

[5] The end of this phrase is almost illegible in the manuscript, so the interpretation is uncertain.

[6] The end of line 15 is hardly legible and only a few scattered words remain of lines 16-19. Lines 20-3 have disappeared. Under these conditions it is impossible to determine the meaning of the paragraph as a whole. According to information furnished by J. T. MILIK, *Dix ans de découvertes dans le désert de Juda*, p. 76 (Eng. edn., p. 114), an as yet unpublished fragment from cave IV allows us to complete lines 15-17 as follows: 'The stupid, the mad, the foolish, the demented, the blind, the crippled, the lame, minors: none of them shall enter in the midst of the Community, for the holy Angels [are in the midst of it].' Cf. *Rule Annexe*, II, 3-8.

[7] The end of a quotation the first words of which have disappeared at the foot of the preceding page.

a man will undertake to be converted to (2) the Law of Moses, for by it all things are carefully taught. And the exact detail ⟨of the⟩ times of the blindness (3) of Israel with regard to all these (ordinances), this is what is carefully taught in the 'Book of the divisions of the times (4) according to their jubilees and their weeks (of years)'.[1]

And on the day on which a man undertakes to be converted (5) to the Law of Moses, the Angel of Hostility will depart from him if he fulfils his promises. (6) For this reason Abraham circumcised himself on the day on which he knew.[2]

And concerning that which He said, *Whatever comes out of thy lips* (7) *thou shalt observe*[3] by fulfilling it, every oath of obligation by which a man has undertaken (8) to practise some point of the Law, let him not ⟨violate⟩ it even at the price of death. Everything in which (9) a man has undertaken to depart fr[om the L]aw, let him not do it even at the price of death.

Concerning the oath of a woman

(10) Concerning the oath of a woman.

As for that which He sai[d, *It is for*] *her husband to annul her oath*,[4] let (11) no husband annul the oath (of his wife) without knowing whether it should be fulfilled or annulled. (12) If this oath is of a kind to violate the Covenant, let the husband annul it and let him not fulfil it.

And likewise for the father of the woman.[5]

Concerning voluntary gifts

(13) Concerning the ordinance relating to voluntary gifts.

Le[t] nothing obtained unlawfully be vowed to the altar. And also,

[1] An obvious reference to the *Book of Jubilees*, whose title in the Ethiopian version begins: 'This is the history of the division of the days of the Law, and of the testimony, of the events of the years, of their weeks (of years), of their jubilees, during all the years of the world.' *Jubilees* was one of the sect's essential books; the Qumran caves have yielded fragments of nine manuscripts of this work.

[2] Probably the day on which he realized that circumcision, the sign of the Covenant with Israel, would deliver him from the power of the evil angels: this is very likely an a¹lusion to the story of his circumcision in *Jubilees*, XV, part of which runs as follows (verses 31-2): 'For there exist many nations and many peoples, and all are His; and over them all He has set spirits with authority to lead them astray from Him. But over Israel He has set neither angel nor spirit, for He is their sole master, and He will preserve them and will deliver them from the hand of His angels and spirits.' Abraham's example, cited here, presupposes a parallelism between circumcision, considered as a sign of entry into the Covenant, and voluntary àdherence to the sect of the Covenant.

[3] Deut. xxiii. 24. For the duty to fulfil 'the oath of obligation', cf. Num. xxx. 3. In the *Rule* (V, 8), the oath of entry into the Covenant is called the 'oath of obligation'. JOSEPHUS (*War*, II, § 141) notes that the Essene must keep to his oath 'even if violence unto death be used against him'.

[4] Num. xxx. 9 (*Septuagint* and *Vetus Latina*). In Num. xxx. 7-16, the Law authorizes the husband, under certain conditions, to annul the oaths and vows of his wife; the present ordinance restricts this right to undertakings that might violate the Covenant.

[5] In Num. xxx. 4-6, there is mention of pledges made by an unmarried woman: her father may annul them. In the sect, the father's right is subject to the same restriction as the husband's.

(**14**) let [not the pr]iests accept from Israel [anything obtained unlawfully].[1]

Let [no] man consecrate the food (**15**) [of his house to G]od; for it is as He said, *They hunt each other with anathema*.[2]

And [l]et no man (**16**) conse[crate] anything at all [. . .] his property (**17**) he shall consecrate [. . .] shall be punished (**18**) whoever vows [. . .] (**19**) to the judge [. . .] (**20-23**) . . .[3]

---

[1] An interdict on offering any stolen goods upon the altar.

[2] Mic. vii. 2. The Hebrew word BHRM can have a double meaning — 'with the net' or 'with anathema'. In the biblical passage the meaning is certainly, 'they hunt each other with the net', but the author makes a pun on the word and understands it here as 'with anathema', wishing to stigmatize — as J. M. LAGRANGE recognized (*RB*, 1912, p. 240, n. 1) — 'the custom of *Korban*, by which a man dispensed himself from performing certain duties, among them the duty to provide food for his parents, under the pretext that the object was consecrated; it was a genuine theft by anathema, cf. Mark vii. 11'.

[3] Only scraps of sentences remain of lines 16-19; lines 20-3 have disappeared completely.

CHAPTER V

THE SCROLL OF THE WAR RULE

Description of the scroll; general character, analysis and date of the book. — Translation: Introduction and principal Rule; Rule Annexe.

In its present state the scroll called 'The War of the Sons of Light against the Sons of Darkness' consists of nineteen columns each containing seventeen to eighteen lines, but a few lines are missing from the foot of each column, perhaps only four or five. The beginning of the book has been preserved but we lack the end; moreover, even those parts which have survived are holed and torn in many places. In the main the script is very clear and legible.[1]

This book, as I recognized as early as 1950 from the fragments published at that time,[2] is essentially a collection of military regulations, the War Rule of the Sons of Light. It is concerned with the war which the 'sons of light' (i.e. the Essenes themselves) were to fight at the end of time against the 'sons of darkness', i.e. against the wicked as represented by all the heathen nations (the *goyim*) and more precisely, the 'Kittim'.

The theme of the final war against the nations and their defeat appears many times in the Bible itself, especially in the book of Ezekiel (xxxviii-xxxix) and in Daniel. It occupies a fundamental place in the speculation of the Qumran sect which gives singular precision to the ancient biblical dream of the universal dominion of the holy race and to the idea of a holy war destined to ensure this dominion for Israel. The war envisaged by these military rules was not a purely imaginary one: the nations and the Kittim against whom the battle was to be fought were not fictitious enemies, and the

---

[1] The complete scroll is published in the posthumous work of E. L. SUKENIK, *Ozar ham-Megillôt hag-genuzôt* (Jerusalem, 1954; Eng. edn. entitled *The Dead Sea Scrolls of the Hebrew University*, 1955), plates 16-34, 47; this is essentially a collection of plates accompanied by a transcription into printed Hebrew characters. Shortly afterwards, an important study of the same scroll was published by Y. YADIN, *Megillat Milḥemet benē or bibenē hōshek* (Jerusalem, 1955). This work consists of a full introduction and commentary; (it is shortly to be published in English). See also, in *Qumran Cave I* (Oxford, 1955), no. 33, pl. XXXI, two fragments from the same scroll collected in 1949 from cave I; cf. *RB*, lxii, 1955, pp. 600-1.

[2] See *Aperçus préliminaires* . . . , p. 98 (Eng. edn., p. 80).

Hebrew scroll expresses a hatred for them which is real, sacred and fanatical. Every sectary, every Essene, was essentially a soldier, a warrior for this future war; he had to be constantly on the alert for the 'Day of Vengeance'.

This warlike aspect of Essenism is closely bound to the eschatological perspectives of the Bible; but as manifested in both the *War Scroll* and in the Pseudepigrapha which formed an integral part of the sect's library, it obviously reflects the profound influence of Zoroastrian concepts. According to these, the world is radically divided into the two camps of Light and Darkness, Good and Evil, Truth and Falsehood. The member of the sect of the Covenant was essentially a soldier in the army of Light; the whole Community was conceived and organized as a divine militia whose members were not only to fight against Evil day by day, but also — and above all — in the great War of God at the end of time when Evil was to be destroyed for ever.

This final struggle was not to be fought between earthly warriors alone, between the sectaries of the Covenant on one side and the Kittim on the other; all the heavenly powers, all the angels good and evil, were to join in the battle. The 'Great Angel' (XVII, 6) i.e. the Spirit of Good, the Prince of Light, was to be sent to the aid of the army of Good in which the elect were to fight side by side with the angels of light. As for the army of the Kittim, it is explicitly called 'the army of Belial'; Belial himself, the Angel of Darkness, was to march at its head escorted by all the evil spirits. The aim of such a war was to be not only the defeat of the earthly adversaries of Israel, but also the final destruction of the forces of darkness, the end of the dominion of wickedness, the dawn of the eternal and exclusive rule of Light and Justice.

Engaged in this immense and truly apocalyptic drama in which the destiny of the visible and invisible worlds was to be decided for ever, the sons of light were to know a time of unspeakable distress; but they would at the same time have the joy of displaying for the attainment of final victory all their valour and all their virtues as soldiers of God. The *War Rule* found at Qumran was to prepare them for this supreme combat, to encourage them and inflame their zeal. The holy war is described concretely and in detail; the many regulations in the book provide, carefully and minutely, for everything that had to be done to place Israel on a war footing and to enable it to overcome the most powerful of enemies. But in reality

the author of the scroll was an enthusiastic visionary, an extraordinary Utopian: it is a grandiose and chimerical dream that he
elaborates, rather than any really practicable programme. But were
there ever idealists more exalted than the Essenes?

Analysed briefly, the work appears to consist of a general introduction (col. I), a principal war rule (cols. II-XIV) and a war
rule annexe (cols. XV-XIX). In my opinion the work is therefore
a composite one, like the scroll of the *Rule*, which also consists of a
principal section followed by a *Rule Annexe* and then by a collection
of blessings.

The principal war rule deals successively with divine service,
leadership, mobilization, the plan for world conquest which was
apparently to follow after the defeat of the Kittim, the trumpets,
the standards, the commander's staff, the line formations and
weapons of the infantry, infantry manœuvres, the cavalry, the ages
of the various military categories, the purity of the camp and the
qualities required of the combatants, the role of the priests and
Levites during the battle, the war 'towers', and ambush. This first
war rule ends with speeches and prayers: the High Priest's exhortation and supplication before battle, the blessings and curses to be
pronounced during battle and the hymns of thanksgiving to be
sung when battle was ended.

The second war rule is another recension, probably written by a
different author. It draws its inspiration largely from the first (or
from the documents on which this was based); it even repeats whole
passages from it. But in fact it is a new composition, presenting
divergences on a number of points; it sets out to describe the various
stages of the final battle in another way. The beginning has disappeared in the lacuna at the foot of column XIV, but at the beginning of column XV we have what seems to be the last sentences
of an address proclaiming the outbreak of war. Then follows a
description of the various stages of the great military exploit: the
High Priest's exhortation in the camp before battle, the first assault,
the relief of the first line which has suffered losses, the calling out of
the second line with another exhortation by the High Priest, the
second assault leading to the defeat and pursuit of the enemy, the
evening prayer asking for a prolongation of the day in order to
complete the pursuit; and finally the hymns of thanksgiving to be
offered next day.

Who exactly were these 'Kittim' against whom the 'sons of

light' were to fight? The word 'Kittim' appears in the *Commentary on Habakkuk*, where it describes a race of conquerors, of detested invaders. As soon as the scroll was published in 1950, I advanced and maintained the theory that the Kittim described there were the Romans, since certain points in the description of these Kittim can apply only to them. The *War Rule* appears to confirm this theory. Indeed however great the part played by biblical reminiscence, as well as by pure imagination, in its broad outline the work most strikingly reflects the art of war as practised by the Roman legions; it was from this art of war that the Jewish visionary drew his inspiration when he described the army of the sons of light, and not from that of the Seleucids. I cannot go into this in detail here, but many of the notes accompanying the translation establish, I think, significant parallels only explicable if the Jewish author lived in the Roman epoch, during the time, that is to say, when Roman troops occupied Palestine and Syria and it was easy to observe them and obtain information about them.[1] Consequently the word 'Kittim' in this scroll must, as in the *Commentary on Habakkuk*, apply to those Romans who had become masters of almost the entire world and under whose yoke Jerusalem herself had fallen.

The date of the work, in its present form at least, must therefore, in my opinion, be placed later than 63 B.C. It should be observed, moreover, that in column I the author draws his inspiration from the last two chapters of the biblical book of Daniel, which he even quotes textually. Since it is generally accepted that Daniel was composed in 165 B.C., during the wars of the Maccabees against the Seleucid king Antiochus IV, the *War Scroll* can only have been written after that date: a considerable lapse of time was necessary for the Essene author to have been able to consider the book of Daniel as a canonical text. On the other hand, certain allusions in the first lines of the scroll appear to suggest that the work was composed, like the *Damascus Document*, during the Community's exile in the land of Damascus, though it was probably written a little while after this other work.

Whatever its exact date, it is certain that the *War Rule of the Sons*

[1] In the work of Y. YADIN mentioned above (p. 164, n. 1), the reader will find an exhaustive study of the arms and tactics described in the Hebrew scroll, together with a detailed demonstration of the Roman thesis. I myself suggested and outlined this theory before Yadin's work was published, particularly in my paper read on January 29th, 1955, at a meeting of the Société Ernest Renan (see *RHR*, cxlix, 1956, pp. 121-3), and in my lecture on April 22nd, 1955, to the 8th International Congress of the History of Religions held at Rome (see *Numen*, ii, 1955, pp. 180 f.).

of Light was considered by the sectaries of Qumran as one of their basic books. Evidence of this is provided by the fact that in addition to the scroll found in 1947, the Qumran caves have yielded the remains of four other manuscripts of the book. The military descriptions which it contains make of it an extremely curious work, not without interest to historians concerned with ancient wars. But its importance for us resides primarily in the doctrinal concepts with which it is imbued. These come to light at every turn, not only in the numerous addresses and prayers inserted into the *War Rule*, but also in the introduction (col. I), and even in the description of the weapons and engines of war: I have in mind the various inscriptions on the trumpets, standards and javelins of these mystic warriors, and the angels' names given to the war 'towers'. The *War Scroll* is thus a very important source of knowledge as regards Essene theology and spirituality: which is not surprising, considering that this war was to be, in the strongest sense of the word, a Holy War — war against the infidel, the supreme duty of the believer, like the *jihād* of Islam.

One other point. If the Kittim, whom the Hebrew scroll describes as the chief enemy, were in fact the Romans — as I think they were — this work shows what deep and exasperated hatred was felt for them among certain Jewish circles from the very beginning of their occupation of Palestine. The *Commentary on Habakkuk*, dating from more or less the same epoch, reveals a similar hostility, as do also the *Psalms of Solomon*, which are loaded with allusions full of bitter hatred for the Roman Pompey. The *War Scroll* is pervaded with hope of a marvellous victory which would break the yoke of the accursed Romans, and of a military conquest which would subject all the nations of the world to the rule of the elect of Israel. Warlike dreams such as these seem after a time to have generally quietened down among the Essenes, who prudently deferred their realization until later, until the moment appointed by God. But at about the same time, at the beginning of the Christian era, these dreams passed over in all their virulence to the newly founded sect of Zealots, the savage adversaries of Roman rule. Thus is explained the violence and desperation of the Jewish uprisings which the Romans drowned in blood, particularly between A.D. 66 and 70, and from A.D. 132 to 135, under Vespasian and Hadrian.

The following translation is based exclusively on the text of the scroll found in 1947; the fragments discovered in 1952 of other manuscripts of the same work are still unpublished. They may help us to complete some of the lacunae, and any variants they show will no doubt permit us to improve the interpretation of the work. I am omitting some very mutilated passages of practically no interest (especially those at the foot of the columns).

TRANSLATION[1]

I (1) For the m[an of understanding.] War [rule.] Beginning.

INTRODUCTION

The first war of the sons of light

The conquest of the sons of light shall be undertaken firstly
against the lot of the sons of darkness, against the army of Belial,
against the band of Edom and Moab and of the sons of Ammon
(2) and the mul[titude of the sons of the East and] of Philistia,
and against the bands of the Kittim of Asshur and their people
(who shall come) to the aid of the wicked of the Covenant,
sons of Levi and sons of Judah and sons of Benjamin.
The Deportation of the desert shall fight against them;
(3) fo[r war] (shall be declared) on all their bands
when the Deportation of the sons of light returns from the desert of the
to camp in the desert of Jerusalem.[2]   [peoples

---

[1] In general, the present translation is the same as the very fully annotated one published by me in *RHR*, cxlviii (1955), pp. 24-43 and 141-80: I would refer specialists desiring philological details to this translation. In the present instance, I have reduced notes to a minimum; on the other hand, I have added a few corrections to my earlier translation. The translation which appeared in *RHR* is dated June 1955; since then other translations have been published: J. VAN DER PLOEG (*VT*, v, 1955, pp. 373-420); H. BARDTKE (*TLZ*, 1955, nos. 7-8, cols. 401-20); M. BURROWS (*The Dead Sea Scrolls*, 1955, pp. 390-9, fragmentary translation); T. H. GASTER (*The Dead Sea Scriptures in English*, 1956, pp. 281-306). I would also like to draw attention to the interesting contribution of K. G. KUHN, in *TLZ*, 1956, no. 1, cols. 26-30, and to the recent work of J. CARMIGNAC, *La Règle de la Guerre des Fils de Lumière contre les Fils de Ténèbres* (Paris, 1958).

[2] This mention of 'the Deportation of the sons of light' and 'the Deportation of the desert' is partly due to the fact that the sons of light (the members of the Essene sect) were fundamentally committed to the mystic ideal of desert life (see *Rule*, VIII, 12-16) and lived in 'camps' set up in desert places far from the cities. Also, having been driven out of Judaea by the persecution of the High Priest and compelled to live in exile in the land of Damascus, they were in fact 'deportees', like the Jews of Babylon in the time of Nebuchadnezzar. The war against the sons of darkness will break out, we read, 'when the Deportation of the sons of light return from the desert of the peoples to camp in the desert of Jerusalem'. The expression 'desert of the peoples' appears in Ezek. xx. 35, where it seems to apply to the Syrian desert between Babylonia and Palestine; here, it may refer to a desert region in the vicinity of Damascus, since we know that it was in the 'land of Damascus' that the sect sought refuge. As for the expression 'the desert of Jerusalem', this does not appear in the Bible; is it a synonym of 'the desert of Judah', and does it refer to the Essene establishment at Qumran where the sect hoped to return? If I understand it aright, the first objective of the sons of light as defined at the beginning of the scroll was to be the liberation of the Holy Land. To achieve this, they had first to conquer Palestine's

The final war; the ultimate defeat of the sons of darkness

And after this war (4) the [nations] shall go up from there
[and the king] of the Kittim [shall enter] Egypt.
And in his time he shall set out, the prey to violent fury,
to battle against the kings of the North,
and his anger shall (seek) to destroy and wipe out the horn (5) of [his]
e[nemies].

This shall be the time of salvation for the people of God,
the hour of dominion for all the men of his lot
and of final destruction for all the lot of Belial.
And there shall be (6) im[mense] confusion [for] the sons of Japheth
and Asshur shall fall without help from any man,
and the dominion of the Kittim shall vanish
that wickedness may be crushed without a remnant
and without any survivor (7) for [all the son]s of darkness.[1]

The progress and eternal triumph of light

(8) Then [the sons of righteou]sness shall lighten all the ends of the world
progressively, until all the moments of darkness are consumed.
Then in the time of God His sublime greatness shall shine
for all the times (9) [of the ages] unto gladness and blessing;
glory and joy and length of days
(shall be given) to all the sons of light.[2]

[1] The whole of this paragraph seems to be a transposition of the passage from Dan. xi.
40-5, describing first the invasion of Egypt by the 'King of the North', then the retreat and
defeat of the latter, who was to be vanquished and to die in Palestine itself, not far from
Jerusalem. The 'king of the North', who in Daniel is the Seleucid king Antiochus Epiphanes, is here replaced by the 'king of the Kittim' — if, that is, my conjecture concerning
the beginning of line 4 is acceptable; this expression, 'king of the Kittim', appears again
in XV, 2. Who then is this 'king of the Kittim' who, after invading Egypt, left that country
abruptly in order to 'fight against the kings of the North'? Perhaps it is a reminiscence of
the expedition of the Roman Caesar, who having arrived in Egypt with his troops in
October 48 B.C., had to leave a few months later, in June 47 B.C., to establish order in Asia
Minor and quell the revolt of Pharnacus, king of the Cimmerian Bosphorus. It seems that
it was to be during the course of an analogous expedition that the 'king of the Kittim'
(the Roman chief), penetrating into Palestine, was to encounter the army of the sons of
light, by then become masters of the Holy Land, and was to be annihilated by them.
This was to spell the end of the rule of the Kittim, i.e. the end of Roman dominion.
[2] The fall of Roman power was to inaugurate a new era, the age of the universal
dominion of the sons of light; light would spread over the world little by little, like the
dawn, until the time came for it finally to shine out in all its brilliance.

various neighbours (the list, Edom, Moab, Ammon, sons of the East, Philistia, is taken
direct from Isa. xi. 14; cf. also Ps. lxxxiii. 7-9), and also to fight the 'Kittim of Asshur',
i.e. the Romans of Syria (in 64 B.C. Pompey made Syria a Roman province). The Romans,
in fact, supported 'the wicked of the Covenant' (this expression is borrowed from Dan. xi.
32), the official Synagogue governed at that time by Hyrcanus II, the sect's enemy, whom
the Romans had recognized as High Priest and ethnarch. When the time came for the
final war, the sons of light were first to oust all the wicked Jews and take over power
themselves in the whole of Palestine.

The great Day

And on the day when the Kittim fall
(there shall be) battle and rude slaughter before the God (**10**) of Israel;
for this is the day appointed by Him from former times
for the war of destruction of the sons of darkness.
On this (day) shall approach for tremendous slaughter
the congregation of the gods and the assembly (**11**) of men.
On the Day of Misfortune[1] the sons of light and the lot of darkness
shall battle together for the Power of God
amid the tumult of a vast multitude
and the cries of gods and men.
And it shall be a time (**12**) of distress fo[r al]l the people redeemed by
[God,
and among all their afflictions there will have been nothing to equal it
from its beginning until its end (in) final redemption.[2]
And on the day when they shall battle against the Kittim
(**13**) He shall sa[ve them from slau]ghter in this battle.
For three lots, the sons of light shall be strongest
to overthrow ungodliness,
and for three (lots) the army of Belial shall make answer
to beat into retreat the lot (**14**) [of God].
[And the batt]alions of infantry shall melt the heart,
but the power of God [shall] strengthen the h[eart of the sons of light].
[And in] the seventh lot the mighty Hand of God
shall subject [the sons of darkness to al]l the angels of His empire
and to all the men [of His lot].[3]

THE PRINCIPAL WAR RULE

Of divine service and leadership

.   .   .   .
[the heads] **II** (**1**) of family of the congregation, fifty-two.[4]

[1] This may also be translated: on the Day of 'Him who is', i.e. on the Day of Yahweh.
[2] Cf. Dan. xii. 1: 'At that time shall arise Michael, the great Prince, the protector of the children of thy people. And there shall be a time of distress such as never has been since there was a nation till that time. And at that time, thy people shall be saved, all who shall be written in the book.'
[3] The author describes here the vicissitudes of the final war. Three times the advantage will be with the sons of light, and three times it will pass to the other side, as happens in combat between equal forces; but on the seventh and decisive occasion God Himself will ensure the victory of His own.
[4] The beginning of this chapter, describing the organization of divine service in time of war, has disappeared in the lacuna at the foot of column 1. Note that the figure 52 corresponds exactly to the number of weeks in the year according to the Essene calendar (364 days = 52 weeks; see my *Nouveaux aperçus* . . . , pp. 147 ff. Eng. edn., pp. 109 ff.) A little below, there is mention of 26 classes of priests; but according to 1 Chron. xxiv. 1-9, the priests were divided into 24 classes (also JOSEPHUS, *Antiquities*, VII, 14, 7). This

And as for the chief priests, they shall command after the Chief Priest and his second. Twelve chiefs (of the priests) shall be in (2) perpetual service before God. And the twenty-six chiefs of the classes shall serve together with their classes.

And after them the chiefs of the Levites (to the number of) twelve shall serve perpetually, one (3) for every tribe. And the chiefs of their classes shall serve, each in his turn.

The chiefs of the tribes, and after them (the heads) of family of the congregation, shall serve perpetually at the gates of the Sanctuary. (4) And the chiefs of their classes together with their men subjected to the census shall be in office for their feasts, their new moons, and for the Sabbaths, and for all the days of the year, from the age of fifty years and over.

(5) These[1] shall be in office for the holocausts and sacrifices. They shall prepare incense of pleasant odour to (obtain) the loving-kindness of God; they shall expiate for all His congregation and shall feed before Him perpetually (6) at the table of glory.

As for all these, they shall take command at the time of the year of release; and in the thirty-three other years of the war they shall be 'men of renown, (7) they that are called to the Assembly'.[2]

Of mobilization

And all the heads of family of the congregation shall choose fighting men for all the lands of the nations from among all the tribes of Israel. They shall mobilize (8) able-bodied men for themselves to leave for the army, in accordance with the rules of the war, year by year; but in the years of release they shall mobilize no man to go into the army for it is a Sabbath (9) of rest for Israel.

Of the general plan of war

In the thirty-five years of service, war shall be prepared for six years; and they that prepare it shall be the entire congregation together.

[1] Apparently the priests and Levites.

[2] This paragraph appears to deal with the heads of family in the congregation; the expression describing them as 'men of renown, they that are called to the Assembly' (cf. III, 3-4) is taken from Num. xvi. 2. The year of release falls every seven years (cf. Deut. xv. 1-8; 1 Macc. vi. 53). The war of the sons of light, involving not only the liberation of the Holy Land and the defeat of the Kittim (Romans), but also the conquest of the whole world, will last for altogether forty years. These will be divided as follows: first, six years of preparation (cf. line 9), followed by a first year of release; then 'thirty-three other years of war'. During these thirty-three years, there will be four years of release: in forty years of war, therefore, there will be five years of release and 'thirty-five years of service' (cf. line 9).

---

change is obviously connected with the sect's calendar: the number of classes has been brought into line with the number of weeks ($26 \times 2 = 52$).

(**10**) And the war by divisions shall take place in the twenty-nine other years.[1]

In the first year they shall battle against Aram-Naharaim.

And in the second, against the sons of Lud.

And in the third, (**11**) they shall battle against the remnant of the sons of Aram, against Uz and Hul and Tugar and Mesha which are in Trans-euphrates.

In the fourth and in the fifth, they shall battle against the sons of Arpachshad.

(**12**) In the sixth and in the seventh, they shall battle against all the sons of Asshur and Persia and the Easterners as far as the Great Desert.

In the eighth year they shall battle against the sons (**13**) of Elam.

In the ninth year they shall battle against the sons of Ishmael and Keturah.

And in the ten years which follow these, the war shall be divided against all the sons of Ham (**14**) according to [their clans in the l]ands where they dwell.

And in the ten remaining years, the war shall be divided against all [the sons of Japheth in the l]ands where they dwell.

Of the trumpets[2]

(**16**) [Rule concerning the trumpets.]

[These are the trumpet]s of sounding for all their service [. . .]

. . . .

[1] After deducting the six years of preparation and the five years of release, there remain 'twenty-nine years' for the various campaigns (cf. lines 10-14). The following plan, which distributes the conquest of the whole world into twenty-nine annual campaigns, is plainly inspired by biblical geography: the author preserves both the ancient terminology and the essential lines of the 'table of the peoples' (Gen. x). It should, however, be noted that the order of the first nine campaigns directed against the sons of Shem departs radically from the order recorded in the biblical list (Gen. x. 22-3): the military plan takes geographical and political realities into account and to a certain extent reflects *the political map of the world of the author's own time.* It is, in particular, not by chance that the sixth and seventh campaigns are directed jointly 'against the sons of Asshur and Persia and the Easterners as far as the Great Desert' (line 12): the 'table of the peoples' (Gen. x) mentions only Asshur. That Asshur (here no doubt the ancient land of Assyria) is joined to Persia and the Easterners 'as far as the Great Desert' (doubtless the desert region to the east of the Iranian plateau) presupposes, in my view, the existence of the Parthian empire. On the other hand, the fact that the first campaign is directed 'against Aram-Naharaim', with no mention of Syria proper (with Antioch for its capital), shows that it was considered as having already been conquered; it was at that time a Roman province, and the defeat of the Romans which was to precede the conquest of the world by the sons of light would imply the fall of Syria also. Consequently the conquest could begin with Aram-Naharaim, i.e. Osrhoene, on the confines of the province of Syria.

[2] This chapter on the trumpets is in two parts: (1) a list of the various kinds of trumpets; (2) a list of the inscriptions to figure on them. The beginning of the first list has disappeared in the lacuna at the foot of column II, but the second list, which is intact, allows us to restore the missing part as follows: the trumpets of summons of the congregation, of the summons of the chiefs, of the transmissions, of the men of renown, of the camps and of the departure from the camps. These trumpets of the sons of light were not merely to relay signals; they were to be blown by the priests (cf. cols. VII-IX, XVI-XVIII) and were to possess a divine and magical power like the horns which caused the walls of Jericho to fall in the time of Joshua.

[and the trumpets] **III** (1) of battle formations; and the trumpets of summons of these formations when the gates of battle are opened that the foot-soldiers may go out; and the trumpets of sounding of slaughter; and the trumpets (2) of ambush; and the trumpets of pursuit when the enemy is overthrown; and the trumpets of reassembly when the fighting men return.

On the trumpets of summons of the congregation they shall write, 'Summoned of God'.

(3) And on the trumpets of summons of the chiefs they shall write, 'Princes of God'.

And on the trumpets of the transmissions they shall write, 'Commandment of God'.

And on the trumpets of the men (4) of renown they shall write, 'Heads of family of the congregation'. When they gather in the house of Assembly they shall write, 'Ordinances of God for the Holy Council'.

And on the trumpets of the camps (5) they shall write, 'Bliss of God in the camps of His saints'.

And on the trumpets of departure of the camps they shall write, 'Mighty deeds of God to disperse the enemy and to put to flight all who hate (6) righteousness, and withdrawal of favours from those who hate God'.

And on the trumpets of the battle formations they shall write, 'Formations of the battalions of God for the vengeance of His Anger upon all the sons of darkness'.

(7) And on the trumpets of summons of the foot-soldiers when the gates of battle are opened that they may go out towards the enemy line, they shall write, 'Reminder of vengeance at the hour (8) of God'.

And on the trumpets of slaughter they shall write, 'Mighty Hand of God in the battle to bring down all the slain of unfaithfulness'.

And on the trumpets of ambush they shall write, (9) 'Mysteries of God to destroy ungodliness'.

And on the trumpets of pursuit they shall write, 'God overthrows all the sons of darkness: He will not withdraw His Anger till He has destroyed them'.

(10) And when they return from battle, when they come (to) the line, they shall write on the trumpets of withdrawal, 'God gathers in'.

And on the trumpets of the road of return (11) from the battle waged against the enemy, when they come into the congregation in Jerusalem, they shall write, 'Rejoicings of God in a happy return'.

The standards[1]

(13) Rule concerning the standards of all the congregation for their transmissions.

[1] This chapter on the standards juxtaposes five different sections: (1) a rule for the inscriptions of the standards of the various units (III, 13-17); the end of this part has disappeared in the lacuna at the foot of column III; (2) a second rule which seems to be specially concerned with the inscriptions to be written on the standards of the tribe of

On the great standard which is at the head of all the people they shall write, 'People of God', together with the names of Israel (**14**) and Aaron and the names of the twelve tr[ibes of Israe]l according to their genealogy.

On the standards of the chiefs of the camps of the three tribes (**15**) they shall write [. . . together with the names of the prince of the camp.]

[O]n the standard of the tribe they shall write, 'Banner of God', together with the name of the prince of the tri[be and the names of the chiefs of] (**16**) [its] cla[ns].

[And on the standard of the Myriad they shall write . . . together with] the name of the prince ⟨of⟩ the Myriad and the names of the ch[iefs of its Thousands].

[And on the standard of the Thousand] (**17**) [they shall write . . . together with the name of the chief of the Thousand and the names of the chiefs of] its Hundreds.

And on the standard [of the Hundred they shall write . . . together with the name of the chief of the Hundred and the names of the chiefs of its Fifties.]

.   .   .   .

IV (**1**) And on the standard of Merari[1] they shall write, 'Levy of God', together with the name of the prince of Merari and the names of the chiefs of its Thousands.

And on the standard of the Thousand they shall write, 'Anger of God furious against (**2**) Belial and against all the men of his lot, without any remnant', together with the name of the chief of the Thousand and the names of the chiefs of its Hundreds.

---

[1] The inscriptions to be written on the standards as determined in this second order seem to me to derive, with the help of a subtle and artificial etymology, from the name of each military unit itself, as though this name, or the letters forming it, possessed some mysterious value which the inscription seeks to reveal. The clearest example is the inscription for the standard of the Ten — 'Rejoicing of God upon the ten-stringed harp'. The 'ten-stringed harp' is clearly introduced here to correspond to the name of the Ten. Merari is the name of the third son of Levi, the first two being Gershon and Kohath (cf. Num. iii). The beginning of this second order, which has disappeared at the foot of column III, may have indicated, as J. CARMIGNAC suggests, the inscriptions for the standards of Gershon and Kohath; each of the three Levitical clans constituting the tribe of Levi was divided, like the clans of the twelve other tribes, into Thousands, Hundreds, Fifties and Tens.

Levi (IV, 1-5); the beginning of this part has also disappeared at the base of column III; (3) an order concerning the inscriptions on standards adapted to the various stages of battle — departure, attack, return (IV, 6-8); (4) an order on the same subject, but more complete (IV, 9-14); (5) an order concerning the height of the standards of each unit. In these different sections (except the third apparently), the number of military units is given as eight: the whole congregation (twelve tribes), the camp (three tribes), the tribe, the Myriad (or clan), the Thousand (or battalion), the Hundred, the Fifty and the Ten. For the first four units, this organization draws its inspiration from Num. i-ii and for the four others, from Exod. xviii. 21 (cf. Deut. i. 15). Like the trumpets, the standards possess a mystic significance and efficacy, as the inscriptions to figure on them indicate.

And on the standard of the Hundred they shall write, 'From (3) God (is) the Hand that fights against all perverse flesh', together with the name of the chief of the Hundred and the names of the chiefs of its Tens.

And on the standard of the Fifty they shall write, 'Ended (4) is the existence of the wicked [by] the Might of God', together with the name of the chief of the Fifty and the names of the chiefs of its Tens.

On the standard of the Ten they shall write, 'Rejoicing (5) of God upon the ten-stringed harp', together with the name of the chief of the Ten and the names of the nine men under his command.

(6) And when they go into battle they shall write on their standards, 'Truth of God', 'Justice of God', 'Glory of God', 'Judgment of God', and after these words all the hierarchy of the list of their names.

(7) And when they draw near for battle they shall write on their standards, 'Right Hand of God', 'Moment of God', 'Conflict of God', 'Slaughter of God', and after these words all the list of their names.

(8) And when they return from battle they shall write on their standards, 'God is raised up', 'God is great', 'Praise of God', 'Glory of God', with all the list of their names.[1]

(9) Rule concerning the standards of the congregation.

When they set out for battle they shall write on the first standard, 'Congregation of God'; on the second standard, 'Camps of God'; on the third, (10) 'Tribes of God'; on the fourth, 'Clans of God'; on the fifth, 'Battalions of God'; on the sixth, 'Company of God'; on the seventh, 'Summoned (11) of God'; on the eighth, 'Militia of God'; and they shall write the list of their names together with all their hierarchy.

And when they draw near for battle they shall write on their standards, (12) 'Battle of God', 'Vengeance of God', 'Trial of God', 'Exploit of God', 'Strength of God', 'Reward of God', 'Might of God', 'Extermination of God unto all the nations of vanity'; and they shall write all the list (13) of their names on their standards.

And when they return from battle they shall write on their standards, 'Salvation of God', 'Victory of God', 'Help of God', 'Support of God', (14) '[Jo]y of God', 'Thanksgiving of God', 'Exaltation of God', 'Peace of God'.

---

[1] This third section gives four different inscriptions for each phase of the battle, whereas the following section gives eight — one for each of the eight military units. No doubt the present section has a more limited organization in view, consisting of only four units: the Thousand, the Hundred, the Fifty and the Ten (cf. *Rule*, II, 21-2, and *Damascus Document*, XIII, 1).

(15) [Rule concerning the stand]ards.[1]

The standard of all the congregation shall be fourteen cubits long; the standard of the thr[ee tribes of the camps, thi]rteen cubits; (16) [the standard of the tribe,] twelve cubits; the standard of the Myriad, elev[en cubits; the standard of the Thousand, ten cubits; the standard of the Hund]red, [n]ine cubits; (17) [the standard of the Fifty, eight] cubits; the standard of the Ten, se[ven cubits].

. . . .

Of the commander's staff[2]

V (1) And on the s[taf]f of the Prince of all the congregation they shall write [his] name [and] the names of Israel, Levi, and Aaron, together with the names of the twelve tribes according to their geneal[og]y (2) and the names of the twelve chiefs of their tribes.

Of battle formations[3]

(3) Rule concerning the formation of the fighting battalions.

When the army is at full strength they shall fill a front line with one thousand men. This line shall be compact. And it shall have seven (4) front formations. They shall be arranged in order in each line (according to their) place, one man after the other.

Of infantry weapons

And they shall all hold shields of bronze polished like (5) a mirror. And the shield shall be surrounded with a braided border in the form

[1] This last order concerning the standards determines their length. It is progressively reduced, from 14 cubits for the first standard (of the whole congregation) to 7 cubits for the eighth (of the Ten); it decreases 1 cubit per unit. Note that according to this ingenious rule, the smallest standard measures 7 cubits — this is a mystic number (see below, the 7 lines of infantry, the spear 7 cubits long, the 7 javelins, etc.) — and the largest standard, 14 cubits, the double of 7. The standards of the armies of the sons of light are not described, but as only their length is given, they seem to have been in the shape of a pole, like the *signa* of the Roman legions, and not banners or flags. The inscriptions prescribed must no doubt have figured on medallions fixed to these poles, like those fixed to the *signa*.

[2] The word 'staff' is not absolutely sure; the manuscript is a little damaged at this point. It is nevertheless quite natural that there should be mention of the commander's staff in a military order (cf. Num. xvii. 17-26 = xvii. 1-13 in the English Bible). This is the only mention of the 'Prince of all the congregation' in the present scroll, but this person, the supreme lay leader of the community, appears in the *Book of Blessings* (V, 20-9) annexed to the *Rule*, and also in the *Damascus Document* (VII, 20).

[3] Each line consists of one thousand men, the strength of a battalion. The seven lines (= 7000 men) face the enemy; they appear to be arranged in depth, one behind the other (cf. V, 16). These seven lines seem to constitute the great tactical unit analogous to the Roman *legion*.

of a coupling in interwoven (?) gold and silver and bronze, the work of an artist; (6) and (it shall be adorned) with many-coloured (?) precious stones, the work of an artist goldsmith. The length of the shield shall be two and a half cubits and its width one and a half cubits.[1]

And in their hand (they shall hold) a spear (7) and a sword.

The length of the spear shall be seven cubits, of which the socket and the point (shall measure) half a cubit. And (there shall be) three rings on the socket chiselled (8) in the manner of a braided border in interwoven (?) gold and silver and bronze, a work of artistic design (in the form) of a coupling. The d[e]sign on both sides of (each) ring, (9) all round, shall be of many-coloured (?) precious stones, the work of an artist goldsmith and encruster (?). And the socket shall be carved between the rings in the manner (10) of an artistic column. And the point shall be in white and shining iron, the work of an artist goldsmith and encruster (?). (And there shall be) pure gold at the centre of the point (and it) shall be sharpened towards (11) the extremity.[2]

And as for the swords, they shall be of purified iron refined in the crucible and made white as a mirror, the work of an ar[t]ist goldsmith; and (they shall be adorned) with encrusted (?) figures (12) in pure gold. An attachment (shall be fixed) to its two sides and rectilineal grooves shall be towards the top, two on one side and two on the other. The length of the sword shall be one (13) and a half cubits and its width four fingers; but the belly shall be four thumbs (wide). And (there shall be) four palms to the belly; and the belly, bent (?) here (14) and there, shall be five palms (long). And the hilt of the sword shall be of pure horn, the work of an artist, (adorned with) a many-coloured design in gold and silver and precious stones.[3]

---

[1] One cubit measuring about 17½ in., the height of the shield is consequently 3 ft. 8 in., and its width 2 ft. 2 in. The shield is rectangular, like the *scutum* of the Roman legionaries.

[2] The spear described here measures, therefore, about 10 ft. 2½ in., including the iron (nearly 9 in.). This is the length of a normal spear such as the Roman *hasta*; on the other hand, the 'sarisse' of the Macedonian phalanx measured 20 ft., and even more.

[3] The sword described here (in Hebrew *kidān*) seems to be curved like a scimitar or, better still, like the 'harpe' — an archaic weapon a few examples of which have been discovered in archaeological excavations in the East. The total length of this sword is 1½ cubits (= 2 ft. 2 in.); note that the 'harpe' found at Byblos is about the same length (2 ft. 1½ in.). The width of the sword is given as four fingers (about 3 in.); but the 'belly' (i.e. the curve, or bulge) is a little wider (4 thumbs = 3¾ in.). Moreover, we read that the weapon measures 4 palms (= ⅔ cubit) 'to the belly' — this is the length of the rectilineal part preceding the bulge — and the length of the 'belly' is 5 palms (⅝ cubit); the total length is therefore indeed 1½ cubits (2 ft. 2 in.), as indicated earlier. The description of the *kidān* as given in this paragraph does not allow us, I think, to identify it with the straight sword, the *gladius* of the Roman legionary for example. There is mention several times in the Bible of a weapon called *kidōn* (a variant of *kidān*). Ancient translators have hesitated as to the meaning of the word, rendering it sometimes as sword, sometimes as javelin or spear, and sometimes as shield: the present passage allows us to restore its real sense, the curved sword ('harpe').

Of infantry manœuvres[1]

(16) And when the [. . .] take up (their) position, they shall form the seven lines, one line behind the other [. . .]

. . . .

VI (1) seven times, then they shall return to their position.

And after them, the three battalions of foot-soldiers shall go out and shall take up (their) position between the lines. The first battalion shall cast [tow]ards (2) the enemy line seven javelins of war. And on the javelin's pennant they shall write, 'Flashing spear for the Power of God'. And on the second throw they shall write, (3) 'Bloody darts to bring down the slain by the Anger of God'. And on the third javelin they shall write, 'Flaming sword which devours the wicked slain by the Judgment of God'. (4) All these shall cast seven times, then they shall return to their position.

And after them, two battalions of foot-soldiers shall go out and shall take up (their) position between the two lines. The first battalion (5) shall hold a spear and a shield and the second battalion shall hold a shield and a sword.

They shall bring down the slain by the Judgment of God
and shall cause the enemy line to give way (6) by the Power of God,
to pay to all the nations of vanity the reward of their evil.
And sovereignty shall belong to the God of Israel
and He shall display His valour by the saints of His people.

Of the cavalry[2]

(8) And seven formations of horsemen shall also take up (their) position to the right and the left of the line; their formations shall take up (their) position on one side and on the other, seven hundred (9) horsemen at one

[1] Now follows a description of the movements of the great tactical unit consisting of seven lines, or battalions, each counting 1000 men (cf. V, 3-4). The part missing from the foot of column V must have described the role of the two first battalions, probably composed of archers and slingers. Then the three following battalions go out, armed with javelins — or rather, in my opinion, with *pila*, the typical weapons of the Roman armies, about 5 to 7 ft. long, with a range of 30 to 65 yards, depending on whether they were thrown with a strap or not. Finally the two last battalions go out, one armed with spears, and the other with swords, for the hand-to-hand fighting. It will be noted that such tactics have nothing in common with those of the Macedonian phalanxes whose formation was extremely rigid; without copying them exactly, their flexibility is reminiscent of the tactics of the Roman army.

[2] To each line of infantry (one battalion of 1000 men) is assigned one formation of cavalry. This consists of 200 horsemen arranged on the two flanks of the line: 100 on the right flank and 100 on the left. As the seven lines of infantry are arranged in depth (cf. V, 16), there will consequently be 700 horsemen on the right flank and 700 on the left: altogether 1400 horsemen for 7000 foot-soldiers. This disposition of the cavalry on the two flanks of the army formation conforms to Roman custom. Note also the round shield of the horsemen, the *clipeus* of the Roman cavalrymen.

extremity and seven hundred horsemen at the other. Two hundred horsemen shall go out with the thousand men of the infantry line. And in the same manner (10) (the horsemen) shall take up (their) position at all the camp's ex[tremities].

Altogether (there shall be) four thousand and six hundred (horsemen) together with one thousand and four hundred mounts for the officers of the lines: (11) fifty to a line. And the horsemen, including the mounts of the officers, shall be six thousand (in number): five hundred for each tribe.

All the horses that set out (12) for battle with the foot-soldiers shall be swift-footed stallions, tender-mouthed, long-winded, and of the required age, trained for battle (13) and able to hear the shouts; and they shall all look alike.

And they that ride these horses shall be men suited to fighting and trained to ride. And (14) their age shall be from thirty to forty-five years; but the cavalry officers shall be from forty to fifty years old.

And they (15) sh[all w]ea[r breast-plat]es (?) and helmets and greaves. And they shall hold in their hand round shields and a spear e[ight (?) cubits] long [. . .] (16) [. . .] and a bow and arrows and javelins of war.

And they shall all be prepared [. . .]

. . . .

Of the age required for the various military categories[1]

. . . .

VII (1) And the officers shall be from forty to fifty years old. And the commanders of the camps shall be from fifty to sixty years old. And the quartermasters also (2) shall be from forty to fifty years old. And all those that strip the dead, and plunder, and purify the earth and keep watch over the weapons (3) and prepare the provisions, they shall all be from twenty-five to thirty years old.

Of the purity of the camp and of the moral and physical qualities required of the combatants

And no young boy and no woman shall enter their camps when they leave (4) Jerusalem to go into battle until their return.[2]

---

[1] The beginning of this chapter has disappeared in the lacuna at the foot of column VI: it must have given the age required for the foot-soldiers, which probably began at twenty years. Compare all this passage with the *Rule Annexe* (I, 6-18) which gives the ages required for admittance to the various civil offices, and also with the *Damascus Document* (X, 4-10; XIV, 7-10).

[2] It is clear from this phrase that at the time of the final battle the sons of light would have already conquered Jerusalem (cf. *supra*, I, 3) and that the battle would take place not far from the capital (cf. Dan. xi. 45). All access to the camp was forbidden to young boys and women, doubtless because they were not specially sanctified for war and would defile the camp by their impure presence; also, no debauchery could be permitted the soldiers of God, either with 'young boys' (apparently an allusion to the paederasty which Hellenism threatened to introduce into Jewish custom), or with women.

And no lame man, nor blind, nor crippled, nor having in his flesh some incurable blemish, nor smitten with any impurity (5) in his flesh, none of these shall go with them into battle. They shall all be volunteers for the battle and shall be perfect in spirit and body and prepared for the Day of Vengeance.[1]

And no (6) man who is in a state of uncleanness because of his flux on the day of battle shall go down with them; for the angels of holiness shall accompany their armies.[2]

And there shall be a space (7) of about two thousand cubits between all their camp and the site of the (retiring) place, and nothing shameful nor ugly shall be visible in the surroundings of all their camp.[3]

Of the role of the priests and Levites during battle

(9) And when they form the battle lines facing the enemy, one line facing the other, then from the middle gate towards the space (between) the lines shall go out seven (10) priests from among the sons of Aaron clothed in garments of fine white linen; in tunics of linen and breeches of linen and girded with girdles of linen, of fine twisted linen in purple, violet, (11) scarlet, and crimson, many-coloured, the work of an artist. And they shall wear on their heads a head-dress in the form of a tiara. These shall be their garments for battle and into the Sanctuary they shall not (12) bring them.

The first priest shall walk in front of all the men of the line to strengthen their hands in battle; and in the hand of the six (others) shall be (13) the trumpets of summons and the trumpets of the reminder and the trumpets of clamour and the trumpets of pursuit and the trumpets of reassembly.

And when the priests go out (14) towards the space between the lines, seven Levites shall go out with them having seven horns of ram's horn in their hands. And three officers from among the Levites (shall go) before (15) the priests and the Levites.

And the priests shall sound the two trumpets of sum[mons and reminder . . .] upon fifty shields. (16) And fifty foot-soldiers shall go out from the first gate [. . .] the Levite officers and the troop (17) of a whole line. And a line shall go out in accordance with all this ru[le . . .]

. . . .

[1] Cf. Deut. xxiii. 2 ff. and above all, *Rule Annexe*, II, 3-9, concerning persons to be excluded from the Assembly.
[2] Cf. Deut. xxiii. 11-12, 15.
[3] Cf. Deut. xxiii. 13-15. The present ordinance adds one detail to the biblical text, namely, that the site of the retiring place must be 2000 cubits (about 1000 yards) from the camp. JOSEPHUS (*War*, II, 8, 9), for his part, declares that when the Essenes wished to excrete they chose 'the loneliest places'. This passage does not explicitly formulate the Essene obligation to bury their excrement which Josephus reports, but because of the Deuteronomic law such an obligation is to be taken for granted, and it is implied in the statement that 'nothing shameful' should remain visible in the camp surroundings.

VIII (1) the trumpets shall sound during the (engagement) of the slingers until they have thrown seven (2) times. And afterwards, the priests shall sound for them the trumpets of withdrawal and they shall come to the side of the first line (3) to stand in their place.[1]

Then the priests shall sound the trumpets of summons and (4) three battalions of foot-soldiers shall go out from the gates and shall take up (their) position between the lines; and the mounted men shall be at their side, (5) to the right and to the left. And the priests shall sound a drawn-out sound on the trumpets for battle formation (6) and the sections shall spread out according to their formations, each towards its position. And when they have taken up (their) position in three formations, (7) the priests shall sound for them a second grave and sustained sound for the march towards the (8) enemy line. Then they shall stretch out their hands over the weapons of war and the priests shall sound on the six trumpets (9) of slaughter a sharp and urgent sound during the battle, while the Levites and all the troop of the horns shall send out (10) with one voice an immense warlike clamour to melt the heart of the enemy. Then amid the noise of this clamour (11) the javelins of war shall depart to bring down the slain. They shall silence the sound of the horns (12) and the priests shall sound a sharp and urgent sound on the trum[pe]ts during the battle until they have cast towards the (13) enemy line seven times. And then the priests shall sound on the trumpets of withdrawal (14) a grave, continuous, and sustained sound. It is in accordance with this rule that the priests shall sound for the three battalions.

And when (15) the first (battalion) throws, the [priests and Levites and all the troop of hor]ns shall send out a noise of immense clamour (16) during the batt[le until they have thrown seven times. And afterwards,] the priests [shall sound] for them (17) the trump[ets of withdrawal . . . and they shall ret]urn to their position. (18) [. . .]

· ·

IX (1) and they shall begin to bring down their hand upon the slain. And all the troop shall be silent, ending the noise of clamour, and the priests shall sound the trumpets (2) of slaughter during the battle until the

---

[1] The manœuvre described in this chapter (VII, 9-IX, 9) is essentially the same as that described earlier in V, 16-VI, 6, but new details are added. Despite the lacunae at the foot of columns VII and VIII, we recognize that the two lines to engage first are light infantry (*velites*) — slingers and probably also archers; the three following lines are armed with javelins (*pila*), and the two last (according to VI, 4-5) with spears and swords. Each line goes into action separately; some of them manœuvre in groups of fifty (VII, 16), others form themselves into three 'sections' (VIII, 6). Owing to the lacunae in the text, the details of these movements are not absolutely clear, but the tactics are patently flexible and carefully related to each other like those of the Roman legion, which from the time of Marius consisted of ten cohorts each containing three divisions (*manipuli*). The army, we read, amounts to a total of 28,000 foot-soldiers divided into 7 lines; so here, each line is formed of 4000 men. Since in a legion the line consisted of 1000 men (cf. V, 3), it is no doubt to be understood that battle formations involved *four* legions juxtaposed. The number of horsemen is given as 6000 in all, the number already indicated above (VI, 11).

enemies are overthrown and have turned their neck. And the priests shall sound (the trumpets) during the battle.

(3) And when (the enemies) are defeated before them, the priests shall sound the trumpets of summons and all the foot-soldiers shall go out towards them from the middle (4) of the front lines, and six battalions shall take up (their) position together with the battalion that has attacked: in all, seven lines; twenty-eight thousand (5) fighting men and six thousand horsemen.

All these shall pursue the enemy to destroy him in the battle of God until (6) final destruction. And the priests shall sound for them the trumpets of pursuit; and they shall di[vide] against all the enemy to pursue him utterly. And the cavalry (7) shall return to the places of battle until the final destruction (of the enemy).

And the priests shall sound from afar when the slain fall, and they shall not come (8) to the midst of the slaughter lest they be defiled by unclean blood; for they are holy and they shall not profane the oil of their priestly anointing with the blood (9) of a nation of vanity.

Of the 'towers'

(10) Rule concerning the change of formation of the fighting battalions.[1] They shall prepare the position [. . .] of the catapults (?) and the towers (11) and the bows and the towers. Then with short strides (?) the sections shall go out, while the flanks [advance on the tw]o extremities of the line [to tram]ple down (12) the enemy.

And the shields of the towers shall be three cubits long and their spears shall be eight cubits l[on]g. And the towers (13) shall go out from the line. One hundred shields and one hundred (shall form) the fronts of the tower; [they] shall a[ll] surround the tower in the three directions of the front (14) (to the number of) three hundred shields. And there shall be two gates to the tower, [one] at [the right and o]ne at the left. And on all the shields of the towers (15) they shall write: on the first, Mi[chae]l, [on the second, Gabriel, on the third,] Sariel, on the fourth, Raphael. (16) Michael and Gabriel shall be to [the right (?) and Sariel and Raphael to the left (?)].

Of ambush

(17) [Rule] concerning ambush [. . .][2]

. . . .

[1] Because of the numerous lacunae, this chapter is difficult to interpret. The word 'towers' appears to describe a particular type of compact square battle formation intended both to break an enemy assault more easily, and to smash his defences; they are not war towers or siege engines. When used in a military context, the Latin word *turris* sometimes means a square battle formation. Each 'tower' is formed of 300 foot-soldiers armed with shields and long spears, with 100 men arranged on three sides; the fourth side is open and does not constitute a line.

[2] This chapter has almost entirely disappeared in the lacuna at the foot of column IX.

The exhortation of the High Priest before battle

. . . .

[. . . It is Thou, O God, who didst command us to sanctify] **X** (1) our camp and to preserve ourselves from all that is shameful and ugly,[1] who didst declare that Thou wouldst be in the midst of us,[2] O great and terrible God, to plunder all (2) our enemies be[fore us], and (who) didst teach us this from former times for our generations:[3] 'When you draw near for battle, the priest shall arise and say to the troop, (3) Hear O Israel! You draw near this day to battle against your enemies. Be not afraid! Let not your heart faint! (4) Tre[mble] not! Fear not before them! For your God walks with you to battle for you against your enemies in order to save you. (5) And ⟨the⟩ officers shall tell all those who are ready for battle, willing volunteers, to cling firmly to the Power of God and to send back all (6) whose heart has melted and to cling firmly to all the valiant heroes.

And (it is Thou) who did[st sa]y by the hand of Moses:[4] When the battle comes to pass (7) in your land against the enemy who oppresses you, you [shall] sound the trumpets; and you shall be remembered before your God (8) and shall be saved from your enemies.

O God of Israel, who is like Thee in heaven and on earth
to accomplish works like Thy mighty works,
(9) and like Thy stalwart power?
And who is like Thy people Israel
whom Thou hast chosen for Thyself from among all the peoples of the
[lands;
(10) the people of the saints of the Covenant and of those who are learned
of those with intelligent under[standing . . .]   [in the Precept,
who hear the voice of the venerated (Being)[5]
and see (11) the angels of holiness;
of those whose ear is opened and who hear profound things?

[1] The beginning of the High Priest's exhortation before battle has also disappeared at the foot of column IX. At the beginning of column X, the High Priest recalls various biblical texts relating to Israel's wars; the first sentence, of which only the end remains, refers to Deut. xxiii. 10 ff. (cf. above, VII, 6-7).
[2] Cf. Exod. xvii. 7; xxxiv. 9, etc.
[3] Cf. Deut. xx. 2-9; verses 2-4 are quoted textually (with a few slight variants), but verses 5-9 are summarized and to some extent modified. Judas Maccabee quotes this same passage from the *Torah* in an address to his troops (1 Macc. iii. 56).
[4] Quotation from Num. x. 9.
[5] Who is this 'venerated Being'? Obviously the expression is applicable to God; but in the sect it is also applicable to the Teacher of Righteousness. This phrase is to be compared with the following passage from the *Damascus Document*: 'and (who) have heeded the voice of the Teacher' (B, II, 28); 'and (who) have lent their ear to the voice of the Teacher of Righteousness' (B, II, 32). The parallelism seems to me to suggest that in the present text the 'venerated Being' is the Teacher of Righteousness.

[It is Thou, O God, who hast created] the expanse of the heavens,
the host of heavenly lights (12) and the office of the spirits and the empire
the glo[rious] reservoirs [of water and] clouds.   [of the saints,
(It is Thou) who hast created the earth and the laws of its divisions
(13) into desert and pleasant land,
and all it produces, with [its] frui[ts and seeds (?)],
the globe of the seas and the reservoirs of the rivers and the chasms of the
(14) animals and winged beings,   [deeps,
the shape of man and the gene[rations issued from] his [see]d (?):
the confusion of tongues and the dispersion of the peoples,
the abode of the clans (15) and the division of territories [. . .]
the sacred moments and the circuits of the years and the (16) everlasting
We know these things because of Thy understanding [. . .]   [ages [. . .]
. . . .

XI (1) But Thine is the battle![1]
And by the might of Thy hand their bodies were stretched upon earth
And Goliath of Gath, a valiant giant,   [with no man to bury them.
(2) Thou didst deliver into the hand of David Thy servant;
for he set his trust in Thy majestic Name
and not in the sword and the spear.

For Thine is the battle!
And (3) he struck [down] the Philistines many times by Thy holy Name.
And Thou hast also saved us many times by the hand of our kings
(4) because of Thy mercy
and not according to our works by which we have done evil
nor (according to) our sinful deeds.

Thine is the battle!
From [Thee] comes the power;
(5) truly (the battle) is not ours!
Not our might nor the strength of our hands display valour,
but it is by Thy might and the strength of Thy tremendous valour;
as Thou didst declare to us (6) in former times,[2]
A star has journeyed from Jacob,
a sceptre has arisen from Israel;
and he crushes the temples of Moab
and overturns all the sons of Seth.

[1] The same refrain recurs in lines 2 (*ad finem*) and 4. Cf. 1 Sam. xvii. 47: 'But the battle
is the Lord's.' The beginning of this declamation on the God of battle has disappeared in
the lacuna at the foot of column X.
[2] Quotation from Num. xxiv. 17-19 (with variants). The same passage is recalled in the
Damascus Document (VII, 19-21): there the 'Star' is identified with the 'Seeker of the Law
who came to Damascus', and the 'sceptre' with the 'Prince of the Congregation'.

(7) And he rules from Jacob
and causes the survivors of the city to perish.
And the enemy becomes a conquered land
and Israel displays its valour.

And by the hand of Thine Anointed (8) who see the Decisions
Thou hast announced to us the times of the battles of Thy hands
in which Thou wilt be glorified in our enemies;
in which Thou wilt bring down the bands of Belial, (9) the seven nations
into the hand of the Poor whom Thou hast redeemed[1]   [of vanity
[by the migh]t and fullness of marvellous Power.
And the melted heart Thou hast wrapped in hope;
Thou wilt deal with them as with Pharaoh
(10) and as with the commanders of his chariots in the Sea of Re[eds].
And those whose spirit is broken Thou wilt cause to pass
like a flaming torch in the straw,
devouring the wicked and returning not
until the (11) destruction of the guilty.

And Thou didst in former days announce in these words the time
when Thou wouldst display the might of Thy hand against the Kittim:[2]
And Asshur shall fall beneath the blows of a sword which shall not be that
and a sword (12) which shall not be human shall devour him.   [of a man,
(13) For Thou wilt deliver the [en]emies of all the lands
into the hand of the Poor,
and by the hand of them that are bent in the dust
wilt Thou humble the valiant of the peoples;
to draw down the reward (14) which is due to the wicked upon [the hea]d
[of [their] en[emies]
and to justify Thy judgment of truth in the midst of the sons of men
and to make for Thyself an eternal name in the people whom (15) [Thou
[hast redeemed . . .]
and to be exalted and sanctified in the eyes of the o[th]er [nat]ions.
(16) judgments against God and all his assembly [. . .][3]
(17) For Thou wilt battle against them from heaven abov[e . . .]

. . . .

---

[1] The 'Poor' are the members of the sect; the same expression appears below in line 13.
This name is also given them in the *Commentary on Habakkuk* (XII, 3, 6, 10) and in the
Commentary on Psalm XXXVII where the sect is actually called 'the Congregation of the
Poor'.

[2] The quotation which follows is from Isa. xxxi. 8; it refers to Assyria, but the author
applies it to the Kittim (i.e. in my opinion the Romans), either because Asshur was for
him the symbol of the enemies of God and Israel (just as Rev. xvii gives the name of
Babylon to Rome), or because he actually had in mind the Roman province of Syria.

[3] Allusion to Ezek. xxxviii-xxxix; cf. Rev. xx. 8.

XII (**1**) For the multitude of the saints in heaven is [Thin]e (?)
and the hosts of angels in Thy holy realm to pr[aise] Thy [Name].
And the elect of the holy people (**2**) hast Thou set for Thyself upon
                                                    [ea[rth]
[and the b]ook of the names of all their host is beside Thee in Thy holy
and the [. . .] of the [. . .] in Thy glorious realm;   [abode,
(**3**) and the favours of [Thy] blessi[ngs are for them]
and Thou hast engraved for them Thy Covenant of peace with the burin
                                                    [of life,
that [the sons of light (?)] may reign in all the times of the ages
(**4**) and that Thy [e]lect may chastise [their] adv[ersaries]
(ranked) according to their Thousands and their Myriads
together with Thy saints and angels;
and that they may inherit a stele (?) (**5**) in the battle
[together with] those who will rise from the earth[1] when Thy judg-
and with the vi[ctorious] elect from heaven.   [ments are disputed,

(**7**) And Thou art a ter[rible] God in Thy kingly glory
and the congregation of Thy saints is in the midst of us (for) fina[l]
[Among] us (is) contempt for kings,   [succour.
disdain (**8**) and mockery for the brave!
For Adonai is holy
and the King of Glory is with us accompanied by the saints.
The pow[ers] of the host of angels are among our numbered men
(**9**) and the Valiant of Battle is in our congregation
and the host of his spirits accompany our steps.
And o[ur] horsemen are [like] the clouds
and like the mists of dew which cover the earth
(**10**) and like the shower of rain
which waters in the desired way all its fruits.

Arise, O Valiant One!
Lead away Thy captives, O glorious Man!
Do (**11**) Thy plundering, O Valorous One![2]
Set Thy hand upon the neck of Thine enemies
and Thy foot upon the heap of the slain!
Strike the nations Thy enemies
and let Thy sword (**12**) devour guilty flesh!
Fill Thy land with glory
and Thine inheritance with blessing!

[1] Allusion to the resurrection of the body; cf. Dan. xii. 2.
[2] These epithets are addressed to God; in line 9 He is called 'the Valiant of battle'. The expression 'glorious Man' (*ish*) may seem astonishing, but in Exod. xv. 3, we find 'Yahweh is a man (*ish*) of war'.

A multitude of cattle in Thy pastures,
silver and gold and precious stones (13) in Thy palaces!
O Zion, rejoice greatly!
Appear amid shouts of joy, O Jerusalem!
Show yourselves, O all you cities of Judah!
Open (14) [thy] gat[es] for ever,
for the riches of the nations to enter in!
And let their kings serve thee
and let all thy oppressors bow down before thee
and (15) [let them lick] the dust [of thy feet]!
[O daughters] of my people, break out in cries of gladness!
Adorn yourselves with magnificent ornaments
and rule over the [ki]ng[dom . . .]

. . . .

Blessings and curses to be pronounced during battle

[. . .] **XIII** (1) and his brethren the [pr]iests[1] and the Levites and all the
veteran officers with him, and (2) when they take up (their) position
they shall bless the God of Israel and all His works of truth, and they shall
execrate [Beli]al there and all the spirits of his lot. They shall speak and say:

Blessed be the God of Israel
because of all His plan of holiness and His works of truth!
And bl[ess]ed be (3) all those who [ser]ve Him in righteousness
(and) know Him by faith!
(4) And cu[rs]ed be Belial because of the plan of hostility,
and may he be execrated because of his guilty service!
And cursed be all the spirits of his lot
because of their (5) wicked plan,
and may they be execrated because of their defiled and unclean service!
For they are the lot of darkness
whereas the lot of God is for (6) [eterna]l light.

(7) O God of our fathers,
we will bless Thy Name for ever.
And we, we are an ever[last]ing people,
and Thou madest a Covenant with our fathers
and hast established it with their seed
(8) for everlasting a[g]es.
And a reminder of Thy Grace is in the midst of us
in all Thy glorious testimonies,
to succour the remnant and the survivors of Thy Covenant

---

[1] The chief priest must have been mentioned before the other priests; cf. XVIII, 5.

(9) that they may re[count] Thy works of truth
and the judgment of Thy marvellous lofty deeds.

[O God of] our [fath]ers,
the eternal people is Thine,
and Thou hast caused us to fall in the lot of light (10) unto Thy truth.
And Thou didst appoint the Prince of Light[1] in former times to bring us
and [all the angels of justi]ce [are] in [his lot]   [help,
and all the spirits of truth are in his empire.
And Thou (11) didst create Belial for the Pit,
the Angel of hostility and repudiation,
[together with] his [plan] and with his design,
that wicked deeds and sins might be committed;
and all the spirits (12) of his lot are angels of destruction,
they walk in decrees of darkness
and their [de]sire tends towards darkness in one movement.
And we in the lot of Thy truth shall rejoice
because of Thy (13) mighty Hand,
and we shall be glad because of Thy salvation.
And we shall rejoice with joy
because of [Thy] succou[r and because of] Thy [p]eace!

O God of Israel, who is strong like Thee?
Truly, (14) Thy mighty Hand is with the Poor!
And what angel or prince is like the succour of [Thy marvell]ous inter-
From former times Thou didst appoint unto Thyself   [[vention]?
the Day of grea[t] battle [against dark]ness,
(15) [to save the li]ght in truth and to destroy among the guilty,
to strike down darkness and to raise up light [. . .]
(16) to wipe out all the sons of darkness;
whereas joy (shall be) the [lo]t of the [sons of light . . .]

. . . .

XIV (1) like the fire of His Wrath against the idols of Egypt.[2]

Hymn of thanksgiving after battle

(2) And after they have departed from the slain to enter the camp, they
shall all joyfully intone the hymn of return. And in the morning, they shall
wash their garments and shall cleanse them (3) of the blood of the guilty
carcases. And they shall return to the place where they took up (their)

---

[1] The Spirit of Good, called 'Prince of lights' in the *Rule* (III, 20) and the *Damascus
Document* (V, 18).
[2] Cf. Isa. xix. 1. The beginning of this phrase bringing to an end the discourse begun in
XIII, 2, has disappeared in the lacuna at the foot of column XIII.

position, where they formed the line before the slain of the enemy fell.
And there they shall (4) all bless the God of Israel and shall praise His
Name in joyful unison. They shall speak and say:

Blessed be the God of Israel who keeps favour unto His Covenant
and testimonies (5) of salvation to the people whom He has redeemed!
He has called them that staggered to [mar]vellous [salvation]
but has wiped out the assembly of the nations unto destruction,
leaving no remnant.
He raises in righteousness (6) the discouraged heart
and opens the mouth of the dumb that it may cry out with joy
because of [His] lofty [deeds].
[To] feeble [hands] he teaches battle
and to them whose knees stagger He gives strength to stand
(7) together with strength of loins to those whose back is bent.
And by the humble of spirit [. . . shall] the hardened heart be pun-
                                                              [ished (?);
all the wicked nations shall vanish by (means of) the perfect of way
(8) and none of their valiant men shall remain standing.

And we, the re[mnant of Thy people,]
[shall praise] Thy Name, O God of favours,
who hast kept the Covenant with our fathers,
and during (9) all our generations
lettest Thy favours fall upon the remn[ant of Thy people].
[For] during the dominion of Belial
and amid the Mysteries of his hostility
they have not driven [us] (10) from Thy Covenant;
and Thou hast caused his spirits of [des]truction to depart far from [us];
[and whereas the m]en of his empire [delivered themselves up to ungod-
Thou hast preserved the soul which Thou didst redeem.   [liness][1]
And Thou hast raised up (11) by Thy might those who were fallen;
but the men of high statu[re] Thou hast cut off [. . .]
[and] there is no saviour for all their valiant men
nor any refuge for their nimble men,
and to their respected men (12) Thou hast replied with scorn.
And all their beings of vanity [. . .]

And we, Thy holy people,
shall praise Thy Name because of Thy works of truth,
(13) and we shall exalt [Thy] ma[gnificence] because of Thy lofty deeds

[1] Restored after a manuscript of the *War Scroll* found in cave IV; cf. C. H. Hunzinger,
'Fragmente einer älteren Fassung des Buches Milhamā aus Höhle 4 von Qumrān, *ZAW*,
1957, pp. 131-51.

[during] the seasons and times appointed by the eternal testimonies,
at the [com]ing of day and night
(**14**) and [when] evening and morning depart.[1]
For Thy [glori]ous [kingship] is great,
together with Thy marvellous Mysteries in the heights [of heaven],
to [rai]se up dust unto Thee
(**15**) and to strike down the gods.[2]

(**16**) Be lifted up, O God of gods, be lifted up!
Be praised in the cl[ouds of heaven . . .][3]

. . . .

WAR RULE ANNEXE

Proclamation of war

. . . .

XV (**1**) For it is the time of distress for Isra[el]
[and the moment appoi]nted for the war against all the nations;
and the lot of God (is set) in final redemption
(**2**) and destruction (is determined) for every wicked nation.

In the camp before battle: the High Priest's exhortation

And all the troo[p of fighting] men shall go to camp before the king
of the Kittim and before all the host (**3**) of Belial gathered about him for
the Day [of Destruction] by the sword of God.

(**4**) And the chief priest shall stand, together with his brethren [the
priests] and Levites and all the officers with him, and he shall read into
their ears (**5**) the prayer in time of wa[r and all the bo]ok of the rule of
that time, together with all the words of their hymns of thanksgiving.[4]
Then he shall form (**6**) all the lines there according to al[l the words of
this rul]e. And the priest appointed for the hour of vengeance by the
decision (**7**) of all his brethren shall advance and shall strengthen the
[heart of the fighting] men. He shall speak and say:

[1] The author insists on fidelity to the religious calendar of the sect, an object of major
preoccupation in the various writings of Qumran, as well as on the duty to pray in the
morning and evening; cf. *Rule*, X, 10.
[2] God raises 'dust' towards Him, i.e. men made of dust; he strikes down 'the gods', i.e.
the angels (an allusion to the myth of the fall of the angels told in *Enoch*).
[3] The end of this hymn has disappeared in the lacuna at the foot of column XIV,
together with the beginning of the second Rule, or Rule Annexe. This second Rule seems
to have begun with a discourse proclaiming the outbreak of final war; it is the end of this
proclamation that appears at the top of column XV.
[4] Is this a reference to the 'Thanksgiving Hymns' (*Hōdāyōt*) preserved in one of the
scrolls found at Qumran? I am inclined to think so; it would show how greatly the sons of
light, i.e. the Essene sect, esteemed this collection. It would also indicate that the *War
Scroll*, or at any rate the second Rule, was written somewhat later than the *Hōdāyōt*.

Be strong! Be hardy! Show yourselves men of valour!
(8) Be not afraid! [Fear] not! [Let not y]ou [heart faint]!
Tremble not! Be not afraid before them![1]
(9) Turn not back! [. . .]
For they are a wicked congregation
and all their works are in darkness
(10) and to darkness turns their desi[re . . .]
and their power shall be as vanishing smoke,
and all the assembly (11) of their [mul]titude [. . .]
and all the substance of their being shall quickly wither (12) [. . .]
Gather your strength for the battle of God
for today is the Hour of battle!
(13) [. . .] on all the multitude of Belial
[and anger] upon all flesh.
The God of Israel raises His hand with His marvellous [Migh]t
(14) [over] all the spirits of ungodl[iness],
[and all the Va]liant of the gods gird themselves for battl[e]
[and] the formation[s of the] saints (15) [gather toge]ther for the Day
[of God . . .]

. . . .

XVI (1) until all the conse[crated of Belial] vanish.[2] For the God of
Israel has called out the sword against all the nations and shall display
His valour by the saints of His people.

First assault

(3) They shall put all this rule into force [on] that [day] when they
take up (their) position before the camp of the Kittim. And then the
priests shall sound for them the trumpets (4) of the reminder, and they
shall open the gates of batt[le and] the foot-soldiers shall go out and shall
take up (their) position in sections between the lines. And the priests
shall sound for them (5) the sound 'formations', and the sections [shall
spre]ad out between the lines at the sound of the trumpets until every
man is in his place. Then the priests shall sound for them (6) a second
sound [for the ass]ault. And when they stand by the line of the Kittim at
throwing distance, each man shall raise his hand over his weapons (7) of
war. And the six [priests shall sound the tru]mpets of slaughter, with a
sharp and urgent sound during the battle, and the Levites and all the
troop (8) of horns shall send [out] a loud [war-cry]; and while they raise
their voice, they shall begin to bring down their hand upon the slain

---

[1] Cf. above, X, 3-4 (the exhortation of the High Priest before battle in the principal
Rule).
[2] The 'consecrated' are the soldiers, as in Isa. xiii. 3; cf. Jer. li. 27-8. This line represents
the end of the discourse beginning in XV, 7.

of the Kittim. And all (9) the troop shall be silent, ending the noise [of the clamour, and the priest]s shall sound the trumpets of slaughter for as long as the battle against the Kittim shall last.[1]

Relief of the first line which has suffered losses, and the calling out of a fresh one: the High Priest's exhortation

(11) And when [Belial] girds himself (to come) to the aid of the sons of darkness, and the slain among the foot-soldiers begin to fall by the Mysteries of God, and He tries by them all those who are destined to fight, (12) then the priests [shall] sou[nd the] tru[mp]ets of summons for another relief line to go out to fight. And (these) shall take up (their) position between the lines, (13) but for those who have attack[ed in ba]ttle (the priests) shall sound the withdrawal.

Then the chief priest shall draw near and shall stand before the line and strengthen (14) their heart [. . .] (15) He shall speak and say:

[God has . . .] the h[ea]rt of His people
and has tried [His] el[ect] (?) [. . .] [2]
For you have heard in former times (16) the Mysteries of God [. . .]

. . . .

XVII (1) and He will ensure their wholeness amid the burnings[3]
[. . .] those who are tried in the crucible.
And He will sharpen ⟨their⟩ weapons of war
and they shall not faint until [. . .] (2) ungodliness.
And remember the judgmen[t of Nadab and Abi]hu sons of Aaron
by whose judgment God was sanctified
in the eyes of [all His people],
[whereas Eleazar] (3) and Ithamar He joined to the Covenant
[for ever and e]ver.[4]
(4) Gather up your strength and fear them not!
Their desire turns toward chaos
and their support is in that which i[s] not and [will] not [be];
[for to the God] (5) of Israel belongs all that is and will be,
and [. . .] in the happenings of the ages.

---

[1] This description of the first phase of the battle, as well as that of the second phase (XVII, 10 ff.) makes no mention of the seven lines, nor of the slingers, nor of the four battalions armed with javelins, nor of the three battalions responsible for the hand-to-hand fighting, nor of the cavalry, as the first Rule does (VI, VIII-IX). It even seems that here the same line first of all attacks with javelins and then fights hand-to-hand; which proves that this is a different recension, another rule.

[2] An allusion to losses suffered in the first assault; this is the trial which God has imposed on his saints, cf. Dan. xi. 35.

[3] God will keep his own safe and sound in the midst of fire; cf. Dan. iii.

[4] Allusion to Lev. x. 1-4; cf. Num. iii. 4.

This day is His hour to bend and bring low
the Prince of the empire (6) of ungodliness.
He will send final succour by the power of the Great Angel
to the lot whom He has [re]deemed,[1]
and to the servant of Michael[2]
by the everlasting light,
(7) to enlighten the Co[venant of I]srael with joy.
Gladness and blessing shall belong to the lot of God
to raise up the servant of Michael in the midst of the gods,[3]
and the dominion (8) of Israel shall be over all flesh.
Righteousness shall rejoice [in] the heights
and all His sons of truth shall be glad in everlasting Knowledge.
And you, O sons of his Covenant, (9) gather up your strength in the
until He hastens His hand [for] His trials to cease,   [trial of God
His Mysteries concerning your being!

Second assault; defeat and pursuit of the enemy

(10) And after these words, the priests shall sound for them the formation of the battalions of the line. And the sections shall spread out at the
sound of the trumpets (11) until [each ma]n is in [his] place. [And] the
priests shall sound with the trumpets a second sound for the assault. And
when (12) the [foot]-soldiers have reached throwing distance of [the
li]ne of the Kitt[im], each man shall raise his hand to his weapons of
war. And the priests shall sound the trumpets (13) of slaughter [with an
urgent sound, and al]l the troops of horns shall send out a warlike clamour. And the foot-soldiers shall strike the army (14) of the Kittim; [and
while the noise of the cl]amour [rises,] they shall begin to bring down
(their hand) upon the slain of the Kittim. And all the troop [shall] end
the noise of clamour and the priests (15) shall sound the [trumpets of
slaughter . . .]

. . . .

XVIII (1) [. . .] when the great Hand of God is raised over Belial[4]
and over all the [lo]t of his empire
to strike a final blow

---

[1] The 'Great Angel' is probably the 'Prince of light', the supreme leader of the angels of
light; cf. XIII, 10: 'And Thou didst appoint the Prince of Light in former times to bring
us help.'
[2] This expression means Israel, whose protector is the angel Michael; cf. Dan. x. 13.
21; xii. 1.
[3] Cf. *Assumption of Moses*, X, 8-10: 'Then shalt thou be glad O Israel . . . and God shall
exalt thee and set thee in the starry heavens in their abode. And thou shalt look down from
above, and shalt see thine enemies on earth.'
[4] Lines 1-3 appear to constitute the end of a discourse exhorting the soldiers to pursue
the enemy.

(2) [in the midst of the tumult of a vast multitude]
and the clamour of the saints;
when they pursue Asshur
and the sons of Japheth fall to rise no more
and the Kittim are cut in pieces leaving (3) [no remnants];
[. . .] the Hand of the God of Israel lifted
over all the multitude of Belial.

At that time, the priests shall sound (4) [the six trumpet]s of the reminder and all the battle lines shall gather unto them, and they shall divide against all the l[ines of the Kitt]im (5) to destroy them utterly.[1]

The evening; prayer asking for a prolongation of the day in order to complete the pursuit

[And when] the sun is on the point of setting on that day, the chief priest, together with the priests and [Levites] who (6) are with him and the officer hea[ds of family], shall stand and bless the God of Israel there. They shall speak and say:

Blessed by Thy Name, O God [of god]s,
for (7) Thou hast magnified [Thine elect] marvellously!
And Thou hast kept for us Thy Covenant from former times
and hast opened for us the gates of salvation many times
(8) becau[se of Thy favour and] Thy [mercy] towards us.
O God of jus[ti]ce, Thou hast acted for [the Glory] of Thy Name.
(10) [. . .] and in former times there was never any happening like this.
For Thou didst know (what would happen) in our time,
and on this day there has shone (11) for u[s . . .][2]
[. . .] with us in the final redemption,
to abolish the do[mi]ni[on of the en]emy that it might exist no more;
and Thy mighty Hand (12) [. . .]
[al]l our enemies with a destroying blow.
And now it is urgent for us today to pursue their multitude;
for Thou (13) [. . .]
Thou hast delivered up the heart of the valiant, without any halting.

Thine is the Power and the battle is in Thy hand!
(14) [. . .] and the times depend on Thy will [. . .]

. . . .

[1] This paragraph, like IX, 5-7, deals with the pursuit of the enemy destined to total destruction, *ḥerem*; cf. Deut. vii. 2; xx. 17.
[2] Or 'appeared unto us'; this seems to be a request that God should renew the miracle of Joshua x. 12-14.

[contempt and disdain] **XIX** (1) [for the va]liant![1]
For our Great One is holy
and the King of Glory is with us
and the host of His spirits accompany our steps.
[And our horsemen are like clouds]
(2) [and like mists of d]ew which cover the earth
and like the shower of rain
which waters in the desired manner a[ll its fruits].

[Arise, O Valiant One!
Lead away Thy captives, (3) O Glorious One!]
[D]o Thy plundering, O Valorous One!
Set Thy hand upon the neck of Thine enemies
and Thy foot [upon the heap of the slain]!
[Strike] (4) [the nations, Thine enemies],
and let Thy sword devour flesh!
Fill Thy land with glory
and Thine inheritance with blessing!
A mul[titude of cattle in Thy pastures],
[silver (5) and gold and precious stones in] Thy palaces!
O Zion, rejoice greatly!
Show yourselves, O all you cities of Ju[dah]!
[Appear amid cries of joy, O Jerusalem]!
[Open thy gates (6) for ever]
[for] the riches of the nations [to enter in]!
And let their kings serve thee
and let [all thy oppressors] bow down before thee
[and let them lick the dust (7) of thy feet]!
[O daughters of] my [peo]ple, break out in cries of gladness!
Adorn yourselves with magnificent ornaments
and r[ul]e over the kingdom of (8) [. . .]

The following morning; hymn of thanksgiving[2]

(9) [and then they shall gather in the cam]p that ni[gh]t to rest until morning. And in the morning they shall come to the place in the line (10) [where the va]liant of the Kittim [fell] and the multitude of Asshur

---

[1] Lines 1-8 reproduce, with a few slight variants, the whole of passage XII, 8-16; this is helpful in completing the lacunae, which are very numerous in column XIX. The epetition of the great war hymn, 'Arise, O Valiant One', which in the principal Rule is recited at the beginning of the battle, can only be explained if, in column XIX, the battle is still in progress for the supreme effort of completing the pursuit and extermination of the enemy.

[2] Passage parallel to XIV, 2 ff., in the principal Rule.

and the army of all the nations [. . .] (**11**) [. . .] where they fell by the sword of God.

And the chi[ef] priest shall draw near, [together with his brethren the priests and Levites] (**12**) [. . .] and all the commanders of the lines and their numbered men . . . (**13**) [. . . a]ll [the sl]ain of the Kitt[im, and there they shall p]raise [the] God of [Israel . . .]

. . . .

(Here ends the surviving portion of the scroll of the *War Rule*.)

CHAPTER VI

THE HYMN SCROLL

Description of the scroll; literary *genre* and author. — Translation.

The life of the Essene was devoted entirely to the praise of God. 'I will sing in Knowledge', we read in the *Rule* (X, 9), 'and my whole lyre shall throb to the Glory of God, and my lute and harp to the holy Order which He has made. I will raise the flute of my lips because of His righteous measuring-cord.' Day and night he blessed God; day and night prayers of thanksgiving ascended to God from his heart and lips. Rejoicing in the wonders of creation and keenly aware of the divine grace which had made him one of the Elect, his heart overflowed with gratitude: this gratitude he expressed in fervent canticles. One of the scrolls discovered in cave I at Qumran is a collection of these very hymns of thanksgiving, called in Hebrew *hōdāyōt*, and in Greek 'eucharists'.[1]

This scroll has reached us in rather a bad condition and the frequent lacunae often make interpretation difficult. Eighteen columns have been found in all, as well as sixty-six fragments, some of them tiny. The first columns are the best preserved. Two different hands may be distinguished in the script, the second beginning towards the middle of column XI, but although both are very clear, the writing of the first scribe is the more expert and elegant. Altogether the scroll contains about twenty more or less complete hymns, some of them extremely long, and in addition fragments of varying size of at least twenty others. In its original state the collection probably consisted of a great many more hymns.[2]

[1] The scroll is published complete in the posthumous work of E. L. SUKENIK, *Oẓar ham-Megillōt hag-genuzōt . . .* (Jerusalem, 1954; English edition entitled *The Dead Sea Scrolls of the Hebrew University*, 1955), plates XXXV-LVIII. This is essentially a collection of photographs with an accompanying transcription into printed Hebrew characters. See also, in *Qumran Cave I* (Oxford, 1955), no. 35, plate XXXI, two very short fragments of *Hōdāyōt* no doubt belonging to the same scroll.

[2] It is not always easy to recognize the division between the various hymns, mainly because of the lacunae at the top and bottom of every column. In the eighteen columns, I have distinguished thirty-two hymns which I have indicated alphabetically (A-Z, followed by A'-F'); but in some cases this distinction is rather uncertain. As regards the

But despite the damage inflicted by time, there is no doubt that this scroll is the jewel of all the mystical literature from Qumran. It seems to have been one of the classic and most highly venerated books of the sect; in fact, we learn from the scroll of the *War Rule* (col. XV, line 5) that in the grave and solemn hours immediately preceding the battle against Belial and his fiends, the High Priest was to read 'the prayer in time of wa[r and all the bo]ok of the rule of that time', as well as all the words of their hymns of thanksgiving (*hōdāyōtām*). It may very well be that the present *Hōdāyōt* are the *Hōdāyōt* of the sons of light to which the *War Scroll* alludes. I would point out, moreover, that six other manuscripts of the same collection were found in cave IV: this great number of copies shows how highly rated the book of the *Hōdāyōt* was among the works contained in the Qumran library.

Most of the hymns begin with the words 'I give Thee thanks, O Adonai', and only a few with 'Blessed be Thou'. On the whole, there is an unquestionable resemblance between them and the psalms of the canonical collection, particularly with those which, from the point of view of form criticism ('gattungsgeschichtliche Methode') experts designate as 'songs of individual thanksgiving' ('Danklieder des Einzelnen').[1] But this type of psalm in post-canonical Jewish literature has not been preserved in a completely pure form; it is often contaminated by other types, and as a result the present *Hōdāyōt* must not be judged according to a too strict 'typological' standard. In point of fact, although they all belong to the *Hōdāyōt* type, the hymns collected in this scroll show a very great diversity. They are at the same time spiritual elevations and confessions; their lyricism draws its inspiration not only from the Psalms, but also from Jeremiah, the Lamentations and Job. With their lofty mysticism these songs are outpourings of the soul in which the author expresses in turn his adoration of God, his total submission to the divine will, his love for the Most High God and his hatred of Belial, his despair and his sudden leaps of infinite hope, his mortal anguish at the thought of the imminent end of the world, and his triumphant joy in the dreams of eternal bliss in the bright company of the angels.

[1] See H. GUNKEL — J. BEGRICH, *Einleitung in die Psalmen* (Göttingen, 1933), pp. 265-92; S. MOWINCKEL, *Offersang og sangoffer* (Oslo, 1951), pp. 277 ff., 283 ff.).

'fragments' published as such in Sukenik's work, it is obviously impossible to try to find out exactly how many hymns they represent.

At the source of these mystical effusions appear the characteristic ideas expounded chiefly in the *Rule*. Doctrine of this kind is, of course, intimately nourished on the substance of the biblical books, and the style of the *Hōdāyōt* is as it were interwoven with biblical reminiscence. But however close their bond with ancient Jewish piety, the *Hymns* of Qumran constantly betray new ideas which are obviously connected with the religious world of Zoroastrianism and Hellenistic Gnosis. The psalmist is a 'man who knows', a Gnostic; he possesses a secret revelation reserved to initiates and it is this knowledge that is the principle of his salvation and the source of his joy.

The author constantly uses the word 'I'[1] and voices most movingly the complaint of a just man, unhappy and persecuted. Who was this writer? To my mind, he unquestionably presents himself in several of the canticles as the leader of the sect of the Covenant: he is the Teacher who teaches, the Father who cares for his children and feeds them, the Source of living waters, the Builder of the Community of the Elect, the Gardener of the eternal Planting. How is it possible to avoid concluding that such a person must be the Teacher of Righteousness himself whom the *Damascus Document* and the biblical Commentaries from Qumran (notably the *Commentary on Habakkuk*) present as the founder and lawgiver of the sect, the Prophet *par excellence* whose tragic destiny and exceptional prestige they describe. Several of the hymns of a more general character contain, it is true, nothing specific obliging us to ascribe them to the Teacher of Righteousness; no doubt they may have been written by some teacher or other, or by some anonymous sectary of the Covenant. It is even possible that the hymns in which the Teacher of Righteousness seems to express himself are, in reality, not his own work but that of one of his disciples speaking as it were through the Teacher's mouth. With regard to the Gāthā of the Avesta, it is in the same way open to question whether, in spite of the 'I', the author was Zoroaster himself or one of his very early disciples. A similar hypothesis is not to be excluded with respect to the *Hymns*. But be this as it may, the collection is at least to be considered as an ancient work of the sect, authentically and profoundly stamped with the personality and doctrine of the Teacher.

This being so, the collection of *Hōdāyōt* is of very special im-

---

[1] There are only four exceptions to the use of 'I' (Fragments 10, 18, 47, 55), and there 'we' clearly alludes to the Community.

portance to the historian. In these *Hymns* we are able to hear, either directly from his own mouth or from one of his most authentic disciples, the mystical confessions of faith, and as it were the spiritual testament, of one whom the faith of his followers raised so high and whom, in view of the quality and extent of his work, we must recognize as one of the loftiest figures of religious humanity.

In the following translation it has seemed useful, and even necessary, to arrange the text in lines so as to emphasize the rhythm and poetic character of the *Hymns*. This is, of course, only an experiment, and many other arrangements are possible. The same may be said of the division into stanzas; the Hebrew manuscript only rarely leaves a blank within a hymn to indicate where a stanza ends. I would point out that in the text of the scroll there are frequent subtleties and formidable obscurities; the present translation in no way pretends to resolve all these enigmas for good and all. The lacunae in the manuscript set problems that are difficult and sometimes impossible to solve; wherever they are not too extensive I have proposed a conjectural reading, paying all the time great attention to the length of the gap and to any trace of letters still discernible. Nevertheless it goes without saying that the value of these conjectures varies: a number can be considered as certainly correct, but most of them are merely probable. In several the intention is only to restore the movement of the phrase or verse, and not the words of the vanished text. The title attached to each hymn is an attempt to draw attention to its principal theme or to certain of its essential ideas. But it in no way constitutes an analysis of the poem; the movement of ideas in these compositions is so complex that any such analysis would require several lines.[1]

---

[1] The following translation is reproduced from my work, *Le Livre des Hymnes découvert près de la mer Morte (1 QH). Traduction intégrale avec introduction et notes (Semitica, VII; Paris, 1957).* In the present work I have omitted the translation of the various fragments as well as of some very mutilated passages; the reader will find these in the above-mentioned book. He will also find there the philological notes intended to justify my interpretation. In this book I include only notes giving certain indispensable explanations. I would draw attention to the English translation (often free and paraphrastic) of T. H. GASTER, *The Dead Sea Scriptures in English Translation* (New York, 1956), pp. 122-225; the work of M. BURROWS, *The Dead Sea Scrolls* (New York, 1955), pp. 390-415, gives only a translation of extracts from the scroll. In German, the translation of H. BARDTKE in *TLZ,* 1956, cols. 149-54, 589-604, 715-24, and 1957, cols. 339-48. Also J. LICHT's *The Thanksgiving Scroll. Text, Introduction, Commentary and Glossary* (in modern Hebrew; Jerusalem, 1957). Other bibliographical indications appear in my work, *Le Livre des Hymnes . . .,* pp. 21-3.

TRANSLATION

HYMN A

Divine creation and the destiny of man[1]

I [. . .] (6) [Thou art merciful] and long-suffering in [Thy] judg[ments]
[and] just in all Thy works.
(7) And in Thy wisdom [Thou hast established the world from] former
and before ever creating them Thou knewest   [times,
all the works which creatures would accomplish (8) during all ages for
for [without Thee] nothing is made   [ever;
and nothing is known without Thy will.

It is Thou who hast formed (9) every spirit g[ood and] ba[d]
[together with their ways] and the judgment of all their works.[2]

It is Thou who hast spread out the heavens (10) for Thy glory
[and] hast [created] all [their hosts] according to Thy will
together with the mighty winds according to the laws which governed
before (11) they became [Thine] angels of hol[iness];[3]   [them
and to the everlasting spirits in their dominions
[hast Thou entrusted] the heavenly lights according to their mysterious
(12) the stars according to the paths [which they follow],   [(laws),
[the clouds and the rain] according to the office which they fulfil,
the thunderbolt and lightnings according to the service appointed unto
and the (13) providential reservoirs according to their functions, [them,
[and snow and hailstones] according to their mysterious (laws).[4]

It is Thou who hast created the earth by Thy strength,
(14) the seas and the deeps [and the rivers],
and Thou hast established [all] their [inhabi]tants by Thy wisdom,
and all that is in them (15) hast Thou di[spo]sed according to Thy will.

[And Thou hast cast a lot] for the spirit of man
which Thou hast formed in the world
for everlasting days (16) and unending generations
to ru[le over the works of Thy hands];
[and] Thou hast allotted their service unto them

---

[1] Of the first five lines of column I only a few fragmentary phrases remain.
[2] Recalling the doctrine of the two Spirits.
[3] Cf. Ps. civ. 4: 'Who makest the winds Thy messengers.' (The Hebrew word 'messenger' signifies also 'angel'.)
[4] Compare this stanza with *Jubilees*, II, 1-3; *Enoch*, LX, 11-23. The 'providential reservoirs' are the celestial reservoirs (cf. Ps. xxxiii. 7; Job xxxviii. 22, etc.).

in all their generations according to their times.
And [Thou hast ordained their] ju[dg]ment
(17) in conformity with the seasons of the domi[nion of the two Spirits]
from generation to generation [according to] their [wor]ks.
And the Visitation bringing gladness unto them,
together with (18) ⟨   ⟩ all the blows that smite them,
[Thou hast know]n [from former times],
and hast allotted it unto all their seed
according to the number of everlasting generations
(19) and according to all their unending years.
[And in conformity with Th]y [glorious design]
and by the wisdom of Thy knowledge
Thou hast established their law before (20) ever they were;
all [things have come into being] by command [of Thy will]
and without Thee nothing is made.[1]

(21) These things I have known because of Thine understanding;
for Thou hast uncovered my ear to marvellous Mysteries.
Yet am I but a creature of clay and a thing kneaded with water,
(22) a foundation of shame and fount of defilement,
a crucible of iniquity and fabric of sin,
a spirit of straying, and perverse,
void (23) of understanding,
whom the judgments of righteousness terrify.
What can I say that is not already known,
and what can I utter that has not already been told?
The world (24) is graven before Thee
with the graving-tool of the reminder[2]
for all the unending seasons
together with the cycles of the number of everlasting years
with all their times;
(25) they have not been hidden nor concealed from before Thee.
But how can a man count up his sins,
and what can he answer concerning his iniquities?
(26) And how can he, perverse, reply to the judgment of righteousness?
Thine, Thine, O God of knowledge,
are all the works of righteousness,
(27) the foundation of truth;
but to the sons of men belong the service of iniquity
and works of deceit.

---

[1] As regards both ideas and style, this stanza calls to mind the basic instruction on the Spirits given in the *Rule* (III, 13-IV, 26).
[2] An allusion to the heavenly tablets on which the destiny of the world is written; cf. the expression 'the graven Decree', in the *Rule* (X, 8).

It is Thou who hast created (28) breath on the tongue
and known the words of the tongue
and determined the fruit of the lips before ever they were.[1]
And Thou hast set out words on a measuring-cord
(29) and measured the breathing of breath from the lips
and hast sent out sounds according to their mysterious (laws)
and breathings of breath according to their harmony;[2]
that (30) Thy glory might be made known
and Thy wonders told
in all Thy works of truth and [judgments] of righteousness,
and that Thy Name might be praised (31) by the mouth of all men,
and that they might know Thee
according to the measure of their understanding,
and might bless Thee for ever and ever.
And it is Thou who in Thy mercy (32) and in the greatness of Thy favours
hast strengthened the spirit of man in the face of blows,
[and hast redeemed] and cleansed him from much iniquity
(33) that he might recount Thy marvels in the presence of all Thy
[works.
[And I, I will rec]ount [unto men] the judgments which have smitten
(34) and all Thy marvels unto the sons of men   [me
because Thou hast manifested Thy power [in me . . .]

Hear, (35) O you wise men,
and you that are diligent in knowledge,
and you that are quick!
Be firmly inclined, [O you that are upright of heart]!
Redouble your prudence, (36) O you just!
Put an end to perversity!
Be a sta[y to the poor], O all you perfect of way,
[and to whosoever cal]ls, reply!
Be slow (37) to anger and despise not [. . .]
[But those that are foo]lish of heart cannot understand (38) these things
[. . .]

[1] An allusion to language: God knew words and determined their meaning even before
there were any men to speak them. In the same way, He established in advance, and
before the creation of the world, 'the whole plan', i.e. all the laws and ideas of being (cf.
above, lines 20-1, and *Rule*, III, 15). This doctrine of the pre-existence of the idea and the
word calls to mind Greek philosophy and Philo.

[2] An allusion to poetry and music and their subjection to the laws of measure and
harmony; the psalmist finds their origin in God. This passage may be compared with
Pythagorean speculation on the subject of numbers and harmony. In the verses which
follow, the psalmist explains that poetry and music have as their sole aim the singing of
the glory of God. The *Hōdāyōt* testify to the Essene taste for sacred song.

HYMN B

*The Teacher of Righteousness exposed to the hostility of the wicked
and a sign of contradiction*[1]

II [. . .] (6) my courage softened at the soun[d of their voices,]
and [my strong] endurance (7) in the face of blows.
But to the uncir[cumcision] of my lips
Thou hast given a reply of the tongue
and hast upheld my soul with strength of loins (8) and strong endurance;
and Thou hast confirmed my steps in the realm of ungodliness.

And I have been a snare for sinners,
but healing for all (9) those that are converted from sin,
prudence for the simple
and the firm inclination of all those whose heart is troubled.
And Thou hast made of me an object of shame (10) and mockery for
[traitors,
(but) the foundation of truth and understanding for them whose way is
And I was exposed to the affronts of the wicked,   [straight.[2]
(11) an object of slander upon the lips of the violent;
the mockers gnashed their teeth.
And I was ridiculed in the songs of sinners
(12) and the assembly of the wicked raged against me
and roared like storms upon the seas
when their billows rage
(13) throwing up slime and mud.
But Thou hast made of me a banner for the elect of righteousness
and an interpreter of Knowledge concerning the marvellous Mysteries,
to test (14) [the men] of truth
and to try them that love instruction.[3]

[1] Only a few fragmentary phrases of the beginning of this hymn remain at the top of
column II.

[2] The psalmist is a man who is questioned and contradicted. He knows himself to be the
bearer of a divine revelation to men; those who resist him are sinners, and those who
believe, good. For the first, his coming and ministry are an occasion of sin, but for the
others he is an instrument of healing and salvation. The same will be said later of Jesus
(Luke ii. 34-5): 'Behold, this child is set for the fall and rising of many in Israel; he shall
be a sign that is spoken against, that the secret thoughts of many may be revealed.'

[3] The psalmist — in my opinion, the Teacher of Righteousness — refers here to Isa. xi.
10: 'In that day (the shoot of) the root of Jesse shall be raised as *a banner* in the midst of
the peoples.' This passage from Isaiah is messianic; the shoot of the root of Jesse is the
Messiah (cf. Isa. xi. 1). He will serve as a banner, i.e. as a rallying sign, for the elect. It
is noteworthy that the psalmist applies the biblical text to himself. His preaching constitutes a decisive test permitting the 'men of truth' to be recognized. Further on he affirms
(VII, 12): 'at the time of Judgment Thou wilt declare guilty all them that attack me,
distinguishing through me between the just and the guilty'. Therefore, to be found just,
i.e. to be saved, it was necessary to believe in him. This is the teaching of the *Commentary
on Habakkuk* (VII, 2-3): 'God will deliver them from the House of Judgment because of
their affliction and because of their faith in the Teacher of Righteousness.'

And I was a man of dispute for the interpreters of straying,
[but a man] (15) [of pea]ce for all who see true things;
and I became a spirit of jealousy to all who seek sm[ooth] things.
(16) [And all] the men of deceit roared against me
like the clamour of the roaring of great waters,
and ruses of Belial were [all] (17) their [thou]ghts;
and they cast down towards the Pit
the life of the man by whose mouth Thou hast established the teaching
and (18) within whose heart Thou hast set understanding
that he might open the fountain of Knowledge to all the understanding.[1]
But they bartered it for uncircumcision of the lips
(19) and for the foreign tongue of a people without understanding
that they might be lost in their straying.

HYMN C
Trust in God during persecution

(20) I give Thee thanks, O Adonai,
for Thou hast placed my soul in the sack of life
(21) and protected me from all the snares of the Pit![2]

Violent men have sought my soul
because I leaned (22) on Thy Covenant.
But they are an assembly of vanity
and a congregation of Belial.
They knew not that my being proceeds from Thee
(23) and that Thou wilt save my soul by Thy favours;
for my steps proceed from Thee.
And it is on Thy behalf that they have threatened (24) my life,[3]
that Thou mightest be glorified by the judgment of the wicked
and manifest Thy power in me before the sons (25) of men;
for it is by Thy grace that I stand upright.

And I said, 'The valiant have pitched their camps against me;
they have encircled ⟨me⟩ with all (26) their weapons of war
and have shot out incurable arrows.
And the flaming of spears was like a fire consuming trees,
(27) and the bellowing of their voice like the roaring of great waters,
a flowing whirlwind to destroy a multitude of men.

---

[1] 'The man' alluded to here is the psalmist, who declares himself (line 13) to be 'the interpreter of Knowledge'. By his mouth, we read, God 'established the teaching'. This expression could not apply to one of the sectaries, or even to one of the sect's teachers: it must refer to the great teacher himself, the Teacher of Righteousness.

[2] The Pit of Hell, Sheol.

[3] Persecution itself comes from God and will be turned to the glory of Him who chastises the wicked and saves the just.

They hatch out (28) the Asp and Vanity like rotten eggs
while their billows rear up'.
And whereas my heart melted like water,
my soul seized hold of Thy Covenant.
(29) And the net which they stretched out for me catches their foot;
they have (themselves) fallen into the traps which they hid for my soul.

But my foot stands upon level ground:
(30) outside their assembly I will bless Thy Name!

HYMN D

Trust in God during persecution

(31) I give Thee thanks, O Adonai,
for Thine eye wa[tches] over my soul
and Thou hast delivered me from the envy of the interpreters of false-
(32) and from the congregation of them that seek smooth things! [hood
Thou hast redeemed the soul of the poor one
whom they planned to remove
by shedding his blood (33) because of Thy service;
but [they kn]ew [not] that my steps proceed from Thee.
And they made me an object of contempt (34) and shame
in the mouth of all those that look for deceit.

But Thou, O my God, hast succoured the soul of the poor and needy,
(35) (snatching him) from the hands of one stronger than he,
and Thou hast redeemed my soul from the hand of the mighty,
and in the midst of their outrages Thou hast not left me without courage
(36) to the point of departing from Thy service
for fear of the cruelties of the wi[cke]d
and bartering for folly the firm inclination
(37) [established by Thee in my heart . . .]

HYMN E

The distress of the persecuted; the terrors of the end of the world and the birth of the Saviour-Messiah[1]

III [. . .] (6) [. . . for I was despised by them]
[and they] had [no] esteem for me.

[1] Of the beginning of this hymn there remain only a few fragmentary sentences at the top of column III. *Hymn* E is one of the most important and the most difficult to interpret of the whole collection; the reader will find a detailed commentary of the translation suggested here in my article, *La Mère du Messie et la mère de l'Aspic dans un hymne de Qoumrân*, published in *RHR*, cxlvii, no. 2, 1955, pp. 174-88. Also to be consulted are J. V. CHAMBER-LAIN, *JNES*, xiv, 1955, pp. 32-41, 181-2; J. BAUMGARTEN and M. MANSOOR, *JBL*, lxxiv, September 1955, pp. 188-92; LOU H. SILBERMAN, ibid., lxxv, June 1956, pp. 96-106.

And they made [my] soul like a ship in the depths of the s[ea],
(7) and like a fortified city before [them that besiege it].

[And] I was confused like the Woman about to bring forth[1]
at the time of her first child-bearing.
For terrors (8) and fearful pains have unfurled on its billows
that She who is with child might bring into the world (her) first-born.
For the children have reached as far as the billows of Death,
(9) and She who is big with the Man of distress (?) is in her pains.[2]
For she shall give birth to a man-child in the billows of Death,
and in the bonds of Sheol there shall spring (10) from the crucible of the
a Marvellous Counsellor with his might;[3]   [Pregnant one
and he shall deliver every man from the billows
because of Her who is big with him.[4]

Every womb suffers pain (11) and terrible anguish
at the time of child-bearing,
and terror seizes them that conceived these children;
and at the time of the bearing of her first-born
every terror unfurls (12) over the crucible of Her who is with child.

And She who is big with the Asp[5] is prey to terrible anguish
and the billows of the Pit (are unleashed) unto all the works of terror.

[1] This expression is borrowed from Jer. xiii. 21. The psalmist, who first compares himself to a ship in distress and then to a besieged city, goes on to develop another comparison, that of a woman in childbirth. This is a classic biblical image used to describe
distress and anguish (see for example, Jer. xxx. 6). But he goes a good deal further than
the usual imagery; the woman in travail to whom he compares himself is the woman who
is to give birth at the end of time to the Messiah. In this there are traces of a myth concerning the Mother of the Messiah — developed, no doubt, from Isa. vii. 14, and also from
Mic. v. 2; something of it reappears in Rev. xii. A little further on, the Mother of the
Messiah is compared, as in a diptych, with the Mother of Belial, or Satan, 'she who is
big with the Asp'. These two mysterious women appear to symbolize the congregations
of the just and the wicked. Writing of the birth of the Messiah, the psalmist describes at
the same time all the pains of childbirth which must precede the coming of the new
world (cf. Rom. viii. 23; John xvi. 21).
[2] This can also be translated: 'And She who is big with the Man is in travail, in her
pains.'
[3] This obviously refers to the Messiah, from Isa. ix. 5-6: 'For a child is born unto us and
a son is given unto us. . . . And he has been called Marvellous Counsellor.' Here, the
'crucible' is the womb. The Messiah who is about to be born must be tried and purified
by suffering; the womb from which he springs is a crucible, the crucible of suffering. The
Woman who is to bring him into the world is the congregation of the just, the Church of
the Saints, victim of the persecution of the wicked.
[4] Such is the 'power' of the Messiah: he delivers from the billows, i.e. the waves of
Death, Sheol, perdition. Note that the Mother of the Messiah, i.e. the Community, is
explicitly associated with this redeeming work: 'because of Her who is big with him', we
read. The Messiah is the 'first-born' of this Church (line 8).
[5] Here the Asp is Belial, or Satan, by allusion to the serpent of Gen. iii; cf. Rev. xii. 9.
Note that in line 18 an equivalent expression is used: 'She who is big with Perversity.'

And they shake (13) the foundations of the rampart
like a ship on the face of the waters,
and the clouds roar in a noise of roaring.
And they that live in the dust are, (14) like them that sail the seas,
terrified because of the roaring of the waters.
And their wise men are for them like sailors in the deeps,
for (15) all their wisdom is destroyed because of the roaring of the waters,
because of the boiling of the deeps upon the fountains of the waters.
[And] the waves [are turb]ulent (rearing) into the air
(16) and the billows resound with the roaring of their voice.
And Sh[eo]l [and Abaddon] open in the midst of their turbulence
[and al]l the arrows of the Pit (17) (fly out) in their pursuit;
they let their voice be heard in the Abyss.
And the gates [of Sheol] open [to all] the works of the Asp,[1]
(18) and the doors of the Pit close upon her who is big with Perversity,
and the everlasting bars upon all the spirits of the Asp.[2]

HYMN F

The redemption of the soul and the terrors of the end of the world

(19) I give Thee thanks, O Adonai,
for Thou hast redeemed my soul from the Pit
and from Sheol of Abaddon (20) Thou hast made me rise (20) to ever-
and I have walked in an infinite plain!   [lasting heights,

And I knew there was hope
for him whom (21) Thou hast shaped from the dust
for the everlasting assembly.
Thou hast cleansed the perverse spirit from great sin
that he might watch with (22) the army of the Saints
and enter into communion with the congregation of the Sons of Heaven.
And Thou hast cast an everlasting destiny for man
in the company of the Spirits (23) of Knowledge,
that he might praise Thy Name in joy[ful] concord
and recount Thy marvels before all Thy works.

But I, creature (24) of clay, what am I?
Kneaded with water, for what am I accounted?
And what is my strength?

---

[1] i.e. the creatures of Belial, the damned, who are to be shut up in Sheol for ever.
[2] i.e. the evil spirits, the demons. This is the end of the dominion of Belial and his
fiends, and the advent of the exclusive reign of God and Goodness; cf. *Rule*, IV, 18-19.

For I have stayed in the realm of wickedness
(25) and in the lot of the company of the wretched;
and the soul of the poor one was an exceeding stranger in the midst of the
and overwhelming calamities accompanied my steps   [tumult
(26) while all the traps of the Pit were opened
and all the snares of wickedness spread out
and the nets of the wretched upon the face of the waters;
(27) while all the arrows of the Pit flew out straight to the target
and shot out leaving no hope;
while the cord (of destruction) beat upon the damned
and the destiny of wrath (28) upon the abandoned
and the pouring out of fury upon the hypocrites,
and while it was the time of wrath for all Belial.

And the bonds of Death tightened leaving no escape,
(29) and the torrents of Belial overflowed all the high banks
like a fire consuming all their shores,[1]
destroying from their channels every tree green (30) and dry
and whipping with whirlwinds of flame
until the vanishing of all that drinks there.
It devours all the foundations of pitch
(31) and the bases of the continent;
the foundations of the mountains are prey to fire
and the roots of flint become torrents of tar.
It devours as far as the Great Abyss
(32) and the torrents of Belial pour into Abaddon
and the ⟨recesses⟩ of the Abyss roar out
amidst the roaring of swirling mud.
And the earth (33) cries out because of the calamity fallen on the world
and all its ⟨recesses⟩ howl,
and all that are on it are stricken with fear
(34) and stagger, the prey to great misfortune.
For God bellows with His mighty roaring
and His holy abode resounds with His (35) glorious truth
and the heavenly host lets its voice be heard.
And the eternal foundations stagger and shake
and the host of the Valiant (36) of heaven
brandishes its whip in the world;
and it shall not end until utter destruction,
which shall be final, without anything like it.

---

[1] Translation uncertain; the word may be explained after the Iranian; cf. P. J. DE
MENASCE, *RQ*, no. 1, 1958, pp. 133-4.

HYMN G

Trust in God during persecution

(37) I give Thee thanks, O Adonai,
for Thou hast become a stout rampart unto me![1]

. . . .

HYMN H

The reverses of the Teacher of Righteousness and the final success of his ministry

IV (5) I give Thee thanks, O Adonai,
for Thou hast illumined my face by Thy Covenant
and [. . .]
(6) [. . . and] I have sought Thee
and like a true dawn
at da[ybrea]k Thou hast appeared unto me.[2]

And they, they [have led] Thy people [astray].
(7) [Prophets of falsehood] have flattered [them with their wor]ds
and interpreters of deceit [have caused] them [to stray];
and they have fallen to their destruction for lack of understanding
for (8) all their works are in folly.
For ⟨I was⟩ despised by them,
and they had no esteem for me[3] when Thou didst show Thy power in me.
For they drove me out of my land (9) like a bird from its nest[4]
and all my companions and friends were driven far from me
and they considered me a broken vessel.

And they, interpreters (10) of falsehood and seers of deceit,
devised plans of Belial against me,
bartering Thy Law which Thou hast graven in my heart
for the flattering words (which they speak) (11) to Thy people.
And they stopped the thirsty from drinking the liquor of Knowledge,
and when they were thirsty they made them drink vinegar,
that (12) their straying might be gazed on,
that they might be foolish concerning their feasts,

[1] This hymn continues at the foot of column III (lines 38-9) and at the top of column IV (lines 1-4), but only a few fragmentary sentences remain.
[2] This appearance of God 'at daybreak' (same expression below, line 23) is doubtless connected with the prayer to the sun which the Essenes offered every morning (JOSEPHUS, War, II, 8, 5, § 128).
[3] Cf. Isa. liii. 3 (on the Servant of the Lord): 'He was despised and we had no esteem for him.'
[4] Same image in Psalms of Solomon, XVII, 18.

that they might be taken in their nets.[1]
For Thou, O God, despisest every thought (13) of Belial:
it is Thy counsel that shall remain,
and it is the thought of Thy heart that shall stand fast for ever.

As for them, they are hypocrites;
the schemes are of Belial which (14) they conceive
and they seek Thee with a double heart
and are not firm in Thy truth.
A root is in their thoughts bearing fruits that are poisoned and bitter
(15) and it is with stubbornness of heart that they seek Thee.
And they have sought Thee out among idols
and have set that before their face which causes them to fall into sin,
and they have gone in (16) to seek Thee according to the preaching of
they who are led astray by error.   [prophets of falsehood,

With bar[bar]ian lips and in a foreign tongue
do they speak to Thy people,
(17) causing all their works to be foolish by deceit.
For [they have] not [heeded] Thy [voice]
nor lent their ear to Thy word;
for they have said (18) of the vision of knowledge, It is not true!
and of the way of Thy heart, That is not it!
But Thou, O God, wilt answer them,
judging them (19) in Thy might [according to] their idols
and according to the multitude of their sins,
that they who have fallen away from Thy Covenant
may be taken in their thoughts.
(20) And at the time of ju[dg]ment Thou wilt cut off all the men of deceit
and there shall be no more seers of error.
For in all Thy works there is no folly,
(21) nor deceit [in] the schemes of Thy heart.
But they that are according to Thy soul shall stand before Thee for ever,
and they that walk in the way of Thy heart (22) shall stand fast eternally.

[As for m]e, because I lean on Thee
I shall rise and stand against them that scorn me
and my hand shall be against them that despise me.
For (23) they had no esteem for [me]
[un]til Thou shouldst manifest Thy power in me.

---

[1] An allusion to Hab. ii. 15. There is question there of the Jews who allowed themselves
to be seduced by evil guides, of the errors of these Jews in connection with the celebration
of the feasts, and their subsequent punishment; this passage should be compared with the
Commentary on Habakkuk (XI, 2-8). Cf. below, p. 266, n. 4.

And at daybreak Thou hast appeared unto me in Thy might
and hast not covered with shame the face
(24) of all them that inquired of me,
that gathered in Thy Covenant and heard me,
that walk in the way of Thy heart
and are ranked for Thee (25) in the assembly of the Saints.
And Thou wilt give everlasting victory to their cause
and truth according to justice,
and Thou wilt not allow them to stray in the power of the wretched
(26) according to the scheme which they have devised against them.
But Thou wilt put their fear upon Thy people
together with destruction for all the peoples of the lands,
to cut off at the time of Judgment all (27) who transgress Thy word.

And through me Thou hast illumined the face of many
and caused them to grow until they are numberless;
for Thou hast given me to know Thy (28) marvellous Mysteries
and hast manifested Thy power unto me in Thy marvellous counsel
and hast done wonders to many because of Thy glory
and to make known (29) Thy mighty works to all the living.

What being of flesh can do this,
and what creature of clay has power to do such marvellous things,
whereas he is in iniquity (30) from his mother's womb
and in the sin of unfaithfulness till his old age?
And I, I know that righteousness is not of man,
nor of the sons of men perfection (31) of way;
to the Most High God belong all the works of righteousness,
whereas the way of man is not firm
unless it be by the Spirit which God has created for him
(32) to make perfect a way for the sons of men,
that all His works may know
the might of His power and the greatness of His mercy
to all the sons (33) of His loving-kindness.

And shaking and trembling seized me
and all my bones cracked,
and my heart melted like wax before fire
and my knees slipped (34) like water descending a slope;
for I remembered my faults
and the unfaithfulness of my fathers
when the wicked arose against Thy Covenant
(35) and the wretched against Thy word.

And I said, It is because of my sins
that I am abandoned far from Thy Covenant.
But when I remembered the might of Thy hand
together with the (36) greatness of Thy mercy
I rose up and stood,
and my spirit stood upright in the face of the blows.
For [I] leaned (37) on Thy favours
and on the greatness of Thy mercy.

For Thou pardonest iniquity
and clean[sest m]an of sin by Thy righteousness;
(38) and [the wor]ld [which] Thou hast made belongs not to man.
For it is Thou who hast created the just and the wicked [. . .]
(39) [. . .] I wish to cling to Thy Covenant for [ever . . .]
(40) [. . .] for Thou art Truth and all [Thy works] are righteousness
[[. . .]
V . . . .
[. . .] (2) Thy pardons and the greatness [of Thy mercy . . .]
(3) and [I] was comforted when I knew these things [. . .]
[for everything comes to pass] (4) by command of Thy will
and in Thy ha[nd] is the judgment of all of them.

HYMN I

God's help during exile and trial

(5) I give Thee thanks, O Adonai,
for Thou didst not abandon me when I was in exile among a stran[ge]
[people [. . .]
[For it is not] according to my sin that (6) Thou hast judged me
and Thou hast not abandoned me because of the wickedness of my
but hast succoured my life from the Pit.   [inclination,

And Thou hast set [my soul unto judg]ment
among (7) the lions intended for the sons of transgression,
lions that break the bones of the strong
and drink the blo[od] of the valiant.
And Thou hast set me (8) in a place of exile among many fishers
that stretch a net upon the face of the waters,
and (among) hunters (sent) against the sons of perversity.[1]

---

[1] The allusion is so general that it is almost impossible to identify this 'place of exile'. In Jer. xvi. 16, from which the passage draws its inspiration, there is mention of 'many fishers' and 'many hunters' — expressions employed there to designate the enemies sent by Yahweh to punish the unfaithful Jews.

And there unto judgment (9) hast Thou established me
and hast strengthened the secret of truth in my heart,
and thence (?) (is) the Covenant (come) to them that seek it.[1]

And Thou hast closed up the mouth of the young lions
whose (10) teeth are like a sword
and whose fangs are like a pointed spear
(filled) with serpents' venom.[2]
All their designs were directed to destruction and they lay in wait,
but they have not (11) opened their mouth against me.

For Thou, O God, hadst hidden me[3]
from before the sons of men,
and hadst sealed up Thy Law within [me]
[un]til the time (12) of the revealing of Thy salvation to me.[4]
For Thou hast not abandoned me in the distress of my soul
and hast heard my cry in the bitterness of my soul
(13) and hast heeded the voice of my misery in my groaning.
And Thou hast delivered the soul of the poor one
in the den of the lions
which had sharpened their tongue like a sword.
(14) Thou hast closed up their jaws, O my God,
lest they tear out the soul of the poor and needy,
and hast made their tongue go back (15) like a sword in its sheath,
and Thou [hast] not [abandoned] the soul of Thy servant.

And it is that Thou mightest manifest Thy power in me
before the sons of men
that Thou hast done marvellously (16) unto the poor one.
And Thou hast made him enter into the cruc[ible]
[like go]ld into the works of fire
and like silver refined in the crucible of the blowers
to be purified seven times.

(17) And the ungodly of the peoples have hurled their torments against
they have pounded my soul all day.   [me,
(18) But Thou, O my God, changest the whirlwind to a breeze,

---

[1] The translation 'thence' is unsure. Nevertheless if the phrase is translated as I suggest,
the author of the hymn presents himself as the founder or renewer of the Covenant (which
is perfectly appropriate if he was the Teacher of Righteousness), and gives the place of
exile as the starting-point of his ministry.
[2] An expression borrowed from Deut. xxxii. 33; in the *Damascus Document* (A, VIII,
9 ff.; B, I, 22 ff.), it is applied to the 'kings of the peoples'.
[3] Cf. Isa. xlix. 2 (second Servant Song).
[4] i.e. until God saved him.

and Thou hast delivered the soul of the poor one
like a hu[nter snatching] the prey from the mouth (**19**) of the lions.

HYMN J

*The tribulations of the Teacher of Righteousness; his confidence in the
growth of the 'Shoot' and in the victory of his church*

(**20**) I give Thee thanks,[1] O Adonai,
for Thou hast not abandoned the orphan
nor despised the needy!
For Thy might is [fathomless]
and Thy glory (**21**) immense,
and wonderful Valiant Ones are Thy ministers.
And [Thou hast] set my foot in the sweepings,[2] in the midst of the humble,
in the midst of them that are quick (**22**) unto righteousness,
to cause all the poor of Grace
to arise from the tumult together.[3]

And I, I was the butt of the in[sults of] my [en]emies,
an object of quarrelling (**23**) and dispute to my companions,
an object of jealousy and wrath to those who had entered my Covenant,
an object of murmuring and contention to those I had gathered together.
And [all who a]te my bread
(**24**) lifted the heel against me.[4]
And all who joined my assembly
spoke evil of me with a perverse tongue.
And the men of my [counc]il rebelled
(**25**) and murmured round about.
And they went among the sons of misfortune
slandering the Mystery which Thou hast sealed within me;
but it is in order that my [wa]y might be exal[ted],
and it is because of (**26**) their sin
that Thou hast hidden the fount of understanding
and the secret of truth.

---

[1] In the manuscript, the word 'I give Thee thanks' is marked with dots, and the
words 'Blessed be Thou' are inscribed above the line in another hand; these represent
a variant substituted for 'I give Thee thanks'.
[2] Cf. I Cor. iv. 13: 'We are until now like the sweepings of the world, the refuse of the
universe.'
[3] The psalmist means that the humiliations of his earthly condition will be followed
for him (the Teacher of Righteousness) as well as for 'all the poor' (the sectaries of the
Covenant), by marvellous glory.
[4] Quote from Ps. xli. 10. The same verse is applied to Jesus in John xiii. 18; see also
Mark xiv. 18.

And their heart was nought but misfortunes,
they conceived [schemes of Be]lial.
They opened (27) a treacherous tongue
like serpents' venom[1] which causes thorns to grow,
and like creatures which creep in the dust
they hurled [poison] of asps like arr[ow]s [of the Pit]
(28) impossible to charm.
And it became an incurable pain
and a malignant wound in Thy servant's members,
so that [the spirit] staggered
and (29) strength was consumed
and he could not stand.

And they closed on me in clefts without refuge
and there was no [pl]ace of rest when they foll[owed] after.
And they sounded (30) my quarrel on the harp
and their censure in chorus on stringed instruments.
Amidst devastation and ruin
trembling [seized me]
together with pains like the terror (31) of her who gives birth,[2]
and my heart shuddered within me.
I clothed myself in black
and my tongue cleaved to (my) palate,
for their heart [was filled] with fol[ly]
and their inclination (32) appeared before me to (fill me with) bitterness.
And the light of my face darkened to thick night
and my brightness changed into blackness;
but Thou, O my God, (33) didst open a wide space in my heart.

And to (my) distress they added still more.
They shut me up in the darkness
and I ate the bread of groaning
(34) and my drink was in tears without end.
For my eyes were darkened because of sorrow
and my soul (was plunged) in bitterness every day.
Fea[r] and sadness (35) encompassed me
and shame covered (my) face.
And my br[ead] was changed into quarrelling
and my drink into an enemy that entered my bones
(36) causing the spirit to stagger
and consuming strength.

[1] Same expression used in the preceding hymn (V, 10); see the corresponding note.
[2] Cf. above, III, 7 ff.

They changed the works of God by their transgression
according to the Mysteries of sin.[1]

For [I was] bound with (37) unbreakable cords
and with chains impossible to sunder,
and a stou[t] wall [held me shut up]
[and] bars of iron and door[s of bronze].
(38) [And] my [pri]son was like the Abyss without [. . .]
(39) [and the bonds of Be]lial bound my soul without any [escape . . .]

VI . . . .
[. . .] (2) my heart [was afflicted] because of the blasph[emies . . .]
(3) [in] immense misfortune [and] destruction without [end . . .]

[But Thou, O my God,] (4) hast uncovered my ear
[to the tea]ching of them that reprove with justice [. . .]
[And Thou didst deliver me] (5) from the congregation of [vani]ty
and from the assembly of violence
and didst cause me to enter the council [of holiness . . .]
(6) And I knew there was hope
for them that are converted from rebellion
and that abandon sin by [. . .]
and by walking (7) in the way of Thy heart without any perversion.

And I was comforted for the roaring of the crowd
and for the tumult of ki[ngd]oms when they assemble,
[for] I [kn]ow (8) Thou wilt soon raise up survivors among Thy people
and a remnant in the midst of Thine inheritance,
and that Thou hast purified them that they may be cleansed of (all) sin.
For all (9) their deeds are in Thy truth
and Thou wilt judge them with abundant mercy and pardon
because of Thy favours,
and Thou wilt teach them
according to (the words of) Thy mouth
(10) and wilt establish them in Thy council unto Thy glory
according to the uprightness of Thy truth.

And [Thou hast] created [me] for Thy sake
to [ful]fil the Law,[2]

[1] Same expression in fragment 50 (line 5) of the scroll of the *Hymns*; compare 2 Thess. ii. 7, 'the mystery of ungodliness'.
[2] The word 'fulfil' is a conjecture and remains uncertain. With this reservation, compare with Matt. v. 17: 'Think not that I have come to abolish the Law and the Prophets; I have not come to abolish, but to fulfil.'

and [to te]a[ch by] my mouth (11) the men of Thy council
in the midst of the sons of men,
that Thy marvels may be told to everlasting generations
and [Thy] mighty deeds be [contemp]lated (12) without end.
And all the nations shall know Thy truth
and all the peoples, Thy glory.[1]
For Thou hast caused [them] to enter Thy [glo]rious [Covenant]
(13) with all the men of Thy council
and into a common lot with the Angels of the Face;
and none shall treat with insolence the sons [. . .]
(14) [. . .] and they shall be converted by Thy glorious mouth
and shall be Thy princes in the lo[t of light].

And Thou hast sent out (15) a sprouting
as a flower that shall bloom for ever,
that the Shoot[2] may grow into the branches of the eternal planting.
And its shade shall spread over all [the earth]
[and] its [top] (16) reach up to the hea[vens]
[and] its roots go down to the Abyss.
And all the rivers of Eden [shall water] its [bou]ghs
and it shall become a [mi]ghty (17) forest,
[and the glory of] its [fo]rest shall spread over the world without end,
as far as Sheol [for ever].
[And] it shall be a well-spring of light
as an (18) eternal unfailing fountain.
In its brilliant flames
all the son[s of darkness] shall be consumed,
[and it shall be] a fire to consume all (19) guilty men
unto destruction.[3]

And they that participated in my testimony
have been led astray by the inter[preters of falsehood]
[and have not held fast] to the service of righteousness.
(20) And Thou, O God, hast commanded them to seek profit
apart from their ways

[1] All this passage on the conversion of the Gentiles and their admission to the Covenant
is of particular importance. In the Bible this universalist tendency is specially apparent
in the Servant Songs (Isa. xlii. 4, 6; xlix. 6); the Servant is to be the 'light of the nations'.
[2] This word (in Hebrew *nezer*) recurs in *Hymn* L (VII, 19), and also three times in
Hymn O (VIII, 6, 8, 10). It is borrowed from the famous passage in Isa. xi. 1 concerning
the 'shoot' which is to grow from the stock of Jesse and its roots; the word has the same
obviously messianic significance in these hymns. The 'Shoot' is associated here with the
'everlasting planting', a characteristic expression applied in the writings of the sect to the
Community of the Elect, the Church founded by the Teacher of Righteousness.
[3] The Community of the just will chastise the wicked at the end of time; same teaching
below, VIII, 17-20 (*Hymn* O).

in [Thy] way of ho[liness]
[whe]re [is salvation],
and where the uncircumcised, the unclean, and the thief (21) do not
But they stagger aside from the way of Thy heart   [pass.
and [totter], the prey to misfortune.
And Belial like a counsellor (22) is with their heart
[and in accord]ance with the scheme of ungodliness
they defile themselves with transgression.

[And I, I w]as like a sailor on a ship.
In the fury (23) of the seas were their waves
and all their billows roared against me;
a wind of confusion (blew)
[and there was no] breeze to restore the soul
and no (24) path to direct the way on the face of the waters.
And the Abyss resounded to my groaning
and [my soul went down] to the gates of Death.

And I was (25) like a man who entered a fortified city
and sought refuge in a steep wall
awaiting deliverance.
And I lea[ned on] Thy truth, O my God.
For it is Thou who (26) wilt set the foundation upon rock
and the frame-work on the cord of righteousness
and the plumb-line [of truth] to [tes]t the tried stones
in order to (build) a (27) stout bui[ld]i[ng]
such as will not shake,
and that none who enter there shall stagger.[1]

For no stranger shall enter [there]
[and] the doors shall be so protected that none will be able to (28) enter,
and the bars so stout that none will be able to break them.
No band (of warriors) shall go in there with its weapons of war
until all the de[cree] is fulfilled (29) concerning the battles of wicked-
[ness.[2]

---

[1] Cf. VII, 8-9 (*Hymn* L). This 'building' constructed on rock and impregnable is the
Community of the just, the Church founded by the Teacher of Righteousness. The same
image appears in the *Commentary on Psalm XXXVII* from cave IV (see below, p. 274):
'The explanation of this concerns the Priest, the Teacher of Righteousness whom . . .
God has established to build for Himself the Congregation of truth.' Cf. Matt. xvi. 18:
'and on this rock I will build my Church'.
[2] The Church built by the Teacher of Righteousness must serve the elect as an impregnable refuge during the war against the forces of evil at the end of time. Cf. Matt.
xvi. 18: 'and the gates of hell shall not prevail against it'.

And at the time of Judgment the Sword of God shall hasten
and all His sons of tr[ut]h shall rouse themselves to [destroy] (**30**) un-
and all the sons of transgression shall be no more.[1]   [godliness
And the Valiant One[2] shall bend his bow
and shall raise the siege
[and scatter them] (**31**) abroad without end,
and the ancient gates shall send out weapons of war[3]
and they shall be migh[ty] from one end (of the earth) to [the other].
[And they shall battle] (**32**) [against them]
[and there shall be no] deliverance for the guilty inclination;
they shall trample (them) underfoot unto destruction
leaving no remn[ant].
And (there shall be) no hope in the mighty number [of horsemen]
(**33**) and no refuge for the valiant of battles.

For to the Most High God belongs the [battle . . .][4]
(**34**) And they that lay in the dust have raised up a pole
and the men of vermin have hoisted a banner [. . .][5]

.   .   .   .

HYMN K

The distress of the persecuted[6]

.   .   .   .
VII (**1**) [. . . and I,] I was silent [. . .]
(**2**) [. . . and (my) ar]m was detached from its ligaments
and my foot sank into the mire.
My eyes were stopped that they should not see (**3**) the evil,
[and] my ears that they should not hear the murders.
My heart was bewildered because of the scheme of malice,
for it is Belial (that is seen) when the inclination (**4**) of their being is
                                                      [revealed.

[1] A reference to the supreme struggle of the sons of light against the sons of darkness,
and to the great revenge of God and His elect — the object of ardent hope among the
Qumran sectaries as the whole *War Scroll* testifies.
[2] God, as in the *War Scroll*, XII, 9, 10; cf. Isa. xlii. 13; Zeph. iii. 17.
[3] The elect are as though shut up in a besieged citadel; God will miraculously raise the
siege and the saints will pass over to the offensive, going through the gates of the fortress
with arms which have been stored there as in an arsenal.
[4] The word 'battle' is restored after the *War Scroll* (XI, 1, 2, 4).
[5] The end of line 34, as well as lines 35 and 36, present grave lacunae; the passage as
a whole seems to be inspired by Isa. xxviii. 15-18.
[6] Two lines have completely disappeared from the foot of column VI and one line from
the beginning of column VII. It is impossible to say exactly where *Hymn* J ends, or *Hymn* K
begins.

And all the foundations of my fabric[1] cracked
and my bones came apart,
and my members within me were like a ship[2]
in the furious (5) storm.
And my heart shuddered even to destruction
and a wind of confusion caused me to reel
because of the calamities of their sin.

HYMN L

*The confidence of the Teacher of Righteousness in the triumph of his
cause and in the growth of the 'Shoot'*

(6) I give Thee thanks, O Adonai,
for Thou hast upheld me by Thy might
and hast poured out Thy (7) holy Spirit within me
that I should not stagger!

And Thou hast made me strong before the battles of ungodliness,[3]
and in the midst of all the calamities which they have brought on me
(8) Thou hast not permitted me cravenly to desert Thy Covenant.
But Thou hast set me up as a stout tower,
as a steep rampart,
and hast established (9) my fabric upon rock;[4]
and everlasting foundations serve me for my ground
and all my walls are a tried rampart
which nothing can shake.

(10) [And] Thou, O my God, hast appointed him[5]
to be a branch of the Council of Holiness;

[1] By 'my fabric' the psalmist means his body (also in fragment 47, line 5); in VI, 26, and VII, 8, he uses the same metaphor to describe the Community he has built. It was therefore easy to slip from one idea to the other, from that of the body to that of the Church (cf. Eph. i. 23; iv. 12, 16, etc.).
[2] Same image above, III, 6; VI, 22.
[3] Cf. above, VI, 29.
[4] Cf. above, VI, 26 (and VII, 4).
[5] In the word 'Thou hast appointed him', the pronoun seems to refer discreetly to the 'Shoot' (*nezer*), as the parallelism with VI, 15, suggests — 'that the Shoot may grow into the branches of the eternal planting'. The 'Council of Holiness' and the 'eternal planting' both refer to the Community of the just, the Church founded by the Teacher of Righteousness. The 'Shoot', which this hymn mentions explicitly a little further on (line 19) and which appears three times more in *Hymn O* (VIII, 6, 8, 10), is essentially the sprout from the eternal 'planting', i.e. the Community of the just, but it is also the founder of this Community, the Teacher of Righteousness. In fact the psalmist speaks here, as in the passage as a whole, of himself and his work; that he does it in the third person ('Thou hast appointed *him*') seems to be from a sense of humility and discretion, as though to efface his own individuality behind the high office which he attributes to himself in the economy of salvation.

and Thou [hast instructed me in] Thy Covenant
and my tongue has been as the tongue of Thy disciples,[1]
(11) whereas the spirit of calamities was without mouth
and all the sons of transgression without reply of the tongue.
For the lips (12) ⟨   ⟩ of falsehood shall be dumb;
for at the time of Judgment Thou wilt declare all of them guilty that
distinguishing through me between the just and the guilty.[2] [attack me,

(13) For Thou knowest every scheme of action
and seest every reply of the tongue.
And Thou hast established my heart (14) [like (that) of] Thy [di]sciples
and dost direct my steps in truth
towards the paths of righteousness,
that I may walk before Thee in the realm (15) [of ungodlin]ess
towards the ways of in[finite] glory and bliss
[which] never shall end.
(16) And Thou knowest the inclination of Thy servant,
that right[eousness] is not [of man].
[But] I have [le]aned [upon Thee]
that Thou shouldst lift up [my] hea[rt]
(17) [and] give (me) strength and vigour.
And I have no fleshly refuge;
[and man has no righteousness o]r virtue
to be delivered from si[n]
(18) [and wi]n forgiveness.
But I, I have leaned on Thy abun[dant mercy]
[and on the greatness of] Thy grace.
I will wait until Thou cause (19) [salv]ation to flower
and the Shoot to grow,[3]
by giving strength and vigour
and [by lifting up the heart].

[And] Thou [in] Thy righteousness
hast appointed me (20) unto Thy Covenant.
And I have held fast to Thy truth
and have [clung to Thy Covenant].
And Thou hast made of me a father to the sons of Grace

---

[1] An evident allusion to Isa. l. 4 (Servant Song). The same allusion appears in *Hymn* O (VIII, 36): 'the tongue of the disciples (was given) to me'.
[2] Cf. Mal. iii. 18. The essential word in this phrase is 'through me'; the Teacher of Righteousness makes of his own person a sort of touchstone, and depending on how men have reacted towards him, with faith or incredulity, so will they be recognized at the time of Judgment as the elect or the outcast. Cf. II, 13-14 (*Hymn* B).
[3] Cf. VI, 15 (*Hymn* J): the same formula, and also the same association of the ideas 'to flower', and the 'shoot'.

(21) and as a foster-father to the men of good omen;[1]
and they have opened their mouth
as a ba[be to its mother's breasts][2]
and as a child delighting in the breast (22) of its nurses.

And Thou hast raised up my horn[3] against all who despise me,
and they are scat[tered] that fight me and seek to quarrel with me,
[leaving no re]mnant (23) like chaff driven by the wind;
and my dominion shall be over the sons [of the ear]th.[4]

[And Thou, O] my [Go]d, hast succoured my soul
and lifted my horn (24) on high.
And I will shine with a seven-fold li[ght]
in the E[den which] Thou hast [m]ade for Thy glory.[5]
(25) For Thou art an [ever]lasting light unto me[6]
and hast established my feet on an [infinite] p[lain].

HYMN M

The mystery of divine grace and pardon

(26) I give [Thee thanks, O Adonai],
for Thou hast given me understanding of Thy truth
(27) and hast made me know Thy marvellous Mysteries
and Thy favours to [sinful] man
[and] the abundance of Thy mercy toward the perverse heart!

(28) Who among the gods is like Thee, O Adonai,
and who is like Thy truth?
And when he is judged, who will be ju[s]t before Thee,
since there is no (29) answer to Thy reproof?
All majesty is but wind

[1] Expression drawn from Zech. iii. 8: 'Hear then, O Joshua, High Priest, you and your friends who sit before you; for they are men of good omen. For behold, I bring my servant the Branch (of David).'

[2] The Teacher of Righteousness is a father; he is even like a mother who suckles her children.

[3] i.e. my power; same expression below, line 23.

[4] The idea announced here is very important: the Teacher of Righteousness will rule; he will be conqueror and lord.

[5] Enoch is also transported by God into the garden of Eden; cf. *Jubilees*, IV, 23. The Teacher of Righteousness announces his luminous transfiguration; compare with the scene of the transfiguration of Jesus (Mark ix. 2-8 and parallels). Cf. *Enoch*, CVIII, 11-13: 'Now I will call the spirits of good from among the generations of light and I will transfigure them that were born in darkness. . . . I will bring forth in shining light them that were born in darkness. . . . They shall shine for uncounted ages.'

[6] Cf. Isa. lx. 19-20; cf. Rev. xxi. 23; xxii. 5.

and none can brave Thy fury.
But Thou causest all Thy sons (30) of truth
to enter into pardon before Thee,
[to puri]fy them of their sins
through the abundance of Thy goodness and the greatness of Thy me[r]cy,
(31) to set them before Thee for ever and ever.

For Thou art a God of eternity
and all Thy ways are established from everlasting (32) to everlasting,
and beside Thee there is nothing.
How then is man, this nothing possessing but breath,
to understand Thy marvellous deeds (33) [unless Thou t]e[a]ch [him]?

HYMN N

Predestination and divine grace

(34) [I give Thee thank]s, O Adonai,
for Thou hast not cast my lot among the congregation of vanity
and hast not set my decree in the assembly of hypocrites,
(35) [but because of the abundance of Thy goodness] and the greatness of
[Thou hast call]ed me to Thy grace and forgivene[ss]!   [Thy mercy

For all the judgments of [. . .]
(36) [. . .] perversity and in the decree [. . .]

. . . .

VIII (2) [. . .] Thy righteousness is firm for ever;
for no [. . .] (3) [. . .]¹

HYMN O

The allegory of the 'Shoot'; the Teacher of Righteousness as the source of living waters and the gardener of the 'everlasting planting'; his physical and moral sufferings

(4) I give [Thee thanks, O Adonai],
[for] Thou hast placed me as a fount of rivers in a dry place
and as a spring of waters in an arid land
and as garden [wa]ters (5) [in a wilderness]!²

¹ At the foot of column VII, after line 36 (very mutilated), three lines have disappeared completely. Moreover, at the top of column VIII there remain only a few illegible traces of line 1 and a few words of line 2; the last words of the hymn have disappeared with the beginning of line 3.
² The whole of this phrase calls to mind Isa. xli. 18, which describes the marvellous transformation of the desert into watered land; but in the present hymn, the Teacher of Righteousness is himself the vivifying spring. Cf. John iv. 10, 14; vii. 37-8.

[Thou hast plant]ed unto Thy glory
a planting of cypress and elm mingled with box.[1]
Trees (6) of life are hidden among all the trees by the waters[2]
in a mysterious realm,
and they shall send out a Shoot[3] for the everlasting planting.
(7) And they shall take root before they send [it] out,
and shall direct their root to the stre[am];
and its stock shall freely approach the living waters also,[4]
(8) and it shall become an everlasting fountain.
And in the Shoot, near by, all the beasts of the thicket shall graze,[5]
and its stock shall be trod underfoot by all that pass on (9) their way,[6]
and all the winged birds shall use its branches.[7]
And all the trees by the wa[ters] shall rise up beneath it,[8]

[1] Here begins the allegory of the 'planting' and the 'shoot'; there is mention of the 'planting of Yahweh' in Isa. lxi. 3, and of the 'shoot of the planting of Yahweh' in Isa. lx. 21. The list of trees (cypress, elm, box) is borrowed from Isa. xli. 19; lx. 13.

[2] The 'trees of life' symbolize the saints, the elect. Cf. *Psalms of Solomon*, XIV, 3-4: 'The saints of the Lord shall live by it (the Law) for ever; the paradise of the Lord, the *trees of life*, these are His saints. Their planting is rooted for ever; they shall not be uprooted for as' long as heaven shall last.' Compare *Odes of Solomon*, XI, 15-16: 'Blessed are they, O Lord, that are planted in Thine earth and for whom there is a place in Thy paradise; who grow in the growing of Thy trees and move out from darkness to light!' The expression 'trees by the waters' is borrowed from Ezek. xxxi. 14: 'That no trees by the waters may grow to lofty height . . . for they are all given over to death, to the nether world, in the midst of the sons of men, with those who go down to the Pit.' By contrast to the 'trees of life', therefore, the 'trees by the waters' symbolize the proud, the wicked given over to damnation (cf. lines 9-10: 'And all the trees by the waters shall rise up . . . they shall grow in their planting, but shall direct no root to the stream'). In the divine 'planting', the saints are 'hidden' among the wicked (like the good grain among weeds). But this mingling of the two is provisional; at the end of time, as is explained further on (lines 17-20), the saints 'that were hidden in secret' will destroy the bad trees and nothing but the 'fruitful planting' will remain.

[3] The same term has been encountered already in VI, 15, and VII, 19. According to the teaching presented here in the form of an allegory, the 'Shoot', the Church founded by the Teacher of Righteousness, has itself sprung from an already well-rooted divine 'planting', the 'trees of life'; i.e. apparently, from a congregation of pious Jews living before the appearance of the Teacher of Righteousness. Cf. *Damascus Document*, I, 7-11: '(God) visited them and caused a root of planting to spring from Israel and Aaron to possess His land and grow fat on the good things of His earth. . . . But they were like blind men and like men who groping seek their way for twenty years. . . . And He raised up for them a Teacher of Righteousness.'

[4] This is the 'stock' of the Shoot which, sprung from the trees of life, itself takes root and is watered by the 'stream' in which the living waters flow, to become in its turn an ever-lasting fountain.

[5] The Shoot, i.e. the Church founded by the Teacher of Righteousness, will become an immense tree spreading over the whole earth; cf. VI, 15-17.

[6] This seems to infer that although the Shoot grows and offers protection and happiness to all men, the man (the Teacher of Righteousness) responsible for providing the life-giving sap is disregarded and despised: a fundamental doctrine developed further in lines 10-15.

[7] Cf. Ezek. xxxi. 6, and Dan. iv. 9; cf. Matt. xiii. 32, and parallels.

[8] An allusion to the triumph of the wicked; but this victory will be a temporary one for, in contrast to the 'trees of life', the 'trees by the waters' have only frail roots unwatered by the 'stream' (line 10).

for they shall grow in their planting;
(10) but they shall direct no root to the stream.
And he who causes the Shoot of ho[li]ness to grow into the planting of
has remained hidden with none (11) to consider him,   [truth
and his Mystery has been sealed with none to know it.[1]

And Tho[u, O G]od, hast shut up his fruit
in the mystery of the strong Valiant Ones (12) and of the Spirits of
and of the Flame of whirling fire.[2]   [holiness
He shall not [slake his thirst at] the fountain of life[3]
and shall not drink with the ancient trees (13) of the waters of holiness,
the clouds shall not cause his fruit to prosper with [full]ness (?)[4]
For they have seen without recognizing
(14) and considered without believing
in the fountain of life;[5]
and he was delivered (?) and [. . .] eternal.[6]
And I, I was exposed to the defilements of the (15) unleashed rivers
when they threw up their slime on me.[7]

[1] This is the Mystery of the Teacher of Righteousness; he 'causes the Shoot of holiness to grow' but his own fate is to be unrecognized and despised. The following lines comment on this Mystery of the dishonoured and afflicted Just Man.
[2] This phrase clearly alludes to the Garden of Eden guarded by the Cherubim and the 'flaming sword which turned every way' (Gen. iii. 24). But what is 'his fruit'? It is doubtless the mystical merit which the Teacher of Righteousness, hidden and despised, has acquired to the profit of his work, his Church, the 'planting'. This 'fruit', or merit (the metaphorical use of the word 'fruit' in this sense is common, especially in the New Testament) is kept and put into reserve by God in the mysterious Eden. But although this is the merit and reward of the Teacher of Righteousness on the divine level, on the earthly and visible plane his personal fate is failure and tragic paradox: he is responsible for the growth and prosperity of the Shoot, i.e. the Church, but he himself is 'like a sucker', 'like a root sprung from dry ground', as is said of the Servant of the Lord (Isa. liii. 2).
[3] The subject of the verb is not expressed, which makes interpretation of this phrase a little uncertain; from the context, this subject must be the same as that appearing above, viz. 'he who causes the Shoot of holiness to grow' (line 10), the Teacher of Righteousness: deprived of all the waters of earth and heaven, he is indeed 'like a root sprung from dry ground' (Isa. liii. 2).
[4] The new feature added here, namely the absence of rain and dew, still seems to describe the extreme destitution of the Teacher, a puny shrub giving only sickly fruit. Similarly, the Servant of the Lord 'had no form or comeliness that we should look at him, and no beauty that we should love him: he was despised and rejected of men' (Isa. liii. 2-3).
[5] The 'fountain of life' is the Teacher of Righteousness himself (cf. line 4). Men saw him but did not recognize his high dignity; they came up against his Mystery and did not believe in his mission. Cf. Isa. liii. 1: 'Who has believed what we have heard? And to whom has the arm of Yahweh been revealed?'
[6] This sentence is too mutilated to decipher.
[7] The psalmist alludes to his maltreatment at the hands of his wicked persecutors; cf. II, 12-13 (Hymn B): 'And the assembly of the wicked raged against me, and roared like storms upon the seas when their billows rage, throwing up mud and slime.' In the present hymn the passage 'And I was exposed' is directly linked with the idea preceding it, namely the incomprehension of which the Teacher of Righteousness was the victim.

(**16**) And Thou, O my God, hast put in my mouth
as it were an autumn rain for all [the sons of men][1]
and a spring of living waters which shall not run dry.[2]
(**17**) The pri[nc]es[3] shall not fail to open it,
and they shall become an unleashed torrent ov[er all the ban]ks
and [shall go down] to the fatho[mless] seas.
(**18**) They that were hidden in secret shall suddenly gush forth[4]
[and shall flow like rivers of ever-run]ning [waters][5]
and shall become [an abyss for every tree] (**19**) green and dry[6]
and a pit for every living being.
And the tr[ees by the waters shall sink like] lead
into the might[y] waters,[7]
[and shall be] (**20**) [prey] to fire and be dried up.
But the fruitful planting [shall prosper],
[and it shall become an] everlasting [fount]ain for the glorious Eden
and shall bear fr[uit for ever].[8]

---

[1] This lacuna can also be restored as 'all the sons of righteousness' or an equivalent expression. The phrase 'autumn rain' recalls Joel ii. 23; it is from this passage (and also from Hos. x. 12) that the expression so frequently encountered in the Qumran texts — Teacher of Righteousness — appears to derive. As a matter of fact the same Hebrew word (*mōreh*, *yōreh*) can mean either 'autumn rain' or 'he who instructs, the teacher' (root *yārāh*). Consequently by speaking of the 'autumn rain' which God has put into his mouth, the author himself seems to allude to the title by which he was known by his followers.

[2] The author here returns to the initial theme (line 1).

[3] 'The princes' are the members of the sect as the *Damascus Document* explains clearly (VI, 3, 6); cf., also above, VI, 14 (*Hymn* J), 'and they shall be Thy princes', and the *Commentary on Psalm XXXVII* from cave IV (see below, p. 271), 'the congregation of His elect, who shall be leaders and princes'.

[4] Like the trees of life 'hidden among all the trees by the waters' (line 6). Every one of the elect becomes 'a fount of living waters' like the Teacher of Righteousness himself (lines 1, 16). Cf. John iv. 14: 'But whoever drinks of the water that I shall give him shall never thirst; the water that I shall give him will become in him a spring of water welling up to eternal life'; vii. 37-8: 'If anyone thirst, let him come to me and drink. He who believes in me, as the scripture has said, "Out of his midst shall flow rivers of living water".' (This text quoted by the Evangelist has not been found in the canonical Bible.)

[5] Cf. Ps. lxxiv. 15.

[6] The elect will judge on the Day of Judgment and execute vengeance on the wicked.

[7] Cf. Exod. xv. 10. According to line 6, the 'trees by the waters' symbolize the wicked.

[8] Cf. *Odes of Solomon*, XXXVIII, 17-21: 'My foundations were set by the hand of the Lord, for it is indeed He that planted me. It is He that has set in the root, has watered it, established and blessed it, *and its fruits are for ever*. He has dug it in, and He has caused it to rise up and grow; and He has filled it (with sap) and it has grown great. To the Lord alone is the glory of His planting and growing, of His care, and of the blessing of His lips, of the lovely planting of His right hand, of the beauty of His planting and of the notifying of His thought.'

In the last phrase of the allegory, this abrupt change to the 'I' shows that the psalmist identifies himself with the mysterious personage whose tragic fate he has described; this skilful way of raising the veil only towards the end of an allegory is encountered, for example, in the famous parable of the vine in Isa. v. 1-7.

(21) And Thou hast opened their fountain by my hand[1]
among the [water] courses,
[and Thou hast disposed] their [ranks] in staggered rows
according to a sure measuring-cord,
and the planting (22) of their trees
according to the sun's direction,[2]
to stre[ngthen it and cause] a glorious branch to [gro]w.
If I move my hand to dig (23) its ditches,[3]
its roots sink (even) to the rock of flint
and [estab]lish their stock [securely] within the earth,
and in the season of heat it retains (24) (its) strength.
But if I take away my hand,
it shall be like a juni[per in the wilderness]
[and] its stock like nettles in a salt-marsh,
and in its ditches (25) shall grow prickles and thorns
and it [shall be delivered up] to thickets and thistles
[and all its] border [trees][4] shall change into trees of wild fruits;
before (26) the heat its leaves shall wither.

But no [fountain] has been opened [for me] in the midst of the wa[ters],[5]
[but] a place of exile in the midst of sickness;
and for me the f[ou]nt was (27) of blows.
And I was like a man forsaken
in the tr[ouble and sadness of my soul]
without any strength;
for my chas[ti]sement g[r]ew (28) in bitterness
and in incurable sorrow
so that I had [no power].
[And confu]sion was on me
as (on) those who go down into Sheol,
and among (29) the dead my spirit searched.

---

[1] In this passage, the psalmist explicitly presents himself as the all-powerful gardener responsible for the divine planting; it is 'by his hand' — by the hand of the Teacher of Righteousness — that God ensures the growth of the Church of the saints. The passage calls to mind the parable of the vine of Isa. v. 1-7, but in the present hymn the gardener is the Teacher of Righteousness, God's instrument and intimately associated with Him — not Yahweh Himself.

[2] The divine plantation seems to be described as a tree nursery in which all the plants are carefully set out in rows; the gardener has planted them taking into account the best orientation.

[3] Irrigation ditches.

[4] The expression 'border trees' is rather strange. From the context it seems to mean choice trees, carefully cultivated, as opposed to the 'trees of wild fruits'.

[5] The restoration is uncertain, but the general meaning emerges quite clearly. Whereas the Teacher of Righteousness is a life-giving spring for others, he is himself deprived of these living waters and fated to suffer sickness, exile, and desertion. This is the teaching expounded above, in lines 12-13.

For [my] li[fe] reached to the Pit
[and] my soul fainted [within me]
day and night (30) without rest.
And it grew like a burning fire shut up in [my bones],
and its flame devoured for many days
(31) exhausting (my) strength for (long) times
and destroying my flesh for (long) seasons.
And the billows flew [towards me]
(32) and my soul was oppressed within me unto destruction,
for my strength had vanished from my body.
And my heart ran out like water
and my flesh melted (33) like wax,
and the strength of my loins was prey to terror
and my arm was undone from its ligaments
without any power to move my hand.
(34) [And] my [fo]ot was caught in irons
and my knees slipped like water
and I could make no step;
and walking was forbidden to the nimbleness of my feet
(35) [for my arms were] bound with chains of staggering.

But Thou hast made the tongue in my mouth to grow without going back,
and there was none to [sil]ence (it).
(36) [For the tong]ue of the disciple[s] (was given) to me
to restore the spirit of them that stagger
and to sustain the weary with the word.[1]
The lips of [falsehood] were all of them dumb[2]

. . . .

HYMN P

Trust in God's paternal protection in the midst of distress

IX (1) [I give Thee thanks, O Adonai,]
[for . . .]
(2) [. . .] during the night [. . .]
(3) [. . . and Belial persecuted me] without mercy.
He stirred up (his) zeal in anger
and [smote me] unto destruction.

[1] Cf. Isa. l. 4 (Servant Song); there is an allusion to the same biblical passage in VII, 10 (*Hymn* J). Compare also Matt. xi. 28: 'Come unto me all you who are weary and heavy laden.'
[2] Of the following lines (37-40) only a few fragmentary words and phrases remain. Furthermore, one or two lines have completely disappeared at the bottom of column VIII where the end of the hymn probably figured.

(4) The billows of Death [encompassed me],
and on the couch of my bed
Sheol intoned a mourning
[and sounded] a voice of groaning.
(5) My eyes (were darkened) like smo⟨ke⟩ in the furnace
and my tears (ran down) in torrents
and my eyes were consumed, imploring repose.
[And my spirit] was (6) far from me,
and my life apart.

But from desolation to ruin
and from pain to the blow
and from travail (7) to the billows[1]
my soul considered Thy marvels,
and because of Thy favours Thou hast not rejected me.
From season (8) to season my soul has del[i]ghted
in Thy great mercy,
and I have replied to them that desired to swallow me up
(9) and reproved them that pursued me,
and I have declared my judges unjust;
but Thy judgments I will declare righteous.
For I know (10) Thy truth and have loved my judgment,
and the blows which struck me were pleasant to me.
For I hoped in Thy grace,
and Thou hast put (11) a supplication in the mouth of Thy servant
and hast not threatened my life
nor driven away my gladness.
And Thou hast not deserted (12) my hope
and in the face of the blows Thou hast made my spirit stand fast.

For Thou hast established my spirit
and knowest my meditation.
(13) And Thou has comforted me in my confusion
and in pardon I delight;
and I was comforted for the original sin.[2]
(14) And I knew there was hope in Thy [fav]ours
and expectation in the greatness of Thy might.

For no man is just (15) in Thy ju[dg]ment
nor [innocent in] Thy trial.
Can human born of human be righteous,

---

[1] The billows of Death; cf. above, line 4, and III, 8, 9, 10 (*Hymn* E).
[2] The sin of the first parents in Eden, the cause of man's corruption.

and can man born of man (**16**) have understanding?
And can flesh born of the gui[lty] inclination be glorious,
and can spirit born of spirit[1] be mighty?
Truly, nothing is (**17**) strong like Thy strength
and Thy glory is [price]less
and Thy wisdom is measureless.
and [life] belongs to the me[n of Thy Covenant],
(**18**) but [death] to all them that have departed far from it [. . .]

And it is because of Thee that I [. . .]
[and because of Thy grace that] (**19**) I stand,
and Thou hast not [. . .]
(**20**) And when they meditate against me Thou [. . .]
and if, for shame of the face [. . .] (**21**) for me.
And it is Thou that hast creat[ed the just and the wicked],[2]
[and] Thou wilt [not] allow my enemies to increase against me
as a stumbling-block [. . .]
[but to all] (**22**) the men who fight against [me]
[. . . Thou wilt give sha]me of face,
and ignominy to them that murmur against me.

(**23**) For at the ti[me of Judgment] Thou, O my God [. . .]
wilt plead my cause.
For Thou hast chastised me in the Mystery of Thy wisdom
(**24**) and hast hidden the truth unto the ti[me of Judgment],
[but] then [Thou wilt reveal it].
And my chastisement has become for me
a joy and a gladness,
(**25**) and the blows that have smitten me
(have become) an ev[erlasting] healing [and bliss] without end,
and the scorn of my enemies has become for me a glorious crown,
and my stumbling, (**26**) everlasting might.

For in [Thy] bli[ss . . .]
and my light has shone out in Thy glory.[3]
For (**27**) Thou hast made the light shine out of the darkness
for the po[or and needy],
[and there is healing for the ti]me when I was smitten
and for my stumbling there is everlasting might
and (**28**) unending re[le]ase in the distress of [my] sou[l].

---

[1] This appears to refer to the spirit of man, the carnal spirit.
[2] Cf. above, IV, 38 (*Hymn* H).
[3] Cf. above, VII, 24-5 (*Hymn* L).

[For Thou, O my God, art] my refuge, my stronghold,
my stout rock, my fortress!
In Thee (29) I will shelter from all [the blows of ungodliness]
[and Thou wilt succour] me unto eternal deliverance.
For from the time of my father (30) Thou hast known me,
and from the womb of my mother [Thou hast established me],
[and from the belly] of my mother Thou hast attended to me,[1]
and from the breasts of her that conceived me
has Thy (31) mercy been over me,
and on the bosom of my nurse [Thou hast cared for me . . .]
Thou hast appeared unto me from my youth
(giving) understanding of Thy judgment (to me)
(32) and hast upheld me by certain truth,
and in Thy holy Spirit Thou hast set my delight.
And [Thy hand] has [gui]ded me until this day
(33) and Thy righteous punishment accompanies my [si]ns.
But Thy loving keeping is for the saving of my soul
and over my steps is (34) abundance of pardon
and when Thou judgest me, greatness of [mer]cy;
and until I am old Thou wilt care for me.
For (35) my father knew me not
and my mother abandoned me to Thee;
for Thou art a father to all Thy [sons] of truth
and hast put Thy joy (36) within them
as her that loves her babe,
and as a foster father (bearing the child) in his breast
so carest Thou for all Thy creatures.

HYMN Q

The power of God the Creator and the nothingness of man

(38) [I give Thee thanks, O Adonai,]
[. . .] Thou hast increased until they are numbe[rless]
(39) [. . . I will praise] Thy Name because [Thy] wor[ks] are marvellous
(40) [. . . with]out end [. . .]
(41) [. . .] and prais[e . . .][2]

. . . .

X (1) [. . .] the design of Thy heart [. . .]
(2) [. . . it is Thou who hast created al]l things

---

[1] Same idea in Isa. xlix. 1, 5 (Servant Song).
[2] One line must have disappeared completely at the foot of column IX, and two, it
seems, from the top of column X.

and without Thy will nothing exists.[1]
But none heeds [Thy] wis[dom]
(3) and none considers Thy [mighty deeds].
And what then is man,
he that is but earth [and] (4) potter's [clay]
and will return to the dust,[2]
that Thou shouldst give him understanding of such marvels
and make known to him [Thy] secret of tr[uth]?

(5) For I, I am but dust and ashes;
what shall I meditate unless it please Thee,
and what thought shall I have (6) without Thy will,
and what strength shall I show unless Thou establish me?
And how ⟨shall I understand⟩ unless Thou reflect (7) for me,
and what shall I say unless Thou open my mouth,
and how shall I reply unless Thou teach me?

(8) Behold, Thou art Prince of the gods and King of the venerated
and Lord of every spirit and Master of all creatures,   [beings,
(9) and without Thee nothing is made
and nothing is known without Thy will.
Except for Thyself, nothing exists,
(10) and nothing is mighty beside Thee,
and in the face of Thy glory nothing is,
and Thy power is without price.
And who (11) among Thy great (and) marvellous works
has strength to stand before Thy glory?
(12) For what is he who returns to his dust
that he should have (such) [strength]?
It is for Thy glory alone
that Thou hast created all these things.

HYMN R

*Trust in God who has given Knowledge to the faithful; contempt for
riches and pleasure*

(14) Blessed be Thou, O Adonai,
O God of mercy, [O Thou who art rich] in grace!
For Thou hast given [me] to know [al]l Thy (15) wonderful [pa]rdon
about which I must not be silent by day nor by n[ight . . .]
[And I have hoped] (16) in Thy grace

---

[1] Cf. *Rule* XI, 17.   [2] Cf. *Rule* XI, 22.

because of the greatness of Thy goodness and the abun[dance of Thy
(**17**) For I have leaned upon Thy truth [. . .]   [mercy . . .]
[For nothing comes to pass] (**18**) unless Thou desire it,
and unless [it pleased Thee nothing was made],
[and unless] Thou threaten (there is) no stumbling,
[nor] (**19**) blow unless Thou know it,
and [nothing exists in the face] of Thy [might].

(**20**) And [I,] according to my knowledge
[will meditate] on Thy tru[th the whole day long].
And because I contemplate Thy glory I will recount (**21**) Thy marvels,
and because I have understood a[ll things
I will hope in the grea]tness of Thy mercy,
and in Thy forgiveness (**22**) I will place my hope.
For it is Thou who hast formed the inc[lination of Thy servant]
[and] hast established me [according to] Thy [will].
And Thou hast not put (**23**) my support in gain
and in the riches [of wickedness] my [h]eart [has found no pleasure].¹
And Thou hast not set the creature of flesh to be my strength
(but) (**24**) the hosts of the Valiant.
[The ungodly lean] on abundance of plea[sure],
[on ab]undance of corn and new wine and oil,
(**25**) and because of (their) possessions and fortune they are proud:
[but Thou hast placed me like a gr]een [tree]
by the side of the watercourses,
heavy with leaves (**26**) and bearing many branches.
For Thou hast chosen [trees of life from among the sons] of men
and they all grow fat from the earth.
(**27**) And unto Thy sons of truth Thou hast given under[standing]
[and they shall know Thee for ever and] ever
[and] shall be glorified according to their knowledge,
(**28**) one more than the other.
And likewise, unto the son of ma[n . . .]
Thou hast given an abundant portion (**29**) of the knowledge of Thy truth
and he shall be [gl]ori[fied] according to his knowledge [. . .]
[And the s]oul of Thy servant has loathed [riches] (**30**) and gain
[and has found] no [delight] in pride of pleasures.²
My heart has rejoiced in Thy Covenant
and Thy truth (**31**) fills my soul with delights.
And I have flowered [like a l]ily

¹ This contempt for profit and riches is typically Essene; cf. PHILO, *Q.o.p.l.*, §§ 76-8;
JOSEPHUS, *War*, II, §§ 122, 141.
² This condemnation of pleasure is also a characteristic feature of Essenism; cf.
JOSEPHUS, *War*, II, § 120: 'The Essenes reject pleasure as an evil.'

and my heart has opened to the everlasting fountain
(32) and my support is in the might from above:
but [the wicked bear a fruit] of affliction
which withers before the heat while still in flower.

(33) And my trembling heart was fearful
and my loins were shaken
and my groaning reached the Abyss
(34) and spread also to the dungeons of Sheol.
And I was afraid when I heard Thy judgment of the (35) strong Valiant
and Thy trial of the host of Thy Saints [. . .]¹   [Ones
[. . .] (36) and judgment (shall be passed) on all Thy works
and justice [. . .]²

. . . .

XI (1) in fe[ar . . .]
[and aff]liction [was not hidden] from my eyes
nor sor[row . . .]
(2) because of the meditation of my heart.

HYMN S

God's loving-kindness to His elect

(3) I give Thee thanks, O my God,
for Thou hast done wonderful deeds unto dust
and hast manifested Thy power greatly, mightily,
in a creature of clay!

And I, what am I,
that (4) Thou [shouldst teach] me Thy secret of truth
and give me understanding of Thy marvellous deeds?
And into my mouth Thou hast put songs of thanksgiving
and on to my tongue (5) [a song of pr]aise,
and Thou hast circumcised my lips in the abode of rejoicing
that I should sing Thy favours
and meditate on Thy power all (6) the day long.
I will bless Thy Name always
and recount Thy glory in the midst of the sons of men,
and in the abundance of Thy goodness (7) my soul will delight.

---

¹ The judgment and chastisement of the fallen angels; cf. *Jubilees*, V, 6; X, 7-11; *Damascus Document*, II, 18.
² Only a few fragmentary letters remain of the last four or five lines of column X; moreover, two or three lines have probably disappeared from the top of column XI. The first two lines of column XI after these lacunae seem to give the end of *Hymn R*.

And I, I know that truth is (in) Thy mouth
and righteousness in Thy hand,
and in Thy thought (8) is all knowledge
and in Thy might all power
and all glory is with Thee.
All the judgments of chastisement are in Thy wrath
(9) and abundance of pardon in Thy goodness.
And Thy mercy is obtained by all the sons of Thy loving-kindness;
for Thou hast made known to them Thy secret of truth
(10) and given them understanding of all Thy marvellous Mysteries.

And Thou hast cleansed man of sin because of Thy glory
that he may be made holy (11) for Thee from all unclean abomination
and from (every) transgression of unfaithfulness,
that he may be joined wi[th] Thy sons of truth
and with the lot of (12) Thy Saints;
that this vermin that is man
may be raised from the dust to [Thy] secret [of truth]
and from the spirit of perversity to [Thine] understanding;
(13) and that he may watch before Thee with the everlasting host
and together with [Thy] spirits [of holiness],
that he may be renewed[1] with all [that is] (14) [and] shall be
and with them that know, in a common rejoicing.

HYMN T

From mourning to joy through Knowledge

(15) [I give Thee thank]s, I give Thee thanks, O Adonai!
I will exalt Thee, O my Rock!
And because [Thy works] are marvellous I [will praise Thee]
[and will bless Thy Name] (16) [for ever!]

For Thou hast made me know the secret of truth [. . .]
(17) [and] hast revealed Thy [wond]ers to me,
and I have contemplated [the depth of Thy mysteries]
[unto all the son]s of Grace.
And I have known (18) [that] righteousness is Thine
and that salv[ation] is in Thy favours,
[and that in the heat of Thy wrath
are vengeanc]e and destruction without mercy.
(19) And a fountain has been opened to me
unto bitter mourning [. . .]

[1] Man will be a 'new man'. Concerning the Renewal of the world, see below, XIII, 11-12 (*Hymn* V).

[and] affliction was not hidden from my eyes
(20) when I knew the inclinations of men[1]
and the return of mankind [to dust]
[and their inclination] to sin and to the sorrow (21) of transgression.
And (these thoughts) entered my heart
and reached into [my] bones [to . . .]
and to plunge me into meditation.
(22) Sorrow and groaning upon the funeral harp
(sounded) unto all mourning,
sor[row] and bitter lamentation
until perversity is destroyed.

And [I was healed]
with no blow to render me sick (again);
therefore (23) I will sing upon the harp of deliverance
upon the lyre of jo[y and the lute of glad]ness
and upon the flute of praise without (24) ceasing.
Who among all Thy creatures
can recount [the multitude] of Thy [wonders]?
By the mouth of them all may (25) Thy Name be praised for everlasting
May they bless Thee by the mouth of the humbl[e of spirit]   [ages!
[and may the Sons of Heave]n utter also (26) a voice of rejoicing
and let there be no more sorrow nor groaning nor perversity [. . .]
And may Thy truth shine out
(27) unto everlasting glory and happiness without end!

Blessed be Thou, [O God of knowledge],
who hast given unto [Thy servant] (28) understanding of Knowledge
to comprehend Thy marvels and [Thy wo]r[ks without n]umber
because of the abundance of Thy favours!
(29) Blessed be Thou, O God of mercy and favour,
because of the greatn[ess of] Thy [mi]ght
and the abundance of Thy truth
and the multitude (30) of Thy favours in all Thy works!
Gladden the soul of Thy servant by Thy truth
and cleanse me (31) by Thy righteousness,
even as I have hoped in Thy goodness
and have put my hope in Thy favours!
And by [Thy] forgiveness (32) Thou hast opened my billows[2]
and comforted me in my sorrow;
for I have ⟨leaned⟩ upon Thy mercy.

[1] Or 'human creatures'?
[2] The billows of death which were drowning me (cf. III, 9, 10, 12); God has 'opened' a way for the sectary through the waves, as He did for the children of Israel in the Sea of Reeds.

Blessed be Thou, (33) O Adonai,
for Thou hast done all these things!
And Thou hast put into the mouth of Thy servant [. . .]
(34) and supplication and reply of the tongue.
And Thou hast established for me the activi[ty . . .]
(35) And I had [strength] to [st]a[nd before Thy glory . . .]
(36) And Thou [. . .]¹

HYMN U

God is to be praised at all times; joy and salvation through Knowledge

. . . .
XII (1) [. . . and] Thou hast wide[ned my] soul [. . .]
(2) [. . .] in trust in the abode of hol[iness]
[in ca]lmness and repose
(3) [. . . in] my tent [I will sing] on [the harp]s of salvation
and praise Thy Name in the midst of them that fear Thee
(4) [with blessings and th]anksgiving and prayers,
bowing down and imploring always
from one season to another:²
when the light comes (5) from [its] dwe[lling place]
at its appointed hour in the circuit of the day
according to the laws of the great luminary;
when evening approaches and (6) light withdraws
at the beginning of the dominion of darkness
at the hours of night in its circuit;
when the morning draws near
and (7) (darkness) vanishes before the light
to return to its dwelling-place,
when the night withdraws and day breaks;
always, in all (8) the beginnings of Time,
(in) the fundamental divisions of the length and circuit of the seasons
(which return) at their appointed hour (as established) by their signs
[for all (9) their dominion,
at the appointed and certain hour according to the mouth of God
and the law decreed by Him who is.
And this law shall endure (10) without end;

¹ All the rest of line 36 has disappeared, as well as almost the whole of lines 37, 38 and 39. This *Hymn* T probably ended either on the last line of column XI or at the top of column XII, the first four or five lines of which have completely gone. So we do not know exactly where the following hymn (U) begins.
² In the development which follows (lines 4-9), the psalmist first describes the daily cycle (morning, evening, morning) and then the yearly one. This development calls to mind the passage in the *Rule* concerning the celebration of the sacred times (X, 1-8); the importance given to the cycle of the seasons is characteristic of Qumran mysticism.

and beside it there was nothing
and nothing shall be in the future,
for the God of knowledge (11) established it[1]
and there is none other beside Him.

And I, gifted with understanding,
I have known Thee, O my God,
because of the Spirit (12) that Thou hast put in me;
and I have heard what is certain according to Thy marvellous secret
because of Thy holy Spirit.
(13) Thou hast [o]pened Knowledge in the midst of me
concerning the Mystery of Thine understanding,
and the source of [Thy] powe[r and the fountain of] Thy [goodness]
(14) [Thou hast revealed (to me)]
according to the abundance of grace and destroying zeal.
And Thou wilt bring to an e[nd the dominion of darkness . . .]
(15) [. . . and] the shining of Thy glory (shall be) an ev[erlasting] light
[[. . .]
(16) [. . . and there shall be no more f]ear of wickedness or deceit [. . .]
(17) [. . .] ruin [among] my [st]eps.
For there shall be no m[ore . . .]
(18) [. . . and there] shall be no more oppression.
For before [Thy] wrath [. . .]
(19) [. . .] my disquiet
and there is no just man beside Thee [. . .]
(20) [to] understand Thy Mysteries
and to answer a word [. . .]
[. . .] (21) [in] Thy reproach.
But they shall watch for Thy goodness,
for in [Thy] gra[ce . . .]
[. . .] (22) and they have known Thee
and at the time of Thy glory they shall rejoice.
And in proportion to [their knowledge . . .]
[and] according to their understanding (23) Thou hast made them draw
and they shall serve Thee in conformity with their authority[2]   [near,
according to the divisions [. . .]
(24) without transgressing Thy word.

And [Thou hast] drawn [me] from the dust
and [out of clay] I was sh[aped]

---

[1] Cf. *Rule*, III, 15.
[2] The amount of authority exercised by the sectaries depended on the degree of their
spiritual advancement, and their hierarchic rank on the excellence of their holiness
(cf. *Rule*, V, 20-4). The same doctrine appears above, in X, 27-8 (*Hymn* R): 'they . . . shall
be glorified according to their knowledge, one more than the other'.

(25) as a fount of defilement and ignominious shame,
a container of dust, a thing knea[ded with water],
[. . .] and a dwelling-place (26) of darkness.
And the law of the creature of clay is return unto dust;
at the time of [death the being] of dust will return
(27) to that from which he was taken.
How, dust and [ashes], shall he answer [his Maker],
[and how] understand (28) His [wo]rks?
And how shall he stand before Him who reproves him?
[Behold, Thou hast created the angels of ho]liness
(29) [and the] everlasting [spirits]
and the receptacle of glory
and the fountain of knowledge and migh[t],
[and] even they are (30) [unable] to recount all Thy glory
or stand in the face of Thy wrath,
and none is able to answer (31) Thy reproof!
For Thou art righteous
and before Thee nothing exists.
But what is he that returns to his dust?

(32) And I was silent; what could I say?
It is according to my Knowedge that I speak:
the creature of clay is without righteousness.
What (33) can I say unless Thou open my mouth,
and how can I understand unless Thou give understanding to me?
And what thou]ght] can I have (34) unless Thou uncover my heart,
and how can I make my way straight unless [Thou es]tablish [it]?
[And how] can (35) [my] foo[tstep] be sure [unless Thou] give strength
and how can I raise myself [. . .]   [and might,
(36) And all [. . .][1]

. . . .

HYMN V

The marvels of Creation and the Renewal of the world

. . . .

XIII (1) [. . . Thi]ne is holiness from before e[ternity . . .]
(2) [. . .] and through Thy marvellous Mysteries [. . .]
(3) [. . .] Thou hast shown Thy Hand [by all Thy] works [. . .]
(4) [. . .] truth [in] their works [. . .] but folly [. . .]

---

[1] About three lines have completely disappeared from the bottom of column XII. Of column XIII, only twenty-one lines remain (about half the original number) and they are all more or less incomplete.

(5) [. . .] and eternal grace unto all the peace-[makers]
but the ev[erlasting] Pit [. . .]
(6) [. . .] and everlasting glory [. . . and] perpetual [j]oy
for the work [. . .] (7) [the wi]cked.

And these things [which Thou hast] est[ablished . . .]
(8) all Thy works before Thou createdst them
with the host of Thy spirits and the congregation [of Thy Saints],
[with the firmament and all] (9) its hosts,
with the earth and all its fr[uits],
in the seas and in the deeps [. . .]
[. . .] (10) and an everlasting Visitation.

For it is Thou who hast established them from before eternity[1]
and the work [. . .]
(11) they shall recount Thy glory in all Thy dominion.
For Thou hast caused them to see what they had not known
[by bringing to an end the] former [things]
and by creating (12) things that are new,[2]
by setting aside the former covenants
and by [set]ting up that which shall remain for ever.[3]
For Th[ou art a God of eternity . . .]
and shalt be (13) for ages without end.

And [Thou hast] divi[ded] all these things
in the Mysteries of Thine understanding
to make Thy glory known.
[But what is] he, the spirit of flesh,[4] to understand (14) all these things
and to comprehend [Thy] great secret of truth?
And what is he that is born of woman
amid all [Thy] mighty [works]?
(15) He is but a fabric of dust
and a thing kneaded with water,
[who]se counsel is nothing but [uncleann]ess
ignominious shame[5] and [. . .]
and over whom the perverse spirit rules.
(16) And if he remains in ungodliness
he will beco[me an object of fear for] ever

---

[1] Cf. above, I, 7 (*Hymn* A).
[2] Cf. Isa. xliii. 19, xlviii. 6-7; cf. *Rule*, IV, 25.
[3] This passage brings out clearly the notion of the New Covenant: it was to be a real innovation and the final one. Cf. the fragment published in *Qumran Cave I*, no. 34 *bis* col. II, line 6: 'and Thou hast renewed Thy Covenant for them' (see below, p. 336).
[4] Same expression below, XVII, 25 (*Hymn* D').
[5] Cf. XII, 25 (*Hymn* U).

and a wonder to the generations
and an object of fri[ght to all] flesh!

It is by Thy goodness alone that (17) man is justified,
and by the immensity of Thy mer[cy].
[For] Thou wilt adorn him with Thy brightness
and fi[ll] him [with abun]dance of pleasure,
with (18) everlasting bliss and length of days.[1]
For [Thou hast sworn it]
[and] Thy word shall not turn back.

And I, Thy servant, I know
(19) by the Spirit which Thou hast put in me
[that Thou art truth]
and that all Thy works are righteousness
and that [Thy] wo[rd] shall not turn back,
[and that all] (20) Thy seasons are desti[ned to Thine elect]
[and Thy deeds cho]sen in view of their needs.
And I know [that . . .]
(21) and the wicked [. . .]

HYMN W

The virtues of the sectaries of the Covenant[2]

. . . .
XIV (1) [. . .] in Thy people and [. . .]
(2) [. . .] the men of truth and [. . .]
(3) [. . . they that lo]ve mercy and are strong of spirit,
they that are pure of (4) [heart . . .]
[. . . they that] show [themselves] brave until the [Day] of Thy judg-
[ments
(5) [. . .] and Thou wilt strengthen Thy precepts [in them] to make
(6) [. . . the planting] of holiness unto e[verlasting] generations and all
(7) [. . .] the men of Thy vision.[3]

[1] Cf. *Rule*, IV, 7.
[2] Several lines at the top of column XIV have completely disappeared, and it is not at all certain that, in the Scroll, this column XIV follows immediately on column XIII. The first lines of column XIV only give us the end of a hymn; a new one (X) probably begins on line 8 since there is a blank at the end of line 7, and the word 'O Adonai' on line 8 is very likely preceded by 'I give Thee thanks', as in nearly all the other hymns. As it is, only the ends of the last seven lines of *Hymn* W remain; I have translated these fragmentary phrases line by line without being able to give them any coherent meaning.
[3] This can also be translated 'Thy visionaries'. The expression refers to the prophets of God (cf. *War Scroll*, XI, 8: 'Those who see the testimonies') or, more generally, the members of the sect favoured with divine visions.

HYMN X

The essential duties of the sectary of the Covenant

(8) [I give Thee thanks,] O Adonai,
who hast put understanding into the heart of Thy servant
(9) [that he may do what is good and right before Thee . . .]
and that he may show himself stout-hearted against the cri[mes] of
and that he may bless (10) [Thy Name . . .]   [ungodliness
[and choose all th]at Thou lovest
and loathe all that (11) [Thou hatest]¹
[. . .] of man.
For in accordance with the [ever]lasting Spirits²
(12) [Thou hast cast a lot for all the sons of men]
between goodness and ungodliness,³
[and hast sea]led their reward.

And by Thy understanding I know
(13) that it is by Thy will that [I have] entered [Thy Covenant]
and [received] Thy holy [Spi]rit.
And likewise Thou sendest me forward toward Thine understanding;
and as (14) I draw near I am full of zeal
against all evil-doers and men of falsehood.
For none of them that approach Thee
can rebel against the commands of Thy mouth,
(15) and none that know Thee can hate Thy words.
For Thou art righteous and all Thine elect are truth,
and all perversity (16) [and ungod]liness Thou wilt destroy for ever
and Thy righteousness shall be revealed to the eyes of all Thy works.

(17) [And] because of the abundance of Thy goodness I know,
and I have sworn an oath on my soul⁴
to sin no more against Thee
(18) [and to] do nothing that is evil in Thine eyes.
And likewise I have caused all the men of my assembly
to go forward in the community;
in proportion (19) to his [un]derstanding will I make (each) one progress
and according to the abundance of his portion I will love him.
I will not raise the countenance of the wicked,
nor consider the gi[ft of the ungodly].

---

¹ Cf. *Rule*, I, 3-4.
² These are the two Spirits of good and evil to which all men are assigned; cf. *Rule*,
III, 18 ff.
³ Cf. *Rule*, IV, 26.
⁴ An allusion to the oath exacted from those who entered the sect (*Rule*, V, 7-11;
Damascus Document, XV, 4-XVI, 9; cf. JOSEPHUS, *War*, II, §§ 139-42).

(**20**) [And] I will [not] barter Thy truth for riches
and all Thy laws for a gift;
but in propor[tion to the folly of each] man, (**21**) [so will I hate] him,
and according as Thou settest him aside, so will I loathe him.
And I will not enter the assembly of the m[en of Belial],
of them that have turned far (**22**) [away from] Thy [Covenant].

HYMN Y

The sectary's love for God

(**23**) [I give] Thee [thanks], O Adonai,
according to the greatness of Thy might and the abundance of Thy
from everlasting to ev[erlasting]!   [marvels,
[Thou art merci]ful and rich (**24**) [in upright]ness,
Thou who pardonest them that are converted from sin
and visitest the iniquity of the wicked.
[Thou lovest them that seek Thee] with a generous (**25**) [heart],
but Thou hatest perversity for ever.

And Thou hast favoured me, Thy servant, with the Spirit of Knowledge,
[to love tr]uth (**26**) [and righteousness]
and to loathe all the ways of perversity.
And I will love Thee generously[1]
[and seek] Thee with all my heart.
(**27**) [. . .] for it is by Thy hand that this is,
and without [Thy might has nothi]ng [been made . . .][2]

. . . .

HYMN Z

Divine predestination

XV (**1-8**) . . . .
(**9**) [. . . they shall l]ove Thee always and [. . .]
(**10**) [. . .] and I have loved Thee generously
and with all my heart and soul.
I have purified [. . .]
(**11**) [. . .] and have not departed from all Thy commands,

---

[1] Same expression below, XV, 10 (*Hymn* Z); cf. Hos. xiv. 5.
[2] Of line 28 there remain only a few letters impossible to translate. *Hymn* Y must have
ended either at the foot of column XIV, where several lines have disappeared completely,
or in the missing part at the top of column XV. Of the first eight lines of column XV only
a few letters remain at the beginning of each line.

and I will cling fast to the Many[1] [. . .]
(12) abandoning (none) of all Thy precepts.

And I, because of Thine understanding I know
that [the righteousness of man] is not in the hand of flesh
[and] that man [is not] master of (13) his way
and that mankind cannot strengthen its step.[2]
And I know that the inclination of every spirit is in Thy hand
[and that] Thou hast ordained [the way of every man]
[together with his visitation][3]
(14) before ever creating him.
And how can any man change Thy words?

Thou alone hast [created] (15) the just
and established him from his mother's womb unto the time of good-will[4]
that he may be preserved in Thy Covenant
and walk in all ⟨Thy way⟩,
and that he [may go forward] upon it (16) because of the immensity of
and that he may unloose all the distress of his soul   [Thy mercy,
to (possess) eternal salvation
and perpetual unfailing peace.

And Thou hast raised up (17) his glory from among flesh,
whereas Thou hast created the wicked [for the time of] Thy [wr]ath
and hast set them apart from their mother's womb for the Day of Massacre.
(18) For they have walked in the way which is not good
and have despised [Thy] Co[venant]
[and] their soul has detested Thy [precepts],
and they have not delighted in all (19) Thy commands
and have chosen that which Thou hatest.
Thou hast created all [them that despise] Thy [will]
to execute great judgment against them
(20) in the eyes of all Thy works,
that they may serve as a sign and wo[nder unto] everlasting [genera-
that [all] may know Thy glory and (21) awful might.   [tions][5]

But what is he that is flesh
to understand Thy works?

---

[1] An expression frequently used in the *Rule* and the *Damascus Document* to describe the members of the sect.
[2] Cf. *Rule*, XI, 10.
[3] Cf. *Rule*, III, 13-15.
[4] Cf. Isa. xlix. 8 ('the time of good-will'); lxi. 2 ('the year of good-will').
[5] Cf. Deut. xxviii. 46; Ps. lxxi. 7; the expression 'a wonder unto generations' appears also above, XIII, 16 (*Hymn* V).

[And] can he that is dust establish his steps?
(22) It is Thou who hast formed the spirit
and established its activity[1] [. . .]
and it is from Thee that the way of all the living proceeds.

And I know that (23) no riches equal Thy truth
and [that the revenge of] Thy [men of hol]iness will be terrible.
And I know that Thou hast chosen them from among all (men) (24) and
It is they who will serve Thee, [for ever.
and Thou wilt not acce[pt . . .]
and for the crimes of ungodliness Thou wilt accept no ransom.
(25) For Thou art a God of truth
and Thou [wilt destroy] all perversity [in the world]
[and] there shall be [no more wickedness] before Thee

[And] I, I know (26) that Thine [. . .][2]

. . . .

HYMN A'

From Knowledge to prayer and the service of God

. . . .

XVI (1) [. . .] And I, [I know] (2) because of the ho[ly] Spirit [which
Thou hast pu]t in m[e]
that [. . .] and that m[an] cannot [. . .] (3) [Thy] ho[ly] Spirit.
[Thy glory] fills h[eave]n [and] earth
[. . .] Thy [glo]ry fills [. . .]
(4) And I know that through [Thy] loving-kindn[ess] to man
Thou hast multiplied [. . .]
[. . .] Thy truth shall [rem]ain for e[ver]
(5) and the place of righteousness [. . .] which Thou hast entrusted to
him [. . .]

(6) Because I know all these things
[I] will utter a reply of the tongue,
praying and [entreating]
[and turning back from al]l my sins,
and searching [Thy] Spirit [of Knowledge]
(7) and clinging fast to [Thy] ho[ly] Spirit,
and adhering to the truth of Thy Covenant

[1] Cf. above, XI, 34 (*Hymn* T).
[2] The end of *Hymn* Z has disappeared at the bottom of column XV or the top of column XVI.

and serving Thee in truth and with a perfect heart,
and loving [Thy truth].

(8) Blessed be Thou, O Adonai,
Thou who hast created the [wo]rld
and art gr[eat] in exploits,
Thou whose work is the world!
Behold, Thou hast undertaken to fi[ll Thy servant] (9) with grace
and hast favoured me with Thy Spirit of mercy
and with the [brightness] of Thy glory.

Thine, Thine, is righteousness!
For Thou hast made ever[y spirit]
[with its strength] (10) and understanding;
for it is Thou who hast allotted the spirit of the just.
And I have chosen to cleanse my hands according to [Thy] wil[l]
and the soul of Thy servant has l[oath]ed every (11) work of perversity.

And I know that none is righteous beside Thee;
and I have appeased Thy face
because of the Spirit which Thou hast put [in me]
to accomplish (12) Thy [fav]ours towards [Thy] servant for [ever]
by cleansing me by Thy holy Spirit
and by causing me to go forward in Thy will
according to the greatness of Thy favours [. . .]
(13) [. . . in] the place of [Thy] loving[-kindness]
which [Thou hast] cho[sen] for them that love Thee
and for them that keep [Thy] com[mandme]nts,
[that they may stand] (14) before Thee [for e]ver
[. . . to] mingle with the spirit of Thy servant
and in every wor[k . . .]
(15) [. . .] and that no blow may [be] for him
a cause of stumbling aside from the precepts of Thy Covenant
but [. . .] (16) of gl[o]ry and [. . .]

[. . . for Thou art . . .] and merciful,
lo[ng-suffer]ing [and rich] in grace and truth,
who pardonest the sin [. . .]
(17) and compassionate towards [all the sons of righteousness],
[they that love Thee] and keep [Thy] command[ments]
[and] are converted to Thee with faith and a perfect heart [. . .]
(18) to serve Thee [and to do what is] good in Thine eyes.

Thrust not away the face of Thy servant
[and reject] not the son of [Thy] handmaid [. . .]
(19) [. . .] And I, according to Thy words [I have] called [on Thy
[Name . . .]¹

HYMN B′

Of divine Judgment (?)

. . . .

XVII (1) [. . .] because of (?) that which is short measured [. . .]
(2) [. . .] revealed without fl[ying away . . .]
(3) [. . .] she who devours [. . .]
(4) [. . .] in a dry place and a cause of stumb[ling . . .]
(5) [. . .] they that strike against, suddenly, all at [once . . .]
(6) [. . .] judgment because of (?) the spirit of him who seeks [. . .]
(7) [. . .] Thou wilt cast into [. . .]
[. . .] the commandment because of (?) the spirit of him who stumbles
[. . .]
(8) [. . .] in the blows of Be[lial (?)]²

HYMN C′

The sure salvation of the sectaries

(9) [I give Thee thanks, O Adonai,]
because of the secrets whi[ch Thou hast revealed to Thine elect],
[they w]ho have not been touched by the [. . .]
(10) [. . .] and because of the judgment [Thou] hast cut sh[ort . . .]
[. . . the thou]ghts of wickedness [Thou hast] hastened [. . .]
(11) [. . .] and because of the judgment [. . .]
[Thou hast cleansed] Thy servant of all his rebellions
[through the greatness of] Thy [m]ercy (12) [and the abundance of Thy
[as Thou] hast said by the hand of Moses,³   [goodness];
[Forgiving rebellion] and iniquity and sin
and pardoning [rebellion] and unfaithfulness.

(13) [For fire shall burn up] the foundations of the mountains
and fire shall con[sume] nethermost Sheol.

¹ The end of *Hymn A′* has disappeared with the bottom of column XVI. A dozen lines
or so have completely disappeared from the top of column XVII. The first eight of the
remaining lines, which are all badly mutilated at the beginning and the end, give us a
few scraps of the final section of a hymn whose general theme cannot be stated with
certainty.
² At the end of line 8 is a blank, which probably indicates that a new hymn begins in the
following line.
³ The quotation which follows is taken from Exod. xxxiv. 7 (slightly modified).

But they that ho[pe] in Thy laws (**14**) [Thou wilt deliver],
[and bring aid] to them that serve Thee with faith
[that] their seed [may] be before Thee for ever.
And [Thou] wilt forg[ive them and] raise up (**15**) [a Saviour (?)]
[to redeem them from s]in
and to cast away all their in[iquities]
and to give to them a share of the glory of man
[and] abundance of days.

HYMN D'

Carnal man and justification

(**17**) [I give Thee thanks, O Adona]i,
because of the Spirits which Thou hast put in me![1]
I will [utt]er a reply of the tongue
to recount Thy righteousness
and the long-suffering (**18**) [. . .]
and the works of Thy mighty Right Hand
[and the forgiveness] of the sins of the fathers,
and to p[ra]y and beseech concerning (**19**) [my own transgressions]
[and the perversion] of my deeds and the corruption of [my] h[eart].
For I have been defiled by uncleanness
and I have [walked] aside from [Thy] assembly
and I have not jo[in]ed (**20**) [. . .]

For Thine, Thine, is righteousness,
and unto Thy Name be blessing for eve[r]!
[Practise] Thy righteousness
and redeem (**21**) [the soul of Thy servant],
[and may] the wicked [va]nish [for ever]!
For I have understood that it is Thou
who hast chosen [the just and established] his way;
and Thou (**22**) [hast taught him] understanding [of Thy Mysteries]
[that] he may not sin against Thee
[and to leave] him[2] his humility in Thy teachings;
and by [Thy] secr[ets] Thou hast [strengthened] his heart.

(**23**) [O my God, prevent] Thy servant from sinning against Thee
and from stumbling aside from all the ways of Thy will!

---

[1] Cf. above, XIII, 19 (*Hymn* V): 'By the Spirit which Thou hast put in me', etc. The plural employed here, instead of the singular, appears to allude to the various spirits enumerated in Isa. xi. 2.

[2] A similar expression appears in the *Damascus Document* (V, 6): 'and God left them to him' (God allowed David to retain the merit of his works).

Strengthen [his] l[oins]
[that he may res]ist the spirits (24) [of Belial][1]
[and w]alk in all that Thou lovest,
and that he may despise all that Thou hatest
[and do] what is good in Thine eyes!
(25) [Banish] from my members [all] their [domi]nion,
for Thy servant [possesses] a spirit of fl[esh].[2]

HYMN E'

The divine Covenant

(26) [I give Thee thanks, O Adonai],
[for] Thou hast poured forth [Thy] holy Spirit upon Thy servant
[and hast clea]nsed my heart from [all the rebellions of] my [sin]s![3]
(27) [And I will put my support in no ma]n
and I will look to no human covenant;
[but it is Thy Covenant that I will seek],
[for they that seek] it find it.
(28) [... they that me]ditate upon it and love it
[... shall live for] everlasting ages.[4]

HYMN F'

The Teacher of Righteousness and the Good Tidings

XVIII . . . .
(1) Thy light and Thou hast set up a heavenly li[ght . . .][5]
(2) Thy light unceasing[ly . . .]
(3) For with Thee is the light [. . .]
(4) and Thou hast uncovered the ear of dust [. . .]
(5) because of the design which [. . .]
and they have been confirmed by [the hands] (6) of Thy servant for
[ever.

[And Thou hast proclaimed] Thy marvellous [me]ssages [by his mouth]
that they may shine (7) before the eyes of all that hear them.
[For Thou hast upheld Thy servant] with Thy strong Right Hand

---

[1] The expression 'spirits of Belial' appears in the *Damascus Document*, XII, 2.
[2] The expression 'spirit of flesh' appears also in XIII, 13 (*Hymn* V).
[3] Cf. above, VII, 30 (*Hymn* M); XVII, 11 (*Hymn* C').
[4] Here ends column XVII (there are no traces of letters below line 28) and probably also this little hymn.
[5] The beginning of *Hymn* F' is lost together with the top of column XVIII. Note that column XVIII does not follow column XVII; the column preceding it (to the right) is partially preserved and appears as Fragment 1 of the *editio princeps* (not translated here).

to guide the[m][1] (8) by the strength of Thy might
[. . . and he has called on] Thy Name and grown great in glo[ry].

(9) Withdraw not Thy [great] Hand [from Thy people]
that it[2] may have one that clings firm to Thy Covenant
(10) and stands before Thee i[n perfection].[3]
[For] Thou hast opened a [fount]ain[4] in the mouth of Thy servant
and upon his tongue (11) Thou hast graven [Thy precepts] on a measur-
[ing-cord,
[that he] may proclaim them unto creatures because of his understanding
and be an interpreter of these things
(12) unto that which is dust like myself.[5]

And Thou hast opened [his] fount[ain][6]
to reprove the deeds of the creature of clay
and the transgressions of him that is born (13) of woman,
in conformity with his works;
and to open Thy l[aws] of truth
to the creature whom Thou hast upheld by Thy might,
(14) that according to Thy truth [he may be]
the one who announces good tidings [in the ti]me of Thy goodness,[7]
preaching the gospel to the humble according to the abundance of Thy
(15) [giving them to drink] from the fountain of h[oliness]   [mercy,
[and consoling the co]ntrite of spirit and the afflicted
to (bring them) everlasting joy.

(16) [. . .] . . . he that is born of wo[man]
(17) [. . .] Thy [mercy] and justice

   [1] 'Them' refers to the hearers and followers of the psalmist, who humbly alludes to
himself here as 'Thy servant'; it is he who communicates the divine messages and is
responsible for 'guiding' the sectaries of the Covenant. This 'servant' of God is the
Teacher of Righteousness himself.
   [2] 'Thy people.'
   [3] This person, who by his attachment to the Covenant and perfect life is to be God's
messenger to the holy people, is the psalmist himself, as the context indicates; he is, I
would repeat, the Teacher of Righteousness.
   [4] Cf. above, VIII, 4, 16 (*Hymn* O). Cf. Zech. xiii. 1.
   [5] By using this expression, the psalmist lifts the veil completely on the identification of
the 'servant'; it is indeed himself. Out of humility he declares that he is 'dust' like all those
to whom his message is addressed.
   [6] In the stanza which begins here the Teacher of Righteousness defines his mission as
the preaching of repentance, the teaching of the divine laws, and the announcement of
the Gospel.
   [7] A manifest allusion to the celebrated passage from Isa. lxi. 1-2: 'The Spirit of the
Lord Yahweh is upon me because Yahweh has anointed me; he has sent me to bring
good tidings to the humble . . . to proclaim the year of the Lord's favour . . . to console all
the afflicted.' Cf. Luke iv. 16-22 (Jesus in the synagogue of Nazareth reads this same
passage from Isaiah and then explains the text as applying to himself: 'Today this scripture
which you have heard is fulfilled.')

(18) [. . . unles]s I had seen it.
(19) [. . . and ho]w can I see unless Thou uncover my eyes,
and (how) can I hear (20) [unless Thou uncover my ears]?
[And] my [hea]rt was amazed,
for the word has been opened to the uncircumcised ear
and unto the heart (21) [of man Thou hast taught truth].
And I knew that it was for Thyself that Thou didst these things, O my
God.

For what is flesh?
(22) [Behold, it was in Thy counsel to] do wonders
and in Thy thought to manifest Thy might
and establish all things for Thy glory.
(23) [And Thou hast created all] the host of Knowledge[1]
to recount mighty deeds unto flesh
and the true precepts unto him that is born (24) [of woman].
[And] Thou hast caused [Thine elect] to en[ter] the Covenant with Thee
and hast uncovered the heart of dust
that they be kept (25) [from all evil]
[and escape] from the snares of judgment
unto Thy mercy.

And I, a creature (26) [of clay],
[receptacle of dus]t and heart of stone,[2]
for what am I accounted
that (27) Thou shouldst [pl]ace in an ear of dust [all Thy words of
[truth]
and engrave the everlasting happenings in a (28) [corrupted] heart,
[and] that Thou shouldst convert [him that is born of woman]
and cause him to enter the Covenant with Thee,
and that he should stand (29) [before Thee always]
in the everlasting place where shines the eternal light of the dawn[3]
wi[thout any] darkness

[1] This expression seems to describe the whole angelic world, the 'Spirits of Knowledge'
(III, 22-3). According to Qumran doctrine, this 'host' is more or less confused with the
'heavenly hosts', which in the Bible usually signifies the astral world; in fact the angels —
or at least some of them — were identified with the stars. They are called 'sons of Heaven'
(III, 22), and like the heavens they 'recount the glory of God' (Ps. xix. 2).
[2] The expression 'creature of clay' appears especially in III, 23-4 (*Hymn* F); 'receptacle of dust', in XII, 25 (*Hymn* U). The expression 'heart of stone' is borrowed from
Ezek. xi. 19; xxxvi. 26.
[3] It should be remembered that the Essenes contemplated the 'light of dawn' every
morning at the time of their prayer to the sun.

(30) [for hours of joy withou]t end
and for ages of unfai[ling] bliss [. . .]

(31) [. . .] and I, a creature of dust [. . .]
(32) [. . .] I will open [. . .]¹

---

¹ This is the only word remaining of line 32; of line 33 there remains but one letter. Several lines have disappeared entirely from the foot of column XVIII taking with them the end of the hymn.

CHAPTER VII

THE BIBLICAL COMMENTARIES

The Essene library whose remains have been found in the caves of Qumran contained a number of exegetical works of a particular kind; we call them 'commentaries' for want of a better word. In fact they are interpretations of biblical texts based, not on their natural or historical meaning, but on their secret or mystic significance. The biblical books were thought to refer essentially to the end of time and to be full of instruction concerning the events of that period; it was the task of the commentator to discover, or rather to divine, all these mysterious teachings by means of his superior intuition. The Hebrew word for this divinatory exegesis is *pesher*, a term which recurs constantly in these compositions. The *pesher* is an explanation of the hidden significance, a revelation of the secrets concealed in the divine books, which only inspired commentators, prophets, or initiates were able to discover.

It goes without saying that all concern for an objective interpretation disappears from an exegetical system of this sort. To tell the truth, the text is only a pretext; the commentator tears it out of its context, transposes, transforms, isolates and forces it, in order to make it express his own obsessive ideas. The Essene was convinced that he had already entered the eschatological era and that the end of the world was imminent. Consequently, for him everything in Scripture really alludes to the final violent upheavals expected in the near future and to contemporary events which he thought the prelude to the supreme catastrophe: namely, the unbounded wickedness of the official priesthood, the bloody persecution of the Elect (i.e. of the leader of the sect and his followers), and the invasion and domination of Palestine by the Romans. This is why these themes recur so frequently in the Commentaries.

These biblical Commentaries are constructed as follows. First, a biblical passage is quoted. Its length varies; sometimes a whole verse is given, sometimes part of a verse, and sometimes even a group of verses. Then comes the interpretation with, as an introductory formula, either the words, 'The explanation (*pesher*) of this is that . . .', or, 'The explanation of this word concerns . . .'. Afterwards, another passage is quoted and subsequently interpreted, and so on until the end of the biblical book.

This arrangement calls to mind Philo's account of the meetings at which the Essenes studied the sacred books (*Quod omnis probus*, §§ 81-2): 'They sit in appointed places, the young men below the old, attentive and well-behaved. One of them then takes the books and reads, and another from among the more learned steps forward and explains whatever is not easy to understand in these books. Most of the time, and in accordance with an ancient method of inquiry, instruction is given them by means of symbols.' Then again, the *Rule* states that in every group of ten men there must be 'a man who studies the Law night and day, continually', and that they must all watch for 'a third of all the nights of the year to read the Book' (VI, 6-7). The spirit of these ascetics drew its nourishment therefore from unceasing study of the biblical books: all their speculations, even the newest and boldest, were ingeniously and subtly linked to biblical texts, even when this required a real *tour de force*. For them the Bible was the Book of God, and as such all truth was thought to lie hidden there. The remains of the biblical Commentaries from Qumran are witness to the immense exegetical labour which the Essenes pursued without respite, day and night, for almost two centuries.

These Commentaries are therefore entirely dominated by sectarian outlook and concerns, and as a result they are a mine of valuable information concerning the sect's doctrine and history. Yet it should be emphasized that on account of their particular character, the biblical Commentaries never bother to develop doctrinal themes but are content to indicate them casually and, as it were, furtively. It is up to us to recognize them, and to restore to them all their importance, even when they are only expressed in a few words. This chance discovery is only a small part of an enormous body of literature, and the historian must be keenly attentive to testimony which sometimes discloses in some brief phrase a fundamental point of doctrine.

As regards the contemporary events to which so many passages of the Commentaries allude, it is certainly tiresome that more often than not these allusions are deliberately mysterious and sibylline. Great lovers of the apocalyptic, the Essene writers have in general preserved in their Commentaries that apocalyptical style which likes to conceal the names of the persons referred to, giving them nicknames instead, and to describe historical facts more or less covertly: this sort of thing is found in the book of Daniel, for example, and in the *Book of Enoch*. The unfortunate result is that the present-day interpreter of these ancient Commentaries sometimes finds himself faced with formidable difficulties and obscurities. Yet however well concealed, the allusions were certainly meant to be understood by the reader, and if historians have been able to explain the allusions in Daniel and *Enoch* — or most of them at any rate — it is not unreasonable to hope that with enough perspicacity and patience the same may be done in these Commentaries. The Essenes were riddle-loving soothsayers, and however strange their game may seem to us, we must enter into it. Besides, not everything is expressed enigmatically. As in the apocalypses, there is enough brightness mingled with the shadow to point the way to the truth: and what we learn from the Commentaries is of such importance as to be worth the effort.

Of the biblical Commentaries found at Qumran the most instructive is the famous *Commentary on Habakkuk* found in cave I and published in 1950;[1] it may be recalled that it was with this scroll that the Dead Sea studies were launched. But since 1950, other Essene Commentaries, or rather fragments of Commentaries, have been found and published. In addition to the *Commentary on Habakkuk*, cave I has yielded fragments of a *Commentary on Micah*, a *Commentary on Zephaniah* and a *Commentary on the Psalms*;[2] and in cave IV, fragments of four *Commentaries on Isaiah* have been found, as well as of two *Commentaries on Hosea*, one *Commentary on Nahum* and two *Commentaries on the Psalms*.[3] I should also add that in several of the sect's writings, particularly in the *Damascus Document*, there is implicit reference to Commentaries on other biblical books — on Deuteronomy for example: although these Commentaries are not otherwise known, they must be taken into account. The great number and diversity of the Commentaries discovered or indirectly attested at

---

[1] In *The Dead Sea Scrolls of St. Mark's Monastery*, vol. i (New Haven, 1950).

[2] Published by BARTHÉLEMY and MILIK in *Qumran Cave I* (Oxford, 1955), nos. 14, 15 and 16.

[3] Published by J. M. ALLEGRO in *PEQ*, lxxxvi (1954), pp. 69-75, and *JBL*, lxxv (1956), pp. 89-95, 174-82; lxxvii (1958), pp. 215-21; lxxviii (1959), pp. 144-7.

Qumran leads us to assume that the Essenes worked not only on one or other of the biblical books, but on almost all of them, whether belonging to the *Torah*, the *Nebi'im*, or the *Ketubim*.

I would point out that in these various Commentaries the principal character, the person who in some way haunts the mind of the interpreter, is the Teacher of Righteousness, the august leader of the sect and the prophet *par excellence*, the builder of the Community of the Elect. It is his story, his dramatic story, that the Essene commentators read throughout the whole Bible: he is, so to speak, the centre and key to all ancient revelation, the chief object of faith. Failing a biography of the Teacher, of which no vestige has yet been recovered from the Qumran caves, the biblical Commentaries show how high this holy person stood in the memory and piety ot his followers, and afford us a glimpse of the essential features of his tragic career and mystical destiny.

Below, I give a translation of the whole of the *Commentary on Habakkuk*, and then a translation of the fragments of the other Commentaries, but only in so far as these fragments are of some historical interest.

1. COMMENTARY ON HABAKKUK[1]

I (1) [*The oracle which the prophet Habakkuk saw.*] [*How long, O Yahweh,*] *shall I* [*c*]*all for help and* (**2**) [*Thou wilt not hear, and cry to Thee 'Violence' and Thou wilt not deliver?*] (I, 1-2)

[The explanation of this concerns the exp]ectation of the generation (**3**) [. . .] . . . upon them (**4**) [. . . who c]ry out because of (**5**) [the violence . . .].

[*Why dost Thou make me see wickedness and ga*]*ze* [*on af*]*fli*[*ction?*] (I, 3a)

(**6**) [The explanation of this concerns those who persecute the elect] of God in oppression and unfaithfulness.

(**7**) [*Cruelty and violence are before me; there are quarrels and discord arises.*] (I, 3b-c)

---

[1] The following translation is on the whole the same as that published by me in 1950 in *RHR*, cxxxvii, pp. 129-71. (See also *VT*, i, 1951, pp. 200-15.) I have nevertheless introduced a certain number of modifications taking into account the contributions of Qumran texts published in the meanwhile. I have also profited from the work of my colleagues and from the objections raised on certain points by various writers. Among the many studies on the *Commentary on Habakkuk* which have appeared since 1950, I would mention in particular the work of K. ELLIGER, *Studien zum Habakuk-Kommentar vom Toten Meer* (Tübingen, 1953); see my remarks on this book in *VT*, v (1955), pp. 113-29.

(8) [The explanation of this concerns those who . . .] and l[oa]the the [Law]; and quarrels (9) [. . .] . . . him (10) [. . .]

Because of this, the Law dies (11) *[and justice sees day no more.]* (I, 4a)
[The explanation of this] is that they have despised the Law of God (12) [. . .].

[For the wicked encompas]ses the righteous. (I, 4b)
(13) [The explanation of this is that *the wicked* is the Wicked Priest, and *the righteous*,] the Teacher of Righteousness (14) [. . .].

So justice goes out (15) *[perverted].* (I, 4c)
[The explanation of this . . .] and not [. . .].

(16-17) *[Look among the nations and see, and you will be astounded, bewildered. For I will do a work in your days; you will not believe when]* II (1) *it is told.* (I, 5)
[The explanation of this concerns] those who have betrayed with the Man (2) of Lies; for they [have] not [believed the words] of the Teacher of Righteousness (which he received) from the mouth (3) of God. And (it concerns) those who betra[yed the] New [Covenant];[1] for they did not (4) believe in the Covenant of God [and profaned] His [h]oly Nam[e]. (5) And likewise, the explanation of this word [concerns those who will be]tray at the end (6) of days: they are the violent . . . who will not believe (7) when they hear all the things which will be[fall] the last generation from the mouth (8) of the Priest whom God placed in [the House of Jud]ah to explain all (9) the words of His servants the Prophets, by [whose hand] God has told (10) all that will befall His people and [the nations].

[F]or behold, I rouse (11) *the Chaldeans, that cru[el and has]ty nation.* (I, 6a)
(12) The explanation of this concerns the Kittim[2] w[ho are] quick and valiant (13) in battle, causing many to perish; [and the earth will fall] under the dominion (14) of the Kittim. And the wi[cked will see i]t but will not believe (15-17) in the precepts of [God . . .].

---

[1] The word 'Covenant' has disappeared in the lacuna; the expression 'New Covenant' figures in the *Damascus Document*.

[2] Whereas the prophet Habakkuk foretells and describes the invasion of the Chaldeans who captured Jerusalem in 586 B.C., the Essene commentator, by means of a bold transposition which is the very essence of the *pesher*, relates all these biblical sentences concerning the Chaldeans to a new conquering people, the Kittim. As in the book of Daniel (xi. 30), these Kittim are the Romans who captured Jerusalem in 63 B.C., and subjected Palestine to their rule. For the commentator, this event is the prelude to the end of time. The whole of his description of the Romans and their conquest is that of a contemporary and betrays the violently hostile sentiments of the sect in the first years of the Roman occupation; the *Psalms of Solomon*, written during the same period, testify to the same mood.

[*That goes towards the wide spaces of the earth to capture dwellings which are not its own.*] (I, 6b)

[The explanation of this concerns the Kittim who] advance [through mountains] **III** (**1**) and valleys to strike and plunder the cities of the earth. (**2**) For it is as He said, *To capture dwellings which are not its own.*

It is terrible (**3**) *and dreadful; its justice and greatness proceed from itself.* (I, 7)

(**4**) The explanation of this concerns the Kittim, fear [and dr]ea[d] of whom will extend over all (**5**) the nations. They knot all their evil intrigues with reflection, and with cunning and trickery (**6**) do they walk with all the peoples.

And their horses are swifter than panthers and nimbler (**7**) *than evening wolves. They leap up, and their horsemen, their horsemen (come) from afar;* (**8**) *they fly like an eagle hurtling to devour. They all come for violence. The aspect* (**9**) *of their countenance is (like) the east wind.* (I, 8-9a)

[The explanation of this] concerns the Kittim who (**10**) trample the earth with their horses and beasts. And (**11**) *they come from afar*, from the islands of the sea,[1] *to devour* [al]l the peoples *like the eagle*, (**12**) without satisfaction. And with wrath and [anger in the he]at of fury and (with) angry nostrils (**13**) do they speak to al[l the peoples; f]or it is as (**14**) He said, *The aspect of their countenance is (like) the east wind.*

And it heaps up captives like sand. (I, 9b)

(**15-17**) [The explanation of this concerns the Kittim who . . .].

[*At kings*] **IV** (**1**) *it scoffs and princes are its laughing-stock.* (I, 10a)

The explanation of this is that (**2**) they are insolent to the great and contemptuous of the respected. At kings (**3**) and leaders they jeer, and despise a multitude (of people).

(**4**) *It laughs at every fortress; it piles up earth and captures it.* (I, 10b)

(**5**) The explanation of this concerns the commanders of the Kittim[2] who despise (**6**) the strongholds of the peoples and insolently laugh at them. (**7**) And they surround them with a multitude of people to take them, and from terror and fear (**8**) they deliver themselves into their hands, and they reduce them to ruins because of the wickedness of their inhabitants.

---

[1] The expression 'islands of the sea' frequently means in Hebrew 'sea-coasts' — here, the coasts of Italy.

[2] This expression (*mōshelē Kittim*) describes the Roman leaders, the pro-magistrates *cum imperio* sent by Rome into the provinces and put in command of the armies. Allusion is made here to the art of siege in which the Romans were past-masters.

(9) *Then the wind changed and passed; and it made of its might* (10) *its god.* (I, 11)

The explanation of [this co]ncerns the commanders of the Kittim (11) who by the decision of [their] House of guilt vanish one (12) before the other.[1] One after the other [their] commanders come (13) to lay waste the ear[th. *And i]t* [*made*] *of its might its god.* (14) The explanation of this [. . . a]ll the peoples (15-17) t[o . . .].

[*Art Thou not from former times, O Yahweh my God, my Holy One? We shall not die. O Yahweh,*] **V** (1) *Thou hast appointed him unto judgment and established him, O Rock, unto him who chastised him, with eyes too pure* (2) *to see evil; and Thou canst not bear the sight of affliction.* (I, 12-13a)

(3) The explanation of this word is that God will not destroy His people by the hand of the nations; (4) but God will judge all the nations by the hand of His elect.[2] And it is by the chastisement which the elect will dispense that (5) all the wicked of His people will atone,[3] because they (the elect) have kept His commandments (6) in their distress. For it is as He said, *With eyes too pure to see* (7) *evil.* The explanation of this is that they let not themselves be led astray into lewdness by their eyes during the time (8) of wickedness.

O traitors, why do you look on and keep silence when the wicked swallows up (9) *the man more righteous than he?* (I, 13b)

The explanation of this concerns the House of Absalom (10) and the members of their council who were silent at the time of the chastisement of the Teacher of Righteousness (11) and gave him no help against the Man of Lies who despised (12) the Law in the midst of all their coun[cil].[4]

[1] The 'House of guilt' seems to be the Roman Senate. We are in the last years of the Republic, a period of civil wars and rivalry among the leaders. One after the other they disappeared: Pompey was beaten at Pharsalus in 48 B.C., and Caesar was assassinated in 44 B.C. Then Antony and Octavius appeared, and in 43 B.C. the second Triumvirate was formed, consisting of Octavius, Antony and Lepidus. Peace did not return until 29 B.C. when Octavius was named *imperator* for life by the Senate.

[2] An allusion to the final war in which the elect, i.e. the sectaries, the sons of light, will conquer the Kittim and the nations. This is the theme of the *War Scroll*.

[3] An allusion to the unfaithful Jews, those belonging to the official Synagogue, the enemies of the sect: they will be finally judged and punished by the elect. This is a recurring theme in the various writings from Qumran.

[4] The expression 'House of Absalom' is rather enigmatic: is it the Absalom who was uncle and father-in-law to Aristobulus II and was taken prisoner by Pompey in 63 B.C. (cf. JOSEPHUS, *Antiquities*, XIV, 4, 4, § 71)? Or is it Absalom son of David, the name being used in a purely symbolical way as a synonym for traitor and rebel? The 'House of Absalom' would then be the great Jewish Council, the Sanhedrin composed of Sadducees and Pharisees, and consequently in the eyes of the Essene commentator, of traitors and rebels. I think the 'Man of Lies', identical with the 'Wicked Priest', must be Hyrcanus II. If the 'House of Absalom' is in fact the Sanhedrin, we learn here that the Teacher of Righteousness was tried before this supreme tribunal, that he was accused there by the Wicked Priest and condemned without any intervention on his behalf. The nature of the punishment is not indicated in this passage, but the biblical text uses the word 'swallows

And Thou hast treated men like fish of the sea, (**13**) *like the wriggling brood to rule over it. He catches it al*[*l on the hoo*]*k and draws it out with his seine,* (**14**) *and he gathers it in* [*his*] *ne*[*t. Therefore he sacri*]*fices to his seine; therefore he is joyful* (**15**) [*and exults and burns incense in honour of his net. For through them*]*his portion is fat* (**16-17**) [*and his food lavish.*] (I, 14-16)

[The explanation of this . . .] **VI** (**1**) the Kittim, and they gather in their riches together with all the fruit of their plundering (**2**) *like fish of the sea.* And as for that which He said, *Therefore he sacrifices to his seine* (**3**) *and burns incense in honour of his net,* the explanation of this is that they (**4**) offer sacrifice to their standards[1] and that their weapons of war are (**5**) the object of their religion. *For through them his portion is fat and his food lavish.* (**6**) The explanation of this is that they distribute their yoke (**7**) and their forced labour, their *food,* among all the peoples year by year, (**8**) laying waste many lands.[2]

Therefore he drew out his sword unceasingly (**9**) *to slay the nations without mercy.* (I, 17)

(**10**) The explanation of this concerns the Kittim who slay many people by the sword, (**11**) youths, grown men, the aged, women and children, and (**12**) have no pity (even) on the fruit of the womb.

I desire to take my stand to watch (**13**) *and to station myself upon my stronghold; and I will spy out to see what He will say to me* (**14**) *and what* [*He will reply*] *to my complaints. And Yahweh answered* (**15**) [*and said to me: Write down the vision and make it plai*]*n upon the tablets so that he may read it easily* (**16-17**) [*that reads it*]. (II, 1-2)

[The explanation of this . . .]. **VII** (**1**) And God told Habakkuk to write down the things which will come to pass in (**2**) the last generation, but the consummation of time He made not known to him.[3] (**3**) And as for that which He said, *That he may read it easily that reads it,* (**4**) the explanation of this concerns the Teacher of Righteousness to whom God made known (**5**) all the Mysteries of the words of His servants the Prophets.[4]

For there is yet another vision (**6**) *relating to the appointed time; it speaks of the end and does not deceive.* (II, 3a)

(**7**) The explanation of this is that the final time will last long and will

---

[1] This points clearly to the Romans and their cult of the *signa.*

[2] An allusion to the Roman fisc which weighed heavily on the conquered peoples. As the commentator states, the Romans collected their taxes annually.

[3] No one knows the day or the hour: constant watch must be kept. This is the advice given in the biblical text interpreted here 'I desire to take my stand to watch'.

[4] The Teacher of Righteousness knows all the secrets of divine Revelation; he is the interpreter *par excellence,* the supreme Hierophant of divine Gnosis.

---

up', which means to do away with, to destroy; this seems to suggest that he was condemned to death.

exceed everything (8) spoken of by the Prophets; for the Mysteries of God are marvellous.

(9) *If it tarries, wait for it; for it will surely come and* (10) *will not delay.* (II, 3b)

The explanation of this concerns the men of truth (11) who observe the Law, whose hands do not slacken in the service (12) of Truth when the final time delays for them;[1] for (13) all the seasons of God come to pass at their appointed time according to His decree (14) concerning them in the Mysteries of His Prudence.

Behold, his soul is swollen, it is not upright (15) [*within him.*] (II, 4a)

The explanation of this is that [the wicked] will receive twofold to themselves[2] (16-17) [and will be treated] with[out loving]-kindness at the time of their judgment [. . .].

[*But the righteous will live by his faith.*] (II, 4b)

VIII (1) The explanation of this concerns all those who observe the Law in the House of Judah. (2) God will deliver them from the House of Judgment[3] because of their affliction and their faith (3) in the Teacher of Righteousness.[4]

Moreover, it is riches that lead the proud to betray, and he does not (4) *remain* (*faithful*) *who widens his gullet like Sheol and is insatiable as Death.* (5) *All the nations gathered towards him and all the peoples flocked towards him.* (6) *Will they not all pronounce a satire and make enigmas upon him?* (7) *And will they not say: Woe to him who increases* (*his goods*) *whereas they do not belong to him? How long will he burden himself* (8) *with a pledge?* (II, 5-6)

The explanation of this concerns the Wicked Priest who (9) was called by the name of truth at the beginning of his coming; but when he commanded (10) over Israel, his heart rose up[5] and he abandoned God and

---

[1] The waiting is long, and they win merit who persevere and watch daily for the coming of the 'final time', the supreme Judgment.

[2] A double chastisement, i.e. a severe and merciless punishment.

[3] i.e. from the Tribunal before which mankind will be judged at the end of time.

[4] The Teacher of Righteousness tries the hearts of men; it is faith in him that saves.

[5] The commentator distinguishes two periods in the pontificate of the Wicked Priest: an initial period during which he behaved as a worthy priest of Yahweh, and a second period when as master of Israel he yielded to pride and cupidity. This distinction is best confirmed in the career of Hyrcanus II. Nominated High Priest by Queen Alexandra on the death of Alexander Jannaeus in 76 B.C., he filled his office during the reign of this queen in a purely religious manner and did not concern himself with politics. When Alexandra died in 67 B.C., he became king; but after three months his throne was usurped by his brother Aristobulus II. In 63 B.C., Pompey nominated him High Priest once more, investing him with temporal as well as sacerdotal authority. It is this plurality of offices sacred and profane (from 67 B.C.) that the commentator stigmatizes here. He particularly reproaches him for his love of wealth, his cupidity; on the riches of Hyrcanus, cf. JOSEPHUS, *Antiquities*, XIV, 1, 2, § 6, and XIV, 9, 3, § 163.

betrayed the precepts because (**11**) of riches, and he stole[1] and heaped up the riches of violent men who rebel against God. (**12**) And he took the riches of the peoples, piling up the worst iniquities upon himself, and (**13**) he followed the ways of a[bo]mination in every kind of unclean defilement.

Will there not suddenly rise up (**14**) *people who will [bi]te thee, and will there not arise people who will cause thee to tremble, and wilt thou not become their prey?* (**15**) *Because thou hast plundered many nations all the remnant of the peoples will plunder thee.* (II, 7-8a)

(**16**) [The explanation of this word con]cerns the Priest who rebelled (**17**) [and viola]ted the precepts [of God and persecuted the Teacher of Righteousness.[2] And they s]et upon him to **IX** (**1**) smite him in virtue of the wicked judgments,[3] and evil profaners[4] (**2**) committed horrors upon him and vengeance upon his body of flesh. And as for that which (**3**) He said, *Because thou hast plundered many nations all* (**4**) *the remnant of the peoples will plunder thee*, the explanation of this concerns the last Priests of Jerusalem[5] (**5**) who heap up riches and gain by plundering the peoples. (**6**) But at the end of days, their riches, together with the fruit of their plundering, will be delivered into the hands (**7**) of the army of the Kittim; for it is they (the Kittim) who are *the remnant of the peoples*.[6]

---

[1] Cf. XII, 10: 'he stole the goods of the Poor'. This is a reference to the confiscatory measures ordered by Hyrcanus against the sect of the 'Poor', i.e. the Essenes.

[2] Line 17 at the foot of the column has almost entirely disappeared: because of the extent of this lacuna, any reconstruction of the passage must remain uncertain. The one I suggest introduces the Teacher of Righteousness; the following passage would then allude to his sufferings ordered by the High Priest, ~~Hyrcanus~~ II. Other writers think the translation should read: '[The explanation of this word con]cerns the Priest who rebelled [and viola]ted the precepts [of God, and he was delivered into the hands of his enemies . . .]' In this case, the following passage would allude to the sufferings of the High Priest. It should be noted that in 40 B.C., Hyrcanus II was captured by the Parthians who installed Antigonus in his place; according to Josephus (*War*, I, 13, 9, § 270; cf. *Antiquities*, XIV, 13, 10, § 366) this man 'himself tore off his ears with his teeth, to prevent him, even if he were freed by revolution, from ever being able to recover the supreme priesthood; for no man can be High Priest unless he is free from every bodily blemish'. However vile and cruel this mutilation, the sufferings alluded to in the present passage of the Commentary appear to have been very much graver; in my opinion they were the tortures inflicted on the Teacher of Righteousness during the persecution directed against him and his followers.

[3] The 'wicked judgments' were those by which the Teacher of Righteousness was condemned to torture and death. The Hebrew expression may however also be understood as 'judgments of wickedness', i.e. God's judgment of wickedness; if the passage as a whole alludes to the maltreatment of the Wicked Priest, this would be its meaning.

[4] This can also be translated 'transpiercers, executioners'. Some writers interpret the Hebrew word quite differently and translate the phrase 'And they committed horrors of evil diseases upon him, and revenge upon his body of flesh'; but the translation 'diseases' raises linguistic difficulties and involves a phrase construction which is heavy and forced.

[5] Probably Alexander Jannaeus, Aristobulus II, and Hyrcanus II (perhaps also Antigonus); Josephus speaks particularly of the riches accumulated in the Temple during the time of Hyrcanus II (*Antiquities*, XIV, 7, 2, §§ 110-11). This wealth fell into the hands of the Roman generals Pompey, Crassus, etc., who levied tribute after tribute on Judaea.

[6] For the commentator, the 'end of days' had already arrived; the Roman empire was

(8) *Because of the murder of men and the violence inflicted on the land, the city, and all its inhabitants.* (II, 8b)

(9) The explanation of this concerns the Wicked Priest whom, because of the iniquity committed against the Teacher (10) of Righteousness and the men of his council, God delivered into the hands of his enemies to humble him (11) with a destroying blow in bitterness of soul because he had done wickedly (12) to His elect.[1]

Woe to him who gets criminal gain for his house, setting (13) his nest on high to be safe from the grasp of misfortune! Thou hast resolved on shame (14) for thy house. Many peoples are in extremities and the sinner is thyself. For (15) the sto[ne] cries out [from] the wall [and] the beam from the framework replies. (II, 9-11)

(16-17) [The explanation of this word] concerns the [Prie]st who [. . .] X (1) that its stones might be in oppression and the beam of its framework in robbery.[2] And as for that which (2) He said, *Many peoples are in extremities and the sinner is thyself,* (3) the explanation of this (is that) it is the House of Judgment; for God will dispense (4) His judgment in the midst of many peoples. And from thence He will make him appear for judgment, (5) and in the midst of them He will declare him guilty and will judge him with fire of sulphur.[3]

Woe to him (6) who builds a town on murder and founds a city on crime! Is it not from (7) the Lord of Hosts? The peoples labour for fire (8) and the nations exhaust themselves for nothingness. (II, 12-13)

(9) The explanation of this word concerns the Preacher of Lies[4] who led many astray (10) to build his town of vanity[5] on murder and to found a congregation on deceit (11) for the sake of his glory, that many people might labour in his service of vanity and conceive (12) in [wo]rks of deceit; that their labour might be for nothingness, that they might come

---

[1] An allusion to the persecution of the Teacher of Righteousness and his sect; note that the biblical text speaks of 'the murder of men'; this suggests that it was a bloody persecution. The divine chastisement of the persecutor consisted, as we read here, of humiliating captivity 'in bitterness of soul' — an allusion to Hyrcanus II, who was captured by the Parthians and mutilated by Antigonus (see p. 264, n. 2).

[2] Part of the phrase has disappeared at the foot of column IX; it is probably a reference to the 'stones' and 'framework' of the city of Jerusalem or of the acropolis where Hyrcanus II resided.

[3] The commentator describes the scenes of the Last Judgment. The Wicked Priest will appear before the divine Tribunal and be solemnly condemned; he will be cast into 'fire of sulphur', the instrument of infernal punishment.

[4] This expression, as well as 'Man of Lies', still refers to the Wicked Priest — in my view, Hyrcanus II.

[5] In 47 B.C., Caesar authorized Hyrcanus II to rebuild the walls of Jerusalem destroyed during the siege of 63 B.C. (JOSEPHUS, *Antiquities*, XIV, 8, 5, § 144): the commentator may be alluding to this reconstruction of the capital.

---

the final empire, and the Romans were the last people called to play a part on the stage of human history.

to (**13**) judgment of fire for having insulted and outraged the elect o God.[1]

(**14**) *For the earth will be filled with the knowledge of the glory of Yahweh as waters* (**15**) *cover the se[a].* (II, 14)

The explanation of this word [is that] (**16-17**) when they are converted [. . .] **XI** (**1**) the lie,[2] and afterwards knowledge will be revealed to them *as the waters* (**2**) *of the sea*, abundantly.

Woe to him who causes his neighbour to drink, who pours out (**3**) *his fury* (*upon him*) *till he is drunk, that they may gaze on their feasts!* (II, 15)

(**4**) The explanation of this concerns the Wicked Priest who (**5**) persecuted the Teacher of Righteousness, swallowing him up in the anger (**6**) of his fury in his place of exile.[3] But at the time of the feast of rest (**7**) of the Day of Atonement he appeared before them[4] to swallow them up (**8**) and to cause them to stumble on the Day of Fasting, their Sabbath of rest.

---

[1] The subjects of Hyrcanus are also his accomplices and, like him, they will be condemned to hell fire.

[2] This is the last word of a phrase the remainder of which has disappeared in the lacuna at the foot of column X.

[3] This phrase informs us quite distinctly that the persecution of the Teacher of Righteousness was violent and 'furious': in the words of the text, the Wicked Priest gave free vent to 'the anger of his fury', even going so far as to 'swallow up' his enemy, i.e. — if we give this metaphor its usual meaning in Hebrew — to do away with him, to kill him. Such was the outcome, I think, of the struggle between the High Priest Hyrcanus II and the leader of the Essene sect, namely, the latter's execution. Where was the 'abode of exile' to which the Teacher of Righteousness went for safety, and where he was pursued, tracked down by his enemy? One is inclined to think it was in the Damascus region where we know the sect sought refuge, and where the Teacher of Righteousness himself may have accompanied his followers (cf. *Damascus Document*, VII, 18-19). The expression may also apply to the community house at Qumran in the desert of Judah, though this seems less likely; or perhaps to some other place of which we know nothing. The Teacher no doubt led a rather wandering existence as appears from the book of the *Hymns* (see, for example, IV, 8-9, V, 5-9, 29).

[4] The Hebrew verb used here may also be translated 'he revealed himself to them', with no supernatural implication. But in any case the subject of this verb can only be the Teacher of Righteousness, and not the Wicked Priest as some writers maintain. The victims of this 'apparition' (or 'revelation') were, in fact, the unfaithful Jews, and not the sectaries: in a passage from the *Hymns* (IV, 11-12) the same verse from Habakkuk is applied to the Jews who allowed themselves to be led astray by evil guides, particularly in connection with the celebration of the feasts, and to their eventual punishment. One more detail is added in the present commentary: the date of the chastisement of the unfaithful Jews by the Teacher of Righteousness is given as 'at the time of the feast of rest of the Day of Atonement'. And it repeats, 'on the Day of Fasting, their Sabbath of rest'. The 'Day of Fasting' is the name given in the *Mishnah* to the 'Day of Atonement' celebrated, as it still is, on the tenth day of the month of Tishri. So what was the catastrophe which struck the unfaithful Jews on a Day of Atonement and is represented as some sort of divine retaliation, the revenge of the Teacher of Righteousness on his enemies? I think it was the capture of Jerusalem by Pompey in 63 B.C.; JOSEPHUS reports that this event took place on 'the Day of Fasting' (*Antiquities*, XIV, 4, 3), i.e. on the Day of Atonement, and Strabo confirms this. For their part, the *Psalms of Solomon* testify to the importance which pious Jews imputed to this national catastrophe, and to the religious significance with which it was invested. Writers who make the Wicked Priest the subject of the verb 'appeared' suppose that the commentator is alluding here to some violent scene in which

Thou hast sated thyself (**9**) *with ignominy more than with glory: drink thou also and stagger!* (**10**) *The cup of the right hand of Yahweh will come round to thee and humiliation* (**11**) *will be upon thy glory.* (II, 16)

(**12**) The explanation of this concerns the Priest whose ignominy became greater than his glory. (**13**) For he did not circumcise the foreskin of his heart and walked in the ways of (**14**) drunkenness to quench his thirst. And the cup of the fury (**15**) of [G]od will swallow him up[1] by heap[ing] up his [humilia]t[ion upo]n [him], and the pain (**16**) [. . .].

(**17**) [*For the violence done to Lebanon will cover thee, and the cruelty used against the beasts*] **XII** (**1**) *will stir up* (*the fire*)[2] *because of the slaying of men and the violence done to the land, the city, and all its inhabitants.* (II, 17)

(**2**) The explanation of this word concerns the Wicked Priest inasmuch as he will be paid (**3**) his reward for what he has done to the Poor; for *Lebanon* is (**4**) the Council of the Community, and *the beasts* are the simple of Judah who practise (**5**) the Law.[3] For God will condemn him to destruction (**6**) even as he himself planned to destroy the Poor. And as for that which He said, *Because of the murders* (**7**) *committed in the city and the violence done to the land*, the explanation of this is (that) *the city* is Jerusalem, (**8**) where the Wicked Priest committed abominable deeds and defiled (**9**) the Sanctuary of God; *and the violence done to the land*, these are the towns of Judah where (**10**) he stole the goods of the Poor.[4]

Of what use is the statue that its maker should carve it; (**11**) *the molten image and the deceiving oracle, that he who fashions his images should put his trust in them* (**12**) *whereas he makes dumb idols?* (II, 18)

The explanation of this word concerns (**13**) all the statues of the nations which they have made, to serve them and bow down (**14**) before them. But these statues will not deliver them on the Day of Judgment.

[1] Or, 'will befuddle him, will make him reel like a drunkard'.
[2] Translation uncertain.
[3] 'The simple' are the simple-minded. Their case is studied in the *Rule Annexe* (I, 19-22) and in the *Damascus Document* (XV, 10-11). Although they were not allowed to belong to the 'Council of the Community', they seem in some way to have been able to remain members of the sect if they were faithful to the Law.
[4] 'The Poor', I would repeat, are members of the sect of the Poor, i.e. the Essenes. The Wicked Priest on the one hand 'planned to destroy them' by putting a certain number of them to death, and on the other he 'stole their goods' by confiscating all or part of their possessions. Furthermore he is reproached for having 'defiled the Sanctuary of God'; this allusion is unclear. It may simply be a reference to the various impurities of which the Priest rendered himself guilty by failing to observe the rules of purity as determined by the sect (cf. *Damascus Document*, V, 6 ff.).

the Wicked Priest tried to intimidate the followers of the Teacher and to snatch them from schism. They say that this scene, which would have taken place on the Day of Atonement, would have left no mark on history. On the contrary. I think that the commentator's insistence on this Day of Atonement points to a great historical date, the date of the capture of Jerusalem and of the loss of its independence, as a punishment for the crime committed against the Teacher and the sect of the Elect.

Woe, **(15)** *w[oe, to him who says] to the wood 'Awake', [and 'Waken'] to [the]*
dumb [st]one! **(16-17)** *[Will it give oracles? Behold, it is plated with gold and*
silver but there is no breath inside it. But Yahweh is in His holy Temple:] **XIII**
(1) *let the whole earth be silent before Him!* (II, 19-20)

The explanation of this concerns all the nations **(2)** that serve stone and
wood. But on the Day **(3)** of Judgment God will destroy all those who serve
idols, **(4)** together with the wicked, from the earth.

2. COMMENTARY ON NAHUM[1]

. . . .

[Where is the den of the lions, the pasture of the young lions?] (II, 12a)
[The explanation of this concerns Jerusalem . . . which has become]
(1) a dwelling-place for the wicked of the nations.[2]

For a lion went to enter in, a lion cub, **(2)** *[with none to frighten (it).]* (II, 12b)
[The explanation of this concerns Deme]trius king of Yāwān who
sought to enter Jerusalem on the counsel of those who seek smooth things.
(3) [But he did not enter, for] from Antiochus until the rising of the
commanders of the Kittim [God did not deliver it] into the hand of
the kings of Yāwān. But afterwards it will be trampled under foot **(4)** [by
the Kittim . . .][3]

[1] Four or five columns of this Commentary remain, but only the first and most important has been published: see *JBL,* lxxv (1956), pp. 89-93 and plate 1.
[2] The biblical text actually alludes to Nineveh, the Assyrian capital; by means of an
extremely bold transposition our commentator applies it to Jerusalem: it is Jerusalem
that has become the 'den of lions'. The 'lions' are the conquering heathens ('the wicked
of the nations') who captured Jerusalem and settled there as its masters, particularly the
Romans, who conquered Palestine in 63 B.C.
[3] The 'kings of Yāwān' are obviously the sovereigns of the Hellenistic kingdoms, and in
particular the Seleucid kings; on the other hand, the expression 'commanders of the
Kittim' describes the Roman leaders as in the *Commentary on Habakkuk.* By a very subtle
interpretation of the biblical text, the commentator is able to recognize in this passage an
allusion to the unsuccessful attempt of one of the Seleucid kings, Demetrius by name, to
enter Jerusalem. But which Demetrius was it? Was it Demetrius I (Sōter), who in 161 B.C.
sent his general Nicanor to conquer Judaea and, in collusion with some of the Jews, to
put down Judas Maccabee, the leader of the resistance (cf. 1 Macc. vii. 26 ff.)? Or was it
Demetrius III (Eucaeros) who, at the call of the Pharisees, entered Palestine with his
army in 88 B.C., in the reign of Alexander Jannaeus, and with the help of the rebel Jews
inflicted a heavy defeat on the Hasmonaean king at Shechem, only to find himself obliged
to turn back as a result of the defection of his Jewish allies without having been able to
reach Jerusalem (cf. JOSEPHUS, *Antiquities,* XIII, 14, 2; *War,* I, 4, 5)? The second hypothesis, postulated by Allegro, seems by far the most likely. The allusion to the defeat of
this Demetrius gives the commentator occasion to recall — that is, if my conjecture
concerning the beginning of line 3 is correct — that Jerusalem remained independent,
and was not subject to the Seleucid kings from the time of Antiochus (Antiochus Epiphanes
from whom Judas Maccabee retook the Holy City in 164 B.C.), until the appearance of
the Roman leaders in Palestine. It was then that Jerusalem, taken by Pompey in 63 B.C.,
was 'trampled underfoot' by the Kittim, i.e. the Romans.

The lion tore the limbs of its young and strangled prey for its lionesses.
(II, 13a)

(5) [The explanation of this] concerns the furious Young Lion who smote his great ones and the men of his council (6) [. . .][1]

[It filled] its den [with prey] and its lair with torn flesh. (II, 13b)

The explanation of this concerns the furious Young Lion (7) [who . . . took ven]geance on those who seek smooth things — he who hanged living men (8) [on wood . . . which was not] formerly [done] in Israel;[2] but he who was hanged alive upon [the] wood [. . .].[3]

Behold, I am against [thee], (9) [*oracle of Yahweh of hosts, and I will burn up thy multitu]de [in smoke] and the sword will devour thy young lions; and I will wip[e out] his [p]rey [from the earth].* (II, 14)

(10) [The explanation of this concerns . . .] And *thy multitude* are the bands of his army [. . .] and his *young lions* are (11) [. . .] and his *prey* is the riches which he heap[ed up in the Temp]le of Jerusalem, which (12) [will

---

[1] The 'Young Lion', as Allegro has recognized, is very likely Alexander Jannaeus, the Hasmonaean king (103-76 B.C.). His reign was marked by a revolt of the Pharisees whom he treated with the utmost cruelty.

[2] 'Those who seek smooth things', obviously pejorative, describes the enemies of the sect — the Pharisees, in fact, as above in line 2. JOSEPHUS (*Antiquities*, XIII, 14, 2) reports that after Jannaeus was defeated by Demetrius, he revenged himself by crucifying eight hundred Pharisees; the commentator is alluding to this event. The expression 'hanged living men on wood' is an allusion to punishment by crucifixion; this atrocious torture was not the custom in Israel and was a scandal to the Jews. Should JOSEPHUS's statement be true (*Antiquities*, XII, 5, 4), that Antiochus Epiphanes had crucified Jews in Jerusalem earlier, this does not in any way affect the accuracy of our commentator's observation, 'which had not formerly been done in Israel'. This expression means that crucifixion was contrary to the customs of Israel — crucifixions ordered by a foreigner are not to be taken into account. Note that Jannaeus is nowhere mentioned here as the persecutor of the sect of the Elect, the Essenes; on the contrary, his victims were, I would repeat, 'those who seek smooth things', i.e. the Pharisees.

[3] This short phrase is rather enigmatic. One word, which must be a verb, has partly disappeared at the end; it is probably [YQ]R', '[they will c]all (on him)'. If the word is completed in this way, the phrase refers to someone who suffered punishment on the cross and became an object of invocation. Who can this extraordinary person be? By whom could he have been crucified? There is nothing to lead us to conclude that it was by Jannaeus; his death may have been ordered by a successor of Jannaeus. The phrase may spring from an association of ideas: although crucifixion is a scandal, there is one crucified man who will, on the contrary, become for some an object of prayer. I would emphasize that this exegesis remains hypothetical since the last word of the phrase is unfortunately mutilated. We may, however, recall the famous passage from Zech. xii. 10-xiii. 1: 'Then I will pour out on the house of David and on the inhabitants of Jerusalem a spirit of good will and supplication, and they will turn their eyes towards me, and towards him whom they have pierced. They will utter cries of mourning in his honour as one mourns in honour of an only son; they will weep for him bitterly as one weeps bitterly for a first-born child. Mourning will be as great in Jerusalem on that day as the mourning of Hadad-Rimmon in the valley of Megiddōn. . . . On that day, a fountain shall spring up for the house of David and the inhabitants of Jerusalem to (wash away) sin and defilement.'

be delivered into the hands of the army of the Kittim . . .] . . . Israel will be delivered [. . .][1]

. . . .

3. COMMENTARY ON PSALM XXXVII[2]

Fragment 1

. . . .

[*Fret not yourself because of him who succeeds in his undertakings, (because) of the man who carries out evil designs.*] (verse 7b)
[The explanation of this concerns the wicked who] **I** (**1**) will perish by the sword and by famine and by plague.

Leave anger and forsake wrath and (**2**) *fret not yourself; it leads only to evil. For the wicked will be cut off.* (verse 8a)
The explanation of this concerns all who are converted (**3**) to the Law, who do not refuse to be converted from their wickedness. For all who rebel against (**4**) being converted from their iniquity will be cut off.

But those who hope in Yahweh will possess the earth. (verse 9b)
The explanation of this (is that) (**5**) *those* are the congregation of His elect who do His will.

Yet a little while and the wicked will be no more; (**6**) *I will examine his place and he will be no more.* (verse 10)
The explanation of this concerns all wickedness: at the end (**7**) of the

---

[1] The numerous lacunae throughout the whole passage do not permit us to translate it with any certainty. There is doubtless still a question of the 'furious Young Lion', i.e. Alexander Jannaeus. One would have liked to know how the commentator explained the biblical phrase, 'thy young lions': as the leaders of the royal army, or as the two sons of the king (Aristobulus II and Hyrcanus II)? I have completed the following phrase concerning riches after the *Commentary on Habakkuk*, IX, 4-7; there the 'last Priests of Jerusalem' are stigmatized — in my view, Alexander Jannaeus and his two sons.

[2] Two fragments of this Commentary remain: the first, in which the upper part of two columns is preserved, is published in the *PEQ*, lxxxvi (1954), pp. 69-75 and plate XVIII; the second, in which only the vestiges of one column are preserved, is published in the *JBL*, lxxv (1956), p. 94 and plate 3. Ps. xxxvii of the biblical collection discusses the lot of the just and the unjust: how can the prosperity of the wicked be reconciled with the affirmation of God's justice which is bound to reward every man according to the good or evil which he has done? The happiness of the wicked is ephemeral, replies the psalmist; the wicked will be destroyed, but the just will possess the earth. A psalm of this kind is particularly well suited to the interpretation of the Essene commentator: the just are the members of the sect, and, in particular, the Teacher of Righteousness; the wicked are the sect's adversaries, and, in particular, the Wicked Priest.

forty years they will be wiped out and on the earth not a (8) [wi]cked man will be found.[1]

But the humble will possess the earth and taste the delights of perfect bliss. (verse 11)
The explanation of this concerns (9) [the Congregation of the] Poor who accept the time of affliction and will be delivered from all the snares (10) [of the Pit . . .] all the [. . .] of the earth [. . .] all the deli[ghts].

. . . .

[*Yahweh knows the days of the perfect and their inheritance will abide for ever. They will not be ashamed on the day of misfortune.*] (verses 18-19a)
[The explanation of this concerns] **II** (1) the converts of the desert who will live for a thousand generations . . . [. . . and to them will belong all the glory] (2) of the man[2] and to their seed for ever.

And in the days of famine they will be sa[tisfied; but the wicked] (3) *will perish.* (verses 19b-20a)
The explanation of this [is that] He will cause them to live during the famine at the time [of affliction; but the wicked] (4) who have not gone ou[t of the land of Judah] will perish from famine and plague.[3]

(4a) *And those who love Yahweh will be like the glory of pastures.*[4] (verse 20b)
The explanation [of this concerns] (5) the Congregation of His elect who will be leaders and princes [over all the earth, like shepherds] (6) of sheep in the midst of their flocks.

(7) *They have vanished completely, like smoke.* (verse 20c)
The explanation [of this] concerns the princes [of wickedn]ess who have oppressed His (8) holy people; they will perish like smoke which van[ishes before the wi]nd.

---

[1] Cf. *Damascus Document*, B, II, 13-15: 'Now from the day when the Unique Teacher was taken, until the overthrow of all the fighting men who turned back to the Man of Lies (there shall pass) about forty years.' 'Forty years' is a round figure indicating the duration of one generation: the Last Judgment was therefore expected before the commentator's generation had passed.

[2] The expression 'the converts of the desert' obviously alludes to the members of the sect. Many Qumran texts show that they were 'converts' or 'penitents', and others that they chose to live in the desert (*Rule*, VIII, 13; IX, 19-20). The *War Scroll* (I, 2) calls them 'the Deportation of the desert'. — 'Who will live for a thousand generations'; cf. *Damascus Document*, VII, 6 = B, II, 5. — 'And to them will belong all the glory of the man'; cf. *Damascus Document*, III, 20.

[3] Cf. *Damascus Document*, VI, 5-6.

[4] The last word is a little uncertain. The Masoretic Text reads 'those who hate Yahweh', instead of, 'those who love Yahweh'; because of the variant adopted by the commentator, the simile, 'like the glory of pastures', has here a very different significance from that in the Masoretic Text.

The wicked borrows and does not repay; (**9**) *but the just man has pity and gives. For those whom He bles[ses will pos]sess the earth, but those whom He curse[s will be cu]t off.* (verses 21-2)

(**10**) The explanation of this concerns the Congregation of the Poor who [giv]e the inheritance of all [. . .] (**11**) they will possess the sublime Mountain of Isra[el and] will taste [everlasting] delights [in] His holiness. [But those who] (**12**) *will be cut off* are the violent of the [nations and the wi]cked of Israel, who will be cut off and destroyed (**13**) for ever.

(**14**) *The steps of man are established by Yahweh and He is pleased in all his [wa]ys. Although h[e fall,]* (**15**) *[he throws not himself down to the ground, for Yahweh upholds his hand.]* (verses 23-4)

The explanation of this concerns the Priest, the Teacher of [Righteousness whom] (**16**) [. . . God] established to build for Himself the Congregation [of Truth which shall not shake . . .][1]

. . . .

Fragment 2

. . . .

(**1**) *The wicked watches out for the righteous and seeks [to slay him. Yahweh will not abandon him into his hand and will not] let him be condemned when he is tried.* (verses 32-3)

(**2**) The explanation of this concerns [the] Wicked [Prie]st who la[id hands on the Priest, the Teacher of Righteousness,] to put him to death. [But God . . .] and he wakened (?) him [because of the Spirit (?)] (**3**) which He sent to him. And God will not let [the Wicked Priest go] un[punished for the blood which] he has shed,[2] but [God will] pay him his [re]ward by delivering him (**4**) into the hands of the violent of the nations to execute [vengeance] upon him.[3]

[1] Here we learn explicitly that the Teacher of Righteousness was a priest, and even that he was considered as 'the Priest' *par excellence*; it is he who is given this name in the *Commentary on Habakkuk* (II, 8) and in the *Rule Annexe* (II, 19). He is the man whom God 'established to build' the new Congregation, the Church of the Elect; cf. *Hymns*, VI, 24-7; VII, 8-9.

[2] Lines 2 and 3 are too mutilated for us to interpret them with any certainty. The readings and restorations suggested by Allegro appear on many points very doubtful. At the end of line 2, in particular, instead of WHTWRH, 'and the Law', I prefer the reading WH'YRH, 'and he awakened him' (?), this word being followed by another, a small part of which is just visible in the photograph and which must be the antecedent of the relative clause at the beginning of line 3. I read therefore: '[because of the Spirit (?)] which he sent to him'. Furthermore, towards the end of line 3, instead of SPTW I think we should read SPKM, 'he has shed' (with the pronominal suffix of the third person plural which it is tempting to link to the preceding *damîm*, 'the blood'). I would emphasize once more that because of the condition of the manuscript all this interpretation is merely *possible*; it can only become probable or certain if parallel texts later confirm it.

[3] An allusion to the punishment suffered by the Wicked Priest; cf. *Commentary on Habakkuk*, IX, 8-12 (cf. above, p. 265, n. 1).

[*Trust in Yahw*]*eh and keep to His way, and He will raise thee up to possess* (5) *the earth; and when the wicked are cut off, thou wilt s*[*ee*]. (verse 34)

[The explanation of this concerns . . .] . . . and they will see the judgment of wickedness and [. . .] (6) [. . .].

. . . .

4. ANOTHER COMMENTARY ON PSALM XXXVII[1]

. . . .

(1) *The wicked have drawn the sword and bent their bow to bring down the needy and the poor* (2) *and to slay the upright. Their sword shall enter their own heart and their bows shall be broken.* (verses 14-15)

(3) The explanation of this concerns the wicked of Ephraim and Manasseh who will seek to lay hands (4) on the Priest and the men of his council at the time of trial which will come upon them. But God will re[de]em them (5) from their hands, and then (the wicked) will be delivered into the hands of the violent of the nations for judgment.[2]

. . . .

Besides these vestiges of two Commentaries on Psalm xxxvii from cave IV, many fragments found in cave I prove the existence of another Commentary on the biblical book of the Psalms.[3] These fragments, for the most part tiny, refer to Psalms lvii and lviii; they have almost nothing worth while to offer the historian.

[1] The fragment translated here is published in *JBL*, lxxv (1956), pp. 94-5 and plate 4. It belongs to a different scroll from that of the two fragments translated above.

[2] An allusion to the persecution of the sect. 'The Priest' is the Teacher of Righteousness (cf. above, p. 272, n. 1) and 'the men of his council' are his followers (an analogous expression appears in the *Commentary on Habakkuk*, IX, 9-10: 'the Teacher of Righteousness and the men of his council'). As for the 'wicked of Ephraim and Manasseh', they are 'the wicked of Israel', i.e. the Jewish enemies of the sect, partisans of the Wicked Priest. Although it is said that 'they will seek' to lay hands on the Teacher and his followers, this does not mean that they have never actually done so: this would expressly contradict the information contained in the *Damascus Document*, the *Commentary on Habakkuk*, and the preceding *Commentary on Psalm XXXVII*, which leave no doubt as to the reality of the persecution or its violent and bloody character. The biblical text interpreted here declares in vivid terms that the attempts of the wicked against the just are doomed to failure: although the wicked direct their weapons against the righteous, they will turn back on themselves. In harmony with the text, the commentator stigmatizes the conduct of the persecutors who 'will seek' *without success* to deal a decisive blow at the leader of the sect and his followers. He explains that 'God will redeem them from their hands', i.e. He will grant them *final* deliverance and salvation. Sooner or later, one way or another, the just will be saved; so in the end, the attempts of the wicked will have been in vain. The chastisement promised to the wicked Jews recalls, as regards the terms, the punishment with which the Wicked Priest is threatened in the preceding *Commentary on Psalm XXXVII* (Fragment 2, lines 3-4): 'they will be delivered into the hands of the violent of the nations' — an allusion, it seems, to the national catastrophe of 63 B.C. In fact, all the members of the sect who sought refuge in the region of Damascus escaped this catastrophe.

[3] These fragments are published in *Qumran Cave I*, no. 16, plate XV.

5. COMMENTARY ON ISAIAH

The book of Isaiah, like the Psalms, seems to have been read and interpreted with particular assiduity by the members of the sect. We possess various fragments of four different manuscripts in which the *Commentary on Isaiah* figures.

Of the first manuscript, four fragments remain,[1] extending from Isaiah x. 22 to xi. 5. The text is very mutilated. Fragment A begins: '[... when] they [ret]urn from the desert of the pe[oples ...]', which calls to mind a phrase from the *War Scroll* (I, 3); then it mentions '[the Pri]nce of the Congregation', an expression found in the *Book of Blessings* (V, 20), the *Damascus Document* (VII, 20) and the *War Scroll* (V, 1). There follows the famous text from Isaiah describing, stage by stage, the march of the Assyrian army on Jerusalem; the Essene commentator applies this passage to the great eschatological war at the 'end of days', and the Assyrian invader of the biblical book turns into another conqueror who 'will go up from the plain of Acco to battle against [...]', who 'will be without any like', and who will reach 'as far as the [pre]cincts of Jerusalem'. These scraps do not allow us to recognize with any certainty who this person is; I myself think he is the 'king of the Kittim' mentioned several times in the *War Scroll*.[2] In any case, Fragments B and C explicitly mention 'the Kittim', 'the valiant of the Kittim', the 'war of the Kittim', and 'all the nations', which clearly sets our commentary within the same perspective as that of the *War Rule of the Sons of Light*.

Fragment C ends with the quotation of the famous passage from Isaiah on the new David (xi. 1-5): *There shall come forth a branch from the stock of Jesse and a shoot shall flower from its roots. And upon him shall rest the spirit of Yahweh, the spirit of wisdom and understanding, the spirit of counsel and power, the spirit of knowledge and the fear of Yahweh; and his pleasure shall be in the fear of Yahweh. He shall not judge by what his eyes see, he shall not decide by what his ears hear; he shall judge the weak according to justice, he shall decide according to equity his sentence upon the*

---

[1] Published in *JBL*, lxxv (1956), pp. 177-82, plates 2 and 3.

[2] J. M. ALLEGRO (loc. cit., p. 181) thinks that the commentator has in mind the Messiah, and that it is his triumphal march to Jerusalem that is described. This opinion seems doubtful to me: it would be a very odd thing to make the Assyrian conqueror, the cruel enemy of Jerusalem, a symbol of the Messiah, the deliverer of Israel. Moreover, at the end of line 9, I think I can distinguish traces of the letters BYS, which would give the reading: 'when he goes up from the plain of Acco to battle against Is[rael]'. A reading such as this obviously excludes any possibility of the text referring to the Messiah.

wretched of the land. He shall smite the violent with the rod of his word, and with the breath of his lips he shall slay the wicked . . . Fragment D preserves part of the interpretation of this passage: here is the translation.

(1) [The explanation of this concerns the Shoot] of David who will arise at the en[d of days . . .] (2) [. . .] and God will uphold him by [the Spirit of po]wer [. . .] (3) [. . . a thr]one of glory, a crown of ho[liness], and garments of man[y] colours [. . .] (4) [. . .] in his hand, and he will rule over all the n[ation]s, and Magog (5) [. . . and al]l the peoples his sword will judge (them). And as for that which He said, *He* (6) [*shall not judge by what his eyes see,*] *he shall not decide by what his ears hear*, the explanation of this is that (7) [. . . a]s they teach him, so will he judge, and according to their decision (8) [. . .] one of the priests of renown will go out and in his hand garment[s . . .]¹

The second manuscript of the *Commentary on Isaiah* is represented by a large fragment corresponding to chapter v of the biblical book.² Column II, the first ten lines of which are preserved almost complete, begins with a commentary on verses 8-10 in which the prophet curses the Judaeans guilty of hoarding, and threatens them with the devastation of their realms: '(1) The explanation of this word relates to the end of days, to the devastation³ of the earth by sword and famine; and it will be (2) at the time of the Visitation of the earth.' Then follows the quotation of verses 11-14, in which the prophet curses the Judaeans who live in luxury and thoughtlessness. The commentator explains simply: '(6) They are the men of mockery (7) who are in Jerusalem.'⁴ Then he goes straight on to quote verses 24e-25: '*They are those who have rejected the Law of Yahweh and despised the word of the Holy One of Israel, etc.*' His interpretation of this text is: 'It is the congregation of the men of mockery who are in Jerusalem . . . .'⁵

The third manuscript is on papyrus. The published fragment⁶

¹ As Allegro has explained, this is doubtless to be understood as meaning that the Messiah will judge according to the instruction of *the priests*, and will receive his royal vestments and the other insignia of his sovereignty from them. Compare the whole of this Fragment D with the passage relating to the 'Prince of the Congregation' in the *Book of Blessings* (V, 20-9); cf. above, p. 112-3.

² Published in *JBL*, lxxvii (1958), pp. 215-18, plate 1.

³ With Allegro, I correct HWBT to HRWBT.

⁴ The expression 'men of mockery' is borrowed from Isa. xxviii. 14; it appears in *Damascus Document*, B, II, 11 (cf. A, I, 14: 'the Man of Mockery').

⁵ It is strange that verses 15-24d are entirely omitted.

⁶ In *JBL*, lxxvii (1958), pp. 218-20, plate 2.

begins with the quotation of Isaiah xxx. 15-18, which is interpreted: '(10) The explanation of this word relates to the end of days, concerning the congregation of those who se[ek] smooth things[1] (11) who are at Jerusalem. . . .' Then follows the quotation of Isaiah xxx. 19-21; unfortunately, the commentary on this passage has disappeared.

The fourth manuscript is represented by several fragments only one of which has so far been published.[2] It relates to the following passage from Isaiah (liv. 11b-12): *Behold, I will set thy stones on antimony and establish thee upon sapphires and I will make thy pinnacles of rubies and thy gates of carbuncles and all thy wall of precious stones.* This text is interpreted phrase by phrase, but only the beginnings of the lines have been preserved. It is possible only to recognize that the biblical text is applied to the foundation of the 'Council of the Community', that the sect is also called 'the Congregation of His elect',[3] that it shines 'like the sun in all its brilliance', and that 'the gates of carbuncles' are 'the leaders of the tribes of Israel'.[4]

6. COMMENTARIES ON HOSEA, MICAH AND ZEPHANIAH

A few fragments remain of a *Commentary on Hosea*; part of one of them has been published.[5] This small text bears on v, 14: *For I am like a lion to Ephraim and like a young lion to the House of Judah; I, even I, will rend, I will go, I will carry off and none shall deliver.* Of the commentary on this verse, the following two incomplete phrases remain: '[. . .] the furious Young Lion to [gr]ind him down (?) like the li[on . . .]', and '[. . . the] last Priest who will lift his hand to smite Ephraim [. . .]'. The expression, 'the furious Young Lion', is known from the *Commentary on Nahum*, where it appears to describe king Alexander Jannaeus.[6] But who is the person referred to as the 'last Priest'? Is it the latter-day Priest, the sacerdotal leader of the Sons of Light — i.e. the Teacher of Righteousness, called in other texts 'the Priest'? Or is it the last priest of Jerusalem, the last High

---

[1] The expression 'those who seek smooth things' is encountered in the *Commentary on Nahum* (fragment translated above, lines 2, 7), the *Damascus Document* (I, 18) and the *Hymns* (II, 32); it describes the Jewish enemies of the sect.

[2] In *JBL*, lxxvii (1958), pp. 220-1, plate 3.

[3] The same expression appears in the first *Commentary on Psalm XXXVII* (col. II, line 5); cf. above, p. 271.

[4] To these four manuscripts should be added a tiny fragment of a fifth manuscript from cave III which gives the beginning of another *Commentary on Isaiah* (published in *RB*, 1953, pp. 555-7, and plate XXIV, *b*).

[5] In *JBL*, lxxv (1956), p. 93 and plate 2.　　　　[6] See above, p. 269, n. 1.

Priest, and in the sectarian perspective, the Wicked Priest? Because of the state of the text it is very difficult answer to this question.[1]

A fragment of another manuscript of the *Commentary on Hosea* has also been published.[2] This fragment, which is rather extensive, includes the remains of one column (the ends of a few lines only), and the greater part of the following column; the whole corresponds to verses 7-14 of chapter ii of the biblical book (ii. 5-12 in the English Bible). Column I gives first of all some fragmentary sentences of the commentary on verse 7 — 'and they were pleased . . . and they yielded . . .' — and then bits of the text and interpretation of verse 8: '[*Therefore I will bar her way*] *with thorns*[3] *and* [*she will find*] *her paths* [*no more*]. [The explanation of this is that they have gone astray in folly] and blindness and confusion [. . .] And the time of their unfaithfulness[4] [. . .] They are the generation of the Visitation[5] [. . . the gene]ration of the end [of days . . .] in the time of wrath [. . .]'. The end of column I must have quoted and interpreted verse 9, but only the words, 'on the return from captivity . . .' remain. Here is the translation of column II:

II (1) [*And she did not know that*] *it was I who gave her corn and* [*new wine*] **(2)** [*and oil, and who*] *granted her abundance* [*of silver*] *and gold (which) they* *use*[*d for Baal*]. (II, 10)

[The explanation of this] **(3)** is that [they ate and] were satisfied and forgot God they who [despised] **(4)** His precepts. They cast behind their back[6] those whom He had sent to them, **(5)** His servants the prophets;[7] and they listened to those who led them astray and respected them, **(6)** and because of their blindness they feared them like gods.

(8) *Therefore I will take back my corn at the time when it should be harvested, and my new wine* [*in its season*]. **(9)** *I will take away my wool and my linen which*

---

[1] In the second phrase it is not even certain that the relative pronoun 'who' refers to the name immediately preceding it.
[2] In *JBL*, lxxviii (1959), pp. 144-7 (with a plate).
[3] A phrase of the Masoretic Text has disappeared here: 'and I will encompass her with a wall'.
[4] Cf. *Damascus Document*, B, II, 23: 'at the time when Israel was unfaithful'.
[5] Here, as often in the Qumran writings, the 'Visitation' is the Last Judgment; the Essene commentator believed that this Judgment would take place before his generation had passed. For this reason it is called 'the generation of the Visitation' and (if the text is restored as I have proposed) '[the gene]ration of the end [of days]'. The same belief and eschatological expectation is encountered in the *Damascus Document*, B, II, 13-15, and in the *Commentary on Psalm XXXVII*, Fragment 1, I, 6-8 (*supra*, p. 270-1).
[6] An expression taken from Isa. xxxviii. 17.
[7] Israel rejected the prophets sent by God; this theme is taken up and developed in the Gospels in the form of the parable of the vineyard (Mark xii. 1-12; Matt. xxi. 33-46; Luke xx. 9-19).

served to cover [her nakedness]. (**10**) *Then I will bare her infamy to the eyes of her lo[vers and none]* (**11**) *shall deliver her from out of my hand.* (II, 11-12)

(**12**) The explanation of this is that He has smitten them with famine and nakedness that they may become an object of sham[e] (**13**) and ignominy in the eyes of the nations on which they have leaned.[1] But they (**14**) will not save them from their distress.

I will put an end to all her rejoicings, (**15**) *[her] fe[asts], her [new mo]ons and her Sabbaths and all her solemnities.* (II, 13)

The explanation of this is that (**16**) they will cause [all the f]easts to come on heathen dates.[2] And [joy] (**17**) [will end and] change into mourning for them.

I will ravage [her vines] (**18**) *[and her plantations of fig trees], of which she said, 'It is my wage [which]* (**19**) *my [lovers have given me]'. I will make of them a forest and the be[asts of the fields] shall devour their fruit.* (II, 14)

. . . .

The *Commentary on Micah* is represented by about twenty small fragments.[3] These give little more than scraps of sentences; in them we find the following expressions, most of which have already been met in the other Commentaries: 'the end of days', the 'Preacher of Lies',[4] the 'Teacher of Righteousness', the 'Council of the Community', 'they who are volunteers to join the elect [of God]',[5] 'the last generation', 'the Day of Judgment'.

The *Commentary on Zephaniah* is represented by one fragment only;[6] in it we can distinguish the verses between i. 18 and ii. 2 of the biblical book, as well as the beginning of the interpretation of this passage: 'The explanation [of this concerns . . .] the land of Judah. The wrath [of Yahweh . . .] and they will become [. . .]'.

---

[1] The commentator appears to have in mind the events of 63 B.C. During the siege Hyrcanus II made common cause with the Romans, but they remained the enemies of the Jewish nation, depriving it of its independence and burdening it with tributes.

[2] Translation uncertain. Is it an allusion to the disputes connected with the calendar? Is the commentator reproaching the enemies of the sect, the official Synagogue, for having made their calendar conform to the pagan one, instead of remaining faithful to the traditional Israelite calendar as the Essenes claimed to do?

[3] Published in *Qumran Cave I*, no. 14, plate XV.

[4] The same expression is found in the *Commentary on Habakkuk* (X, 9); cf. *Damascus Document* (I, 14; IV, 19; VIII, 13). It refers to the Wicked Priest, who is also called 'the Man of Mockery' and 'the Man of Lies'.

[5] The expression 'volunteers' applied to the members of the sect, is met several times in the *Rule* (I, 11; V 10; etc.).

[6] Published in *Qumran Cave I*, no. 15, plate XV.

Chapter VIII

THE GENESIS APOCRYPHON

Description of the scroll; analysis, character, and date of the book. — *The Story of Lamech* and *Enoch* CVI-CVII.— Translation: 1. *The Story of Lamech*. 2. *The Story of Abraham*.

Of the seven scrolls found in cave I, the least well preserved is without doubt the work originally called the Apocalypse of Lamech, and now known as the *Genesis Apocryphon*. When it was discovered it was so desiccated, hard and brittle, that no attempt could be made to unroll it without taking very special precautions. Mar Athanasius Samuel, who had transported it to the United States in 1948 together with the three other scrolls which he had acquired, refused to allow American scholars to develop and study it, and the scroll remained unpublished. It was not until 1954, when the State of Israel succeeded in buying the four scrolls, that work was able to start; two Israeli scholars in Jerusalem, Nahman Avigad and Yigael Yadin, were immediately commissioned to publish it. The task of unrolling the scroll was entrusted to an expert, J. Biberkraut, and demanded a great deal of patience and skill. But after this was done, it still remained to disencumber the sheets of leather of all kinds of mess, mostly due to the decomposition of the leather and certain reactions of the ink used — a work of delicate technique without which the reading and deciphering of most of the texts would have been impossible.

Since all this took a great deal of time, the editors wisely decided not to wait until it was completed before informing scholars of the first results of their study. In 1956, a partial edition of the scroll appeared, dealing with five of its columns (the best preserved), and giving a photograph of each, together with the transcription and translation. Furthermore, a general introduction describes the scroll as a whole, analyses its contents (as far as they can be known at the present time), and attempts to determine the character and date of the document.[1] A complete edition will appear later; but the partial

[1] *A Genesis Apocryphon. A Scroll from the Wilderness of Judaea. Description and Contents of the Scroll. Facsimiles, Transcription and Translation of Columns II, XIX-XXII* (Jerusalem, 1956). In modern Hebrew and English. In the present chapter I have turned to account not only the translation suggested by the editors but also the numerous erudite remarks assembled in the introduction.

edition is already of very great interest, and it is impossible to say enough by way of thanks and congratulations to the Israeli scholars for having so speedily and generously allowed Qumran specialists to enjoy the fruit of their first labours, even before they were able to utilize the new texts thoroughly themselves. A fine example of scientific unselfishness!

The complete scroll consists at present of four sheets of leather sewn together. The first, which is about 1½ ft. wide, contains four columns; the second, about 2 ft. 2 in. wide, has five; the third, about 2 ft. 1 in. wide, seven; and the fourth, about 2 ft. 9 in. wide, has six columns — a total of twenty-two columns in all. The first sheet which was on the outside of the scroll must originally have been wider; one column, and perhaps more, has without doubt disappeared before the present column I.[1] If the beginning of the book is lost, it seems that the same can also be said of the end; the fourth and last sheet bears the clearly visible traces of sewing, which suggests that originally there was at least a fifth sheet, now gone.

The scroll has probably suffered so badly because it was not enclosed in a jar like the others. As a matter of fact the state of preservation varies from one column to the next according to the position of each. Since it lay on the ground, those parts of the scroll which were underneath were very much more attacked by damp than those facing upwards. Only the last three columns (the central ones) are almost wholly intact.

Four main sections may be distinguished in what remains of the scroll: (1) The Story of Lamech (cols. I-V); (2) The Story of Noah (cols. VI-XV); (3) The Table of the Peoples (cols. XVI-XVII); (4) The Story of Abraham (cols. XVIII-XXII). The stories of Lamech, Noah and Abraham are generally told in the first person; it is the patriarchs themselves who recount the events of their lives. The general plot of the narrative is borrowed from Genesis, but the biblical account is enriched and embellished by rather extensive and purely imaginary developments related to the midrashic genre: the present scroll is a precious example of the Essene *midrash* and it is interesting to compare it with one or other of the Rabbinic *midrashim*.[2] It differs radically from the genre of the Commentaries (*pesharim*); these, as I have explained in the preceding

[1] Perhaps the fragments which the archaeologists recovered from cave I belong to this missing portion: these are published in *Qumran Cave I*, no. 20 (and plate XVII).

[2] Cf. M. R. LEHMANN, '1 Q Genesis Apocryphon in the Light of Targumim and Midrashim', in *RQ*, no. 2, October 1958, pp. 249-63.

chapter, aim at discovering predictions in the biblical text relating to the end of the world, whereas the *midrashim* endeavour to make the story of the past more vivid and full.

The Israeli editors have given our scroll the title, *A Genesis Apocryphon*; in point of fact it is, as they explain, 'a sort of apocryphal version of stories from Genesis, faithful, for the most part, to the order of the chapters in Scripture'.[1] In this respect the work calls to mind the famous *Book of Jubilees*, which also presents a special and greatly altered version of Genesis. But the affinities between the *Genesis Apocryphon* and *Jubilees* go much further than this common link with the biblical book of Genesis: in the various elements which they add to the biblical account the two stories are often closely parallel, even to the point of using the same terms. It is clear not only that they originate from the same environment, but also that one of them must have served as a source for the other. As the stories of *Jubilees* are generally more concise, the editors of the scroll think that the latter is probably the source and consequently the older of the two; but I think this problem can only be examined really usefully when the remainder of the text of the *Apocryphon* is known in its entirety. In the same way, the dating of this work must be deferred until later. The script seems to indicate a relatively late date (the end of the first century B.C., or the first half of the first century A.D.) but, as the editors rightly remark, the date of the manuscript in our possession is not necessarily the date of the actual redaction of the work.

The *Genesis Apocryphon* is written in Aramaic; from this point of view it is of considerable interest. Compared with the Aramaic of the biblical book of Daniel, which dates from about 165 B.C., the Aramaic of our scroll seems to be a little more recent: certain words and features of the Aramaic of ancient Rabbinical writings already make their appearance there. I would be inclined to place it in the first century B.C.,[2] a period for which literary texts in Palestinian Aramaic have so far been lacking. Thanks to this scroll (and to fragments of other Aramaic scrolls found at Qumran) we now possess examples of the Aramaic tongue as it was written and spoken in Palestine at a time very close to that of the preaching of Jesus and the formation of the New Testament.

[1] Op. cit., p. 38.

[2] On this subject, see the two studies by E. Y. KUTSCHER, 'Dating the Language of the Genesis Apocryphon', in *JBL*, lxxvi (1957), pp. 288-92, and 'The Language of the Genesis Apocryphon: A Preliminary Study', in *Aspects of the Dead Sea Scrolls* (Jerusalem, 1958), pp. 1-35.

But linguistic criteria only permit us to date approximately the Aramaic recension preserved in the scroll. The work may originally have been written in Hebrew and translated into Aramaic later; once again, it would be imprudent to try to settle the question now.

The edition at our disposal gives only the text of five columns, as I have said: column II and columns XIX to XXII. These last four columns are all concerned with the Story of Abraham and correspond to Gen. xii to xv; I give the translation below.

Column II gives part of the Story of Lamech. The text is so mutilated that the account would be almost unintelligible in places were it not for the fact that a parallel story is preserved in the *Book of Enoch* (chapters CVI to CVII). I think it useful to translate this first.[1]

'And after a time, my son Methuselah took a wife for his son Lamech, and she conceived by him and bore a son. And his flesh was white as snow and red as the flower of a rose, and the hair of his head and his locks were white as wool. And his eyes were beautiful; and when he opened his eyes, he lightened all the house like the sun and all the house was very bright. And then he rose from the hands of the midwife, he opened his mouth and spoke to the Lord of righteousness. And his father Lamech was seized with fear before him, and he fled and went to his father Methuselah. And he said to him: "I have brought into the world a child different (from other children). He is not like men, but is like a child of the angels of Heaven. His nature is quite other, and he is not like us. His eyes are like the rays of the sun; his face is brilliant. And it seems to me that he is not mine, but the angels', and I fear that a wonder may be done in his days on earth. And now I beg thee, O my father, and ask thee to go to Enoch our father to learn the truth from him, for his dwelling is with the angels."

Now when Methuselah heard the word of his son, he came to me to the ends of the earth for he had learned that I was there. And he cried out and I heard his voice. And I went to him and said to him: "Here I am, O my son. Why comest thou to me?"

He answered and said to me: "It is because of great disquiet that I come to thee, and because of an astonishing vision that I draw near. And now, O my father, hear me! A child has been born to my son

---

[1] After F. MARTIN, *Le livre d'Hénoch traduit sur le texte éthiopien* (Paris, 1906), pp. 278-83.

Lamech, and there is none like him. His nature is not like the nature of men; his colour is whiter than snow and redder than the flower of the rose, the hair of his head is whiter than white wool, and his eyes are like the rays of the sun. And he opened his eyes and lightened all the house. And he rose from the hands of the midwife and opened his mouth and blessed the Lord of Heaven. His father Lamech was seized with fright and fled to me; he does not believe that he is his, but (believes him to be) the likeness of the angels of Heaven. And behold, I have come to thee that thou make known the truth to me."

Then I, Enoch, answered and said to him: "The Lord will accomplish new things upon the earth. I have already seen this in a vision, and have made it known to thee, that in the time of Jared my father there were those who transgressed the word of the Lord in the heights of Heaven. And behold, they committed sin and transgressed the law. They joined themselves to women; they committed sin with them and married them and had children. Therefore there will be great ruin over all the earth; there will be flood and great ruin for one year. But this child who is born to you will remain on the earth, and his three children will be saved with him when all men die who are on the earth. He will be saved, he and his children. They (the evil angels) will beget giants on the earth, not of spirit but flesh. There will also be a great punishment on the earth and the earth will be purified from all corruption. And now tell Lamech, thy son, that he who is born to him is truly his son; and give him the name of Noah, for he will be a remnant to you, and he and his children will be saved from the destruction which will come upon all the earth because of all the sin and because of all the unrighteousness which will be done on the earth in his days. And after that, a still greater unrighteousness will come than that first done on the earth; for I know the mysteries of the holy ones, for the Lord has shown (them) to me and has made (them) known to me, and I have read (them) on the tablets of Heaven. And on them I have seen it written that one generation will be more wicked than another until a generation of righteousness arises and crime is destroyed and sin disappears from the face of the earth and every good comes upon it. And now go, O my son! Tell thy son Lamech that this child who is born to him is truly his son and (that) it is no lie."

And when Methuselah heard the word of his father Enoch, for he had shown him all things in secret, he returned and made (it) known (to Lamech). And he gave this child the name of Noah, for he was to comfort the earth for all ruin.'[1]

It will be noticed that in the *Book of Enoch* the story of the birth of Noah is told by Enoch himself, whereas in the *Genesis Apocryphon* the narrator is Lamech, Noah's father. But this is only a secondary variant; the story is exactly the same.

Column II of our scroll brings us into the middle of the account: the preceding column must have described the birth of the marvellous child. The translation of column II is followed by that of columns XIX to XXII.

1. THE STORY OF LAMECH

Lamech's misgivings over Noah's birth

. . . .

II (1) Behold, I thought in my heart that the conception was from the Watchers, and that from the Holy Ones was the [. . .] and that to the Giants [. . .][2] (2) And my heart was changed within me because of this child.

(3) Then I, Lamech, hastened and went to Bath-Enosh[3] [my] wi[fe, and I said to her: '. . .] (4) [. . .] by the Most High, by the Lord of greatness, by the King of all ag[es . . .] (5) [. . .] the Sons of Heaven, until thou tell me all in truth whether [. . .] (6) tell me [in truth] and with no lies [. . .] (7) by the King of all ages until thou speak to me in truth and with no lies [. . .]'.

(8) Then Bath-Enosh my wife spoke to me with much heat [and . . .] (9) and she said: 'O my brother! O my lord! Remember my charms![4] [. . .] (10) [befor]e the time, and (may) my breath (remain) in its sheath![5]

---

[1] By good fortune, a fragment of a very similar account of Noah's birth was found in cave I of Qumran: this fragment is written in Hebrew and is published in *Qumran Cave I*, no. 19 (p. 85). Another fragment of the same account has been recovered from cave IV; cf. J. T. MILIK, *Dix ans de découvertes . . .*, p. 33, n. 1. (Eng. edn., p. 35).

[2] An allusion to the myth of the union of the angels with the daughters of men, and of the birth of the Giants. This myth occupies an important place in *Enoch* and *Jubilees*, and is reported in various passages of the writings of Qumran (cf. Gen. vi. 1-4). Lamech fears that his wife, who has given birth to an extraordinary child, must have conceived it as a result of her union with an angel; he believes he has been deceived and adjures his wife to tell him the whole truth.

[3] This is also the name of the wife of Lamech in *Jubilees*, IV, 28; she is not given this name elsewhere.

[4] Or 'my pleasure' (AVIGAD and YADIN). The same word is used again in line 14.

[5] A rather enigmatic word meaning, it seems, the body; it appears also in Dan. vii. 15: 'As for me, Daniel, my spirit within my sheath was anxious.'

As for me, [I will tell thee] all in truth [. . .] (**11**) [. . .].' And then my heart within me was greatly changed.

(**12**) When Bath-Enosh my wife saw that my face upon me was changed [. . .] (**13**) then she mastered her emotion and spoke to me and said: 'O my lord! O my [brother . . . Remember] (**14**) my charms! I swear to thee by the great Holy One, by the King of H[eaven . . .] (**15**) that this seed is truly from thee and this conception is truly from thee and [this] childbearing is truly from thee [. . .] (**16**) and from no other; neither from any of the Watchers nor from any of the Sons of Heav[en . . . Why] (**17**) has thy face upon thee changed like this and altered, and why is thy spirit oppressed like this? [. . . For] (**18**) I speak to thee in truth.'

(**19**) Then I, Lamech, ran to Methuselah my father and [I told] him all, [and I asked him to go to Enoch] (**20**) his father, that he might know all things from him with certainty because he was a friend (of God) [and . . . and that with the Holy Ones] (**21**) his lot had been given and that they told him all things.

And when Methusela[h] heard [my words . . .] (**22**) [he went to] Enoch his father to know from him all in truth [. . .] (**23**) his will, and he went to the East (?) of Parwaim[1] and he found him there [. . .] (**24**) And he said to Enoch his father: 'O my father! O my lord! Thou to whom I [. . .] (**25**) [. . .] and I will speak to thee that thou be not angry with me because I have come here to [. . .] (**26**) terrible [. . .]

. . . .

2. The Story of Abraham

Abraham goes from Bethel to Hebron[2]

XIX . . . .

(**7**) [. . .] and I said: 'Thou art (**8**) for [me the e]verla[sting Go]d [. . .] till now thou hast not reached the Holy Mountain.'[3] And I went (**9**) to [. . .] Then I travelled on towards the south [. . .] until I came to Hebron; [now it was at that time that] Hebron was built. And I dwelt (**10**) [there for two year]s.

Abraham goes from Hebron to Egypt[4]

And there was famine in all this land, and I heard it said that prosperity [. . .] (reigned) in Egypt, and I went (**11**) to [. . .] to the land of

[1] Translation uncertain. I read LH QDMT (instead of L'RKMT).
[2] Cf. Gen. xii. 8-9; *Jubilees*, XIII, 8-10a.
[3] Perhaps Zion. Because of the preceding lacuna this phrase remains enigmatic.
[4] The story of Abraham's journey into Egypt, and of his contentions with Pharaoh about Sarah, extends to column XX, line 32; it is a long midrashic development on Gen. xii. 10-20. In *Jubilees* (XIII, 10b-15a) the episode is, on the contrary, completely abridged, as though the author of this book wished to suppress everything which, from the point of view of nobility of character and loyalty, might cast a slur on Abraham.

Egypt [. . .]. And I [came to] the river Karmōn, one of the (**12**) arms of the river[1] [. . .]. At that time, we [. . .] [and] I [cr]ossed the seven arms of this river which (**13**) [. . .] At that time, we crossed (the boundary of) our land and entered into the land of the sons of Ham, into the land of Egypt.

Abraham's dream: the cedar and the palm tree

(**14**) And I, Abram, had a dream during the night of our entry into the land of Egypt, and I saw in my dream. [And beho]ld, a cedar and a palm tree (**15**) [. . .] and man came and sought to cut down and uproot the cedar and to leave only the palm tree alive). (**16**) And the palm tree cried out and said: 'Cut not down the [c]edar! For cursed be he who fells the [cedar]!' And because of the protection of the palm tree the cedar was left (alive) (**17**) and [was] not [cut down].

And I woke from my sleep in the night and I said to Sarai my wife: 'I have had (**18**) a dream [. . . and I am] afraid [because of] this dream.' And she said to me: 'Tell me thy dream that I may know.' And I began to tell her this dream. (**19**) [Then she asked me the meaning] of the dream [and I said to her:] '(It is) that they will seek to kill me and to leave thee (alive) [li]ke this (palm tree). All the favour (**20**) [. . .] in all [. . . if thou say] of me, "He is my brother", and I will live because of thy protection and my soul will be saved because of thee. (**21**) [But if thou say not of me, "He is my brother", they will seek] to carry thee away from me and to kill me.' And Sarai wept because of my words that night (**22**) [. . .] and Sarai to go to Tanis[2] (**23**) [. . .] in his soul that no man might see her [. . .]

Abraham is visited by the three princes of Egypt

And after these five years (**24**) [came] three men from among the great ones of Egyp[t . . .] from Phara[oh] of Tan[is] concerning my business (?) and concerning my wife, and they gave (**25**) [. . .] possessions and wisdom and truth. And I read (?) before them [. . .] (**26**) [. . .] during the famine which [. . .] and they came to insist (?) until [. . .] (**27**) [. . .] with abundant food and with drink [. . .] the wine (**28-33**) [. . .]

. . . .

The three princes of Egypt describe Sarah's beauty to Pharaoh

XX (**1**) . . . .
(**2**) '[. . .] How [beautiful . . .] and (how) beautiful is the shape of her countenance! And how (**3**) [. . . fi]ne is the hair of her head! How fair

---

[1] As in *Jubilees*, the Nile is considered here as forming the frontier between Israel and Egypt. The 'seven arms' of the Delta are also mentioned by HERODOTUS (II, 17); here, the river Karmon seems to be the most easterly arm.

[2] In Hebrew, *Ẓō'an*; today, *Sān* in Lower Egypt. In the passage which follows, the king of Egypt is called 'the Pharaoh of Tanis'.

are her eyes and how agreeable is her nose and all the brightness (4) of her countenance [. . .] And how lovely is her bosom and how beautiful all her whiteness! Her arms, how beautiful they are, and her hands, how (5) perfect, and (how) [gracious] (is) all the appearance of her hands! How fair are her palms, how long and slender are the fingers of her hands! Her feet, (6) how beautiful they are, and how perfect are her legs! No virgin, no bride that enters into the marriage chamber will ever be more beautiful than she. Beyond all (7) women is she full of beauty and her beauty prevails over the beauty of all women. And with all this beauty there is much wisdom in her. And the slenderness of her hands (8) is so fair!

Pharaoh orders Sarah to be abducted; Abraham's prayer

When the king heard the words of Horkanosh[1] and his two companions which they all three uttered from one and the same mouth, he was greatly enamoured of her and commanded (9) immediately that she be brought to him. As soon as he saw her he marvelled at all her beauty; he took her as a wife for himself and sought to kill me. But Sarai said (10) to the king: 'He is my brother.' So I profited thereby; because of her, I, Abram, was left (alive) and was not killed. But I, Abram, wept (11) many tears, as also did Lot the son of my brother, on the night when Sarai was taken from me by force.

(12) I prayed on that night, and implored and entreated, and full of affliction I said while my tears flowed: 'Blessed be Thou, O Most High God, my Lord, for all (13) ages! For Thou art Lord and Sovereign of the world, and hast power over all the kings of the earth to judge them all. And now (14) I lodge complaint before Thee, O my Lord, against Pharaoh of Tanis, king of Egypt, because my wife has been taken far from me by force. Judge him for me, and let Thy great Hand be seen (15) against him and all his house, and let him have no power this night to defile my wife (who is) separated from me; that thus they may know Thee, O my Lord, that Thou art Lord of all the kings (16) of the earth.' And I wept and was silent.

Pharaoh's sickness

On that night, the Most High God sent a spirit of chastisement to smite him and all his household, an (17) evil spirit[2] which smote him and all his household; and he could not approach her. Moreover, he knew her not for as long as he was with her, (18) during two years.

[1] The name of Pharaoh's prince is only mentioned in *Genesis Apocryphon*.
[2] The editors have translated 'a pestilential wind', 'an evil wind'; the Hebrew word (*ruaḥ*) can in fact signify either 'wind' or 'spirit'. But there is a question here of an 'evil spirit', a spirit of sickness rather than an 'evil wind'; in line 29, Abraham lays his hands on Pharaoh to drive out both the sickness and 'the evil spirit' which causes sickness.

At the end of two years, the scourges and plagues became grievous and strong against him and all his household. And he commanded (**19**) all [the sages] of Egypt to be called, and all the wizards, together with all the physicians of Egypt, that they might cure him and his (**20**) household of this scourge. But all the physicians and wizards, and all the sages, could not cure him, for this spirit smote them all (**21**) and they fled.

The healing of Pharaoh

Then Horkanosh came to me and asked me to come and pray for (**22**) the king and to lay my hands on him that he might live. For in a dream [. . .]. And Lot said to him: 'Abram my uncle cannot pray for (**23**) the king for as long as Sarai his wife is with him. And now go and tell the king to send back his wife to her husband and (Abram) will pray for him that he may live.'

(**24**) When Horkanosh heard the words of Lot, he went to the king and said: 'All the scourges and plagues (**25**) with which my lord the king is smitten and chastised are because of Sarai, the wife of Abram. Let Sarai be restored to Abram her husband (**26**) and he will drive this plague from thee, together with the spirit of purulence.'[1] And (the king) called me to him and said to me: 'What hast thou done to me concerning [Sara]i? Thou saidst to me, (**27**) 'She is my sister', whereas she is thy wife; and I took her as a wife for myself. Behold thy wife who is with me! Go and depart from (**28**) all the province of Egypt! And now pray for me and my household that this evil spirit may be driven far from us!' And I prayed for [him and for] his princes, (**29**) and I laid my hands[2] on his [he]ad. And the plague departed from him, and the evil [spirit] was driven [far from him], and he lived. And the king arose and said to me (**30**) [. . .]. And the king swore to me by an oath which [. . .] (**31**) [. . .] And the king gave her[3] much [silver and go]ld, and many garments of byssus and purple [. . .]

---

[1] Read ŠHLNY' (and not ŠHLNP'); cf. P. GRELOT, 'Sur l'Apocryphe de la Genèse (XX, 26)', in *RQ*, no. 2, October 1958, pp. 273-6.

[2] Here the laying on of hands is an exorcism: the evil spirit is expelled from the body of the sick man who is thus healed. The same rite for the healing of the sick is described in the New Testament; cf. Mark v. 23: 'My little daughter is at the point of death. Come lay your hands on her that she may be made well and live'; vi. 5: '. . . he laid his hands upon a few sick people and healed them'; vii. 32 (the healing of the deaf mute); viii. 23-5 (the healing of the blind man); xvi. 18: 'they (the disciples) will lay their hands on the sick and will heal them'; Luke iv. 40-1: 'And he laid his hands on every one of them and healed them. And demons also came out of many, crying "Thou art the son of God!"?'; xiii. 13 (the healing of the woman with a curved spine); Acts ix. 12, 17-18 (the healing of Saul by Ananias); xxviii. 8 (the healing of the father of Publius by Paul). In the *Genesis Apocryphon* it is interesting to see Abraham in the role of exorcist and healer; according to JOSEPHUS (*War*, II, 8, 6, § 136), the Essenes were particularly expert in the art of healing the sick.

[3] To Sarai, apparently. Pharaoh also gave her Hagar as a slave, a detail absent from Genesis but appearing later in various Jewish legends.

(32) before her and also Hagar and [. . .] for me, and he appointed men to go with me who would take me out [. . .].

Abraham and Lot leave Egypt and go to Bethel[1]

(33) And I, Abram, departed with exceedingly great flocks, and also silver and gold, and I went up from [Egyp]t; [and Lot], (34) the son of my brother, went with me. And Lot also acquired many flocks, and he took for himself a wife from among [the daughters of Egypt. And I camped with him] XXI (1) [in] every place where I had camped, until I came to Bethel, the place where I had built the altar. And I built it a second time (2) and offered burnt offerings upon it and an oblation to the Most High God. And there I called on the Name of the Lord of ages and praised the Name of God. And I blessed (3) God, and offered thanksgiving there before God for all the flocks and possessions which He had given to me, and for His goodness to me, and for having caused me to return (4) to this land safe and sound.

Lot leaves Abraham and settles at Sodom[2]

(5) After that day, Lot parted from me because of the deeds of our shepherds. And he departed and settled in the valley of Jordan, taking all his riches (6) with him: and I myself added much to his possessions. As for him, he grazed his flocks and came to Sodom. And at Sodom he bought[3] a house for himself (7) and dwelt in it. And I lived on the mountain of Bethel. And I was angry that Lot, the son of my brother, had parted from me.

Abraham explores the land as far as Euphrates[4]

(8) And God appeared to me in a night vision and said: 'Go up to Ramath-Hazor[5] which is to the north (9) of Bethel, the place where thou dwellest, and lift up thine eyes and look to the east and the west and the south and the north. And behold all (10) this land which I give to thee and to thy seed for ever!' And the next day I went up to Ramath-Hazor and from this height I saw the land; (11) from the river of Egypt[6] to

---

[1] Cf. Gen. xiii. 1-4; Jubilees, XIII, 15b-16.
[2] Cf. Gen. xiii. 5-13; Jubilees, XIII, 17-18.
[3] Reading WZBN instead of WYBN, 'and he built for himself'.
[4] Cf. Gen. xiii. 14-18; Jubilees, XIII, 19-21.
[5] Today, Tell 'Azur, five miles north-east of Bethel. This is the highest point of central Palestine (3300 ft.), and the extensive view stretches from the Mediterranean to Transjordan and the mountains of Hebron. This mention of Ramath-Hazor in the story of Abraham is proper to the Genesis Apocryphon.
[6] The Nile, called below 'Gihon'. Our author considers it as forming the southern frontier of Israel.

Lebanon and Sanir,[1] and from the Great Sea[2] to Hauran, and all the land of Gebal as far as Kadesh,[3] and all the Great Desert (**12**) which is to the east of Hauran and Sanir as far as Euphrates.[4] And He said to me: 'I will give all this land to thy seed and they shall inherit it for ever. (**13**) And I will multiply thy seed like the dust of the earth which no man may count; neither shall thy seed be numbered. Arise, go and depart, (**14**) and see how great is the length of this land and how great its width. For I will give it to thee and to thy seed after thee, for ever.'

(**15**) And I, Abram, departed to travel and see the land. I began to journey from the river Gihon,[5] and I went along by the sea until (**16**) I came to the Mountain of the Bull.[6] Then I journeyed from the shore of this Great Sea of Salt and went along the Mountain of the Bull eastward in the breadth of the land (**17**) until I came to the river Euphrates.[7] Then I journeyed along the Euphrates until I came to the Red Sea[8] in the east. Then I went along (**18**) the Red Sea until I came to the gulf of the Sea of Reeds[9] which issues from the Red Sea. Then I journeyed to the south until I came to the river Gihon. (**19**) Finally I returned and came to my house safe and sound; and I found all my people in good health. Then I departed and returned to the oaks of Mamre, which is at Hebron, (**20**) just north-east of Hebron. And there I built an altar. And I offered a burnt offering on this altar and an oblation to the Most High God. And there I ate and drank, (**21**) I and all my household. And

---

[1] Mount Hermon, at the southern extremity of Anti-Lebanon.

[2] The Mediterranean, called below (line 16) 'the Great Sea of Salt'.

[3] The 'land of Gebal' is the land of Seir (cf. below, line 29), between the Dead Sea and the Gulf of Akaba. Kadesh is situated in the Negeb, to the south of Beersheba.

[4] The 'Great Desert', stretching east of Hauran and Mount Hermon to the Euphrates, is the Syrian desert. According to our author, the Euphrates forms the northern and eastern frontiers of Israel; this conception seems to derive from Gen. xv. 18: 'To your descendants I give this land *from the river of Egypt to the Great River, the river Euphrates.*'

[5] The Nile. This was both the beginning and the end of Abraham's journey (line 18); the patriarch sets out to follow (from south to north, then from north to east, and finally from east to south, the various boundaries of the land given to him.

[6] In Aramaic, *Ṭur Ṭōrā*; probably to be identified as Mount Amanus, or more exactly as that part of the mountain which the Greeks called 'Mount Tauros' (not to be confused with the Taurus Mountains). Amanus, which overlooks the Gulf of Alexandretta, marks the northern extremity of Abraham's journey; he has travelled along the Mediterranean coast from the Nile to Mount Amanus.

[7] From the Mediterranean coast Abraham travels diagonally to the east, leaving Amanus behind him; he crosses northern Syria from west to east to rejoin the Euphrates in the region of Carchemish.

[8] The Indian Ocean, as in *Jubilees*. This is also the meaning of the term 'Red Sea' (Erythrean Sea) in Herodotus; it is into the Red Sea, he notes, that the Euphrates and the Tigris flow. According to this geographical representation Abraham, by travelling along the Euphrates to the east, i.e. by descending the river, naturally arrives at the Red Sea.

[9] This term, which is also the biblical one, describes the sea known today as the Red Sea; for our author, the 'Sea of Reeds' is a gulf running directly out of the 'Red Sea' (i.e. the Indian Ocean) in a northerly direction. From the 'Sea of Reeds', Abraham, 'travelling to the south' (i.e. towards the southern regions of Palestine), rejoins the Nile, his starting-point.

I sent a message to invite Mamre and Arnam and Eshkol,[1] the three Amorite brothers, my friends; and they ate together (22) with me and drank with me.

Abraham's victory over the four kings[2]

(23) Before those days, Chedorlaomer king of Elam, Amraphel king of Babylon, Ariok king of Cappadocia,[3] Tideal king of the nations — (24) which is Mesopotamia[4] — came and made war on Bera king of Sodom, and on Birsha king of Gumram,[5] and on Shinab king of Admah, (25) and on Shemyobed[6] king of Zeboyim, and on the king of Bela. All these were joined together to fight in the Valley of Siddim. Now the king (26) of Elam, together with the kings who were with him, prevailed over the king of Sodom and his allies, and they imposed a tribute on them. For twelve years (27) they paid their tribute to the king of Elam, but in the thirteenth year they rebelled against him. Then in the fourteenth year the king of Elam put himself at the head of all (28) his allies, and they went up by the way of the desert[7] and they smote and plundered from the river Euphrates (onward). They smote the Rephaim who were at Ashteroth-(29)Karnaim, and the Zumzamim who were at Ammon,[8] and the Emim [who were at] Shaveh-Hakeriyoth, and the Horites who were in the mountains of Gebal,[9] until they came to El-(30)Paran which is in the desert. And they returned [and came to . . . and smote the . . . who were] at Hazazon-Tamar.

(31) And the king of Sodom came out to meet them, together with the king [of Gumram and the ki]ng of Admah and the king of Zeboyim and

---

[1] These three names, which appear again below (col. XXII, lines 6-7) are taken from Gen. xiv. 13, 24; but in these two biblical verses the name Arnam is given as Aner.

[2] This section is parallel to Gen. xiv. to which it is very closely linked both in style and contents; the story in the *Genesis Apocryphon* is even told in the third person as in the Bible, and no longer in the first person singular as in the preceding sections. In fact the additions and modifications are so relatively insignificant that it may almost be regarded as a simple paraphrase of the biblical text in the targumic manner. Chapter xiv of Genesis is generally thought to be an interpolation of fairly recent date and already midrashic in style; the author of the *Genesis Apocryphon* saw no need to add new midrashic developments to this ancient *midrash*. Note that the parallel section in *Jubilees* (XIII, 22-9) is, on the whole, a very brief summary of the biblical account; but the commentary on the institution of the tithe-offering is proper to it (verses 25-7).

[3] The title, 'king of Cappadocia (KPTWK)', replaces 'king of Ellasar' in the biblical text.

[4] This explanation of the title 'king of the nations' is added to the biblical account.

[5] This is the form given to the name 'Gomorrah' in the scroll (see also below, line 32). Is there any connection here with the name of Qumran itself, in which the initial *q* is probably a transcription of an Arabic guttural better rendered by a *g*, and whose final *n* may, according to the usual process, have taken the place of an original *m*?

[6] Instead of Shemeber in the biblical account.

[7] That is to say, of the Great Desert (cf. above, line 11); the four kings came direct from the Euphrates, crossing the Syrian desert from east to west.

[8] Instead of 'the Zuzim in Ham' in the biblical account.

[9] Instead of 'the Horites in their Mount Seir' in the biblical account. Cf. above, line 11 ('and all the land of Gebal as far as Kadesh').

the king of Bela. [And they fought] a battle (32) in the Valley o[f Siddim] against Chedorla[omer king of Elam and the kings] who were with him. And the king of Sodom was defeated and he fled; and the king of Gumram (33) fell into the pits[1] [... and] the king of Elam [carried off] all the possessions of Sodom and (34) [Gumram ...] and they took Lot, the son of the brother **XXII** (1) of Abram, who dwelt at Sodom with them, and also all his goods. Now one of the shepherds (2) of the sheep which Abram had given to Lot escaped from captivity and came to Abram: Abram then dwelt (3) at Hebron. He told him that Lot, the son of his brother, had been taken prisoner, together with all his possessions, but that he had not been slain; and that (4) the kings had taken the way of the Great Valley[2] to their province, and that they were taking captives and plundering and smiting and slaying, and that they were going (5) towards the province of Damascus. And Abram wept over Lot, the son of his brother. Then Abram took heart again and rose (6) and chose from among his servants three hundred and eighteen picked men, trained for battle; and Arnam (7) and Eshkol and Mamre went with him. He pursued them until he came to Dan; and he found them (8) camping in the Valley of Dan. And he threw himself upon them in the night, attacking them from four sides; and he slew (9) among them in the night and vanquished them. He pursued them and they all fled before him (10) until they came to Helbon[3] which is to the north of Damascus. And he rescued from them all whom they had taken captive, (11) and all they had taken as plunder, and all their possessions. He also delivered Lot, the son of his brother, and all his possessions and all (12) the captives which they had taken he gave back. And the king of Sodom heard that Abram had given back all the captives (13) and all the booty, and he went up to meet him; and he came to Salem, which is Jerusalem. Now Abram was camping in the Plain (14) of Shaveh, which is the Plain of the King, the Valley of Beth-Kerem.[4] Then Melchizedek king of Salem brought (15) food and drink to Abram and to all the men who were with him: now he was the priest of the Most High God. He blessed (16) Abram and said: 'Blessed be Abram by the Most High God, Lord of Heaven and earth! And blessed be the Most High God (17) who has delivered them that hate thee into thy hand!' And (Abram) gave him the tithe of all the possessions of the king of Elam and his allies.

---

[1] The biblical account tells how the kings of Sodom and Gomorrah both fell into the pits of bitumen, which makes it difficult to understand how the king of Sodom is able to reappear towards the end of the story. Here it is specified that the king of Gomorrah alone fell into the 'pits', whereas the king of Sodom fled.

[2] i.e. the valley of the Jordan (the Ghor).

[3] Instead of Hobah in the biblical account, a name found nowhere else. Helbon, named in Ezek. xxvii. 18, is identified as the village of Halbun, 15½ miles north of Damascus.

[4] The words 'the Valley of Beth-Kerem' are an addition to the biblical text; this site is mentioned in the *Mishnah* and may be Ramath-Rahel, as Y. AHARONY suggests.

(18) Then the king of Sodom drew near and said to Abram: 'My lord Abram, (19) give me the persons belonging to me who are captive with thee, whom thou hast rescued from the king of Elam. As for the goods, (20) they are all of them left to thee.' Then Abram said to the king of Sodom: 'I lift up (21) my hand today to the Most High God, the Lord of Heaven and earth. From a thread even to a sandal-strap, (22) I will take nothing of thine lest thou say, "From my possessions comes all the wealth of (23) Abram" — with the exception, however, of what the young men who (24) are with me have already eaten, and with the exception of the portion of the three men who went with me: they are masters of their portion to give it thee.' And Abram restored all the possessions and all (25) the prisoners and gave them to the king of Sodom; and all the prisoners who were with him, who came from this land, he released (26) and sent them all back.

Announcement of the birth of Isaac[1]

(27) And after these things, God appeared to Abram in a vision and said to him: 'Behold, ten years (28) have passed since the day of thy going out of Haran: two years hast thou spent here, and seven in Egypt, and one (29) since thy return from Egypt.[2] And now examine and count all thy possessions, and see how they have grown (to be the) double of (30) all thou didst take away with thee on the day of thy departure from Haran. And now, fear not! I am with thee, and I will be for thee (31) a stay and a strength. I will be a shield over thee, and thy halo (?) without thee will be a stout (shelter) for thee.[3] Thy riches and possessions (32) shall grow exceedingly.' And Abram said: 'My Lord God, my riches

[1] Cf. Gen. xv. 1-4; *Jubilees*, XIV, 1-3. The story must have continued in the following column on a sheet of leather which has now disappeared. Note that this account is still given in the third person as in the preceding section.

[2] For the seven years passed by Abraham in Egypt, see above, XIX, 23 (five years), and XX, 18 (two years). The total of ten years, counted from his departure from Haran, corresponds exactly to the chronology of *Jubilees*. Abraham arrives in Canaan at the beginning of the first year of the seventh week of the fortieth jubilee (XIII, 8); he goes down to Egypt in the third year of that week, and remains there for five years before Sarah is taken from him (XIII, 11), i.e. until the end of the seventh year and of the fortieth jubilee; he returns to Hebron in the third year of the first week of the forty-first jubilee (XIII, 16), so his stay in Egypt lasted another two years. Finally the apparition in which God announces the birth of a son occurs in the fourth year of the same week (XIV, 1); altogether, therefore, ten years have passed. This correspondence between the chronology of the *Genesis Apocryphon* and *Jubilees* justifies the editors' conjecture as regards the lacuna at the beginning of line 10 of column XIX: 'two years' (the length of Abraham's first stay at Hebron).

[3] A difficult passage; my translation is uncertain. I think the word 'SPRK is a noun (with a pronominal suffix), a transcription of the Greek word *sphaira*, 'sphere' (hence 'halo'), a transcription attested for example in Syriac. 'SPRK can also be considered a noun of Iranian origin: *sparak* (Persian *sipar, siparak*), 'shield', according to the excellent suggestion made to me by the librarian of the University of Tübingen, Walter MÜLLER. In that case, the passage should be translated: 'I will be a shield over thee, and an *aegis* which will serve as a stout (protection) without thee.'

aud possessions are great. But what good to me is (33) all that? For when I die quite naked, I will depart without children and one of my servants will be my heir. (34) Eliezer son of [. . .] will be my heir.' And God said to him: 'He shall not be thine heir, but one who shall come **XXIII** [(1) from out of thy bowels . . .]

. . . .

CHAPTER IX

APOCRYPHA AND PSEUDEPIGRAPHA

The problem of the origin of the Apocrypha and Pseudepigrapha of the Old Testament. — Fragments of Tobit, Ecclesiasticus and the Epistle of Jeremiah — Fragments of *Jubilees* and *Enoch*. — Fragments of the *Testaments of the Twelve Patriarchs*.

The scrolls and scroll fragments studied in the preceding chapters by no means represent the sum total of the non-biblical writings discovered in the various caves of Qumran; besides these, there exist an enormous number of fragments of varying size, most of them still unpublished, and even two scrolls (from cave XI) about which we so far know no more than their titles. But within the limits of our present information, some comprehensive idea of all this literature must now be given.

I will first discuss the various relatively recent Jewish writings with which we were already familiar, works called — by Protestants anyway — the 'Apocrypha and Pseudepigrapha of the Old Testament'.[1] The common characteristic of these writings is that they were not accepted into the canon of inspired Scripture by the Synagogue, but enjoyed considerable prestige in the primitive Church. Taking ancient Christian tradition into account, the Roman Catholic Church has even defined some of these Jewish books as canonical, describing them as 'deutero-canonical', whereas those accepted into the Jewish canon are known by her as 'proto-canonical'. Among Protestants, on the other hand, only the 'proto-canonical' books are recognized as canonical; the 'deutero-canonical' books are described as the 'Apocrypha of the Old Testament'. Consequently the other works belonging to this class of Jewish literature, qualified 'Pseudepigrapha' by Protestants, are styled 'Apocrypha' by Catholics. In the present book I am adopting the Protestant terminology, which has the advantage of indicating the non-adherence of both groups to the official canon of the Synagogue.

Already in 1950, in my *Aperçus préliminaires sur les manuscrits de la*

---

[1] There are two great classical collections of these: E. KAUTZSCH, *Die Apocryphen und Pseudepigraphen des Alten Testaments* (Tübingen, 1900), and R. H. CHARLES, *The Apocrypha and Pseudepigrapha of the Old Testament* (Oxford, 1913).

mer Morte (pp. 115 f.), I felt it right to draw attention to these famous
'Apocrypha and Pseudepigrapha'. 'A number of writings', I wrote
at that time, 'whose Essene origin was formerly considered by
serious scholars to be at least very probable, can equally be connected with the sect of the New Covenant. Thus, in the first place,
the *Book of Jubilees.* . . . Another example is the *Apocalypse of Lamech*,[1]
one of the Dead Sea Scrolls; it is certainly connected with the writings
of *Enoch*, which are thus themselves brought into relation with the
sect of the New Covenant. Now the Essene origin of *Enoch* was
suspected long ago. Besides *Jubilees* and *Enoch*, I am convinced that
many other writings among the 'Pseudepigrapha of the Old Testament' should be ascribed to the sect of the New Covenant — and at
the same time to the Essenes — in particular, the *Testaments of the
Twelve Patriarchs*, to which the *Damascus Document* makes many
allusions, the *Assumption of Moses*, the *Psalms of Solomon*, and indeed
certain of the 'Apocrypha'. All questions of literary and historical
criticism relative to this literature must be thoroughly re-examined.
Here is a whole mass of documents the historical study of which
presented extreme difficulty because the allusions they contained
were mostly undecipherable. Now new light has been thrown on
the religious history of the last two centuries B.C.; a thousand details
in the writings of this period now become intelligible, emerging at
last from chaos.'[2]

What of these views today? What has, in fact, been found in the
Qumran caves of this vast and important body of literature?

As regards the 'Apocrypha', I have already drawn attention
(p. 3) to the discovery of manuscripts of two of these works: Tobit
and Ben Sira (or Ecclesiasticus). The book of Tobit, whose original
Semitic text was lost, and which had only survived in the ancient
versions, is represented at Qumran by fragments of four different
manuscripts found in cave IV: three are written in Aramaic and one
in Hebrew. These fragments are still unpublished, but J. T. Milik,
who has studied them, recognizes that the text of the Qumran
manuscripts corresponds to the long recension attested by *Sinaiticus*,
a Greek manuscript of the fourth century A.D., and *Vetus Latina*, and
not to the short recension represented by two other Greek manu-

---

[1] I would remind the reader that this is known today as the *Genesis Apocryphon*.
[2] See also my *Nouveaux Aperçus* . . . (1953), pp. 63 f. (Eng. edn., pp. 38 f.)

scripts, the *Alexandrinus* and the *Vaticanus*. According to this writer, the language of the original was Aramaic rather than Hebrew.[1]

As for Ecclesiasticus, two Hebrew fragments of this work have been recovered from cave II. As is known, it had been transmitted mainly in a Greek version, and the major portion of the original Hebrew text, which had disappeared, was recovered towards the end of the last century in the Cairo *geniza*, the *geniza* in which the *Damascus Document* was found. We are assured that the text of the fragments from cave II is almost identical with that from the Cairo *geniza*. The presence of Ecclesiasticus in the Qumran library is extremely interesting. In 1953 I wrote the following:[2] 'The literary problem posed by this work is complex; it seems that not all of it dates from exactly the same time or derives from the same environment. It is possible that once accepted by the sect of the Covenant, the original work — written by a pious priest in about 200 B.C., but manifesting a piety which is quite down to earth — was subjected to a certain number of additions recognizable by their more mystical character. It would then be necessary to distinguish, bit by bit, what was contributed by the first writer and what should be attributed to a later redactional layer. The case would be analogous to that of Ecclesiastes (*Koheleth*), in which many modern critics discern a primitive kernel, and additions in quite another spirit intended to complete or even rectify the assertions of the first writer.' At that time it was not yet known that Ecclesiasticus figured in the sect's library; now that the fact is established, it is no doubt opportune to examine closely my earlier hypothesis concerning the composition of this book and its partly Essene origin.

To the remains of Tobit and Ecclesiasticus must be added the Greek papyrus fragments found in cave VII, of a third 'Apocryphon', the Epistle of Jeremiah;[3] this work has been preserved in the Septuagint and, in the common opinion of scholars, was originally written in Greek. The existence at Qumran of such a Greek writing is particularly instructive.

Generally speaking, the presence of these various Apocrypha in the Qumran library when they were excluded from the official canon of the Synagogue, shows that Essene Judaism accepted a scriptural canon which was appreciably more open and liberal than

---

[1] *Dix ans de découvertes* . . ., p. 29. (Eng. edn., p. 31.)
[2] *Nouveaux Aperçus* . . ., p. 103, no. 142. (Eng. edn., p. 73, n. 44.)
[3] Cf. *RB*, 1956, p. 572. In the Latin Vulgate, the *Epistle of Jeremiah* is annexed to the Book of Baruch (itself apocryphal).

that prevailing in Rabbinico-Pharisaic Judaism. Now by accepting these Apocrypha, the primitive Church proved itself to a certain extent heir to the Essene canon: this seems to be another indication, and a by no means negligible one, of the close bonds which existed in the beginning between the Church and Essene Judaism.

Among the 'Pseudepigrapha' which were equally in favour in the ancient Church there are so far three whose remains have been discovered in the Qumran caves: *Jubilees*, the *Book of Enoch* and the *Testaments of the Twelve Patriarchs*. In 1950, only one fragment of *Jubilees* from cave I had been found and identified: there was still nothing of *Enoch* or the *Testaments*. In 1951, a fragment of *Enoch* appeared. A little later I ventured to write:[1] 'Nothing has so far been found of the *Testaments*, but we may expect to discover fragments of this too. This work, in fact, contains many references to the writings of *Enoch*, and its literary and doctrinal affinities leave very little doubt as to its real origin.' Today we possess these expected fragments at last.

First of all a word about *Jubilees*. The *Damascus Document* (XVI, 2-4) refers to this work — which is also called the *Little Genesis* — explicitly. It had only survived in an Ethiopian version published a century ago and, partially, in a Latin version; now, we have the fragments of at least nine manuscripts of its original Hebrew text.[2] A number as large as this immediately shows what importance was imputed to it by the Qumran sectaries. In the previous chapter I have described its close affinities with the *Genesis Apocryphon* — whether this served as its source, or on the contrary, derived from it. In any case it was a basic book, and a detailed analysis of its religious ideas is the best introduction to Qumran research today.

No less a sectarian classic must have been the *Book of Enoch*; this work had also come down to us in an Ethiopian version and, partially, in a Greek version. Its prestige in the primitive Church exceeded that of all the other Pseudepigrapha; a passage from it is even explicitly quoted in the Epistle of Jude (verses 14-15); and the *Epistle of Barnabas*, one of the most ancient Christian writings, goes so far as to introduce a quotation from *Enoch* with a formula reserved

---

[1] *Nouveaux Aperçus* . . ., p. 63. (Eng. edn., p. 38.)

[2] Two from cave I (published in *Qumran Cave I*, nos. 17 and 18), two from cave II, and five from cave IV.

to quotations from the Bible: 'For Scripture says . . .' (XVI, 5).
Actually the *Book of Enoch* is composite; it is made up of several books
which were originally independent. It even includes several passages
from an ancient *Book of Noah*. Cave I has yielded several fragments of
a Hebrew manuscript which correspond precisely to these passages
from the *Book of Noah* inserted into *Enoch*.[1] Furthermore, cave IV
has furnished a number of *Enoch* fragments belonging to ten Aramaic
manuscripts: five of these are related to the first and fourth sections
of the present *Book of Enoch* ('Journeys' and 'Visions'),[2] four to the
third section ('Book of the Heavenly Luminaries'),[3] and one to the
fifth ('Apocalypse of Weeks' followed by some supplements).[4]
Of the second section ('Similitudes'),[5] no fragment has so far been
found; nothing has been recognized anyway. From this negative
fact some writers have felt able to conclude that this section of the
'Similitudes' is not of Essene or Jewish origin, but was written and
incorporated into the *Book of Enoch* by a Christian author. 'This
absence', writes J. T. Milik, 'cannot be fortuitous. The similitudes
(of *Enoch*) must therefore be the work of a Judeo-Christian of the
second century A.D. . . .'[6] A momentous conclusion such as this is by
no means imperative; I must here explain why.

First it should be pointed out that the study of the manuscript
fragments is still in progress. The inventory that has been drawn up
is still only a provisional one. In 1955, *eight* Aramaic manuscripts
of *Enoch* had been located;[7] in 1957, their number had risen to *ten*.[8]
May we not suppose that in time to come remnants will be found,
among the still unidentified fragments, of an eleventh manuscript
corresponding to the 'Similitudes' section, or at least attesting one
or other of the doctrines peculiar to that section? Besides, even if,
when the search has ended, nothing of this kind should have been

---

[1] The fragments are published in *Qumran Cave I*, nos. 19 and 19 *bis* (pp. 84-6, 152).

[2] At Qumran, these two sections, which correspond to chapters I-XXXVI and
LXXXIII-XC, seem with chapters CVI-CVII (fragments of the *Book of Noah*) to have
formed a separate work. A fragment of manuscript *b* and another of manuscript *d* of the
work thus composed are published by J. T. Milik in *RB*, 1958, pp. 70-7.

[3] At Qumran, this section, which corresponds to chapters LXXII-LXXXII, seems
also to have formed a separate work. A fragment of manuscript *a* of this second Enochian
work is published in *RB*, 1958, p. 76.

[4] At Qumran, this section, which corresponds roughly to chapters XCI-CVIII, seems
to have formed a third separate work.

[5] Chapters XXXVII-LXXI.

[6] *Dix ans de découvertes* . . ., p. 31. In the English edition (p. 33) the last sentence has
been significantly altered: 'The "Similitudes" are probably to be considered the work of
a Jew or a Jewish Christian of the first or second century A.D.'

[7] Cf. *RB*, 1956, p. 60 (communication dated August 28th, 1955).

[8] *Dix ans de découvertes* . . ., pp. 30-1. (Eng. edn., p. 33).

found, argument *a silentio* would have no decisive value seeing that the relics recovered from Qumran cannot pretend to represent the total number of manuscripts forming the Essene library: it is chance that has saved part of them while leaving the rest to sink to destruction. Statistical reasoning can only be applied here with the greatest reserve and extreme prudence.

It is indeed recognized that the 'Similitudes' must originally have formed a separate book of a very particular nature. It was the 'Book of the Messiah', and its speculations on the person and role of the Messiah, and even the titles given to him of 'Son of Man' and 'Elect', plainly distinguish it from the other sections of *Enoch*. It has even been noticed that in a passage alluding to the writings thought to have been composed by the patriarch Enoch (IV, 16-25), the author of *Jubilees* seems to be ignorant of the 'Similitudes'. It is possible that this Enochian book was not written, or did not appear, until later, some time after the others. But it is going rather far to declare for this reason that the work is a Christian composition, and that it dates from the second century A.D. Today, as before the Qumran discoveries, the question of the origin of the book of the 'Similitudes' must be examined essentially by means of internal criteria. For a long time scholars have wondered whether the work is Jewish or Christian; several critics have even tried to distinguish in it a Jewish part and a Christian one. The reason for this is that the book's most characteristic Messianic conceptions reappear with astonishing accuracy in the New Testament itself; some writers clearly find it distasteful to have to accept that any Jewish sect before Jesus Christ could profess such doctrines. It is impossible to tackle so difficult a problem here. I will say only that the theory of a purely Jewish origin is the one most generally accepted today: it is supported, among others, by Abbé F. Martin[1] on the Roman Catholic side, and by A. Lods[2] on the Protestant. The great Scandinavian scholar, S. Mowinckel, has quite recently expressed the same opinion.[3] J. T. Milik's view is retrograde and without justification and I consider it very weak.

---

[1] *Le Livre d'Hénoch traduit sur le texte éthiopien* (Paris, 1906), pp. xci ff.

[2] *Histoire de la littérature hébraïque et juive* (Paris, 1950), pp. 880-2.

[3] *He That Cometh* (Oxford, 1956), pp. 354 f. Cf. also O. CULLMANN, *Christologie du Nouveau Testament* (Neuchâtel-Paris, 1958), p. 121: 'There is no need at all to accept this hypothesis (of Christian interpolations), to which recourse has been made too easily, anyway, in explaining later Jewish writings — sometimes for apologetical reasons and to underline the distance separating them from primitive Christian writings. On the contrary, an acknowledgment of existing affinities should urge us to look for the novelty of

Let us now turn to the *Testaments of the Twelve Patriarchs*. These twelve patriarchs, the twelve sons of Jacob, were each thought to have addressed an edifying discourse to their children before dying. The work is consequently in twelve parts. It is chiefly known to us through a Greek version, but also through an Armenian version and a Slavonic one. There are very considerable divergences between the various versions, and also between the various manuscripts of each version, and scholars are badly hampered in their attempts to reconstruct the original text of the work written initially in Hebrew or Aramaic.

Cave I, first of all, has yielded fragments of an Aramaic manuscript of the *Testament of Levi*, one of the sections of this work.[1] It should be noted that it is to this *Testament of Levi* that the *Damascus Document* alludes (IV, 15), though this allusion may be to some other ancient recension and not to the recension of the *Testament* attested by the versions. As a matter of fact, more than fifty years ago important Aramaic fragments of an ancient *Testament of Levi* were recovered from the Cairo *geniza*: the text of these is parallel to that of our versions but much longer. Furthermore, one of the manuscripts of the Greek version of our *Testaments* (that from Mount Athos) includes an interpolation attesting the same long text as that of the Aramaic *Testament of Levi*. This interpolation, which is quite extensive, partly corresponds to the Aramaic fragments from the *geniza*, but also extends beyond them, thereby restoring in Greek a new piece of the long recension of the *Testament of Levi*.

Now among the fragments from cave IV, J. T. Milik has recognized the remains of three Aramaic manuscripts of this recension of the *Testament of Levi*.[2] Several of these relics correspond to various passages in the Aramaic fragments from the *geniza*, and to the passage preserved in Greek only in the manuscript from Mount Athos. Others do not check with any of the known passages (in Aramaic or Greek) of the Greek recension of the *Testament of Levi*,

[1] These fragments are published in *Qumran Cave I*, no. 21.
[2] See *RB*, 1955, pp. 398-406: in this article the surviving fragment of the second of these three manuscripts is published. On the Aramaic *Testament of Levi*, see also P. GRELOT, 'Le Testament araméen de Lévi est-il traduit de l'hébreu?' in *REJ*, xiv (CXIV), 1955, pp. 91-9, and 'Notes sur le Testament araméen de Lévi' in *RB*, 1956, pp. 391-406.

the Gospel where it really lies. What I say here applies also to present-day comparison of the Qumran texts with the ideas expressed in the New Testament.'

but are parallel to chapters XIV to XVII of the *Testament of Levi* in the collected *Testaments of the Twelve Patriarchs*.[1]

It should be added that more recently the same writer has recognized a fragment of the *Testament of Naphtali* written in Hebrew.[2]

These various finds are of cardinal interest to the study of the *Testaments*. In the Middle Ages this work enjoyed considerable popularity due to the Latin version which Robert Grosseteste, Bishop of Lincoln, rendered from the Greek manuscripts. This Latin version was later translated into French and published in Paris in 1555 under the title, *Testament des Douze Patriarches, enfants de Jacob*. In 1698, Grabe edited the Greek text for the first time.[3] This author then expressed the opinion that the work had been written by a Jew in pre-Christian times, but had been subjected to the interpolations of Christian copyists. This opinion was much disputed. In his *Dictionnaire des Apocryphes*, vol. i (Paris, 1856), p. 854, Abbé Migne, for example, declares: 'This apocryphal composition appears to have been written towards the end of the first century A.D., or at the beginning of the second; it is evidently the work of a Jewish convert who ascribes to the children of Jacob the most obvious Messianic prophecies. . . . To the divinity of Jesus Christ this work bears very fine witness, highly important because of its antiquity. . . . The author was well versed in the knowledge of Scripture, from which he reproduces, not without success, both the spirit and the most striking expressions. . . . ' So two opposing theories already confronted each other. According to the one, the *Testaments* are a genuinely Jewish work into which Christian interpolations were introduced later; according to the other, they are an authentic Christian work written by a Jew converted to Christianity. At the beginning of this century the admirable labours of the eminent Oxford scholar, R. H. Charles, threw a great deal of light on this debate, and convinced most critics of the essentially Jewish nature of the work, the Christian interpolations being strictly limited and confined to dogmatic Christology.

Nevertheless a young Dutch scholar, M. De Jonge, has recently

---

[1] J. STARCKY (*RB*, 1956, p. 66), for his part, reports the existence of 'three manuscripts at least' representing 'an apocryphon analogous to the Testament of Levi'. These seem to be different manuscripts from those mentioned by J. T. MILIK; so what is this other work 'analogous to the *Testament of Levi*'?

[2] *Dix ans de découvertes* . . ., p. 32. (Eng. edn., p. 34.)

[3] *Spicilegium Patrum* (Oxford, vol. i, pp. 145-253).

revived the problem.[1] He does not deny that the author of the *Testaments* borrowed from Jewish works, but holds that these Jewish borrowings were altered, transformed and completed by a Christian author who was a 'compiler and not an interpolator'. This theory, which agrees with the one supported by Abbé Migne a hundred years ago, received a warm welcome from some writers. J. T. Milik, in particular, rallied — in the essentials at least — to the view of De Jonge. 'Some confirmation of the thesis defended by De Jonge', he writes,[2] 'results from the fact that no fragments of the *Testaments of the Twelve Patriarchs* have been found among the Qumran manuscripts; given the extreme richness and variety of the latter, a pre-Christian and Palestinian origin of this apocryphon seems, for this reason, to be practically excluded.' And again:[3] 'We are therefore inclined to ascribe to the *Testaments of the Twelve Patriarchs* an origin analogous to that of the *Book of Enoch*. A Judeo-Christian of the second century,[4] having before him one or other of the *Testaments* already existing, composed a work of the same kind for the twelve Patriarchs. That they were all written by one man is seen in the repetition of the same literary *schema*: each testament consists of a pseudo-historical introduction, a parenetic section, and a messianic and apocalyptic conclusion. . . . On the doctrinal level, the theme of the two Messiahs should be noted; for the author these seem to have been realized in a single person. Other elements bear a Christian stamp and cannot easily be considered interpolations; which confirms our hypothesis that the *Testaments of the Twelve Patriarchs* are of Christian origin.'[5]

What is to be thought of a theory such as this? It should first be noted that De Jonge took no account of the Essene texts when he wrote his book: neither of the *Damascus Document* nor of the Qumran manuscripts (except for two furtive references in the notes on page 164). And yet, as Milik himself states,[6] 'the Essene character of the *Testaments* is incontestable': the great doctrinal and moral themes of

---

[1] *The Testaments of the Twelve Patriarchs. A Study of their Text, Composition and Origin* (Assen, 1953).

[2] *RB*, 1955, pp. 297-8.

[3] *Dix ans de découvertes* . . ., p. 32. (Eng. ed., pp. 34 f.) Fr. J. DANIÉLOU expresses a similar opinion in his *Théologie du Judéo-Christianisme* (1958), p. 24.

[4] In the English edition of his book MILIK writes: 'A Jew or Jewish Christian of the first or second century . . .' (p. 34). Cf. above, p. 299, n. 6.

[5] In the English edition MILIK again shows more of a *nuance*: 'Other elements bear a Christian stamp, and since they cannot easily be considered as interpolations, they suggest a Christian rather than a Jewish origin for the Testaments . . .' (p. 35).

[6] *RB*, 1955, p. 298.

the Qumran sect appear on every page of the *Testaments*. What a remarkable paradox it is that the old theory of Christian authorship should be revived at the very moment when, by extraordinary good luck, the historian has at last at his disposal documents which authentically reveal how close, on the whole, Essene mysticism was to the spirituality and dogmas which Christianity was to propagate — documents which even oblige us to reconsider the question of the Christian interpolations in the *Testaments*! We cannot, of course, deny the possibility of such interpolations in the different versions of the work, which were all transmitted by Christian copyists; but the Qumran documents, particularly in what they teach of the existence and career of the Teacher of Righteousness, undoubtedly prompt us to limit their number and importance rather than to augment them.[1] What is one to say, then, of a theory which attributes the complete work to a Christian writer?

Today we possess numerous fragments from the Qumran caves of two authentically Jewish Testaments: the *Testament of Levi* and the *Testament of Naphtali*, both closely connected with those of our Greek collection of *Testaments*. And in the *Testament of Levi* appear even the famous chapters XIV to XVII which it had been especially tempting to consider as later additions to the original work, as Milik himself notes.[2] Really, what more can one reasonably demand in favour of the theory of a pre-Christian origin, given the state in which the Qumran library has come down to us? From the fact that only two of the twelve *Testaments* have been discovered and identified, Milik jumps to the conclusion that the other ten were entirely conceived and written by a Christian. Here again, this hasty judgment is, in my opinion, most unwise. Are we sure that among the Qumran fragments, whose study is still incomplete, the remains of *Testaments* other than those of *Levi* and *Naphtali* will not be found? J. Strugnell, for instance, has reported fragments from cave IV in which sapiential passages appear: he has explicitly suggested that these passages may belong to works like *Jubilees* or the *Testaments of the Twelve Patriarchs*.[3] Let the supporters of this theory of Christian authorship at least

[1] On this subject, see the remarkably penetrating study of M. PHILONENKO, 'Les interpolations chrétiennes des Testaments des Douze Patriarches et les Manuscrits de Qoumrân' in *RHPR*, 1958, pp. 309-43, and 1959, pp. 14-38; these two articles have been combined to form an independent work (Paris, 1960).

[2] *RB*, 1955, p. 399. In my *Nouveaux Aperçus* ... (pp. 63-84; Eng. edn., pp. 38-57) I tried to show that these chapters — whose eventual discovery at Qumran no one could foresee — allude to the Teacher of Righteousness and his time.

[3] *RB*, 1956, p. 65.

wait for the identification of the fragments to be finished before concluding as they do! If fragments of only the Testaments of *Levi* and *Naphtali* have been recognized so far, might this not be because they are the ones most easy to identify, since we already have an Aramaic text of the first and a Hebrew text of the second? Research is more difficult and takes longer when one has to recognize an Aramaic or Hebrew text known only in its Greek version.

This also should be noted. It is known that the *Damascus Document* offers numerous parallels, not only to the Testaments of *Levi* and *Naphtali* but also to those of *Reuben, Simeon, Judah, Zabulon, Dan, Gad, Asher, Joseph* and *Benjamin*; to be convinced, one has only to consult the index of parallels established by C. Rabin in his edition of the *Damascus Document*.[1] Is this not at least indirect proof that the complete work, with its twelve parts, already existed in the sect before the Christian era? The work transmitted by the version — the *Testament of Levi* anyway — is doubtless presented in a generally shorter form than that attested by the Qumran text; but may not this abridgement, if it really is an abridgement, have been composed by an Essene? The Jews were very able at writing summaries: does not the author of ii Maccabees present his work as an abridgement of a study in five books written by Jason of Cyrene? And among the Essenes themselves, are not certain passages of the *Book of Jubilees* an abridgement of the *Genesis Apocryphon*: if, that is, it is accepted that this *Apocryphon* served as a source?[2] The origin of our Greek version of the *Testaments* is certainly obscure; but nothing seems to authorize the assumption that they, any more than the 'Similitudes', were written by a Christian.

---

[1] *The Zadokite Documents*, p. 83.   [2] See above, p. 281.

CHAPTER X

FRAGMENTS OF EXEGETICAL WRITINGS

Biblical exegesis at Qumran. — *The Sayings of Moses.* — *Florile-gium.* — *The Patriarchal Blessings.* — *Testimonia.*

In their Qumran solitude the members of the Essene Community were fervent readers of the Bible. 'They shall be separated from the midst of the habitation of perverse men', says the *Rule* (VIII, 13-16), 'to prepare the way of "Him" (God); as it is written, *In the wilderness prepare the way of (Adonai), make straight in the desert a highway for our God.* This (way) is the study of the Law which He has promulgated by the hand of Moses, that they may act according to all that is revealed, season by season, and according to that which the Prophets have revealed by His holy Spirit.' The essential purpose of their retreat into the desert and their life there was to study the Law and the Prophets; in Hebrew, this study is called *midrash*, 'research, exegesis'. The Teacher of Righteousness is himself named *par excellence* the 'Seeker (*dōresh*) of the Law', the 'Interpreter'. I have shown (page 57) how the study of the Law was organized within the sect: in each group of ten, there had to be 'a man studying the Law night and day, continually', and every night the sectaries, divided into three groups, watched in relays and kept a permanent vigil 'to read the Book, study the Law, and bless in common'.

The biblical Commentaries, discussed in an earlier chapter, are one of the most characteristic achievements of this immense exegetical labour. But the Qumran caves have restored the remains of other examples of exegetical writings and it is these that I intend to present now.

First there is the scroll of the *Targum of Job* discovered in 1956 in cave XI. Nothing precise is so far known about this work except that it was rejected by the official Synagogue and condemned as heretical. Its presence in the Essene library suggests that it was written by an Essene.

The Essenes also composed *paraphrases* of the biblical books: various fragments from cave IV derive from paraphrases of Genesis and Exodus, and others from a paraphrase of Samuel.[1]

[1] Cf. *RB*, 1956, p. 63.

To these must be added fragments found in cave I of a scroll which the editors have called *The Sayings of Moses*.[1] It is really a sort of free paraphrase of Deuteronomy, comparable in genre to *Jubilees*. The writer also draws on Leviticus and avails himself here and there of midrashic traditions. The preserved fragments belong to the first columns of the scroll; the text is unfortunately very incomplete and full of lacunae. Here is the translation.

God speaks to Moses[2]

I (**1**) [God called] Moses [in the fortieth] year after the departure of [the children of I]srael [from out of the land of E]gypt, in the eleventh month, (**2**) on the first day of the month,[3] and said to him:

'[Call together] all the congregation and go up t[o Mount Nebo] and remain there, thou (**3**) and Eleazar son of Aaron. Exp[ound to the heads of fa]mily of the Levites and to all the [priests], and proclaim to the children (**4**) of Israel, the words of the Law which I commanded [thee] on Mount Sinai to proclaim to them. [Proclaim] all of them into their ears: (**5**) what I [requ]ire of them is good. And [call] heaven and [earth to witness against] them; [f]or they will not [lo]ve [me] (**6**) as I have commanded [them], neither they nor their sons, [all] the days during which they will [live upon the ear]th. For I foretell (**7**) that they will abandon me and will choose [the idols of the] nations and their abominations and horrors, and that they will serve (**8**) idols which will be (for them) a pit[fall and] a snare. And they will vio[late all the ho]ly [assemblies] and the Sabbath of the Covenant [and the feasts,] all that (**9**) I have commanded thee this day [that] they should [d]o. [So I will smi]te them with a great [affliction] in the midst of the land which they go [to poss]ess in crossing (**10**) the Jordan. And then all the curses will come upon them and will pursue them until they perish and (**11**) are destroyed: and they will know [that] for them the truth has been accompl[ished].'

Moses speaks to Eleazar and Joshua[4]

Then Moses called Eleazar son (**12**) [of Aaron] and Josh[ua son of Nun and said to them]:

---

[1] These fragments are published in *Qumran Cave I*, no. 22, plates XVIII and XIX.

[2] God commands Moses to ascend Mount Nebo and proclaim there before Israel the laws already decreed by Him on Sinai; in Deut. xxxii. 48 Moses does not ascend Nebo until after he has proclaimed the laws, and then only in order to die there: the proclamation takes place in the plain. This discourse which God addresses to Moses draws its inspiration more particularly from Deut. xxxi. 28-9.

[3] The same date as that given in Deut. i. 3.

[4] This discourse is full of various reminiscences of Deut. xxvii. 9-10; vi. 11; viii. 14; ix. 1; xxx. 20.

'Speak all (?) [these words to the people]. [Be silent] II (1) Israel, and hear! [Become] this day [a peo]ple for God thy [God], and k[eep my precepts] and testimonies and [commandm]ents which (2) [I] command thee to [accomplish] this day [a]s thou goest to cross the Jordan that I may [give] thee [citi]es great (3) [and beauti]ful, and houses filled with eve[ry kind of possessions, vines and olives] which thou [hast] not [planted, and] excavated [cis]terns which thou (4) hast not dug, so that thou mayest eat and be satisfied. [Take care] that thy [hear]t be not raised up and that thou for[get] not that which I command thee this day. (5) [For] this it is that will obtain for thee life and length of days.'

Moses speaks to the people[1]

[Then] Moses [called the children of I]srael and [said to them]:

'[Behold], forty (6) years (have passed) since our departure from out of the land of [Egypt, and this] day [has Go]d [our] God [uttered these wor]ds from His mouth, (7) [all] His [ordi]nances and all [His] ordi[nances].[2]

[Ho]w [can I carry alone] your burden [and your l]o[ad, and settle your disputes]? Therefore (8) when I have fulfilled the [establishment of the] Covenant and the proclamation of the way in which you must walk, [appoint wise men who] will apply themselves to explain (9) [to you and to] your [children] all these words of the Law.

In your own interest, wa[tch with greatest] care [to fulfi]l [them, lest there ki]ndle and burn against you the wrath (10) [of your God], and lest he stop the heights of heaven from pouring rain upon you and the [waters] be[low from] bringing you (11) [harv]est.'

Law concerning the sabbatical year[3]

And Moses s[aid again] to the children [of Israel]:

'Behold the commandments which God has commanded you to observe (12) [. . .]

III (1) [Every seventh y]ear [thou shalt observe] the Sabbath [of the earth. Whatever the] ear[th shall bring forth by herself during her Sabbath shall serve thee] for food; [thee and the cattle and the] wil[d beasts] (2) [shall it serve for fo]od. [And whatever shall be in ex]cess shall be for [the poor of] thy [brethren] who are in [the land]. No man shall s[ow his field nor] cut [his vine]; (3) [no man shall reap the fruit of the seed fallen from his former harvest nor] gather in [anything].

---

[1] The first paragraph (introduction) recalls Deut. ii. 7 (cf. viii. 2, 4), iv. 1: the second (the institution of the 'wise men'), Deut. i. 12-13: the third (the threats), Deut. xi. 17.
[2] Text uncertain; dittography?
[3] Cf. Lev. xxv. 1-7 and Deut. xv. 1-3.

[Observe] all these [words of the] Covenant (4) [. . .] Thou shalt also remit debts in that year. (5) [Every creditor who has lent something to] a man or [who holds a pledge on his brother], shall can[cel it from] his neighbour; for (6) [remission of debt is proclaimed] in honour of God you[r God]. [Repayment shall be required] of the str[anger but] not [of a brother]. For during [that] year (7) [Go]d [will bless you, pardoning your] faults.'

Law concerning the Feast of Atonement[1]

[And Moses said again:]

'[. . .] (8) [. . . eve]ry year [in the seventh month on the tenth day] of the month (9) [. . .] on that day [. . . For] your [fa]thers [we]re wanderers (10) [in the desert] until the tenth day of the [seventh] month [. . .][2] On the tenth [day] of the month (11) [all work shall be] forbidden; and on the tenth day of the month they shall make atonement [. . .] of the month (12) [. . .] they shall take [. . .] IV (1) and in the congregation of the gods [and in the assembly of the ho]ly ones[3] and in [. . .] their [. . . for the children of Isra]el and for the ea[rth].[4] (2) [And he shall] ta[ke its blood and] pour it upon the earth [. . .] (3) [. . . and they shall make at]onement for them [. . .]'

[And] Moses [said again]:

'You shall do [. . .] (4) [. . . ever]lasting precepts for [your] generations [. . .] And on the day [. . .] (5) [. . .] the [priest] shall take [. . .] the children of Isra[el] (6-7) [. . .] (8) [. . .] on the book of [. . .] me, the priest [. . .] (9) [. . .] and he shall lay his hands [. . .] (10) [. . .] (11) [. . .] of the two r[ams (?) . . .] (12) [. . .]

. . . .

These *Sayings of Moses* show how ingeniously the Essene interpreters regrouped scattered passages from the Bible in order to make them explain and complete each other. They were not afraid to modify the general arrangement of the biblical book more or less seriously, nor to add new elements and delete old ones from the text. This remarkable freedom sprang from no lack of respect, but from the

---

[1] The text becomes very broken; it allows us to do little more than recognize that it concerns the ritual for the Day of Atonement: cf. Lev. xxiii. 26-32 and xvi. 7 ff.

[2] This restoration is MILIK's; if it is correct, the origin of the feast is explained as being a commemoration of the day on which Israel's wanderings in the desert ended. This point is absent from the Bible. In *Jubilees* (XXXIV, 12-13, 18) the origin of the feast is connected with the recollection of the day on which Jacob received Joseph's mantle soaked in the blood of a goat and wept for the death of his son.

[3] The 'gods' and 'holy ones' are the angels.

[4] This should doubtless be preceded by the words 'they shall make atonement'; the idea that the members of the sect offer expiation not only for Israel but also 'for the earth' is found again in the *Rule* (VIII, 6, 10; IX, 4).

naive conviction that, however audacious it may appear to us, their studious exegesis in no way betrayed the biblical book. In their eyes, the resulting new compositions were vested with an authority of the same order as that belonging to the inspired books because their exegesis was itself inspired. Thus originated the *Book of Jubilees*, which is a second Genesis, and the book of *The Sayings of Moses*, which is a second Deuteronomy, and no doubt many more works of the same kind which have not survived.

The study of the Bible, to which the people of Qumran devoted themselves with a passion equal to their virtuosity, has produced some more very curious works, a few examples of which have been recovered from the Qumran caves. I must now speak of three documents from cave IV to which their editor, J. M. Allegro, has given the provisional titles, *Florilegium*, *The Patriarchal Blessings* and *Testimonia*.

Twenty-one fragments of *Florilegium* have been recovered; skilfully pieced together, they restore one column almost entire, and a small portion of a second column.[1] J. M. Allegro explains that the scroll from which these fragments derive 'was apparently devoted to a collection of *midrashim* on certain biblical texts, compiled perhaps for their common eschatological interest'. I would remark at this juncture that the word *midrash*, which appears once in the document itself (I, 14), must not be accepted here in the exact and limited sense it usually has in Rabbinic literature, where it describes stories depending on 'haggadic' tradition, but as I have indicated earlier (p. 306), in the broad and general sense of 'research, exegesis'. In fact the 'interpretations' figuring in our piece are essentially of the same type as the biblical Commentaries (*pesharim*) studied in chapter VII. It would be preferable, therefore, to avoid the word *midrashim*, which is equivocal, and to call them instead *pesharim*, a term pointing direct to the genre of the Qumran Commentaries.

The difference between the *Florilegium* and the Commentaries studied earlier is that the latter are concerned with the whole of one or other of the biblical writings, whereas the former presents a selection of various passages and accompanies each one with a commentary. In the preserved fragment, the three following

[1] This document was first published partially in *JBL*, lxxv, 1956, pp. 176-7, and then as a whole in the same review, lxxvii, 1958, pp. 350-4, with a photograph.

passages are successively quoted and interpreted: (1) 2 Sam. vii. 10b-14a (this passage is divided into three short sections); (2) Ps. i. 1; (3) Ps. ii. 1-2. The first passage is extracted from the prophecy of Nathan concerning the future of the Davidic dynasty; very likely part at least of the beginning of this prophecy (2 Sam. vii. 8-10a) figured in the column, now lost, preceding our present column I. But we have no idea at all which biblical passages were quoted and interpreted before the verses from 2 Samuel or after the verses taken from Psalms i and ii.

It is consequently very difficult to recognize the idea governing the choice of biblical passages in this *Florilegium*. There was talk at first of a 'messianic *Florilegium*', but as we can see from our piece, the texts chosen have not all a properly messianic significance. To speak of 'their common eschatological interest' is rather vague, since all the Qumran Commentaries are dominated by eschatological preoccupations. In the surviving section of the *Florilegium* the commentator is concerned more precisely with the Community itself as the representative of the new Israel; he describes its composition, its present and future trials, and its hope in the coming of the Davidic Messiah. It was, I think, in view of this theme — offered no doubt as a subject of meditation during some study session or liturgical reunion of the sect — that various passages from the Bible were assembled.

In the commentaries accompanying each biblical quotation the author of *Florilegium* sometimes cites other biblical texts taken from Exodus, Amos, Isaiah and Ezekiel. But these scriptural references are really secondary. They only indirectly form part of the *Florilegium* and merely reveal the erudition and virtuosity of the Essene interpreters.

Now follows the translation of the recovered piece of the *Florilegium*.

. . . .

I (1) [. . . into the ha]nd of [his] enem[ies].

And no son of perversion [shall oppress it agai]n[1] as formerly, from the day when (2) [*I established judges*] *over my people Israel.* (2 Sam. 10b-11a)

This is the House which [will be built at the e]nd of days;[2] as it is

---

[1] The reference is to Israel, as the beginning of the verse indicates.

[2] The Community of the Covenant itself, called in the *Rule* 'House of holiness for Israel' (VIII, 5) and 'House of perfection and truth in Israel' (VIII, 9). In the *Hymns* it is compared to a 'fabric' founded on rock (VI, 25-7; VII, 8-9). This Community built by the Teacher of Righteousness (*Commentary on Psalm XXXVII*, see above, p. 272) gathers together the elect for the 'end of days', the eschatological period which has already begun.

written in the Book of (3) [Moses, *In the sanctuary, O Adonai,*] *which Thy hands have established, Yah[w]eh will reign for ever and ever.*[1] It is the House into which will enter (4) [neither the ungodly nor the defiled], ever; neither the Ammonite, nor the Moabite,[2] nor the half-breed,[3] nor the stranger,[4] nor the sojourner, ever, but they that are called saints. (5) Yah[w]eh [will reign (there) for] ever; He will appear above it constantly, and strangers will lay it waste no more as they formerly laid waste (6) the sanctua[ry of I]srael because of their sin. And He has commanded a sanctuary (made by the hands) of man to be built for Himself, that there may be some in this sanctuary to send up the smoke of sacrifice in His honour (7) before Him among those who observe the Law.[5]

And concerning that which He said to David, *I* [*will give*] *thee* [*rest*] *from all thine enemies* (2 Sam. vii. 11b), (the explanation of this) is that He will give them[6] rest from al[l] (8) the sons of Belial who will seek to cause them to stumble that they may destroy them and [swallow] them [up], just as they came with a plot of [Be]l[ia]l to cause the s[ons] (9) of ligh[t] to stumble and to devise wicked plots against them, deli[vering] his [s]oul to Belial in their wi[cked] straying.[7]

---

[1] Quotation from Exod. xv. 17c-18; this is why I have completed the phrase with the words, 'in the Book of Moses' at the beginning of line 3.

[2] Cf. Deut. xxiii. 4 (English Bible: xxiii. 3).

[3] Cf. Deut. xxiii. 3 (English Bible: xxiii. 2).

[4] Cf. Ezek. xliv. 9. — Cf. *Hymns*, VI, 27.

[5] In this phrase, the interpretation of the two Hebrew words *miqdash 'ādām* is uncertain. If it is translated, as here, 'a sanctuary (made by the hands) of man' — this is ALLEGRO's translation ('a man-made sanctuary') — the allusion is, of course, to a material sanctuary: we may think of the sanctuary of the future Jerusalem, where undefiled sacrifice will be offered to God once more, or to a sanctuary which the Essenes may have erected at Qumran itself. But it may also be taken to mean 'a sanctuary of men' — a spiritual sanctuary, a sanctuary 'built in men' — and the whole phrase be translated, 'And He has commanded a sanctuary of men to be built for Himself, that in this sanctuary may be sent up, as smoke of sacrifice in His honour (7) before Him, the works of the Law'; cf. Eph. ii. 19-22, and 1 Pet. ii. 4-5. On the sect's attitude to sacrifice, see *Rule*, IX, 3-5, and my note 1 on p. 93.

[6] The sons of light, the members of the sect.

[7] An allusion to the maltreatment of the members of the sect by their persecutors; to 'cause them to stumble' does not mean, 'to cause them to waver in their faith', as some writers have tried to explain with regard to the *Commentary on Habakkuk* (XI, 8), but as line 8 clearly shows, to try to destroy them. The words 'deli[vering] his [s]oul to Belial' are difficult to interpret. First of all, who is the person referred to? Whereas the plural has been used until now (applying to all the members of the sect in general), we have here the singular — in Hebrew, *nafshō*, 'his soul': (it can also be translated, 'delivering *him* to Belial'). Does this enigmatic singular allude to the Teacher of Righteousness, the leader of the Community, as Allegro suggests? For my own part, I do not see how it can be explained otherwise. The Teacher is once described in the *Hymns* (VII, 10) in the same way, with the same discretion and mystery. The Pythagoreans, it should be remembered, used simply *autos*, 'he', when mentioning their teacher; from a similar concern, the Essenes also forbore to pronounce the name of their teacher. Though they usually refer to him as the 'Teacher of Righteousness', the simple 'he' (or 'himself') was enough to describe him. If, therefore, this passage alludes to the Teacher, what do the words 'delivering him to Belial' mean? As Allegro again suggests, I think they should be con-

(**10**) [*And*] *Yahweh* [*de*]*clares to thee that He will build thee a house; and I will raise up thy seed after thee, and I will establish his royal throne* (**11**) [*for ev*]*er. I wi*[*ll be*] *a father to him and he shall be my son.* (2 Sam. vii. 11c, 12b-c, 13, 14a)

This is the Branch of David[1] who will arise with the Seeker of the Law[2] and who (**12**) will sit on the throne of Zion at the end of days; as it is written, *I will raise up the tabernacle of David which is fallen.*[3] This tabernacle (**13**) *of David which is fallen* (is) he who will arise to save Israel.[4]

(**14**) In[ter]pretation of *Blessed is the man who has not walked in the counsel of the wicked.* (Ps. i. 1)

The explanation of this word concerns those who have departed from the way [of ungodliness]; (**15**) as it is written in the book of the prophet Isaiah concerning the end of days, *And then when* [*the* (*divine*) *Hand seized* (*me*), *He removed me from walking in the way of*] (**16**) *this people.*[5] And they of whom it is written in the book of the prophet Ezekiel, *The Lev*[*ites who strayed far from me to follow*] (**17**) *their* [*i*]*dols,*[6] they are the sons of Zadok who se[ek their own] counsel[7] and fol[low the works of] their [han]ds[8] outside the Council of the Community.

[1] This expression, which we have already encountered in the *Commentary on Isaiah* (see p. 274), and which we shall meet again in the 'Patriarchal Blessings' (see p. 315), obviously alludes to the Davidic Messiah, the King-Messiah; it is taken from Jer. xxiii. 5; xxxiii. 15 (cf. Zech. iii. 8; vi. 12).

[2] i.e. the Teacher of Righteousness, as in the *Damascus Document* (VI, 7; VII, 18). A very important passage concerning the return of the Teacher of Righteousness at the end of time; it confirms the assertion appearing in the *Damascus Document*, 'Until the coming of the Teacher of Righteousness at the end of days'.

[3] Quotation from Amos ix. 11. The same quotation appears in *Damascus Document*, VII, 16, but there, curiously enough, the 'tabernacle of David' is the Law.

[4] The same function is attributed to the Branch of David in Jer. xxiii. 6: 'In his days, Judah will be saved and Israel will dwell securely' (cf. Jer. xxxiii. 16). Cf. Luke xxiv. 21: 'We had hoped that he (Jesus) was the one to redeem Israel. . . .'

[5] Quotation from Isa. viii. 11.

[6] Quotation from Ezek. xliv. 10.

[7] The 'sons of Zadok' alluded to here are either the Sadducees proper, the enemies of the members of the Covenant, or those sectaries (cf. *Damascus Document*, IV, 3-4) who were insubordinate and unfaithful (cf. *Damascus Document*, B, II, 8-13).

[8] 'The works of their hands' are their idols (in the figurative sense, as in *Rule*, II, 11, 17, i.e. whatever causes them to fall into sin). But the restoration of these two words is very uncertain, as is also the preposition 'outside'.

---

sidered parallel to the formula of excommunication appearing in 1 Cor. v. 5: '(I have decided) to deliver this man to Satan for the destruction of his body'; cf. 1 Tim. i. 20: 'I have delivered these men to Satan.' We would then learn from this passage that the Teacher of Righteousness was excommunicated by his enemies, the leaders of the official Synagogue; this would cause us little surprise given the Teacher's radical opposition to this body. On the penal level, excommunication pronounced by the High Priest, the leader of the nation, could have only the gravest consequences; the present passage is obviously to be added to all the others in the various Commentaries alluding to the persecution of the Teacher of Righteousness by the Wicked Priest and to the punishment which he suffered.

(**18**) [*Why*] *are the nations* [*in tumult*] *and why do the peoples* [*plot in vain?*
The kings of the earth] *rise up* [*and the pr*]*inces take counsel together against
Yahweh and against* (**19**) [*His Anointed*]. (Ps. ii. 1-2)

[The ex]planation of this word [is that the kings of the na]tions [will
rise against] the elect of Israel at the end of days; **II** (**1**) that is, at the
time of trial which will co[me upon them . . .][1]

(**2**) of Belial, and a re[mnant] will be left [. . .]

(**3**) Moses, that is, the [. . .]

. . . .

The work provisionally called *The Patriarchal Blessings* is only
known to us at present from a small fragment seven lines long,
nearly all of them incomplete, relating to the famous chapter xlix
from Genesis in which Jacob predicts to each of his twelve sons the
destiny of the tribe of which he is the ancestor, and more precisely,
the oracle concerning Judah. The published fragment[2] is a commentary on verse 10; I give a literal translation of this verse after the
Masoretic Text.[3]

> *The sceptre shall not be taken from Judah
> nor the commander's staff from between his feet
> until Shiloh comes,
> to whom the obedience of the peoples is due.*

This biblical quotation does not appear in our fragment but must
have been given at the end of the preceding column where it was
probably followed by the usual introduction, 'The explanation of
this is that . . .'. I translate the text of this piece as follows:

. . . .

[The explanation of this is that] (**1**) a monarch will [not] be wanting
to the tribe of Judah[4] when Israel rules, (**2**) [and] a (descendant) seated on
the throne will [not] be wanting to David.[5] For *the* (*commander's*) *staff* is the
Covenant of kingship,[6] (**3**) [and] the *feet* are [the Thou]sands of Israel.

---

[1] Same expression in the fragment of the second *Commentary on Psalm XXXVII* (see above,
p. 273).

[2] See *JBL*, lxxv, 1956, pp. 174-6.

[3] In this text, as everyone knows, the word 'Shiloh' is particularly enigmatic; the
versions give differing variants. We do not know exactly what reading was adopted by the
Essene commentator.

[4] This can also be translated 'to the sceptre of Judah'; the author appears to be playing
on the double meaning of the Hebrew word *shebeṭ* ('sceptre' or 'tribe').

[5] Quotation from Jer. xxxiii. 17 (the text is a little different).

[6] In the *Damascus Document* (VI, 7) on the other hand, we read 'The rod is the Seeker
of the Law' (i.e. the Teacher of Righteousness); but there a different biblical passage is
interpreted.

Until the Messiah of Righteousness comes, the Branch (4) of David;[1] for to him and to his seed has been given the Covenant of the kingship of his people for everlasting generations, because (5) he has kept [. . .] the Law with the members of the Community. For (6) [. . .] is the synagogue of the men [of mockery . . .][2]

. . . .

This piece is very valuable because it shows us the biblical texts on which the Essene community based its hope in the coming of a King-Messiah, a Davidic Messiah who would liberate Israel and ensure her everlasting dominion. Another document called *Testimonia*[3] throws new light on the messianic beliefs of the sect. It consists of a simple sheet of leather, measuring roughly 9 in. long and 6 in. wide, and contains thirty lines of script; this sheet was independent and did not form part of a scroll. The document has reached us whole, except for a small fragment whose disappearance deprives us of the beginning of lines 25 and 29. The text is clearly divided into four sections which are indicated not only by a blank on the last line of each section, but also by a sign in the shape of a hook inscribed in the margin at the beginning of each new section.

The first three sections consist entirely of biblical quotations; the fourth is also a quotation, but one taken from an apocryphal book of the sect called the *Psalms of Joshua*, the remains of which have equally been found in cave IV. Here is the translation of this curious document.

(1) And Adonai[4] spoke to Moses in these words:
Thou hast heard the words (2) which this people have spoken to thee; all they have said is good. (3) Ah, if only they could have this same heart to fear me and

---

[1] This double expression is inspired by Jer. xxiii. 5: 'I will raise up for David a *righteous Branch*; he shall reign as true king, and he shall have understanding; and he shall execute law and justice upon the earth.' Cf. xxxiii. 15: 'I will cause a *Branch of Righteousness* to spring forth for David, and he shall execute law and justice upon the earth.' The expression 'Messiah of Righteousness' is obviously connected with this passage; it calls to mind the expression 'Teacher of Righteousness', common at Qumran, and 'Elect of Righteousness', in the Similitudes of *Enoch*. As for 'Branch of David', this appears in two other fragments (see above, p. 313, n. 1).

[2] 'The synagogue of the men [of mockery]' is no doubt the official Synagogue, the enemy of the sect. That it is mentioned here to explain the two last words of the biblical quotation, which are usually translated 'the obedience of the peoples', shows either that the commentator understood the words quite differently, or that he had another text.

[3] Published in *JBL*, lxxv, 1956, pp. 182-7, and plate.

[4] In place of the divine tetragrammaton (YHWH), the text has here, as also below in line 19 and in a few other Qumran manuscripts, a row of four dots; this was probably read 'Adonai' as in the *Qere* of the Masoretic Text.

keep all (4) *my commandments always, to be happy, they and their children, for ever!*[1] (5) *I will raise up from among their brethren a prophet like thee. I will put my words* (6) *into his mouth and he shall say all that I will command him. Whoever* (7) *will not listen to my words which this prophet shall utter in my name, I myself will* (8) *call him to account.*[2]

(9) *And he*[3] *spoke his oracle in these words. 'Oracle of Balaam son of Beor, and oracle of the man* (10) *whose eye is perfect; oracle of him who hears the words of God and has knowledge of the Most High, who* (11) *gazes on the vision of the Almighty, who falls down and his eye is uncovered. I see him but not now;* (12) *I behold him but not near. A star has journeyed from Jacob and a sceptre has risen out of Israel, and he shall crush* (13) *the temples of Moab and overthrow all the sons of Sheth.'*[4]

(14) *And of Levi he*[5] *said: 'Give to Levi thy Thummim and thy Urim, to thy follower whom* (15) *thou didst try at Massah and with whom thou didst quarrel at the waters of Meribah; who said to his father* (16) *and mother, "I know thee not", and who knew not his brothers and knew not his children.* (17) *For he has kept thy word and observed thy Covenant. And they shall cause thy ordinances to shine for Jacob,* (18) *and thy Law for Israel; they shall set incense in thy nostrils and whole burnt offerings upon thine altar.* (19) *Bless, O Adonai, his might, and be pleased with the work of his hands. Crush the loins of his adversaries and enemies* (20) *that they may rise no more.'*[6]

(21) When Joshua had finished offering praise and thanksgiving with his psalms, (22) he said:
'Cursed be the man who builds that city!
At the cost of his first-born (23) *shall he found it,*
and at the cost of his youngest shall he set up its gates.[7]
Behold, an accursed man, a (fiend) of Belial,
(24) will arise to be a fow[ler's n]et to his people
and destruction to all his neighbours.
And [his sons] will arise (25) [on that d]ay
[that they] both may be instruments of violence.
And they will rebuild the (26) [city of Jerusalem]
[and will s]et up for it a wall and towers
to make it a stronghold of ungodliness.
(27) [And they will commit crimes] in Israel
and a horrible thing in Ephraim,
and in Judah (28) [. . .]
[And they will com]mit a profanation in the land
and a great shame among the children (29) [of Israel].

[1] Quotation from Deut. v. 28-9.   [2] Quotation from Deut. xviii. 18-19.
[3] Balaam.   [4] Quotation from Num. xxiv. 15-17.
[5] Jacob.   [6] Quotation from Deut. xxxiii. 8-11.
[7] Quotation from Joshua vi. 26. Note that after 'that city', the Masoretic Text adds 'Jericho'; but this word is absent from the Septuagint. Its omission makes it easier to apply this biblical verse to the city of Jerusalem.

[And they will shed blo]od like water
on the ramparts of the daughter of Zion
and within the precincts (30) of Jerusalem.'

The biblical quotations constituting the first three sections of this document are manifestly related to the triple aspect of messianic expectation among the Qumran sectaries — expectation of the Prophet at the end of time, of the lay Messiah, and of the priestly Messiah. This triple aspect is clearly expressed in this short phrase from the *Rule* (IX, 10-11): '. . . until the coming of the Prophet of the Anointed of Aaron and Israel'.[1] In this text, the 'Prophet' is without doubt the supreme Prophet, the Prophet 'similar to Moses' promised to Israel in Deut. xviii. 18; that is to say, in the same passage that figures in the first section of our *Testimonia*. As for the 'Anointed of Aaron and Israel', they correspond to the two 'Anointed' of the celebrated vision of Zech. iv. 1-14, the High Priest and the lay leader; this page from Zechariah is certainly at the basis of the doctrine of the two Messiahs — the Messiahs of Aaron and Israel — elaborated by the sect. In the Qumran writings the 'Messiah of Israel', i.e. the lay Messiah, the King-Messiah, is also called 'the Prince of the Congregation': it is to him that the sceptre belongs, and the *Damascus Document* (VII, 20-1) expressly applies to him the text from Num. xxiv. 17 quoted in the second section of the *Testimonia*.

This document, in its first three sections anyway, appears as a small collection of fundamental biblical texts, or 'testimonies', relating to messianic beliefs. Allegro has correctly compared it to the collections of *testimonia* which scholars have for some time recognized as having been used in the writings of the primitive Church. The first section of the Qumran document juxtaposes and combines two different passages from Deuteronomy, a method of composite quotation found also in the New Testament. It should be noted that the text from Deuteronomy referring to 'the Prophet similar to Moses' (xviii. 18) is applied to Jesus in Acts iii. 22.

As I have said, the whole of the fourth section is a quotation from the *Psalms of Joshua*, an apocryphal book of the sect. This text alludes to three accursed people, a father and his two sons, who were guilty of committing acts of gravest wickedness in Jerusalem and the Holy Land. I will show later that these allusions have, in my view, a very

---

[1] See above, p. 94, n. 3.

precise relevance and are directed to specific historical persons, contemporaries and adversaries of the Teacher of Righteousness and his
sect. An essential question is why the Essene writer should have
copied, on the same page and following the messianic *testimonia*, the
passage from the *Psalms of Joshua* calling down curses on the sinister
trio and stigmatizing their abominable deeds. Allegro has shrewdly
noticed that in the first three sections each of the messianic *testimonia*
ends with a threat against the unbelievers and enemies who would
rise against the Prophet, the predicted Messiah: '*Whoever will not
listen to my words which this prophet shall utter in my name, I myself will
call him to account*'; '*He shall crush the temples of Moab and overthrow all
the sons of Sheth*'; '*Crush the loins of his adversaries and enemies that they may
rise no more*'. If there is some coherence in our document between the
quotation from the *Psalms of Joshua* and the biblical quotations preceding it, it consists precisely in this, I think, that the three accursed
persons upon whom the menaces of the biblical texts fall are really
the enemies of the Prophet, of the double Messiah to whom these
texts refer — they are, that is to say, 'antichrists'.

But if the three wicked men — who, as I will show later, were in
fact the enemies of the Teacher of Righteousness — were considered
'antichrists', must it not be accepted that the Teacher himself was
thought to be the Prophet, the Messiah foretold by Scripture? This
curious work would then prove that the Teacher of Righteousness
was venerated as the supreme hero of the eschatological age, as one
endowed with the triple quality of Prophet, lay Messiah and priestly
Messiah; the faith of his followers transferred to his august person
the various messianic functions formerly attributed to three separate
characters.[1] I would mention that the historian Josephus made the
Hasmonaean High Priest, John Hyrcanus, the beneficiary of a similar
transference of powers. 'He was the only one', Josephus writes, 'to
unite three great advantages: the government of his nation, the
sovereign pontificate, and the gift of prophecy.'[2]

The messianic beliefs of the Qumran sect are really very complex;
they did not remain fixed and immutable for two centuries. In fact
they appear in the Qumran texts in a variety of forms testifying to

---

[1] The hymn preserved in the *Testaments of the Twelve Patriarchs* (Testament of Levi,
XVIII) testifies, in my view, to the same process of messianization of the Teacher of
Righteousness: see my *Nouveaux Aperçu* . . .) pp. 78-84 (Eng. edn., pp. 51-7.)
[2] *War*, I, 2, 8, § 68. Cf. *Antiquities*, XIII, 10, 7, §§ 299-300: 'He had already been
judged worthy by God of the three highest favours: power over his people, the office of
High Priest, and gift of prophecy.'

numerous experiments and considerable evolution. Although the Teacher of Righteousness was *at times* considered the one complete Messiah, the 'Anointed of Aaron and Israel', *at others* he was, I think, recognized as the sacerdotal Messiah only — the office of lay Messiah, King-Messiah, being then relegated to a person still to come. In a matter such as this, there was room for speculation of every sort within the Essene sect, speculation which varied according to circumstances and according to the inspiration of their great prophets and doctors. At the present time the scholar can do no more than suggest a provisional outline; he must principally set out to uncover the messianic doctrine contained in every published writing and fragment. Only when he has all the documents at his disposal, and has succeeded, if this is possible, in classifying them chronologically, can he attempt to draw an overall picture of the multiple aspects and evolution of messianic belief in the sect of Qumran.

CHAPTER XI

FRAGMENTS OF APOCALYPTICAL, LITURGICAL AND OTHER WRITINGS

Apocalypse of Pseudo-Daniel. − Prayer of Nabonidus. − Other apocalyptical fragments; *The Book of Mysteries.* − *A Description of the New Jerusalem.* − Fragments of liturgical writings; *Angelic Liturgy; Prayer for the Feast of Weeks.* − Fragments of hymnic, sapiential and juridical writings; *mishmaroth*; horoscopes; fragments in cryptic script.

The Essenes in their harsh solitude at Qumran directed all their thought towards the invisible realities; they were avid for visions, revelations and apocalypses. In that inhuman desert they already lived in the company of the angels, and the heavens opened to reveal to them their hidden mysteries. As we read in the various passages of their writings, they were 'men of vision',[1] 'they who see the angels of holiness, whose ear is opened and who hear profound things'.[2]

They were assiduous readers of the book of Daniel, that great apocalyptical work dating from the time of the persecution by Antiochus Epiphanes, whose edifying stories and mysterious visions had supported the faith and hope of the pious of Israel — the Hasidim fighting at the side of Judas Maccabee against the Syrian armies for the establishment of the Kingdom of God. Not only did the author of the *War Rule* visibly draw his inspiration from a passage from Daniel,[3] but vestiges of seven manuscripts of this biblical apocalypse have been found in the Qumran caves.[4] Furthermore, we already know that the *Book of Enoch*, that primary work of all Jewish apocalyptical writings, was one of the sect's great classics (see above, pp. 298 ff.): a dozen or so 'Enochian' manuscripts are represented in the finds from cave IV. But Essene predilection for this apocalyptical genre is shown in many other compositions whose fragments have been recovered from Qumran.

First there are the fragments of three Aramaic manuscripts found in cave IV, the remains of a work unknown till now and thought,

---

[1] *Hymns*, XIV, 7.   [2] *War Scroll*, X, 10-11.   [3] See above, p. 167.
[4] Two from cave I (published in *Qumran Cave I*, nos. 71-2), four from cave IV, and one from cave VI.

like the book of Daniel, to describe the revelations of Daniel, the Jewish seer said to have lived at the time of the Babylonian exile.[1] In this work, Daniel speaks before the king and his courtiers; in a vast historical tableau he relates the whole history of the world from the age of Noah and the Flood to the Hellenistic era, i.e. the author's own time, considered then as the beginning of the eschatological age. In the surviving fragments there are allusions to the capture of Jerusalem by Nebuchadnezzar; to a 'first kingdom' — which, as in Dan. ii. vii, must be the kingdom of Babylon; to a certain 'Balacros' (perhaps the Seleucid king Alexander Balas who reigned from 152-145 B.C.); and to another person with a Greek name (perhaps '[Demet]rios').

These pointers, which are still more or less uncertain, seem to indicate that the author wrote his apocalypse towards the end of the second century B.C., at about the same time as the writing of the Vision of the Animals in *Enoch* (LXXXV-XC) and the Apocalypse of Weeks (XCIII). But this provisional dating will obviously have to be revised if allusions are eventually found in the work relating to the last Seleucid kings or to Roman domination.

Within the same 'pseudo-Danielic' cycle must be included a very strange work, of which five small fragments have been recovered, again from cave IV.[2] Four of them correspond to the beginning of the scroll where the title of the work appears as, 'Words of the prayer spoken by Nabunai, king of the la[nd of Ba]bylon . . .'. Most probably king 'Nabunai' is, as Milik believes, Nabunaid (or Nabonidus), the last king of the neo-Babylonian dynasty (555-539 B.C.). According to this writing, Nabunai stayed in 'Teiman' for seven years; now it is known that Nabonidus was obliged for political reasons to live on the oasis of Teima for seven or eight years. The *Prayer of Nabonidus* is written in Aramaic. The prayer itself was inserted into a narrative written entirely in the first person and thought to have been composed by the king himself. But the text of the prayer has not come down to us; we have little more than the first lines of the first column of the scroll — and these with lacunae —

[1] Some of these fragments have been published by J. T. MILIK in *RB*, 1956, pp. 411-15.
[2] Published by J. T. MILIK in *RB*, 1956, pp. 407-11, with photograph, and 415 (*Addendum*).

together with a minute fragment of some other part of the book. Here is the translation I propose for column I.[1]

I (1) Words of the prayer spoken by Nabunai, king of the la[nd of Ba]bylon, [the great] king, [when he was smitten] (2) with a malignant inflammation by decree of the M[ost High Go]d at Teiman.

[With a malignant inflammation] (3) was I smitten for seven years, and [my] cou[ntenance] (?) no longer resembled that [of the sons of men (?).[2] But I prayed to the Most High God] (4) and an exorcist forgave my sins:[3] it was a Jewish [man], one of [the exiles.[4] He said to me:] (5) 'Tell this in writing[5] to give honour and pr[aise and glory] to the Name of the [Most High] G[od.' And I wrote this.]

(6) 'I was smitten with a mal[ignant] inflammation at Teiman [and my countenance (?) no longer resembled that of the sons of men (?)], (7) For seven years [I] prayed to [all] the gods of silver, gold, [bronze.

---

[1] This translation differs on numerous points from Milik's. His has been adopted with no appreciable alteration by M. BURROWS, *More Light on the Dead Sea Scrolls* (New York, 1958), p. 400, and H. BARDTKE, *Die Handschriftenfunde vom Toten Meer. Die Sekte von Qumran* (Berlin, 1958), p. 301; but it seems to me to require careful revision.

[2] Translation uncertain. MILIK suggests 'And I was banished far [from men]': but the verb ŠWY can scarcely mean 'banish'.

[3] MILIK: '[But when I had confessed my sins] and faults, (God) granted me a diviner.' He corrects LH, 'to him', to LY, 'to me', which is admissible but, as we shall see, certainly unnecessary. In any case the translation '(God) granted me a diviner' seems quite impossible: (1) it obliges us to supply the subject (God) entirely, which is really strange; (2) it gives the very unusual meaning 'to grant' to the verb *shebaq*, 'to abandon, leave'. In the phrase as MILIK understands it, there should be a verb like *yehab* 'to give' or better still *shelah* 'to send'. As for the noun which MILIK translates 'diviner', namely, *gazir*, this word is often found in Daniel where its exact significance is uncertain. It has been translated 'astrologer' and 'haruspex', but the translation 'exorcist' has also been advanced (FURLANI, *Atti della Accademia Nazionale dei Lincei*, 1948, pp. 177 ff.). In the present context this last interpretation seems preferable since there is a question of a sick man to be healed, and in consequence, according to ancient ideas, a man in the clutches of sin and the devil. I take *gazir* to be the subject of the verb *shebaq*, and the first word in the line ('my sins') to be the object of the same verb, which here can only mean 'to pardon, forgive'—a sense fully attested in both Judeo-Aramaic and Syriac. So I translate 'and an exorcist forgave my sins', which is irreproachable linguistically. This formula is to be compared with the one in Mark ii. 5 (also Matt. ix. 2)—'Thy sins are forgiven'. (Note that in the Syriac version of the Gospels, the verb used is, in fact, *shebaq*.) I would add that in the phrase as understood in this sense, the word LH, 'to him, for him', which follows the verb *shebaq*, may simply be an expletive, a usage well known in Aramaic and Hebrew (*dativus ethicus*): if so, there is no point in correcting LH to LY, as MILIK proposes. If, however, it still seems preferable to make this correction, the sentence then reads 'an exorcist forgave *me* my sins' (cf. Luke iv. 20 'Thy sins are forgiven *thee*'). In both cases the meaning remains the same.

[4] Probably Daniel; cf. Dan. v. 13: 'Thou art Daniel, one of the exiles of Judah . . . ?'

[5] Word for word, 'Tell and write . . .'; these two verbs are in the imperative. MILIK reads them in the perfect tense: 'he (the diviner) gave the explanation and reported it in writing . . .'. But the text as a whole suggests that, like Nebuchadnezzar in Dan. iii. 31-iv. 34, it is the king himself, not the diviner, who is going to write the story. Consequently, the end of line 5 should be completed 'And *I* wrote this', not 'And *he* wrote this', and line 7 should be translated '*I* prayed', and not 'thou didst pray'.

iron,] (8) wood, stone, and clay,[1] for [I thou]ght th[ey] were gods[2] [. . .]

. . . .

Unfortunately the rest of the account is missing. Probably king Nabunai, after invoking the false gods in vain, then addressed his prayer to the true God, the Most High God. As a result, a Jewish exorcist — probably Daniel — 'forgave his sins' and in consequence healed his sickness. In line 1 of the small isolated fragment we read, in effect, '. . . and I was healed without them',[3] which should no doubt be understood as 'without the help of the false gods'. On the other hand, in line 4 of the same fragment we read, '[. . . and I said to him,] "How like thou art to. . .".' Perhaps it is at this point in the story that the king begins to realize that the Jewish exorcist who has cured him is the famous Daniel.

Such a story calls to mind the history of king Nebuchadnezzar told in the book of Daniel (iii. 31-iv. 34). For seven years the king is sick and is separated from his people; then he is miraculously cured and proclaims in writing, to the glory of the Most High God, the wonders that have been worked in him. More than one scholar has thought that originally the story concerned Nabonidus, and that his name was later replaced by that of Nebuchadnezzar. Our *Prayer of Nabonidus* doubtless shows that this hypothesis is not entirely without foundation; it proves that in the cycle of legends relating to the wise man Daniel, there was an ancient account identifying the sick king of Babylon, the recluse, with Nabonidus — which is closer to history. It is nevertheless true that the canonical book of Daniel explicitly names Nebuchadnezzar as the hero of the episode and that if there was a substitution it was intentional.[4]

But because the Qumran writing introduces Nabonidus, and in so doing follows a tradition which is at the same time more ancient and accurate, we must not jump to the conclusion that the account of the illness and healing of the king as described in this writing is itself older than the more or less parallel account in Daniel, and that

---

[1] The same enumeration appears in Dan. v. 4, 23 (except for the last word, 'clay').

[2] The phrase must have continued, 'gods that are true, that act, gods that heal'.

[3] And not 'And furthermore, I had a dream' as MILIK translates. The verb 'ḤLMT is here in the *huphal*, from the root ḤLM II, 'to be healthy' (and not ḤLM I, 'to dream').

[4] In Dan. v there is again mention of Nebuchadnezzar; Belshazzar is described, not as the son of Nabonidus but as the son of the Nebuchadnezzar who deported the Jews after the capture of Jerusalem and who was deposed and 'driven from the midst of men' (Dan. v. 11, 13, 18, 22).

it served it as a source, as Milik suggests.[1] On the contrary, the Qumran story, in its present recension anyway, seems to me to be of later date than the book of Daniel. As far as can be judged from the little that remains of it, one has the impression that the author of the *Prayer of Nabonidus* more or less drew his inspiration from various passages of the biblical book, and that his work as such stems from a later phase of the development of the Danielic cycle, the phase of additions and supplements to which belongs, for example, the Prayer of Azariah inserted into Dan. iii. As a literary parallel we may also mention the Prayer of Manasseh, which appears in some manuscripts of the Greek Bible and must be of rather recent date.

Although the story told in the *Prayer of Nabonidus* calls to mind the sickness of Nebuchadnezzar in Daniel, it is in reality distinguished from the latter on more than one point (even apart from the different names given to the central character). Here the king's illness is 'a malignant inflammation', whereas in Daniel he suffers from a sort of madness which causes him to live like an animal. Here the place of retirement is Teiman, whereas in Daniel it is left entirely vague. Here the king invokes first the pagan gods and then the Most High God, but in Daniel there is no mention of any prayers offered by the king. Here the cure is due to the intervention of an exorcist (very probably Daniel), whereas in the biblical book it occurs spontaneously at the end of seven years.

The structure of the two stories is so different that in order to explain what they have in common we can do little else than refer to some distant common source. This source may first have been exploited independently by the biblical writer; he may have substituted Nebuchadnezzar for Nabonidus, and suppressed, in consequence, the mention of Teima (or Teiman), and reshaped the story to his own liking. Later, the author of our *Prayer of Nabonidus*, wishing to rewrite the story of the miraculous cure of the king of Babylon, would have borrowed from ancient tradition the name of Nabonidus and perhaps a few other features as well. From then on, he would have composed a second story which, despite the resemblances, did not contradict the biblical account since there the hero is Nebuchadnezzar.

One of the most original features of the Qumran account is the intervention of an exorcist in the healing of the king. The Essene writer seems to have been entirely responsible for this detail. There

---

[1] *Dix ans de découvertes . . .*, p. 34. (Eng. edn., p. 37.)

is also an account of healing in the *Genesis Apocryphon*; there the sick man is Pharaoh and the healer Abraham. The latter behaves like a genuine exorcist since he cures the king of Egypt, who has been attacked by some purulent malady, by laying his hands on him and expelling the evil spirit (XX, 21-9).[1]

In the *Prayer of Nabonidus*, the healer — who, as I have said, was very likely Daniel — is also an exorcist; he is even given this title in the text.[2] Nothing is said of the way in which this exorcist proceeded; what is remarkable is the formula employed in the narrative, 'and an exorcist forgave my sins'. In the context, a formula such as this is obviously equivalent to 'and this exorcist healed me of my sickness'. In the Synoptic Gospels Jesus says in the same way to the paralytic, 'My child, thy sins are forgiven', meaning that he is cured. As the Scribes are scandalized by such a statement, Jesus explains to them: 'Which is easier to say to the paralytic, "Thy sins are forgiven", or "Arise, take thy pallet and walk"?' And thereupon he ordered the sick man to rise, take up his bed and return to his house.[3]

The comments which the Gospel story attributes to the Scribes on this occasion are particularly instructive: 'How can this man (Jesus) speak so? He blasphemes! Who can forgive sins but God alone?'[4] These comments reflect Pharisaic sentiment; they would have been quite out of place among the Essenes. Our *Prayer of Nabonidus* shows clearly that the Essenes believed that a properly qualified exorcist possessed the power to remit sin, and at the same time expel sickness; Jesus in the Gospel speaks like Daniel in the Qumran writing. Moreover, the *Damascus Document* appears to attribute to the 'overseer' (*mebaqqer*) power to forgive sins within the Essene community. 'He will loose all the chains that bind them ...' (XIII, 10); what chains can these be but the chains of sin?[5] There was therefore doctrinal conflict between the Pharisees and the Essenes with regard to forgiveness of sins; Jesus's declaration is in line with Essene doctrine.

Many other fragments reveal the sectaries' partiality for apocalyptical literature. There is in particular an apocalypse of Michael

---

[1] See above, p. 288, n. 2. [2] See above, p. 322, n. 3, on the word *gazir*.
[3] Mark ii. 1-12 (cf. Matt. ix. 1-8; Luke v. 17-26).
[4] Mark ii. 7 (cf. Matt. ix. 3; Luke v. 21). [5] See above, p. 157, n.4

whose exact title reads, 'Words of the book which Michael spoke to the angels', as well as an apocalypse of jubilees showing affinities, we are told, with chapter XVII of the *Testament of Levi* in the *Testaments of the Twelve Patriarchs*.[1] But so far nothing has been published of these two writings.

Then again, in a number of fragments recovered from the caves there is mention of the heavenly tablets, the tablets on which destiny is inscribed. Here is the translation of one of them written in Aramaic.[2]

. . . .

(1) thy seed, and all the just shall survive and . . . [. . .]
(2) perversity and there shall be no more lies [. . .]
(3) And now take the precious tablets, for [. . .]
(4) [in al]l my afflictions, and whoever shall be brought in [. . .]
(5) [. . .] the tablet . . . [. . .]

. . . .

A fragment such as this is enigmatic in its brevity. To whom is the discourse addressed? To Noah, the hero of the Flood? And is the speaker Enoch himself?[3] In any case, a phrase like 'and there shall be no more lies' brings to mind the end of time when all perversity is to disappear for ever from the world and only the just are to survive. It is the very doctrine expounded in the instruction on the two Spirits in the *Rule* (IV, 18-23):

But in His Mysteries of understanding and in His glorious wisdom
God has set an end for the existence of Perversity,
and at the time of the Visitation He will destroy it for ever.
Then Truth shall arise in the world for ever . . .

This basic theme of Qumran eschatology is taken up and developed in an important work written in Hebrew whose remains have been discovered in cave I[4] and also in cave IV;[5] it has been given the title *Book of Mysteries*. Here is the translation of column I of the principal fragment of this apocalypse, found in cave I.

[1] See above, pp. 354 ff.
[2] Published by M. TESTUZ in *Semitica*, v (Paris, 1955), p. 38 and plate I.
[3] Cf. *Enoch*, LXV.
[4] Published in *Qumran Cave I*, no. 27, plates XXI-XXII.
[5] The fragments found in cave IV derive from at least two manuscripts; cf. *RB*, 1956, p. 61. In addition, fragments have been reported of an Aramaic manuscript reproducing a more or less similar work; cf. ibid., p. 66.

. . . .
I (1) [...] (2) [...] the mysteries of sin
(3) [...] and they (the wicked) have not known the Mystery to come
and have not understood past things,
and they (4) have not known that which would befall them,
and have not saved their soul from the Mystery to come.

(5) But this is the sign for you that (these things) shall come to pass.[1]
When the children of Perversity are shut up,[2]
then Wickedness shall retire before Righteousness
as [da]rkness retires before (6) the light,
and as smoke vanishes and [is] no more,
so shall Wickedness vanish for ever
and Righteousness appear like the sun, the (7) norm of the world.
And all those who hold the marvellous Mysteries (unjustly)[3] shall be no
and Knowledge shall fill the world,   [more;
and then Foolishness shall be no mo[re].
(8) This word is certain to come to pass
and this oracle is truth.
And by this may it be known to you that (this oracle) is beyond recall.[4]
Do not all (9) the peoples hate Perversion?
Yet it is spread by them all.
Does not Truth's praise (issue) from the mouth of all the peoples?
(10) (Yet) is there a lip or tongue that clings to it?
Which nation loves to be oppressed by (one) stronger than itself?
(11) (Yet) which nation has not oppressed another?[5]
Who would wish to see himself stripped of his goods by a criminal?
(Yet) where is there any man who (12) has not stripped [another] of his
                                                                  [goods?

. . . .

All that remains of column II are the beginnings of a few lines
which seem to deal with the fate of the just and the unjust. Here
below, the wicked prosper and the just are unfortunate: how pain-

---

[1] The sign announcing that the time of final and everlasting triumph of God is near:
this sign is the very excess of wickedness itself.
[2] At the end of time, the demons and the wicked, the whole brood of Belial, will be
imprisoned in Hell; cf. *Hymns*, III, 17-18.
[3] An allusion to the story of the evil angels who transmitted the divine secrets to men;
cf. *Enoch* LXV, 6, 11.
[4] The passage which follows describes the deep, and in some way innate, badness of
mankind, the universal rule of perversity and injustice. Even though man may wish to do
good, he inevitably does evil (cf. Rom. vii. 14-24). The universal wickedness reigning
today is the sign that God will soon put an end to it for ever.
[5] In the text, this phrase follows 'Who would wish to see himself stripped of his goods
by a criminal?' The sense invites the rearrangement made here.

ful it is for the good to be aware of this apparent injustice! But this paradoxical situation is only a temporary one; at the end of time everything will be put in order. The sectary waits with feverish impatience for the day when accounts will finally be settled and begs God for signs to assure him that the time is near. This need for signs of the coming of the Day of Judgment is expressed with particular insistence in *4 Ezra*, one of the most important of Jewish apocalyptical works. The angel Uriel is authorized to reveal some of them (V, 1-13): 'As for the signs, behold a time shall come when the inhabitants of the earth shall be seized with great fear. The way of Truth shall be hidden and the place of faith barren. Wickedness shall be greater than thou seest it now, and greater than thou hast heard tell of in times past. . . . Reason shall be seen no more and understanding shall be shut up in its storehouse; many shall seek it and shall not find it. Iniquity and fornication shall multiply upon the earth. One land shall ask another, saying: "Has justice with equity passed in the midst of you?" And the answer shall be: "No." . . . Behold the signs which I have been permitted to discover. . . .'

A passage such as this, and others too, shows remarkable affinities with the part of the *Book of Mysteries* translated above. I would specially draw attention to the idea that human nature bears within itself the principle of evil; the Qumran writing develops this idea by showing that even though his mind conceives goodness and loves it, every man, every nation, in practice abandons itself to evil. The author of *4 Ezra* complains to God of man's sad condition (III, 20-2): '. . . Thou hast not taken away their evil heart that Thy law might bear fruit within them. For it is because of having borne this evil heart that Adam, the first one, disobeyed and fell, and also all who are born of him. This frailty has become lasting. The law is in the heart of men but it meets there with evil seed; thus, that which is good has vanished and that which is bad remains.' When all the recovered fragments of the *Book of Mysteries* are known, this Essene apocalypse may appear as one of the sources used by the writer of *4 Ezra*, or at least one from which he took his inspiration.

Another type of apocalypse is represented at Qumran by a work written in Aramaic called *A Description of the New Jerusalem*. About twenty minute fragments have been found in cave I, and fragments probably belonging to the same work have been recovered from caves IV and V, and above all from cave II.[1] To judge by the fragments from caves I and II, the only ones published so far,[2] the work describes the future Temple, giving very precise measurements, and lays down the liturgical laws to be followed there. It is set within the framework of a vision: a heavenly personage, no doubt an angel, reveals the future edifice to the seer, the objects contained there and the cult to be observed. The inspiration for a work such as this undoubtedly springs from the famous vision of the new Temple at the end of the biblical book of Ezekiel (chapters xl-xlviii). It reveals, or confirms, that although the Essenes remained separate from the Temple of Jerusalem, which they considered as having been defiled by the official priesthood, they maintained a profound interest in it and in the cult and, as true 'sons of Zadok', dreamt of a messianic future when, in the new Holy City and in a purified and restored Temple, the elect would celebrate with fervour and punctuality the holy and authentic liturgy of the God of Israel.

Their taste for divine worship is further attested by various liturgical collections whose remains have also been found. In particular, three hundred fragments are reported to have been recovered from cave IV of a manuscript on papyrus giving the set forms of morning and evening prayer for every day of the month.[3] Another manuscript, also from cave IV, is concerned with the liturgy of the sect's baptismal rites,[4] and fragments of a *Liturgy of the Three Tongues of Fire* have been found in caves I and IV.[5]

Besides these, I must mention a work of considerable importance concerning the liturgy of the 'Sabbath burnt offering'; cave IV has restored the fragments of at least four manuscripts of this document. At the moment, only two passages are known,[6] but they both reveal

[1] Among the four scrolls taken from cave XI is an apocalypse reported to be a description of the New Jerusalem.

[2] See *Qumran Cave I*, no. 32, plate XXXI, and *RB*, 1955, pp. 222-45, plates II and III.

[3] Cf. *RB*, 1956, p. 67.   [4] Cf. ibid., p. 66.

[5] See *Qumran Cave I*, no. 29, and *RB*, 1956, p. 64.

[6] These two passages were presented by J. STRUGNELL, one of the members of the team responsible for the publication of the manuscript fragments found in the caves, in his report to the Third International Congress for the Study of the Old Testament at Oxford on September 4th, 1959; the complete text is published in the *Proceedings* of the Congress (*Supplements to Vetus Testamentum*, vii, 1960, pp. 318-45) under the title, 'The Angelic Liturgy at Qumran (4Q Serek Šîrôt 'ôlat haššabbāt)'. The author, whose Oxford paper I heard, has had the kindness to give me a copy of the manuscript sent to the printers so that I could take into account the new Qumran fragments in the present English edition

the very characteristic development of Qumran speculation on the subject of the angels, a development which will cause no surprise since we know, thanks to Josephus (*Jewish War*, II, § 142), that the Essenes were especially proficient in the knowledge of the 'names of the angels'. The two passages in question carry us even further into the world of the heavenly spirits than do the other Qumran writings — already so rich in evidence of the sect's angelology — and disclose their mysterious and ineffable liturgy.

The first passage is a sort of poem on the seven 'Chief Princes' — the title given here to the highest dignitaries in the angelic hierarchy — and on the 'seven words' of blessing to be proffered in favour of all the angels subordinate to them, and in favour of all the perfect on earth who, as members of the sect of the elect, form one society with that of the heavenly beings. Full of grandiloquence and redundancy, this poem seems originally to have consisted of eight stanzas. The first seven were devoted to each of the seven 'Chief Princes', and the eighth to all of them collectively; but the first three stanzas have disappeared, and only a few scraps of the beginning of the eighth remain. In each stanza the formula, 'he shall bless . . . with seven words . . .', occurs three times, but is amplified every time in some new way with variations which, in spite of the inevitable repetition of certain words, show a genuine virtuosity. The structure of the various stanzas is, without being rigorously uniform, remarkably polished and studied, and I have tried to bring this into relief by arranging the translation in verse form.[1]

. . . .
[The fourth] (**17**) among the Chief Princes[2] shall bless in the name of
al[l] that wa[lk in upr]ightness   [the [Ki]ng's maje[sty]
   with [sev]en words of ma[jesty],
and he shall bless the foundations of ma[je]sty
   with seven (**18**) [marvellous] words,

[1] This translation is based on the text of 4Q Sl 39, completed here and there with the help of 4Q Sl 38 and 40, according to the transcription proposed by J. STRUGNELL. I have not had the photographs at my disposal; these are to appear in the publication itself.
[2] The expression is taken from Ezek. xxxviii. 2, 3, xxxix. 1, where it is applied to 'Gog, chief prince of Meshek and Tubal'.

of my book; I am most grateful to him. According to STRUGNELL, the work from which the two passages are taken appears to have as its general title, 'Rule relating to the canticles of the Sabbath burnt offering'. The four manuscripts in which this work survives are provisionally listed as 4Q Sl 37-40 (Sl being an abbreviation of Strugnell).

[and] he shall bless all the god[s¹ that exa]lt [His] tr[ue] knowledge
  with seven words of righteousness
    that (they may obtain) [His g]lo[rious] mercy.

The fifth (**19**) of the [Chief] Prin[ces] shall bless in the name of [all] His
  all who know the Mysteries of the per[fect]ly pure beings   [wonders
  with seven wo[rds] of [His] sublime (**20**) truth,
[and he shall bless] all that are quick to do His will
  with seven marvellous [w]ords;
and he shall bless all who confess Him
  with seven [wor]ds of majesty
    (**21**) that (they may all obtain) marvellous majesty.

The sixth of the Chief Princes shall bless in the name of the Powers of the
  all beings powerful in understanding   [gods
  with the seven (**22**) words of His marvellous Powers,
and he shall bless all that are perfect of way
  with seven marvellous words
    that (they may be) for ever with the (**23**) everlasting beings,
and he shall bless all who hope in Him
  with seven marvellous word[s]
    that (they may obtain) the return of His gracious mercy.

The seventh of the Chief Princes (**24**) shall bless in the name of His
  all the holy among the foundations of Knowledge   [holiness
  with the seven words of [His] marvellous holiness,
and he shall bless all who exalt (**25**) His judgment
  with seve[n] marvellous [wor]ds
    that (they may be) stout shields,
and he shall bless all the predes[tined] of justice
  who praise His glorious kingship [for] everlasting [ages]
    (**26**) with seven marvellous words
      that (they may obtain) eternal bliss.

And all the [Chief] Princes [. . . shall ble]ss [. . .] the [G]od of gods
  in [the name of . . .]
[and] all [the . . .]

. . . .

It is extraordinarily interesting to find in this poem such clear
evidence of the conception of a supreme angelic Heptad. This con-

¹ 'Gods' (*elīm*) signifies here, and also below in lines 21 and 26, as very frequently in
the various Qumran writings, the divine eternal beings, the angels. In line 17, they are
called 'foundations of majesty' (after 4Q Sl 40), or 'founders of majesty' (after 4Q Sl 39).

ception appears in the book of Tobit (xii. 15): 'I am Raphael, one of the seven holy angels that offer the prayers of the saints and stand before the glory of the Holy One.' The *Book of Enoch*, according to its Greek recension anyway, gives the names of the seven angels (XX) and alludes to a group of seven angels in three other passages (LXXXI, 5; LXXXVII, 2; XC, 21). We find the same allusion in the *Testament of Levi* (VIII, 1-2), in the Slavonic *Enoch* (*2 Enoch*, chapter VIII), and also in Rev. (i. 4, 20; iii. 1; iv. 5; viii. 2, 6).

The origin of this angelic Heptad no doubt already appears in Ezek. ix. 2, where six men appear before the prophet, and in the middle a seventh clothed in white linen and carrying in his girdle the writing-case of a scribe. One is inclined to associate this mysterious person with Nabu, the scribe-god, and the whole group of seven men with the seven planetary gods of the Babylonian pantheon.[1] In any case the great angelic Heptad of Jewish apocalyptical tradition shows evident connections with astrological speculation, and more precisely with a representation of the seven planets and the seven heavens. The book of Revelation writes of the seven stars and, at the same time, of the seven angels and seven spirits of God. The 'archons' of Gnosis, to the number of seven, are obviously associated with the seven planets; each is assigned to one of the seven heavens.[2] In the *Hebrew Book of Enoch* (*3 Enoch*) we read of the seven chief angels, the princes of the seven heavens (chapters XVII-XVIII); each has under his command 496,000 myriads of angels. The Qumran fragment on the seven 'Chief Princes' does not explicitly associate them either with the seven planets or with the seven heavens but testifies to an already very advanced stage in the evolution of an angelological doctrine

One other feature of the poem on the seven chief princes needs to be emphasized, namely the accent laid, with reference to the angelic world, on the idea of Knowledge (see lines 18, 19, 21, 24). In the *Hymns* (III, 22) the angels are similarly called 'spirits of Knowledge'. As a matter of fact, the idea of Knowledge, Gnosis, impregnates the whole of Qumran thought and mysticism, as I have shown above (p. 46). As some writers guessed earlier, the Essene sect even appears to have been the initial source of that mysticism and

[1] Cf. W. BOUSSET, *Die Religion des Judentums im späthellenistischen Zeitalter* (Tübingen, 3rd edn., 1926), p. 325.

[2] Cf. H. CH. PUECH, art. Archontiker, in *Reallexicon für Antike und Christentum*, i (1950), cols. 633 ff.

Jewish esotericism which developed so remarkably during the Middle Ages, particularly in the Kabbala.

Now the very earliest Jewish mysticism was, as Professor G. G. Scholem has emphasized, the mysticism of the Throne, or divine Chariot, the mysticism of *Merkabah*. 'The throne-world is to the Jewish mystic what the *pleroma*, the "fullness", the bright sphere of divinity with its potencies, aeons, archons and dominions is to the Hellenistic and early Christian mystics of the period who appear in the history of religion under the names of Gnostics and Hermetics. The Jewish mystic, though guided by motives similar to theirs, nevertheless expresses his vision in terms of his own religious background. God's pre-existing throne, which embodies and exemplifies all forms of creation, is at once the goal and the theme of his mystical vision.'[1] Professor Scholem has even suspected that the beginnings of the Jewish *Merkabah* mysticism may go back to the Essenes.[2] The second fragment which I am to present brings unexpected confirmation to this way of thinking, since it is none other than a description of the divine Chariot; the description is, of course, based on Ezek. i. x, but it is enriched with several new features, thereby showing that the divine Chariot was already a chosen theme of meditation among the Essenes. Here is the translation of the passage.[3]

. . . .

(2)[. . . the Minis]ters of the glorious Face[4] in the Abo[de of the God] of Knowledge fall do[wn] before the [Cheru]bim[5] and utter bl[ess]ings

---

[1] G. G. SCHOLEM, *Major Trends of Jewish Mysticism* (London, 1955), p. 44.

[2] op. cit., p. 43.

[3] This translation is based on the text of 4Q Sl 40, 24 (according to the transcription proposed by J. STRUGNELL); it is unsure on certain points, but examination of the photograph of the document will permit improvement here and there.

[4] This expression refers to a higher category of angels, apparently those called the 'Angels of the Face' in *Jubilees* (I, 27), *Enoch* (XL, 2); cf. at Qumran, *Hymns*, VI, 13, and *Book of Blessing* (Q S^b), IV, 23. In the present passage, these angels are distinct from the Cherubim (line 2) and from the 'angels of holiness' (line 4) and from the 'spirits of supreme holiness' (line 5); the 'angels of holiness' are mentioned in *Jubilees* (II, 2; XXXI, 14) and *Enoch* (*passim*), and also in the *War Scroll* (VII, 6; X, 11).

[5] The Cherubim are mentioned in the description of the divine Throne in Ezek. x; they are identical with the four 'living creatures' (*ḥayyōt*) of Ezek. i. According to the translation proposed here, these Cherubim receive the homage of the 'Ministers of the glorious Face'; the latter are therefore inferior to the Cherubim. In 3 *Enoch*, XVIII, we read that every angel 'falls upon his face' in the presence of an angel hierarchically superior. The passage can also be translated '[. . . the Minis]ters of the glorious Face, in the Abo[de of the God] of Knowledge. Before Him the [Cheru]bim fall down', etc. In this case it is the Cherubim, not the Ministers of the Face, that make obeisance. But if, as in the description in Ezekiel, the Cherubim are themselves the supports of the divine Throne, it is difficult to imagine them in an attitude of prostration.

while the sound of the divine wind rises[1] (3) [. . .] and there is a tumult of shouting while their wings cause the sound of the divine [win]d to rise. The Cherubim above the heavens bless the likeness of the Throne of the Chariot[2] (4) [and] acclaim the [majes]ty of the firmament of light beneath the seat of His glory. And when the wheels turn, angels of holiness come and go between (5) His glorious wheels like visions of fire. Spirits of supreme holiness surround them, visions of streams of fire[3] similar to scarlet; and (6) [sh]ining creatures clothed in glorious brocades, many-coloured marvellous garments, more (brilliant) than pure salt, spirits of the living [G]od, unceasingly accompany the glory [of] the (7) marvellous Chariot.[4] And the sound of the wind of blessing (is mingled) with the tumult of their marching, and they praise Holiness while they return on their steps. When they rise, they rise marvellously; and when they alight (8) [and are s]till, the sound of joyous shouting ceases in all the camp of God and also the win[d] of [d]ivine blessing, [and] a voice of praise (9) [. . .] from the midst of all their battalions in [. . . and] all the numbered ones[5] cry out, e[a]ch, each, in [his] pla[ce . . .]

. . . .

A description such as this is assuredly most instructive as regards the history of Jewish speculation on the Throne and the divine Chariot. In the Ethiopian book of *Enoch* (XIV, 18-23; LXI, 10; LXXI, 7-8) and also in the Slavonic *Enoch* (*2 Enoch*, IX) the description essentially concerns the Throne; there is no allusion to the Chariot except for the mention of the *Ophanim*, the Wheels, beside the Cherubim and the Seraphim. In Rev. iv, there is mention of the Throne alone. The *Apocalypse of Abraham*, on the

---

[1] This feature, which recurs in lines 3, 7 and 8, is absent from the Ezekiel account; it is borrowed from the vision of Elijah on Horeb (1 Kings xix. 12).

[2] The expression 'the likeness of the Chariot' appears in 1 Chron. xxviii. 18; and the phrase 'the Throne of the Chariot' in *3 Enoch*, XLVI, 7. Note that the term 'chariot' has no place in Ezekiel, which speaks only of a 'throne'; this throne is described rather as a sort of palanquin borne by the four 'living creatures', but it also owes something to a chariot because it has wheels. Later, Ben Sira (XLIX, 8) speaks explicitly of a Chariot: 'Ezekiel gazed on the vision of glory which the Lord showed him on the Chariot of the Cherubim.' It is also the accepted term (*Merkabah*) in the whole of Jewish tradition.

[3] These 'streams of fire' seem to be taken from the description of the divine Throne given in Dan. vii. 10; but the fire itself, and the scarlet (*hashmal*), come from the description in Ezekiel.

[4] The exact Hebrew text reads, '[of] the Chariots' (MRKBWT). Is this simply a royal plural in place of the singular? Such an interpretation is possible. Nevertheless I would point out that there is mention in the *Testament of Job* (XXXIII, 9) of 'the chariots of the Father' (passage quoted by M. PHILONENKO in *Semitica*, viii, 1958, pp. 48-9), and that in *3 Enoch*, XXIV, the many Chariots of God are described at length.

[5] This expression appears often in the *War Scroll* (II, 4; XII, 8; XIX, 12) where it applies to the members of the sect, the soldiers of the army of the sons of light. Does it refer here also to the sectaries, who, each in his place, join the angels in acclaiming the divine Chariot? Or are these the members of the heavenly host? The lacunae on line 9 do not permit us to answer this question with any certainty.

other hand, speaks explicitly of a Chariot (XVIII, 11-12):[1] '...
Behind the Living Creatures I saw a Chariot with wheels of fire; each
wheel was full of eyes all around, and on the wheels was a throne at
which I gazed. It was covered with fire and fire flowed all round
about it....' In the same way, we read in the *Apocalypse of Moses*
(XXXIII):[2] '...Eve looked towards heaven, and she saw a
Chariot of light approach, drawn by four shining eagles. No man
born from the womb of woman can describe its magnificence nor
look it in the face. Angels went before it. They came to the place
where Adam, your father, stood. Then the Chariot stopped, and
between your father and the Chariot were Seraphim. I see censers of
gold and three gold cups, and the angels come with the incense,
censers, and cups. They blew on them so that the smoke of the incense encompassed the heavens. The angels bowed down and worshipped God, saying, 'O holy Jael! Pardon! He is thy likeness and
the creation of thy holy hands....' This description already shows
great freedom of speculation on the *Merkabah*. The Qumran fragment comes to confirm this evidence; even before the fall of the
Second Temple, the reveries of ancient Jewish Gnosis on this marvellous and fascinating theme had attained a development beyond
all expectation.[3]

Very important also among the liturgical books of the Essenes is
a collection of prayers to be recited at certain feasts: some fragments,
still unpublished, were found in cave IV[4] and others in cave I.[5] In
one of the latter, we read: 'Prayer for the Day of Atonement.
Remem[ber, O A]donai ...' Another gives a fairly extensive part
of a prayer apparently associated with the feast of Weeks (Pentecost).
Here is the translation.

.   .   .   .

I (5) [... Thou wilt distinguish between the jus]t and the unjust
and wilt deliver up the wicked for our ransom
and the tr[ait]ors (6) [for our redemption],[6]

---

[1] The following quotation comes from the German translation by P. RIESSLER in *Alt-
jüdisches Schrifttum ausserhalb der Bibel*, 1928, p. 28.
[2] The following quotation comes from the German translation by P. RIESSLER, op. cit.,
p. 151.
[3] Compare the Qumran fragment with the passages from the *Hebrew Book of Enoch*
(III *Enoch*) concerning the *Merkabah*; on these passages, see H. ODEBERG, *III Enoch or The
Hebrew Book of Enoch* (Cambridge, 1928), pp. 170-4. — The date of III *Enoch* is very much
disputed. Some writers tend to consider it rather recent, but the Qumran fragment
studied here suggests an earlier date — as regards the basic doctrine anyway.
[4] Cf. *RB*, 1956, p. 66.   [5] See *Qumran Cave I*, nos. 34 and 34 *bis*.
[6] Cf. Isa. xliii. 3.

[and Thou wilt smite] unto destruction all them that oppress us.
And we, we shall confess Thy Name for ever
(7) [. . .] since for this Thou hast created us.
And behold, [we say] to Thee,
'Blessed (8) [be Thou, O Adonai . . .]
. . . .

II (1) [. . . Thou hast created] the great heavenly light for the [day]-time
[and the little heavenly light for the night . . .]
(2) [. . .] without transgressing their statutes.
And they all [. . .]
(3) [. . .] and their dominion covers the whole world.
But the seed of man has not heeded
all that Thou hast given him in heritage,
and they have not known Thee (4) [when]ever Thou hast spoken,
and they have done wickedly in all things
and have not heeded Thy very great power.
Therefore Thou hast rejected them,
for Thou lovest not (5) per[versit]y
and the wicked cannot live in Thy presence.
But Thou hast chosen for Thyself a people in the time of Thy good-will,
for Thou hast remembered Thy Covenant.
(6) And Thou hast [appointed] them to be set apart from all the peoples,
as a holy thing, for Thyself,[1]
and Thou hast renewed for them Thy Covenant[2]
(founded) on the vision of Glory[3]
and the words (7) of Thy holy Spirit,
upon the works of Thy hands
and the Writing of Thy Right Hand,[4]
causing them to know the glorious teachings
and everlasting ascensions (8) [. . .]
[and Thou hast raised up] for [the]m a faithful Shepherd[5] [. . .]
. . . .

Very closely related to this kind of prayer are the religious hymns.
Besides the scroll of the *Hymns* studied earlier (chapter VI), the

[1] An obvious reference to Israel; but to the real Israel, the sect.
[2] The idea of a renewal, or restoration, of the Covenant appears also in the *Book of Blessings* (III, 26; V, 21), and the concept of an eschatological Renewal, in the *Rule* (IV, 25) and the *Hymns* (XIII, 11-12). Moreover, the sect actually called itself 'the Covenant', and the 'New Covenant'.
[3] The vision of God on Sinai; cf. Exod. xxiv. 16-17.
[4] The tables of the Law written by the hand of God; cf. Exod. xxxii. 16.
[5] The Teacher of Righteousness (cf. *Damascus Document*, I, 11). The lacuna can also be restored 'And thou wilt raise up' (instead of 'And thou hast raised up'). There would then be a question of the expectation of the Davidic Messiah.

Qumran caves I,[1] II and IV, have restored the remains of several other collections. To these must be added the *Psalms of Joshua*, fragments of which have been found in cave IV; a quotation from this work appears in *Testimonia* (see above, pp. 315 ff.). Despite the fact that so far no trace of them has been found at Qumran, I must also mention the famous *Psalms of Solomon*, whose ideas and style betray, in my opinion, their Essene origin, and a curious collection of five psalms attributed to David whose affinities with the Qumran *milieu* seem equally incontestable; these have been preserved in Syriac.[2]

Nor was the so-called 'Wisdom' literature absent from the Qumran library. Cave I has yielded a few remains of a sapiential work;[3] another manuscript of the same work is represented by some important fragments from cave IV. In the latter cave, moreover, fragments — some of them very extensive — have been found of four manuscripts of a sapiential work perhaps identical with the preceding one, as well as the vestiges of four or five other manuscripts of an equally sapiential character. In addition, I would point out that another manuscript of the same nature contains a series of beatitudes addressed to those who observe the commandments, together with a description of the torments reserved to the wicked.[4]

Besides the Code of the *Damascus Document*, juridical literature from cave IV is represented by collections of ordinances whose fragments, corresponding to four different manuscripts, will teach us more about Essene *halakhah*. To them must be joined a collection of sentences pronounced by the sect's tribunal on specified persons: the names of these persons are given as well as the offences imputed to them.

A group of manuscripts from cave IV is of particular value to the study of the Essene calendar. These manuscripts, to which Milik has given the name *mishmaroth* ('service duties'), deal with the weekly

---

[1] See *Qumran Cave I*, nos. 36-40.

[2] The Syriac text of these psalms will be found with translation and commentary in the study of M. NOTH, 'Die fünf syrisch überlieferten apocryphen Psalmen' in *ZAW*, 1930, pp. 1-23. As far back as 1952 I recognized the Qumran character of this small collection, and some time ago invited Marc PHILONENKO to examine it from this point of view; while waiting for his work to appear (in *Semitica*, ix), M. DELCOR's 'Cinq nouveaux psaumes esséniens?' may be consulted in *RQ*, no. 1 (July 1958), pp. 85-102.

[3] Published in *Qumran Cave I*, no. 26.   [4] Cf. *RB*, 1956, pp. 64-5, 67.

service of the sacerdotal families; several of them establish a synchronism between this weekly service, the religious calendar of the sect (a solar calendar consisting of twelve months of thirty days, plus one day per term, i.e. a total of 364 days), and another calendar of the lunar-solar type (consisting of twelve months of twenty-nine and thirty days alternately, i.e. a total of 354 days — plus one intercalary month of thirty days every three years). It also gives the list of the various yearly liturgical feasts in relation to the priests' weekly turn of office.[1]

To all these documents so different in character must be added a Hebrew work found in cave IV containing horoscopes:[2] strangely enough, the script in this work runs from left to right, and not, as is the rule in Hebrew, from right to left. Essene partiality for cryptic scripts is revealed in various manuscripts from caves II and IV which testify to the use of several secret alphabets. One of these manuscripts contains astronomical observations; another has for its title, '[Words] of the man of understanding addressed by him to all the sons of the dawn'; and another, 'Interpretation of the Book of Moses'.[3]

This survey gives some idea of the variety and abundance of the writings in the Qumran library. When all its remaining fragments are at last published, how much new light they will throw on the peculiarities of the mysterious Essene sect!

[1] See J. T. MILIK, *Dix ans de découvertes . . .*, pp. 71-3. (Eng. edn., pp. 108-11.)
[2] Already reported above, p. 52. On this work, still unpublished, see MILIK, op. cit., pp. 38, 78-9. (Eng. edn., pp. 42, 119.)
[3] Cf. *RB*, 1956, p. 61.

CHAPTER XII

THE HISTORICAL BACKGROUND OF THE WRITINGS FROM QUMRAN

The problem; the various opinions. — 1 . The Kittim. — 2. The Wicked Priest.

In the preceding chapters, particularly those devoted to the *Damascus Document* and the biblical Commentaries, I have several times expressed my opinion on a fundamental problem constantly met by interpreters of the new texts — the problem of the chronological framework, of the historical environment in which the persons and events mentioned in the texts are situated. This is a matter of some difficulty because, as I have already explained, the style of these Essene books is generally sibylline and content to make more or less ambiguous allusions to people and events. Given this deliberate obscurity, it is not very surprising that present-day historians find themselves somewhat perplexed: they are faced with a complex ensemble of allusions and enigmas to which they have to find the key.

As early as 1950, when I suggested that the Qumran sect should be identified as the Essenes described in the first century A.D. by Philo of Alexandria, Flavius Josephus and Pliny the Elder, I felt able to maintain as an hypothesis that the basic events referred to in the *Commentary on Habakkuk* and the *Damascus Document* took place in the first century B.C. The Teacher of Righteousness, I explained, began his ministry towards the end of the second century B.C.; this ministry continued during the whole of the reign of Alexander Jannaeus (103-76 B.C.) and during the reign of Alexandra (76-67 B.C.). It was during the dramatic period of the war between the two sons of Jannaeus, Hyrcanus II and Aristobulus II (67-63 B.C.), in a violent persecution directed against the sect, that the Teacher was condemned and executed and the sectaries, shortly before the capture of Jerusalem by Pompey (63 B.C.), fled to the land of Damascus. This Damascus exile lasted during the whole of the pontificate of Hyrcanus II (63-40 B.C.), then the sect resettled in Judaea, and in particular in Qumran. About a hundred years later, at the time of the great Jewish War (A.D. 66-70), the Essenes again left their home in Qumran after hiding their sacred books in the near-by caves.

This was a first attempt to place the newly discovered documents as exactly as possible, in spite of the mystery surrounding their historical indications. It opened the way to a number of similar attempts, and a great many other hypotheses were then advanced. Some writers, for instance, maintained that the Qumran sect was posterior in time to the birth of the Christian Church. G. Vermes, for example, suggested A.D. 100;[1] G. R. Driver, the sixth century;[2] Zeitlin, the ninth; and P. R. Weiss, the time of the Crusades! Today these various hypotheses are definitely ruled out; the archaeological excavations carried out at Khirbet Qumran between 1951 and 1958 make it quite clear that the Jewish community responsible for the manuscripts found in the caves abandoned its settlement on the shores of the Dead Sea at the time of the great Jewish War, or more exactly — as Father R. de Vaux has established as being very probable — in June A.D. 68. So this was when the scrolls were concealed; which obviously fixes a *terminus ad quem* for the copying of the manuscripts and, *a fortiori*, for the redaction of the works.

But the excavations, by themselves, do not permit us to determine with certainty the *terminus a quo*, and all sorts of theories are possible. Coins found on the site of Qumran suggest, it is true, that the community did not begin to establish itself there until about the end of the second century B.C., and that except for a temporary absence whose date and precise duration are difficult to determine archaeologically, it remained there until the great Jewish War. But I readily admit that this fact does not exclude the possibility that the sect may have existed prior to its settlement at Qumran, and that certain of its writings may refer essentially to events which took place during this earlier period. In point of fact, even taking into account only those conforming to the archaeological conclusions, opinions are still very varied. For some, the historical background is essentially the *pre-Maccabaean* period prior to 168 B.C.; for others, the *Maccabaean* (or *Hasmonaean*) epoch, between 168 and 63 B.C.; for others still, the *Roman* period, from 63 B.C. onward. And what a number of candi-

---

[1] In his book entitled *Les manuscrits du désert de Juda* (1953; in English: *Discovery in the Judean Desert*, 1956) this author has developed the theory of a pre-Christian (Maccabaean) origin.

[2] This writer, having abandoned his first hypothesis, now places the history of the Qumran sect in the first century A.D., and identifies the sectaries as Zealots.

dates there are to the title 'Wicked Priest': Menelaus, Alcimus, Jonathan, Simon, John Hyrcanus, Alexander Jannaeus, Hyrcanus II, Joezer ben Boethus, etc.!

Faced with so many contrary views, must we yield to scepticism, as some do, and give up the idea of any precise hypothesis? I do not think so. At the beginning certain writers, more preoccupied with denominational apologetics than with historical truth, invented a chronological system which would have, before all else, what was to them the advantage of excluding all possibility of Jewish influence on primitive Christianity. But now that it is established that, whatever the exact date of the ministry of its founder the Teacher of Righteousness, the Jewish community was indisputably present in Judaea at the time of the birth of Christianity, preoccupation of this kind is pointless. Nevertheless, although it has become less acute the problem of the historical background to the Qumran writings still remains extremely important and deserves to be examined with the greatest care. Now that several texts have been published which were unavailable at the start of research, it seems opportune to return to this inquiry once more in order to see, by the light of these other texts, whether my initial hypothesis is still tenable or should be discarded. Let me say immediately that in fact it seems to call for only a few minor modifications.

I will confine myself to two principal questions, one concerned with general history, and the other with Jewish political history. (1) Are the Kittim mentioned in the writings of Qumran Seleucids, or Romans? (2) Who is the Jewish priest described in the texts as the 'Wicked Priest', the contemporary and persecutor of the Teacher of Righteousness?

1. THE KITTIM

In the *Commentary on Habakkuk*, the word 'Kittim' occurs frequently as the name of a race of invaders and conquerors substituted, by audacious transposition, for the Kasdim (Chaldeans) named and described in the biblical text. These Kittim were evidently contemporaries of the author, who recognizes in their invasion a preamble to the end of the world.

What does this word 'Kittim' mean? In its proper sense, it first applied to the people of Kition in Cyprus; then its meaning widened more and more in the Jewish language to include Cypriots in general, then the inhabitants of the various islands of the eastern Mediterranean, then the Macedonians, as is seen in 1 Maccabees (i. 1; viii. 5), and finally the Romans. This latter sense is attested from the middle of the second century B.C. in the book of Daniel. Predicting events of the reign of Antiochus Epiphanes, the prophet writes: 'Ships of the Kittim shall come against him and he shall be afraid' (xi, 30). All interpreters agree that this is an allusion to the embassy of C. Popilius Laenas, an envoy of the Roman Senate who, in 168 B.C., compelled Antiochus Epiphanes to leave Egypt. The Septuagint version makes no mistake as to the precise meaning of this phrase, translating it 'And the Romans shall come'; the Latin Vulgate, also, translates it *et venient super eum trieres et Romani*. In the first century of the Christian era, Josephus attests this very wide significance of the word 'Kittim'. 'Chetimos', we read (*Jewish Antiquities*, I, 6, 1), 'occupied the island of Chetima, today called Cyprus; whence the name given by the Hebrews to all islands, and to most of the peoples living beyond the sea.' The appellation 'Kittim', in the sense of Romans, is preserved in the Targums and in various Jewish writings of the Middle Ages.

When research first started, certain writers suggested that 'Kittim' in the *Commentary on Habakkuk* should be understood in the sense of Macedonians, as in 1 Maccabees — or more precisely in the sense of Seleucids. As we know, the Seleucids of Syria were the successors to Alexander the Great, the Macedonian; it was these Macedonians, the Macedonians of Syria, whom the commentator had in mind. He therefore wrote his commentary well before the Roman epoch, and probably in the time of Antiochus Epiphanes. But it should be observed that there is no evidence at all of such an employment of the word 'Kittim' to describe the kingdom of the Seleucids or some other kingdom sprung from the empire of Alexander. Moreover the general description which the commentator gives of the Kittim, with their victorious *élan* and the universality of their conquest, agrees very poorly with the Seleucid kingdom at about the time of Antiochus Epiphanes. After the defeat at Magnesia, the treaty of Apamea in 188 B.C. ushered in its final decline, and from then on its power weakened and it was Rome, to which the Seleucids were compelled to pay heavy tribute, that gained more and more mastery over the Orient.

Opposing this Seleucid theory, I tried in 1950 to show that in the *Commentary on Habakkuk*, as in Daniel, the Kittim are the Romans.

This thesis rapidly won the approval of a great many historians; but the Seleucid theory still has its supporters, among them Professor H. H. Rowley of Manchester University who remains its resolute champion.[1] However, the majority opinion is not necessarily the best, and for this reason I think it worth while to recall the arguments which seemed to me to necessitate the adoption of the Roman theory.[2]

The most impressive argument is the one arising from the following words in the *Commentary on Habakkuk* (VI, 3-5): '. . . The explanation of this is that the Kittim sacrifice to their standards, and that their weapons of war are the objects of their religion.' These words plainly indicate that the Kittim worshipped their military standards. Now no historian of classical antiquity can be mistaken on this point. On the one hand the cult of the military standards in the Roman legions is solidly attested by a great deal of indisputable evidence; on the other there is nothing whatever of this kind with regard to the Seleucid armies. Since I raised the problem almost ten years ago, the supporters of the Seleucid theory have not been able to produce a single text or document showing that the Seleucid army worshipped their standards. Among the Roman armies, on the other hand, the fact has always been recognized and can be denied by no one, so clear and abundant are the proofs. This detail, plainly indicated by the commentator, is for me the distinguishing feature.

Some, it is true, object that the cult of the *signa* is only explicitly attested in the Roman legions from the time of the Imperial epoch; they explain that this cult did not come into being until that moment, by virtue of the imperial cult itself when the emperor was represented on the standards. I think this allegation is wrong. A fresco such as the one at Doura-Europos, for example, proves that worship was offered even to standards without any effigy of the emperor. On the other hand, several texts exist which show that the cult of the *signa* goes back as far as the Republican era. In reality the origins of the cult are lost in the mists of time. Besides, even though it were established that such a cult was only practised under the emperors, logically this would constitute no argument in favour of the Seleucid thesis. The Kittim would still remain Romans; we should just have

[1] See his recent article, 'The Kittim and the Dead Sea Scrolls', in *PEQ*, July-December, 1956, pp. 1-18.
[2] Cf. *Aperçus préliminaires . . .* (1950), pp. 39-42. (Eng. edn., pp. 28-31.) *Nouveaux Aperçus . . .* (1953), pp. 33-61. (Eng. edn., pp. 14-37.)

to conclude that the author of the *Commentary on Habakkuk* wrote his work during the Imperial epoch beginning with the reign of Augustus. We should only move still further from the age of the Seleucids.

A second argument in favour of the Roman thesis is this. The Kittim, we read, 'come from afar, from the islands of the sea, to devour the peoples like the eagle, without satisfaction' (III, 10-12). The *Habakkuk* text interpreted here reads simply, '(They come) from afar; they fly like the eagle swift to devour.' As we see, the commentator retains the words 'from afar' but adds the detail 'from the islands of the sea'. These two words, deliberately introduced, must not pass unnoticed; they indicate, in effect, the distant habitat of those ravening invaders. In Hebrew, the word 'islands' is, as we know, frequently applied to peninsulas and even sea coasts. If the Kittim are Romans, the expression fits admirably. The far-off maritime country from which the terrible conquerors poured into the world was Italy, a peninsula in the western Mediterranean some 1250 miles distant from Palestine. Let us at this point recall Josephus's definition: 'The name Chetim (=Kittim) is given by the Hebrews to all islands, and to most of the peoples living beyond the sea.'

But if the reference were to the Macedonians of Syria, the Seleucid sovereigns, how very inapt these words would be! For a Palestinian, Syria is not a distant but a neighbouring country. Moreover, although the Seleucid empire possessed sea coasts, notably those of ancient Phoenicia, it stretched far inland to the north and the east; its domain was part of the Asiatic continent. Why should 'the islands of the sea' be mentioned as the characteristic starting-point of Syrian conquest, when the Seleucid kings waging war in Asia Minor, Euphrates, Persia, Palestine and Egypt more often than not had to travel overland from their capital, Antioch, which was not a maritime city.

And this is the third argument. In the *Commentary on Habakkuk* (IV, 5, 11, 12), the leaders of the Kittim are called *mōshelīm*, a Hebrew word signifying literally 'commanders' (in Latin *imperantes*); these leaders were also warriors in control of a powerful army. Applied to the Roman leaders, the expression *mōshelē Kittim*, 'commanders of the Kittim', is entirely appropriate: it fits perfectly those pro-magistrates *cum imperio* who were sent by Rome into the provinces and placed in command of the armies. But if the writer had in mind the Seleucid monarchs, why did he not call them 'kings'? This is the title constantly given to them and to the Ptolemaic monarchs in the book of Daniel when it describes prophetically the history of the Hellenistic period.

Actually, these observations on the title *mōshelē Kittim* which I formulated in 1950 have recently received what appears to be undeniable confirmation. In the fragment of the *Commentary on Nahum* published by J. M. Allegro (see above, p. 268), we find this important passage (on Nahum ii. 12b): 'The explanation of this concerns Demetrius king of Yāwān, who sought to enter Jerusalem on the counsel of those who seek smooth things. But he did not enter, for from Antiochus until the rising of the commanders of the Kittim, God did not deliver it into the hands of the kings of Yāwān. But afterwards it will be trampled underfoot by the Kittim. . . .' As Allegro has suggested, this 'Demetrius king of Yāwān' is most likely Demetrius III (Eucaeros). Others prefer to identify him as Demetrius I (Sōter).[1] Be this as it may, it is quite clear that in this passage the Seleucid king Demetrius III, or Demetrius I, is called 'king of Yāwān', and the Seleucid kings collectively 'kings of Yāwān'. Furthermore, is it not apparent in the same passage that the expression 'commanders of the Kittim' obviously refers to leaders other than the 'kings of Yāwān', and consequently the Seleucid kings; that it refers to another historical period than that made famous by the name of Antiochus — doubtless Antiochus IV (Epiphanes) — and that it can therefore only allude to the new invaders of Palestine, to the Roman leaders that is to say, and in particular to Pompey, who — as we may recall — captured Jerusalem in 63 B.C.?

I would mention at this point that the expression 'king of Yāwān' is borrowed from the book of Daniel (viii), where it is applied to Alexander the Great as well as to the 'four kings' who shared his succession between them and 'arose from his nation': the sovereigns, no doubt, of the four kingdoms Macedonia, Thrace, Syria and Egypt which issued from the empire of Alexander. So in this expression, the name Yāwān describes, besides Ionia — or more generally Greece — the whole of Asiatic Greece, all the Hellenized Orient. When we read in Zech. ix. 13, 'I will raise up thy sons, O Zion, against the sons of Yāwān', the sons of Yāwān in this text are probably the Seleucids or, more precisely, Antiochus Epiphanes,

[1] On these two identifications, see above, p. 268, no. 3.

against whom the Jews rose in revolt at the call of the Maccabees. By giving the title 'kings of Yāwān' to Demetrius and Antiochus, the *Commentary on Nahum* conforms to this biblical terminology.

But it is not the only book of the Qumran sect in which the expression occurs; we meet it again in the *Damascus Document*. This book, as we may recall, contains several allusions to a particularly grave and tragic historical event which was considered by the members of the sect as an act of divine vengeance, as God's punishment of the unfaithful Jews. Now in one passage (A, VIII, 11-12; cf. B, I, 23-4), the person responsible for carrying out this memorable punishment is described thus: '. . . and *the head of asps* is the Chief (*rō'sh*) of the kings of Yāwān who came to wreak vengeance upon them'. Who is this 'Chief of the kings of Yāwān' who invaded Judaea to punish the guilty Jews? It is extremely important to elucidate, if possible, this allusion to an essential historical fact. In 1950 I suggested that the person so described was the Roman Pompey, the conqueror of Jerusalem in 63 B.C.[1] I returned to the problem in an article which appeared in 1955[2] and which I will take the liberty of summarizing here.

Who more than Pompey merited this title of 'Chief of the kings of Yāwān'? Let us be quite clear as to what it means. According to the usual sense of the word *rō'sh*, it signifies that the chief in question was in command of the kings of Yāwān, i.e. that they were under his orders and obliged to obey him; there is nothing to lead us to assume that he must himself have been one of the kings of Yāwān. If the expression refers to the great Roman leader, it should first be remembered how insistently the author of 1 Maccabees, in his famous eulogy of the Romans (viii. 1-16), emphasizes the fact that the Romans, 'none of whom wore a crown', and who were governed not by a king but by a 'Council' (the Senate), vanquished and overthrew the kings. This supremacy of republican Rome over the kings of the whole world is the *leitmotiv* of the whole section: 'They have prevailed over the kings, over them that are near and them that are far. . . . All whom they wish to succour and to reign, reign; all whom they wish to depose, they depose. . . .' Is it not evident in this passage that, owing to his conquests, the Roman has become the 'chief of the kings'?

[1] Cf. *Aperçus préliminaires* . . ., p. 70. (Eng. edn., p. 56.)
[2] In *Semitica*, v (Paris), pp. 41-57, article entitled, 'Le chef des rois de Yâwân dans l'*Écrit de Damas*'.

But the *Damascus Document* is not alluding to the Romans in general; it has Pompey himself in view. This is why the expression it uses is defined 'Chief of the kings of Yāwān', i.e. chief of the kings of the Hellenized Orient. Pompey was, in fact, by virtue of the *imperium* delegated to him by the Roman Senate, lord of the kings of the Orient. The *lex Manilia*, passed in 66 B.C., entrusted him with the task of conducting the war against Mithridates king of Pontus, and Tigranes king of Armenia, and vested him with extraordinary powers. This war, declares Cicero in his *De Imperio Pompei* (§§ 64, 66), was 'the Asiatic war against the kings' (*bellum Asiaticum regiumque*); and to 'conquer the armies of the kings' (*exercitus regios superare*), Pompey received all power 'in Asia, Cilicia, Syria, and in the kingdoms of the nations of the interior'. After conquering Mithridates, he held in 64 B.C. a 'veritable court of kings', according to the expression of Th. Reinach, at Amisos on the Black Sea. There, on his own authority, he settled the political condition of the ancient kingdom of Pontus and its dependencies, distributing territories and crowns at his whim. Soon afterwards he annexed Syria, thereby sanctioning the disappearance of the Seleucid dynasty. Then he went to Judaea, captured the Jewish king Aristobulus II, and after taking Jerusalem in 63 B.C., installed his rival Hyrcanus II in his place. In 61 B.C., the great triumph of the conqueror of the Orient took place in Rome, with several vanquished kings in attendance.

Despite the vicissitudes of his career, from 59 to 49 B.C. Pompey wielded his own personal authority over an Orient on which he had imposed the law of Rome: the Orient remained his fief. Lucanus, in the verses of *Pharsalus*, has brought this Great Pompey, this remarkable chief of the kings of the Orient, magnificently to life. The poet describes as being under Pompey's command at Pharsalus, 'the tetrarchs, kings, mighty tyrants, and all the purple enslaved by the Latin iron' (VII, 226-7). Then after the defeat, he evokes the power of the vanquished leader who but lately commanded kings and distributed kingdoms: 'Look on the kings with a tranquil eye and not in supplication; look on the cities which thou hadst and the kingdoms which thou gavest' (VII, 708-10). In spite of his reverses, the kings of the Orient remained faithful to him: 'Even though overthrown by destiny and driven from the field of battle, the Great (Pompey) did not see the submission of the kings taken from him by Fortune; the lords of the earth, they who hold the sceptres of the Orient, remain the companions of his exile' (VIII, 206-9).

To the end, therefore, Pompey the Great appeared, in the eyes of the poet, surrounded by a docile escort of the kings of the Orient. Can we hope for a better paraphrase of the Hebrew writers' formula, 'Chief of the kings of Yāwān', than that provided by these Latin texts?

On the other hand, does this title fit Antiochus Epiphanes, to whom some authors would like to apply it? At about the time of this monarch, the 'kings of Yāwān' were, besides the king of Syria himself, the kings of Macedonia, Egypt, Pergamus, Bithynia and Pontus. But in what sense can Antiochus Epiphanes have been called the 'chief' of these kings? On the plane of international politics, his reign was marked by humiliating set-backs. He invaded Egypt in 168 B.C. for the second time, only to have to leave it on an injunction from Rome; by the will of Rome his cherished dream of ruling over Egypt finally crumbled. No, the 'Chief of the kings of Yāwān' was not this Seleucid whose reign was, on the whole, already in decline, and who in any case, even though he did have the upper hand of the king of Egypt for a short time, was never the lord of the *kings* of the Hellenized Orient.

If, as I hope I have shown, the *Damascus Document* really alludes to Pompey and his invasion of Judaea, we find in another contemporary Jewish work explicit evidence of the profound impression these same events of 63 B.C. made on the Jews: I refer to the *Psalms of Solomon*. For the subject under discussion, this is a work which, more than any other, should be read and re-read. Psalm II describes the occupation of Jerusalem by Pompey, presenting it as a chastisement for the sins of the Jews, and also Pompey's death, the punishment of that potentate's pride; Psalm VIII again describes the occupation of Jerusalem as well as the sins which led to the punishment; and Psalm XVII takes up the same themes once more. As all modern critics agree, the *Psalms of Solomon* are dominated by the memory of Pompey and the events of 63 B.C., but they never refer to him by his proper name; he is called simply 'the Sinner' (II, 1), 'the Dragon' (II, 25), 'He who comes from the end of the earth, He who smites mightily' (VIII, 15), 'the Ungodly One' (XVIII, 11). Nor does the *Damascus Document* name Pompey; but how fortunate its author was in the discovery of the formula, 'Chief of the kings of Yāwān', used to describe him there — a formula ingeniously extracted from the text of Deuteronomy (xxxii. 33) in the subtle manner of the *pesher* — defining as excellently as it does, above all from the point of view of an Oriental, the exceptional authority wielded by the great Roman Chief over the Hellenized Orient, all of whose kings became as it were his clients or vassals!

It is within the historical perspective of the *Damascus Document* and the *Psalms of Solomon* that, in my opinion, the following famous and difficult passage from the *Commentary on Habakkuk* should be placed (XI, 4-8): 'The explanation of this concerns the Wicked Priest who persecuted the Teacher of Righteousness, swallowing him up in the anger of his fury in his place of exile. But in the time of the feast of rest of the Day of Atonement, he (the Teacher of Righteousness) appeared before them (or manifested himself to them) to swallow them up and to cause them to stumble on the Day of Fasting, their Sabbath of rest.' Since 1950 I have demonstrated several times that this passage alludes to the capture of the Temple of Jerusalem by Pompey, a tragic event which, according to Josephus, actually took place on 'the Day of Fasting' of the year 63 B.C. I cannot reproduce that demonstration here. I will say only that if the *Damascus Document*, like the *Psalms of Solomon*, testifies to the exceptional importance with which this event was invested in the eyes of the sectaries of the Covenant, it is even more likely that the *Commentary on Habakkuk*, apparently written in about 40 B.C., should allude to it also. The event which occurred on the Day of Atonement and 'swallowed up' the guilty Jews was, I think, the same as that with which the name of Pompey is linked, that 'Chief of the kings of Yāwān who came to wreak vengeance on them'.

Thus everything combines to lead to the theory identifying the Kittim with the conquering Romans. The name of these Kittim appears frequently in another writing from Qumran, the *War Rule of the Sons of Light* (cf. chapter V), where they are represented as the chief enemies of the sons of light. Who are these Kittim? The provisional publication in 1948 of a few short passages from the *War Scroll* led to a serious mistake in that the editor reported the occurrence of the double expression, 'Kittim of Asshur' and 'Kittim of Egypt': consequently these expressions seemed to apply respectively to the Macedonians of Syria (the Seleucids) and the Macedonians of Egypt (the Ptolemies). But the publication of the complete scroll in 1954 showed that the expression 'Kittim of Asshur' appears only once, at the very beginning of the scroll (I, 2); everywhere else they are called just 'Kittim'. Above all, contrary to what had been said, the expression 'Kittim of Egypt' makes no appearance at all in the text. This reads simply, after a lacuna: '[. . .] the Kittim in Egypt' (I, 4). There is nothing to make us think that there is any question here of the Ptolemies; the passage — which, it seems, should be completed '[and the king] of the Kittim [will enter] into Egypt' — can very well allude to the presence and domination of the Romans in Egypt. As for the 'Kittim of Asshur', why not, as Dr. Y. Yadin suggests, translate this 'the Romans of Syria'? In 64 B.C. Pompey turned Syria into a Roman province, and from then on it was ruled by a Roman governor assisted by several legions. These 'Kittim of Asshur' were not Seleucids but Romans settled in Syria. As a result a grave and entirely artificial difficulty vanishes, a difficulty that has weighed heavily on the problem of the identification of the Kittim ever since research began. In my opinion the word 'Kittim', in *all* the writings from Qumran known today, applies to the Romans, in accordance with the terminology inaugurated in the second century B.C. by the book of Daniel.

As regards the book of the *War Rule* in particular, this sense of the word 'Kittim' is indirectly confirmed by the fact that on more than one point the book reflects the art of war as it was practised by the Roman legions. I will confine myself to a reference to the book devoted to the *War Scroll* by Dr. Yadin, who independently of myself, and as a result of very thorough research, has come to the same general conclusion, namely that the Jewish work, in its present form anyway, originated during the Roman epoch 'at the time', as I have written earlier, 'when the Roman troops were present in Palestine and Syria, and when it was easy for a Jew to observe them and to obtain information about them' (p. 167). This being so, the word 'Kittim' in the *War Scroll*, as in the *Commentary on Habakkuk* and the *Commentary on Nahum*, must describe the Romans themselves.[1]

If these observations concerning the Kittim in the Qumran documents seem admissible, the question of the historical setting already

---

[1] The title 'king of the Kittim' met in the *War Scroll* (XV, 2; cf. I, 4) constitutes no objection to the identification of the Kittim with the Romans. Even during the Republican epoch the Orientals, the Jews, could quite easily have given this title to a dictator as authoritative as, for example, Caesar, as I have explained in *RHR*, cxlviii, 1955, p. 30, n. 1. H. H. ROWLEY (*PEQ*, July-December 1956, p. 5) complains that I have contradicted myself with regard to this title 'king of the Kittim'; my distinguished critic, an indomitable supporter of the Seleucid thesis, has doubtless omitted to read my explanation. I maintained, it is true, that the expression 'commanders of the Kittim' applied strictly to the Roman leaders and not to the Seleucid kings; but I have never claimed that the title 'king of the Kittim' could not describe the Roman emperor or, before the Imperial epoch, some dictator of the Republican era.

becomes appreciably clearer. To come to still closer grips with the problem it remains for us to inquire into the identity of the 'Wicked Priest', the persecutor of the sect and its leader.

2. THE WICKED PRIEST

I have already referred to the disquieting diversity of hypotheses advanced on this question. It would be long and tedious to discuss them in detail, and I think it more worth while to try to justify as thoroughly as possible my own hypothesis identifying the Wicked Priests as the Hasmonaean High Priest, Hyrcanus II.

Broadly speaking, if my preceding observations about the Kittim are judged admissible, and if, in particular, it is agreed that the capture of Jerusalem by Pompey in 63 B.C. constituted an essential date for the sect — as, I think, appears chiefly in the *Damascus Document* — the Hyrcanus II hypothesis has an immediate chronological advantage in that this High Priest lived at the end of the era of Hasmonaean independence and at the beginning of the Roman occupation. But this hypothesis seems to me to be further recommended by detailed arguments, both more numerous and better than those of its rivals.

The first of these arguments is drawn from the following passage in the *Commentary on Habakkuk* (VIII, 8-13): 'The explanation of this concerns the Wicked Priest who was called by the Name of truth at the beginning of his coming; but when he commanded over Israel, his heart rose up and he abandoned God and betrayed the precepts because of riches. . . .' It should first be noted that the commentator's 'Priest' is certainly a High Priest, one or other of the High Priests of the Hasmonaean dynasty. He says, in effect, that the Wicked Priest 'commanded (*māshāl*) over Israel'; so this Priest was at the same time a temporal sovereign. It is as temporal sovereign that in another passage (X, 9-13) mention is made of 'his city' — of Jerusalem, his capital — and of the many people who 'labour in his service' — the Jews, his subjects. But it should also be observed that in the career of the High Priest alluded to, the commentator distinguishes two successive phases: the 'beginning of his coming', when he was 'called by the Name of truth', when, that is to say, he behaved as a worthy priest of Yahweh; and the phase in which he came to exercise temporal authority and when, as master of Israel, he yielded to pride and cupidity. In the first phase, therefore, this High Priest fulfilled a religious office alone, without temporal power; it was only during the second phase, from the time when he 'commanded over Israel', that his conduct altered and he behaved as a 'Wicked Priest'.

This career in two acts is, I think, a feature of essential interest to the problem of the identification of the Wicked Priest. Among the members of the Hasmonaean dynasty, only Hyrcanus II had a career corresponding exactly to this allusion in the Commentary. I would briefly recall that, nominated High Priest in 76 B.C. on the death of his father Alexander Jannaeus, his function was at first a purely religious one until the death of his mother Alexandra who, as queen, had herself assumed the temporal power. It was not till her death in 67 B.C. that Hyrcanus II was proclaimed king, thereby opening the second phase in his career when he 'commanded over Israel'. This phase continued, after a brief interruption due to the usurpation of his office by his younger brother Aristobulus II, until 40 B.C., when he was taken prisoner by the Parthians. So his long pontificate did in actual fact comprise two periods: the first of nine years, without temporal authority, the second of twenty-seven years (including the time when Aristobulus II occupied the throne) when Hyrcanus was also political leader of Israel, first as king and then as ethnarch.

Another point is clearly indicated in the *Commentary on Habakkuk* (IX, 9-12): 'The explanation of this concerns the Wicked Priest whom, because of the iniquity committed against the Teacher of Righteousness and the men of his council, God delivered into the hands of his enemies in order to humble him with a destroying blow, in bitterness of soul, because he had done wickedly to His elect.' This humiliating captivity, and the bitterness of soul which overwhelmed the captive, accord perfectly with the history of Hyrcanus II. In 40 B.C. he was deposed and taken prisoner by the Parthians, who installed Antigonus in his place; Josephus reports (*Jewish War*, I, 13, 9, § 270; cf. *Jewish Antiquities*, XIV, 13, 10, § 366) that the new High Priest 'himself tore off his ears with his teeth, so that even if a revolution should restore him to liberty, he would never be able to recover the High Priesthood; for no man can be High Priest unless he is free from all bodily blemish'. We know that Hyrcanus II, led away captive by the Parthians, returned later to Jerusalem at Herod's request and that the latter had him assassinated in 30 B.C. It is possible, of course, to cite other High Priests who, during the Hasmonaean period, were 'delivered into the hands of their enemies': Menelaus, Jonathan, Simon, Aristobulus II, Antigonus. But to identify the Wicked Priest, this feature must be added to the preceding one, and only in Hyrcanus II are all the necessary conditions fulfilled.

A passage from the *Commentary on Nahum* probably alludes to the father of this Hyrcanus II, Alexander Jannaeus:[1] 'The explanation of this concerns the furious Young Lion who . . . took vengeance on those who seek smooth things — he who hanged living men on wood . . . which was not formerly done in Israel. . . .' In all likelihood the event referred to here is, as Allegro has recognized, the bloody repression which Jannaeus carried out, after his defeat by Demetrius III, against the Pharisees who had allied themselves to the Seleucid king. Josephus reports that he avenged himself by crucifying eight hundred Pharisees (*Jewish Antiquities*, XIII, 14, 2). These are the Pharisees, the victims of Jannaeus's cruelty, whom the *Commentary on Nahum* designates as 'they who seek smooth things', an expression whose plainly pejorative character is only comprehensible if the sect of Qumran was distinct from the sect of the Pharisees, and even opposed to it.

But — and this should be carefully noted — in our passage, Jannaeus, blameworthy and scandalous though his conduct was, is not stigmatized as being himself the persecutor of the Qumran sect (in my view, the Essenes). Although he undoubtedly was a wicked priest, the title Wicked Priest is not given to him but is reserved — as is seen in the *Commentary on Habakkuk* in particular — to the Wicked One *par excellence*, the man who laid hands on the Teacher of Righteousness and persecuted his followers, namely Hyrcanus II.[2]

---

[1] Cf. above, p. 269.

[2] I would repeat once again that in my opinion the Teacher of Righteousness began his ministry in about 104-103 B.C. and died in about 65-63 B.C.; so, before the Roman period, he was a contemporary of Alexander Jannaeus and certain key works of the sect, such as the *Rule* and the book of the *Hymns*, may have originated at that time. Allusions to the reign of Jannaeus like those in the *Commentary on Nahum* should therefore cause no surprise. Although Jannaeus was not actually the 'Wicked Priest', it is not at all impossible, as I have shown earlier (*Nouveaux Aperçus* . . ., p. 76, n. 12; Eng. edn., p. 49, n. 12) that the Teacher of Righteousness and his sect were already at odds with this High Priest whose conduct and politics must have appeared scandalous in the eyes of the pious Essenes, and to whom they must have been antagonistic.

The same estimate is, I believe, borne out in a short apocalypse preserved in the *Testament of Levi* (chapter XVII). Here is the translation.

And as you have heard tell concerning the seventy years,
hear tell also concerning the priesthood.
For to every jubilee shall correspond a priesthood.

And during the first jubilee, the first Anointed to the priesthood shall be
and he shall speak to God as to a father,   [great;
and his priesthood shall be fully with the Lord,
and in his joyful days he shall arise for the salvation of the world.

In the second jubilee, the Anointed shall be promoted because of the
and his priesthood shall be honoured   [mourning of a loved one,
and he shall be glorified by all.

As for the third Priest, he shall vanish sadly.

And the fourth shall be in sorrows,
for iniquity shall be heaped upon him in abundance
and all (the children of) Israel shall hate one another.

The fifth shall vanish into darkness:
likewise also the sixth and the seventh.

Now in the seventh (jubilee), there shall be a defilement
(such) that I cannot speak of (it) before men;
for they shall know it who shall commit it!
Because of this they shall be taken captive and shall be plundered,
and their land and possessions shall be destroyed . . .

There is, I think, no doubt that this apocalypse envisages definite historical reality — seven priests following one after another, succeeding one another as in a dynasty. Which sacerdotal dynasty can this be? It has a holy and glorious beginning, and a miserable and criminal end: does this not suggest, first and foremost, that the author has in mind the Hasmonaean dynasty which began so well with Judas Maccabee, continued honourably under Jonathan, fell into decadence with Simon and John Hyrcanus, and completed its decline with Aristobulus I, Alexander Jannaeus and Hyrcanus II, the three priests who dared assume the title of 'king'? To the last one — Hyrcanus II — a particularly atrocious sacrilege is imputed, which I believe to have been the persecution of the sect, or more precisely the execution of its leader, the Teacher of Righteousness. Other passages from the *Testament of Levi* (chapters X, XIV-XVI) allude to the same crime and to the exemplary chastisement which fell on the guilty City, namely, the capture of Jerusalem by Pompey. I cannot here justify in detail the whole of my interpretation of this apocalypse; I have tried to do this elsewhere with the necessary elaboration.[1] But if it seems admissible, it will be agreed that these passages from the *Testament of Levi* harmonize perfectly with the facts given in the Qumran Commentaries. The Wicked Priest *par excellence* is Hyrcanus II; but his father and predecessor, Alexander Jannaeus, is also considered an evil priest, a son of darkness who 'vanished into darkness'.

In support of this interpretation I can now cite another document, the one known as *Testimonia*, translated and interpreted above (p. 315-9). The fourth section of this document consists, it will be remembered, of a quotation from an apocryphal book of the sect called the *Psalms of Joshua*, in which there is clear allusion to three accursed persons, a father and his two sons, the elder and the younger. The author of the *Psalms of Joshua*, like the authors of the biblical Commentaries, certainly has in mind real historical characters who through their wickedness, or by direct attack, opposed the Teacher of Righteousness or obstructed the success of his mission. He cleverly chooses a verse from the biblical book of Joshua (vi. 26) in which a father and his two sons, the elder and the younger, are associated in a common malediction in connection with the building of a city. The biblical verse refers to the city of Jericho, but the name of Jericho is omitted from the quotation which is explicitly applied to Jerusalem. Transpositions such as this are common in the Qumran Commentaries. The three stigmatized persons are therefore directly associated with Jerusalem itself, the capital of the land of Israel. First the father is described as an 'accursed man', a 'fiend of

---

[1] In *Semitica*, iv (1952), pp. 35-53, article entitled 'Le *Testament de Lévi* et la secte juive de l'Alliance'; see also *Nouveaux Aperçus* . . . (1953), pp. 63 ff. (Eng. edn., pp. 38 ff.) Since these two publications, I have been induced slightly to modify my initial hypothesis concerning the identification of the Wicked Priest. Instead of recognizing this title as applying sometimes to Aristobulus II and sometimes to Hyrcanus II, the two rival brothers, I think now that all the allusions to the Wicked Priest are directed solely and exclusively to the elder brother, Hyrcanus II. This simplification alters nothing of the essential chronological framework.

Belial' who is a snare 'for his people' as well as 'destruction to all his neighbours'. Then attention is turned to his two sons, 'instruments of violence' who, after their father, will commit grave wickedness in Israel. They will rebuild and fortify Jerusalem which will become a 'stronghold of iniquity', but all this will be accompanied by bloodshed: 'And they will shed blood like water upon the ramparts of the daughter of Zion and within the precincts of Jerusalem.'

Who is this accursed father? And who are the two sons even more ill-fated than he? I think, like Allegro, that it is difficult not to recognize them as Alexander Jannaeus, with his elder son Hyrcanus II, and his younger, Aristobulus II. The famous rivalry between the two brothers is well known through Josephus. Moreover, in a text of Diodorus of Sicily (XL, frag. 2) there is explicit mention of the violence and 'wicked murders' committed by both of them. The allusion to the reconstruction of Jerusalem may well be connected with the authorization given by Caesar to Hyrcanus II in 47 B.C. to rebuild the walls of the capital. I would remind the reader of this passage from the *Commentary on Habakkuk* (X, 9-13): 'The explanation of this word concerns the Preacher of Lies who led many astray to build his city of vanity in murder (literally, in blood). . . .'

So the document of the *Testimonia* brings us to the same events and the same characters as the preceding texts.[1] I would add that the tragic period of the rivalry between the two brothers is, as R. H. Charles recognized, very likely alluded to once more in two passages from the *Testaments of the Twelve Patriarchs*. The first (*Testament of Judah*, XXI, 6 - XXIII) is a long diatribe against the exactions of the 'kings': '. . . And the Lord will cause them to be divided one against the other, and there will be continual war in Israel. And my kingship shall be destroyed by strangers. . . .'[2] The second passage (*Testament of Zabulon*) is more explicit: '. . . I have learned in the Scripture of my fathers that in the last days you will

[1] J. T. MILIK suggests that the accursed father should be identified as Mattathias, and the two sons as Jonathan and Simon (*Dix ans de découvertes dans le désert de Juda*, 1957, p. 57, n. 1 and p. 104; Eng. edn., pp. 63 f., 81 f.); but this interpretation is obviously forced and paradoxical. How could Mattathias, the holy and heroic priest who gave the signal for the revolt against the invading wickedness, the father of the glorious hero of national liberation, Judas Maccabee, how could he be an 'accursed man, a fiend of Belial, a fowler's net to his people'? As for Jonathan and Simon, his second and fifth sons, what connection can they have with the two accursed sons, who are distinctly described as the eldest and the youngest sons?

[2] An allusion to the suppression of the Hasmonaean sovereignty by Pompey in 63 B.C.; Hyrcanus II was reinstalled as head of the Jewish State, not as 'king', but as High Priest and ethnarch.

depart from the Lord, and will be divided in Israel, and that you will follow two kings and will accomplish every abomination and adore every idol. And your enemies will take you captive, and you will be ill-used among the nations, with many infirmities and tribulations.'[1] The 'two kings', whose supporters are engaged in relentless war, are the two sons of Jannaeus, Hyrcanus II and Aristobulus II.

Thus everything converges on the great event of 63 B.C., on Pompey, and on Hyrcanus II. And here to end with, is a fragment from cave IV, still unpublished but partly disclosed by J. T. Milik,[2] in which 'Hyrcanus' (no doubt Hyrcanus II) is explicitly mentioned, and also 'Emilios', i.e. Emilius Scaurus whom Pompey sent to Jerusalem in 65 B.C. at the time of the war of the two brothers, and whom he made governor of Syria in 62 B.C. All these indications accumulate and reveal little by little, and with growing probability, the historical background of the writings of Qumran upon which I have tried to throw as much light as I can.

---

[1] An allusion to the national catastrophe of 63 B.C.; many Jews were led into captivity.
[2] See *VT*, Supplement IV (1957), p. 26.

Chapter XIII

THE TEACHER OF RIGHTEOUSNESS

The anonymity of the Teacher of Righteousness; his earthly career. — 1. The Prophet. — 2. The Man of Sorrows. — 3. The Head of the Church.

The Teacher of Righteousness is without doubt the most astonishing of the revelations of the Dead Sea Scrolls. The place he occupies in the writings of Qumran is such that in almost every chapter I have had occasion to speak of him, of his work, of his tragic career, of the intense piety surrounding his person, and of the essential role which the faith of his followers ascribed to him in the economy of salvation.

His name is unknown. As a mark of respect, his adherents refrained from uttering it or writing it, just as the Jews then did with regard to the name of Yahweh. It is no doubt to this that Josephus alludes in his account of the Essenes (*Jewish War*, II, 8, 9, § 145): 'The name of the Lawgiver is, after God, a great object of veneration among them, and if anyone blasphemes against the Lawgiver he is punished with death.' Here, I think, the Lawgiver is not Moses; the name of Moses appears constantly in the sect's writings without any mystery or circumlocution. But nowhere is the name of the sect's lawgiver divulged; he is simply called 'the Teacher', 'the Unique Teacher', and above all, 'the Teacher of Righteousness'. He is also referred to as 'the Priest', i.e. the Priest *par excellence*, 'the Seeker of the Law', 'the Star', 'the Lawgiver'; but never is there any betrayal of the secret of his name, a name shrouded in venerable mystery, a name which human lips are unworthy to pronounce.

So for us the Teacher of Righteousness is Ignotus. Despite this stubborn anonymity, various attempts have been made to identify him with some known person in Jewish history. Names have been suggested such as that of Onias III, a High Priest who incurred the hostility of the usurper Menelaus and was murdered at Daphne, near Antioch, in 171 B.C. Jose ben Joezer has been mentioned, a priest and doctor of the Law reported by Rabbinic tradition to have been crucified at the instigation of the High Priest Alcimus in

162 B.C.;[1] Judas the Essene, whose activity as a diviner in the time of Aristobulus I (104-103 B.C.) is reported by Josephus; Onias the Just, said by Josephus to have died, stoned by the mob in the camp of Hyrcanus II in 62 B.C.;[2] Menahem ben Judah, a Zealot leader who was summarily executed in A.D. 66; and there are others.

For my own part, I hesitate to support any definite identification of the Teacher; enough for me to try to identify his enemy, the 'Wicked Priest'. If he really was Hyrcanus II, the various hypotheses concerning the Teacher collapse except the one identifying him as Onias the Just. This hypothesis would accord perfectly with the general chronological setting which has seemed to me since 1950 to be the one most likely. However, it is not without some difficulties, and for this reason I consider it wiser not to commit myself on this point.[3]

Actually this question of the identification of the Teacher of Righteousness is not all-important; what interests us more is his career, and the lofty role which he claimed for himself on the religious and mystical plane, or which his followers attributed to him.

His career, as the *Damascus Document* and the biblical Commentaries allow us to picture it, can be summarized in a few lines. The Teacher of Righteousness was a priest. A zealous reformer and an ardent mystic, he was the resolute enemy of the official priesthood which he reproached for their contempt of the Law and for their impiety. He broke with official Judaism and the service of the Temple, which he considered defiled, and drew a number of priests and laymen into schism after him. Surrounded by his followers in the solitude of Qumran, he then organized the community of the New Covenant, which, in opposition to the 'Congregation of perverse men' — his name for the official Synagogue — was to represent

[1] This identification was proposed recently by E. STAUFFER, 'Der gekreuzigte Thoralehrer', in *Zeitschrift für Religion- und Geistesgeschichte*, 1956, fasc. 3, pp. 250-3; see by the same author, *Jerusalem und Rom* (Bern, 1957), pp. 128-32.

[2] This theory has been brilliantly supported by Roger GOOSSENS, 'Onias le Juste, le Messie de la Nouvelle Alliance, lapidé à Jérusalem en 65 av. J.-C.', in *La Nouvelle Clio*, no. 7 (July 1950), pp. 336-53.

[3] In my view, what causes difficulties is the fact that the place and method of execution of this Onias the Just, as reported by Josephus, do not correspond to the information which the biblical *Commentaries* from Qumran seem to give of the tragic end of the Teacher of Righteousness. On the other hand, the connection with Hyrcanus II, and even the date of Onias's death (a little before 63 B.C.), accord very well with the facts which, I think, emerge from the Qumran writings. Is it possible that the Josephus account refers to a partly legendary tradition substituted for the historically more exact tradition reflected in the Qumran documents?

the true Israel, the Israel of God. Such a reformer provoked, of course, the hostility of the Jewish authorities whose disgrace and depravity he unceasingly denounced, and who could not but react more or less violently. In fact, the Qumran documents frequently mention a bloody persecution which raged against the sect, a persecution 'by the sword', in the course of which the Teacher of Righteousness was finally arrested, judged, maltreated and very probably put to death.[1]

But although our knowledge of the earthly history of the Teacher of Righteousness is very imperfect — this is also the case with very many other founders of sects and religions, such as Zoroaster, Pythagoras and Buddha — we are better informed as regards his mystical personality. I will say nothing here of his messianic quality proper: for this I would refer the reader to the many passages in the preceding pages where I have touched on the question of messianism in the Qumran sect in connection with the various writings studied.[2] With the help of the biblical Commentaries, and above all the *Hymns* which were published not long ago and are still little utilized, I would like to outline the figure of the great hero of the Essene sect as Prophet, Man of Sorrows and Head of the Church.

1. THE PROPHET

According to the *Commentary on Habakkuk*, the Teacher of Righteousness was 'the Priest whom God placed in [the House of Jud]ah to explain all the words of his servants the Prophets' (II, 8-9). 'God', the author writes (VII, 4-5), 'made known' to him 'all the Mysteries of the words of His servants the Prophets.' Similarly, in the *Hymns* he is called 'an interpreter of Knowledge concerning the marvellous Mysteries' (II, 13); he was 'the foundation of truth and understanding' (II, 10), 'the man by whose mouth' God established 'the teaching' and 'within whose heart' He 'set understanding, that he might open the fountain of Knowledge to all the understanding'

---

[1] This point was greatly disputed at the start of research; but the idea of the martyrdom of the Teacher of Righteousness gains more and more adherents. Writers who have identified the Teacher, either as Onias III (assassinated), or Jose ben Joezer ('the crucified Doctor of the Law' as E. Stauffer writes), or Menahem (executed) — not to mention the supporters of Onias the Just! — can clearly not object to this theory. Abbé A. MICHEL, whose other views are certainly very different from mine, has even seen fit to write: 'The violent death of the Teacher of Righteousness seems to me undeniable, and I willingly give M. Dupont-Sommer the credit for having been the first to bring this out into relief' (*Le Maître de justice . . .*, 1954, p. 271); I thank him for his courtesy.

[2] See especially, pp. 317-9.

(II, 17-18). One could cite many more *Hymns* passages on this theme; here are a few. 'And through me Thou hast illumined the face of many . . . for Thou hast given me to know Thy marvellous Mysteries . . .' (IV, 27-8); 'for Thou hast given me understanding of Thy truth and hast made me know Thy marvellous Mysteries . . .' (VII, 26-7); 'And Thou, O my God, hast put in my mouth as it were an autumn rain for all [the sons of men], (VIII, 16); 'Thou hast opened a [foun]tain in the mouth of Thy servant, and upon his tongue Thou hast graven [Thy precepts] on a measuring-cord, [that he] may proclaim them unto creatures because of his understanding, and be an interpreter of these things unto that which is dust like myself' (XVIII, 10-12).

This 'interpreter' versed in all the Mysteries of Knowledge was the great Doctor of Essene Gnosis, the Hierophant *par excellence*. But he was also the Prophet, in the biblical sense of the word. The Spirit of God was in him, as is said in many passages: 'And I, Thy servant, I know by the Spirit which Thou hast put in me . . .' (XIII, 18-19); 'And Thou hast favoured Thy servant with the Spirit of Knowledge . . .' (XIV, 25); 'for Thou hast upheld me by Thy might and hast poured out Thy Holy Spirit within me . . .' (VII, 6-7); 'For Thou hast poured out [Thy] holy Spirit upon Thy servant . . .' (XVII, 26).

The expression 'Thy servant' recurs in these passages with such insistence that one cannot fail to compare them with the celebrated poems known as the 'Songs of the Servant of the Lord' in the book of Isaiah, in which Yahweh presents the mysterious Prophet, His Servant, thus (Isa. xlii. 1):

> Behold my Servant whom I uphold,
> my Chosen, in whom my soul delights;
> I have put my Spirit upon him,
> He will proclaim his law[1] to the nations.

Defining the mission of Jesus as prophet and saviour, the primitive Christian Church explicitly applied these Songs of the Servant of the Lord to him; about a century earlier, the Teacher of Righteousness applied them to himself. Here, for example, is what the Teacher declares: 'And Thou [hast instructed me in] Thy Covenant and my tongue has been as the tongue of Thy disciples . . .' (VII, 10). And again: 'For [the tong]ue of the disciples (was given) to me to restore the spirit of them that stagger and to sustain the weary with the

---

[1] This is the reading of the first scroll of Isaiah found in cave I; the Masoretic Text reads, 'the law'.

word . . .' (VIII, 36). Here is an obvious echo of the words of Isaiah in the third 'Servant Song' (L, 4):

> The Lord Yahweh has given me the tongue of the disciples . . .
>   to sustain the weary with the word.
> He wakens each morning, he wakens my ear,
>   that I may hear as the disciples.

And when the Teacher of Righteousness declares that God has given him the mission to be according to His truth 'the one who announces good tidings [in the ti]me of Thy goodness, preaching the gospel to the humble according to the abundance of Thy mercy, [giving them to drink] from the fountain of ho[liness and consoling the co]ntrite of spirit and the afflicted' (XVIII, 14-15), is this not a direct allusion to that other passage from the 'Servant Songs', which Jesus equally applies to himself (Isa. lxi. 1-2)?

> The Spirit of the Lord Yahweh is upon me
>   because Yahweh has anointed me.
> He has sent me to bring good tidings to the humble,
>   to tend them that are contrite of heart . . .
> to proclaim the year of Yahweh's good-will
>   and the day of vengeance of our God,
> to comfort all the afflicted . . .

Furthermore, in the second Song the Servant proclaims (Isa. xlix. 1; cf. 5):

> Yahweh has called me from the womb;
> from the bowels of my mother he named my name.

Now on the lips of the Teacher, this theme of the Prophet's pre-destination[1] becomes (IX, 29-31):

> For from the time of my father Thou hast known me,
> and from the womb of my mother [Thou hast established me],
> [and from the belly] of my mother Thou hast attended to me,
> and from the breasts of her that conceived me
> has Thy mercy been over me . . .

Speaking of the sectaries gathered round him, the Teacher of Righteousness once uses the expression 'those who had entered into *my* Covenant' (V, 23); elsewhere he usually says '*Thy* Covenant'. But if he says '*my* Covenant', it is because he considered himself to be truly the leader of the divine Covenant.

[1] Cf. also Jer. i. 5.

How did he conceive his mission as leader of the divine Covenant? This is what he himself says on the subject in a very important passage (VI, 10-13):

> And [Thou hast] created [me] for Thy sake
> to [ful]fil the Law
> and [to te]a[ch' by] my mouth the men of Thy council
> in the midst of the sons of men . . .
> And all the nations shall know Thy truth,
> and all the peoples, Thy glory.
> For Thou hast caused [them] to enter Thy [glo]rious [Covenant]
> with all the men of Thy council
> and into a common lot with the Angels of the Face

His mission was therefore a double one: not only was he to restore the true Covenant of Israel, but also to bring salvation to the nations. Now this was equally the twofold mission of the Servant of the Lord (Isa. xlix. 6):

> It is little that thou shouldst be my Servant
> to restore the tribes of Jacob
> and lead back the remnant of Israel:
> I have made thee the light of the nations
> that my salvation may reach to the end of the earth.

This is what we read again in Isa. (xlii. 6; cf. xlix. 8): 'I have made thee the Covenant of the people, the light of the nations.'

So the Teacher of Righteousness, the champion and mediator of the New Covenant, was as it were a new Moses; in the eyes of his followers he was, as many critics now recognize,[1] the Prophet similar to Moses whose coming is announced in Deut. xviii. 18, 19: 'I will raise up from among their brethren a prophet like thee. I will put my words in his mouth and he will say all that I command him. And whoever will not listen to my words which this prophet shall speak in my name, I myself will call him to account.'[2] The Teacher of Righteousness was conscious of being himself this Prophet who tries the hearts of men: such is the theme of an entire hymn in which he presents himself as the sign of contradiction (II, 6-19). 'And I have been a snare for sinners, but healing for all those that are converted from sin', he declares (II, 8-9). His role was 'to test [the men] of truth and to try them that love instruction' (II, 13-14). On the

---

[1] Already in 1950 in my *Aperçus préliminaires* . . ., p. 81 (Eng. edn., p. 66), I described the Teacher as a 'new Moses'.

[2] This essential text figures at the beginning of the *Testimonia*; see above, p. 315.

Day of Judgment, it would be 'through me' that God would 'distinguish between the just and the guilty' (VII, 12): the just would be the man who had believed in him, and the guilty, the incredulous. It is the same teaching as that expounded in the *Commentary on Habakkuk* (VIII, 1-3): God, we read, will deliver the just from the House of Judgment, 'because of their affliction and their faith in the Teacher of Righteousness'.

2. The Man of Sorrows

If the Teacher of Righteousness as Doctor and Prophet cannot fail to be compared to the Servant of the Lord, how much more must this be so in his capacity as the suffering just man, disgraced, persecuted and beaten? He is indeed the replica of that Man of Sorrows whose tragic destiny, and whose valour in the face of blows[1] and final exaltation are described in the fourth 'Servant Song' (Isa. liii. 12). We know from the *Commentary on Habakkuk* that the Teacher was persecuted by the 'Wicked Priest', ill-treated and executed. The *Hymns* tell us in a singularly living and concrete way of his unceasing struggles and reverses, and of the persecutions by his enemies. He appears there as a man continually opposed and harried, a man who had to leave his country and his relations and friends (IV, 8-9; V, 5), and who was even betrayed by his own (V, 22-5). His destiny was to be a 'man forsaken' (VIII, 27), 'in bitterness and incurable sorrow' (VIII, 28). Like the Servant of the Lord, men had 'no esteem' for him (IV, 8, 23);[2] like the Servant, he was overwhelmed by blows and sickness (VIII, 26-7).[3]

In the midst of all his trials, the Teacher of Righteousness was aware of God's support: his courage was intrepid and his confidence in the help of God unflinching. He declares (VII, 7-8):

And Thou hast made me strong before the battles of ungodliness,
and in the midst of all the calamities which they have brought upon me
Thou hast not permitted me cravenly to abandon Thy Covenant.
But Thou hast set me up as a stout tower, as a steep rampart . . .

Never does he despair; never does he remain silent when he must deliver his message (VIII, 35):

But Thou hast made the tongue in my mouth to grow without going back,
and there was none to [sil]ence (it).

[1] Cf. also Isa. l. 6 (third 'Servant Song').
[2] Cf. Isa. liii. 3.   [3] Cf. Isa. liii. 3-4.

Similarly, the Servant of the Lord says (Isa. xlix. 2): '(Yahweh) has made my mouth a cutting sword.' And again (Isa. l. 7):

> But the Lord Yahweh will help me:
> therefore was I not insulted,
> therefore I have set my face like flint
> and knew that I should not be ashamed.

In the midst of blows, the Teacher knows that God manifests His power in him (IV, 8, 23, etc.). Not only is he resigned like the Servant of the Lord (Isa. liii. 7), but he is full of joy: 'For.... I have loved my judgment and the blows which struck me were pleasant to me' (IX, 10). And again: 'And my chastisement has become for me a joy and a gladness, and the blows that have smitten me (have become) an e[verlasting] healing [and bliss] without end, and the scorn of my adversaries has become for me a glorious crown, and my stumbling, everlasting might' (IX, 24-6).

His soul was uplifted by magnificent hope. Like the Servant of the Lord, convinced that 'his cause is with Yahweh and his reward with God' (Isa. xlix. 4), the Teacher of Righteousness waited with heroic confidence for deliverance and final victory (VII, 23-5):

> [And Thou, O] my [G]od, hast succoured my soul
> and lifted my horn on high.
> And I will shine with a sevenfold l[igh]t
> in the E[den which] Thou hast [m]ade unto Thy glory.
> For Thou art an [ever]lasting light unto me.

This luminous transfiguration of the Teacher exceeds the reward promised to the Servant of the Lord (Isa. liii. 11): 'Because of the affliction of his soul, he shall see the light and shall be satisfied.'[1] Not only will the leader of the Community of the Sons of Light 'see the light', but he will himself become wholly light.

But before this supreme exaltation, the earthly destiny of the Teacher was horribly dramatic: the Saviour-Messiah was to be born in distress, in 'the waves of Death'. Such is the theme developed in one of the *Hymns* (III, 7-18) revealing the highest summits of messianic speculation attained by the Essene sect. Another passage (VIII, 4-15) evokes the great Mystery of the Teacher of Righteousness: he whom God chose to be the instrument of the great work of salvation remains unknown, unrecognized, wretched and, to repeat

---

[1] This is the reading of the two manuscripts of Isaiah found in cave I; it conforms to that of the *Septuagint*. The Masoretic Text suppresses the word 'the light'.

the expression of the 'Servant Songs', 'like a young plant', 'like a root out of dry ground' (Isa. liii. 2). Yet it is through him that man is healed (*Hymns*, II, 8-9): 'And I have been . . . healing for all those that are converted from sin, prudence for the simple, and the firm inclination of all those whose heart is troubled.' The Servant of the Lord also brought healing: 'By his bruises we are healed' (Isa. liii. 5). In the humiliations and sufferings of the Teacher lies the deepest of Mysteries (*Hymns*, VIII, 11); God willed that in these sorrows the Teacher should build his glorious Church.[1]

3. THE HEAD OF THE CHURCH

The *Commentary on Psalm XXXVII* found in cave IV[2] interprets verses 23-4 as follows: 'The explanation of this concerns the Priest, the Teacher [of Righteousness whom God] established to build for Himself the Congregation [of truth . . .].' Thus the sect founded by the Teacher of Righteousness is an edifice, a building. It is of this building — of his Church that is to say — that he speaks in this passage from the *Hymns* (VI, 25-7):

> For it is Thou who wilt set the foundation upon rock
> and the framework on the cord of righteousness
> and the plumb-line of tr[uth] to [tes]t the tried stones,
> in order to (build) a stout bui[ld]i[ng]
> such as will not shake
> and that none who enter there shall stagger . . .

This is echoed in another passage (VII, 8-9):

> And Thou hast established my fabric upon rock
> and everlasting foundations serve for my ground
> and all my walls are a tried rampart
> which nothing can shake.

The Teacher says 'my fabric' because this Church is his work, and also because he in some way identifies himself with it. In other passages[3] he calls it 'the Shoot' (*nezer*), from a word borrowed from

---

[1] It has been observed that nowhere in the *Hymns* does the Teacher present his sufferings as serving to atone for the sins of others; the Servant of the Lord, on the contrary, 'was pierced for our rebellions, pounded for our iniquities . . . he bore the sin of many and made intercession for sinners' (Isa. liii. 5, 12). The remark is correct; but it is impossible to overlook the fact that the doctrine of atonement for the sins of others was fundamental to the sect (see *Rule*, VIII, 6, 10; IX, 4; *Sayings of Moses*, III, 11; IV, 3). The Teacher of Righteousness must have professed the same doctrine himself.

[2] See above, pp. 270-2.   [3] Cf. VI, 15; VII, 19; VIII, 6, 8, 10.

Isaiah (xi. 1); he develops an allegory of the greatest interest on this theme of the messianic 'Shoot' (VIII, 4-11).

The theme of the 'Shoot' is closely associated with that of the 'everlasting Planting';[1] this latter expression is also taken from Isaiah (lxi. 3), from the passage in which the Servant of the Lord declares that he has been sent to bring good tidings to the humble and to comfort all the afflicted. The term is encountered not only several times in the *Hymns* to denote the Essene Church, but again in the *Rule* and the *Damascus Document*. A passage from the *Hymns* (VI, 15-17) describes the growth of the divine tree as follows: '... Its shade shall spread over all [the earth, and] its [top] reach up to the hea[vens and] its roots go down to the Abyss. And all the rivers of Eden [shall water] its [bo]ughs and it shall become a [mi]ghty [forest]; [and the glory of] its [fo]rest shall spread over the world without end, as far as Sheol, [for ever]'. This is what the Church of the Teacher of Righteousness believed itself to be: it wished to be universal, present in the whole world, everlasting. It felt itself in communion with Eden, and even with Sheol.

In another passage of the *Hymns*, the Teacher of Righteousness describes himself as the Gardener of the divine Planting (VIII, 21-6); it prospers through his care, but if he abandons it, it will perish. Yet he is more than the Gardener who ensures the watering of the divine Planting by digging its channels; he it is who, from inside, causes 'the Shoot of ho[li]ness to grow into the planting of truth' (VIII, 10). He is the sap, the very life of the Church — his Church.

---

[1] Cf. VI, 15; VIII, 6, 10.

Chapter XIV

ESSENISM AND CHRISTIANITY

Jewish apocalyptical writings, Essenism and Christianity. — John the Baptist and the sect of Qumran; Jesus and the Teacher of Righteousness. — The primitive Church and Essenism: affinities and borrowings; contrasts. — Conclusion.

In *l'Avenir de la Science*, Ernest Renan, then aged twenty-five and already absorbed by plans for the great critical history of the beginnings of Christianity which he wished one day to write, expressed himself thus: 'A history of the Origins of Christianity written by a critic following the sources would certainly be a work of some philosophical importance. Well, with what should we construct this marvellous history which, executed scientifically and definitively, would revolutionize thought? With profoundly insignificant books such as the *Book of Enoch*, the *Testaments of the Twelve Patriarchs*, the *Testament of Solomon* and, generally speaking, the apocrypha of Jewish and Christian origin, the Chaldean paraphrases, the *Mishnah*, the deutero-canonical books, etc. On that day, Fabricius and Thilo who prepared a satisfactory edition of these texts, Bruce, who brought back the *Book of Enoch* from Abyssinia, Laurence, Murray and A.-G. Hoffman who elaborated the text, will have advanced the work more than Voltaire flanked by the whole of the eighteenth century. Thus from this broad viewpoint of the knowledge of the human spirit, the most important works can be those which at first sight one would judge the most insignificant. . . .'

These lines were written more than a hundred years ago. What would the illustrious historian have said if he had had in his hands authentic Hebrew and Aramaic fragments of this *Book of Enoch* and the *Testaments of the Twelve Patriarchs*, recovered by wonderful good fortune from their ancient hiding-places? Above all, what would he have said if, in addition to these works which certain of the Christian Churches had preserved, he had known the top-secret archives of the Jewish sect in which this same *Book of Enoch* and so many other apocalyptical writings were elaborated? In his *Vie de Jésus*, Renan reaffirms, not without reason, that these Jewish apocalypses 'are of the highest importance to the history of the development of messianic theories and to the understanding of Jesus' conception of the Kingdom of God'. And he adds: 'The *Book of Enoch*, in particular, was much read in Jesus' entourage. Some of the sayings ascribed to Jesus by the Synoptic Gospels are presented in the Epistle attributed to Saint Barnabas as being from *Enoch*. . . .' Indeed, what would Renan have said if he had been introduced, as we are today, to the very source of these apocalyptical works, into the highly mystical and fervent environment in which they originated?

Through an admirable presentiment, the same historian explicitly connected the Essenes with this *milieu* in which the apocalypses germinated. We read again in the *Vie de Jésus*: 'Essenism, which seems to have been directly related to the apocalyptic school, originated at about the same time, and offered as it were a first rough sketch of the great discipline soon to be instituted for the education of mankind. . . .' He means, of course, Christianity, which with highly accurate intuition he places exactly in line with the apocalyptic school and Essenism. The outstanding interest of the Dead Sea Scrolls lies precisely in the fact that they reveal this Essenism, until now so enigmatic and mysterious — the Essenism that presents us with 'as it were a first rough sketch' of the institution of Christianity. It should not be forgotten that the Essene sect was strictly esoteric in character; according to Josephus, the new member swore never to reveal any of the sect's doctrines 'even if subjected to violence unto death', and the Qumran documents echo this rule of secrecy. In an unhoped-for manner, the Dead Sea Scrolls disclose, authentically, the very doctrines and rites whose divulgence was so severely proscribed. Thanks to the discovery of these long-buried manuscripts, the Essene sect is now better known than it could have been even to the contemporaries of Essenism — to all who were not actually initiates — and this includes Philo of Alexandria and Flavius Josephus!

After Renan, eminent critics did not omit to draw attention to the affinities existing between the teachings contained in certain of the 'Pseudepigrapha of the Old Testament' and those of primitive Christianity. R. H. Charles, who was one of the greatest experts in all this literature, maintained almost fifty years ago that the *Testaments of the Twelve Patriarchs* were 'a product of the school that prepared the way for the New Testament'. The Sermon on the Mount, he wrote, 'reflects in several instances the spirit, and even reproduces the very phrases of our text (of the *Testaments*); many passages in the Gospels exhibit traces of the same text, and St. Paul seems to have used the book as a vade-mecum.... The main, the overwhelming value of the book lies not in this province, but in its ethical teaching, which has achieved a real immortality by influencing the thought and diction of the writers of the New Testament, and even those of our Lord. This ethical teaching, which is very much higher and purer than that of the Old Testament, is yet its true spiritual child, and helps to bridge the chasm that divides the ethics of the Old and New Testaments'.[1] When Renan, in one of the passages quoted above, qualifies as 'profoundly insignificant' writings such as *Enoch* and the *Testaments of the Twelve Patriarchs*, there can be no mistaking his true appreciation, for on the same page he declares that these writings are only insignificant 'at first sight', and that for the really profound and perspicacious they rank among 'the most important works' since they combine to illumine and solve one of the greatest problems to haunt the mind of the historian and thinker, the problem of the genesis of Christianity.

In the Introduction I have mentioned that other saying of Renan, 'Christianity is an Essenism that has largely succeeded'. At the end of the present book, in which it has been my purpose to assemble and translate the 'Essene writings from Qumran' — those writings through which Essenism emerges from the shadows and stands fully revealed — the reader no doubt expects me to lead him back to the essential problem: exactly what connection is there between Essenism and Christianity? I have touched on this problem several times since 1950,[2] but as the published documents multiply it becomes more and more vast and complex. It would be impossible for me to discuss it here with any thoroughness. A task such as this would require at least one whole book; and this would still be provisional since many of the texts taken from the Qumran caves are as yet unknown. In this last chapter I will therefore confine myself to a few reflections born of long commerce with Qumran literature, reflections whose only aim is to emphasize in a general way the exceptional interest of the new documentation for the historical study of Christian origins.

---

[1] *The Apocrypha and Pseudepigrapha of the Old Testament* (1913), pp. 282, 291-2.
[2] See especially, *Aperçus préliminaires* . . ., pp. 119-22 (chapter IX: La 'Nouvelle Alliance' juive et la 'Nouvelle Alliance' chrétienne) — Eng. edn., pp. 97-100; *Nouveaux Aperçus* . . ., pp. 191-213 (chapter IX: La Communauté de l'Alliance et les origines chrétiennes) — Eng. edn., pp. 147-66.

Nearly a century after the appearance of the Teacher of Righteousness, quite near to the monastery of Qumran, at the time when it was inhabited by Essenes, in the same desert of Judah, there rose another prophet, John the Baptist. 'He preached in the desert of Judah', reports Matthew (iii. 1-6), 'saying, "Repent, for the Kingdom of Heaven is at hand. For this is he of whom the prophet Isaiah has said, *A voice crying in the wilderness: prepare the way of the Lord, make straight his paths. . . .*" Then Jerusalem went out to him, and all Judaea, and all the region of Jordan, and they were all baptized by him in the river Jordan, confessing their sins.'

Of course, this preaching of repentance, baptism, confession of sin, this expectation of the Kingdom of God, the quotation from Isaiah about preparing the way of the Lord,[1] even the same desert of Judah in which the prophet's voice sounded, is all very reminiscent of the Community of Qumran. Was John the Baptist really a member of the Essene Community? For a time, perhaps; but during his ministry he distinctly spoke of himself as an independent prophet. The baptism he administered was 'the baptism of John'; his disciples formed a distinct group, 'the disciples of John'. Yet although this group was not properly speaking Essene, it was at least inspired by the same ideal and the same mystical *élan*, and at the voice of its prophet the flame, which for more than a century had been lit at Qumran and continued to burn there, spread with fresh ardour throughout the whole of Palestine.

Then appeared Jesus the Nazarene. Gospel tradition expressly links him with John the Baptist. It reports that he came from Galilee in Judaea to be baptized by John in the waters of the Jordan, and that after his baptism he retired into the same desert of Judah to be tempted by the devil. He, too, gathered disciples about him. During the whole of his ministry he was exposed to the hostility of official Judaism, to the hatred and intrigues of the Sadducees and Pharisees. He was hunted down, at times compelled to seek refuge outside his own country, and at the time of the supreme crisis he was abandoned by his own and even betrayed by one of them. He was arrested in Jerusalem on the orders of the High Priest, condemned and put to death under Pontius Pilate. After his death his disciples regrouped round Peter, and out of their faith was born the Christian Church.

Clearly the earthly destiny and work of Jesus remind us on more

---

[1] The same quotation appears in the *Rule* (VIII, 14).

than one point of the Teacher of Righteousness, the great prophet of the Essene sect; at the distance of about a century the same story is repeated. What is more, Jesus, like the Teacher of Righteousness before him, applied to himself the mysterious Isaiah oracles relating to the Servant of the Lord.[1] This common reference to the Servant is highly significant in that it establishes a particular relationship between the two prophets which is quite unique.

However, I think it would be a mistake to argue from these affinities and similarities, remarkable and striking though they are, that the Gospel account is simply the story of the Teacher of Righteousness rewritten, and that it is pure fiction with Jesus merely a mythical double of the Essene prophet; or that the Teacher of Righteousness was, as some have tried to show, identical with Jesus himself. Side by side with the resemblances there are differences no less incontestable which, in my view, preclude any confusion of the two men. Here are some of them.

The Teacher of Righteousness was a priest of the tribe of Levi; Jesus was not a priest but a layman from the tribe of Judah. The Teacher of Righteousness was revered as the Priest-Messiah, the Messiah of Aaron; Jesus was recognized as the Messiah of Israel, the King-Messiah, son of David. The Teacher of Righteousness, founder of the Community of Qumran, exercised his ministry essentially in Judaea; Jesus was a Galilean and preached mainly in Galilee on the shores of Lake Tiberias. The Teacher of Righteousness was a scholarly teacher so superstitiously venerated by his followers that, like the disciples of Pythagoras, they did not utter his name; Jesus was a familiar teacher, approached freely by his disciples and even by the crowd, and there was nothing secret or mysterious about his name. Judging by the monachal rule which he imposed on his followers, the Teacher of Righteousness was a severe ascetic, charitable no doubt, but also as hard on himself as he was on others, who regarded all contact with sinners as a defilement. Jesus mingled more with everyday life, was more human. 'John (the Baptist)', he declared, 'came neither eating nor drinking, and they said, "He has a demon"; the Son of man came eating and drinking and they said, "Behold a glutton and a drunkard, a friend of publicans and sinners".'[2] The Teacher of Righteousness was the exponent of a mysterious Gnosis elaborated with the help of the highest wisdom then circulating in the world and reserved to

---

[1] See above, p. 362.   [2] Matt. xi. 18-19.

initiates; Jesus was above all a popular preacher, sprung from humble people and expressing himself in simple language with comparisons full of freshness and life.

At the outset of Christianity there was therefore a new Prophet, a new Messiah, whose existence and originality I, for one, have never dreamt of denying. But, this point established, the documents from Qumran make it plain that the primitive Christian Church was rooted in the Jewish sect of the New Covenant, the Essene sect, to a degree none would have suspected, and that it borrowed from it a large part of its organization, rites, doctrines, 'patterns of thought' and its mystical and ethical ideals. Many of these borrowings must, I think, have been apparent in the preceding chapters to all with some knowledge of the Christian New Testament and more or less acquainted with the problems of the history of Christian origins.

In France as elsewhere, several works have already appeared on this question of the influence of the Jewish sect from Qumran upon the early Church. All of them, even those whose authors are most careful to safeguard the unrivalled authority of the Christian religion, punctiliously draw attention to the many parallels emerging from a comparative study, whether it be with regard to the community life and constitution of the primitive Church, with the very conception of the Church, with the fundamental rites of baptism and the Eucharist, with the Sermon on the Mount, with the writings of the Apostle Paul and the Johannine Gospel, with the fundamental doctrines of justification and predestination, or with beliefs relative to the Messiah and the end of the world. I cannot here do more than mention these various lines of research in which historians and theologians are now engaged side by side.[1] But according to Pro-

[1] On this subject, consult in particular the collective work edited by Kr. STENDAHL, *The Scrolls and the New Testament* (New York, 1957). This is a collection of fourteen studies written by a team of theologians, Protestant (W. H. Brownlee, O. Cullmann, W. D. Davies, S. E. Johnson, K. G. Kuhn, Bo Reicke, Kr. Stendahl), and Catholic (R. E. Brown, J. A. Fitzmyer, K. Schubert, E. Vogt), joined by a Jewish writer (N. N. Glatzer). Each of these various studies approaches some great problem of New Testament exegesis in the light of the writings of Qumran; together, they give striking proof of the interest roused by the new documents among New Testament specialists, and of the vast fields of new research in which they must now engage. They extend to all the books of the New Testament, and also to many other writings of primitive Christian literature (*Didache, Hermas*, etc.). The contributions assembled in the work of Kr. STENDAHL are not all of equal value and betray sensibly different leanings. The most remarkable, I think, is that of STENDAHL himself with which the collection opens: 'The Scrolls and the New Testament: An Introduction and a Perspective' (pp. 1-17). In it he develops the

fessor W. F. Albright, one of the most highly qualified American orientalists, 'The new evidence with regard to the beliefs and practices of Jewish sectarians of the last two centuries B.C. bids fair to revolutionize our approach to the beginnings of Christianity.'[1]

Scholars have recently even gone so far as to maintain, with regard to the date of the Last Supper, that Jesus and his disciples did not follow the calendar of the official Synagogue for the celebration of the religious feasts, but adopted an entirely different one, the same calendar as that regulating the liturgical life of the Community of Qumran.[2] This thesis has been approved by several Catholic writers. If it is admissible, nothing shows the effective contacts of the primitive Christian group with the sect from Qumran more clearly: by borrowing the Essene calendar, which imposed dates for the holy days at variance with the official calendar, and which in consequence necessitated a religious life apart, Jesus and his disciples revealed their close affinities with the sect of the Essenes.

Nevertheless, it is essential to note that although the early Church made numerous borrowings from Essenism, they were never entirely passive ones. Owing to the initiative and spirit of its founder, Jesus

---

[1] *BASOR*, Supplem. Studies nos. 10-12 (1951), p. 58.
[2] See A. JAUBERT, *La date de la Cène* (Paris, 1957).

---

theory that the essential difference between the Essene sect and the Christian sect, a difference that is merely relative, resides in 'the degree of anticipation' of the eschatological perspective, of the messianic expectation in which the faith of both was situated. 'The Christian Church' — he explains — 'was one act ahead of the Essenes. . . . We have found that even where the claims and the tenets differed, this was not a difference in ideas or in the structure of thought but that there were at some points different degrees of fulfilment, different claims as to how much of the ultimate consummation was present as a gracious and joyous anticipation of the one great event which to Christians and Essenes alike was yet to come.' The author — a Christian — speaks ironically of the preoccupation of present-day Christians for whom the 'paramount problem is to prove that there is something new in Christianity, something never heard of before'; of those Christians who wish Jesus to be 'the inventor of Christianity', and the Church, 'the guardian of his patent and copyright'. 'In the New Testament' — he writes — 'the major concern is the diametrically opposite one: to make clear that all is "old", in accordance with the expectation of the prophets.' I will quote one more passage: 'It is hard to see how the authority of Christianity could depend on its "originality", i.e. on an issue which was irrelevant in the time when "Christianity" emerged out of the matrix of Judaism, not as a system of thought but as a church, a community. But one may hope that Christianity of today is spiritually and intellectually healthy enough to accept again the conditions of its birth. It is true to say that the Scrolls add to the background of Christianity, but they add so much that we arrive at a point where the significance of similarities definitely rescues Christianity from false claims of originality in the popular sense and leads us back to a new grasp of its foundation in the person and events of its Messiah.'

the Nazarene, and owing also to the circumstances of its historical development, institutions rites and beliefs underwent an evolution in Christianity which was often considerable. So Christianity is not properly speaking Essenism, even though initially it depended on it.

It is even necessary to point out that there are a number of features in primitive Christianity which seem to indicate deliberate opposition to certain characteristic aspects of classical Essenism as we know it from the Qumran documents. But it is a recognized fact in the history of religion that when a new sect comes into being it distinguishes itself from the old sect from which it emerges by certain innovations which are directly opposed to it, and yet at the same time betray its source of origin: this is the law of all dissidence. Even though the historian may, in a sense, be led by the importance of the resemblances and borrowings to consider the primitive Church as a 'para-Essene' sect, a sort of derivative or variety of Essenism, he feels in no way disposed to set aside or underestimate the differences, and even the contrasts, between the Church and classical Essenism. His research can even lead him to discern with far greater clarity and accuracy than was formerly possible not only the common ground, but also the distinction and the peculiar characteristics of the personality of Jesus, or of what he was thought to be by the primitive Christian community born of faith in him.

I would like briefly to give some examples of these contrasts. First, with regard to hierarchy and discipline, the Essene congregation was organized as a militia in which each man was awarded his order number every year, in full assembly — a place in the hierarchic rank in accordance with his seniority and merits — and in which every one of the brethren owed strict obedience to whoever was officially placed above him.[1] Jesus, on the other hand, declares: 'The first shall be last and the last shall be first';[2] 'Whoever would be first among you must be the servant of all.'[3] With these words he abolishes at one blow the whole official hierarchy forming the backbone of Essene society. Whoever they are, men are not qualified to say who is first and last in the sight of God; on God alone, and on His grace and favour, depend the rank and merit of all men. 'Am I not allowed to do what I choose with what belongs to me? Would my goodness make you jealous?' says the master of the vineyard to one of the workers from the first hour.[4]

---

[1] See above, p. 47.
[2] Matt. xx. 16.
[3] Mark x. 44.
[4] Matt. xx. 15.

Another example: Essene society possessed a complete and highly perfected judicial machinery with tribunals, judges, trials and a detailed code fixing extremely severe penalties for every infringement of the law.[1] Jesus rebelled against such a system. 'Judge not', he said, 'that you be not judged. As you judge, so shall you be judged; the measure you give will be the measure you get.'[2] Of course the institution of the Essene tribunals proceeded from a praiseworthy and vigilant concern for the observance of the sect's rules, and for the maintenance of unfailing fervour in community life. But what inconvenience, and what abuses, this mutual and indiscreet supervision must have caused. Every member was to be reported for the smallest fault! And above all, should not the office of judge in a spiritual society, be left to God, to Him who alone sounds the hearts and minds of men?

At Qumran, communication of the doctrines of Gnosis, the revelation of the Mysteries, was rigorously reserved to the initiates, to those who had attained the required degree of understanding and wisdom.[3] 'For the man of understanding' is a phrase frequently met at the head of the sect's writings. The 'simple', those without understanding, had no right to Knowledge. The privilege accorded to the 'understanding' ran the risk of engendering in them intolerable spiritual pride. Jesus abolished it with a firm hand: 'I bless Thee, O Father, Lord of heaven and earth, who hast hidden these things from the wise and the understanding and hast revealed them to children. This is so, O Father, because Thou hast decided it in Thy loving-kindness.'[4]

At Qumran, admittance to the Congregation's meetings was forbidden to 'every person smitten in his flesh, paralysed in his feet or hands, lame or blind or deaf or dumb, or smitten in his flesh with a blemish visible to the eye'.[5] According to the Gospel parable, on the contrary, those called to the feast in the Kingdom of God are 'the poor, the lame, the blind and the maimed'.[6]

At Qumran, the Law ruled in all its rigour, and a detailed jurisprudence protected it from any complacent interpretation or criminal laxity; the laws concerning the observance of the Sabbath were

[1] See above, p. 48.
[2] Matt. vii. 1-2; cf. Luke vi. 37: 'Judge not and you shall not be judged; condemn not and you shall not be condemned; forgive and it shall be forgiven you.'
[3] See above, pp. 46-7.
[4] Matt. xi. 25-6; Luke x. 21.
[5] *Rule Annexe*, II, 5-7 (see above, pp. 107-8).
[6] Luke xiv. 15-24; cf. Matt. xxii. 1-10.

particularly harsh.[1] Without abolishing the Sabbath law, or any of the Mosaic laws, Jesus called for a more humane and liberal casuistry. 'The Sabbath', he said, 'was made for man, and not man for the Sabbath.'[2] He scandalized the Pharisees by allowing his hungry disciples to pull the ears of corn for food on the Sabbath, and he himself worked various cures on that day.

In all these instances, and in others still, we therefore see Jesus making a direct stand against certain of the failings and excesses of Qumran Essenism. He did not, of course, repudiate Essenism altogether, for there is a great deal of evidence to show his deep affinities with the Essene *milieu* and his perfect agreement with the fundamental doctrines and spirituality of the sect. But in the name of a purer and more inward religion, he reacted against the excesses, rigidities and formalism from which classical Essenism had not been able entirely to protect itself. By liberating souls from a certain sterile constraint, he aimed at leading them with a more complete and spontaneous impetus towards the same essential ideal, the love of God and man.

The theory attributing an Essene origin to Christianity is, I repeat, no new idea. As I have reminded the reader in the Introduction, it was very widespread in the eighteenth century among the philosophers of the Enlightenment. It always had its supporters, but during the whole of the nineteenth century and the first half of the twentieth it generally came up against a very lively repugnance on the part of Christian historians, Catholic and Protestant alike. A few years ago, for example, one could read this sort of thing among these historians: 'Essenism has left no traces in Christianity, either in its doctrine or in its institutions: it had no more influence on its founder than it had on its propagators.'[3] Or again: 'The Essenes seem to have remained wholly foreign to the work of Jesus and the apostles. We shall therefore not need to say much about them; moreover, little is known of this sect.'[4]

Today a negative attitude such as this is quite impossible. To measure the distance travelled, it is enough to quote these lines from the pen of Fr. J. Daniélou in a little work published in

[1] See above, p. 57.   [2] Mark ii. 27.
[3] L. MARCHAL, article 'Esséniens' in *Supplément au Dictionnaire de la Bible*, ii (Paris, 1933), col. 1131.
[4] Fr. Jules LEBRETON, l'*Église primitive* (Paris, 1934), p. 49.

1957; they will serve to end this book. 'By informing us', he writes, 'of the immediate environment in which Christianity came into being (i.e. the Essene *milieu*), the Qumran discoveries resolve a considerable number of problems which exegesis had not been able to solve. . . . The utilization of all these documents, and the comparisons to which they will lead, will doubtless considerably augment the number of solved enigmas. It can therefore be said that this is the most sensational discovery ever made.'[1]

[1] *Les Manuscrits de la Mer Morte et les Origines du Christianisme* (Paris, 1957), p. 123.

APPENDICES

I

THE COPPER SCROLLS DISCOVERED IN CAVE III[1]

March 1952 saw the discovery in cave III of various manu-script fragments and, in addition, a document of a particular type. It consists of three sheets of very thin copper, each measuring 12 in. wide and 32 in. long; originally these copper sheets were riveted end to end, forming a strip 8 ft. long. On them is engraved a lengthy text in square Hebrew script set out in several columns. One of the sheets had become detached and had rolled in on itself; the two others formed a single scroll.

These scrolls had become greatly oxidized and extreme care was necessary in order to avoid the irremediable deterioration of the inscription engraved on their inner face. From 1952 various chemists were consulted, in particular Dr. Corwin of Johns Hopkins University in Baltimore; but the copper was so corroded that it was evidently impossible to make it flexible enough to unroll it without causing serious damage.

An entirely different process had to be considered therefore, in which each sheet would be cut into several pieces so as to reveal the inner surface without injuring the inscription. The scrolls, as such, had no artistic value: they could be sacrificed without very great regret should this be necessary for the decipherment of the in-scription in which their whole interest lay. With the permission of the Jordan Government, the small scroll was brought to England in July 1955 and entrusted to a specialist, Professor H. Wright Baker of the College of Technology at Manchester, so that he could proceed with the planned dissection. He used an extremely fine, small circular saw mounted on an apparatus specially designed for the purpose and provided with all the technical devices necessary. The operation was begun on September 30th, 1955, and succeeded perfectly; by November 26th, J. M. Allegro, a Hebrew scholar from the University of Manchester, was able to send the results of his

[1] Cf. my article in *RHR*, cli (1957), pp. 22-36.

decipherment of the scroll thus opened to G. Lankester Harding, the Director of the Jordan Department of Antiquities. Shortly afterwards, at the beginning of January 1956, the other scroll consisting of two copper sheets also arrived in Manchester and was immediately treated in the same way. Professor Baker divided it into eighteen sections, while beside him Allegro proceeded with happy enthusiasm to make a preliminary decipherment which he communicated at once to Lankester Harding. In April 1956, the precious documents were returned to Jordan.[1]

The complete inscription engraved on the two scrolls comprises about three thousand letters. It is arranged in twelve columns, each containing thirteen to seventeen lines: eight columns in the large scroll, where the inscription begins, and four in the small, which continues and ends the text. In its general lay-out and dimensions the document is reminiscent of the leather scrolls, the 'volumes' found at Qumran. Only the material is different: consequently the various sheets were riveted to each other instead of being sewn as in the leather scrolls.

Before the inscription was known, scholars were inclined to think that this long strip of copper was a sort of placard or poster set up in a convenient place in the community house at Qumran, and engraved with some important text commemorating, for example, the foundation of the monastery or the sect, or recalling its essential rules. It was supposed that at the time of the great Jewish War in A.D. 68 when the Essenes were obliged to quit their *laura* at Qumran, they hid their library in the neighbouring caves and at the same time detached and concealed the great copper inscription.

However, Professor K. G. Kuhn, at present professor at the University of Heidelberg, went to Jerusalem in October 1953 and was able to examine the famous copper scrolls in the Palestine Archaeological Museum. Though he was obviously unable to read anything of those parts of the inscription which were hidden in the interior of the scrolls, he applied himself with legitimate curiosity and laudable patience to deciphering a certain number of letters and words sufficiently visible from the outside and appearing in relief. As a result of this reading, which was still very partial, he came to what was at first sight the astonishing conclusion that the copper scrolls give 'a

---

[1] Professor H. WRIGHT BAKER has explained the technique of his work in an article entitled, 'Notes on the opening of the "bronze" scrolls from Qumran', published in the *Bulletin of the John Rylands Library*, xxxix, no. 1, September 1956, pp. 45-6 (4 plates).

description of the hiding-places of the riches, objects of value, and movable possessions of the Essene community'.

The sect, he explained (*RB*, 1954, p. 204), 'practised common ownership of property. Whoever entered, transferred his private fortune to the common one (*Rule*, VI, 19). This was administered by "the overseer in charge of the revenues of the Many" (*Rule*, VI, 20; cf. Josephus, *Jewish War*, II, 8, 3, §§ 122 f.). Since the Essenes lived a very frugal life and were simple and hard-working, it is easy to assume that in time the common funds became very considerable. It may also be supposed that, as is always the case with religious orders, pious foundations contributed to the enlargement of this fortune. Now at the onset of the great revolt the Essenes did not abandon the seat of their order in a sudden panic: we can see this by the care with which they packed and concealed their entire library and perhaps, to this end, even made a new and careful revision of their manuscripts beforehand. This being so, they certainly did not neglect the order's fortune and valuables. Once their manuscripts were hidden, they would have placed their movable fortune and valuables in a place of safety. We are even entitled to think that they did this with still more care than for the library, since the fortune would be indispensable in making a new start in the future. I therefore consider it possible that the "overseer" may have concealed or buried everything of value and drawn up an inventory of these things. This catalogue was indestructibly engraved on copper and was itself also hidden in a cave, so that in case of the death of the "overseer" and of the other members informed of the hiding-place, the surviving members of the community might one day, thanks to this catalogue on copper, be able to rediscover the fortune.'

It is right that we should pay homage today to Professor Kuhn's perspicacity. Though the text of the inscription as a whole is still kept secret, an official announcement was made by G. Lankester Harding and Fr. de Vaux on June 1st, 1956, simultaneously in Jordan, France, Great Britain and the United States; it was read on the same day before the Académie des Inscriptions et Belles-Lettres. It states, on the basis of a provisional decipherment made by Fr. J. T. Milik, that the inscription on the copper scrolls is in actual fact a list of hiding-places, a catalogue mentioning about sixty deposits of gold and silver and also of boxes of incense, with detailed indications as to the site of each deposit. These sites, it adds, are dispersed over a region stretching from Hebron to Mount

Gerizim near Nablus, but most of them seem to be in the vicinity of Jerusalem. The exact locations are, however, 'naturally difficult to identify today, as the toponymy of the region has undergone considerable changes since the first century A.D.'.

A few brief extracts have been translated and published as examples and to show the nature of the document. Here is the text of these extracts after Fr. Milik's translation (the Hebrew text is still unpublished):

No. 3 (col. I, lines 6-8): 'In the great cistern which is in the peristyle court, in a recess at the bottom, hidden in a hole opposite the upper opening: nine hundred talents.'

No. 11 (col. II, lines 10-12): 'In the cistern which is below the rampart, on the eastern side, in a hollow of the rock: six hundred bars of silver.'

No. 52 (col. XI, lines 1-4): 'Close by, below the southern corner of the portico, at the tomb of Zadok, under the column of the exedra: a box of incense in pine-wood and a box of incense in cassia-wood.'

No. 62 (col. XII, lines 10-12): 'In the near-by pit, on the northern side, in a cavity opening to the north with tombs at its opening, there is a copy of this document with the explanation, measurements and all the details.'[1]

These few examples certainly give the impression that we are faced with real deposits, carefully described and scrupulously indicated. But the report of June 1st expressly dismisses this interpretation: the inscription, it says, is nothing but a collection of traditions relating to places where ancient treasure was supposed to have been hidden. It continues as follows: 'It is difficult to understand why the Essenes of Qumran were so much concerned with these stories of hidden treasure, and especially why they saw fit to engrave them on copper, which at that time was a costly metal. It is also curious to learn from the last paragraph (no. 62) that there was a second copy of this document giving explanations which we should very much like to know. . . . The total sum of silver and gold thus listed amounts to some two hundred tons. This clearly fantastic figure, added to the

---

[1] Cf. J. T. MILIK, *The Biblical Archaeologist*, xix, 3, September 1956, pp. 62-3. In no. 52, instead of 'a box of incense in pine-wood and a box of incense in cassia-wood' I prefer to read, 'a vase of pine-sap (DM', literally 'tear') and a vase of cassia-sap'; they would then be liquid perfumes, not incense. Compare this with the 'alabaster vase of perfume of pure nard, very costly' mentioned in the Gospels (Mark xiv. 3; cf. Matt. xxvi. 7; Luke vii. 37; John xii. 3).

depths at which the deposits are said to have been buried — up to 15 or 20 ft. deep — casts serious doubt on the reality of these stories. At all events, this guide to hidden treasure is the most ancient document of its kind to have been found, and is of interest to the historian of folk-lore.'

In my opinion, this conclusion immediately gives rise to serious objections; the authors of the report seem to be aware of them themselves. How is it possible to imagine that an Essene, a member of a mystical brotherhood distinguished by its love of poverty and contempt for riches, a man who had renounced all his possessions to enter the order, derived any pleasure from stories of hidden treasure or found enjoyment in counting up all this 'mammon of unrighteousness'? Is it really possible to think of an Essene abandoning himself to dreams so absolutely contrary to the whole of his life's ideal? Or must we suppose that he went mad, that he fell victim to a morbid obsession in which all these treasures of gold and silver, treasures accursed yet unconsciously desired, shimmered before his imagination? But even if this were so, why should this raving Essene decide to inscribe such reveries on copper, whereas the holy books themselves were only copied on leather or papyrus? Moreover, how was he able to obtain copper, a relatively costly metal, and prepare the sheets and rivet them himself, without his brethren knowing about it? The hypothesis formulated by the authors of the report seems to me to be in absolute and monstrous opposition to the context of the discovery, to all that we know of the seriousness and austerity characterizing the Qumran sect, and of their spirit of poverty. I do not believe that the inscription is the futile copy of some fantastic story of hidden treasure. It is a document drafted with all the baldness of book-keeping, and the reason for its having been engraved on resistant material, and kept in two copies, is that it is an important archive, not of invented riches, but of very real ones.

As we have seen, it is objected that the depth of some of the hiding-places described is most improbable: I am afraid the cogency of this observation escapes me. It is said again that the total of the deposits of gold and silver mentioned in the inscription — about six thousand talents — is 'obviously fantastic'. Is it really so obvious? It should be recalled, for example, that on the capture of Jerusalem in 63 B.C., Pompey demanded immediate tribute of 'more than ten thousand talents' (Josephus, *Jewish Antiquities*, XIV, 4, 5, § 78); and that a little later Crassus carried off two thousand talents which

Pompey had left in the Temple, and in addition, gold 'for eight thousand talents' (Josephus, *Jewish Antiquities*, XIV, 7, 1, §§ 105-9).

J. M. Allegro has not published his decipherment of the inscription on the copper scrolls; no doubt he has not been authorized to do so. But in a recent work (*The Dead Sea Scrolls*, 1956, p. 184) he disagrees with the theory expressed in the Jerusalem report, and does not hesitate to assert that it is 'indeed an inventory of the Sect's most treasured possessions, buried in various locations'. With the proviso that the complete text when published contributes nothing unexpected, I believe we can rally to this opinion of Allegro who knows the document.

I would emphasize straight away that if this opinion is confirmed, the inscription on the copper scrolls is not just a rather frivolous and misleading fairy tale, but a document of value offering us precious information about the sect.

We learn from it, first of all, that the Essene order was very rich. It was a community of 'the Poor', of course, but although each individual member cultivated the spirit of poverty, the community, as such, had the right to possess great property. From generation to generation it was enriched by the fortune brought in by each new member, and doubtless also by the numerous donations and legacies made by pious souls. All these contributions accumulated continually whereas there was no great expenditure. This fortune was, as both Josephus and the *Rule* tell us, administered by a functionary specially appointed for the purpose; no doubt his administration was scrupulously prudent and honest. It should be noted, too, that the *Rule* is extremely precise and severe with regard to any damage caused by one of its members to the 'possessions of the community' (VII, 6-8). It is not surprising that the riches of the Essene order were a temptation to the state treasury, the authorities in Jerusalem; we learn in fact from the *Commentary on Habakkuk* that at the time of the persecution of the sect, the 'Wicked Priest' — in my opinion the High Priest Hyrcanus II — confiscated all, or part, of these riches. It is explicitly said that the Wicked Priest 'stole the goods of the Poor' (XII, 9-10). 'The Poor' is the name, or one of the names, by which the members of the sect called themselves; and an attack such as this on the community treasure cannot have been the least of the grievances which 'the Poor' must have borne against the accursed persecutor.

But if the inscription on the copper scrolls allows us to picture how solidly the Essene brotherhood, with all its ingots of silver and gold, was rooted in this world, it can no doubt also tell us of the extent of that brotherhood. In point of fact, the deposits seem to have been made in the various cities of Palestine where there were houses belonging to the order, houses affiliated to the Qumran mother-house. Josephus reports that the Essenes formed colonies 'in every city' (*Jewish War*, II, 8, 3, § 124),[1] and Philo of Alexandria states that 'they lived in a number of towns in Judaea, and also in many villages and large groups' (*Apologia pro Judaeis* in Eusebius of Caesarea, *Praeparatio Evangelica*, viii, 11, § 1).[2] The places indicated in the inscription must therefore constitute, as it were, the map of the Essene establishments: it was among these that the bursar-general, anxious to divide the risks, distributed the property of the order for each of them to conceal in some near-by hiding-place. This prudent administrator then engraved on the copper scrolls, in dupli-cate, the inventory of the treasure thus dispersed and carefully hid the two documents, one in a cave in the vicinity of the mother-house, the other somewhere else. It is not without interest to observe that the deposits are spaced from Hebron in the south to Mount Gerizim in the middle of Samaria, and that most of them are situated in the neighbourhood of Jerusalem. This suggests that the Essene houses were distributed over the whole of Judaea, and even as far as Samaria. The reader will note the presence of Essenes among the Samaritans, those schismatics whom the Jews, generally, treated with the utmost contempt.

Recently Dr. Ch. Rabin suggested that the treasures mentioned in the copper scrolls belonged, not to the Qumran sect, but to the Temple of Jerusalem (*Jewish Chronicle*, June 1956). Professor Kuhn, following the report of June 1st, 1956, returned to the question of the copper scrolls with which he was occupied in 1953. In an article in the *Theologische Literaturzeitung* (1956, no. 9, cols. 542-6), he first recalls, not without legitimate satisfaction, the conclusions arrived at in his earlier research, conclusions so brilliantly confirmed, in essentials at least, by the decipherment of the complete inscription. He then very pertinently questions the opinion that the inscription — the 'whimsical product of a deranged mind', in Fr. de Vaux's words — is devoid of any historical value. Finally, without categori-cally retracting his previous thesis that these are Essene deposits, he formulates the hypothesis, as Rabin does, that the inventory may allude to deposits from the Temple of Jerusalem: the mass of gold

---

[1] Cf. above, p. 28. [2] Cf. above, p. 24.

and silver indicated in the inscription would be 'quite thinkable', he explains, in connection with this Temple, 'one of the most esteemed and wealthy of the whole of the ancient world'.

It seems to me, on the contrary, extremely difficult to imagine that the Jewish authorities would have entrusted the duty of concealing the Temple treasure to the Essenes, or that, if such a proposition were made to them, the Essenes would have felt able to accept it. Although the riches of the Essene order were, in the eyes of its members, blamelessly pure and holy, they regarded the riches accumulated in the Temple very differently. From their sectarian viewpoint, the Temple wealth was the fruit of shameless plunder, as appears in the *Commentary on Habakkuk* (IX, 4-7). How could they have consented to defile their hands with these unclean riches, to hide them for the sole profit of the official priesthood which they looked on as fallen and unworthy?

But even though conceding that, faced with the grave peril menacing the entire Jewish nation, the Essenes may have succeeded in silencing all their resentment and scruples, Kuhn's hypothesis meets with yet another objection, which, moreover, the author himself records quite frankly: 'Josephus says nowhere that the riches of the Temple were hidden in secret places outside Jerusalem; on the contrary, the Jewish historian's data speak on the whole against such an opinion.' And in point of fact, the account of the capture of the Temple by the soldiers of Titus, which is given in much detail, makes it clear that the treasure had not left the Temple at that moment (August 6th, A.D. 70). Here are the texts: 'Whilst the Temple burned, the soldiers carried off all the booty. . . . They also burnt down the treasury chambers where there was an immense quantity of money, countless vestments, and all sorts of ornaments, and in a word, all the opulence of the Jewish nation, for the rich had transported there the precious objects from their houses' (*Jewish War*, VI, 5, §§ 271, 282). And again: 'All the soldiers had such huge spoils that the gold pound was sold in Syria for half its former value' (*Jewish War*, VI, 6, § 317).

Trying to reconcile his new hypothesis with this formal evidence, Kuhn explains that 'if they had hidden the Temple treasure, or a large part of it, outside Jerusalem before the Roman siege, it would certainly have been kept so rigorously secret that quite possibly, and even probably, Josephus knew nothing about it'. A flimsy argument! Josephus himself points out that soon after the capture and burning of the Temple, a fresh batch of sacred treasure which had escaped pillage was handed over to Titus by one of the priests anxious to preserve his life; it had no doubt been concealed by him in some hiding-place, but *in the Temple itself*, not outside Jerusalem, nor even outside the precincts of the Temple, as is plain from Josephus (*Jewish War*, VI, 8, §§ 387-91): 'At this time, one of the priests, named Jesus son of Thebuthi, having received from Caesar a sworn assurance that his life would be preserved on condition that he delivered up certain objects of the sacred treasure, went out and passed over the Temple wall two candlesticks similar to those in the sanctuary, and tables, bowls, goblets, all made of solid gold and very massive. He also handed over the veils, the vestments of the High Priests garnished with precious stones, and many other articles intended for worship. Phineas, the guardian of the Temple treasure, was also taken; he laid out the tunics and girdles of the High Priest, a great quantity of purple and scarlet held in reserve to repair the veil of the Temple, besides much cinnamon, cassia and other aromatic spices which were mixed together and burnt daily to the honour of God. He also gave the Romans many other precious things and a great number of sacred ornaments. This procured for him, although he had been taken by force, the pardon reserved to deserters.'

It is interesting no doubt to notice the mention of aromatic spices in the inventory, particularly cassia, which also figures in one of the deposits described in the copper inscription. But the passage from Josephus by no means proves that the Temple riches, or even part of them, were entrusted to the Essenes for concealment; on the contrary, it gives the impression that no such precautions had been taken. Kuhn also cites the following text mentioning the 'mopping up' in the city by the Roman soldiers after it had been captured (*Jewish War*, VI, 9, 4, §§ 429-32): 'They also sought out all who had taken refuge underground, and digging into the ground, they killed all the Jews they met with. They found there more than two thousand men who had killed themselves by their own hands or killed each other, or who had in a greater number succumbed to hunger. A fearful smell of corpses struck those who entered. Many withdrew immediately; many penetrated inside, driven by cupidity, treading underfoot the piled-up bodies. They found many precious things in the trenches; the love of lucre rendered lawful every means of satisfying it. . . .' But there is nothing to indicate that the 'precious things' found by the Roman soldiers in the underground passages of the city had anything to do with the Temple treasure; they were most likely the private possessions of Jews who had hidden them in order to preserve them from pillage.

Kuhn's hypothesis gives rise to another grave objection. It is most probable that, as Fr. de Vaux has very soundly established (*RB*, 1954, p. 233), the Qumran buildings were attacked and destroyed by the Romans in June, A.D. 68. So it was on this date that the Essenes abandoned their Qumran *laura*, having previously hidden in the near-by caves everything they wished to save: their holy books, and also the famous copper scrolls. If the deposits mentioned in these scrolls refer to Essene property, it is easy to explain that at about the time when the Romans were approaching Jericho and the Dead Sea (Josephus, *Jewish War*, IV, §§ 450, 477, 486), the leaders of the community of Qumran, aware of the grave menace threatening the monastery, decided to send all or part of the order's riches into the regions of Hebron and Jerusalem where the Romans had not yet reached. But if it is the Temple treasure, we have to accept that it was evacuated and handed over to the Essenes at least some time before the abandonment of Qumran, before June, A.D. 68, that is. Now at that moment Jerusalem was not yet invested, and the Holy City must have appeared to the Jews as the safest place of refuge. Would it have even occurred to the Temple authorities to disperse the Temple wealth outside the precincts of Jerusalem, which was the most strongly protected city in Palestine and which they were determined to defend to the end? Was it not a far greater risk to remove the sacred treasure, to hide it in the outskirts of Jerusalem where, in the event of siege, the soldiery would obviously be able to search and ferret around for months on end? In fact there is, as we have seen, not the least sign in Josephus that the Temple leaders carried such a dispersion into effect: it was in the 'treasury chambers', in the very precincts of the Temple, that the Roman soldiers seized its wealth or the riches consigned to its care.

It may perhaps be objected that if the Essene order had really possessed the two hundred tons of precious metal mentioned in the copper inscription, it would have held such enormous power as to make it the rival of the Jerusalem priesthood and as it were a State within the State. We are certainly rather surprised to learn that the Essene brotherhood grew so rich: but has not the accumulation of riches been the fate of more than one religious order, in

Christianity, Islam and Buddhism alike? As for the power of the Essene order, the esteem it enjoyed, its influence on the Jewish world, no one today would dream of denying it. Moreover, there is nothing to make us think that, however great the Essene fortune, it exceeded that of the Temple. True, we are unable to make any exact calculation of the Temple fortune at the time when it was pillaged by the legionaries of Titus, but the passages from Josephus quoted above show plainly that these riches were immense. After plundering the Temple, the Roman soldiers, as we have seen, poured out gold so profusely in Syria that the price of the gold pound dropped by half! In any case, even if the deposits described in the Qumran inscription turn out to be Temple treasure, it would have to be recognized that the total fortune of the Temple greatly exceeded these four thousand to four thousand five hundred talents hidden outside Jerusalem; they would only have formed part of it, since the Romans laid hands on considerable riches in the Temple itself.

So Professor Kuhn's new theory appears as unprofitable as it is unlikely. It is better to abide by his initial hypothesis which nothing so far seems to have weakened. I think the inventory found in the Qumran cave is, quite simply, an inventory of the property of the community of Qumran.

Postscript. J. T. Milik has recently published in *RB*, 1959, no. 3, pp. 321-57, and no. 4, pp. 550-75, a complete translation of the inscription engraved on the copper scrolls, together with a 'topographical commentary' and various 'notes on Palestinian epigraphy and topography' connected with his decipherment of the inscription. Unfortunately, we have not been given the essential, namely a photograph of the document and the Hebrew text itself: Milik is reserving this for the *editio princeps*, i.e. vol. iii of the series, *Discoveries in the Judaean Desert*. This volume is unlikely to appear before 1961 or 1962. Given the extreme difficulties which the reading and interpretation of the inscription entail, difficulties on which the author himself insists (pp. 328 f.), we cannot, without being able to verify its merits, consider the translation he gives us now as sufficient ground upon which to base any conclusions. His 'topographical commentary', especially, seems very erudite and ingenious, but on the whole extremely fragile; moreover, the author himself warns us in all fairness of 'the hypothetical character of almost all the identifications proposed'. We shall obviously have to wait until we know the Hebrew text.

Despite the grave uncertainties which, as he himself admits, are involved in his decipherment and interpretation of the text, Milik clearly reaffirms the theory maintained in the report of June 1st, 1956, namely that 'the bronze catalogue merely describes imaginary treasure deriving from Jewish folk-lore of the Roman epoch'. As for the origin and date of this catalogue, instead of attributing its composition, as he did in the beginning, to some member of the Essene community at Qumran, therefore in not later than A.D. 68, he now declares that a more profound study of the document leads him to prefer 'the period between the two Jewish wars against the Romans, in round figures, let us say, the year 100': the text would then have nothing whatever to do with the Essenes. It should be noted that Milik has been led to modify his first translation appreciably; thus, the final paragraph of the catalogue (col. XII, lines 10-13), which he first translated (see *supra*, p. 382) 'In the near-by pit, on the northern side, in a cavity opening to the north with tombs at its opening, there is a copy of this document with the explanation, measurements, and all the details', now becomes: 'In the gallery of the Smooth Rock to the north of Koḥlit which opens to the north and has tombs at its opening: a copy of this document, with explanations, measurements, and a detailed description.' In this new translation, where the author previously read 'in a cavity', there now appears a toponym, 'Koḥlit', which according to him figures in three other passages of the catalogue.

This mention of 'Koḥlit' (KḤLT), which at first escaped the author's attention, now seems to him most revealing. He thinks he can relate it to the 'Spring of Koḥel' (KḤL) in a curious Jewish work of the Middle Ages called the *Treatise of the Vessels*. This 'treatise' is a detailed and manifestly fictitious description of the treasures of the Temple of Solomon, indicating the places where they were hidden at the time of the capture of Jerusalem by the Babylonians in 586 B.C.: Baghdad, Borsippa, 'En Koḥel, Babylon, and Tell Baruk. Actually the name 'En Koḥel (Spring of Koḥel) does not appear in the text of the Hebrew 'treatise' edited by A. Jellinek (*Bet ha-Midrasch*, Leipzig, 1853, ii, pp. xxvi f., and 88-91): this printed text reads KTL., not KḤL. But Milik thinks he can correct this KTL to KḤL. He explains that a collection of marble plaques has recently been found at Beirut on which is engraved, after the biblical book of Ezekiel, the aforementioned *Treatise of the Vessels*; this latter work is preceded by a short account which states that the vessels of the sanctuary were hidden at 'En Koḥel, on the western slopes of Mount Carmel. Milik at once identifies the 'En KTL of Jellinek's text with this 'En KḤL of the Beirut document. He does not say whether this last document also reads, 'En KḤL, in the passage from the *Treatise of the Vessels* where the Jellinek text reads, 'En KTL, doubtless because he himself has been unable to ascertain it. This is really tiresome, for the correction he suggests is some-what uncertain: in the *Treatise of the Vessels*, 'En KTL, mentioned as being between Baghdad and Borsippa on the one hand, and Babylon on the other, seems also to be situated in Babylonia, where-as in the short account proper to the Beirut document, 'En KḤL is expressly located on Carmel in Palestine. Can this account, which does not belong to the *Treatise of the Vessels*, represent a legendary tradition different from that attested by the work itself?

However this may be, it nevertheless seems essential to observe that in the copper scroll from Qumran it is by no means certain that the word KḤLT has anything to do with the 'Spring of Koḥel' in the inscription on the Beirut plaques. In none of the four passages where Milik reads this word KḤLT does the word 'spring' occur. Moreover, in the first of these passages (col. I, lines 9-10), we distinctly read 'On the tell of KḤLT'. Milik translates it 'On the hill of Koḥlit'; but the Hebrew word TL really means a mound of debris, a 'tell' and not a hill in general. So Koḥlit seems to be a place-name (Milik himself draws attention to a 'Koḥlit which is in the desert', a Beit Kaḥil near Hebron, a Khirbet Kuḥlat near Beersheba), and not the name of a spring. Furthermore, is the reading KḤLT really certain in the three other passages? In the last of these Milik seems at first to have read BḤLT, since he trans-lated it 'in a cavity'. It is odd that Koḥlit, this alleged spring on Carmel, should figure in four different places in the catalogue: in column I (lines 9-12), then in column II (lines 12-15), then in column IV (lines 11-12) and, finally, in column XII (lines 10-13), in quite disparate geographical contexts. Why such a capricious dispersion?

The real interest of the parallelism established by Milik between the inscription on the copper scroll from Qumran and the *Treatise of the Vessels* is, I think, quite the reverse of what the author intends: it brings out in full relief the complete contrast between the two documents. On the one hand we have an exact and detailed inventory, a piece of accountancy in the driest style, with detailed indications concerning the nature and quantity of the deposits and the site of each hiding-place; on the other hand we have an absolutely fantastic list of treasure, and hiding-places as desperately vague as 'in a tower in the land of Babylon in the city called Baghdad'. Or again 'in the place called Borsippa'. Whereas the Qumran inventory, when mentioning the hiding-places of vessels, indicates really plausible, modest quantities — 'twenty vessels', 'six hundred and nine vessels' — the *Treatise* counts vessels by 'one hundred and twenty myriads', 'two hundred myriads', etc. As for the gold and silver, in the Qumran documents the total of the deposits amounts to some four thousand five hundred talents. But the sums mentioned in the *Treatise* are extravagant; for instance, 'a million talents of silver and one hundred thousand talents of gold'. Who can help seeing the difference? The comparison is eloquent: the Qumran catalogue has absolutely nothing in common with stories of hidden treasure from Jewish, Arab, or any other folk-lore, except that these stories necessarily include figures and place-names also. We must therefore resolutely dismiss the unfortunate explanation advanced in the report of June 1956: Milik, by trying to justify it, has dealt it its death-blow.

Now if, as I have maintained in these pages (written in December 1956), this really is a genuine inventory, a memorandum, and not a fictitious composition, what property and treasure does it refer to? Is it the treasure of the Community of Qumran, as Professor Kuhn first suggested, and as J. Allegro believes? Or is it the treasure of the Temple of Jerusalem (the Second Temple), as Professor Kuhn has recently maintained? I prefer the first opinion, albeit provisionally and without committing myself (see *supra*, p. 384). For the time being I will refrain from taking up any position in the matter. Allegro, who has been acquainted with the document since 1956 and has studied it at first hand, is himself bringing out in the summer of 1960 a work entitled *The Treasure of the Copper Scroll*; it will include a complete facsimile, a transcription of the Hebrew text, an English translation and detailed notes. By presenting us with the document itself, a work such as this will allow each of us to approach the study personally. It may be that in going thoroughly into the problems raised by the still enigmatic inscription Allegro will have been led to modify his first opinion to a certain extent. While awaiting the

publication of his book, he has kindly let me know that he resolutely maintains, against Milik, the theory of a genuine inventory,
and also that the particular interpretation which he suggests concerning the copper scrolls is in no way opposed to the general thesis
of an Essene origin of the Postcript writings from Qumran.

[J. M. Allegro's book has now appeared (Routledge & Kegan
Paul, London, 1960; 191 pages, 10 photographs and 31 line draw-
ings). It reveals the complexity and difficulty of the manifold
problems involved in the study of the copper scroll and at the same
time makes a valuable contribution towards their solution. Nevertheless, before attempting a thorough study of this still highly enigmatic
document myself, I think it imperative to await J. T. Milik's publication of the complete work in volume III of *Discoveries in the Judaean
Desert*. This will contain, in particular, photographs of the entire
inscription. (Allegro gives only a copy of the text.)]

II

ARE THE QUMRAN SCROLLS OF KARAITE ORIGIN?

When the fragments of the *Damascus Document* from the Cairo *geniza*
were published in 1910, several writers expressed the opinion
that this work was written in the Middle Ages and emanated from
the Karaite sect: thus, A. Büchler,[1] W. Bousset[2] and A. Marmor-
stein.[3] It should be recalled that the Karaite sect appeared in
Judaism at the beginning of the Middle Ages; it had as its founder a
certain Anan who lived in the eighth century; it was distinguished
by its rejection of Rabbinical jurisprudence and by its direct recourse to the text of the Law. To support their theory, the champions
of the Karaite origin of the *Damascus Document* cited certain striking
similarities in doctrine and language between this work and Karaite
writings. The date of the two Cairo manuscripts by which the
Damascus Document was then known did not contradict this thesis
since they were themselves not ancient but dated from the Middle
Ages (tenth and twelfth centuries approximately).

Professor S. Zeitlin of Dropsie College (Philadelphia) also sup-

[1] 'Schechter's Jewish Sectaries' in *JQR*, N.S. iii, 1912-13, pp. 429-85.
[2] *TR*, 1915, pp. 51-8.
[3] 'Eine unbekannte jüdische Sekte' in *Theologisch Tijdschrift*, lii, 1918, pp. 92-122.

ported this theory about thirty years ago.[1] The discovery of the
Dead Sea Scrolls, and among them as I have said (pp. 115-6) various
fragments of this same *Damascus Document*, has done nothing to
shake his conviction: according to him, not only is this work of
medieval and Karaite origin, but so are all the Dead Sea discoveries.
The *Damascus Document*, he declares, was written 'by Karaites for
the purpose of propaganda, to show that the Karaites were an
ancient sect, and that they originated even before the destruction
of the first Temple'. As for the *Rule* and the *Commentary on Habakkuk*,
they are not only similar to the Zadokite Fragments (his name for
the *Damascus Document*), but 'are products of one period' and 'were
written by men of that period, i.e. the Middle Ages'.[2] Ever since
1949 Zeitlin has defended this thesis unceasingly in the *Jewish
Quarterly Review*, whose editor he is, with an obstinacy and aggressive-
ness which cannot, unfortunately, take the place of proof. The Dead
Sea Scrolls, he repeats, are from the Middle Ages; they have no
shred of importance for biblical exegesis, or for the history of ancient
Judaism, or for the history of Christian origins.[3]

Alas, it becomes more and more evident that the Dead Sea Scrolls
are of ancient date, much earlier than the Middle Ages and the
Karaites; since their discovery, the thesis of a Karaite origin of the
Damascus Document, which despite very serious objections did have
some chance before, has now become quite groundless. To sustain
this theory today, and even aggravate it by including all the scrolls
and fragments from the Qumran caves, is to close one's eyes to
the facts.

Zeitlin's theory is no longer credited in the scientific world, and
for good reason; but the author continues to complain bitterly that
his arguments have never been refuted. 'Indeed they have!' answers
Fr. de Vaux, very rightly.[4] 'All his arguments have been refuted,
not by reasoning but by facts, against which the best arguments
in the world are valueless. I would ask Professor Zeitlin to read —
or to read more closely — the reports of the archaeologists whom
he derides. If he had done so, he would not all the time confuse
the Qumran discoveries with those of Murabba'at and Mird. . . .
He would learn that caves III, V, VII, VIII, IX and X were
discovered by archaeologists and not by Bedouin, that the fragments

---

[1] *JQR*, 1926, pp. 385-6.
[2] *The Zadokite Fragments* . . . (Philadelphia, 1952), pp. 5, 23; cf. p. 29.
[3] See his latest work, *The Dead Sea Scrolls and Modern Scholarship* (Philadelphia, 1956).
[4] *RB*, 1957, pp. 636-7.

found by the archaeologists in caves I and IV complement the scrolls and fragments sold by the Bedouin as coming from these same caves; he would learn, too, that there is a site called Khirbet Qumran, whose buildings are dated by coins, whose pottery is identical with that of the caves, whose ostraca carry the same script as the cave scrolls. He would learn much, but he does not want to learn: he has decided that the manuscripts *cannot* be ancient. These manuscripts *are* ancient, and consequently all discussion with Zeitlin is impossible. It is a pity, for if he knows medieval Jewish literature as well as he says he does, he could tell us about the survival or revival of the vocabulary, customs and doctrines of the Community of Qumran, especially among the Karaites.'

If only he would abandon his fruitless obstinacy, Zeitlin is certainly one of those who could do most useful work in determining the exact connections linking medieval Karaism across the centuries with ancient Essenism. 'It is a very remarkable fact', I wrote in 1953,[1] 'that in the Essene cemetery of Qumran the bodies were buried with their heads to the south. This is also a custom observed by the Karaites to this day. Another striking fact is that in the prayers which the Karaites still recite, mention is expressly made of the Teacher of Righteousness, a term so typical of the documents of Qumran: "And may God send us the Teacher of Righteousness to guide the hearts of the fathers towards their children!" At present no definite conclusion can be drawn, but most certainly we have here a line of investigation which must be explored with the greatest care.'

III

ARE THE QUMRAN SCROLLS OF JUDEO-CHRISTIAN ORIGIN?

When studying the *Damascus Document* fifty years ago, the Rev. G. Margoliouth had quite a different idea; according to him this work is Christian or, more exactly, Judeo-Christian.[2] The 'Messiah of Aaron and Israel' is John the Baptist; the Teacher of Righteousness, Jesus.

---

[1] See my *Nouveaux Aperçus* . . ., p. 107. (Eng. edn., p. 76.)
[2] See 'The Sadducean Christians of Damascus', in *The Expositor*, xxxvii (1911), pp. 499-517; xxxviii (1912), pp. 213-35; 'The two Zadokite Messiahs', in *JTS*, xii, 1911, pp. 446-50.

The idea of a Judeo-Christian origin has been revived in connection with the Dead Sea Scrolls by J. L. Teicher of the University of Cambridge.[1] For this writer, as earlier for Margoliouth, the Teacher of Righteousness is Jesus. And Teicher adds that the Wicked Priest is Paul, the Apostle of the Gentiles and the hated enemy of the Judeo-Christians, i.e. Christians come from Judaism and still faithful to the Law. The Qumran documents, he explains further, were written after A.D. 70, when the Judeo-Christian community — or more exactly the Ebionite community — was reorganized outside Judaea. As for the manuscripts we possess, they were copied during the second century, or at the beginning of the third, and were hidden in A.D. 303 during Diocletian's persecution.

Teicher's theory does not seem to have won much support. Like Zeitlin's, though less seriously, it runs glaringly counter to archaeological findings, which establish that the sect quitted the Qumran monastery and concealed its books in the caves during the Jewish War in A.D. 68. Furthermore, many points in the documents themselves take us back, as I have tried to show (chapter XII), to a pre-Christian period, to the time of the Hasmonaean dynasty. Besides, the identification pure and simple of the Teacher of Righteousness as Jesus the Nazarene is difficult to maintain given the marked and numerous differences between the two (see above, pp. 372-3). And what are we to think of the identification of the Wicked Priest as the Apostle Paul, when — not to mention other objections — it is evident that Paul was not a priest?

But erroneous though his essential thesis may be, Teicher's research is not without interest. It stresses the notable and striking resemblances between the sect of the scrolls and ancient Christianity, the Teacher of Righteousness and Jesus the Teacher from Galilee, and shows that a remarkable kinship existed between primitive Christianity and the people of Qumran. Teicher has penetrated these affinities; his fault is that he has wanted to demonstrate, radically and systematically, that there is identity where there is only resemblance, a resemblance explained quite simply by the priority of the Jewish sect and by the influence it exerted on nascent Christianity.

Teicher is particularly impressed by the fact that the Qumran sectaries, like the Judeo-Christians — whom for that reason Christian

[1] *JJS*, ii (1951), pp. 67-99, 115-43; iii (1952), pp. 53-5, 87-8, 111-18, 128-32, 139-50; iv (1953), pp. 1-13, 49-58, 93-103, 139-53; v (1954), pp. 38, 93-9; etc.

heresiologists knew as 'Ebionites' — called themselves 'the Poor', *ebiōnīm*. It is excessive to conclude from this, as he does, that 'the Poor' of Qumran and 'the Poor' of Christianity are identical; what is true is that the Judeo-Christians chose the name 'the Poor' precisely because they were the direct heirs to that Essene spirituality which proclaimed the eminent dignity of the poor and of the virtue of poverty.

As a matter of fact, this is not the only bond linking the Ebionites in a very special way with the Jewish sect of the Covenant: Ebionite beliefs show a close resemblance on more than one point to those of Qumran, particularly with regard to the 'Prophet of truth', and in places they may even help us to grasp their sense and bearing better. An extremely fruitful field of research extends in this direction.[1] Sprung direct from the Christian community of Jerusalem, the Ebionites are witnesses of the Christian faith in its most primitive form, 'authentic heirs of the apostolic group'.[2] When they left Jerusalem in A.D. 70, 'they preserved their ancient customs and traditions in their new home', as has been rightly said;[3] although these customs and traditions did not remain static over the years, but underwent various developments not without importance, at least they were not subjected to the influence of Pauline Christianity and remained independent of the evolution of the great Church. It is clear that if we wish to discover the features common to Essenism and Christianity in their purest and most primitive form, we should look for them on the Christian side among the Ebionites, rather than among the documents proceeding from the great Church.

IV

ARE THE QUMRAN SCROLLS OF ZEALOT ORIGIN?

Recently Cecil Roth advanced another opinion, namely that the Qumran writings are of Zealot origin. In the same way that Zeitlin

---

[1] See, for example, O. CULLMANN, 'Die neuentdeckten Qumrantexte und das Judenchristentum der Pseudoclementinen', in *Beiheft zur ZNW*, xxi, 1954, pp. 35-51; J. A. FITZMYER, 'The Qumran Scrolls, the Ebionites, and their Literature', in *The Scrolls and the New Testament* (New York, 1957), pp. 208-31.

[2] M. SIMON, *Les premiers Chrétiens* (Paris, 1952), p. 124.

[3] J. THOMAS, *Le mouvement baptiste en Palestine et Syrie . . .*, p. 159.

and Teicher, at the time of research into the *Damascus Document*, both had predecessors for their present-day hypotheses, so C. Roth's theory was in some way foreshadowed by Fr. M. J. Lagrange. The sectaries of Damascus, the latter explained, were Galileans, Zealots, 'in the broad sense of the word at least'. At the time of the war of Hadrian (A.D. 132-35), the Zealots deserted Bar-Kokhba, the lay leader of the insurrection, and formed themselves into an independent sect abroad. The *Damascus Document* dates from approximately A.D. 200. Obviously there could have been no question of any influence of the Jewish sect over Christianity at that date: 'Since the overseer (of the *Damascus Document*) is really like a Christian bishop of the Syriac *Didascalia*', concludes Fr. Lagrange, 'one is tempted to say that it was Christianity, which had already spread everywhere by the time of Hadrian and the final Jewish catastrophe, that served as model. Furthermore, it was from the Christians that the sect borrowed its title of the new covenant, and above all, its very pressing recommendations to assistance and charity.'[1]

This opinion, which is not devoid of apologetical bias, is very different from the one which the same author advanced twenty years earlier in an article full of the most perspicacious remarks.[2] In that article he noted very judiciously that the *Damascus Document* 'belonged to the same group as the *Testaments of the Twelve Patriarchs*, *Jubilees*, the *Book of Enoch*' and that the new document was interesting principally because it informed us 'that apocalypses in the style of *Enoch* or *Jubilees* were not the reveries of isolated individuals, but the manifestos of a compact and active group'. This group from which the apocalypses and the *Damascus Document* derive, was not, he explained, either the Sadducees or the Pharisees, but 'messianic reactionaries'.[3] He expressly refused to identify the sectaries of Damascus with the Zealots, an hypothesis which he qualified at that time as a 'mirage'. 'One should hear at least once', he wrote, 'that appeal to liberty which was the distinguishing mark of the Zealots. One can hardly conceive them as being so resigned, waiting so passively for the help of God. And finally, the Zealots do not appear to have had any special regard for the descendants of Aaron and Levi.'

[1] *Le Judaïsme avant Jésus-Christ* (Paris, 1931), pp. 330-7.
[2] 'La secte juive de la Nouvelle Alliance au pays de Damas', in *RB*, 1912, pp. 321-60.
[3] This identification is very vague: the author ought to have named here the Essenes whom Josephus described, together with the Sadducees and Pharisees, as the third great Jewish sect! But he had, a little off-handedly, dismissed them too soon; cf. above, p. 146.

Fr. Lagrange's reflections on the Zealot hypothesis retain their value today. They have not, however, prevented their author from eventually adopting the opinion against which he had so excellently fought. Nor have they prevented C. Roth from becoming its champion with regard to the Dead Sea discoveries.[1] According to this historian the essential event in the history of the sect, namely the putting to death of the Teacher of Righteousness, took place in A.D. 66 precisely. The Wicked Priest responsible for the Teacher's death was a certain Eleazar ben Hananiah, who was then the captain of the Temple guard; and the Teacher himself was Menahem ben Judah, one of the Zealot leaders at the beginning of the great Jewish War. Josephus reports that this Menahem wanted to take the lead in the insurrection against the Romans. One day he even had the audacity to make a solemn entry into the Temple clothed in royal costume and escorted by his partisans in arms, but Eleazar, the captain of the Temple guard, fearing for his own authority, opposed this manifestation with force and dispersed Menahem's supporters. Menahem himself was obliged to flee and, overtaken on the hill of Ophel, was summarily executed. This, according to Roth, was definitely the Teacher of Righteousness whose career and tragic end are described in the Qumran writings, and particularly in the *Commentary on Habakkuk*. This identification, continues our author, entails a very serious consequence. 'If the Teacher of Righteousness of Qumran literature is Menahem, the Zealot leader, the mystery of the sect of Qumran is solved: they were, as Joseph Klausner supposed, Zealots.'

As a matter of fact, the identification proposed by Roth meets with a number of objections, among them this: the Qumran documents establish with certainty that the Teacher of Righteousness was a *priest*. I would remind the reader of just one text from the *Commentary on Psalm XXXVII*: 'The explanation of this concerns the Priest, the Teacher of Righteousness whom God established to build for Himself the Congregation of truth. . . .'[2] Now according to Josephus, Menahem was the son of the famous Judas the Galilean, the founder of the Zealot party in about A.D. 6; it is nowhere stated that either this Judas the Galilean, or his son Menahem, was of

---

[1] See, for instance, his two studies, 'Le point de vue de l'historien sur les manuscrits de la mer Morte', and 'Les rouleaux de la mer Morte et l'insurrection juive de l'an 66', in *Évidences*, no. 65 (June-July 1957), pp. 37-43, and no. 70 (March 1958), pp. 13-18; and also his little book, *The Historical Background of the Dead Sea Scrolls* (Oxford, 1958).

[2] Cf. above, p. 272.

sacerdotal lineage, and nothing leads us to think they were. This fact alone is enough to undermine the author's whole argument.

Without refuting point by point the subtle explanations with which the distinguished historian attempts to make the story of this Menahem agree with what we learn from the Qumran literature,[1] I insist on one basic remark: though the Qumran writings agree perfectly with what we know of the Essenes, they scarcely lead us on the whole to think of the Zealots. As we have seen, Fr. Lagrange (first opinion!) had already pointed this out with regard to the *Damascus Document* alone; his view is amply confirmed by the new material. The Zealots were characterized above all by their spirit of active, direct and immediate resistance to the occupying Romans; theirs was a terrorist organization whose frequent use of the dagger earned for them the title 'Sicarii'. They were not, of course, brigands in the ordinary sense of the word, as Josephus would have us think, and these fanatical patriots, or the best among them anyway, were probably animated by an ardent religious faith and professed a doctrine not on the whole inferior to that of the Pharisees to whom Josephus explicitly compares them. But there is a vast difference between this and making them an essentially mystical sect tending towards Gnosis and its Mysteries, towards an ideal of penance and atonement, poverty and chastity, humility and gentleness, like the sect of Qumran. Read again, for example, the Penal Code inserted into the scroll of the *Rule* (VI, 24-VII, 25). Among the many offences envisaged, not one indicates a genuinely Zealot environment, i.e. a group of men whose predominant concern was for immediate armed struggle. On the contrary, this Penal Code is manifestly the code of a community of monks anxious above all to achieve salvation and to practise perfection.

I do not, however, overlook the fact that among the Qumran scrolls there is a *War Rule of the Sons of Light*. The sectaries considered themselves the militia of God and waited eagerly for the Day of Judgment when they would have to fight, weapons in their hands, against the Kittim and all the 'sons of darkness'; this dream and expectation are indisputably attested by the Qumran documents, and there is no question of hiding or denying the fact. But what seems to me to distinguish the Qumran sect from the Zealots is that

---

[1] I refer the reader to the detailed discussion of C. Roth's thesis which I published in *Évidences*, no. 68 (December 1957), pp. 27-36; no. 70 (March 1958), pp. 19-20; no. 73 (September-October 1958), pp. 38-9.

for the Essenes this armed war was a still distant ideal, postponed to some mysterious date, the Day of God, whereas for the Zealots it was a present duty suffering no delay. Clearly, on the practical level a difference of this kind was of prime importance: the Zealots were for effective immediate fighting and, pending the coming of the great war, for guerilla tactics and assassination.

It should be noted here that the Essene dream of a Holy War, the eschatological war destined to exterminate the wicked from the earth and to inaugurate the Kingdom of God and goodness, probably went through various phases. The *War Rule* reflects, I believe, an epoch in their history when the sect was being persecuted by the High Priest Hyrcanus II and was intoxicated by hopes of vengeance. But with the coming of Herod the Great, who is said by Josephus to have shown the Essenes much esteem and consideration, their attitude to established power changed, and on the practical level they adopted a general attitude of calm and submission — though without, on the ideal level, renouncing their expectations or their desire for the Day when the wicked would be crushed and the just victorious. It was during this new phase of their history, I think, that there developed among them the pacificism on which Philo insisted in the first century A.D., and that the undertaking was introduced into the formula of their oath of initiation to show 'constant loyalty to all, but above all to those in power, for authority never falls to a man without the will of God', according to the expression reported by Josephus (*Jewish War*, II, 8, 7, § 140).[1]

It was for the very reason that the Essenes were at that moment generally more sober, uninvolved in active politics and absorbed in following a holy and heavenly life, that a new sect sprang into being whose essential aim, in reaction against the spirit of submissiveness which was then an Essene duty, was revolt, armed and bloody insurrection against the authority of Rome and its agents. These Zealots threw off the yoke and tolerated no other master but God. But they were not Essenes; although some of them had belonged to the Essene sect, henceforth the sect could only reject them, and they went to swell the ranks of the new party of the Sicarii.[2]

[1] On this evolution and its consequences, see my *Aperçus préliminaires* . . ., p. 114. (Eng. edn., pp. 93-4.)

[2] Hippolytus's account of the Essenes seems to link them with the sect of the Zealots. He says that the Zealots were a later derivation of Essenism, and that the Essenes of the primitive observance refused to have anything to do with them; cf. above, p. 32, n. 5. This passage from Hippolytus is rather obscure; perhaps we should simply understand from it that at various times the Zealots made a certain number of recruits from among the Essenes.

Besides, the *War Rule* cannot be a Zealot book, as C. Roth maintains. The type of warfare it describes is nothing like Zealot warfare,
i.e. guerilla warfare, but ranked battle fought by strong forces and
conforming to the tactics of the Roman legions. Would a Zealot
writing between A.D. 66 and 73 — in accordance with Roth's theory
— ever have dreamt of conducting war so differently from the war
his sect was obliged to wage? Dr. Y. Yadin, the author of a masterly
commentary on the *War Rule*, places its date in the first century B.C.,
as I myself do: that is, before the creation of the Zealot party. There
is, in my opinion, no indication that we should, like C. Roth, date
it from the first century A.D. But the zeal for the Holy War which
formerly inspired this work passed in all its virulence into the new
sect of the Zealots, whilst the Essenes preferred to wait in recollection and prayer for the time appointed by God for the Day of
Vengeance.[1]

Against the Essene theory C. Roth has formulated the following
objection. The famous account of the Essenes written by Pliny the
Elder is given in the present tense, and is followed by a brief account
concerning the town of Engedi, where allusion is made to the
destruction caused by the Jewish War. The description of the
Essenes must therefore also refer to the post-war period. Now
excavations at Qumran have shown that this site was destroyed in
the course of the war; consequently, Roth concludes, it is clear that
the sect formerly established at Qumran, as well as the scrolls found
in the near-by caves, have nothing to do with the Essenes of whom
Pliny speaks. Thus collapses one of the major arguments on which the
Essene theory rests.

The objection is clever; but it was noticed long ago that the
value of the present tense in Pliny's description is one of a 'descriptive
present' taken, no doubt, from some earlier account, and that the
use of this present tense in no way implies that the Essenes actually
lived on the shores of the Dea Sea at the time when Pliny was
writing. This, for example, is how P. E. Lucius, in his classic book,

---

[1] Cf. above, p. 168. — What was the Essene attitude at the time of the great Jewish
Revolt in A.D. 66? Josephus tells us that a certain 'John the Essene' was one of the generals
who conducted operations against the Romans, and that this person perished in battle
(*War*, II, 20, 4; III, 2, 1-2); other Essenes, and perhaps even those who lived at Qumran,
may have given way to the pressure of circumstances and joined the movement which was
drawing the whole nation after it. The question remains obscure. If the Essenes, wholly or
in part, did rally to the insurrection and abandon their former attitude, such a sudden
change at the moment of the supreme crisis of the Jewish nation would cause no surprise
to the historian.

Der Essenismus in seinem Verhältniss zum Judenthum (Strasburg, 1881) explains things. 'Unless we are quite mistaken', he writes (p. 33), 'we have in Pliny's account a description of the Essene order before A.D. 70. The fact that at the beginning of the 'seventies Pliny still supposes this order to exist, means absolutely nothing. Solinus, Pliny's summarist in the second half of the third century, speaks even more distinctly of the Essenes as though they still lived in Judaea; and similarly Josephus and the Rabbis suppose the whole situation in Palestine to be exactly as it was before the war.' These lines of Lucius, nearly eighty years old, have the advantage that on the subject of Pliny's text they present the view of a cautious historian totally independent of our present-day opinions. They show, anyway, that Roth's interpretation is far from imperative.

Moreover, since this author appeals to archaeological data, I would add that the thesis he maintains is in manifest conflict with the conclusions of the archaeologists. If it is established that the Qumran centre was destroyed during the war (in June, A.D. 68 according to Fr. de Vaux), it is very difficult to accept that the persecution and death of the Teacher of Righteousness, which according to Roth's Zealot thesis, happened during the autumn of A.D. 66, could in so short a time have been related as events of the past and have occupied a central place in the various biblical commentaries found at Qumran. All this literature on the Teacher, so profoundly considered and so carefully elaborated on the basis of biblical texts, must have required a fairly long lapse of time, much longer than twenty months or so.

V

ARE THE QUMRAN SCROLLS OF PHARISAIC ORIGIN?

Prior to the Dead Sea discoveries, the theory of a Pharisaic origin of the *Damascus Document* was supported by several writers, among them W. H. Ward,[1] E. Meyer,[2] A. Bertholet,[3] L. Ginzberg,[4]

---

[1] 'The Zadokite Documents', in *The Bibliotheca Sacra*, lxviii (1911), pp. 429-56.

[2] 'Die Gemeinde des neuen Bundes im Lande Damaskus. Eine jüdische Sekte aus der Seleukidenzeit', in *Abhandlungen der preussischen Akademie der Wissenschaften*, 1919 (Phil.-hist. Klasse 9).

[3] 'Zur Datierung der Damaskusschrift', in *Beihefte zur ZAW*, xxxiv, 1920, pp. 31-7.

[4] *Eine unbekannte jüdische Sekte* (New York, 1922).

F. Hvidberg[1] and Joachim Jeremias.[2] This theory has recently been
revived by Chaim Rabin with regard to the whole of the Qumran
literature. He first outlined his views in his remarkable edition of the
Damascus Document,[3] and then developed and completed them in a
small and very compact work which certainly merits attentive
reading;[4] it is a personal and original work testifying to a deep
knowledge of Rabbinical sources and the Qumran writings.

Rabin first of all recognizes that the Essene theory is today 'almost
universally accepted', but disagrees with it. It has led, he says, 'to
widespread and somewhat unexpected consequences. Not only are
ever larger sections of pseudepigraphal literature being attributed to Essene authors, but we already hear of an "Essene Bible
text" and the "Essene scribal art". It is thus all the more important
to give the fullest consideration to other possibilities of identification
of the Qumran sect'. So here he is in search of other 'possibilities'!
He recalls the early works of Ward and Ginzberg tending to identify
the *halakhah* of the *Damascus Document* as Pharisaico-Rabbinical
jurisprudence, and, astonished that nobody has yet attempted a
similar demonstration for the new documents as a whole, he himself undertakes to do this with the sole aim of developing the
hypothesis that they are of genuine Pharisaic origin.

Actually Saul Liberman, a great expert in Talmudic literature,
had already explored these paths before Rabin;[5] but he merely
pointed out some analogies between the Qumran sect and the type
of Pharisaic brotherhood known as *ḥabūrāh*, and took good care not
to identify the one with the other. Rabin's attempt is a good deal
bolder and much more systematic. According to him the Qumran
community was a continuation of the Pharisaic *ḥabūrāh* of the first
century B.C., 'an organization within which people could trust each
other in matters of tithing of produce, ritual purity of food, and other
halakhic matters affecting everyday contact between individuals'
(p. viii). But Rabin establishes an explicit distinction between this
ḥabūrāh — a pure expression of primitive Pharisaism — and Rabbinic

---

[1] *Menigheden af den nye Pagt i Damascus* (Copenhagen, 1928).
[2] *Jerusalem zur Zeit Jesu*, II, B (Leipzig, 1929), pp. 130-4.
[3] *The Zadokite Documents* (Oxford, 1954). I have already had occasion (pp. 144-5)
to discuss Rabin's views as expressed in this work; in the present appendix, I discuss the
author's thesis in the wider and more developed form which he subsequently gave to it.
[4] *Qumran Studies* (Oxford, 1957).
[5] 'Light on the Cave Scrolls from Rabbinic Sources', in *Proceedings of the American
Academy for Jewish Research*, xx (1951), pp. 395-404; 'The Discipline in the so-called Dead
Sea Manual of Discipline', in the *JBL*, lxxi (1952), pp. 199-206.

Judaism as represented in Tannaitic literature. This Rabbinic Judaism, he explains, moved away from its primitive purity in that it had to make wide concessions in order to adapt legislation to an extended recruitment. These concessions were the cause of schism between Pharisees of the old observance and the Rabbis of the new persuasion. Both groups considered themselves the authentic heirs to the great Pharisaic tradition. But the first — to which members of the Qumran sect adhered — came off worst in the struggle between the two movements; it was to Rabbinic Judaism that the future belonged. Rabin places the opposition of the Qumran community 'at the point of transition between Pharisaism and Rabbinic Judaism', i.e. during the first century A.D.; he does not suggest a more precise date, nor does he identify any of the various personalities alluded to in the scrolls.

I will say at once that this representation of the historical background of the Qumran community is extremely fragile. There is in reality, no trace in Rabbinical sources of hostility towards the Pharisees; no writer has ever reported conflict between the Pharisees and the Rabbis, much less bloody conflict 'by the sword', as the Qumran documents have it. On the contrary, it has always been accepted that Rabbinic Judaism, of the Tannaitic period and later, was a continuation of Pharisaic Judaism. If there was an appreciable evolution from one to the other, it operated with sufficient suppleness and in conformity with the circumstances. Of course there existed diverse tendencies within Pharisaism as within Rabbinism; but there is nothing to indicate that at a given moment in the course of the first century A.D. there was violent and murderous schism. Pharisaism concerned itself to adapt the jurisprudence of the Law to make it acceptable to the whole nation and not to the members of a brotherhood alone, but this preoccupation seems to have existed almost from the beginning, and even constitutes as it were the characteristic of the Pharisee party: their hold on the people was so great, reports Josephus,[1] 'that all divine things, prayers and oblations and sacrifices, are done according to their interpretation', and the Sadducees, when they came to power, were obliged to 'concede all that the Pharisees say in order not to make themselves unbearable to the crowd'. This is distinctly said of the Pharisees, and not of the Rabbis, and hardly authorizes us to think that the extension and adaptation of Pharisaic rules to the nation as a whole

[1] *Antiquities*, xviii, 1, 3-4.

began only in the first century A.D., and was essentially the work of the Rabbis in conflict with the Pharisees. This struggle, this bloody struggle, seems to me to be entirely imaginary.

Moreover it is clear that Rabin's theory tallies but poorly with Qumran chronology. The author honestly admits that he 'is inclined to place the date of the sect after the destruction of Jerusalem' (p. 66), the most likely period for the conflict he imagines to have taken place between the ancient ḥabūrāh and Rabbinism. But this would contradict the archaeological data, and to escape the dilemma Rabin is led to antedate the trouble by fifty years or so: but it is all artificial and forced. As a matter of fact, even this back-dating is insufficient. Archaeology shows that the Qumran site was occupied by the community of the scrolls from the end of the second century B.C. to A.D. 68, and as I have shown (chapter XII), the Wicked Priest, the enemy of the Teacher of Righteousness, must have been a member of the Hasmonaean dynasty. Rabin's ingenious construction is entirely out of true and without foundation.

Furthermore, although it is right to point out certain affinities between Qumran *halakhah* and Pharisaic *halakhah*, the discrepancies ought also to be mentioned. Ginzberg, although a supporter of the Pharisaic thesis, did not omit to do this with regard to the laws of the *Damascus Document*. The prohibition of polygamy, for example, which the *Damascus Document* justifies by means of biblical texts, and, based on analogous reasoning, its extension of the laws of incest to include marriage with a niece, are, he declares, 'a decidedly heretical doctrine'. In the *Damascus Document* again, the rules relating to witnesses in a case involving a capital offence contradict Talmudic jurisprudence, and the sacrificial laws are, he says, 'distinctly schismatic' in character.

But there is something more serious. The existence in the Qumran sect of a special religious calendar brings it into radical opposition to the sect of the Pharisees. As everyone knows, nothing marks the distinction between sects more surely than the question of the calendar which on the practical level is of extreme importance. Ginzberg considered the allusion in the *Damascus Document* to the book of *Jubilees* and its calendar (XVI, 2-4) as a later interpolation, but the Qumran writings prove that the sect had its own calendar, very similar to that of *Jubilees*, and held to it most firmly. This means that it was separated from the Pharisees 'by an abyss', to repeat an expression of Fr. Lagrange apropos of the calendar of *Jubilees*.[1] If

[1] *RB*, 1912, p. 355.

Ginzberg had known of the new documents, no doubt his opinion regarding the nature of the sect of Damascus would have altered entirely. Nowadays it is impossible to speak of an interpolation. Rabin (pp. 77-81) admits that the Qumran sect adopted the calendar of *Jubilees*, but says that it did so later and, so to speak, incidentally. But in fact this is not at all the impression obtained from the Qumran writings. For them, this calendar question seemed absolutely fundamental, and knowledge of the authentic calendar was in their eyes one of the loftiest revelations granted them.

I cannot here examine each chapter of Rabin's work in detail,[1] but I will say a few words about the first chapter entitled 'The Noviciate'. Rabin has diligently assembled a few scraps of information collected here and there from Talmudic sources on the procedure for admission into the Pharisaic *ḥabūrāh*, and with the help of this rather scanty information he first outlines this procedure and then compares it, point by point, with the procedure described in the Qumran texts. He then notices an exact and precise correspondence between this outline and the Qumran procedure, whereas the comparison between the same Qumran procedure and that attested by Josephus as having been practised among the Essenes seems to him to reveal important divergences. But whilst Josephus's description is open to little criticism, the way in which Rabin presents both the Pharisaic and the Qumran procedures is highly unreliable. Everything is cleverly arranged to fit the conclusion he has in mind. This is very properly pointed out by K. Smyth in an otherwise kind review of Rabin's book:[2] 'There is also a general criticism of Rabin's method. He first synthesizes several items from Qumran into a certain pattern. The items are, on his own admission, "relatively unimportant". With this pattern in mind, he emphasizes those points of Essenism which contrast with it, and builds up from Rabbinical sources a pattern which will correspond to his Qumran synthesis. This method is only valid if the first, the Qumran synthesis, is fully representative and solidly certain; and if the second, the Rabbinic, is not composed of too many doubtful and originally disparate elements.' The forced and artificial nature of Rabin's demonstration could not be exposed more clearly. I will give one example only. Josephus informs us without ambiguity that final

---

[1] The reader can consult J. M. BAUMGARTEN's detailed review in the *JBL*, lxxvii (1958), pp. 249-57.

[2] *J. Sem. S.*, iii (1958), p. 198.

admission into the Essene sect entailed the swearing of an *oath*; this essential point is clearly attested at Qumran, but not at all in the Pharisaic *ḥabūrāh*, where Rabbinical texts speak only of an *undertaking*. Rabin brushes aside this nevertheless essential difference: it is obviously antithetical to the identification of the Qumran sect with the Pharisaic brotherhood whereas, on this question of the oath of initiation, the sect of Qumran is in agreement with what Josephus tells us of the Essenes (see above, pp. 45-6).

In short, Rabin's fault is that he applies himself mainly to trivialities which are often uncertain, while leaving essential observations to one side. Alas, he fails to see the wood for the trees![1] It would, however, be unjust not to pay homage to the author's erudition. And after all, we must be grateful to him for having tried, despite the difficulties of the task, to breathe life into the Pharisee hypothesis. If his attempt has come to grief it is because no success can be found along that path. The Qumran documents, which are decidedly unamenable to any annexation to Pharisaism, offer specialists in Rabbinic studies another more fruitful and much more interesting task — that of determining, with the help of a comparative study of the Qumran writings and Rabbinic sources, the connection between the two sects, Essene and Pharisaic, and the doctrinal and literary influence which the one was able to exert upon the other. Without doubt Rabin is one of the persons most competent to carry out such a task.

VI

ARE THE ESSENES A MYTH?

The sectaries of Qumran are consequently neither Karaites, Judeo-Christians, Zealots, nor Pharisees. The idea of making them Sadducees, in the proper sense of the word, which tempted some writers with respect to the *Damascus Document*, can hardly be revived by anyone, so evident is it that our 'sons of Zadok' were, on the contrary, the bitterest enemies of that party of mundane priests who

---

[1] Fr. LAGRANGE made almost the same reproach, worded somewhat maliciously, to Ginzberg (*Le Judaïsme avant Jésus-Christ*, p. 331): 'We do not dispute the Rabbinical competence of Mr. L. Ginzberg who has made the Pharisaic character of the sect predominate, but this criticism itself seems to slip into the failing with which Jesus reproached the Pharisees; it swallows a camel and strains a gnat. . . .'

believed neither in resurrection nor in the angels, and whose conduct seemed abominable to them. Who were they then? Every argument except one leads to an impasse: they were the Essenes whose customs and beliefs are described by Philo and Josephus, and who are said by Pliny to have lived on the western shore of the Dead Sea, upstream from Engedi. Positive arguments in favour of the Essene theory abound. On the other hand, a negative argument of no small value arises from the failure of all the other attempts at identification made by a few isolated scholars since the Qumran discoveries; their mutually destructive hypotheses have in fact met with little echo. Thus everything leads today to the Essene thesis, a thesis 'almost universally accepted', as Rabin himself states.

But did these Essenes really exist whom the recent discoveries have so suddenly returned to a place of honour and in whom the whole world is now interested? Are they not a myth, a pure creation of the mind like the chimera of mythology, or like those monsters with which ancient geographers peopled the antipodes? The human imagination is so rich in invention of every kind. Were these Essenes ascetics? Monks? Prior to Christianity? Come, come! Judaism could never have produced such a thing! There are, of course, the ancient accounts of Philo, Josephus, Pliny and Hippolytus, but a fig for all their scribbling! With a little ingenuity, nothing is easier than to see in them a mere tissue of fantastic blunders and later interpolations, empty of historical value. But if the Essenes never existed, how about the scrolls found in the Qumran caves? Jewish books of every kind, brought from no one knows where, to be hidden because out of use or heterodox! And what about the cemetery, buildings and cisterns of Khirbet Qumran? Like the books, the dead are from no one knows where; the buildings sheltered the diggers and guardians of the cemetery, and the cisterns served to wash the corpses and purify the cemetery visitors! So everything is marvellously explained. There were never any Essenes at Qumran or anywhere else in the world.

This is the great, the supreme revelation made recently which is to direct Qumran studies into the right path at last, studies which for ten years have gone astray amid anachronistic theories. This is indeed a sensational revelation! For as many years as there have been historians to inquire into the Essene problem, never has one of them, even the most hypercritical, even thought of denying the existence of the Essenes! Over the centuries, discussion has focused on the veracity of such and such a point asserted by ancient writers, on the character and essence of Essenism, on the nature of the foreign influence to which it may have been subjected, on the importance of its role in the Jewish world, and last but not least, on its connection with primitive Christianity; but never on the very reality of Essenism. It was left to H. E. Del Medico radically to exterminate the Essene sect in two recent works: *L'énigme des manuscrits de la mer Morte* (1957), and *Le mythe des Esséniens* (1958). This is definitely the best way to rid us for ever of the theory of the Essene origin of the Dead Sea Scrolls.

Before the publication of these books the author was little known. A book published by him in 1950, *La Bible cananéenne découverte dans les textes de Ras Shamra*, is scientifically so feeble that G. R. Driver, for example, one of the finest British Semitic scholars, does not even mention it in the copious bibliography of his book, *Canaanite Myths and Legends* (Edinburgh, 1956), devoted to the same subject; and C. H. Gordon, one of the most highly qualified American scholars, makes not the smallest reference to it in his classic work, *Ugaritic Manual* (Rome, 1955), where, none the less, about one hundred and twenty writers are quoted. The preface to *La Bible cananéenne* informs us that 'M. Del Medico was born in Istanbul of a Venetian family to which belonged such illustrious scholars as Elie Del Medico (1460-1497), the teacher of Pico della Mirandola . . .'. He is to be congratulated on his ancestry and full of esteem for his person I would sincerely have liked to say nothing of his work if it had not succeeded in disturbing some people. A few, it is true, claim that the author only wished to enliven the austere debate on the Dead Sea Scrolls with a little humour and fantasy, with a sort of innocent farce after the manner of *Donogoo*. But this is not quite certain, so I think it worth while to enlighten the reader a little.

Without going into all the details, let us see from one example what is to be thought of his translation. Let us take a short passage in Greek from Hippolytus's account of the Essenes. It should obviously be translated: 'They (the Essenes) do not forbid marriage (*to gamein*), but themselves keep apart from marriage (*gamou*). As for the women who wish to join the same sect, they do not receive them. . . .' Clearly, there is a question here of the Essene attitude to marriage and to the ban on the admission of women into the order. Here is what this nevertheless so limpid text becomes in Del Medico's translation: 'They forbid them to fornicate, as they themselves abstain from fornication. As for the women, although they must be attentive to their benevolent counsel, they do not trust them. . . .'[1] Our translator merely confuses marriage (*gamos*) with fornication (*porneia*)! Moreover he omits the negative in the first phrase, and misinterprets almost every word in the second. Thereupon he declares that in mentioning the Essenes, Hippolytus really wished to speak of the *ḥazanim* (superintendents) of the synagogues, and it is this grotesque misapprehension that has passed into Josephus's account of the Essenes, itself the work of later interpolators, etc. Unbelievable!

From such extremely whimsical translations Del Medico can hardly avoid reaching extravagant conclusions. Whereas, even though some of them are more or less composite, the Qumran writings clearly manifest an identical source of origin, he with incredible offhandedness dissects the text, lopping off here a 'Zaddukite' bit, there a Rabbinical bit, and a little further on, a Zealot bit; and in this curious amalgam he recognizes nothing of Essene origin. This is real bad luck! But anyway, there never were any Essenes. . . .

The proof of their non-existence, especially at Qumran, rests in the fact, he explains, that the region of Qumran is quite simply 'uninhabitable'.[2] Let us hear what Fr. de Vaux has to say.[3] 'M. Del Medico . . . thinks that Khirbet Qumran, where he has never been, is an uninhabitable place. And, again, his reason for that statement is simple: there are too many insects because there are no birds, and there are no birds because they could not fly owing to the air pressure in an area which is more than 1000 ft. under sea level.[4] Truly, this is not serious. Adding up all my visits down there, I have spent one year at Qumran, and I am still alive. It is not always comfortable but one can get on with the mosquitoes. And there certainly are birds. I have eaten partridges shot near our camp, and pigeons nesting in the caves. I have seen ravens and small eagles circling over our refuse pit; all sorts of birds were crossing in the sky. No, there can be no doubt, a group of several men once lived in that region.'

Del Medico argues from the condition of the manuscripts.

[1] *L'énigme des manuscrits de la mer Morte*, pp. 88-9. In *Le mythe des Esséniens*, p. 111, the translation of the first phrase is slightly modified: 'They forbid them to have sexual intercourse, as they themselves abstain from sexual intercourse. . . .' This changes nothing of the sense (or rather, nonsense).

[2] *L'énigme des manuscrits* . . ., p. 101.

[3] *The Listener*, June 19th, 1958, p. 1007. See also *RB*, 1959, pp. 95 f.

[4] Cf. DEL MEDICO, *L'énigme des manuscrits* . . ., p. 11.

According to him, several of the scrolls from cave I were partly burned, deliberately, before being hidden in the caves. This shows, he assures us, that they were heterodox and were concealed for that reason.[1] The author has not seen the scrolls of which he speaks, neither the *Commentary on Habakkuk*, nor the *Rule*, nor the *War Scroll*. Now it is an indisputable *fact* that, contrary to Del Medico's allegation, these scrolls bear not the slightest trace of combustion. I have seen them in the hall of the Hebrew University where they are kept and exhibited. I have examined them most carefully in the company of Dr. Yadin and other Israeli archaeologists, and can assert that we noticed no sign whatsoever of their having been burnt. Thus, where we have facts which are ordinary, extremely simple and easy to observe or verify, M. Del Medico invents. If there is any myth in this affair is not the myth-maker M. Del Medico?

Let us therefore put away his two unprofitable books and be serious once more; the subject invites it more than any other. For the Qumran manuscripts confront us with one of the greatest problems which the historian, contemporary man, has to face: the problem of the genesis of Christianity, of that two-thousand-year-old institution which has left so deep a mark on the civilization of the Western world, and which remains one of the highest expressions of the mystical instinct of man.

[1] op. cit., pp. 53 ff.

BIBLIOGRAPHY

A chronological list of the author's principal publications (books and articles) in the field of Qumran studies is given below for the benefit of readers wishing to follow the development of his research since 1949.

1949

Manuscrits hébreux de Palestine, in *Revue Archéologique*, xxxiv (1949), pp. 79-82.

La grotte aux manuscrits du désert de Juda, in *Revue de Paris*, July 1949, pp. 79-90.

1950

Observations sur le Commentaire d'Habacuc découvert près de la mer Morte. Paper read before the Académie des Inscriptions et Belles-Lettres on May 26th, 1950. 8vo, 32 pages. Paris, Adrien-Maisonneuve, 1950.

Le Commentaire d'Habacuc découvert près de la mer Morte: traduction et notes, in *Revue de l'Histoire des Religions*, cxxxvii (1950), pp. 129-71.

La 'Règle' de la Communauté de la Nouvelle Alliance: extraits traduits et commentés, in *Revue de l'Histoire des Religions*, cxxxviii (1950), pp. 5-21.

Lumières nouvelles sur les manuscrits découverts près de la mer Morte, in *La Nouvelle Clio*, no. 7 (July 1950), pp. 330-5.

Aperçus préliminaires sur les manuscrits de la mer Morte. 8vo, 128 pages, with a map and 10 photographs. Paris, Adrien-Maisonneuve, 1950. — English edition: *The Dead Sea Scrolls. A Preliminary Survey.* Oxford, Blackwell, and New York, Macmillan, 1952.

1951

Observations sur le Manuel de Discipline découvert près de la mer Morte. Paper read before the Académie des Inscriptions et Belles-Lettres on June 8th, 1951. 8vo, 32 pages. Paris, Adrien-Maisonneuve, 1951.

Le Maître de justice fut-il mis à mort? in *Vetus Testamentum*, i, 3 (1951), pp. 189-99.

La Nouvelle Alliance juive et le Maître de justice, in *Revue de Paris*, August 1951, pp. 91-104.

1952

Contribution à l'exégèse du Manuel de Discipline X, 1-8, in *Vetus Testamentum*, ii, 3 (1952), pp. 229-43.

413

La sainteté du signe 'noun' dans le Manuel de Discipline, in *Bulletin de l'Académie royale de Belgique (Classe de Lettres)*, v, 38 (1952), pp. 184-93.

Découvertes nouvelles dans le désert de Juda, in *Revue de la Pensée juive*, no. 10 (1952), pp. 66-77.

L'instruction sur les deux Esprits dans le Manuel de Discipline, in *Revue de l'Histoire des Religions*, cxlii (1952), pp. 5-35.

Le Testament de Lévi (XVII-XVIII) et la secte juive de l'Alliance, in *Semitica*, iv (1952), pp. 33-53.

1953

Nouveaux Aperçus sur les manuscrits de la mer Morte. 8vo, 222 pages, with a map and 5 photographs. Paris, Adrien-Maisonneuve, 1953. — English edition (with a supplement): *The Jewish Sect of Qumran and the Essenes*. London, Valentine, Mitchell & Co., and New York, Macmillan, 1954, xii-195 pages.

1954

Le problème des influences étrangères sur la secte juive de Qoumrân (Saint-Cloud Congress, 1954), in *Revue d'Histoire et de Philosophie Religieuses*, xxxv (1955), pp. 75-94.

Le couvent essénien du désert de Juda, in *Revue de Paris*, November 1954, pp. 101-14.

1955

Quelques remarques sur le Commentaire d'Habacuc à propos d'un livre récent, in *Vetus Testamentum*, v, 2 (1955), pp. 113-29.

La Mère du Messie et la Mère de l'Aspic dans un hymne de Qoumrân, in *Revue de l'Histoire des Religions*, cxlvii (1955), pp. 174-88.

Le 'Chef des rois de Yâwân' dans l'Écrit de Damas, in *Semitica*, v (1955), pp. 41-57.

Les manuscrits de la mer Morte; leur importance pour l'histoire des religions, in *Numen*, ii (1955), pp. 168-89.

Les recherches sur les manuscrits de la mer Morte (1948-1955) avec référence spéciale aux rouleaux récemment publiés en Israel, in *Les Manuscrits de la mer Morte. Colloque de Strasbourg 1955* (Paris, Presses Universitaires de France, 1957), pp. 1-23.

'Règlement de la guerre des fils de lumière': traduction et notes, in *Revue de l'Histoire des Religions*, cxlviii (1955), pp. 25-43, 141-80.

1956

Bref aperçu sur les manuscrits de la mer Morte appartenant à l'Université hébraïque et récemment publiés en Israel, in *Revue de l'Histoire des Religions*, cxlix (1956), pp. 121-3.

On a passage of Josephus relative to the Essenes (*A.J.*, xviii, § 22), in *Journal of Semitic Studies*, i (1956), pp. 361-6.

Les notices de Philon d'Alexandrie sur les Esséniens, in *Évidences*, no. 54 (January-February 1956), pp. 19-26.

Les notices de Josèphe et Pline l'Ancien sur les Esséniens, in *Évidences*, no. 55 (March 1956), pp. 27-34.

L'origine essénienne des rouleaux de Qoumrân, in *Évidences*, no. 56 (April 1956), pp. 11-25.

Le rouleau de la *Règle*, in *Évidences*, no. 57 (May 1956), pp. 9-23, and no. 58 (June-July 1956), pp. 27-39, 49.

L'Écrit de Damas, in *Évidences*, no. 59 (August-September 1956), pp. 13-37, and no. 60 (October-November 1956), pp. 25-36.

1957

Le rouleau de *La Guerre des fils de lumière*, in *Évidences*, no. 62 (January-February 1957), pp. 32-47.

Le rouleau des *Hymnes*, in *Évidences*, no. 63 (March 1957), pp. 19-32.

Le Livre des Hymnes découvert près de la mer Morte. Traduction intégrale avec introduction et notes. 8ᵛᵒ, 120 pages (*Semitica*, vii). Paris, Adrien-Maisonneuve, 1957.

Les rouleaux de cuivre trouvés à Qoumrân, in *Revue de l'Histoire des Religions*, cli (1957), pp. 22-36, 142-4.

Les Commentaires bibliques trouvés à Qoumrân, in *Évidences*, no. 65 (June-July 1957), pp. 19-28.

Le milieu historique des rouleaux de Qoumrân, in *Évidences*, no. 67 (November 1957), pp. 27-33.

Les rouleaux de Qoumrân sont-ils d'origine zélote? in *Évidences*, no. 68 (December 1957), pp. 27-36.

1958

L'importance des manuscrits de la mer Morte, in *Évidences*, no. 69 (January 1958), pp. 37-43.

Réponse à M. Cecil Roth, in *Évidences*, no. 70 (March 1958), pp. 19-20.

Sur le passage de Pline l'Ancien relatif aux Esséniens, in *Évidences*, no. 73 (September-October 1958), pp. 38-9.

Les problèmes des Manuscrits de la mer Morte, in *Diogène*, April 1958, pp. 70-99.

1959

Les Écrits esséniens découverts près de la mer Morte. 8ᵛᵒ, 446 pages. Paris, Payot, 1959.

Remarques linguistiques sur un fragment araméen de Qoumrân ('Prière de Nabonide'), in *Comptes rendus du Groupe linguistique d'Études chamito-sémitiques*, viii (1959), pp. 47-50.

Exorcismes et guérisons dans les écrits de Qoumrân, in *Proceedings of the Third International Congress for the Study of the Old Testament (Supplements to Vetus Testamentum*, vii; Leiden, E. J. Brill, 1960), pp. 246-61.

Publications relating to the Dead Sea Scrolls are multiplying throughout the world at an ever-increasing pace; it would be out of the question to present a complete list of them here. Instead, I refer the reader to *Bibliographie zu den Handschriften vom Toten Meer* (Berlin, 1957) by CH. BURCHARD. This almost exhaustive bibliography ends at the beginning of 1957, but the author continues to bring it up to date in the successive issues of *Revue de Qumran*. In the following list, I indicate only a few general works, presented chronologically and chosen as representative of the differing opinions and trends in this field of studies.

1951

KAHLE, P., *Die hebräischen Handschriften aus der Höhle* (Stuttgart, 1951).

1952

BARDTKE, H., *Die Handschriftenfunde am Toten Meer* (Berlin, 1952).
ROWLEY, REV. H. H., *The Zadokite Fragments and the Dead Sea Scrolls* (Oxford, 1952).

1953

VERMES, G., *Les Manuscrits du désert de Juda* (Paris, 1953). English translation: *Discovery in the Judean Desert* (New York, 1956).

1954

MOLIN, G., *Die Söhne des Lichtes* (Wien, 1954).

1955

BURROWS, M., *The Dead Sea Scrolls* (New York, 1955).
VINCENT, ABBÉ A., *Les Manuscrits hébreux du Désert de Juda* (Paris, 1955).
WILSON, EDMUND, *The Scrolls from the Dead Sea* (New York, 1955).

1956

ALLEGRO, J. M., *The Dead Sea Scrolls* (Penguin Books, 1956).
DAVIES, A. POWELL, *The Meaning of the Dead Sea Scrolls* (New York, 1956).

FRITSCH, CH. T., *The Qumran Community* (New York, 1956)
GASTER, T. H., *The Dead Sea Scriptures in English translation* (New York, 1956).
KAPELRUD, A. S., *Dødehavs-rullene* (Oslo, 1956).
LAMADRID, A. G., *Los Descubrimientos de Qumran* (Madrid, 1956).

1957
Les manuscrits de la mer Morte. Colloque de Strasbourg, 1955 (Paris, 1957).
HOWLETT, D., *The Essenes and Christianity* (New York, 1957).
MILIK, ABBÉ J. T., *Dix ans de découvertes dans le Désert de Juda* (Paris, 1957). English translation: *Ten Years of Discovery in the Wilderness of Judaea* (London, 1959).
RABIN, CH., *Qumran Studies* (Oxford, 1957).
VAN DER PLOEG, FR. J., *Vondsten in de woestijn van Juda. De Rollen der Dode Zee* (Utrecht, 1957). English translation: *The Excavations at Qumran: a survey of the Judaean Brotherhood and its ideas* (London, 1958).
YADIN, Y., *The Message of the Scrolls* (London, 1957).

1958
Aspects of the Dead Sea Scrolls (Jerusalem, 1958).
BARDTKE, H., *Die Handschriftenfunde am Toten Meer (Band II). Die Sekte von Qumran* (Berlin, 1958).
BURROWS, M., *More Light on the Dead Sea Scrolls* (New York, 1958).
CROSS, F. M. (Jr.), *The Ancient Library of Qumran and Modern Biblical Studies* (New York, 1958).
ROTH, C., *The Historical Background of the Dead Sea Scrolls* (Oxford, 1958).
SCHUBERT, K., *Die Gemeinde vom Toten Meer* (Munich-Basle, 1958). English translation: *The Dead Sea Community* (London, 1959).

1959
ALLEGRO, J. M., *The People of the Dead Sea Scrolls in Texts and Pictures* (New York, 1958; London, 1959).
HABERMANN, A. M., *Megilloth Midbar Yehuda. The Scrolls from the Judaean Desert edited with Vocalization, Introduction, Notes and Concordance* (Jerusalem, 1959).
VAN DER PLOEG, FR. J., BARTHÉLEMY, FR. D., et al., *La secte de Qumrân et les Origines du Christianisme* (Bruges, 1959).
KOSMALA, H., *Hebräer-Essener-Christen. Studien zur Vorgeschichte der frühchristlichen Verkündigung* (Leiden, 1959).

INDEX

I. Alphabetical Index
of the Translated Qumran Writings[1]

[1] Abbreviations used by specialists are in brackets.

[1] Italicized references correspond to biblical quotations in the Qumran writings, and the figures in brackets to footnotes.

2. APOCRYPHA AND PSEUDEPIGRAPHA OF THE OLD TESTAMENT

A. APOCRYPHA (DEUTERO-CANONICAL BOOKS)

B. PSEUDEPIGRAPHA

3. NEW TESTAMENT

III. Index of Authors